↑
Hadassah
Medical Center

St. George's
Cathedral

Hebrew
University

NABLUS RD.

STREET OF THE PROPHETS

RUSSIAN
COMPOUND

Central Prison

Church of the
Holy Sepulcher

Police
HQ

Barclay's
Bank

Law Courts

GPO

Police
Station

OLD CITY

Western
Wall

al-Aqsa
Mosque

Dung Gate

PRINCESS
MARY RD.

MAMILLAH RD.

Jaffa
Gate

David's
Citadel

Police
Barracks

MAMILLAH RD.

Palace
Hotel

French
Consulate

HEBRON RD.

Zion
Gate

Secretariat
Annex

King David
Hotel

JULIAN'S WAY

YMCA

Windmill

**YEMIN
MOSHE**

Valley of Hinnom

David Brothers
Building

**GERMAN
COLONY**

HEBRON RD.

BETHLEHEM RD.

N
E
W
S

Government
House

Allenby
Barracks

0   MILE   ½

0   METERS   500

Also by Bruce Hoffman

The Evolution of the Global Terrorist Threat:
From 9/11 to Osama bin Laden's Death (coeditor)

Inside Terrorism

The Failure of British Military Strategy
Within Palestine, 1939–1947

ANONYMOUS SOLDIERS

ANONYMOUS SOLDIERS

THE STRUGGLE FOR ISRAEL
1917–1947

BRUCE HOFFMAN

NEW YORK   ALFRED A. KNOPF   2015

THIS IS A BORZOI BOOK
PUBLISHED BY ALFRED A. KNOPF

Copyright © 2015 by Bruce Hoffman
Map copyright © David Lindroth Inc.

All rights reserved. Published in the United States by Alfred A. Knopf,
a division of Random House LLC, New York, and distributed in Canada
by Random House of Canada Limited, Toronto,
Penguin Random House companies.

www.aaknopf.com

Knopf, Borzoi Books, and the colophon are registered trademarks
of Random House LLC.

Library of Congress Cataloging-in-Publication Data
Hoffman, Bruce, [date] author.
Anonymous soldiers : the struggle for Israel, 1917–1947 /
Bruce Hoffman.
pages ; cm
"This is a Borzoi book."
ISBN 978-0-307-59471-6 (hardcover);
ISBN 978-1-101-87466-0 (eBook)
1. Palestine—Politics and government—1917–1948.
2. Counterinsurgency—Palestine—History—20th century.
3. Palestine—History—1917–1948.
4. World War, 1939–1945—Palestine.
5. Zionism—Palestine—History—20th century.
I. Title.
DS126.H634 2015   956.94'04—dc23   2014018177

Jacket image: Ruined wing of the King David Hotel, Jerusalem,
July 24, 1946 © Imperial War Museum (E 31975), London
Jacket design by Stephanie Ross

Manufactured in the United States of America
First Edition

For you again, D.

And, this time for M., N., S., and A., too.

Also, in memoriam: David Hoffman, 1921–2009

Contents

Preface

Does terrorism work? Its targets and victims steadfastly maintain that it does not, while its practitioners and apologists claim that it does. Scholars and analysts are divided. Given the untold death and destruction wrought by terrorists throughout history, the question has an undeniable relevance that has only intensified since the September 11, 2001, attacks. Yet a definitive answer unaccountably remains as elusive as a universally accepted definition of the phenomenon itself.[1]

"Terrorists can never win outright," Prime Minister Ian Smith of Rhodesia confidently declared in 1977. Following the 1983 suicide truck bombing that killed 241 U.S. military service personnel in Lebanon, President Ronald Reagan defiantly proclaimed that "the main thing" is to show that terrorism "doesn't work . . . [and] to prove that terrorist acts are not going to drive us away." Margaret Thatcher described the attempt by the Provisional Irish Republican Army (PIRA) to kill her at the 1984 Conservative Party Conference as illustrative not only of a failed attack but of a fundamentally futile strategy. And in July 2006, Prime Minister Ehud Olmert of Israel promised that his government "will not give in to blackmail and will not negotiate with terrorists when it comes to the lives of Israel Defence Force soldiers."[2]

Scholars have made similarly sweeping claims. The Nobel laureate Thomas Schelling observed in 1991 that despite considerable exertion, terrorists mostly have little to show for their efforts except for fleeting attention and evanescent publicity. In the wake of the September 11, 2001, attacks, the historical novelist cum military historian Caleb Carr consolingly averred, "The strategy of terror is a spectacularly failed one." And in a 2006 article unambiguously titled "Why Terrorism Does Not Work," the political scientist Max Abrahms argued that terrorism was also tactically ineffective. "The notion that terrorism is an effective coercive instrument," he concluded, "is sustained by either single case studies or a few well-known terrorist victories."[3]

Yet if terrorism is so ineffective, why has it persisted for at least the past two millennia and indeed become an increasingly popular means of violent political expression in the twenty-first century? The sense of personal empowerment and catharsis articulated by Frantz Fanon in *The Wretched of the Earth*, based on his experiences in Algeria during that country's struggle for independence against France, only partially explains terrorism's enduring attraction to the alienated and disenfranchised, the "so-far powerless [and] would-be powerful," described some forty years ago by Frederick J. Hacker, a psychiatrist like Fanon.[4] It is necessarily incomplete because individual motivations are only one side of a coin that also must address organizational dimensions and imperatives and the collective mind-set that they reflect.

Hence, much as statesmen and scholars may trumpet terrorism's ineffectuality, it is nonetheless widely accepted that terrorist violence is neither irrational nor desperate but instead entirely rational and often carefully calculated and choreographed. Terrorism is thus consciously embraced by its practitioners as a deliberate instrument of warfare, a pragmatic decision derived from a discernibly logical process. As the doyenne of terrorist studies, Martha Crenshaw, explained in her seminal 1981 article on the causes of terrorism, "Campaigns of terrorism depend on rational political choice. As purposeful activity, terrorism is the result of an organization's decision that it is a politically useful means to oppose a government . . . Terrorism is seen collectively as a logical means to advance desired ends."[5]

Terrorism's posited ineffectiveness as a coercive strategy—confined to a handful of case studies or to infrequent and entirely sui generis successes—thus hardly squares with the terrorists' own fervent and abiding faith in the efficacy of their violence, its intractable persistence over the course of history, or indeed the disproportionate influence that even a small number of well-known victories has had in inspiring imitation and emulation by successive generations of terrorists.[6]

In other words, the handful of supposed exceptions may be far more important and far more compelling than the perceived rule. And even if terrorism's power to dramatically change the course of history along the lines of the September 11, 2001, attacks has been mercifully infrequent, terrorism's ability to act as a catalyst for wider conflagration or systemic political change appears historically undeniable. The assassination of the archduke Franz Ferdinand by a young Bosnian terrorist in June 1914 and the cross-border Palestinian terrorist attacks that led to the 1967 Arab-Israeli Six-Day War are arguably examples of the former, while the struggles for independence won by Ireland in 1922, Cyprus in 1960, and Algeria in 1962 are among the examples depicting the latter.[7]

The list goes on: Rhodesia is now Zimbabwe; the U.S. Marines soon departed Lebanon; Sinn Féin's Martin McGuinness, a former PIRA terrorist, has been the deputy first minister of Northern Ireland since 2007; and that same year Israel freed five of its imprisoned terrorists in exchange for the bodies of two kidnapped Israeli sergeants. Hezbollah's significant role in Lebanon further challenges arguments about terrorism's strategic futility. Indeed, neither Sinn Féin nor Hezbollah could ever have acquired the power, influence, and status both enjoy today if not for its terrorist antecedents.

The political violence that plagued Palestine when it was ruled by Great Britain presents an ideal case with which to examine and assess terrorism's power to influence government policy and decision making. Prior to 1948, the land that eventually became the Jewish state of Israel was administered by Britain under the terms of the mandate awarded it in 1922 by the League of Nations. Charged with preparing this territory for eventual independence, Britain was regularly subjected to violent pressure by both Arab and Jew alike. Arab rioting and attendant anti-Jewish violence and terrorism during the 1920s led to more widespread insurrection in the late 1930s. Then, during the 1940s, two Jewish terrorist organizations—the Irgun Zvai Le'umi (National Military Organization) and the Lohamei Herut Yisrael (Fighters for the Freedom of Israel), known to Jews by its Hebrew acronym, Lehi, and to the British as the Stern Gang—arose to challenge Britain's rule over Palestine.

The terrorist campaigns waged by both these organizations, it should be emphasized, were only one facet of a broader confrontation that dominated Anglo-Zionist relations throughout the mandate's final decade. Palestine's Jewish community and Britain came into conflict over a number of issues involving the rights of Jews—immigration to Palestine; the purchase of land and construction of settlements; the acquisition, importation, and storage of weapons; the organization and training of civilian self-defense forces—and, most fundamentally, over Palestine's political future. The struggle for Jewish statehood employed almost every means possible: diplomacy, negotiation, lobbying, civil disobedience, propaganda, information operations, armed resistance, and terrorist violence.

But the Palestine case is especially valuable in understanding the impact that terrorism can have on government policy and decision making. The

Jewish terrorist campaign was arguably the first post–World War II "war of national liberation" to clearly recognize the publicity value inherent in terrorism; the violence was often choreographed for an audience far beyond the immediate geographic locus of the terrorists' struggle. The lessons with respect to government policy responses and tactical counter-measures are equally profound. Modern Western nations' fear of foreign terrorist infiltration and radicalization of an indigenous minority popula-tion, for instance, echoes concerns sixty years ago about the spread of Jewish terrorist activities from Palestine to Britain and Europe.

Many of the security challenges that Britain subsequently encountered in Malaya, Cyprus, and Kenya during the 1950s and in Northern Ire-land throughout the closing decades of the twentieth century and that the United States and Britain together have faced in Iraq and Afghanistan since 2001 were also present in Palestine throughout the period of Brit-ish rule. Highly professional military forces, in some cases flushed with recent hard-fought victories on conventional battlefields, were perplexed by their failure to swiftly suppress and ultimately defeat numerically infe-rior, poorly armed, enigmatic adversaries. They chafed at highly restric-tive rules of engagement in densely populated urban areas and often had grave difficulties in obtaining the cooperation of the local population. Intelligence collection and analysis were similarly frustrating and often inadequate; policing was largely accorded a low priority, and consequently training was poor and personnel numbers deficient; proficiency with local languages was frequently a problem; and civil-military relations were strained and coordination fractured.

Since the late 1970s, a more complete understanding of the events and processes that led to Britain's decision in 1947 to surrender the mandate and leave Palestine has emerged as a result of the declassification of many critical state documents from that time. The British Public Records Act of 1958 stipulates that official records will be made available to the pub-lic thirty years after their creation—unless they are either still in use by government ministries or deemed by those ministries to be of sufficient sensitivity that they must be retained.

Accordingly, three decades after Britain left Palestine, a variety of cabinet papers, minutes, and memorandums became available along with correspondence from the Colonial, Foreign, Prime Minister's, and War Offices, among other government ministries. The material included reports and analyses prepared by individual departments and the reflections of the senior officials who reviewed and commented on them, telegrams and letters exchanged between ministers in London and their subordinates overseas, the war diaries of military forces deployed to Palestine, the records of the colonial police service, and so on. The array of personal papers deposited in private archives by many of the dramatis personae involved in the formulation and execution of British policy in Palestine during the mandate filled in more of the details, as did official documents of various kinds found in both Israel and the United States.

As a young doctoral student, I spent several years researching this subject during the late 1970s and early 1980s. I examined material in the Public Record Office at Kew, London, as well as in collections of private papers scattered throughout England, consulted archives in Israel and the United States, and interviewed many former British statesmen, soldiers, and police involved either in governing Palestine or in crafting British policy for the mandate, along with past members of the Irgun and Lehi (my doctoral thesis was submitted to the Faculty of Social Studies at Oxford University in 1985).

I was always conscious of the material at the Public Record Office to which public access was denied. Notations attached to numerous files in archival registries stated that they were either closed for fifty years or "retained by department." Equally frustrating were the fleeting glimpses of individual intelligence reports and analyses occasionally found in the files of other ministries or departments that had somehow escaped vetting and exclusion. These lacunae were perhaps most conspicuous with respect to the records of Britain's intelligence and security services and those of the Palestine Police Force's intelligence arm, the Criminal Investigation Department (CID).

The centrality of intelligence to understanding history has long been the focus of research by the renowned Cambridge historian Professor Christopher Andrew. "Secret intelligence in twentieth-century Britain," he wrote in the preface to *Her Majesty's Secret Service: The Making of the British Intelligence Community*, "has varied greatly in both quantity and quality but the historian of national and international politics can never afford to ignore it. Any analysis of government policy, particularly on foreign affairs and defence, which leaves intelligence out of account is bound to be incomplete. It may also be distorted as a result."[8]

I subsequently moved on to the study and analysis of more contemporary issues of terrorism and counterterrorism, often on behalf of the U.S. government while employed for some twenty years at a prominent think tank. Nonetheless, I always carried with me the nagging thought that the work for my doctorate, as Professor Andrew's admonition implied, was incomplete and thus was best regarded rather as a work in progress—to be amended at some future time.

The opportunity to undertake this work finally presented itself about a decade ago as a result of three developments. First, starting in the late 1990s, the British Security Service (MI5) made available at the Public Record Office—renamed the National Archives in 2003—the first tranche of documents pertaining to its early history. This was the start of subsequent, often annual releases of hitherto highly classified intelligence reports, analyses, interrogations, intercepts, diaries, and other communications. Second, in 2002 the service selected Professor Andrew, by now a cherished friend and mentor, to write its official history—the magisterial book published in 2009, to coincide with the service's centenary, titled *The Defence of the Realm: The Authorized History of MI5* (and in the United States as *Defend the Realm*). Professor Andrew's work on this project continued the flow of additional files, including many pertaining to Palestine. The KV series, as the Security Service's papers are designated, I soon discovered, yielded a treasure trove of new information on Palestine, among which were handwritten minutes to memorandums by Winston Churchill and correspondence sent to MI5 signed by H. A. R. "Kim" Philby, the notorious cold war spy.

Over the next seven years I made several visits to the archives at Kew. I also revisited private papers collections in Britain and archives in both Israel and the United States—where I found a large amount of newly donated papers and recently declassified documents. As the participants in the struggle over Palestine in the 1940s aged and, in many cases, passed away, either they or their heirs had increasingly deposited at university libraries and research centers hitherto unknown and unavailable material in the form of long-forgotten official papers and personal diaries. The papers of John J. O'Sullivan, a senior British intelligence officer who served in Palestine and was at the vortex of virtually all the investigations into all the major terrorist attacks both in Palestine and elsewhere between 1944 and 1947, proved invaluable especially with respect to the assassination of Lord Moyne in Cairo in 1944, the bombings of Jerusalem's King David Hotel and the British embassy in Rome in 1946, and the kidnapping and lynching of two British field intelligence sergeants the following year. In addition, the discovery in Israel of the long-mislaid intelligence files of the Palestine Police Force, now housed at the Haganah Archives in Tel Aviv, also provided insight.

The result is the research presented in *Anonymous Soldiers*, which takes its name from the title of a poem written by Abraham Stern that subsequently became the Irgun's and then Lehi's anthem. The book is divided into three parts.

The first part, comprising chapters 1 through 6, covers the period of time from Britain's conquest of Palestine in 1917, toward the end of World War I, to the early years of World War II. It attempts to depict the reasons behind the emergence of a Jewish underground in response to Arab violence and terrorism and traces its evolution into a counterterrorism strike force that eventually turned its weapons on Britain as well.

The second part, chapters 7 through 10, focuses on wartime Palestine: the split that produced rival Jewish terrorist factions; their relations with the mainstream, official Zionist movement; and the growing polarization of the Jewish community from the British government that led in turn to the escalation of Jewish terrorism, now directed solely against the British government.

The final part, chapters 11 through 19, chronicles the war that Britain fought in Palestine following World War II. It was during this time that a concatenation of powerful forces, including Jewish terrorism, combined to render Britain's continued rule of Palestine untenable. These chapters, accordingly, focus on terrorism's role in the momentous events that led to Britain's decision to abandon the mandate. An epilogue assesses the lessons of this struggle in the context of both terrorism's subsequent trajectory and the challenges faced by governments in countering this menace.

Neither this book nor its author makes any pretension to providing a definitive history of the Zionist struggle against British rule or the entire spectrum of factors that led to the creation of the State of Israel. Rather, as might be expected from someone who has spent his entire career studying terrorism and counterterrorism, this book considers those specific dimensions of this story in light of the broader question raised at the beginning of this preface: how terrorism affects government policy and decision making and whether terrorism is an effective weapon with which to achieve fundamental political change. *Anonymous Soldiers* thus recounts the history of this struggle mostly through the eyes of the British statesmen, soldiers, officials, policemen, and others variously charged with administering the mandate, policing it, and crafting policies for, or making decisions about, it.

Bruce Hoffman
Washington, D.C.
May 2014

ANONYMOUS SOLDIERS

CHAPTER 1

To Die for Our Nation

On May 14, 1948, at 8:00 a.m. sharp, General Sir Alan Gordon Cunningham, the high commissioner for Palestine and Trans-Jordan, emerged from his residence at Government House in Jerusalem to inspect an honor guard of the Highland Light Infantry. On the balcony above, a solitary bagpiper played a mournful lament. The sound of gunshots could be heard in the distance as Jewish and Arab snipers traded fire: the first Arab-Israeli war had already started. A bugle then sounded, and the honor guard came to attention. The Union Jack was lowered, and three decades of British rule in Palestine ended.[1]

The night before, in a farewell address over the Palestine Broadcasting Service, Cunningham had struggled to strike an optimistic note. "I have never believed, and do not believe now," he said, "that the seed of agreement between Jew and Arab does not exist, even though in all our efforts we have failed to find the soil in which it would germinate." He took one last walk around the beautiful gardens that ringed the building that had been both his residence and his office for the past two and a half years. Situated on the infelicitously named Jabal el Muqabbar, the biblical Hill of Evil Counsel, Government House was justly renowned for its spectacularly panoramic views—overlooking the new city to the west, the walled Old City and Mount Scopus to the north, the Mount of Olives to the east, and the Judaean desert and Dead Sea beyond. Soldiers, statesmen, diplomats, and the country's Arab and Jewish elites had once mingled there. On this melancholy morning it would not have escaped Cunningham's notice that no representative from either community had come to bid him farewell.[2]

A black four-ton, bulletproof, armor-plated Daimler limousine awaited Cunningham out front in the compound's majestic driveway. The vehicle had been specially built during the London Blitz for King George VI to tour the city's bombed-out neighborhoods. The prime minister, Clement Attlee, had sent it to Jerusalem for Cunningham's use. Until today, he had refused to ride in it, but British army intelligence believed that there were plots by Jewish and Arab extremists alike to assassinate him. The five-mile route to Qalandia airstrip, accordingly, was lined with troops and tanks, while Spitfire fighter aircraft and Lancaster heavy bombers flew overhead. The high commissioner inspected another honor guard before boarding a Royal Air Force (RAF) Dakota for the short flight to Haifa. Within an hour of landing, Cunningham had been whisked to the Haifa docks, again amid tight security, and piped aboard HMS *Euryalus*. At midnight, the Royal Navy battle cruiser set sail, and, as Cunningham had said in his last broadcast the previous night, "the final page of the history of the British Mandate in Palestine . . . turned."[3]

It had all begun so differently thirty-one years earlier, when another British general found success and fame in Palestine. But General Sir Edmund Allenby's victorious march to Jerusalem had in fact begun with a defeat half a world away. In April 1917, as World War I ground to an uncertain conclusion, General Allenby held command of the British Third Army during the Arras offensive. Allenby "clumsily" attempted, and failed, to break through German lines. For his unimaginative tactics, and for the heavy loss of life that resulted from them, Allenby was stripped of his command and transferred from the Western Front to the Middle East.[4]

Allenby was inconsolable, regarding his reassignment to a "peripheral war theatre" as a "demotion and punishment for failing in France." He was now in charge of the British-led Egyptian Expeditionary Force (EEF), which was locked in battle with the German-led Ottoman Turkish army. Allenby's predecessor had already been repelled twice at Gaza in April 1917 by Ottoman forces; Allenby was now working to an impossible timetable to take Jerusalem by Christmas.[5]

Three months after he arrived in the region, Allenby initiated the third, and final, battle for Gaza. In a stunning coup de main, he divided his force, sending mounted and infantry divisions to strike at the enemy's weaker, eastern flank. Thundering across the desert, his Australian, New Zealand, and British cavalry swept into Beersheba, cutting off the reinforced Turkish garrison in Gaza. Five weeks later, Jerusalem fell to Allenby's troops. Indeed, whatever his failings were in the static warfare of the Western Front, as a cavalryman himself Allenby was clearly in his element in the desert.[6]

Allenby entered Jerusalem on December 11, 1917. The weather, he wrote to his wife, was perfect for the occasion: "iced sunshine, with no wind." Postcards from the time show men of his Sixtieth Division lining the route down Jaffa Road and a contingent of Australian cavalrymen gathered in front of Jaffa Gate, the southwest entrance to Jerusalem's Old City, forming the honor guard that greeted Allenby as he rode by. Perhaps the most iconic photograph depicts Allenby making his official entry through Jaffa Gate on foot, an event that was carefully stage-managed and choreographed for its maximum symbolic value. Weeks earlier, Field Marshal William Robertson, the Chief of the Imperial General Staff (CIGS), Britain's most senior military officer, had sent the following instructions to Allenby:

> In the event of JERUSALEM being occupied, it would be of considerable political importance if you, on officially entering the city, dismount at the city gate and enter on foot. German emperor rode in and the saying went round "a better man than he walked."
> Advantage of contrast in conduct will be obvious.[7]

Accompanied by his staff officers, representatives of Britain's French and Italian allies, and Major T. E. Lawrence, the famed Lawrence of Arabia, Allenby walked the short distance to David's Citadel, where he read a proclamation placing Jerusalem under military administration. Interpreters then translated it into Arabic, Hebrew, French, Italian, Greek, and Russian for the crowd of Jerusalemites who had come to witness this historic moment. "The people of the city assembled in some considerable numbers and appeared to be pleased at our arrival," Allenby wrote the following day to the Reverend Rennie MacInnes, the Anglican bishop of Jerusalem. Seventy-five years later, Anna Grace Lind, who as a twelve-year-old had watched the procession from a balcony near Jaffa Gate, recalled how "we were all so excited to see the British coming in."[8]

Short of men, it was not for another ten months that Allenby was able to resume his offensive. But on October 30, 1918, after a few weeks of fighting near Megiddo, the biblical site of Armageddon, the Turks surrendered. Palestine, that "peripheral war theatre," was the crowning achievement of Allenby's career. He was promoted to field marshal a year later, awarded a viscountcy, appointed high commissioner of Egypt, and voted £50,000 (roughly the equivalent of $3.4 million today) by Parliament in appreciation.[9]

Allenby's conquest of Palestine ended four centuries of rule by Turkey's Ottoman Empire. The country had suffered terribly during the four years of war. In addition to the fighting that had ravaged Palestine's landscape and economy, famine, locusts, and military requisitioning had depleted livestock and denuded crops and forests alike. Palestine's population had shrunk by perhaps as many as 100,000 people from its prewar level of roughly 700,000 inhabitants, the result of death from both warfare and disease, forced conscription, and cruel civilian deportation.[10]

The problems facing Allenby and his army in administering Palestine were thus formidable. Accordingly, in April 1918 responsibility for the country's governance passed from the chief political officer attached to the EEF to a more formal, but still provisional, entity called the Occupied Enemy Territory Administration (OETA), pending the country's ultimate disposition.[11]

But Britain's rule of Palestine, however glorious its beginnings, was undermined from the start by two separate commitments that it had made to two peoples who both considered that country historically their own—the Arabs and the Jews. During the war, just weeks before Allenby marched into Jerusalem, the British government had issued the Balfour Declaration. That statement of British policy was in fact a letter sent on November 2, 1917, by the foreign secretary, Arthur Balfour, on behalf of the British government, to Lord Rothschild, a president of the English Zionist Federation. "I have much pleasure in conveying to you, on behalf of His Majesty's Government, the following declaration of sympathy with Jewish Zionist aspirations which has been submitted to, and approved by, the Cabinet," Balfour had written. "His Majesty's Government view with favour, the establishment in Palestine of a national home for the Jewish people, and will use their best endeavours to facilitate the achievement of this object, it being understood that nothing shall be done which may prejudice the civil and religious rights of existing non-Jewish communities in Palestine, or the rights and political status enjoyed by Jews in any other country." The hard strategic realities of a war that had dragged on with no clear resolution loomed behind the declaration's benevolent prose and altruistic intent. Prominent among these was the hope of favorably influencing Jewish opinion in the United States so that America would enter the war and in Russia in hopes that country would not conclude a separate peace with Germany. In addition, Palestine's strategic location both as adjacent to Egypt and the Suez Canal and as a land bridge across the Middle East to Britain's empire in India and the Far East had always figured prominently in British geopolitical calculations about the region.[12]

Throughout the process of seizing Palestine from the Ottomans and garnering Jewish support for the larger war effort, however, the cabinet had not bothered to consult with its Arab allies, anticipating little or no negative reaction to these portentous decisions. As events would shortly demonstrate, this was a grave omission.[13]

Although the Balfour Declaration pledged Britain to safeguard the civil and religious rights of Palestine's majority Arab population, this qualification failed to allay Arab fears that the Jews, with Britain's assistance, would eventually turn Palestine into a Jewish state. Critically, nothing had been said about the Arabs' political and economic rights. In addition, this new statement of policy contradicted a previous British commitment to support the Arabs' self-determination in return for their military assistance against Turkey. Between July 1915 and March 1916 a series of ten letters between Sir A. Henry McMahon, the high commissioner of Egypt, and Sharif Hussein of Mecca, who would lead the Arab Revolt and become Britain's most important ally in the region, had spelled out this commitment, even though the correspondence did not constitute a formal treaty. The British government subsequently argued that the McMahon-Hussein agreement had not been meant to apply to Palestine in any case. Accordingly, Palestine's Arabs came to fear that they would be cheated not only of Britain's promises of self-determination but of their homeland as well.[14]

The delicacy of navigating between two peoples' historical, cultural, religious, and political claims to the same land was beyond the capacity of many British officials in OETA. Not only were they generally unsympathetic to Zionism, but their predisposition favoring the Arab claim poisoned relations with Palestine's Jewish community. The anti-Semitism common to the British upper and officer classes of the time likely played a role as well. This antipathy toward the Jews and Zionism became so obvious that, following a visit to Palestine in 1920, the director of military intelligence reported to his superiors in London that OETA's military and civilian officials were "unanimous in expressing their dislike of any policy favoring the Jews, and [harbor] serious fears of the consequences of such a policy."[15]

Meanwhile, Arab political discontent in Palestine was contributing to an increase of attacks on isolated, rural Jewish agricultural settlements. The problem was not new and indeed had become so serious before the war that in 1907 a group of neighboring Jewish settlements in the Galilee had founded an illegal, and therefore by necessity clandestine, "watchman's guild." They named the group Bar Giora, in reference to the Hebrew warrior who had led the first Jewish revolt against ancient Israel's Roman occupiers. Bar Giora successfully defended the handful of settlements under its aegis, and two years later it was reorganized into a countrywide security force and renamed Ha-Shomer (the Watchman). During the war, however, the Ottomans began to more actively suppress these illegal activities and forcibly conscripted many of Ha-Shomer's members into the Turkish army. The group, consequently, disintegrated.[16]

The self-defense issue had lain dormant since then, until a series of Arab raids on Jewish settlements in the upper Galilee region of northern Palestine between late 1919 and early 1920 prompted renewed concern. The Yishuv (Hebrew for "settlement," but the word used since the 1880s to refer to the Jewish community in Palestine) was further unnerved by growing reports of Arab threats to urban Jews as well.[17]

One of the first people to publicly articulate this concern was Vladimir "Ze'ev" Jabotinsky. Acclaimed as a brilliant orator, essayist, ideologue, and poet, Jabotinsky emerged as among the most vociferous and militant of the Zionist leaders and thinkers during the period between the two wars. Born in Odessa in 1880, he subsequently studied in Switzerland and for a longer period in Italy, where he became enamored with the writings of leading figures of the Risorgimento—the strident nationalist movement that achieved Italy's unification in the late nineteenth century.[18]

The pogroms that convulsed Russian Jewry from 1903 to 1905 both awakened and account for Jabotinsky's fervent Zionism. He hurriedly organized makeshift Jewish self-defense units for his native city, collecting money, raising recruits, and obtaining weapons. Although his efforts likely blunted anti-Semitic violence in Odessa, the infamous pogrom in Kishniev, then the capital of Bessarabia (now Moldova), galvanized Jabotinsky, who was henceforth transformed into "a professional Zionist [and] a travelling agitator." As a journalist in Egypt covering World War I, Jabotinsky learned that Ottoman authorities had forcibly deported hundreds of young Jewish men from Palestine. Seized with the idea of creating a Jewish legion that would both help British forces liberate Palestine and endow Zionism with needed political capital, Jabotinsky lobbied tirelessly in London for its creation. His efforts resulted in the formation of the Zion Mule Corps, which participated in the ill-fated invasion of Turkey at Gallipoli in 1915, and three Jewish battalions of Royal Fusiliers that served under Allenby in the EEF. Their modest contribution to the war effort, however, was overshadowed in Zionist eyes by their symbolic value as uniquely Jewish military units.[19]

Jabotinsky believed that a properly armed and organized Jewish self-defense force was now required to replace the more informal and, in his view, archaic Ha-Shomer. He further argued that this new force should be not a clandestine body but an official paramilitary force enjoying the full recognition, and cooperation, of the British. An Arab attack on the northern village of Tel Hai in March 1920, in which six Jews were killed, infused the self-defense issue with new urgency. Among the dead was Captain Joseph Trumpeldor, a Jewish war hero who had once trained to become a dentist but had gone on to co-found the Zion Mule Corps with Jabotinsky. Wounded at Gallipoli, Trumpeldor had previously lost his left arm fighting in the 1904–5 Russo-Japanese War, and his valiant defense of Tel Hai against a large force of Bedouin brigands became a source of both anxiety and inspiration for the Yishuv. The anxiety was caused by renewed concerns over British assurances of protection, and the inspiration was a result of Trumpeldor's reported last words, "It is good to die for one's country."[20]

Meanwhile, a group of demobilized Jewish legionnaires and members of various youth sports groups in Jerusalem became impatient and formed their own secret paramilitary unit that they called the Haganah (Defense) and asked Jabotinsky to serve as their commander. He agreed, provided that the group allowed him to obtain permission from the authorities for its establishment. Senior OETA officials, however, feared that such an organization would further incite the already restless Arab population and therefore rejected Jabotinsky's request. Nonetheless, the group continued to drill and train every evening, supplemented by weekend hikes where Haganah ex-servicemen instructed their units in both field craft and the use of hand grenades. Arms, meanwhile, were procured at high cost from an Armenian gunrunner in the Old City. Jabotinsky was emphatic that any provocation of the Arabs was to be avoided. However, in keeping with his muscular, aggressive Zionist ideology, he counseled, "If an Arab walks up to you and insults you, do not answer; never strike first; but if he hits you once, hit back twice as hard."[21]

Throughout March 1920 tension rose in Jerusalem as rumors circulated that the Arabs planned to use the forthcoming Muslim Nebi Musa festival as a pretext to attack Jewish targets in Jerusalem. Despite the protests of Jabotinsky and other Jewish leaders, who worried that the predominantly Arab police force was neither properly trained nor sufficiently numerous to handle any unrest, OETA officials maintained that no additional security measures were needed. The 1919 holiday, despite similar Jewish fears, had passed without incident, Sir Ronald Storrs, the military governor of Jerusalem from 1917 to 1920 and its civilian governor until 1926, reasoned. Indeed, he was so confident of this outcome that in keeping with Ottoman traditions, he agreed to provide a military band to accompany the traditional procession.[22]

The potential dangers of the 1920 event were clear to Jabotinsky. Fifteen months earlier, he had warned, "Arab impudence is growing daily. Not forty-eight hours pass but some inciting speech is heard . . . concluding in a call to the 'Arab sword' . . . The Palestine authorities are acting in a manner which clearly tells the Arabs that the [Balfour] Declaration need not be fulfilled." On March 12, he told Dr. Chaim Weizmann—the Zionist leader who had been instrumental in the Balfour Declaration's issuance and was then president of the Zionist Organization, the preeminent Jewish political organization created in 1897 by Zionism's founding father, Theodor Herzl—that "the pogrom is liable to break out here any day."[23]

As April 4, the date of that year's Nebi Musa celebrations, approached, Jabotinsky and the Haganah senior command put into effect their defensive plan. Jerusalem was divided into four sectors, each with a commander reporting directly to Jabotinsky based at a command headquarters situated on Jaffa Road. Early that morning anonymous Arabic-language notices were circulated in Jerusalem proclaiming, "The Government is with us, Allenby is with us, kill the Jews; there is no punishment for killing Jews." By mid-morning, a large Arab crowd had gathered just outside Jaffa Gate. Egged on by tendentious speakers who addressed them from the balcony of the nearby Arab Club, the crowd began to chant the rhyming Arabic couplet "Palestine is our land, the Jews are dogs!" Then 'Aref al-'Aref, the nationalist firebrand and newspaper editor, shouted, "If we don't use force against the Zionists and against the Jews, we will never be rid of them." The crowd replied, "We will drink the blood of the Jews." As is often the case when mobs are worked to a frenzy, the accounts of who struck the first blow or provided the initial provocation are confused and contradictory. Frances Newton, an English missionary who lived in Palestine from 1889 until 1938, claims that a Jewish spectator spat at one of the Islamic banners that a celebrant was carrying. Regardless of the precise cause, the mob went wild. Even Newton, who refused to accept that the riots might have been premeditated and unequivocally blamed "Zionist influence" as their cause, admits that "innocent Jews suffered" grievously.[24]

Edward Keith-Roach, a young British civil servant, was just leaving Sunday services at the Church of the Holy Sepulcher, located in the center of the Old City, when a nearby crowd caught his attention. There was lots of shouting and "sticks . . . being brandished. A stone was thrown and hit a Jew. In the twinkling of an eye the street was in a turmoil. Seeing an Arab about to attack another old Jew, I called upon an Arab policeman to help him, but the policeman just faded away and so did the Arab." At that moment, Storrs was walking out of St. George's Cathedral, just a few blocks north of the Old City in East Jerusalem, where he had attended

Easter Matins service with his parents, who were visiting from England. Storrs's Arab butler approached and whispered that there had been serious trouble at Jaffa Gate. "It was as though he had thrust a sword into my heart. Even now the mere memory of those dread words brings back the horror of the shock," Storrs recalled twenty years later.[25]

Jabotinsky and Pinchas Rutenberg, a moderate Zionist leader who had also played a pivotal role in the creation of the Jewish Legion during the war, had been desperately searching for the governor. Having finally tracked Storrs down at his office just as he returned from church, they asked permission to deploy armed Haganah paramilitaries to defend the inhabitants of the Old City's isolated Jewish Quarter, which was situated far from the nearest police station and thus vulnerable. Storrs dismissed the request out of hand and assured both that the police would deal with any trouble. Unbeknownst to him, the Arab police had already abandoned their posts and had joined the attacks on Jews and looting of Jewish property. As the violence spiraled out of control, the British authorities imposed a curfew and ordered British troops onto the streets to restore order. The rioting, however, continued for another four days. In the end, five Jews lay dead and 216 injured. Almost all the Jewish casualties had occurred in the Old City. British troops posted at the entrance had barred the way to the Haganah units that had attempted to come to the Jews' defense. Four Arabs had also been killed and 23 wounded. "The Easter riots were, alas, only the first eruption of the volcano," Newton sadly noted.[26]

The Nebi Musa disturbances above all confirmed the collision course that British policy for Palestine was on, at least so far as Anglo-Zionist relations over security matters were concerned. The Yishuv and its leaders bitterly criticized OETA for failing to anticipate the violence and for its inadequate response. Officials in OETA reacted by blaming the Jews, whose presence and activities in Palestine, they maintained, had alarmed the Arabs and provoked their wrath. Relations were further strained when police, acting on OETA's orders, arrested Jabotinsky and nineteen other Haganah members. They were charged with illegal possession of firearms and ammunition and for conspiracy to commit unlawful acts. They were tried, convicted, and sentenced to prison terms of three years each with Jabotinsky receiving a fifteen-year sentence and ordered deported from Palestine upon his release. The Yishuv was shocked, not only because Jabotinsky and the defendants had acted in self-defense, but also because the two Arab leaders convicted of instigating the riot, the aforementioned

'Aref al-'Aref and a colleague, Haj Amin al-Husseini, had received only ten-year prison sentences each. Both men avoided imprisonment by fleeing to Trans-Jordan.[27]

The most important effect of the riots on the Yishuv, however, was to marshal support behind the formal establishment of a proper Jewish self-defense force. With Jabotinsky now in prison, there was no one with his stature or credibility to oppose the establishment of a clandestine entity completely independent of government control. Accordingly, the remaining Haganah leaders met on June 12, 1920, to found the Irgun ha-Haganah ha-Ivrith b'Eretz Yisrael (Hebrew Defense Organization in Palestine, known simply as the Haganah). The creation of an independent, armed Jewish underground represented its founders' belief that only by relying on themselves would the Jewish population of Palestine ever be secure. Among them were Yitzhak Ben-Zvi, who would become Israel's second president, and Eliahu Golomb, who would oversee the Haganah's evolution over the following two decades and transform it from a modest self-defense militia into a capable fighting force.[28]

The volatile character of Arab discontent, the unreliability of the police, and the marked hostility of the British authorities to unilateral Jewish defensive measures, its founders reasoned, compelled the Yishuv to respond in this manner. Perhaps more important, however, was that they specifically conceived the new defense force as the nucleus of a future Jewish army in a future Jewish state. Apart from the belief that this necessitated it be independent of any foreign control, the Haganah's creators concluded that like any army in a democracy it should be under elected civilian control. At the time no such representative Zionist entity existed in Palestine, but the establishment in December 1920 of the Histadrut (Ha-Histadrut Ha-Klalit shel Ha-Oudim, General Federation of Jewish Workers; known simply as the Histadrut) redressed this situation, and it therefore was agreed that the Haganah would be supervised by the Histadrut's elected executive board. That decision, however, only widened the cleavage separating Jabotinsky, given his long-standing opposition to the Histadrut's ideology. Thus the prospect of retaining his support for a fundamentally clandestine Jewish paramilitary force vanished with both the new group's underground orientation and its close association with the Zionist labor movement.[29]

The Nebi Musa disturbances were also a watershed in Britain's rule of Palestine. Reaction in London was sharply critical of OETA's performance. Complaints were voiced in the capital's most influential newspaper, *The Times*, on April 27, 1920, and by the Foreign Office as well. Lord Curzon, the foreign secretary, told Allenby that with the country under military control the riots "ought never to have happened." Colonel Richard Meinertzhagen, OETA's chief political officer, was especially displeased. Going outside the military chain of command, he fired off a long dispatch to Curzon that assailed senior OETA officials for their active hostility to Zionism and for their failure both to anticipate the riots in the first place and to contain the violence once it had started. Curzon showed it to the prime minister, David Lloyd George, and, according to Meinertzhagen, "They acted on my advice within twenty-four hours of its receipt."[30]

Although no formal peace treaty with Turkey had yet been signed and the newly created League of Nations had still not officially recognized Britain's rule of Palestine, Lloyd George and Curzon agreed that the provisional military regime should be replaced by a properly constituted civilian administration. They selected Sir Herbert Samuel, a prominent British Zionist and former member of the cabinet, as its head and urged him to leave for Palestine as soon as possible.[31]

Samuel arrived in Palestine aboard the HMS *Centaur* on June 30, 1920, and was welcomed with a seventeen-gun salute and RAF ceremonial fly-past. A talented parliamentarian who had been elected to Westminster in 1902, Samuel was the first practicing Jew to serve in a British cabinet. A lifelong Liberal Party member, Samuel was instrumental in framing the legislation passed by the Liberal government between 1905 and 1914 that laid the foundation of the modern British welfare state. He also devised the critical compromise formula that kept the cabinet intact on the eve of World War I. It was Samuel, in fact, who a year later had first raised with cabinet members the idea of enlisting Jewish support in the war and then had pushed for the government's endorsement of Zionist aspirations contained in the Balfour Declaration.[32]

Samuel stepped ashore wearing the British proconsul's official attire of white uniform, plumed helmet, and ceremonial sword. The waiting Jewish crowd was described by his private secretary as "messianic" with adulation. Palestine's Arabs were more subdued. Indeed, intelligence reports suggested that an attempt might be made on Samuel's life. Accordingly, he was transported in an armored car to the railhead in Lydda, where Samuel proceeded to Jerusalem aboard a special protected train. Storrs was present at the welcoming ceremonies and accompanied Samuel to Jerusalem. The governor of Jerusalem had taken the extraordinary precaution of arming himself with a cocked and loaded Browning automatic pistol, to be used, he later explained, "in case of emergency."[33]

Samuel assumed office the following day. Because Palestine was to be designated a "mandated territory" by the embryonic League of Nations, Lloyd George decided that Samuel's title should be "high commissioner" and not "governor," as was the case with Britain's colonial possessions. Palestine otherwise was organized exactly along crown colony lines. Hence, by 1921 the Colonial Office had assumed direct responsibility from the Foreign Office for the country's governance. The post of civil (later, chief) secretary was created, as were a commandant (later, inspector general) of police and prisons and the heads of the various other public service departments: health, education, and agriculture. A new legal system, which incorporated many of the Ottoman statutes, was implemented under the direction of a legal secretary (later, attorney general). Palestine was divided geographically into ten administrative districts (which were later consolidated and reduced to three), each supervised by a district commissioner and an assistant district commissioner. All district commissioners and heads of department were British; their staffs, however, were variously composed of Britons, Arabs, and Jews. The high commissioner's office and that of his administration were located in the Kaiserin Augusta Victoria Hospice. Like Government House, which would replace it in 1931, the hospice, situated between Mount Scopus and the Mount of Olives, overlooked Jerusalem—but from the northwest.[34]

Samuel moved quickly to try to heal the wounds from April's violence and to prove his impartiality to Palestine's Arab and Jewish communities. During his first week in office, he pardoned Jabotinsky and his imprisoned comrades as well as al-Husseini and al-'Aref. In September, the new Palestine administration promulgated an immigration ordinance establishing an annual monthly quota of 16,500 certificates for Jewish families seeking to settle in Palestine. In reality, however, the quota went grievously unfilled. A lack of jobs and housing, coupled with the Zionist Organization's meager funds, discouraged immigration at a critical moment in the Yishuv's history when the gates were essentially wide open.[35]

Despite amounting to only a fraction of the allowable quota, the arrival of these new immigrants quickly stoked Arab unease and undermined Samuel's good intentions. This was made abundantly clear in December 1920, when the Muslim-Christian Association (MCA), a representative body of Palestinian Arabs, held its Third Palestine Arab Congress in Haifa. Resolutions were passed denouncing the Balfour Declaration as contravening the "Laws of God and Man" and protesting governmental facilitation of its pro-Zionist terms. Although Samuel downplayed the resolutions' significance as the mere venting of accumulated frustrations, at the same time he was greatly dismayed by War Office plans to further reduce the Palestine garrison from the twenty-five thousand troops in the country at the time of the Nebi Musa disturbances to below even the existing complement of seventy-two hundred men. Indeed, the fact that many of the most senior positions in the Palestine administration were filled by Jews—the high commissioner, the legal secretary (Norman Bentwich), the director of immigration (Albert Hyamson), and the principal assistant secretary (Max Nurock)—did little to mitigate Arab fears and ensured that it would not be long before they again exploded in anti-Jewish violence.[36]

A collective sigh of relief was breathed in Jerusalem and London when the next year's Nebi Musa festivities peacefully concluded. But the country's crowded urban geography, coupled with its newly volatile political climate, meant that even a small spark could rapidly turn into a major conflagration. In this respect, the new Jewish city of Tel Aviv and the geographically contiguous ancient Arab port city of Jaffa uneasily coexisted beside each other much like the country's Jewish and Arab populations. Once a modest, though pleasant, coastal enclave known as much for its fragrant orange groves as its busy harbor, Jaffa had already begun to surpass Gaza as the region's most important—and prosperous—city toward the end of the nineteenth century. For Arabs as well as Jews, Jaffa was a place of uncommon beauty. "The bride of the sea in her sweet fragrance and perfume of blooming oranges and lemons" was how Hana Malak, an expatriate Arab Christian Jaffan, described the place of his birth, while it was "the maritime beauty" of the Mediterranean Sea to the Jewish novelist and later Nobel laureate S. Y. Agnon.[37]

A thriving economy and vibrant culture existed there. From 1911, for instance, all three of Palestine's most important newspapers had their main offices in Jaffa. But to David Ben-Gurion, the preeminent Zionist leader of his time and Israel's first prime minister, who arrived in Jaffa from his native Poland in 1907, the city had considerably less charm. Jaffa was "not very pretty," he recalled. "As in any oriental city, the streets are narrow and winding. An awful dust hangs over the marketplace, for there are no paving stones. I saw an uglier exile in Jaffa than in Plonsk [Ben-Gurion's dreary birthplace]," and he swiftly decamped for a rural settlement seven hours away.[38]

A Jewish watchmaker from Jaffa named Akiva Weiss had the idea in 1906 to build "the first Hebrew city" in modern times just up the coast, to the north. Like Ben-Gurion, Weiss despaired of living in what he also regarded as Jaffa's dirty and unsanitary conditions and consequently believed that more Jews would be encouraged to immigrate to Palestine if they had a clean, sanitary, and aesthetically pleasing "Hebrew urban centre" in which to live. Sixty Jewish families formed an association to achieve this goal, and in 1909 construction commenced. Tel Aviv's population expanded quickly and grew from 550 residents in 1911 to 3,604 in 1920 and by 1921 had nearly quadrupled. Jews, however, still lived in Jaffa, accounting for more than a third of its 42,000 inhabitants that same year. The "confrontation between Jaffa and Tel Aviv," according to the Middle Eastern historian Mark LeVine, "was a key theme in Arab literature of the period." In short, Jaffa and neighboring Tel Aviv were a tinderbox waiting to be set alight.[39]

Unlike the Nebi Musa disturbances, the precise circumstances that ignited the riots in Jaffa on May 1, 1921, are well known. A small group of Jewish communists defied a government ban and held a noisy May Day parade through the few streets of Tel Aviv calling for the creation of a "Soviet Palestine." At some point, their procession collided with a larger, legally sanctioned demonstration organized by some Jewish socialists. A scuffle ensued, and the police intervened to disentangle the two groups by pushing the communists into an open space of sand dunes that separated Tel Aviv from Jaffa. As this otherwise minor and easily containable street clash among Jews unfolded, Arabs from Jaffa, armed with sticks, gathered to watch, before themselves deciding to join the melee. The police responded quickly and effectively, forming a cordon to separate the Arabs and the Jewish communists. Not content to go home, with their ardor for violence whetted, the Arab mob turned around and descended back into Jaffa, looting Jewish shops and assaulting Jewish shopkeepers and passersby. The rioters had ample targets.[40]

The Arab police once again joined the rioters or simply abandoned their posts. One senior Arab officer decided that the start of violence was an opportune moment to return home for lunch and clean his belt of some blood that had spattered it. Just as the Old City of Jerusalem's steep, narrow, and twisting alleyways had abetted the violence there the previous year, Jaffa's labyrinthine Old Town was well suited to sudden acts of anonymous violence and uncontrolled mayhem. Familiarity with the alleys and knowledge of rooftops afforded the miscreants both easy access to victims and a ready means of escape. The mob thus set upon a building where newly arrived Jewish immigrants were temporarily housed, raping and butchering its residents. The bloodshed continued throughout the day, as some Jews retaliated, attacking Arab targets. With nightfall, the disorders abated, leaving a grim toll of death and destruction. Twenty-seven Jews and three Arabs lay dead, and more than a hundred Jews and thirty-four Arabs were wounded.[41]

The new day brought renewed violence. Rioting spread from Jaffa to the suburb of Abu Kabir, where six more Jews were killed, and thence to the surrounding countryside. Both the Palestine government and the Haganah were stunned by the outbreaks and caught equally unprepared. Only days earlier, the Haganah had actually removed weapons from its Jaffa armory to protect the exposed Jewish settlements in the Galilee. Similarly, all the government's preparations and precautions had been focused on Jerusalem, where trouble had always previously flared. Not until May 3 did Samuel declare martial law. Troops were then rushed to Jaffa to restore order, and the Arab police there were disarmed. In a belated show of force, Royal Navy destroyers from the Suez Canal Zone were dispatched to Jaffa and Haifa. But after three days of carnage, events had gone too far to contain the bloodlust elsewhere. Some twenty-five thousand Muslim pilgrims had gathered in nearby Ramle for a festival at the tomb of Nebi Saleh, a seventh-century companion of the Prophet Muhammad. The following day they attacked the Jewish towns of Petah Tiqva, Rehovot, Hadera, and Kfar Saba, farther north. A lone RAF plane bombed and strafed the marauding Bedouin at Petah Tiqva. British military and police reinforcements together with Jewish settlers repulsed the remaining attacks. On May 7 the violence finally ended. A total of forty-seven Jews had been killed and 146 injured. Arab casualties were forty-eight dead and 73 wounded.[42]

Samuel's policy of studied impartiality, based on the hope that Palestine's Arabs would reconcile themselves to the concept of a Jewish national home in their country, was yet another victim of the violence. Not for the first time, a high commissioner had learned that goodwill and the best of intentions were completely inadequate in the face of sectarianism and atavistic fears of dispossession. Characteristically, his inclination was to conciliate rather than punish. The mob's singling out of the immigrant hostel as a target and the unmitigated brutality of the assault upon it convinced Samuel and his advisers that the new immigrants were the crux of the problem. As Keith-Roach later reflected, the Arabs resented and disliked the " 'new' Jews [who] were very different from the 'old' ones who had lived quiet lives" and were less politically active and aggressive, less boisterous, and indeed less numerous. Samuel, accordingly, announced a temporary suspension of Jewish immigration. The Yishuv denounced it as craven capitulation both to violence and to the threat of further violence. The colonial secretary, Winston Churchill, though publicly supportive, privately thought it spineless and mistaken. The press in London were equally condemnatory. "The stoppage of Jewish immigration into Palestine after the Jaffa riots is doubtless a temporary measure, but its wisdom is open to serious doubt," an editorial in *The Times* opined. Even the Arabs were not sated. Hailing the decision as a victory, they nonetheless continued to boycott Jewish shops in Jaffa. Arab boatmen also refused to bring ashore any travelers from ships docked in the harbor until a doctor examined and certified them not to be Jewish.[43]

Undeterred by either criticism or calumny, Samuel persisted in a dual-track strategy designed, on the one hand, to mollify Arab discontent and, on the other, to strengthen the government's powers to suppress lawlessness and deal more firmly with troublemakers. As subsequent events would show, the latter track proved the more successful of the two. Enacted in July, the Ordinance for the Prevention of Crime empowered the high commissioner to impose collective fines, or decree some other form of collective punishment, on groups of people or entire villages adjudged guilty of participating in, or abetting, civil disorder.[44]

With respect to the first track, however, Samuel's good intentions went tragically awry. As a result of the violence, the high commissioner decided to confirm the appointment of Haj Amin al-Husseini as mufti (Islamic religious leader) of Jerusalem and president of the Supreme Muslim Council. The council was the Muslim administrative entity responsible for community affairs that the Palestine government itself had created as the Arab counterpart to the Zionist Organization to represent Muslim interests much as the Zionist Organization represented the Yishuv's. The rationale behind putting a known rabble-rouser, one of the two Arab leaders convicted in absentia of fomenting the 1920 Nebi Musa disturbances, in these two key posts is alone questionable. Indeed, according to Keith-Roach, al-Husseini's "sole qualifications for the post were the pretensions of his family plus shrewd opportunism." But as Samuel's mostly laudatory biographer Bernard Wasserstein notes,

> Samuel could not, of course, foresee the Mufti's later role as the leader of the Palestine Arab revolt between 1936 to 1939, as organizer of an anti-British coup in Iraq in 1941, as broadcaster for the Nazis from Berlin, and as a Pied Piper who led his people into defeat, exile, and misery . . . Samuel never intended that the Mufti should become the single most powerful figure in Arab Palestine. That aggrandizement occurred gradually, and the plenitude of the Mufti's power became visible only after Samuel's departure from Palestine. Nevertheless, Husseini's earlier record in the 1920 riots might have given Samuel pause for thought.[45]

The appointment of the twenty-six-year-old al-Husseini had been championed by Storrs and his adviser on Arab affairs, Ernest Richmond, who would later resign over what he claimed was the administration's partiality toward the Jews. Storrs doubtless saw advantage in balancing the recent election of a member of the rival Nashashibi family as Jerusalem's mayor with an al-Husseini as mufti—these being among Arab Palestine's leading families. Al-Husseini certainly had the family pedigree for such an appointment: his grandfather, father, and elder brother had occupied the same post under the Turks. He also had a pedigree for challenging Zionism. His father had emerged as a vehement critic of Jewish immigration while serving as mufti at the end of the nineteenth century, arguing that all Jews who had arrived after 1891 should be pressed to leave of their own volition or face deportation. Further, in addition to his religious studies as a student at Cairo's prestigious al-Azhar University in 1912, the younger al-Husseini had organized a Palestinian student society to protest Zionism. In a meeting with Samuel arranged by Storrs, al-Husseini had promised the high commissioner that he would use his family's influence to ensure that the 1921 Nebi Musa festival remained peaceful. The fact that the festival did pass without incident likely also weighed favorably in Samuel's decision. Here, too, Samuel appears to have been misled by the articulate and persuasive al-Husseini. A distinguished Israeli historian of the Palestinian nationalist movement, Yehoshua Porath, subsequently unearthed evidence that although al-Husseini might have kept his word so far as Jerusalem was concerned, he was directly connected to the 1921 Jaffa disturbances.[46]

In a final sop to the Arabs, on June 3, in honor of the King's Birthday, the high commissioner sought to clarify the "unhappy misunderstanding" contained in the Balfour Declaration regarding British support for the establishment of a Jewish national home in Palestine. According to Samuel, this had been intended to suggest not that all Jews could immigrate to Palestine but that "some among them, within the limits that are fixed by the numbers and interests of the present population, should come to Palestine in order to help by their resources and efforts to develop the country, to the advantage of all its inhabitants." In practice, this meant that henceforth the number of Jewish immigrants allowed into Palestine would be determined on the basis of the contribution they would make to the country's economy. Samuel's formula was subsequently codified as policy in the white paper that the government issued on June 3, 1922.[47]

Named after the colonial secretary, the "Churchill White Paper" incorporated Samuel's ideas that in fact derived from a Colonial Office memorandum drafted nine months earlier that the high commissioner had mostly reframed and fleshed out. The white paper, however, was thus a critical restatement of British policy for Palestine. It was released only weeks after Churchill had defeated a House of Commons motion that sought to completely repudiate the mandate's terms and, as such, reverse the commitment contained in the Balfour Declaration. The new policy statement reaffirmed Britain's commitment to the establishment of a Jewish national home in Palestine and indeed the Jews' historical connection to the land. However, it also specifically upheld, and clearly highlighted the salience of, Arab rights in Palestine, stating that the government did not intend that the Jewish home should comprise the entire country. But even these concessions masquerading as clarifications failed to satisfy the Arabs. The Fifth Palestine Arab Congress, held in Nablus the following month, rejected the white paper in its entirety. The Jews, relieved that the Balfour commitment had not been completely jettisoned, acceded to the new policy—albeit with some privately voiced reservations.[48]

On July 22, 1922, the League of Nations formally granted the mandate for Palestine to Britain. The Arabs protested the mandate's establishment on the grounds that it violated not only the pledges of independence they had received from Britain in the 1915–16 McMahon-Hussein correspondence but also Article 22 of the League of Nations Covenant promising self-determination to "certain communities formerly belonging to the Turkish Empire." They particularly objected to the terms of Articles 2 and 6, which committed Britain to both establishing the Jewish national home in Palestine and facilitating Jewish immigration and land purchase.[49]

Worse still, Samuel had intended that the new policy not be seen either as blaming the victim by punishing the Yishuv for provoking Arab unrest or as conveying the impression to the Arabs that government policy could be influenced by violence. Instead, he hoped that Arab anxieties might be calmed without seriously harming Jewish immigration. Each community, however, drew its own conclusions. For the Yishuv, it was the beginning of the end of Britain's commitment to the Balfour Declaration. Even while disagreement continued over exactly how the Yishuv's defenses should be organized, a consensus was growing that the Jews could no longer rely completely on the British to protect them. The Haganah therefore now commenced in earnest the secret importation of arms to Palestine. A fund for this purpose was organized in London by Moshe Shertok (who later Hebraized his name to Sharett), Israel's first foreign minister and second prime minister, and David Hacohen, who was later elected to Israel's Knesset (parliament). For Palestine's Arabs, the lesson was equally clear. Whatever doubts they might previously have had were erased. The British government, they were now convinced, could indeed be threatened and coerced by violence into granting further political concessions.[50]

CHAPTER 2

The Seeds of Terror

For the next eight years, violent Arab protest ceased. There had been a flare-up in Jerusalem on November 2, 1921—the Balfour Declaration's fourth anniversary—when rioting erupted. But, unlike with previous incidents, the police were more effective, and the violence subsided. Even so, four Jews and an Arab died. The Ordinance for the Prevention of Crime—which embodied the military-oriented model of law enforcement derived from Britain's recent experiences in Ireland—coupled with improved policing, partly accounts for this development. The influx of experienced police officers from the disbanded Royal Irish Constabulary (RIC), and its notorious auxiliary force known as the Black and Tans, greatly strengthened the embryonic Palestine Gendarmerie. Indeed, almost the entire British section of the police consisted of former RIC personnel. In 1926, the Palestine Gendarmerie was reorganized and formally reconstituted as the Palestine Police Force (PPF). The emergence of a professional police force, staffed by men with extensive experience in controlling civil disorder, prompted London to reduce the military presence in Palestine to just one RAF squadron and two companies of armored cars.[1]

But the more significant factor accounting for the country's placidity was the traditional Arab elite's temporary reassertion of its control over the younger and more violent radicals who were inexorably transforming the Palestinian nationalist movement. Following the government's tough crackdown on Arab troublemakers in the wake of the 1921 riots, the elder leadership's counsels of patience and faith in negotiation prevailed over the movement—at least for the time being.[2]

These years were arguably the most tranquil the mandate would know. A "period of appeasement and development during which it seemed legitimate to hope that the two communities would settle down side by side" was how a 1946 analysis described it. Within months of the riots, for example, Tel Aviv's mayor, Meir Dizengoff, had expressed those same sentiments. "It cannot be denied that a kind of state of war exists between the Jews and our Arab neighbors," he accepted, "but it is, however, a peaceful war, a competition between different ideas and conceptions [and] between different kinds of energy and manners of life and work."[3]

Such expressions of optimism were seemingly validated by the 1927 countrywide municipal elections, which passed without incident, thus giving rise to hopes that an elected parliament representing all Palestine's peoples might yet be established. The "illusion that all was going well" in Palestine was also sustained by the unprecedented investment, population growth, building construction, and infrastructure development that occurred throughout the first decade of British rule. Nowhere was this more obvious than in the country's three major metropolitan centers: Jerusalem, Jaffa–Tel Aviv, and Haifa.[4]

Jerusalem was the heart of the British enterprise in Palestine. Nearly a century before, in 1839, Britain had been the first Western state to establish a consulate in the holy city, thus beginning a Victorian-era obsession with both Jerusalem and the Holy Land. Societies like the Palestine Exploration Fund (PEF) were established to champion British religious and archaeological interests. The PEF's activities often overlapped with Britain's less ethereal geostrategic, military, and imperial interests in the Holy Land, and it thus became a "front for intelligence work" immediately before World War I. The Wilderness of Zin Survey, an archaeological project that a young T. E. Lawrence helped undertake between 1912 and 1914, was, according to one historian, "nothing but a cover" for mapping work done by British military intelligence. The intense interest in the sacred sites aroused by biblical study inevitably led to a concomitant determination to protect and preserve the Old City's history and beauty.[5]

A town planning ordinance provided both for the restoration and renovation of the Old City and its holy properties and for the establishment in the new city of industrial, commercial, and residential zones as well as a "green belt" that encircled Jerusalem and preserved its stunning natural beauty. A modern road network was built, an electric power system was created, street lighting was installed, public gardens were laid out, and for the first time in centuries there was a clean and reliable water supply.[6]

In 1926 construction began on one of the city's most spectacular structures: the YMCA building with its soaring phallic tower. The noted American architect Loomis Harmon, who was simultaneously drawing the plans for New York City's Empire State Building, had designed it. Five years later another Jerusalem architectural icon opened across the street, which was then called Julian's Way and is now known as King David Street: the grandly imposing and luxurious King David Hotel. Office buildings, factories, shops, religious institutions, and sports facilities as well as houses and military installations were all products of the city's sudden construction boom. The massive Allenby Barracks complex in south Jerusalem, on the Hebron Road, was Jerusalem's largest military facility, and its garrison underpinned the local economy. Finally, some fifty new neighborhoods—two-thirds of them Jewish—were built.[7]

If Jerusalem was the heart of the British enterprise in Palestine, Tel Aviv was the central nervous system of the Jewish one. Described by one contemporary visitor as "the pulse beat of the entire land," by 1930 Tel Aviv consumed 80 percent of capital invested in Palestine and accounted for 60 percent of all Jewish industry and 70 percent of Jewish productivity. Nearly two-thirds of Jews employed in Palestine worked in Tel Aviv. In his farewell speech upon stepping down as high commissioner in 1925, Samuel paid homage to Tel Aviv's iconic status, describing it as "Palestine's city of wonders. One may compare it with the miraculous cities of the tales of the Arabian Nights, which blossom overnight in the desert." The economic depression that affected Palestine between 1925 and 1928 only seriously impacted Tel Aviv for one year—1926. By that time, the city's municipal budget had already overtaken Jaffa's and was the country's largest. In 1929, one visitor accurately summed up Tel Aviv as that "dream city washed ashore right near Jaffa."[8]

Haifa was different. Like Jerusalem, it was a place where Muslims, Christians, and Jews lived. But unlike that city, Haifa had no shrines of any significance associated with Islam, Christianity, or Judaism. People from each of those communities were thus attracted to the city (in nearly equal proportions, according to the 1928 census) for material, rather than spiritual, or even historical, reasons. Its thriving deepwater harbor, relatively temperate climate, and stunning, mountainous beauty proved a sufficient draw to Arabs, Jews, and Britons alike. Employment opportunities abounded, not only at the port, but with the civil service at the rail yards and surrounding workshops. The building of the oil pipeline from Kirkuk, Iraq, which terminated at Haifa, begun in 1932 and completed two years later, created still more jobs. Not surprisingly perhaps, Haifa's population underwent a fivefold expansion from 1918 to 1939 (eighteen thousand people to more than a hundred thousand). Where Jews were only a quarter of the population in 1922, nine years later they were a third. New Jewish neighborhoods, accordingly, multiplied between 1920 and 1923 on Mount Carmel and along the shoreline below. New Arab neighborhoods, mostly populated by Christians, were also established in the same areas. For the British, however, Haifa was valued most for geostrategic purposes. It was the first or last port of call linking the Mediterranean Sea by land to Britain's important imperial and trade interests in Trans-Jordan, Iraq, Iran, and India. Haifa's excellent naval facilities and proximity to Alexandria and the Suez Canal also gave the Royal Navy additional strategic depth from which to defend the vital waterway to the empire's outposts farther afield in Africa, South Asia, and the Far East.[9]

In sum, 1922 to 1928 was a uniquely halcyon period in Palestine. But the main reason for the country's quiescence, though not fully grasped at the time, sowed the seeds for the resumption of intercommunal violence—this time on an even grander scale. The aforementioned economic depression in Palestine had been triggered by the Polish currency crisis of 1925. This necessarily affected the financial prospects and economic comfort of the lower-middle-class Polish Jews who accounted for the bulk of Zionist immigrants during the 1920s. Fully 42 percent of immigrants settling in Tel Aviv, for example, came from Poland, thus earning the city the sobriquet Little Warsaw. Jewish immigration to Palestine thus fell from a record-setting 34,386 persons in 1925 to a little more than a seventh of that total during 1929. In fact, Jewish *emigration* exceeded immigration between 1926 and 1929. With so few Jews arriving and many more leaving, Arab restiveness was temporarily held in check. But impatience and frustration were growing among a younger, more activist generation of Palestinian nationalists. They watched anxiously as the Yishuv nonetheless experienced a net 50 percent population increase under British rule as their elders' nonviolent approaches failed to secure any definitive repudiation of Britain's support of Zionism.[10]

"Modern Arab politics," one historian of the Middle East has written, "depends in large measure upon a 'street,' an urban mob that can be summoned at will and given its marching orders, whether these be to provide a demagogue with a vocal and approving audience, [or] to intimidate political rivals." Between 1928 and 1929, Haj Amin al-Husseini, the mufti of Jerusalem, summoned such a mob in Palestine for exactly these purposes. In doing so, he infused the Palestinian nationalist movement with an emotive religious component that both energized and radicalized his followers. Further, through his mobilization of both the urban masses and the rural fellaheen (peasants or agricultural workers) around a common religious issue, al-Husseini was able to circumvent the traditional Arab leadership and thereby consolidate his position as the movement's preeminent head. He pressured the British for more political concessions, and the question of Palestine, until then a local dispute confined mostly to that country, was elevated to a pan-Arab, region-wide Islamic issue.[11]

The catalyst for the turmoil that would engulf Palestine at the close of the 1920s was a minor dispute that erupted over Jews' bringing chairs and benches with them while worshipping at Jerusalem's Western Wall. The Western Wall is Judaism's most sacred landmark, constituting the only remaining part of the Second Temple's outer wall built by King Herod around 19 B.C.E. but destroyed by the Romans in 70 C.E. For two thousand years since, Jews have mourned the temple's destruction and the exile from Zion that followed, and for at least the past millennium they have venerated and prayed at the wall. Muslims revere this same spot as well. Called the Buraq Wall (Ḥā'iṭ Al-Burāq), it forms the western boundary of the Temple Mount or Noble Sanctuary, Islam's third-holiest shrine, erected in the seventh century on the site of the Jews' destroyed Second Temple. Muslims believe that Muhammad tethered his horse, Buraq, at the wall before embarking on his *mihraj*, or ascent to heaven.[12]

The wall's religious pedigree apart, the prevailing consensus in 1920s Palestine was that it belonged to Muslims. Indeed, the pavement opposite had long been settled by Moroccan Muslims who attended to visiting pilgrims and maintained the surrounding area. Jews were allowed access to the wall by sufferance and custom rather than legal right. Adherence to the religious status quo had been clearly defined from the day British rule over Palestine began.[13]

To Muslims, the Jews' efforts to alter the status quo by bringing chairs and benches to the wall, however modest, were a harbinger of further designs to rebuild the Jewish temple. Years of constant bickering and recrimination were then unhelpfully electrified when the chief rabbi of the European (Ashkenazi) community issued a broadly worded decree calling for the temple's resurrection. Armed with this edict, a group of Jewish worshippers in September 1928 decided on Yom Kippur to place a larger than customary ark in front of the wall and to fasten a screen to the wall and the pavement in front of it to separate the male and female congregants, per Orthodox tradition. After the Muslim guardian of the site complained, Keith-Roach, who was then deputy district commissioner of Jerusalem, asked that the screen at least be removed before the Jews' morning prayers the next day and alerted the British police inspector on duty at the wall to ensure this was done. Morning found the screen still in place, so the police forcibly removed it—along with a rabbi who stubbornly clung to the prohibited item. Howls of protest erupted from both Jews and the Supreme Muslim Council. As the most powerful quasi-governmental, representative institution in Palestine, the council was responsible for most Arab community affairs, and Haj Amin al-Husseini was its president. In the aftermath of the contretemps over the screen, he adroitly exercised his political clout as head of the council while exploiting his religious authority as mufti to transform the dispute into a major issue. Within days, Haj Amin organized a mass rally at the al-Aqsa Mosque. A detailed memorandum to the government followed, and meetings were held between al-Husseini and senior British officials. Financial contributions were solicited as far afield as India to support the campaign to preserve Muslim access to the Noble Sanctuary, and leaflets in Palestine linked to the Supreme Muslim Council summoned the faithful to its defense.[14]

Meanwhile, Zionist agitation was becoming more feverish as well. Newspapers representing a cross section of the Yishuv's political spectrum repeatedly criticized British officials for their acceptance of Muslim claims to the wall. Even the moderate daily *Ha'aretz* proclaimed that the Yishuv's patience had been exhausted. A committee for the defense of the wall chaired by a leading Jewish scholar was established, and urgent telegrams were sent to community organizations and prominent Jews abroad soliciting financial, political, and moral support.[15]

At the center of this gathering storm was none other than Jabotinsky. Although Samuel's commutation of his prison sentence in 1920 also nullified the deportation order issued by the British military tribunal, Jabotinsky had been expelled from Palestine the following year on charges of incitement to violence during the 1921 disorders. The general quiescence in Palestine afterward had persuaded Lord Plumer, Samuel's successor as high commissioner, to allow the Zionist leader to return—on the condition that he abstain from politics. Jabotinsky thus arrived in Palestine that October—just as the controversy over the wall was heating up. His employment as an insurance agent, which was necessary to secure an entry visa, proved to be very short-lived. In November, Jabotinsky announced that he had been named editor in chief of *Doar Ha-yom*—the most militant of the Hebrew newspapers engaged in the dispute over the wall. Under Jabotinsky's editorship, it was poised to become even more aggressive.[16]

The newspaper provided Jabotinsky with an invaluable platform at a critical time in his political life. Five years earlier, he had resigned from his elected position on the Zionist Organization's executive committee. Its acceptance of the 1922 white paper and what Jabotinsky derided as its "minimalist" approach to Zionism had laid bare the ideological chasm separating him from his fellow Zionists. Jabotinsky insisted that a Jewish state would only be established through a "maximalist" interpretation of Britain's commitment to Zionism—that is, by ensuring Britain's full compliance with the Balfour Declaration's inalienable principles. Foremost among these, Jabotinsky argued, was an aggressively expansionist conception of a Jewish state that would in fact encompass both sides of the Jordan River. Jabotinsky also believed in a policy that would actively "liquidate the Diaspora" and encourage Jewish immigration to Palestine on a larger, more intensive scale. Accordingly, he demanded that Britain rescind the policy limiting Jewish immigration to Palestine (Jabotinsky's abiding, if misjudged, faith in the compatibility of British strategic interests in the eastern Mediterranean with Zionist aims in Palestine underlay his pursuit of these policies). Finally, with respect to the Yishuv's self-defense, Jabotinsky disdained the mainstream Zionists' emphasis on self-reliance and again insisted that Britain be pressed to faithfully fulfill its commitment to Zionism, which, he argued, included providing for the Yishuv's defense in concert with an officially sanctioned Jewish self-defense force.[17]

Perhaps Jabotinsky's most fundamental disagreement with mainstream Zionists, however, was over whether there could ever be any kind of modus vivendi with Palestine's Arabs. In a seminal 1923 article Jabotinsky declared that Zionism's aims would only ever be achieved through the construction, in cooperation with British arms, of an "iron wall that the indigenous population could not break." This separation of Arab and Jew was as obvious, Jabotinsky argued, as it was necessary. "It is impossible to dream, now and in the foreseeable future," he wrote, "of a voluntary agreement between Jews and the Palestinian Arabs . . . As long as the Arabs harbor even a glimmer of hope that they could get rid of us, no sweet talk or enticing promises will motivate the Arabs to abandon this hope, precisely because they are not a mob but a living nation."[18]

In order to attain these political aims, and thereby "revise" a Zionist ideal that Jabotinsky believed had been diluted and corrupted, he founded a new political party in 1925, the World Union of Zionist Revisionists, known as the Revisionist Party. Its youth wing was called Histadrut ha-Noar ha-Zioni ha-Activisti al Shem Joseph Trumpeldor (Organization of Zionist Activist Youth in the Name of Joseph Trumpeldor), more commonly referred to as Brit Trumpeldor or simply by its acronym, Betar. The word "Betar" carried the additional significance as the name of the site of the legendary Hebrew warrior Bar Kochbar's last stand against the Romans in 135 c.e. Affiliates were soon active throughout Poland and neighboring eastern European countries.[19]

The first Betar training school opened in Tel Aviv in 1928. Instruction consisted of military preparedness exercises, political awareness seminars, and attention to personal appearance. Among the new wave of Jewish immigrants who arrived in Palestine during 1929 were many Betar and

Revisionist Party members; it was a group of these Betarim who would trigger the violence that swept Palestine in August 1929.[20]

After a year of Arab and Jewish agitation and mounting tension, Palestine was primed to explode. The catalyst was one of the regular demonstrations that a Jewish committee in defense of the wall had organized. On August 14 some six thousand people gathered in Tel Aviv to denounce the government to chants of "The wall is ours!" That same evening, another crowd of around three thousand Jews converged on the wall for a prayer meeting and vigil that lasted until midnight. The following morning, the pious Jews coming to worship at the wall were joined by some three hundred Betarim wielding truncheons. The demonstrators raised the Jewish flag, stood in silence for two minutes, then sang the Zionist anthem, "Ha-Tikva" (The hope; now Israel's national anthem), and then dispersed. The British commission of inquiry appointed to investigate the violence that followed would later single out this incident as its cause.[21]

Word of the Jewish demonstration spread quickly among the Arabs the next day, Friday, the Muslim day of prayer. The Supreme Muslim Council quickly organized a protest to follow services at the al-Aqsa Mosque. At least two thousand worshippers, proclaiming, "There is no God but God; the religion of Mohammed came with the sword," attended the rally and then descended from the Noble Sanctuary to the wall, setting fire to Jewish prayer books and other devotional items. The next day, as both communities seethed with resentment and recrimination, some non-observant Jewish boys bored by the Sabbath were playing soccer on a field in Jerusalem's Bukharan quarter, which bordered the Arab neighborhood of Sheikh Jarrah. When an errant kick sent the ball into an Arab's tomato garden, one of the boys went to retrieve it, and a fight erupted. Several people were injured, and the Jewish youth who had gone to retrieve the ball was stabbed. He died three days later, on August 20.[22]

The funeral took place the following morning, and inflammatory eulogies crying for vengeance whipped up an estimated two thousand mourners who had gathered before the government hospital at the Russian Compound. The crowd then attempted to march down the adjacent Jaffa Road, Jerusalem's central artery, toward the Old City but did not get very far before encountering a double cordon of police drawn up in front of the Central Post Office. Refusing to halt or disperse, the procession had to be beaten back by baton-wielding police on horseback and on foot.[23]

"In Jerusalem there is great excitement," the August 22 edition of the

Arab newspaper *Falastin* (Palestine) observed. "The atmosphere is tense, and it is apprehended that tomorrow (Friday, August 23rd) when many fellaheen assemble for prayers in Jerusalem a substantial answer will be given to these incidents." The Hebrew-language press was similarly rife with rumors of impending Arab attacks designed to blunt a Jewish attempt to occupy the Noble Sanctuary. Belatedly, the Palestine government intervened to defuse the situation. The timing of this latest crisis could not have been worse. Both the high commissioner, Sir John Chancellor, and Attorney General Norman Bentwich were away on leave. It thus fell to the chief secretary, Sir Harry Luke, as acting high commissioner, to persuade both the mufti and the chief rabbi to arrange for sermons to be given on Friday and Saturday that would restrain their respective congregants. But it was too late. Already that day, there were reports of Arabs from surrounding towns and villages converging on Jerusalem armed with clubs, sticks, and other simple weapons.[24]

Friday prayers at the al-Aqsa Mosque on August 23 began inauspiciously. The *khatib*, or preacher, entered. He was attired, as usual, in the traditional green cloak worn by Muslim prelates in Jerusalem. As was also typical, he was preceded by a *kavass* (guard), who loudly struck the ground with his stave to announce the start of the service. What was atypical was the drawn sword that the *khatib* ostentatiously displayed. Sheikh Sa'ad el Din mounted the pulpit. After praising and thanking God, he called upon the faithful to defend Islam from the Jews and their plots to seize the Noble Sanctuary. "If we give way an inch to the Jews in regard to their demands at the Wailing Wall," he inveighed,

> they will ask for the Mosque of Aqsa; if we give them the Mosque of Aqsa they will demand the Dome of the Rock; if we give them the Dome of the Rock they will demand the whole of Palestine, and having gained the whole of Palestine they will proceed to turn us Arabs out of our country. I ask you now to take the oath of God the Great to swear by your right hand that you will not hesitate to act when called upon to do so, and that you will, if need be, fight for the Faith and the Holy Places to death.

The packed congregants raised their hands in unison and swore this pledge. "Then go," the sheikh instructed them, "pounce upon your enemies and kill that you in doing so may obtain Paradise."[25]

Around 12:30 p.m., Major Alan Saunders, the acting commandant of the PPF and one of its original and longest-serving British officers, received word that a large and unruly crowd of Arabs was leaving the Noble Sanctuary and heading in the direction of Jaffa Gate. About ten minutes later he saw a young Orthodox Jew run past with an Arab mob in pursuit. British police officers intervened, and the Jews' pursuers were driven off, but within minutes they were overwhelmed by hundreds of rioters streaming through the gate toward the Orthodox Jewish Mea Shearim neighborhood.[26]

Shouting, "The country is our country and the Jews are our dogs," and, "The religion of Mohammed came with the sword," the Arabs descended on the quarter with sticks, clubs, swords, and a handful of rifles. The Arab police again mutinied and joined the onslaught, at the end of which twenty-nine Jews lay dead and forty-three injured. Thirty-eight Arabs had also died: twenty-six from bullet wounds inflicted by the security forces. Fifty-one others were wounded.[27]

The beleaguered police and handful of troops on hand in Palestine could do little to stem the violence. Successive government fiscal crises since 1922 had impacted the police more severely than any other arm of the Palestine government; the force was thought to be a quarter of its required establishment on the eve of the 1929 riots. The British police contingent comprised roughly a fifth of the approximately fifteen hundred officers in the PPF, while the entire British military contingent in Palestine consisted of fewer than a hundred soldiers with six armored cars and five or six flight-worthy aircraft. As the violence intensified, Luke telegraphed the Colonial Office in London requesting that at least a battalion of troops (that is, six hundred men) be sent from Egypt to Palestine without delay. He also wired the Royal Navy base at Malta asking for naval assistance. In the meantime, fifty Oxford University theology students, studying in Jerusalem over their summer vacation, were enrolled as special police constables. The first military reinforcements, a contingent of sixty men, arrived in Palestine about 5:00 p.m. on Saturday, August 24, but by then the violence had spread beyond Jerusalem.[28]

For at least four hundred years, the small Jewish enclave in Hebron had lived in peace with its Arab neighbors. One of four holy cities in Judaism (Jerusalem, Tiberias, and Safed are the others), Hebron is the site of the biblical Cave of the Patriarchs, a place sacred to Jews, Christians, and Muslims alike, where Abraham, Sarah, Isaac, Rebecca, Jacob, and Leah are believed to be buried. The five hundred or so Orthodox, apolitical and mostly non-Zionist, Jews who lived there had remained blissfully aloof from the nationalist ferment that had gripped Palestine for most of the preceding decade. Indeed, according to two Jewish survivors, even as news of the violence that had convulsed Jerusalem reached Hebron on Friday afternoon, the anxious Jewish community took comfort from the assurances received from their Arab neighbors that "there could never be a pogrom" in Hebron because the city had remained so quiet during all prior disturbances. Hebron's Arabs had told Raymond Cafferata, the assistant district superintendent and the only British police officer in the city, the same thing. A letter written by the Hebron residents Aharon Reuven Bernzweig and his wife, Breine Zuch Bernzweig, to their children only days later describes the tragic chain of events that unfolded over the next twenty-four hours. It corresponds with the testimony Cafferata gave before the Shaw Commission the following November.[29]

Friday afternoon in Hebron was tense but quiet. News began to trickle in of the violence in Jerusalem. Groups of Arabs were reportedly roaming Jerusalem's streets and had beaten several Jews. Cafferata, accordingly, instructed the Jewish community to stay inside and lock their doors. "Suddenly, just one hour before candle lighting," the Bernzweigs recounted, "pandemonium broke loose. Window panes were smashed on all sides. In our building, they broke every window and began throwing stones inside. We hid ourselves. They were breaking windows in all the Jewish homes. Now we were in deathly fear." But just as the Jews began to panic, mounted police arrived, and, according to the Bernzweigs, "all became still outside. We thought our salvation had come." As soon as he had learned of the attacks, Cafferata ordered his meager force of eighteen mounted Arab police and fifteen elderly Arab foot patrolmen—who, he later recalled, were "practically useless" because of their age—to the Jewish quarter and to the city's outskirts, respectively, to report any suspicious traffic coming from Jerusalem. He also contacted police headquarters in Jerusalem and urgently requested reinforcements. None, however, could be spared. Although there were fewer than three dozen policemen to contend with a population of twenty-four thousand Arabs in Hebron and another sixty thousand in the surrounding area, the patrols that Cafferata had deployed proved effective, and there were no further incidents that night. But any hope that the worst had passed was soon shattered.[30]

Early Saturday morning, cars packed with Arabs brandishing long iron bars, big knives, and axes, and screaming that they were going to slaughter Jews in Jerusalem, raced up and down Hebron's streets. Mounted on horseback, Cafferata cautiously eyed the crowd now gathering before him. Suddenly two Jewish yeshiva students appeared. In an instant, the mob was after them. Cafferata intervened, shooting two Arabs and emptying his pistol before the swarming mass enveloped both him and the two students. The latter were mercilessly stoned to death, while Cafferata was knocked off his horse. Jumping to his feet, he ordered the handful of policemen beside him to form a firing line and shoot into the crowd. Although some of the rioters dispersed, others, shouting, "On to the Ghetto," simply rushed past Cafferata and his men. Just after 8:00 a.m., the first sounds of a massacre in progress were heard. "Screams pierced the heart of the heavens," the Bernzweigs recalled. Cafferata took off in pursuit. In his report to headquarters, he described what happened next:

> On hearing screams in a room I went up a sort of tunnel passage and saw an Arab in the act of cutting off a child's head with a sword. He had already hit him and was having another cut, but on seeing me he tried to aim the stroke at me, but missed; he was practically on the muzzle of my rifle. I shot him low in the groin. Behind him was a Jewish woman smothered in blood with a man I recognized as a police constable named Issa Sherif from Jaffa in mufti. He was standing over the woman with a dagger in his hand. He saw me and bolted into a room close by and tried to shut me out—shouting (in Arabic) "Your Honour, I am a policeman." . . . I got into the room and shot him.[31]

The carnage went on for another two and a half hours before Cafferata and his men were able to restore at least a semblance of order. Hebron would account for the largest toll of Jewish deaths and injuries in the violence that continued for another week. Sixty-four Jews lay dead, and fifty-four others were wounded. Only one had been killed by a bullet; all the others had variously been stabbed, hacked, bludgeoned, or stoned to death. Had some Arab families not hidden or protected their Jewish neighbors, Cafferata later reflected, "not a Jewish soul in Hebron would have been saved." That was how the Bernzweigs survived.[32]

But the Jewish community in Hebron was no more. The remaining 435 persons were evacuated three days later "practically naked and barefoot," having lost everything. Following the Six-Day War in 1967, a group of politically far-right Orthodox Jews, led by Rabbi Moshe Levinger and calling themselves Gush Emunim (Bloc of the Faithful), reestablished a continuing Jewish presence in Hebron's Jewish quarter that has been a source of contention in contemporary Palestinian-Israeli relations since. As for Cafferata, he was awarded the King's Police Medal for gallantry and thereafter was known as "the Man of Lead" for having single-handedly stood down seven hundred rioters that Saturday morning and rescued Hebron's Jews.[33]

The rest of Palestine, meanwhile, was collapsing into anarchy that same Saturday morning. Just as the anti-Jewish violence was abating in Hebron, it was gathering momentum outside Motza, a village to the west of Jerusalem. A crowd of Arabs descended on a house belonging to a Jewish family, killing the father and mother, their two daughters, a son, and two guests before setting it and an adjacent stable on fire (one son escaped). Farther north, Arab mobs tried to storm the police barracks in Nablus and attacked Jews in the town of Beisan (now called Bet Shean). By noon, the situation throughout the country was so perilous that the PPF informed Luke that the police could no longer accept responsibility for public security. An RAF group captain, the most senior military officer then present in Palestine and Trans-Jordan, assumed command of all security force operations. In hopes of dampening any further incitement, the Palestine government also ordered the suspension of all newspapers. Only in Jaffa and Haifa, however, were the police successful in preventing any escalation of the anti-Jewish violence.[34]

Astonishingly, it was not until Tuesday, August 27, that any meaningful number of reinforcements had either set out for or arrived from Egypt and Malta. These included three battalions of troops (approximately eighteen hundred men), a company of armored cars, an RAF squadron, and five warships with landing parties equivalent to a battalion in strength. They did not, however, make it in time to save the Jews of Safed. Another ancient Jewish city of piety and learning, Safed is perhaps best known as the spiritual center of Kabbalah, or Jewish mysticism. Like Hebron, it had been seemingly immune to the violent political currents that had continually swept through Palestine in recent years. By August 29, nearly a week had passed without incident since the disorders had commenced in the south. It might have been reports that a detachment of British troops was en route to Safed to protect its small Jewish population that inflamed the city's ten thousand Arab residents, but whatever the case, that morning an Arab mob rushed into the Jewish quarter and within twenty minutes had killed fifteen Jews and injured thirty-three others. As in Hebron, it was a young British police officer, Assistant Superintendent J. A. M. Faraday, who saved the day. The lone Briton among a small contingent of Arab police, his prompt intervention averted further bloodshed. The troops arrived two hours later, but even their presence could not prevent the looting and burning of Jewish homes that continued until the end of the month. As at Hebron, the report of the Palestine government's director of health cited the ferocity of the attacks on Safed's Jews as evidenced by the multiple injuries sustained from knives, sticks, staves, clubs, and other blunt instruments.[35]

What had begun eleven months earlier as a dispute over some furniture being brought to the Western Wall ended in August 1929 with the deaths of 133 Jews and injuries to 339 others. Arab casualties were nearly as high—116 killed and 232 wounded. However, whereas the former were the victims of lawlessness and wanton bloodletting, the latter were mostly inflicted by government security forces attempting to maintain order. At least twenty Jewish communities across Palestine had come under Arab attack. This unprecedented violence was a turning point in the history of both British rule and Arab and Jewish relations.[36]

For the British, the 1929 riots necessitated yet another investigative commission, another white paper, and another clarification of government policy at the expense of Zionism. The Shaw Commission, named for its chairman, a distinguished colonial judge, arrived in Palestine only weeks after the disturbances. Its report was issued the following March and concluded that the Arab violence was "neither provoked, premeditated, nor directed against the British Administration." Instead, it was prompted by Arab fears of Jewish political and economic domination that would lead to the loss of their land and livelihood. "Excessive" Jewish immigration in 1925 and 1926 and attendant land purchases, the commission's members believed, had heightened these concerns and set in motion the tragic chain of events that culminated in the widespread violence.[37]

The mufti and the Arab Executive (AE)—the committee established in 1920 by Palestine's Arab leaders to represent their community—were exonerated from any complicity in either planning or inciting the disturbances. The report, however, blamed both for fostering the climate of hatred and vituperation that had led directly to the disorders (in a written dissent published as an annex to the report, one of the commission's members, a Labour MP named Henry Snell, pointedly disagreed with this conclusion and placed the onus of responsibility on the mufti). The Palestine government was also held blameless for its response once the rioting had begun. The report made several recommendations, the most important of which was that the British government issue a clear statement of policy pledging itself to safeguard the rights of Palestine's non-Jewish communities—especially with respect to Jewish immigration and land purchase. Another recommendation called upon the government to issue a clear statement regarding its policy on Jewish immigration as well as to conduct a review of how the annual quotas were determined. It further recommended that "non-Jewish interests" also be accorded some voice in immigration policy.[38]

Although the report generally satisfied the Arabs, the Arab Executive argued that it should also have called for the cessation of Jewish immigration, a ban on Jewish land purchase, and the establishment of a democratic government in Palestine based on proportional representation. The Yishuv bristled at being blamed and punished for the violence directed against it. The official Zionist response to the report, however, chose to emphasize the need for a clear and expanded government commitment to protect the Yishuv alongside the initiation of an official program whereby Jews would be trained and armed in their own defense. One of the report's positive outcomes for the Yishuv, accordingly, was the subsequent establishment of a Jewish special auxiliary constabulary within the PPF, complete with sufficiently stocked armories.[39]

The League of Nations' Permanent Mandates Commission took an especially dim view of the report, rejecting its conclusion that the disturbances were not premeditated and that they therefore could have been neither anticipated nor prevented. The British government and the Palestine administration were faulted not only for ignoring "the social and economic adaptation of the Arab population to the new conditions due to Jewish immigration" but for having stationed insufficient security forces in Palestine, thus failing to provide "the essential condition for development of the Jewish National Home, security for persons and property." The British government was nonplussed by the criticism and simply ignored it.[40]

The Shaw Commission Report also set in motion a complete overhaul of the PPF. The riots had clearly revealed the damage done to the police by cutbacks in funding. The police's failure either to prevent or to contain the riots, however, was also the product of the force's Arab contingent and its inadequate intelligence apparatus. As had happened in 1920 and 1921, many Arab police not only had made no effort to stop the violence but had joined the attacks on Jews. This disgraceful behavior was somewhat mitigated by the gallant performance of the force's relatively new British Section. Although for the time being there was no formal reversal of policy, it was obvious that in the future the British Section would be primarily responsible for public security. Indeed, more than twice as many British as Palestinian recruits (523 versus 221) entered the force following the riots. To redress the PPF's overall manpower deficiency, the Colonial

Office granted permission for the immediate recruitment of an additional fifteen British and thirteen Palestinian senior officers and more than five hundred British and two hundred Palestinian constables.[41]

The other problems undermining the police force's performance were less easily dealt with because their amelioration required changes in the police force's policy, orientation, and structure. The Colonial Office, accordingly, asked Herbert Dowbiggin, the inspector general of police in Ceylon (now Sri Lanka), to undertake a comprehensive assessment of the PPF and make recommendations on its reorganization.[42]

With respect to the force's British contingent, Dowbiggin sought to engage them more in the day-to-day policing duties of crime prevention and patrolling. He hoped that this would better integrate the British police with their Arab and Jewish counterparts and also give them a better understanding of the country's populace and local conditions. In addition, Dowbiggin recommended that the number of police stations be increased from 88 to 116 and that army units be co-located with police. He believed this was necessary both to buttress the defenses at isolated posts and to facilitate the rapid deployment of a well-armed intervention force to nip any trouble in the bud. Accordingly, two British infantry battalions totaling some fifteen hundred men along with twelve aircraft and seven armored cars were permanently stationed in Palestine.[43]

Dowbiggin, though, was especially scathing in his criticism of the police force's criminal investigation department (CID), describing it as the "weakest spot in the Force." He blamed it for the police force's failure to appreciate the depth of Arab discontent or to anticipate the violence that it ignited. As the department specifically charged with the acquisition, analysis, and dissemination of political intelligence, the CID had also been faulted by the Shaw Commission for failing to furnish the PPF with the information that should have warned of the disturbances. Dowbiggin concluded that this was because the department was too narrowly focused on monitoring actual subversive political activities as opposed to fully understanding the country's religious and social dynamics.[44]

The changes to intelligence gathering and analysis that Dowbiggin mandated were systemic and far-ranging. The CID was to be reorganized into specific sections responsible for both criminal investigation and countering subversion.[45]

The broader policy implications of the Shaw Commission Report, fortunately for the Yishuv, proved less durable. A new government white paper—known as the Passfield White Paper—followed in October 1930. It further clarified Britain's obligations to Palestine's Arab and Jewish communities, revising the Jewish immigration quota to include a condition that it not adversely impact Arab employment. The white paper also committed the government to fulfill the Arab leadership's long-standing demand for a proportionally representative legislative council and to facilitate some limited, future immigration of non-Palestinian Arabs to the country. The Passfield White Paper is noteworthy for two reasons. First, it again confirmed the impression among Palestine's Arabs that government policy could indeed be influenced by violence. Second, its provisions were never implemented. Four months later, Prime Minister Ramsay MacDonald wrote to Weizmann assuring him that Jewish immigration would continue without either government interference or any reference to Arab job prospects—in effect reversing the Passfield White Paper. It is not surprising, therefore, that the Arabs termed this additional clarification of policy the MacDonald "Black Letter."[46]

Meanwhile, courts sitting in Palestine were busy adjudicating the cases of some 700 Arabs accused of murder and looting and of about 160 Jews who, despite claiming to have acted in self-defense, had been charged with murder. Fifty-five Arabs were convicted of capital crimes and nearly half that number sentenced to death, as was one Jew. However, the high commissioner commuted the sentences to life imprisonment for all but three Arabs, who were hanged in June 1930. The condemned men were heralded by their co-religionists as "heroes, martyrs, and victims of imperialism."[47]

For Palestine's Arabs, the disturbances were regarded as the first tangible manifestation of an uprising against Britain's support of Zionism. The rapidity with which the entire country was summoned in the name of Islam and in defense of Jerusalem's Noble Sanctuary was not lost on the mufti and his acolytes. "Instead of abstract nationalist slogans about self-determination, majority rights, etc.," the historian Yehoshua Porath explains, "they now had a concrete symbol which was clearly understood by the Muslim masses." The effective fusing of religion and politics enabled Haj Amin to burnish his reputation and position himself as the Palestinian Arabs' preeminent leader. Arab disquiet would henceforth neither abate nor be sated by anything short of Britain's unambiguous disavowal of the Balfour Declaration.[48]

"The events of August last cannot easily be forgotten," the Shaw Commission Report had warned. Indeed, nearly a century later, the 1929 riots and the Hebron massacre in particular are still looked upon by many Jews as a watershed in the history of the Yishuv, in its relations with Palestine's

Arabs, and in the lineage of Jewish self-defense efforts that eventually resulted in the birth of the State of Israel and establishment of the Israel Defense Forces. It was now clear that the Yishuv could no longer remain dependent on British guns and bayonets for its protection; it required a fully trained, suitably prepared, and well-armed self-defense force of its own.[49]

The outbreak, magnitude, and rapid escalation of the disturbances had caught the Jewish leadership as completely off guard as it had the British. The Zionist Executive, for instance, had departed Palestine in late July to attend the biennial Zionist Congress in Zurich, Switzerland, and thus were also away during the worst of the violence. The Haganah had nonetheless swung into action as soon as the rioting had erupted in Jerusalem. Its commanders requested permission from Luke to arm five hundred of its fighters and deploy them in defensive positions throughout the country. The chief secretary refused, citing the government's view that any Jewish action was likely to provoke further Arab violence. The Haganah commanders, however, ignored him and did whatever they could to defend the Yishuv. The group's shortcomings were evidenced by the large number of Jewish casualties.[50]

The Haganah, the Yishuv's leaders concluded, clearly lacked sufficient quantities of arms and ammunition. Training had been rudimentary and too informally organized, run by small teams of volunteers who arranged meetings and exercises under the guise of youth sports and other recreational programs. Upon returning to Palestine, Ben-Gurion, the Histadrut's director, pressed for the allocation of additional funds to the Haganah, arguing that the "self-defense forces saved the Yishuv from destruction. The riots' first lesson to the Yishuv and Zionism is the consolidation and strengthening of the Haganah." It was agreed to reorganize and centralize the Haganah command, to increase funding of the group, and to improve recruitment procedures and training. Civilian control of the Haganah passed from the Histadrut, which could no longer afford to underwrite the costs of a self-defense force, to the recently created Jewish Agency, the political institution established by the Zionist Organization earlier in 1929 to oversee Jewish immigration, land purchase, and settlement in Palestine.[51]

The issue of Jewish self-defense nevertheless continued to be the politically partisan issue it had become when the Haganah had first associated itself with the Histadrut eight years before. Many Betarim belonged to the Haganah, and during the 1929 disturbances they had defended the Yishuv either in that capacity or as independent Betar units. The ideological differences separating the Labour socialists from the Revisionists proved irreconcilable, and in 1931 a dispute arose between Haganah headquarters and its Jerusalem commander, Abraham Tehomi, a staunch Revisionist Party member. Tehomi's ideological affiliation, coupled with his stubborn independence and aggressive interpretation of Haganah defense policies, had brought him into repeated conflict with his superiors. Their disagreements finally exploded in April, when Tehomi, accusing the Haganah of discriminating against its nonsocialist members, quit. A majority of the Jerusalem detachment followed him and, armed with weapons taken from the Haganah's local armory, announced the formation of a new Jewish self-defense force that they called the Haganah-Bet (*bet* being the second letter in the Hebrew alphabet). Members of the Haganah unit in Tel Aviv along with students from that city's Betar school also joined the new group, as did some similarly disgruntled Haganah members from Haifa and Safed.[52]

The Haganah-Bet, however, did not officially align itself with the Revisionist Party. Although its members were overwhelmingly Revisionists or Betarim, the party did not exercise direct influence over the new organization, nor did Jabotinsky occupy any formal position. Instead, a civilian board representing all the Yishuv's nonsocialist political parties was created to provide guidance and advice. Tehomi was appointed the Haganah-Bet's commander. Recruits continued to be drawn from various local sports clubs, like the Maccabee association, but also from students at Jerusalem's new Hebrew University. The new force's training generally resembled that of the original Haganah—marching drills, field exercises, conditioning, and the use and care of small arms. But unlike the Haganah, the Haganah-Bet did not see itself as a self-defense force. And it therefore did not limit its training to defensive tactics only. Instead, the Haganah-Bet provided instruction in more offensively minded operations, including sabotage, bomb making, and hit-and-run attack—in other words, the core tactics of terrorism.[53]

CHAPTER 3

Red Days of Riots and Blood

Palestine had always exhibited a remarkable ability to reset itself back to some semblance of normality following each violent spasm of unrest and upheaval. The aftermath of the 1929 riots similarly brought a return to the tense tranquillity that passed for civility under British rule. There were no new serious outbreaks of violence for the next seven years. This was also a time when the country prospered and the benefits of British governance were arguably most evident to Palestine's inhabitants. Investment in building and infrastructure was transforming the country both economically and aesthetically. In Jerusalem, such architectural gems as Government House and the King David Hotel were constructed between 1929 and 1931 and remain among the lasting examples of this burst of public and private construction. The pipeline linking the oil fields in Kirkuk, Iraq, with the newly built refinery at Haifa was completed soon after, thus further reinforcing that port city's—and in turn Palestine's—economic and strategic importance to the British Empire.[1]

Government district officers were especially active throughout this period, providing services in health, education, urban development, and agriculture to Palestine's populace. Those responsible for rural areas often made their rounds on horseback, sometimes accompanied by a doctor, calling at villages and arranging for medical care, the building or staffing of schools, the allocation of government money to dig new wells, the building and repair of roads, and help with agriculture. The latter category embraced a vast array of government benefits that were routinely provided free of charge to Arab villages and Jewish settlements alike. It "was a tremendous lovely life to lead in the open air doing what we were there for," Stewart Perowne, an Education Department official, recalled. The incidence of smallpox and cholera was greatly reduced, and the availability of chlorinated water and pasteurized milk in the more developed areas of the country increased appreciably. The number of children attending government schools doubled, creating a new problem—overcrowding. The country's British rulers might therefore be forgiven the conceit that the new decade heralded a new era of peace and prosperity for Palestine in contrast to the bloodshed and disorder of the previous one.[2]

In November 1931, Lieutenant General Sir Arthur Wauchope succeeded Chancellor as high commissioner. Wauchope, the only one of Palestine's seven high commissioners ever to be reappointed to a second term, was also perhaps the most colorful and eccentric. The new high commissioner was also remarkable for his complete and utter lack of favoritism between Arab and Jew. Wauchope, for instance, used his own money to fund agricultural projects for Arab villages, including an experimental hill fruit cultivation station, and was never more pleased than when he was called a "friend of the fellah [Arab peasant]." In addition, Wauchope personally paid for the construction of new schools for Arab children. He was also intensely interested in Jewish agriculture and the development of kibbutzim (rural farming communities) and demonstrably sympathetic to the Zionist cause. "Apart from helping us on immigration," Ben-Gurion recalled, "Wauchope seemed to have a deeper understanding than any other High Commissioner of what we were trying to do in Palestine, that we were not only trying to develop a country but also revive our nation."[3]

At the same time, the high commissioner also maintained good relations with the mufti, who he believed exercised a moderating influence over the Arab community. Wauchope had standing instructions that letters from the mufti were to be answered the same day—and the reply dispatched by hand via special messenger. He also repeatedly turned a blind eye to the Supreme Muslim Council's money problems and sloppy bookkeeping. Finally, Wauchope reportedly never once threatened to cut off government funding when seditious sermons were preached in mosques under the council's aegis.[4]

Adolf Hitler's ascent to power in Germany, however, would have a profoundly destabilizing effect on Palestine. On January 30, 1933, the Nazi Party leader was sworn in to office as *Reich* chancellor. It was not long before the aggressive persecution of the country's Jews commenced; by the end of the year, accordingly, thirty-seven thousand Jews had left Germany—including the nearly seven thousand who immigrated to Palestine.[5]

The German refugees constituted almost a quarter of the record thirty thousand Jewish immigrants, mostly from Poland, who arrived in Palestine during 1933. This figure was in fact greater than the total of the previous six years combined. The number of refugees settling in Palestine increased to forty-two thousand during 1934 and peaked at sixty-two thousand the following year. The country's Jewish population thus expanded by more than 80 percent between 1933 and 1935. Jews now made up 27 percent of Palestine's total population of 1.3 million people compared with just 16 percent in 1931. Jewish land purchases from Arabs increased commensurately. Between 1930 and 1932, for instance, Jews bought from Arabs an average of nineteen thousand dunams—a unit of measurement used during the Ottoman Empire equaling slightly less than a quarter of an acre—per year of land. This nearly doubled in 1933 (to thirty-seven thousand dunams) and again in 1934 (to sixty-two thousand dunams). In 1935 alone Jews acquired seventy-three thousand dunams. Palestine's Arabs, meanwhile, watched these developments with grave concern as the new immigrants and their money transformed their land.[6]

In point of fact, Arab restiveness and resistance to the Zionist enterprise had never abated. It was not long after the 1929 riots that word of continued anti-Jewish violence reached Jerusalem. A police intelligence report for the week ending October 19, 1929, stated that an Arab gang rumored to number some four hundred men was terrorizing Jews in the Safed area. The gang, which was known among Arabs as the Green Hand, actually consisted of no more than about twenty-five men. Significantly, they considered themselves mujahideen—or holy warriors, thus underscoring the fusion of religion and nationalism into the powerful rebellious force that the 1929 riots had achieved. A more detailed report followed a week later that revealed an organized campaign of sedition abetted by the Supreme Muslim Council and funded by the Arab Executive. A combined force of army and police eliminated the Green Hand early in 1930. That was the good news. The bad news was that the authorities had determined it was actually a prototype of sorts to test the waters for resuming the inchoate revolt that the 1929 riots had started. Although this initial experiment had failed, Chancellor worried that similar groups would follow.[7]

Chancellor's prediction initially proved inaccurate. Whatever plans for renewed rebellion were being made in the countryside, it was the increased pace of Jewish immigration and concomitant land purchase that preoccupied the mostly urban-based Arab leadership for the next three years. Hitler had been in power less than a month when the Arab Executive met to discuss how the Arabs might make their displeasure with the government's abandonment of the Passfield White Paper known. Their concerns were indeed well-founded; just when Nazi persecution was escalating, MacDonald's "Black Letter," reaffirming Britain's support for Zionism, had in effect flung open the gates of Palestine to Jews seeking to flee Germany and neighboring countries. Editorials and stories in the

Arab press painted a dire picture of ongoing and increasing Jewish immigration, and in March 1933 the Arab Executive issued a sternly worded manifesto criticizing the British government's decision to permit "the discarded Jews outcast by Germany" to immigrate to Palestine. But the Arab leadership was again coming to the conclusion that words alone would have little effect and therefore called for a mass protest to be held in Jerusalem on October 13, 1933.[8]

Just past noon on the appointed day, a crowd that the police estimated to number about two thousand people assembled at the Temple Mount. The plan was to march in protest to the government offices just outside Damascus Gate. The police, however, were ready and waiting. A cordon of some sixty men, including twenty mounted police, had drawn up outside the city walls to meet the procession as soon as it left the Old City. The officer in command repeatedly warned the demonstrators to disperse, but the crowd continued to surge forward, egged on by a cadre of more militant, younger leaders who had seized control of the march. The police charged, their baton blows met with successive volleys of stones. Within an hour, the melee was over with neither the police nor the marchers having sustained serious injury.[9]

The Arab Executive was disappointed. It had hoped to attract a broad cross section of city and country Arabs alike from throughout Palestine. Very few protesters not already resident in Jerusalem, however, had bothered to come. Accordingly, the Arab leadership announced that another demonstration would be held two weeks later, this time in Jaffa. Both sides now had ample time to plan. The biggest challenge that the police faced was the budgetary constraints that had deprived it of even proper riot-control gear. Accordingly, Harry Rice, the CID's chief, instructed one of his staff to come up with a solution. The young corporal returned a couple of hours later with fifty ordinary baking pans each twenty inches in diameter. His clever idea was to weld handles with padded straps onto the pans, thus turning them into shields. The transformation was hastily effected in the PPF's Jerusalem workshop, and the makeshift shields were dispatched to Jaffa in advance of the scheduled protest.[10]

Friday, October 27, was the Muslim holy day. A larger number of worshippers than usual packed Jaffa's mosques that morning. The tension, almost imperceptible to begin with, had risen with the heat of the day as a large crowd continued to gather in the main square, beneath its distinctive Ottoman-era clock tower, awaiting the end of prayers. Sensing trouble, shopkeepers quickly shuttered their businesses, and passersby hurried away. Shortly after noon, the mosques emptied, and suddenly thousands of men were pouring into the square. Facing them was a line of some sixty police, wearing steel helmets and armed with truncheons and the baking pan shields. A screen of twenty dismounted Bedouin constables from the PPF Camel Corps headquarters in Beersheba were positioned in front of the police line with an additional forty officers mounted on horseback behind. The official estimate put the crowd at seven thousand people— with fewer than a hundred police arrayed against them. The officer in charge was Deputy Superintendent Faraday, who had distinguished himself four years earlier in Safed, when he had saved that town's Jewish community during the 1929 riots. Standing in the ranks, in command of one of the PPF's detachments, was also Assistant Superintendent Cafferata, the hero of Hebron. He was ordered to lead the first baton charge in hopes of dispersing the crowd. It had no effect; three or four more charges were launched before complete pandemonium broke out.[11]

Colin Imray, a young police recruit manning the cordon, recalled the chaos around him: "Stones came from everywhere and seemed to hit friend and foe alike." Faraday now realized that the grievously outnumbered police were rapidly losing control and were also unable to extricate their injured comrades from the mob. Accordingly, at 12:20 Faraday ordered a fifteen-man police firing party waiting in reserve into the square. He again told the crowd to disperse. When it refused, Faraday issued the command to open fire. It took three successive volleys to disperse the mob; a fourth volley was directed at Arab gunmen shooting at the police from a café. Two hours passed before order was completely restored. By that time, one Arab policeman lay dead, and fifty-six other officers had been wounded, three seriously. Twenty-six demonstrators had been killed and nearly two hundred others injured. "It was an awful day," the British constable A. L. Abraham later wrote. "Little did we realize what the years ahead would bring."[12]

Word of the events in Jaffa quickly spread. That same evening an Arab mob numbering some two thousand people rioted in Haifa, assaulting Jews and repeatedly stoning the police struggling to maintain order. Gunfire was again required to quell the disturbances. Even still, the disorders continued the next morning. When they finally ended, four Arabs had lost their lives, and sixteen police had been wounded. Another Arab demonstrator was shot dead by police that same day in Nablus, where things had also gotten out of hand. There were two more spasms of rioting in Jerusalem on October 28 and 29 before the police finally regained control— with the assistance of two squadrons of RAF fighter aircraft deployed from Egypt that repeatedly buzzed the crowd before it finally dispersed.[13]

In contrast to previous disturbances, the police had performed remarkably well, as the report from the inevitable commission of inquiry that followed attested. It was the Arab leadership, however, who drew the most important lessons from the disturbances. This was the first time that the protests had been organized and not spontaneous, proving that the Arab leadership was able not only to mobilize the masses but also to control them. The implications of this newly found power, coupled with the new self-confidence it bred, would shortly be revealed on a far more extensive and consequential scale. For the moment, however, the disorders had clearly depicted the depth of Arab anger over Jewish immigration and land purchase and, even more so, the sense of betrayal and unconcealed hostility felt toward the government. This was an especially dire development. For the first time Zionism became equated with British imperialism, spawning an enmity that would henceforth be directed with equal fervor against both.[14]

Indeed, having concluded that no change in British policy would be achieved through the traditional leadership's strategy of strikes and demonstrations, much less by negotiation and entreaty, a more radical younger generation of Arab nationalists now pressed for outright confrontation. They found common cause with both an increasingly militarized Muslim clergy and the more extreme elements of an emerging pan-Arab movement that sought to link Palestine's fate with like-minded independence movements in Egypt and Trans-Jordan. The collective zeitgeist was perhaps best summed up by Rashid al-Haj Ibrahim, one of Haifa's most prominent bankers, a pan-Arabist, and leader of the newly founded al-Istiqlal (Independence) Party. Addressing a clandestine meeting of fellow militants early in 1933, Ibrahim forcefully presented the case for armed revolt. "The Jews are advancing on all fronts," he declared. "They keep buying land, they bring in immigrants both legally and illegally, and they have even invaded Trans-Jordan. If we cannot demonstrate to them convincingly enough that all their efforts are in vain and that we are capable of destroying them at one stroke, then we shall have to lose our holy land or resign ourselves to being wretched second-rate citizens in a Jewish state." When asked exactly how he proposed to achieve this, Ibrahim unhesitatingly replied, "By doing what we did in 1929, but using more efficient methods. We have learned from our mistakes and they will not recur." A geriatric local imam and itinerant marriage registrar named Sheikh 'Izz al-Din Abd al-Qadir al-Qassam would become the unlikely leader of the organized revolt that Ibrahim had promised.[15]

On paper at least, there was little in al-Qassam's background that would suggest his lasting historical importance as the legendary Palestinian martyr-hero he remains today. He was born sometime during the 1870s or early 1880s to an impoverished family who lived in a small Syrian village. His father was a teacher in the local *kuttab* (an Islamic elementary school often attached to a mosque) that the younger al-Qassam attended before entering Cairo's al-Azhar University. It was in Egypt that his political consciousness appears to have awakened. Al-Qassam became involved with the nationalist movement protesting British rule, but upon graduation he moved to Turkey to work as a religious teacher. Al-Qassam, however, soon returned to Syria. In 1911, Italy invaded Libya, and he again became immersed in radical politics. Declaring resistance to the invasion a jihad, al-Qassam raised funds to support the struggle and recruited 250 volunteers to go fight in Libya. At the start of World War I, al-Qassam had joined the Ottoman army and after receiving the standard infantry training served as chaplain to a unit quartered near Damascus. He subsequently fought as a guerrilla in the ill-fated 1919–20 uprising against France's occupation of Syria. Sentenced to death in absentia by a French military court, al-Qassam fled to Haifa via Beirut in 1921 and shortly afterward was appointed imam of the newly opened, Supreme Muslim Council–funded al-Istiqlal Mosque.[16]

He quickly achieved renown as a popular and galvanizing cleric. A fiery and impressive orator with the credentials of a learned teacher and theologian and the street cred of a warrior blooded in battle against the Western invader, al-Qassam swiftly gained status and stature within the community. His tireless ministering to the poor and the unfortunate further solidified al-Qassam's reputation. He established a night school for illiterate working-class adults and devoted himself to guiding at-risk youths to lives of piety and devotion. These good deeds, however, were increasingly overshadowed by his growing involvement in radical, nationalist Palestinian politics. Together with Ibrahim, al-Qassam in 1928 founded the Haifa chapter of the militant Young Muslim Men's Association and six years later succeeded his close friend as its president. Al-Qassam's appointment as marriage registrar for the Galilee enabled him to cement his network of contacts and expand his circle of admirers beyond the city to the rural heartland. His official duties also provided al-Qassam with the perfect cover to recruit new fighters to the struggle, establish clandestine guerrilla cells, cache arms and supplies, oversee military training, and generally lay the foundation for the violent uprising he planned to lead when the time was right.[17]

Al-Qassam also appears to have been a Salafist embracing a literal and austere form of Islam that inextricably linked politics to religion and regarded rebellion and the defense of Muslim lands against Western encroachment as a personal obligation. Al-Qassam and his followers dressed in traditional Muslim attire and grew their beards long according to Qur'anic injunction. His men proudly claimed for themselves the respected title of "sheikh" and also swore *bayat* (a personal oath of allegiance) to al-Qassam, who ensured that the rebellion he was planning would be considered theologically legitimate by obtaining from the mufti of Damascus a fatwa sanctioning attacks on both Britons and Jews.[18]

For al-Qassam, the struggle against Palestine's British rulers and Jewish interlopers alike was divinely decreed. Clandestine meetings therefore began with religious instruction before moving on to practicalities, including training in firearms and bomb making. Al-Qassam was scathing in his dismissal of the mainstream Muslim establishment's passivity and cowardice. "You are a people of rabbits," he inveighed from his pulpit, "who are afraid of death and scaffolds and engaged in prattle. You must know that nothing will save us but our arms." He routinely criticized the Arab Executive for its bluster and the mufti of Jerusalem and Supreme Muslim Council for spending money on restoring mosques rather than purchasing weapons.[19]

By the early 1930s, al-Qassam's subversive activities had crystallized in the form of a secret association calling itself the Black Hand. Numbering in the several hundreds, its purpose was to kill as many Jews as possible and spread terror among the Jewish populace across northern Palestine. What remains unclear is whether this group or a dissident splinter was responsible for the spate of Jewish settlers murdered between April 1931 and December 1932. Regardless, by 1935 al-Qassam had made sufficient preparations for the sustained rebellion he had long believed was necessary to rouse the masses and challenge what he regarded as the insufficiently militant Arab leadership. Only in this manner, he believed, would the collapse of British rule and attendant demise of Zionist dreams for Palestine be achieved. On November 6, 1935, al-Qassam left Haifa to implement his battle plan. The timing appears to have been influenced by the accidental discovery only a few weeks earlier of a large amount of arms and ammunition concealed in a consignment of cement on the Jaffa docks. The intended recipient had a Jewish surname and an address in Tel Aviv; Arab press reports claimed this was incontrovertible evidence that the Jews were arming themselves to seize control of the country. Al-Qassam had thus decided the time had come to start the rebellion.[20]

He took to the hills with a small band of followers. There are conflicting accounts whether the gang prematurely tipped its hand by shooting a Jewish police sergeant or crossed paths with a police patrol hunting for fruit thieves. Regardless, in the gun battle that followed, a Jewish police officer was killed, and a manhunt was launched. Al-Qassam and his followers hid in caves for nearly two weeks. As the chill and damp of winter set in, it cannot have been a comfortable existence. Moreover, depending on which year he was in fact born, al-Qassam was in either his late fifties or his early sixties, hardly an age suited to an existence of living life in the rough, on the run. On November 20 or 21, acting on information supplied by an informer, the police surrounded a cave near the Arab village of Ya'bad in which the rebel band was hiding. In the four-hour gun battle that ensued, al-Qassam and two of his band were killed and five others captured. Two were able to escape.[21]

Almost immediately, this otherwise inconsequential clash became the stuff of legend. Stories circulated about the gang's piety: how they were all found with Qur'ans in their pockets; how they faithfully prayed five times a day despite being relentlessly hunted; how they passed their time in hiding deep in Qur'anic study; and how a talisman had been found in the folds of al-Qassam's turban that read,

> *O God save me from the terrible armoury of the infidel*
> *O God let your religion win and go victorious*
> *O God protect me in my coming adventure.*[22]

Four thousand people attended al-Qassam's funeral, where he was hailed as a martyr. Classes in Arab schools throughout Palestine were suspended in his honor. David Ben-Gurion, the newly elected chairman of the Jewish Agency Executive Committee, observed these developments with grave unease. Al-Qassam's last stand at Ya'bad, he argued, was the Arab version of Tel Hai, with al-Qassam cast in Trumpeldor's heroic role. "This is the first time the Arabs have seen that a man could be found ready to give his life for an idea, and this will undoubtedly be a very important educational factor for the Arab masses, and at all events for their youth," Ben-Gurion predicted. "There is no doubt that this episode will now bring about further attempts at terrorism."[23]

Ben-Gurion's assessment was soon validated. Although al-Qassam had been neither elected nor appointed to any position of national leadership or authority, his example at once roused to consciousness and militarized what had hitherto been at best an ill-formed and spasmodic protest movement. The appeal of al-Qassam's uncompromising hostility toward Britain's continued governance of Palestine and support for Zionism blazed across the class and social distinctions that had long divided Palestinian Arab society. In effect, al-Qassam endowed the movement with a new ideological and nationalist focus solidified by the powerful force of militant Islam. He transformed what had hitherto been a mostly spontaneous, inchoate, poorly organized, and uncoordinated struggle into a clearly articulated—albeit nascent—revolution. As the Palestinian-American historian Philip Mattar notes, al-Qassam "achieved more in death than he did during fifteen years of preaching." Indeed, it was al-Qassam's loyal followers—the so-called Qassamiyyun—who, within months of his death, set alight the most serious and protracted challenge to British rule over Palestine and the greatest threat yet posed to the Yishuv: the 1936–39 Arab Rebellion.[24]

On April 15, 1936, a Qassamiyyun gang blockaded a stretch of road between Nablus and Tulkarm. After robbing the occupants of ten automobiles, they stopped a bus and held up its Arab and Jewish passengers, assuring the former that their money would be well spent in helping to fund the brigands' rebellious activities. Almost as an afterthought, they ordered three Jews off the bus and shot them. One was killed outright and the other two wounded, one mortally.[25]

The following evening, members of the Haganah-Bet murdered two Arab workers near Petah Tiqva in reprisal. The country's already highly charged atmosphere had been further electrified earlier in the day when trouble erupted at the funeral of one of the Jewish victims. Mourners had clashed with police and roughed up several Arab passersby. Rumors, however, quickly spread that the Arabs had in fact been killed and not just beaten. For two tense days there was no further trouble. But then, on April 19, Jaffa exploded in violence. Arab gangs assaulted Jews both there and in neighboring Tel Aviv. The police, apparently taken by surprise, were initially overwhelmed. They were forced to fire into the crowd to disperse it, but it was not until an RAF armored car squadron arrived from Ramle late in the afternoon that order was finally restored. Nine Jews lay dead, and ten more were wounded. After more than a year of increasing Arab agitation and mounting tension, the Palestine government moved swiftly to contain any further violence, imposing a curfew on Jaffa and Tel Aviv and invoking the Palestine (Defence) Order in Council, essentially proclaiming a state of emergency throughout the country. The next day, however, Arabs killed five more Jews, and two Arabs were shot dead by police. Meanwhile, Arabs in Jerusalem, Jaffa, Nablus, Haifa, and Tulkarm independently decided to go on strike, thus paralyzing commerce in those cities. Pressure was now building across Palestine for the Arab leadership to declare a general, nationwide strike.[26]

On April 25, delegates from all the major Arab parties and factions gathered in Jerusalem. They agreed to establish the representative Higher Arab Committee, comprising eight leaders, along with subsidiary local committees, that now superseded the Arab Executive by assuming responsibility for directing the protests. Haj Amin al-Husseini was elected its chairman, and a statement was issued vowing to continue and expand the de facto local strikes into a countrywide work stoppage until the "British Government makes a fundamental change in its present policy in Palestine in a manner which will be manifested by the stoppage of Jewish immigration." The committee also called for the prohibition of Jewish land purchase and the creation of a truly representative national government. "The present position is very critical," Haj Amin told Wauchope. "The Arabs were of the strong belief that the continuation of the present policy will lead them to immediate annihilation. They find themselves compelled, moved by their struggle for existence, to defend their country and national rights."[27]

The Arab Rebellion had now officially begun. Arab workers throughout the country went on strike, all Arab businesses closed, Arab public and private transport stopped, and classes in Arab schools were suspended. Idle strikers and students alike milled about the streets, staged protest marches, and brazenly intimidated shopkeepers who defied the committee's ban on commerce.[28]

From the start, the Higher Arab Committee walked a thin line between encouraging civil disobedience and abetting violence. The mufti embodied this duality. For at least the previous two years he had played a pivotal behind-the-scenes role in the plans for the uprising. Although Haj Amin had repeatedly spurned al-Qassam's demands to launch a countrywide revolt, he had not been idle. Eschewing immediate action, he had instead devoted his efforts to careful preparations, instructing his young followers to begin stockpiling arms and commence clandestine weapons training. The mufti had also formally assumed command the previous summer of the subversive al-Jihad al-Muqaddas (Holy War Organization) that his nephew had previously founded.[29]

Wauchope nonetheless persisted in his belief that Haj Amin was a moderate who had a calming effect over his more radical followers. Even as the mufti and the Higher Arab Committee imposed a reign of terror over Palestine during May and June 1936, the high commissioner stubbornly clung to this position. It was yet another indication of the continued incompetence of police intelligence despite the lesson of the 1929 riots and the Dowbiggin reforms. Keith-Roach, for example, recounts how in May, Wauchope naively gave permission to Haj Amin al-Husseini and the Higher Arab Committee to tour the country with the expectation that they would allay antigovernment sentiment and not further stoke it. The mufti in fact agitated for an intensification of the campaign of civil disobedience. "Incendiarism, attacks on railways and roads, bomb throwing at police and shooting became rife" as a result of the tour, a British army intelligence assessment concluded.[30]

Indeed, the two weeks that followed the mufti's rabble-rousing excursion were among the most violent and destructive that Palestine had yet known. The locus of the unrest now also shifted from Palestine's urban centers to its rural heartland. Rebel gangs burned down Jewish-owned wheat fields and uprooted more than fifteen thousand trees from Jewish-owned orchards and citrus groves. They destroyed government telephone and telegraph poles and repeatedly sabotaged the Kirkuk–Haifa oil pipeline. Jews traveling by bus or car were routinely shot at, and outlying Jewish settlements were attacked, as were isolated police barracks and military posts. In the cities, meanwhile, the violence also persisted. There were forty-one bombings in Jaffa alone and another thirty-five in Haifa. Jews were shot at while leaving a Jerusalem cinema and going to classes at Hebrew University. Thousands of Jaffa's Jewish residents were forced to abandon their burned-out homes and move elsewhere.[31]

In just weeks the rebellion had transformed itself from an urban riot and general strike to a countrywide, rural guerrilla war. Yet when Wauchope finally allowed the police to arrest sixty-one leading Arab nationalists on sedition-related charges, he specifically excluded the mufti and other committee members from the dragnet. The police and the army chafed at the administration's dilatory response to the disorders and the restrictions imposed on them. The high commissioner, however, brushed aside their complaints, explaining to the colonial secretary, William Ormsby-Gore, "It is understandable that soldiers and many others want to apply more drastic methods. Extreme methods might be best to meet our present difficulties but the bitterness so engendered would have deplorable results in the future."[32]

Wauchope's unyielding faith in conciliation over suppression in fact arguably had precisely the opposite effect: provoking more violence fueled by the rebels' perception of governmental weakness rather than sagacity. The high commissioner failed to grasp that the mantle of leadership of the Arab community had passed from the traditional ruling elite of long-established elders to a new generation of impatient, radicalized youths. It was the *shabaab* (young guys) who had effectively seized control of the nationalist movement and were driving the rebellion forward. Regardless of whether this was a product of Wauchope's innate recalcitrance or the inadequacy of the police intelligence he was provided, it was a major miscalculation that would have dire repercussions. "Critical days were allowed to pass without energetic action on the part of the Administration, and the initiative gradually passed into the hands of the strikers," observed John Marlowe, the pseudonym of a British resident of Palestine named Jack Collard, who later wrote two of the earliest accounts of the British mandate's violent history.[33]

Thus procrastination born of wishful thinking condemned Palestine to three more years of unremitting violence. What Wauchope, however, correctly understood was the depth of the Arabs' commitment to their rebellion. "I knew it was useless to argue that Jewish immigration has hitherto been the cause of material benefit to the Arab people," Wauchope told the colonial secretary, "for the Ulemas [Muslim scholars with authority in religious and legal matters] and the Arabs are not thinking of material profit or loss, nor of the past: they are all dominated by the fear of what may happen in the future if immigration be not stopped and their minds are not open to argument."[34]

The escalating rebellion had also laid bare the insufficient number of British police and military forces in Palestine. Following the 1929 riots, London had decided to permanently station two battalions of infantry and an RAF armored car squadron. This was eventually supplemented by an additional squadron as well as four more armored car sections. But in reality, the number of British troops available for internal security operations—when those deployed on static guard duties and involved in noncombat support and logistics tasks were subtracted—amounted to little more than a thousand men. The effective strength of the PPF was no better, and there were no funds to maintain any kind of proper forces in reserve. Government control over the countryside was therefore illusory at best. "The situation was . . . like the Wild West in the days when the west was wild and Indians might come rushing out of the wilder wild at any moment," Brigadier H. J. Simson recalled. "In Palestine the Arabs play the part of Indian still."[35]

Some of these problems might have been substantially mitigated or avoided altogether had the effective police intelligence apparatus that Dowbiggin had envisioned for Palestine following the 1929 riots materialized. Unfortunately, despite the massive overhaul and reforms that he had recommended, the CID once again failed in its mission of providing timely and accurate intelligence that might have either better anticipated the rebellion or enabled the police to respond more effectively once it had begun. Accordingly, nearly a month had passed before Wauchope asked that reinforcements be dispatched to Palestine. Their impact was marginal. The high commissioner asked for more troops on May 22, and within two weeks the number of military forces in the country had doubled to approximately three thousand men. It was, however, too little and too late. As an army assessment astringently noted, "By then, the Arab part of Palestine was in incipient rebellion, bomb throwing ambushes, firing on military camps, incendiarism and cutting of telegraph line being general."[36]

June brought no respite to the spreading lawlessness as larger bands of fifty to seventy Arab marauders, led by their Qassamiyyun commanders, roamed the countryside, attacking at will. Additional reinforcements were rushed from Egypt so that the Palestine garrison was now four times larger than it had been just two months before. Military forces in Palestine now numbered nearly seven thousand men, yet the administration's initial hesitancy and then its continued vacillation only fanned the flames of insurrection. On June 12, Wauchope was finally persuaded to lift the restrictions he had placed on offensive military action. He also agreed to allow the extraordinary powers previously granted to the government under the Palestine (Defence) Order in Council to be implemented. These gave the government the right to impose collective fines, institute curfews, detain people for an unspecified period of time without charge, censor the press, deport political undesirables, and seize and use buildings and road transport as needed. Later that month the Order in Council was cited to legally sanction the destruction of more than two hundred Arab homes and businesses in Jaffa's labyrinthine Old City after it had been transformed into a rebel stronghold and no-go area for the security forces. British army sappers used hundreds of pounds of gelignite to cut wide swaths through formerly narrow alleyways. "Goodbye, goodbye, old Jaffa," the headline in *Al-Difa'* lamented. "The army has exploded you." Nearly six thousand Arabs were made homeless and rendered destitute. But even these extreme measures proved ineffective. Moreover, within weeks the regulations under the Order in Council were no longer being enforced after the Higher Arab Committee had complained of their severity. Instead, new restrictions were placed on the military's use of deadly force.[37]

Meanwhile, the rebels' targets broadened to include their fellow Arabs as well as Jews and British security forces. Old scores were settled and long-standing vendettas eagerly avenged. Security continued to deteriorate throughout August into September, even though there were now thirteen thousand troops in Palestine—the equivalent of more than an army division. Although Arab gangs had by then killed more than three hundred people (nearly two hundred of whom were their fellow Muslims) and wounded thirteen hundred others, no rebel brought before the Palestine courts had yet been sentenced to death. As Palestine slid deeper into anarchy, Wauchope finally accepted that the time for restraint had passed. On September 7 he authorized new security regulations. These measures in essence amounted to the invocation of martial law but without its actual declaration and full implementation. Their purpose was to serve notice on the Arabs that the security forces would no longer be restrained in their suppression of the uprising. Lest there be any doubt, Wauchope personally delivered this message to the Higher Arab Committee the following week.[38]

The Higher Arab Committee was in a bind. The entire First Infantry Division had just been redeployed to Palestine, bringing the total number of troops now to some twenty thousand men and thus ensuring the newly arrived general officer commanding (GOC), Lieutenant General Sir John Dill, the resources he required to crush the rebels and restore order. Continuing the revolt thus risked total defeat. But the Arab leadership had boxed itself into a corner by repeatedly demanding that the government suspend Jewish immigration as a nonnegotiable precondition for ending the strike. Its options were further constrained by the Arabs' dire economic circumstances. Five months of work disruption and enforced idleness had shattered Palestine's economy, and with the citrus crop ready for harvest a critical window of opportunity for gainful employment and the recouping of lost wages would disappear if the committee did not act quickly. A timely, face-saving intervention materialized on October 11 in the form of an appeal from the rulers of Iraq, Saudi Arabia, Trans-Jordan, and Yemen calling on their Palestinian brothers to end the strike and "rely on the good intentions of our friend, Great Britain, who has declared that she will do justice." The following day, the fighting stopped, the country returned to work, and the first phase of the Arab Rebellion ended.[39]

No one, however, could derive much satisfaction or comfort from this respite. The Arabs had achieved little despite tremendous exertion and much suffering. Their only solace was that the rebel bands active in the hills remained intact. For the British, there was no pretending that this latest development represented any kind of triumph for the forces of law and order. Even though there were now twelve times as many British troops in Palestine as there had been at the rebellion's start, Wauchope still refused to authorize either the stern measures or the active operations that would bring the unrest to heel once and for all. "The fact remains that Martial Law never was declared," Dill complained. "Policy changed and instead of a policy of intensive measures a policy was pursued of help-ing the Higher Arab Committee to stop resistance to government uncon-ditionally . . . An opportunity had, in fact, been missed of re-establishing British authority in the country." Worse still, by brooking the Arab kings' collective intervention, the British had allowed Palestine to become a genuinely pan-Arab issue, exciting the interest and ensuring the contin-ued meddling and intervention of the surrounding countries in its inter-nal affairs. Blame for this inevitably fell on Wauchope, whose persistent faith in Arab moderation and tireless conciliatory efforts were regarded by Whitehall as having squandered any immediate prospects of defeating the rebellion. Ormsby-Gore would later describe the high commissioner as "a dear little man, admirable while the going is good, but hardly the charac-ter to ride out a storm." The British military establishment's assessment of Wauchope's performance was harsher. In a letter to his designated suc-cessor as GOC, the future field marshal and penultimate viceroy of India, Archibald Wavell, Dill described the high commissioner as someone who "loves greatly, administers with knowledge and imagination, but . . . does not rule." Some junior officers were even more dismissive, deriding Wau-chope as a "washout" and as "ga-ga"—slang for someone who has lost his mind through senility.[40]

Like a deer in the headlights, the Yishuv, meanwhile, had no idea which way to jump. From the start, Weizmann had correctly grasped the existen-tial threat that the Arab Rebellion posed to the Jewish national home. "On one side, the forces of destruction, the forces of the desert, have risen, and on the other stand firm the forces of civilization and building. It is the old war of the desert against civilization, but we will not be stopped," he had declared on April 23, 1936. But other leading Zionists argued that such fears were not only exaggerated but counterproductive—ascribing to the Arabs an ideological cohesiveness and degree of coordination that did not exist. Berl Katznelson, a lifelong Zionist-socialist, founding father of the Labor Party, and the editor of the leading Hebrew-language daily newspaper *Davar*, for instance, dismissed any talk of an Arab "rebellion" as nonsense. Katznelson couldn't discern any distinct nationalist movement orchestrating the disorders. "In all these terrorist manifestations," he wrote, "one might find evidence of personal dedication to religious fanaticism and xenophobia, but we cannot discern anything else . . . Can this be described as nationalism? Let's not believe it for a moment!" This view reflected that of the high commissioner and other British officials as well and indeed many in the Yishuv who were also inclined to downplay both the dimensions and the consequences of the rebellion.[41]

Ben-Gurion, however, would have none of it. "There are comrades among us who see only one enemy, the government," he responded. "In their opinion, there is no uprising or revolt by the Arabs . . . I have a hard time understanding the astonishing blindness of people like [them]." In a letter to the Labor Party Central Committee in August 1936, Ben-Gurion expressed his bafflement with what he regarded as a willful denial of the facts. "The Arabs fight with arms and strikes, terror and sabotage, mayhem and destruction of property . . . What more must they do to make their acts merit the name of rebellion and uprising?"[42]

Despite the magnitude of this latest threat to the Jewish national home, Ben-Gurion remained firmly convinced that the mainstream Haganah's long-standing policy of *havlaga* (restraint) must be adhered to without exception. His view was that the Arabs had discredited themselves and their cause by their resort to indiscriminate violence. This was a grave miscalculation, Ben-Gurion argued, that could be used to Zionism's advantage—provided that the Yishuv resisted the temptation to retaliate and exact revenge on the Arabs. In a speech delivered in Jerusalem on April 19, Ben-Gurion made no bones about his utter contempt for, and complete rejection of, the anti-Arab violence that had followed the funeral of one of the Jewish victims of the attack on the Nablus–Tulkarm road three days earlier. "What happened in Tel Aviv," he declared, "beating up shoe-shine boys, breaking into a closed Arab shop, is a violation of that which is holy . . . I understand and empathize with all the bitterness voiced here . . . but owing to the very gravity of the situation we must maintain clarity of thought as well as the moral and political principles which guide Zionism and the Yishuv . . . If attacked we must not exceed the bounds of self-defense."[43]

The "moral and political principles" Ben-Gurion cited were embodied in the code of conduct that attended the Haganah's policy of *havlaga* called *tohar ha-neshek* (purity of arms). This encapsulated the moral conviction that the Haganah's weapons could be kept "pure" if used for defensive purposes only. In this manner, the Yishuv sought to place its use of force on a higher moral plane than the Arabs'—and, not incidentally, also favorably impress the British. Ben-Gurion made precisely this point to Wauchope in a letter he co-wrote with Moshe Shertok, the head of the Jewish Agency's political department. It was not fear or weakness that restrained the Yishuv from striking back at the Arabs, they explained, but "solely . . . a deep moral persuasion."[44]

To the men and women of the Haganah-Bet these debates were nothing more than a rehashing of the fundamental cleavage of opinion that had led to the group's estrangement from the Haganah in the first place. For them, concepts such as *havlaga* and *tohar ha-neshek* had been rendered moot by this new, profound threat to the Jewish national home. Accordingly, they pressed Jabotinsky and Tehomi for permission to retaliate against the Arabs on a more organized and systematic scale. Incidents such as the bomb thrown by Arab terrorists onto the playground of a Jewish school in Jaffa that injured seven children doubtless fed their demands. The fact that Arab shooting at Jewish neighborhoods from the Jaffa–Jerusalem train ceased following a Haganah-Bet reprisal attack that killed one Arab passenger and wounded five others also intensified the militants' demands for more aggressive operations. Frustrated by Tehomi's refusal to countenance retaliation, many in the Haganah-Bet began to ask why a separate fighting force was needed if it was going to blindly follow mainstream Haganah policies. Indeed, there had already been a string of unsanctioned reprisal operations during which Haganah-Bet fighters had killed another three Arabs and injured nine more.[45]

But both Jabotinsky and Tehomi remained resolutely opposed to any deviation from the policy of *havlaga*. For more than a decade Jabotinsky had pinned his faith and hopes on establishing an officially sanctioned, aboveground Jewish defense force. The Arab Rebellion, he believed, would finally persuade the British to realize his dream. Accordingly, Jabotinsky argued that taking the fight to the Arabs now risked undermining any opportunity to achieve lasting Anglo-Zionist military cooperation. It was left to Tehomi to ensure that the Haganah-Bet complied with this edict. To that end, special Haganah-Bet "military tribunals" were convened to punish any breaches of discipline.[46]

Tehomi's commitment to *havlaga*, however, went well beyond the narrow considerations that motivated Jabotinsky. At this time of grave national crisis, the Haganah-Bet commander had actually come to doubt the entire rationale behind the existence of two separate Jewish paramilitary forces performing the same function. Tehomi was convinced that their continued separation not only was illogical but created a dangerously enervating duplication of effort when total national unity was required. The Haganah-Bet leader and some of his commanders therefore decided to approach the Haganah and the Jewish Agency to discuss merging the two groups under a single command. On August 6, 1936, they drafted a unification agreement that provided for the amalgamation of the Haganah-Bet into the Haganah and for the Haganah-Bet's "unconditional acceptance" of Jewish Agency authority and subservience to a single commander that the Jewish Agency Executive would appoint. The document further stipulated that Haganah-Bet members who either refused to comply with the merger or failed to abide by its terms would be deemed "criminals" and dealt with accordingly.[47]

None of this was acceptable to Jabotinsky. Apart from the fact that Tehomi had not consulted him, the Revisionist Zionist leader remained adamant that a unified Jewish self-defense force must represent the Yishuv's entire political spectrum and not be dominated by, or exclusively at the command of, one party—for example, the Labor Zionists. But Jabotinsky was also conflicted by his fervent belief in the need for unity at this time of profound threat and his belief that only Britain could provide the training and assistance required to transform their rudimentary paramilitary organizations into the bona fide Jewish military force he had long envisioned. His famous treatise, commanding Jewish youths to "learn to shoot" as they had once learned their ABCs, reflected Jabotinsky's view that this fundamental requirement was not the provenance of one political party or another but a national imperative. "Of all the necessities of national rebirth," he wrote, "shooting is the most important . . . We are forced to learn to shoot and it is futile to argue against the compulsion of a historical reality."[48]

A meeting was held between Tehomi and Jabotinsky in Vienna that failed to resolve their differences. They met again in December 1936 in Paris, where, after a marathon six-hour session, Tehomi obtained Jabotinsky's approval to continue the negotiations to merge the two Haganahs. Jabotinsky, however, insisted that any reconstituted body be truly pluralistic and genuinely representative of "a united Zion and united Yishuv." He remained concerned that unification should not entail complete subordination to the Jewish Agency. Jabotinsky therefore obtained from Tehomi a signed statement acknowledging that the Haganah-Bet commander served at the pleasure of the president of the Revisionist Party and was therefore beholden to follow Jabotinsky's guidance and instructions.[49]

Tehomi returned to Palestine disconsolate. Although he admittedly had Jabotinsky's permission to press ahead with the negotiations for merger, he had in fact been given little latitude and no real authority. Of more immediate consequence, however, was the problem of the Haganah-Bet militants who were both unwavering in their disdain for *havlaga* and opposed to any discussion of unification. As a precaution, Tehomi ordered that eleven local commanders with access to Haganah-Bet armories be reassigned to other duties. He was especially concerned about the loyalty of the Jerusalem detachment's commander—a twenty-six-year-old former yeshiva student and Hebrew University dropout named David Raziel, who six years earlier had followed Tehomi when he himself had left the Haganah to found the Haganah-Bet.[50]

CHAPTER 4

Terror Against Terror

On November 11, 1936, the Royal (Peel) Commission arrived in Palestine. The idea behind this latest august governmental body charged with divining a lasting political solution for the country had been Wauchope's. As the general strike and attendant unrest spread throughout the country, the high commissioner had been desperate to find some way to assuage Arab discontent. Because the Higher Arab Committee refused to send a delegation to London to discuss their grievances, Wauchope came up with the idea of a royal commission to break the impasse. But the Higher Arab Committee had rejected even this gesture and refused to call off the strike until all Jewish immigration to Palestine stopped. Lacking any viable alternative to suppressing the rebellion except through the continued application of military force—which London now feared would adversely impact Anglo-Arab relations across the region—the government of Prime Minister Stanley Baldwin warmly embraced Wauchope's proposal. The Royal Commission's terms of reference were quickly agreed to, and Lord Peel, a well-known Tory and past secretary of state for India, was appointed chairman. The commission was directed to ascertain the reasons behind the violence that had erupted in April 1936; determine whether Britain was properly fulfilling its obligations to both Arabs and Jews under the terms of the mandate; assess whether either community had legitimate grievances about how the mandate had been or was being implemented; and, in the event these grievances were justified, "make recommendations for their removal and for the prevention of their recurrence."[1]

The cabinet, however, had persisted in the fiction that the Royal Commission should not be perceived as rewarding violence. Accordingly, it had delayed the commissioners' departure until the Arabs called off their strike. The Arab kings' intervention, coupled with the Higher Arab Committee's announcement of the strike's suspension on October 11, had removed this obstacle, and the commission departed England early the following month. On that same day, the Palestine government announced the allocation of eighteen hundred Jewish immigration certificates for the half-yearly schedule ending in March 1937. The Higher Arab Committee was livid and declared its intention to boycott the commission—urging all Palestinian Arabs to do the same. The Yishuv was similarly dismayed. Though grateful that the government had not entirely suspended immigration, as the Arabs had demanded, the Jewish leadership was upset by this considerable diminishment of the semiannual quota. Moreover, they recalled with no small amount of trepidation the policy reversal that had followed the last commission that had come to Palestine following the 1929 riots. Mindful of the need to present its case as vigorously as possible to avert an identical outcome, the Jewish Agency decided to appear before, and cooperate with, the Royal Commission in hopes of favorably influencing its final report and recommendations.[2]

The commission held thirty public and forty private hearings between November 1936 and January 1937. In addition, the commissioners traveled throughout the country gaining a broad perspective on the mandate's operation and the country's political, religious, social, and economic condition. According to Keith-Roach, "The commission had made a deep impression. It listened, heard, and cross-examined. The dignity, the courtesy, the searching questions, the promptitude and the accuracy of the transcript of questions and answers had won respect and everyone who met its members was loud in their praises." Even the Higher Arab Committee was persuaded by the Arab kings to testify before the commission. "The commission left with everyone's goodwill," Keith-Roach approvingly noted.[3]

It was not long, though, before rumors surfaced that the Royal Commission would likely recommend the partition of Palestine into separate Arab and Jewish states. Accordingly, the unresolved issue of a unified Jewish self-defense force assumed new urgency given that the anticipated Jewish state would require a properly organized army to replace the two clandestine paramilitary forces performing duplicative functions. Tehomi, of course, was already completely on board. It was Jabotinsky who still required convincing. Both Ben-Gurion and Eliahu Golomb pressed him to approve the draft agreement that Tehomi had negotiated the previous summer. Indeed, for the Jewish Agency, the mainstream Haganah, and Tehomi himself, the need for unity was greater than ever given that Tehomi in any event was losing control of some elements within the Haganah-Bet. One of his chief lieutenants, Moshe Rosenberg, was suspected of removing weapons from an armory without authorization and accused of robbing a bank, presumably to fund a breakaway splinter.[4]

Then, in mid-March 1937, there was a new outbreak of Arab violence.

Over the course of four days, six Jews were murdered in four separate incidents. Although isolated and geographically disparate, the attacks were a tragic reminder of how easily Jewish blood was spilled and how quickly events might again spiral out of control. Worse still, the discontent swelling within the Haganah-Bet's ranks since Tehomi had returned from Paris now triggered a dangerous spate of unsanctioned retaliation. The most serious incident involved three Haganah-Bet members who, having been rebuffed by their commander, decided to take matters into their own hands. One built a bomb that he gave to the other two, who traveled by motorcycle to the Arab village of Yazur, located along the Tel Aviv–Jerusalem road. Pulling up in front of a busy café, the rider hurled the explosive inside before fleeing. Although no one was killed, several people were seriously wounded and the coffeehouse completely destroyed.[5]

On April 15, 1937, Golomb addressed the Histadrut Executive. He declared that in this time of crisis the anomalous existence of two paramilitary forces performing identical functions could not continue. Moreover, the risk of further acts of vengeance necessitated that control over all Jewish military activities be exercised by one central body. "We must see to it," Golomb demanded, "that there is one united group." But it was already too late. Earlier in the month, Jabotinsky had been presented with a new set of conditions governing the merger that he had rejected out of hand. Ben-Gurion now issued an ultimatum to the Haganah-Bet: either submit to the authority of the Yishuv's official institutions or suffer the consequences.[6]

Tehomi had in any case come too far to be deterred by Jabotinsky's rejection of the merger and heeded Ben-Gurion's demand. He pressed ahead with unification even as a majority of Haganah-Bet commanders objected. On April 9 a letter arrived from Jabotinsky reminding Tehomi of the commitment he had made in Paris and ordering him to desist from merging the two groups. He refused, and the following day a group of younger Haganah-Bet officers issued a statement announcing Tehomi's expulsion from the group and the creation of a new organization that they called the Irgun Zvai Le'umi (National Military Organization), often referred to simply as the Irgun or by its Hebrew acronym, Etzel.[7]

The unification issue was not as simple as the mere reconciliation of two different paramilitary units performing identical functions. The political and ideological disagreements separating the two Haganah organizations were formidable, reflecting the "minimalist" and "maximalist" policies of their respective political masters. The Jewish state that the Royal Commission was rumored likely to propose comprised an even smaller portion of Palestine than most Zionists were prepared to accept. After considerable debate and discussion, the Zionist Organization—and the various socialist-labor groups under its aegis—had nonetheless agreed to accept the commission's anticipated recommendation as a basis for further negotiation. The Revisionist Party, however, and the organizations under its umbrella, rejected the plan outright and unequivocally demanded a Jewish state encompassing the land on both sides of the Jordan River—that is, not only the entirety of Palestine's current geographic borders, but that of Trans-Jordan as well.

Jabotinsky was suspicious that the Jewish Agency's renewed merger overtures were a plot to stifle dissent within the Yishuv and thereby facilitate the acceptance of the Royal Commission scheme in advance of its announcement. Accordingly, the breakdown of negotiations and estrangement in relations that resulted in the formation of the Irgun were perhaps inevitable. Golomb claimed that about half of the Haganah-Bet's three thousand members left with Tehomi and joined the Haganah. Irgun sources, however, state that no more than a thousand and perhaps only a few hundred people actually defected—and that many had second thoughts and subsequently joined the Irgun.[8]

Jabotinsky appointed Robert Bitker, a thirty-year-old Russian émigré who had led the Betar detachment in China's Shanghai International Zone, as commander. Abraham Stern, a brilliant classicist from Hebrew University and one of the hard-core junior Haganah-Bet officers who had opposed Tehomi, was appointed secretary. Another Russian émigré, Moshe Rosenberg, was named chief of staff, and David Raziel was left in charge of the Jerusalem detachment. Jabotinsky, according to his biographer Joseph Schechtman, would exercise "supreme moral authority in all major Irgun matters." In practical terms, because the British forbade Jabotinsky to return to Palestine, he would have no role or authority over the Irgun's day-to-day operations or in the appointment or promotion of officers other than the commander. In addition, no overt or formal ties were established between the new group and the Revisionist Party, freeing Jabotinsky to pursue the party's political aims without publicly associating himself with the illegal Irgun. Nonetheless, it is clear that Jabotinsky regarded the Irgun as a part of, and subordinate to, the Revisionist Party. The Jewish Agency similarly concealed its actual relationship with the Haganah—which was, of course, also an illegal organization. But where the Haganah was directly subordinate to the Yishuv's elected civilian leadership in the Vaad Le'umi (Jewish National Council) and to its appointed representatives in the Jewish Agency, and therefore ultimately accountable to the Yishuv, the Irgun was completely independent and therefore accountable neither to the Revisionist Party nor to any popularly elected civilian leadership or, for that matter, to anyone except Jabotinsky himself.[9]

On April 23, Raziel and Stern distributed a statement to their fellow Irgunists defining the new organization's mission. "To those faithful to the oath!" it began.

Today there exists in the land two organizations: one leftist subject to the authority of the left, which to our great misfortune a portion of our people joined; and the second is Etzel in the land of Israel which continues in its role of fighting for the honor and life of the nation and its revival. We believe in the mission/destiny of the movement and in its power to bring into existence from anew complete independent life within the historical borders of the Hebrew state.

We believe in the sacrifice of battle and the sacrifice of the Israeli youth that sets as its goal the strength and independence of the core of the Hebrew strength.

Anonymous soldiers!

The core of Hebrew strength stands loyal to every order and to every sacrifice.

From these ranks only death do us part![10]

The Royal Commission's 404-page report was published on July 7, 1937. "It is the most exhaustive and fairest document ever written about Palestine," Keith-Roach observed, "a model that every person in public life should read." As everyone in Palestine surmised, the commission recommended partition.[11]

Palestine's Arabs rejected the report in its entirety. On July 23 the Higher Arab Committee wrote to both Ormsby-Gore and the League of Nations' Permanent Mandates Commission to express its "repugnance to the whole of the partition scheme." It instead demanded that Britain terminate the mandate, grant Palestine full independence, and immediately ban all Jewish immigration and land purchase. The Arab leadership found the report's recommendation of population and land transfers between the proposed Arab and Jewish states—if necessary, at the point of British bayonets—especially repellent. Muslims outside Palestine, especially in India, also condemned the partition proposal, thus threatening to turn Muslims elsewhere against Britain.[12]

The Yishuv was not pleased with the report either. The proposed Jewish state comprised less than a fifth of Palestine and was thus much smaller than even the diminutive state that the Jews had been led to expect. However, although its very modest territorial dimensions were completely unacceptable, a confluence of urgent concerns argued against outright rejection. The consolidation of the Nazis' power in Germany, coupled with growing persecution of Jews, the likely renewal of the Arab Rebellion given that community's unmitigated opposition to the partition plan, and the Yishuv's fear that Britain's commitment to the Jewish national home might erode further, compelled the Zionist leadership to accept the Royal Commission's recommendations, albeit with serious reservations. Jewish acquiescence to the Royal Commission's plan was made conditional upon negotiations to increase the size of the proposed Jewish state.[13]

Rather than having resolved, much less defused, the causes that had triggered the Arab Rebellion, the Royal Commission's report had the opposite effect. It simply confirmed everyone's worst fears of the inevitability of some new clash as each party to the dispute—Arab, Jew, and Briton alike—prepared for the next round of bloodshed. Accordingly, in July 1937, a new government statement on Palestine was issued which warned that any new outbreak of violence would quickly be suppressed. For the next two months, however, the country remained deceptively quiet. It was the Qassamiyyun who would again be responsible for the volcanic explosion that followed and thereby provided the spark that marked the start of the Arab Rebellion's second, considerably more violent phase.[14]

Lewis Andrews, the acting district commissioner for the Galilee, was among the most popular British officials in Palestine. A fluent Arabic and Hebrew speaker, he had first come to the country twenty years earlier as a young soldier serving under General Allenby. After the war, Andrews worked in OETA before joining the Palestine government as an administrator and then development officer. A native of Sydney, Australia, he rose quickly in the Palestine civil service and had played an important role in facilitating the Royal Commission's travels around Palestine the previous winter. Andrews, however, was reputed to be "a friend of the Zionists" and "an Arab hater" who would in any event have certainly incurred Arab displeasure because of his meticulous documentation of Arab land sales to Jews—including, allegedly, many transactions involving prominent members of the Arab Executive and the Supreme Muslim Council. Indeed, the forty-one-year-old husband and father of three small children knew that he was a marked man. In mid-September, Andrews had told his deputy, Christopher Pirie-Gordon, that he was expecting an attempt on his life and even named the village from which he believed the assailants would come.[15]

Undaunted by these threats, Andrews and his police bodyguard arrived on September 26 at the Anglican church in Nazareth, where he regularly worshipped and served as church warden, shortly before the evensong service scheduled to begin at six o'clock. They had just parked their car at the bottom of a narrow lane leading up to the church when Pirie-Gordon pulled up next to them. Andrews and Pirie-Gordon were engaged in conversation as they walked up the lane, with Constable Peter McEwan following close behind, when Andrews noticed a group of four seemingly ordinary fellaheen loitering up ahead. Something about the Arabs suddenly alarmed Andrews, who shoved Pirie-Gordon aside and shouted at him, "Run for your life!" The four Arabs immediately produced revolvers and started shooting. Constable McEwan was hit first but managed to return fire before losing consciousness. Andrews raced toward the church and had just reached the steps to the courtyard when he was struck down. The gunmen reportedly continued to pour fire into Andrews's lifeless body before turning their attention to the fleeing Pirie-Gordon, who tripped and fell to the ground, where he lay still until the shooting ceased. Convinced that they had killed Pirie-Gordon as well, the assassins then made good their escape. The assistant district commissioner was the only survivor.[16]

With Andrews's murder the Palestine government was finally roused to consciousness. The assassination of the highest-ranking British civil servant in Palestine to date was seen as a declaration of war on Britain—which is exactly what the Arab extremists responsible for it had intended. Within the week, the government enacted the harsh security measures approved by the cabinet earlier in the year in anticipation of any resumption of violence, including the dissolution of the Supreme Muslim Council. Haj Amin was removed from his official posts as its president and chairman of the General Waqf Committee. A warrant was issued for his arrest and that of all the Higher Arab Committee's leaders—each of whom was also served with deportation orders. The mufti, however, was able to avoid capture by remaining safely within the sacred confines of the Noble Sanctuary on the Temple Mount, where he had taken refuge since July, when a previous arrest warrant had been issued. A standoff had followed whereby the British authorities, fearful that any attempt to forcibly seize him might trigger an international incident, had arrayed police officers around the

Temple Mount on permanent watch. Their efforts, however, were to no avail. Under cover of darkness on the night of October 12, Haj Amin disguised himself in Bedouin clothing—although some accounts claim he had dressed as a woman—and climbed down the Temple Mount's outer wall, where a car was waiting to spirit him to Jaffa, from which he went by ship to Lebanon. He was never to return to Palestine but for a brief visit to East Jerusalem thirty years later. The majority of Haj Amin's colleagues on the Higher Arab Committee and its subordinate local committees were less fortunate. Five committee members were arrested and placed aboard two Royal Navy ships waiting in Haifa harbor to transport them to exile in the Seychelles islands. Two hundred others were also swept up by police and imprisoned. The mufti's brother and trusted confidant, Jamal al-Husseini, however, also evaded capture and escaped to Syria.[17]

The successful apprehension of so many of the rebellion's key political figures had been facilitated by the news blackout that William Battershill, the chief secretary and, in Wauchope's absence, the officer administering government, had imposed under the Order in Council's draconian powers. This had also enabled him to order the suspension of all telegraph and telephone service throughout Palestine and hence prevent news of the arrests from being communicated. Nonetheless, even though the entirety of the rebellion's political leadership was either in custody or in exile, its military commanders remained at large.[18]

On the evening of October 14, Palestine would be brought to its knees by a coordinated series of rebel attacks throughout the country. Shortly after dusk, Jewish buses came under Arab attack outside Jerusalem. About the same time, a basket concealing two bombs was found in a Jerusalem café popular with British police, and shortly afterward the evening train from Haifa to Jerusalem was assaulted. Battershill immediately imposed a curfew on Jerusalem, but the locus of the violence merely spread elsewhere. Daybreak brought only a temporary respite, as Arab raiders had attacked the country's main airport at Lydda, burning down the buildings housing customs, passport, and communications offices. The Arab Rebellion had clearly started anew.[19]

The contrast to the Palestine administration's dilatory response and lenient policies of the previous eighteen months, however, could not have been more striking. For more than a year, Wauchope had prevented the execution of rebels convicted of capital offenses as part of his efforts at conciliation—even though their victims had included soldiers and police as well as civilians. Dill, while GOC, had complained bitterly of this, and Simson's account of the rebellion's first year was now in British bookstores.

Simson was unsparing in his criticism of the Palestine administration's feckless performance during the rebellion's first year. Hence, the pressure from London on the administration to deal decisively with the new outbreak of violence was irresistible. The Colonial Office's announcement on October 29 that Wauchope would retire earlier than expected paved the way for a dramatic change. It was unveiled less than two weeks later when Battershill revealed details of new amendments to the Order in Council. Military tribunals—presided over by a field officer along with two more junior officers—would replace civilian courts to judge crimes involving the discharge of firearms, illegal possession of arms, bombs, and other weapons, and acts of sabotage and intimidation, with the first two categories punishable by death. All sentences were to be subject to confirmation by the GOC—from which there would be no right of appeal.[20]

The Irgun, meanwhile, had also made plans of its own to respond to any renewed Arab violence. Around the time of the first anniversary of the Arab Rebellion's start the previous April, Jabotinsky had sanctioned the more aggressive policy proposed by the group's new commanders. "Do not restrain yourselves," he had told them. But at a meeting subsequently held in Alexandria between Jabotinsky and Bitker, accompanied by his two key lieutenants, Rosenberg and Stern, to finalize these arrangements, the Zionist leader had expressed second thoughts. As Schechtman explains, the "necessity and inevitability of such a course appeared obvious . . . for Jabotinsky it was in more than one respect a difficult decision to make. Though recognizing the bitter political justification for retaliation, he had grave doubts as to the moral aspect of such a course, which was bound to affect not only Arab terrorists, but also such Arabs—men, women and children—who were not directly responsible for indiscriminate killing of Jewish men, women and children."[21]

At the end of the day, Jabotinsky's decision came down to the fact that he felt it was not his place to impose limits on Irgun operations or to dictate the circumstances in which force should be used when he was living safely abroad while Irgun fighters were risking their lives to protect the Yishuv. A revised agreement, accordingly, was concluded that authorized the Irgun to mount whatever retaliatory and offensive operations its commanders deemed necessary. As long as these were infrequent and limited, there was no need to consult Jabotinsky. However, in the event that the Irgun high command decided that more extensive and systematic operations were required, Jabotinsky's express consent would be obtained before proceeding. A simple telegram signed with the name "Mendelson" would signal his assent.[22]

The ink was hardly dry on the agreement when yet another reshuffle of the Irgun high command occurred. Although Bitker was a fine soldier, he lacked both the experience and the temperament to lead an underground movement. Moreover, as a newly arrived immigrant, he could not communicate with his subordinates in Hebrew, nor did he possess the intimate knowledge and understanding of the region required for someone in that position. Sensing that he was out of his depth, Bitker had already proposed that he step down as commander and be replaced by Rosenberg, his deputy and chief of staff. Before Bitker could do so, however, unhappiness within the group over his leadership and judgment boiled over. In October, the Irgun general staff and its Revisionist Party counterparts dispatched an emissary—a young South African journalist and member of Betar named Samuel Katz—to Poland to explain the situation to Jabotinsky. The Zionist leader approved the shake-up, appointing Rosenberg to succeed Bitker and elevating Raziel to the number two slot while retaining command of the group's Jerusalem detachment.[23]

Irgun operations commenced on November 11 with the bombing of an Arab café in reprisal for the killing of five Jewish farmers outside Jerusalem forty-eight hours earlier. Two persons were killed and five wounded, two seriously. The Palestine government immediately imposed a curfew on the city, and for the next two days a tenuous quiet prevailed. Then, at seven o'clock on November 14, a day henceforth known as Black Sunday, the Irgun struck in both Jerusalem and Haifa. In a series of coordinated attacks seven Arabs were murdered and eight others wounded. Among the casualties were three women.[24]

These operations marked a significant milestone in the Irgun's violent history. Not only had the group evidenced impressive command and control in the execution of six coordinated assaults in two different cities, but it firmly established Raziel's position as one of the organization's most capable commanders. In his postmortem report to the Irgun high command, Raziel explained how the targets had been carefully selected after detailed reconnaissance.[25]

The Irgun attacks were roundly assailed by Britons, Jews, and Arabs alike. The Jerusalem city council and representatives from Jewish and Arab business associations denounced the group, as did both the Arabic- and the Hebrew-language press. The Jewish Agency publicly accused the Irgun of "marring the moral record of Palestine Jewry, hampering the political struggle and undermining security." Raziel's reply to this criticism was contained in his analysis of the operation's political and military implications that was circulated within the group and embraced as the seminal explication of the Irgun's strategy. "The shame of restraint has been removed," he declared. "And not only honor was saved here, but . . . the results of the actions are already beginning to show. He who saw the faces of the Arabs on 'Black Sunday' and in the days following is able to describe for himself what fear fell on them. All of their insolent heroism that in the past year and a half pierced their eyes disappeared suddenly at once."[26]

Raziel was convinced that there was no option for the Yishuv but to transition from what he termed "passive defense" to "active defense." To his mind, "all of these thoughts lead to one conclusion: he who does not want to be defeated has no choice but to attack . . . He needs to charge his enemy and to break his force and his will." The Irgun commander decried passivity as the failed policy of the "Left"—not only of Zionism's labor-socialists in the Jewish Agency and the Haganah, but also of their gentile social democratic counterparts in Germany and Austria who had supinely acquiesced to Hitler's repressive policies and spinelessly accepted Nazi domination. Indeed, rather than being deterred by either official condemnation or popular vituperation, the Irgun became more emboldened while burrowing deeper underground. Internal discipline was tightened and stringent security measures adopted to thwart identification and infiltration.[27]

The group's secretive recruiting practices evidence this. An Irgun training document described the qualities sought in recruits: "a spirit of sacrifice and love for the nation and fatherland, whether he is able to . . . think and decide for himself, and to use his own initiative." Only existing members could recommend potential candidates. The Irgun then conducted a thorough background check of the candidates, including inquiries about their political views, friends and associates, and characters. If a candidate successfully passed this vetting, he was told to present himself at a secret meeting place. The candidate would be admitted only after giving the correct password and then was brought into a pitch-black room where a flashlight was shone directly into his eyes. A specially convened board of examiners would question him about his reasons for wanting to join the Irgun and warn of the dangers that membership in an illegal, underground organization entailed. Finally, the candidate was asked about his attitudes toward Jewish self-defense and to explain the key difference that distinguished the Irgun from the Haganah. If the candidate's answers and explanations satisfied the examiners, one of his hands was placed on a Bible and the other on a pistol. He was then ordered to repeat the following oath:

In full cognizance, without any outside pressure, I hereby swear to be a loyal soldier of the Irgun Zvai Le'umi in the Land of Israel guarding its property, soul and national honor and helping to revitalize the entire nation on the land of its forefathers. I hereby take upon myself complete obedience, without refusal and complete silence regarding everything that I know and will know of the matters of the Irgun. I hereby accept upon myself to listen to my commanders and to fulfil all of their orders in every place and in every time. May the Guardian of Israel help and supplement me.[28]

Against all logic, London had once again permitted the Palestine garrison to shrink to a dangerously inadequate level. In contrast to the two divisions of troops on hand a year earlier, only two "experienced but rather weary" infantry battalions remained—a difference of some fourteen thousand men. Accordingly, Wavell, the new GOC, had no artillery, no armored vehicles (apart from a single company of RAF armored cars), and no cavalry. Moreover, the same rural Arab guerrilla bands that Wauchope had prevented Wavell's predecessor, Dill, from pursuing the previous year had regrouped and resumed their attacks in the northern part of the country. The situation in Palestine's cities was little better. In December 1937, for example, an English schoolteacher living in Jerusalem complained to her sister that "conditions here are definitely growing worse, & are even now in some ways more difficult than in times of actual rioting, for with the present campaign of murders . . . no one feels safe."[29]

The police were both of little help and part of the problem. Indeed, it was the PPF's inability to anticipate the rebellion's eruption and dimensions that had necessitated the army's massive intervention in the first place. The police force's meager capabilities were further strained by the continued unreliability of its Arab section. Despite the lessons of the 1929 riots and Dowbiggin's attempt to reform the CID, that department remained grievously understaffed at precisely the moment when its services were desperately needed. The number of officers assigned to intelligence duties had neither grown nor been given priority between 1930 and 1936. In 1936, for example, the entire CID comprised just twenty-six British and thirty-nine Palestinian officers. The following year saw the addition of only one Briton, whose presence was offset by the departure of a Palestinian.[30]

Battershill, as acting high commissioner, pondered all these developments with mounting unease. Palestine was again spiraling out of control. A new approach was required, and for Battershill the solution clearly involved improving the police force's performance. The army, as events across the previous two decades had repeatedly shown, came and went, with troop strength ebbing and flowing depending on the country's state of upheaval. But the police should have provided the consistent presence required to maintain order as well as the early warning capability needed to nip any trouble in the bud. The PPF had done neither. Hence, Battershill concluded that the services of an outside expert were again required. He specifically requested someone with long experience of India who was knowledgeable about ethnic violence and civil insurrection as well as counterterrorist operations. Ormsby-Gore selected Sir Charles Tegart.[31]

Tegart was perhaps the archetypal British colonial policeman. An Irishman by birth, he had joined the Indian Police Service in 1901 at age twenty and within five years had been promoted to deputy commissioner of police in Calcutta and in 1923 to commissioner. Known as the "Man of Iron" because of his efficiency in "putting down revolution and murder in Bengal," Tegart—uniquely perhaps among senior Colonial Service officials at the time—was also strongly pro-Zionist.[32]

Tegart and his chosen assistant, Sir David Petrie, arrived in Palestine in December 1937 and submitted their report the following month. In contrast to Dowbiggin's three-hundred-page tome of eight years earlier, Tegart and Petrie's assessment totaled no more than sixty-five pages— together with twenty-eight crisply presented recommendations. The report was thus the antithesis of Dowbiggin's in every way. Tegart and Petrie argued for nothing less than the reversal of all Dowbiggin's reforms and for the PPF's complete reconceptualization back to the more militarized organization that Dowbiggin had sought to eliminate. Tegart's fundamental conclusion was a stark rebuke to his predecessor's core values of colonial policing. Given his experience in putting down riots and suppressing terrorism and the parallels Tegart drew between the security conditions in India he knew so well and those he encountered in Palestine, his emphasis was diametrically opposed to the unarmed "civilian in uniform" that was Dowbiggin's colonial model.[33]

First and foremost, Tegart and Petrie called for the reorientation of the British section's mission. They regarded any British officers assigned to traffic or clerical duties as a gross misuse of manpower and urged transferring them, as the only truly reliable and responsible members of the PPF, to public security duties. In this respect they advocated the abandonment of Dowbiggin's fully integrated police force. In contrast to Dowbiggin's emphasis on demilitarizing the police, Tegart and Petrie proposed the creation of a sufficiently staffed rapid-response strike force composed entirely of British personnel. They did not completely oppose the existence of joint British-Palestinian police units in all circumstances. Indeed, they thought that an irregular rural force employed exclusively on patrol and security duties could only function effectively if it included Palestinian officers. But this would be a unique unit, staffed by a "tough type of man, not necessarily literate, who knows as much of the game as the other side." Tegart and Petrie also made the seemingly self-evident argument that the traditional blue PPF uniform should be replaced by khaki drill.[34]

As in Dowbiggin's assessment, however, the CID absorbed the lion's share of Tegart and Petrie's criticism. Inadequate training, poor command, and insufficient staffing, they concluded, had completely undermined its efficiency and effectiveness. Their main recommendation was to obtain the appointment of someone genuinely skilled in and knowledgeable of police intelligence techniques and analysis. The person from the Indian Police Service that Tegart and Petrie had in mind was not available, so Arthur Giles, then assistant commandant of the Suez Canal police and a distinguished veteran of the Egyptian Police Service, was recruited instead. Giles, known by the Egyptian honorific Giles Bey, was regarded as an "authority on Middle East matters after a lifetime in the maelstrom of Arab affairs." He took up his appointment as the head of the Palestine CID in March 1938. In addition to longer and improved training, Tegart and Petrie recommended that the CID be reorganized. The report did indeed have the galvanizing effect on the CID that the authors intended. By the end of the year, its ranks had expanded tenfold to include 237 British and 236 Palestinian officers.[35]

But perhaps Tegart's most enduring legacy was the specially designed fortified police barracks known as Tegart forts—many of which are still used today in both Israel and Palestine and, as one historian of the Palestinian-Israeli conflict notes, "have become as much part of the landscape of the Holy Land as the rocky hills and stone houses." Tegart intended the structures to serve as liaisons between the police and the army to better coordinate security operations. Built of reinforced concrete, each fort contained living quarters for bachelors as well as married couples; jail cells; interrogation rooms; and a full range of entirely self-contained personnel services, including recreational facilities, a laundry, kitchen, and mess hall. The forts were strategically situated at vital choke points along roads and rail lines, in and around villages, and close to the eponymous fifty-mile-long Tegart Wall of double- and, in certain critical places, triple-layer barbed-wire fence built at considerable expense along Palestine's borders with Lebanon and Syria.[36]

Another Tegart innovation was the creation of so-called Arab Interrogation Centres, where specially trained and selected police officers (mostly Arabs) used water boarding and what Keith-Roach termed other "third degree" measures until the detainees, in his words, "spilled the beans." Douglas Duff, a veteran of the Black and Tans in Ireland, who had come to Palestine in 1922 as one of the original members of the Palestine Gendarmerie before rising through the PPF's ranks to become police inspector for Jerusalem, described the process in chilling detail:

> This method . . . had the merit, from the investigators' viewpoint, of leaving no traces for doctors to detect. The victim was held down, flat on his back, while his head was clamped immovably between cushions that left no marks of bruising. It is not pleasant to talk about and even unpleasanter to admit having witnessed. Usually, we British officers remained discreetly in the background, not wishing to have the shirts of our garments soiled, but we were ready to benefit by information wrung by our subordinates from the wretched suspects or criminals.

The aphorism for torture used by British police of giving someone a good "duffing up" was reputedly coined in reference to the same Douglas Duff. In any case, when Keith-Roach learned that such a center was operating in Jerusalem, he went to Wauchope and had it closed.[37]

On March 1, 1938, Wauchope left his beloved Palestine for the last time. His successor as high commissioner, Sir Harold MacMichael, arrived three days later. A more stunning contrast in personality, temperament, and outlook would be hard to imagine. Where Wauchope was ebullient, vivacious, and generous, MacMichael was austere, aloof, and reserved. A Cambridge classicist who had spent most of his career in the Sudan Political Service, MacMichael was described as withdrawn and introspective. The Yishuv despised him. Ben-Gurion recalled MacMichael as a "nasty person, arrogant and bureaucratic, a real disaster for the Jews, Palestine and the British." In *Ben Gurion Looks Back*, the Jewish leader explained why: "He was dreadful. Very bad indeed. I don't say this because he was opposed to us, which he was. There were others who did not see eye to eye with us but whom we could respect as persons. McMichael [sic] was different. He was petty-minded, arrogant, bureaucratic, full of himself and his power; he behaved as a potentate towards 'natives'; and, which was the most grievous sin in a man of affairs, he had a closed mind . . . I cannot recall a single [meeting] which was not distasteful."[38]

For the British—both in Palestine and especially in London—MacMichael was a breath of fresh air. His appointment was greeted warmly and enthusiastically from the start, and his popularity among British civil servants in Jerusalem never waned. Indeed, with the selection of so accomplished a colonial administrator, steeped in Arab culture and fully conversant in the language, London was sending a clear message to its wayward mandate. The policy in force since the Balfour Declaration was no longer manageable. The Royal Commission's partition scheme was now dead. The Foreign Office and Chiefs of Staff warned vehemently against any solution that alienated the Arabs in both Palestine and surrounding countries and would in turn undermine Britain's influence and prestige throughout the region. And the Colonial Office and the Palestine administration were increasingly concerned about having to implement a policy rejected by the majority of the country's population in the face of mounting bloodshed and continued unrest. Britain's ebbing support for the Zionist enterprise would soon be enshrined in a new government policy. MacMichael as such was cast as the government's hatchet man, a role to which he would quickly prove well suited.[39]

One of MacMichael's first duties was to determine the immigration schedule for the March to September 1938 time frame. This he fixed at three thousand persons—a total less than half that assigned for the preceding six-month period. The effect was that Jewish immigration to Palestine, which before the Arab Rebellion had reached a record level of sixty-two thousand persons in 1935, continued to decline to less than half that number in 1936 and to only a fraction of it in 1937 and again in 1938. However unintentionally, the government had once more signaled to the Arabs that violence paid. That Britain's newly evolving Palestine policy incontrovertibly entailed the placation of Arab opinion—and that MacMichael had been specifically chosen to implement it—was again demonstrated only a few weeks later with the arrest of three young Jews charged with attacking an Arab bus.[40]

A string of Arab attacks on Jewish travelers along the Tiberias–Safed road as it passed near the settlement of Rosh Pinna had claimed the lives of ten Jews. Plans were made, but subsequently shelved, by the local Betar contingent to punish the Arabs, who lived in a nearby village, believed to have been responsible for the incidents. Then an especially gruesome attack occurred. Four more Jewish travelers were killed—two women and a child among them. Two young Betarim from Rosh Pinna, Shalom Zurabin and Abraham Shein, resolved to defy their commanders' orders and avenge the deaths. They recruited a slightly older Betar member named Shlomo Ben-Yosef, a twenty-two-year-old illegal immigrant from Poland who had recently arrived in Palestine. Their plan was to ambush an Arab bus on which they thought the men responsible for the attacks used to travel to their jobs in Tiberias. At three in the morning on April 21, the three Betarim broke into the group's armory and removed two pistols and several hand grenades. Shein and Zurabin would shoot at the bus as it slowed along a sharp curve, and Ben-Yosef would then throw the grenade at the vehicle.[41]

From the start, however, the plan went awry. As the Arab bus came into view, Ben-Yosef struck a match to light the grenade's fuse. Suddenly a Jewish car sped past, the men hesitated, and in those few seconds the opportunity to launch their assault vanished. Undeterred, the three Betarim lay in wait until another Arab bus approached. This time Shein and Zurabin opened fire, while Ben-Yosef tossed the grenade in the bus's direction. It failed to explode. Amid screams of fear and panic from the uninjured passengers, the bus driver accelerated and quickly disappeared behind the bend as Ben-Yosef and his companions walked forlornly back to Rosh Pinna. It was their misfortune to stumble into a police patrol searching for illegal immigrants. They were arrested and subsequently charged with three counts of violating the emergency regulations imposed under the Order in Council: illegal possession of firearms and explosives; the illegal discharge of said firearms; and the use of an explosive all with the intention of causing death and destruction. Each carried the death penalty. They were tried by a military court in Haifa on May 24.[42]

Contemporary accounts depict an almost surreal quality to the trial. Three young men were facing execution for an attack in which no one had been injured and no damage had been done. Nearly a thousand Arabs had been arrested and charged with similar offenses, yet only two had in fact been executed. But with Arab violence again escalating and a new high commissioner in place with the remit to restore order in Palestine, the government was determined both to crack down harshly on lawbreakers and to visibly demonstrate its impartiality toward Jew and Arab alike. Indeed, by the end of the year, the death sentences imposed on fifty-three Arabs would be carried out. The defense attorney that the Revisionist Party retained for the three men struggled to distinguish their feckless act of retribution and self-defense from the other acts of sedition and violence endemic to Palestine at this time.[43]

On June 3, 1938, the court found the accused guilty. Zurabin, who had pleaded insanity, was ordered confined to a mental institution. Shein and Ben-Yosef were sentenced to hang. Appeals were immediately filed on their behalf. Messages begging for clemency poured in from Jewish organizations in Europe, Britain, and the United States; from the Polish government (Ben-Yosef was a Polish citizen); from the chief rabbis of the British Empire and Palestine; from churches and synagogues in Palestine and elsewhere; and from Ben-Yosef's impoverished, elderly mother, who beseeched the authorities to at least stay the execution until she could travel to Palestine to see her son for the last time. An editorial in *The Manchester Guardian* also called on the government to show mercy. At a mass rally in London, Jabotinsky blamed Britain for failing to protect the Yishuv and punishing two young men instead.[44]

On June 24, Lieutenant General Sir Robert Haining, the new GOC, commuted Shein's death sentence to life imprisonment because he was not yet eighteen years of age. Ben-Yosef was hanged five days later. Given the extenuating circumstances of Ben-Yosef's crime, the government's determination to make an example of him, and what struck many in the Yishuv as an unseemly rush to judgment—whereby trial, sentence, appeal, and execution took place in little more than a month—Ben-Yosef assumed in right-wing Zionist circles, according to one sympathetic observer, the hallowed status of a "martyr for the cause of liberty." Certainly, the Irgun, Betar, Jabotinsky, the Revisionist Party, and others in Palestine and elsewhere regarded him as such. For example, a young member of Betar in Hungary named Dov Gruner, who two years later illegally immigrated to Palestine and would eventually acquire renown as an Irgun fighter, prophetically wrote to his girlfriend, "It is a shame that Ben Yosef had to go to the gallows to create a Jewish state, and it is more of a shame that others will have to follow him. But it is on the necks of the Ben Yosefs that a free Jewish state will one day rise."[45]

Accounts of Ben-Yosef's composure, courage, and steadfast commitment to Revisionist Zionism's ideals while awaiting execution contributed to his hagiography. Rosenberg, the Irgun's commander, who visited Ben-Yosef the day before his execution, reportedly told a friend, "Either he doesn't understand what he faces, or he is so brave that he does not fear death." A letter reputedly written by Ben-Yosef to his friends in the Betar cell back in Poland to which they had all belonged suggests he was fully cognizant of his fate: "I am going to die tomorrow, despite this I am happy. Why? Because for a period of ten years I gave all of my strength to Betar and I am proud to be the first Betar member on the gallows . . . I believe that after my death they will not restrain themselves." Ben-Yosef reportedly told a group of Jewish journalists who called on him that same evening, "Do not console me. I need no consolation. I am proud to be the first Jew to go to the gallows in Palestine. In dying I shall do my people a greater service than in my life. Let the world see that Jews are not afraid to face death." Various sources relate how Ben-Yosef had carved slogans in poor Hebrew on the walls of his prison cell. They included "Death is nothing compared to the homeland"; "What is a homeland? It is something for which to live, to fight, and to die"; "I was a servant of Betar until the day of my death"; and the title of a well-known poem of Jabotinsky's that was Betar's anthem, "To Die or to Conquer the Mountain." His final words were reportedly "Long live Jabotinsky, long live the Jewish state on both banks of the Jordan River." He went to his death singing "Ha-Tikva." Jabotinsky's wife claimed to have seen her husband cry for the first time in her life. Jabotinsky himself later declared, "Ben Yosef has taught me the meaning of Zionism."[46]

The execution traumatized the Yishuv. The Revisionist Party distributed handbills and pamphlets calling for demonstrations, strikes, and the closure of all Jewish-owned businesses and cinemas in mourning. Protesters in Tel Aviv clashed with police and denounced the government as well as the Jewish Agency for failing to prevent the execution. The administration responded by imposing a curfew on that city as well as on the Jewish sections of Jerusalem to prevent the protests from escalating. Although the Mapai (the dominant Zionist Labor-Socialist political entity in Palestine) and Histadrut had publicly spoken out against Ben-Yosef's death sentence on moral grounds, Zionist leaders such as Ben-Gurion had refused to condemn the execution. According to two of Ben-Gurion's biographers, the Jewish Agency's executive director believed that the life of a Jabotinsky acolyte, who had defied the Yishuv's official policy of *havlaga*, was not worth a confrontation with the British. He ordered the removal of the black flag flying in mourning over the Histadrut's headquarters building and then resigned from its executive committee in protest against the organization's stance on Ben-Yosef. Ben-Gurion maintained that the Revisionists had orchestrated the crisis and sacrificed Ben-Yosef simply to further their aims and generate popular sympathy and support. At the same time, he thought the government's decision to go ahead with the execution was a colossal strategic blunder in terms of its relations with the Yishuv. MacMichael, Ben-Gurion later observed, "was both inept and malicious, and he showed this soon after his arrival when he recommended the hanging of Shlomo Ben Yosef . . . This single act," the Zionist leader argued, "contributed more than anything else to the growth of the dissident terrorist organization, Etzel."[47]

Indeed, the new high commissioner's hopes of appeasing the Arabs with

Ben-Yosef's execution failed. In a report to Malcolm MacDonald, the new colonial secretary, MacMichael noted how much the Arabs had seemed to enjoy seeing Britain placed in the difficult position of responding to Zionist complaint and opprobrium. "It was one of the worst miscarriages of justice in the history of British Colonial administration," Marlowe later reflected.

> It had not even the excuse of expediency. As a means of demonstrating that the Administration was not pro-Jew, it was superfluous. As an attempt to impress Arab opinion it was undesirable. As a demonstration of firmness it was ludicrous; all it demonstrated was the Administration's extraordinary and discreditable desire to curry favour with the Arabs. The effect of the execution was to increase the Arabs' contempt, the Jews' dislike, and many other people's disgust for the Administration. Members of the Administration were immoderately pleased about it, and seemed to think that they had scored a notable triumph.[48]

The alienation of Jabotinsky, who for nearly a quarter of a century had placed his faith in Britain as the Jews' only true patron and defender in the world, was profound. At a rally held in London on June 30, he ominously warned, "The Jews are beginning to ask themselves whether Ben Yosef's way is not the best one. We know from history that martyrs become prophets and bombs become altars." And just a few days later, during a secret meeting with Golomb, the Haganah's commander, Jabotinsky hinted at a dramatic change in Irgun policy. "If I were a terrorist in Eretz Israel," he had reportedly stated, "I would have felt the urge, after Ben Yosef's trial, to do something against England . . . This had touched me so much that I am seriously considering a complete change in our orientation towards England." Jabotinsky in fact had already taken that fateful step. As the final preparations were being made to hang Ben-Yosef, he had sent a telegram to Raziel, the Irgun's chief of staff: "If final, invest heavily," signed "Mendelson."[49]

Jabotinsky had made another important decision with Ben-Yosef's execution. Frustrated by Rosenberg's hesitancy and unimaginative strategy, he demanded the Irgun commander's resignation. Jabotinsky then instructed the four members of the high command to select a successor from among themselves. They chose Raziel. He accepted on the condition that he be regarded as the "first among equals." "For a man such as you I have waited fifteen years," Jabotinsky told Raziel when they finally met for the first and only time in February 1939.[50]

Born near Vilna (now Vilnius), Lithuania, in 1910, Raziel was descended from a religiously devout and learned family of rabbis. As a student at Hebrew University, he soon joined a right-wing student society called Brit El-Al, where he met a charismatic and brilliant fellow student named Abraham Stern. In 1932, Raziel was suspended from the university for disrupting a speech he disagreed with given by the incumbent professor of international law and former attorney general for Palestine, Norman Bentwich.[51]

Raziel had served in the Haganah's Jerusalem detachment during the 1929 riots, but two years later he sided with his mentor, Tehomi, in the split that resulted in the creation of Haganah-Bet. Raziel was thus one of the founding members of the Irgun and by 1935 was so completely immersed in all aspects of the organization that he left the university. That same year, at Tehomi's request, Raziel and Stern wrote a 256-page textbook of Jewish military preparedness and another on military operations.[52]

Raziel's views and plans thus accorded perfectly with the prevailing sentiment within the Irgun. He had, moreover, already distinguished himself as the Irgun's Jerusalem detachment commander and demonstrated his skills as a field commander in orchestrating the coordinated attacks that convulsed Palestine on Black Sunday the previous November. Most of all, he was resolutely opposed to *havlaga* and advocated a more aggressive, offensive strategy to deter Arab violence. Ben-Yosef's execution had shaken him profoundly. In a collection of essays memorializing the martyred youth, Raziel had contributed the chapter titled "Those Who Die Will Redeem the Homeland." In it, Raziel revealed his own personal philosophy—which would also become interwoven with the Irgun's. "There can be no struggle for national freedom," he wrote, "that is not accompanied by sacrifices, conflicts and the slaying of heroes . . . Rise up from the dust!" he commanded the Yishuv. "There are those who are dying to redeem you!" He heralded Ben-Yosef specifically as "the first victim of a Jewish National Liberation Front, a sacrificial lamb"—whom Raziel now vowed to avenge.[53]

There had been a new outbreak of Arab violence on the day of Ben-Yosef's execution. In a matter of hours, twenty-one Jews had been killed. Then, that evening, a bomb tossed into a wedding reception in Tiberias injured seven more, including three children. The next day, Raziel and Stern met with two senior Revisionist Party officials—Joseph Katznelson, a close associate of Jabotinsky's, and Benjamin Eliav, one of Betar's founding members—to discuss the Irgun's response. Raziel and Eliav argued that with Ben-Yosef's execution the Yishuv was at war with Britain and that offensive operations should commence at once against government as well as Arab targets. Stern and Katznelson took a more cautious line, maintaining that the Yishuv was under attack from the Arabs, not Britain, and therefore the Irgun should focus on Arab targets for the time being. "We must create a situation," Katznelson urged, "whereby killing an Arab is like killing a rat, where Arabs are dirt, thereby showing that we and not they are the power to be reckoned with" in Palestine. Katznelson's view carried the day, and plans were now laid for a new Irgun offensive.[54]

About an hour after sunrise on Monday, July 4, an Irgun unit raked Tel Aviv's Carmel Street with gunfire and hurled hand grenades at a group of Arabs gathered near the entrance to a British army encampment. Five persons were wounded, two seriously. Twenty minutes later, a second Irgun team struck diagonally across town near the central train station, killing one Arab and badly wounding two others. The dead and the injured were still being removed from Carmel Street when an Irgun time bomb exploded, injuring several more Arabs. Panic ensued in nearby Jaffa as ambulance and police sirens wailed and an unruly crowd gathered. The government immediately imposed a curfew, ordering all shops closed as British military units and armored cars fanned out across the city. In Jerusalem, meanwhile, attacks had also commenced at daybreak. Two squads of Irgun gunmen opened fire on separate groups of Arabs near the city center and on the city's northern outskirts, wounding four persons. Minutes later, a third squad attacked an Arab bus as it passed within sixty feet of the central police station near the main market in west Jerusalem. Under covering fire, an Irgunist ran up to the vehicle and tossed a bomb inside, killing four persons and wounding six others—four grievously.[55]

The Arabs had their revenge that same evening, when an attack on a Jewish settlement near Tulkarm claimed the lives of four Jews. The next morning, a Jewish merchant and his son were slain in their shop in Jerusalem's Old City, and on July 6 an Arab terrorist threw a bomb into a Tel Aviv train, killing a Jewish woman and seriously wounding four Jewish men. *The Times* termed these three days of bloodshed "the worst outbreak of terrorism yet recorded" in Palestine.[56]

On the evening of July 6, however, the violence crossed a new threshold. Around 6:00 an Irgunist disguised as an Arab porter made his way through Haifa's crowded central market carrying two metal milk churns. He casually set the churns down next to a stall across from a police station and left. Approximately an hour later a tremendous explosion ripped through the market as the time bomb concealed in one of the churns detonated, releasing a lethal fusillade of steel nails in all directions. Then the second bomb exploded. Panic ensued as suddenly shots rang out from every direction. It took the police half an hour to restore order, but the violence both continued and spread to Jerusalem and Tel Aviv.[57]

In less than two weeks, this sustained wave of Irgun attacks had claimed the lives of more than sixty Arabs and injured at least three times that number. But rather than paralyzing the Arabs with fear or inaction and deterring them from further violence, the Irgun operations seemed only to incite greater bloodshed, locking both communities into a vicious upward spiral of intercommunal butchery that refused to abate. Spontaneous rioting broke out in Haifa following the first round of attacks on Monday, claiming the lives of two Jews in addition to that of Weizmann's brother-in-law, one of the architects of Jerusalem's stunning, newly opened Central Post Office on the Jaffa Road. The Zionist elder statesman issued a public appeal for restraint on both sides and pointedly condemned any resort to reprisal.[58]

His plea fell on deaf ears. Less than a week later, again on the Muslim holy day, the Irgun carried out another lethal bombing. A forty-pound explosive was left in the Arab vegetable market, just inside Jaffa Gate and opposite a mosque. It was timed to explode just as midday services concluded and the street would be filled with departing congregants and shoppers. The blast killed twenty Arabs and wounded more than thirty others. The carnage continued when, less than seventy-two hours later, three Arabs were found shot dead outside Tel Aviv and in retaliation Arabs killed four Jewish laborers near Ramat Ha-Kovesh. Indeed, within forty-eight hours, twelve Jews had been murdered and more than thirty others wounded. The Irgun's aggressive new strategy, however, was proving counterproductive in other ways as well. An intelligence assessment prepared for Shertok by Eliyahu Sasson, head of the Jewish Agency's Arab department, detailed how the group's terrorist campaign was driving hitherto moderate Arabs into the rebels' arms—much to the delight of the rebellion's leadership.[59]

As the violence from both sides intensified, Haining ordered the Black Watch onto the streets of Jerusalem to assist the beleaguered police, who were now suffering through daily sixteen- to eighteen-hour shifts. He also requested the dispatch of two battalions of reinforcements from Egypt. In addition, the HMS *Repulse* landed a company of Royal Marines in Haifa who were immediately deployed on curfew duty. Approximately six thousand troops were now in Palestine—a thoroughly inadequate number given the country's worsening security. Quickly grasping the magnitude and dire implications of the situation, the War Office instructed the Fifth Infantry Brigade based at Aldershot, England, to prepare to depart for Palestine—although it would not arrive for at least another six weeks.[60]

Of all Palestine's major cities, Tel Aviv was arguably unique. Conceived and developed as the first truly Jewish city in modern times, it generally felt safer and more secure to Jews than mixed metropolises such as Jerusalem and Haifa. Saturday evening, July 23, began much like any other. Crowds strolled along Tel Aviv's lengthy, palm-lined boulevards. So popular was this routine that a Hebrew word—*l'hizdangeff*—derived from the name of the city's first mayor, Meir Dizengoff, and one of its central thoroughfares, was coined to describe the process of walking down Dizengoff Street. At twenty minutes past seven, a car packed with explosives blew up outside the nearby oceanfront San Remo Hotel. Twenty-three Jews, ranging in age from fourteen to sixty, were injured.[61]

Less than thirty-six hours later the Irgun struck again in Haifa. Once more, an Irgun fighter disguised as an Arab porter arrived at the same central market early on the morning of July 25 with a delivery of pickles. Hidden in a large can were sixty pounds of high explosive again wrapped with steel nails. More than three times the size of previous bombs, this device was designed, in the words of the Irgun's official historian, "to harvest blood on a scale that had not been experienced since the outbreak of the [Arab Rebellion] in 1936 and that would leave a long echo in the streets of the world." The bomber left the can at a spot about sixty feet from the scene of the July 6 incident and then boarded an Arab bus. He was miles away when it exploded forty-five minutes later. Fifty-three Arabs were killed and forty-five wounded, seven of whom subsequently died of their injuries. This incident would stand as the single greatest casualty toll inflicted on one day in Palestine throughout the entire Arab Rebellion. A riot ensued as an enraged Arab crowd attacked Jewish passersby. The police had to stage multiple baton charges to disperse the rioters. By the time order was restored, four Jews lay dead, and ten others had been injured. Thirteen Arabs had also been hurt in the baton charges. At 8:15 a.m. the government declared a curfew. For the remainder of the day, all businesses and banks in Haifa were closed, court proceedings were suspended, and residents were confined to their homes.[62]

These bomb attacks were different from any that the Irgun had previously carried out or that the Arabs had experienced. The fundamental objective of the market bombings had been wanton, mass, indiscriminate killing. Although low-level Irgun operations continued in Tel Aviv, Kfar Saba, Ramat Gan, and Petah Tiqva, among other places, the organization's taste for the dramatic, spectacular, and stunning blow had been whetted. An internal circular boasted that since July the Irgun had inflicted three times as many casualties on Arabs as Arabs had on Jews. The Irgun high command bragged that the Arabs had sustained more casualties in the previous few weeks than the Yishuv had experienced since the start of the Arab Rebellion more than two years before. At the same time, the Irgun's commanders were aware that the group had crossed a red line with the series of bomb attacks on innocent civilians shopping in crowded market-places or exiting mosques after services. One member of the Irgun team responsible for the second Haifa bombing had been "arrested" by the Haganah and, despite repeated entreaties, had still not been released (he was eventually handed to the police). The Irgun high command accord-ingly ordered the tightening of internal force security procedures. "All of the people of the Irgun are asked to exercise caution and to prevent idle conversations," one directive decreed. "Always remember that there are many lurking ears."[63]

The Yishuv, in whose defense the Irgun claimed to have acted, was unsparing in its criticism. Newspaper editorials in *Davar* and *Ha'aretz* respectively denounced the group for its "shameful and calamitous" actions and for daring to "gamble with the fate of the Jewish community." The official Zionist organizations were no less vehement in their criti-cism, going so far as to warn that the Irgun's weapons would eventually be turned against its fellow Jews. An article on the importance of *hav-laga* published on July 28 in the London-based *Jewish Chronicle* alluded to this prospect. Nor were such broadsides empty words. Two weeks ear-lier Golomb had traveled to London specifically to advise Jabotinsky of the dire consequences should the Irgun continue along its self-appointed path of vengeance. Jabotinsky replied that any Haganah action taken against the Irgun in Palestine would necessarily have serious repercus-sions throughout the Diaspora, suggesting that a Jewish civil war would not be confined to Palestine. As the threats of Haganah intervention grew louder, Jabotinsky held a press conference in mid-August in Warsaw, where he proclaimed, "This danger is unfortunately real. Already at the beginning of July I heard the same threat from a man who is very close to the security service of the Jewish Agency (Golomb); he made it perfectly clear to me that, should they not succeed in achieving unity on the hav-laga question, the elements who are under the influence of the Agency would use their arms against the Revisionists." Jabotinsky recounted other pointed threats that had been made to senior Revisionist Party officers in Tel Aviv. These were not "empty phrases," he continued, but "an attempt at an internal Jewish pogrom" that would be resisted in Palestine and else-where in the Diaspora. According to Jabotinsky, police sweeps, aided by leftist "riff-raff"—the Haganah—had already resulted in the incarceration of hundreds of Betarim. Members of the Irgun had also been seized by the Haganah and reportedly subject to brutal interrogation. Meanwhile, Arab terrorism continued apace.[64]

Raziel caustically dismissed the editorials and other criticism of the Irgun's actions. "They can kiss my . . . ," he reportedly told a fellow Irgun member, promising to continue to deliver "bouquets" to the Yishuv's Arab enemies. The next delivery arrived in the Jaffa vegetable market on August 26— another Friday. The operation was a carbon copy of the July 25 Irgun bombing of the Haifa market. A young Irgunist disguised as an Arab vendor left behind a time bomb, again concealed in a large can of pickles packed with nails that exploded at seven in the morning. Twenty-four Arabs were killed and nearly forty wounded. An enraged crowd chanting anti-British slogans decrying the government's inability to protect them torched the local branches of the Barclays and Anglo-Palestine Banks. A British businessman was also assaulted and his car set afire. A mob menacingly proceeded up Tel Aviv's King George V Avenue (now King George Street), looting shops before police were able to restore order and enforce a daytime curfew.[65]

Raziel's defiant actions pushed the Yishuv to the brink of civil war. Two days later, the Irgun and the Haganah agreed to meet and once more attempt to bridge the ideological and operational chasms that separated them. On September 19, 1938, an agreement was reached. Unlike the 1936 unification experiment, it was decided this time that there would be no formal merger of the two organizations. Thus, while the Irgun would retain its complete organizational independence, for operational purposes it would agree to participate in and abide by the decisions of a joint Haganah-Irgun committee that would consider all matters concerning the Yishuv's defense. Final ratification of the pact was made dependent upon Jewish Agency approval. Ben-Gurion, however, refused to countenance the agreement and threatened to resign if the Jewish Agency approved it over his opposition. "The only condition on which [the Irgun] can be brought into our ranks," he insisted, "is for it to be willing to accept the political discipline of the Zionist Executive." As he had done two years before, Jabotinsky rejected any agreement that involved subjugating Zionist Revisionist ideology to labor-socialism. Thus yet another attempt to reconcile the two competing Jewish paramilitary forces into a unified command collapsed. Although the threatened civil war never materialized, from this point forward the Irgun and the Haganah went their separate ways.[66]

CHAPTER 5

Dark Nights of Despair

By the fall of 1938, Palestine was coming apart at the seams. The British army's adoption of mobile columns to harass the rebel bands and cut off their escape routes had proven stunningly effective but frustratingly evanescent. The Arab guerrillas had suffered severe losses in back-to-back defeats at Jenin and the Galilee the previous March, but this had still failed to break the rebellion. Instead, the survivors had regrouped and dispersed into smaller units that deprived the army of the massed forces that it had previously so effectively targeted. Although the rebellion had always essentially been acephalous, its new disposition confounded Haining and his officers. "There are practically no major leaders controlling the gangs, and the various minor leaders," he reported, "are practically completely independent and . . . there is no central organization whose destruction would cause the rebellion to collapse."[1]

Accordingly, no more than a thousand to fifteen hundred Arab guerrillas had been able to impose a reign of terror over the northern half of the country. Armed gangs roamed the hills, venturing into undefended towns and villages where they established shadow governments and parallel administrative structures that dispensed rough justice and collected taxes. Those Arabs who resisted were murdered. Others—landowners and merchants as well as ordinary shopkeepers—were routinely blackmailed or kidnapped for ransom. Arab government clerks and other functionaries together with Arab police either voluntarily or through coercion provided the rebels with information that enabled them to stay one step ahead of the security forces. Governance, commerce, and communications thus ground to a halt. Trains could travel only by day and even then under heavy military guard. Telephone and telegraph lines were regularly vandalized.[2]

Haining had no choice but to redeploy his forces on static guard duties—over the railways and roads and in the cities and towns. The army's new strategy of permanently occupying villages had commenced in late May. Twenty small communities in northern Palestine were thus permanently garrisoned in platoon strength by some forty men. Their mission, the GOC explained to the War Office, was

(a) To deny the village and its neighborhood to the gangs as a source of food, shelter, and recruitment;
(b) To assist the civil authorities to regain control of the area;
(c) To protect, and gain the confidence of, the law-abiding among the inhabitants;
(d) To assist in opening up the more inaccessible parts of the country by road-making, patrols, etc.[3]

By August, Haining could report that the new program had mostly achieved its objectives. Indeed, it was so popular that the leaders of other villages had come forward with requests to be included, though the continued shortage of troops made it impossible for the GOC to comply. Nonetheless, the village occupation strategy was not without its problems. The Arab gangs, deprived of the opportunity to victimize these protected villages, instead found new—now less well-defended—targets for attack, with Haining citing an upsurge in sabotage of roads and railways and particularly of the Kirkuk–Haifa oil pipeline. In fact, the GOC's new strategy was something of a boon rather than an impediment for the guerrillas. With the army and the police shackled to villages or assigned to protect roads and railway lines, the rebel bands were free to raid and plunder wherever they pleased. Indeed, a staggering 5,708 terrorist incidents would be recorded for 1938—a figure more than twelve times the previous year's tally.[4]

For the moment, no help either was forthcoming or could be expected from London. A succession of international crises in the Far East with Japan, in the Mediterranean and East Africa with Italy, and with Germany over the Nazi annexation of Austria had served to underscore Britain's limited military strength and feeble strategic position in multiple theaters. Hence, for more than a year, both the Chiefs of Staff and the Treasury had been complaining that the ongoing military commitment in Palestine was adversely impacting Britain's military strategic interests elsewhere.[5]

The remainder of the fall brought no relief to the beleaguered Palestine government and its security forces. The country was in open rebellion and governmental authority at a nadir. Government facilities rather than Jewish settlements bore the brunt of guerrilla attacks, with the railway and post offices favored targets. Violence was now pervasive, and no part of Palestine was spared in contrast to only a few months earlier when the rebellion had been confined to just a handful of cities and the country's northern regions. The uprising, the high commissioner reported, "has unquestionably become a national revolt involving all classes of the Arab community in Palestine and enjoying considerable support from the

Arabs outside. While there are still a number of foreign volunteers it is no longer the fact that the majority of the armed men are foreigners; on the contrary they are 'locals' and moreover there have been several instances of the villages turning out *en masse* to assist a gang which is engaged with Government forces."[6]

So profound was the breakdown of security that the government's authority actually stopped at the walls of Jerusalem's Old City. No one who was not an Arab dared venture inside, where shopkeepers were at the mercy of the rebels, who stole, looted, and vandalized with impunity. The Temple Mount functioned as their local headquarters—without any visible interference from the police or the military.[7]

This all began to change later in October as a result of the Munich Agreement. The settlement reached by Britain, France, Italy, and Germany, had permitted the dismemberment of Czechoslovakia, but for the time being also averted war. Accordingly, the British military forces being held in reserve in the U.K. could now be deployed to Palestine. Within weeks, the British garrison had expanded in size from the two infantry brigades left behind after the 1937 drawdown to two full divisions, totaling some forty-five thousand men, including twenty thousand troops organized in eighteen infantry battalions along with two cavalry regiments, a battery of howitzers, various armored car units, and some seven hundred RAF personnel.[8]

Their first order of business was to reoccupy Jerusalem's Old City. Over the preceding months, the rebels had steadily bolstered their ranks with the arrival of additional fighters from the surrounding countryside. Their commanders had then embarked on a new campaign of intimidation and defiance of the government, setting fire to the police station near Jaffa Gate and hoisting the rebel flag over the Old City's ramparts. On October 18 the Palestine government announced that jurisdiction over Jerusalem had been formally handed to the military. Using Arab civilians as human shields, British troops forcibly entered the Old City and within a week had cleared it of rebel forces. The Temple Mount, as a religious site, remained off-limits to the security forces so as not to provoke an international incident. Accordingly, many Arab fighters were able to find refuge there before escaping under cover of darkness.[9]

The Palestine administration also imposed new security measures on the country, including strict controls on all movement by civilians whether via road or rail. No one was allowed to travel anywhere without both a government-issued identity card and a special permit. A dusk-to-dawn curfew was also imposed on all vehicular traffic in rural areas. By November, the army had essentially reoccupied the entire country, and Palestine was once again under government control. "From this time on," Haining reported to London, "it became increasingly difficult for the remnants of the rebel gangs to find any security or rest."[10]

Haining's success in Palestine, however, had created new problems for Britain elsewhere. The harsh methods used to suppress the revolt had provoked criticism in Egypt and Iraq as well as in India. Given that Britain in 1938 had more Muslim subjects than any country in the world, with some twenty million in India alone, this was a matter of no small consequence. The Chiefs of Staff and the Committee of Imperial Defence were already closely monitoring German and Italian efforts to turn Muslim opinion against Britain. Indeed, the increasing likelihood of war with Germany despite the Munich Agreement's pledges to the contrary made achieving lasting peace in Palestine of paramount strategic importance to Britain. In the event of war troops involved with internal security duties in the mandate would be more urgently needed for home defense or deployment to Europe. Additional reinforcements would also be required from India. But if Italy entered the war on Germany's side and blocked British access to the Suez Canal from either the Mediterranean or the Red Sea, these forces would have to travel overland across the Middle East, through Palestine. Continued fighting there would impede their movement. Accordingly, a major reassessment of British policy for Palestine was in motion that MacDonald intimated to Haining on October 15 would entail "political moves in the next few weeks which will make a contribution towards ultimate peace."[11]

These "political moves" inevitably focused on the Royal Commission's recommendation for Palestine's partition into separate Arab and Jewish states. The Foreign Office had always opposed partition on the grounds that it could only be imposed by force, thus necessitating a military commitment beyond Britain's means to fulfill while incurring the enmity of Arabs in Palestine and in surrounding countries, and of Indian Muslims as well. This was also the position of the War Office and the Chiefs of Staff. Accordingly, the viability of partition was ultimately decided on the basis of the negative effect that its implementation would have on Anglo-Arab and Anglo-Muslim relations, not only in Palestine, but across the region. The report of the commission chaired by Sir John Woodhead to examine the challenges of implementing the Royal Commission's recommendations presented the government of Prime Minister Neville Chamberlain with an opportunity to abandon partition once and for all.[12]

The Woodhead Commission Report was published in early November. The government seized upon its inability "to recommend boundaries which will afford a reasonable prospect of the eventual establishment of self-supporting Arab and Jewish States" as sufficient justification to jettison partition. A white paper issued the same day explained that the "political, administrative and financial difficulties involved in the proposal to create independent Arab and Jewish States inside Palestine are so great that this solution of the problem is impractical." Accordingly, the government announced that a conference would be held in London early in 1939 to consider Palestine's future. Representatives from Palestine's Arab and Jewish communities as well as from surrounding Arab states would be invited. However, should the conference not produce agreement "within a reasonable period of time," the government reserved the right to impose on Palestine a policy of its own devising.[13]

The London Conference began on February 7, 1939. Britain was determined that its outcome should assuage Arab discontent and thus ensure peace in Palestine at a time when British military commitments were strained by the exigencies of home, continental, and imperial defense. To this end, the foreign secretary, Lord Halifax, told the cabinet, the British delegation's intention would be to avoid "arousing antagonism with the Arabs." The Arab delegation—which included four of the five Palestinian leaders whom the Palestine government had exiled to the Seychelles fifteen months earlier along with representatives from Egypt, Iraq, and Saudi Arabia—was unyielding in its demands for the mandate's termination, complete independence, and an end to Jewish immigration and land purchase.[14]

The government's attitude toward the Jews, meanwhile, was influenced not just by British strategic priorities but by what the Israeli historian Yehuda Bauer has called a "matter-of-fact inclination to view the Arab cause as more logical and correct" than Zionist claims to Palestine. "The conclusion," he argued, "was clear enough—there was no escaping the sacrifice of the Jewish cause on the altar of preparation for a second world war." The cabinet justified this policy on the grounds that in a war with Germany the Jews had nowhere else to turn but to Britain for help. Chamberlain had been brutally frank on this point. "It was of immense importance," he explained to the cabinet, "to have the Moslems with us. If we must offend one side, let us offend the Jews rather than the Arabs."[15]

For more than a month the talks continued. Neither side was prepared to accept the British proposals to resolve the impasse. Weizmann recalled the "atmosphere of utter futility which dominated the Conference." On March 15, Europe was again plunged into crisis when German troops, in defiance of the Munich Agreement, occupied Prague. That same day, the British government announced that if agreement on Palestine was not reached soon, it would declare the conference closed and impose a solution of its own. Two days later the conference ended.[16]

The new policy was unveiled in the white paper issued on May 17. It declared that the Royal Commission's proposal to partition Palestine into "self-supporting, independent Arab and Jewish States . . . had been found to be impracticable." This realization also accorded Britain the opportunity to clarify the "ambiguity of certain expressions in the Mandate, such as the expression 'a National Home for the Jewish people.'" To this end, the statement of policy continued, the government therefore now "declare[s] unequivocally that it is not part of its policy that Palestine should become a Jewish State." Instead, Palestine should remain a unitary entity—"a State in which the two peoples in Palestine, Arabs and Jews, share authority in government in such a way that the essential interests of each are secured." Britain would grant Palestine independence at the end of a ten-year transition period. Jewish immigration was to be strictly regulated at a maximum rate of ten thousand persons per annum over the next five years but thereafter would be dependent upon Arab consent. In view of what the white paper termed the "Jewish refugee problem" in Europe, however, Britain would allow an additional twenty-five thousand immigrants to settle in Palestine. Restrictions were also placed on Jewish land purchase in Palestine—including a complete prohibition covering about two-thirds of the country—although these would not take effect until February 1940. After that date, Jews would be entitled to purchase land without restriction in only about 5 percent of Palestine.[17]

The Higher Arab Committee denounced the white paper as unacceptable in a statement issued from Beirut on May 30. Its objections centered on the proposed transition period to independence, which was dismissed as unnecessarily long, and on the continuance of any Jewish immigration and land purchase.[18]

"All in all, the White Paper was a failure," the German historian of Palestine Gudrun Krämer notes. "It enraged the Zionists without satisfying the Arabs." The Chamberlain government in fact grossly miscalculated the intensity of the Yishuv's reaction. MacDonald had been especially optimistic. In April, for example, he had suggested to the cabinet that there would be a rough patch of perhaps two to three months, during which "Dr. Weizmann would no doubt try to exercise his moderating influence" and any lingering protests would then abate. Accordingly, the colonial secretary had confidently told his colleagues, the cabinet did not need to take seriously the threat of Jewish resistance. He was not alone in this assumption. MacMichael thought the Yishuv too economically weak to confront the government for any sustained period, while British army intelligence in Palestine similarly discounted the likelihood of any trouble from the Jews.[19]

On May 18 an oath was taken in synagogues and other public gathering places across Palestine. "No sacrifice will be too precious in order to set [the new policy] at nought," its adherents pledged. Protests and rallies took place in Jerusalem, Tel Aviv, and Haifa. A demonstration in Tel Aviv organized by the Irgun erupted in rioting as a crowd numbering in the thousands ransacked the district government's building and set fire to the Immigration Department and Land Registry offices. In Jerusalem, the Immigration Department was also attacked and gutted by fire. The following night renewed rioting in Jerusalem resulted in the fatal shooting of a British police officer and injuries to at least two hundred protesters. Afterward, community leaders accused the British police of deliberately preventing the arrival of ambulances of the Red Shield of David, the Jewish first aid society, to treat the injured.[20]

Scenes of Jews battling British soldiers and police in the streets of Palestine were unprecedented. Haining was furious. The following morning he summoned Ben-Gurion and five other Jewish leaders to his office and angrily told them that there would be "no . . . mincing matters" in the event of renewed unrest. Ben-Gurion subsequently replied in writing on the group's behalf. After expressing regret over the police officer's death, he explained,

> With all due deference I must, however, take exception to your statement this morning that the blood which may be shed will be on the heads of the Jews . . . The Jewish demonstrations of yesterday marked the beginning of Jewish resistance to the disastrous policy now proposed by His Majesty's government. The Jews will not be intimidated into surrender even if their blood be shed. In our submission the responsibility for what may occur in this country in the course of enforcing the new policy will rest entirely with the Government.[21]

The Jewish Agency's formal response to the white paper, which was presented to the high commissioner later that same month, contained an identically defiant message. The agency immediately began to implement its active program of resistance to the new policy. As Ben-Gurion explained, "It's either the Mandate or a Jewish State. Britain has definitely come out against a Mandate, so it must be a State." The two most critical means to achieve this objective would entail an intensification of efforts to bring Jewish immigrants to Palestine illegally and the Haganah's transformation into a full-fledged underground army. Accordingly, the program embraced the following specific measures:

- non-cooperation with any government agency or office charged with implementing the White Paper;
- defiance of all laws and regulations pertaining to immigration and land purchase;
- acquisition and stockpiling of weapons—and resistance to government efforts to disarm the Yishuv;
- the building of fortifications and development of nascent naval and air power capabilities;
- training Jewish youth for military and national service;
- the establishment of two separate Haganah streams—a "legal" one (e.g., the Supernumerary Police) and illegal one (e.g., special commando units);
- the establishment of a clandestine press and attendant information operations capabilities;
- the development of a Jewish shadow government with the intention of eventually seizing power when the time was judged propitious;
- the institution of Jewish control over Jerusalem and Tel Aviv; and
- the continued development of local Jewish industries, including arms manufacturing.

These steps necessarily marked a profound change in Anglo-Zionist relations. The time for self-defense and restraint had passed. The Yishuv was at war with Britain.[22]

Ben-Gurion, accordingly, insisted that the Haganah now have a proper budget—provided by both the Zionist Congress and the Jewish Agency Executive and not just by the shadow tax called the *Kofer ha-Yishuv* (the Yishuv ransom) routinely skimmed off sales of luxury items, restaurant bills, cigarettes, and so on, as had previously been the case. He also created clear lines of command and control whereby the Haganah would answer directly to the Yishuv's elected civilian leadership—with Ben-Gurion in effect acting as civilian defense minister. All Jewish adults between the ages of eighteen and thirty-five would be required to serve within its ranks, and Haganah units would be assigned either to local defense or to national defense missions while also maintaining a "semi-regular army" of some fifty-seven battalions.[23]

Perhaps the most far-reaching change, however, would involve the abandonment of *havlaga*. Bowing to mounting pressure within the Haganah for more aggressive operations, Ben-Gurion ordered the creation of a dedicated commando unit referred to as the Special Squads. The hand-picked members of these elite operational teams reported directly to him, thus completely bypassing the Haganah's newly restructured chain of command. The Special Squads' mission would be to attack select British government and economic targets as well as carry out retaliatory strikes against the Arabs. They were also given responsibility for dealing with Jewish informants working for the British authorities. Plans were actually developed for the Special Squads to assassinate British government officials and assault Government House, the police headquarters in downtown Jerusalem, other PPF facilities around the country, and the government printing office. The fundamental differences between the Irgun and the Haganah thus seemed to fade with the Special Squads' establishment. Moreover, the squads served an important cathartic purpose for the Haganah at an especially desperate and uncertain time: they maintained internal discipline and cohesion and discouraged defection to the Irgun.[24]

The Special Squads' existence, however, was short-lived. They were disbanded in September shortly after Britain declared war on Germany. Their record was accordingly commensurately modest: the sinking of a PPF launch used to intercept illegal immigrants arriving by sea; the sabotage of the Kirkuk–Haifa oil pipeline; the firebombing of some police vehicles in Jerusalem; and a raid on a Bedouin village near Haifa. For Ben-Gurion, all these activities were nonetheless of vital importance to the Yishuv, thus further solidifying a common purpose and communal ethos of self-sacrifice and commitment. In addition, they served notice on Britain that it would pay a high price for what was regarded as the betrayal of the Balfour Declaration contained in the 1939 white paper.[25]

On a personal level, these events also elevated Ben-Gurion's stature and leadership within the Yishuv. According to his biographer, Ben-Gurion emerged as its preeminent figure during this time. "His image as a daring leader," Shabtai Teveth writes, "took root in the public mind, and his charisma—which was to grow steadily in direct proportion to the intensifying struggle for the establishment of the state—began to manifest itself. There is no doubt that the days of the White Paper were his finest hour." For a man who had only graduated from high school and always lacked the polish, education, and sophistication of a Weizmann or a Jabotinsky, this was a remarkable achievement.[26]

The Irgun's response to the white paper's announcement was suddenly derailed when police arrested Raziel on the morning of May 19. Hanoch Kalay, his deputy, replaced him as interim commander, but it took another week for the Irgun to react. In a calculated snub to the official Zionist leadership, four Irgunists stole the car belonging to Weizmann's brother, which they then used to gun down Arab passersby as they drove along a busy Haifa street. Eight persons were killed and three wounded. A week later the group attacked an Arab village using a plan that Raziel had previously conceived. Three Irgun teams totaling some twenty-five men converged on the village from three directions under cover of darkness. In the ensuing confusion, four women were killed and a child wounded. Jabotinsky was furious. He demanded that the men responsible be punished and that warnings henceforth be issued to avoid harming women, children, and the elderly. Kalay scoffed at these suggestions but assured Jabotinsky that the Irgun would be more careful in future.[27]

That same night, the Irgun also bombed Jerusalem's Rex Cinema. Although only two of its four bombs exploded, eighteen persons were injured, including ten Arabs, a young Jewish couple, and three Arab and three British policemen. In reprisal, Major General R. N. O'Connor, the Jerusalem district commander, ordered the indefinite closure of all Jewish cinemas, coffeehouses, and restaurants and the cancellation of the philharmonic orchestra concert.[28]

On June 2 the Irgun attacked government targets, destroying the telephone exchanges in three different parts of Jerusalem that severed nearly half of the city's phone lines, including communications at police and military headquarters. But this was only the beginning. A few hours later, a powerful time bomb exploded in an Arab market near Jaffa Gate. Five Arabs were killed, including a policeman, and nineteen others injured. O'Connor now ordered the suspension of local Jewish bus services as punishment. In defiance, the Irgun pressed ahead with its campaign of shooting Arabs and mining roads, footpaths, and orchards in and around Arab villages. Following the Irgun's murder of another Arab passerby in Jerusalem, O'Connor ordered his troops to cordon off the city's Jewish neighborhoods and conduct house-to-house searches for terrorist suspects and weapons caches. This was the first time that Jewish neighborhoods experienced the same security operations that had routinely been applied to Arabs during their rebellion.[29]

The Irgun's propaganda campaign and public information efforts now also shifted into high gear. Slogans with the Irgun's motto, "By blood and fire Judea fell, and by blood and fire Judea shall arise," began to appear on the walls of Jerusalem, Tel Aviv, Haifa, and various other Jewish areas.

The group's clandestine radio station also commenced broadcasting. "We shall retreat before nothing," a typical broadcast from this time period asserted, "for our souls revolt against slavery in which there is no danger, against life in which there is no honor, against peace which has no freedom." The broadcast would then close with the Irgun's anthem, "Hayalim Almonim" (Anonymous or unknown soldiers), sung suitably *grave maestoso*, per its composer's instruction. Derived from a poem written by Abraham Stern earlier in the decade, "Hayalim Almonim" proclaimed,

We are the anonymous soldiers without uniform
Surrounded by fear and the shadow of death.
We have all been conscripted for life;
From these ranks, only death will free us.

Refrain:
In the red days of riots and blood,
In the dark nights of despair,
In the cities and villages our flag we will raise,
And on it: defense and conquest!

We are not conscripted by the whip like multitudes of slaves,
In order to spill our blood in foreign lands.
Our desire: to be forever free men!
Our dream: to die for our nation.

[Refrain]

From all directions a great many obstacles,
A cruel fate has been placed in our path;
But enemies, spies, and prisons
Will not be able to stop us.

[Refrain]

And if we fall in streets and in the houses
And we will be buried quietly in the night,
In our places will come thousands of others
To defend and to guard forever.

[Refrain]

With the tears of bereaved mothers,
And with the blood of innocent babies,
Like cement we will use our bodies as building blocks
To establish the structure of the homeland.[30]

In addition, the Irgun circulated handbills, posters, and pamphlets explaining its aims and motivation. Each had the Irgun logo prominently emblazoned across the top—depicting a hand gripping a rifle against a background of a map representing both Palestine and Trans-Jordan, which the Revisionists erroneously claimed constituted the original British mandate—beneath the words "Rak Kach" (Only thus).[31]

Throughout June 1939 the Irgun launched a succession of shootings, bombings, road minings, and various acts of sabotage and vandalism against British and Arab targets alike. These incidents, however, paled in comparison to the Irgun's bombing, for the third time, of Haifa's vegetable market. The blast, which was heard as far as a dozen miles away in Acre, killed 20 Arabs, among them 8 women and 2 children. Twenty-seven persons were wounded. Three years of Irgun terrorism, amounting to some sixty separate attacks, had by now claimed the lives of more than 250 Arabs and injured hundreds more.[32]

The Yishuv recoiled in horror. *Davar* warned that the Irgun's actions perilously threatened to reignite the Arab Rebellion just when it was on the verge of defeat. A headline in a Histadrut-owned newspaper read, "Terrorism in Its Despicableness." Ben-Gurion issued a statement on behalf of the Jewish Agency that condemned these "foolish and tasteless acts of sabotage [which] do nothing except to help our enemies. These shenanigans of crime and death," he declared, "stain our just war, undermine the legitimacy of our activities and give a hand to our enemies."[33]

The Irgun dismissed this criticism as further evidence of the Jewish Agency's serial political miscalculations and the Haganah's operational impotence. "Arabs use terror as a means in their political fight—and they are winning," an Irgun communiqué retorted. "Meanwhile the leaders of the Jewish Agency do nothing but talking and analysing and going back and forth in their own steps. A hitting fist," it concluded, "must be answered by two hitting fists—a bomb explosion has to be replied with two bomb explosions."[34]

The febrile pace of Irgun attacks—and their sanguinary results—inevitably brought intensified scrutiny from the authorities. The Jewish section of the PPF's CID had redoubled its efforts to penetrate the group either with its own agents or with Jewish informants. By July 1939, accordingly, seventy-four of the ninety-five Jews detained under the Order in Council's emergency regulations were categorized as "Revisionists"—members of the Revisionist Party, Betar, or the Irgun. A deadly cat-and-mouse game thus emerged between the police and the Irgun throughout that summer. Inspector Ralph Cairns, the head of the CID's Jewish section, oversaw PPF operations against Jewish terrorists. One of the few British police officers fluent in Hebrew, Cairns had acquired notoriety within the Irgun for his alleged torture of prisoners. The Irgun accordingly had warned Cairns that he would be killed if he continued to mistreat captured Irgun fighters.[35]

Cairns knew that he was a marked man. He therefore wore a bullet-proof vest, was always armed, and never went anywhere without his friend and colleague Inspector Ronald Barker, the head of the CID's Arab Section. Nonetheless, an Irgun surveillance team was able to discover where he lived, and plans were made to assassinate Cairns. On the night of August 25, an Irgun team planted an explosive device between two trees along the walkway to Cairns's residence. The following afternoon, Cairns and Barker alighted from their car and turned toward the house. As they passed between the trees, an Irgun operative detonated the mine, killing both men. The Irgun claimed credit for the murders twenty-four hours later in a communiqué announcing that Cairns had been found guilty of torturing prisoners by a special Irgun tribunal. He had ignored repeated warnings to stop and therefore had been executed. The message concluded with a warning to "every secret police officer—even if he is British—who dares to abuse a Jewish prisoner [you] will die!"[36]

The police, though, had their revenge five days later when a massive raid on an Irgun safe house in Tel Aviv resulted in the arrest of the group's entire high command, including Kalay, Abraham Stern, and three other officers. The loss of these men completely shattered the organization. But even this grave setback was incomparable to the cataclysmic events unfolding in Europe.[37]

On September 1, Germany invaded Poland. Two days later Britain declared war on Germany. World War II had begun.

The outbreak of war placed the Jewish community in Palestine in a quandary. Although the menace to Jewry inherent in a German victory far outweighed the Yishuv's hostility toward Britain, it did not diminish Zionist opposition to the white paper. However, any program of active resistance to the white paper and to British rule over Palestine, along the lines approved by the Jewish Agency in April, would inevitably hamper Britain's prosecution of the war against Nazi Germany. At the same time, Britain's enforcement of the white paper closed one of the few avenues of salvation open to European Jewry. The Yishuv's political leadership therefore decided to steer a middle course between these two imperatives: it offered its undivided support for the British war effort, and it continued to press for the white paper's repeal. This tension was palpable in the joint statement issued by the Jewish Agency and the Vaad Le'umi on September 3 pledging the Yishuv's support for Britain. Ben-Gurion neatly encapsulated the crux of this contradictory policy when he declared, "We shall fight with Great Britain in this war as if there was no White Paper, and we shall fight the White Paper as if there was no war."[38]

The following day, Jabotinsky, in his capacity as president of the New Zionist Organization, wrote to Chamberlain to affirm his and the organization's loyalty to Britain. On September 10 the Irgun similarly proclaimed its support for Britain and publicly announced the suspension of all antigovernment activities for the duration of the war.[39] This decision was not without controversy. With the entire high command in jail, full consultation had been impossible. Raziel had been able to draft only an outline of the statement, which was then smuggled out of his prison cell within the British army base at Sarafand, outside Tel Aviv, by a sympathetic Jewish police sergeant. Stern was resolutely opposed to the cease-fire and was apparently taken by surprise when it was publicly announced. This created an irreparable breach in his long friendship with Raziel that would eventually have far-reaching consequences for the Irgun, Britain, and the Yishuv.[40]

For their part British officials had already taken Jewish support of the British war effort for granted when they had conceived the white paper. The propensity by 1939 to regard the Jews as a less troublesome and therefore less important factor than the Arabs in Britain's Middle East policy had of course been the driving force behind the white paper.[41] This depreciation of the Jews' political importance in turn encouraged an impression among some senior British civilian and military officials of the Jewish people as an emotional, bleating, and even craven race. Weizmann later recalled sadly, "In those days before the war, our protests, when voiced, were regarded as provocations; our very refusal to subscribe to our own death became a public nuisance, and was taken in bad part." Addressing the House of Commons during a debate on the white paper, the Labour MP Colonel Josiah Wedgwood alluded to the prevalence of such prejudice among British officials, citing "the attitude, which we all share, of liking people who stand up and fight for their rights . . . The Arabs stand up and fight and massacre . . . [while] the Jews are always complaining and begging for justice . . . The attitude of supplication, of being on your knees, has a very bad effect upon the respect of all nations for the Jews."[42]

These British officials were also fully cognizant of the hopes and ulterior motives behind the pledges of Jewish support. Zionists of all stripes—the Jewish Agency, the Vaad Le'umi, the Revisionist Party, and the Irgun—were all of one mind in the expectation that Britain would reward their loyalty and support at the end of the war at least by rescinding the white paper and perhaps even by establishing a Jewish state in Palestine. Chamberlain's careful reply to a letter from Weizmann assuring the government of the Yishuv's allegiance to Britain illustrates this. The prime minister's noncommittal response simply states, "You will not expect me to say more at this stage than that your public-spirited assurances are welcome and will be kept in mind." A minute written on October 11 by Harry Maurice Eyres, the consul in the Foreign Office's Eastern Department, more clearly alludes to the assumption implicit in Chamberlain's reply. "They all [the Jews] seem to think that the defeat of Germany will necessarily entail the establishment of a Jewish State in Palestine," he observed, "which is unfortunate."[43]

CHAPTER 6

The Shadow of Death

The crowd sitting in the lobby of Jerusalem's King David Hotel on October 24, 1939, must have been startled by the arrival of heavily armed police escorting a man shackled hand and foot in chains. Earlier that day, David Raziel had been taken from his jail cell at the Sarafand military base and brought to the hotel. There, he was delivered into the custody of Pinchas Rutenberg, the president of the Vaad Le'umi. A well-known Labor Zionist and the founder of the Palestine Electric Company, Rutenberg was intent on harmonizing relations between the official Zionist institutions and both the Revisionists and the Irgun and thus presenting to the British a united front of Jewish support.[1]

Rutenberg was doubtless also concerned about a second, contradictory Irgun proclamation that had been released hours after the group announced its truce with Britain the previous month. "Treacherous and idle hands are directing the potential energy of the people into unsuitable channels," the communiqué had declared. "IZL [Irgun] soldiers will not spill their blood for concepts of democracy, justice or European culture aimed *merely* at the defense of *foreign* interests and totally incapable of bringing our redemption any nearer." Rutenberg was therefore keen to clarify this inconsistency and obtain from Raziel a reaffirmation of the Irgun's commitment to stand beside Britain in the war. The Irgun leader complied, the police removed his shackles, and after five months in jail Raziel was a free man.[2]

As the rival proclamations showed, the organization that Raziel now resumed command of had become both less unified and more extreme in his absence. Without the overriding imperative of fighting the Arabs, with Jabotinsky still exiled from Palestine and now living in the United States, and with Raziel in prison, long simmering disputes over leadership, policy, and strategy had surfaced. A dissident faction led by Abraham Stern objected to the Irgun's perceived subordination to the Revisionist Party. An underground movement, Stern and his followers argued, can only truly be effective when it is completely free from political influence or pressure.

He and his followers had also lost confidence in Jabotinsky's leadership and especially his misplaced faith in Britain. Indeed, Stern openly styled himself as the movement's chief ideologue and presumptive leader and criticized Jabotinsky and his policies as dangerously anachronistic. These internal tensions had exploded in public with the Irgun's decision to suspend its revolt—which had caught Stern and the other dissidents by surprise and thus prompted their bitter riposte later that same day.[3]

Like Jabotinsky, Raziel believed that Nazi Germany was the Jews' preeminent enemy and that there was no option but to support Britain. Indeed, immediately following his release, Raziel had issued a public statement reasserting the Irgun's loyalty. Privately, he told his followers, "I believe in the victory of England, which will be weakened at the end of the war, and then we will be able to enter into an open war if she still has not fulfilled her word. At the present time, a war against Britain would be suicide." Stern and his fellow dissidents still disagreed. Both Britain and Germany were equally enemies of the Jewish people, they argued. There was no difference between the British, who closed the gates of Palestine to the Jew, and the Nazis, who persecuted him.[4]

That Raziel alone had been freed while Stern and the other Irgun commanders remained jailed added yet another corrosive element to their increasingly troubled relations. The final break came when Stern learned that Raziel had obtained his freedom by agreeing to spy for British police and military intelligence. In addition, Raziel had promised that the Irgun would assist the British military with clandestine operations in the Middle East, the Balkans, and the Baltic States. The British would pay for the information and also had promised to free the remaining imprisoned Irgunists, stop censoring Irgun and Revisionist Party publications, and allocate to the Irgun a quarter of the immigration certificates in the next quota. Raziel would claim that he had made the deal to secure the release of the Irgun detainees but that the police had refused to free Stern and four other Irgun senior officers.[5]

As the Irgun's involvement with the authorities grew, Stern and the remaining imprisoned Irgunists became angrier. Accordingly, when they were finally released on June 18, 1940, they had already resolved to remove Raziel from command. At a meeting held in Tel Aviv the following day, they confronted the Irgun leader. Stung by accusations of treachery, Raziel resigned and returned to Hebrew University and the study of philosophy. Stern was selected to replace him.[6]

Within the week, on June 26, 1940, the Irgun released a new statement explaining Stern's vision for the revitalized group. After expressing regret for the "days of confusion and lost senses" that had recently paralyzed the organization, Stern outlined the reconfigured organization's four core principles:

- the "establishment of the Kingdom of Israel in its historical borders";
- unceasing resistance both to the "occupying army" and to British rule of Palestine;
- complete noncooperation with the British war effort, including refusing to serve in the British armed forces; and
- noncooperation with the official Zionist institutions, especially the Haganah, because of their support of British war aims.[7]

There was one contingency, however, that Stern and his loyalists had apparently failed to take into account: Jabotinsky's displeasure. Having been alerted by alarmed Revisionist Party elders in Palestine to the changes taking place in the Irgun, Jabotinsky sent telegrams to Raziel and Stern on July 17, 1940. He instructed Raziel to resume command of the Irgun and ordered Stern to subordinate himself to Raziel's leadership. But events had gone too far to reverse the schism that now permanently divided the Irgun. Defeatism, Stern told his followers, "is destroying everything we now aspire to achieve." Raziel was equally critical of his former best friend. In a letter he wrote to Hillel Kook, a Lithuanian-born Revisionist Party figure who had changed his name to Peter Bergson when he moved to America with Jabotinsky the previous year, Raziel described Stern as a "delicate playboy hovering over this base, earthly world in holy piety, almost not touching the impurity of this world with his angel's wings," who was in fact an unscrupulous "super-demagogue . . . who so distorts the facts that the borders of reality mean nothing to him."[8]

Raziel's scathing depiction of Stern encapsulates the paradoxes of a man who was variously described by those who knew him as a poet, a scholar, a dandy, a womanizer, a dreamer, and a zealot. Eliahu Lankin, who knew both men well, said Stern was "more of a dreamer, poet, idealist and patriot than a man of action, [who] had a sensitive soul and a keen mind, but he did not excel in the skills of leadership and organization. He was not a good revolutionary commander." In his memoir, Yitzhak Yezernitzky (also spelled as Jeziernicky), who later, as Yitzhak Shamir, would serve as Israel's prime minister from 1983 to 1984 and again from 1986 to 1992 and was among Stern's most devoted disciples, provides this portrait of Stern: "exceedingly intelligent, erudite (he translated Homer into Hebrew), unusually good-looking, polite and very controlled . . . He was

also somewhat of a dandy, very well-dressed, always in a suit with a tie—
even in Palestine, where the tone was set in those days by men in shorts,
open-necked shirts and sandals. He sounded and behaved like a young
university professor."[9]

Fluent in both Greek and Latin, Stern had been an outstanding clas-
sics student at Hebrew University, where he and Raziel had first met. "He
didn't look like a terrorist or a man of violence," Samuel Merlin, a former
secretary to Jabotinsky and leading Revisionist Party official, recalled. Yet,
beyond any doubt, Stern passionately embraced the same self-righteous
conceit shared by visionaries who have employed terrorism through the
ages: a belief that daring and dramatic acts of violence could change the
course of history. This idée fixe completely estranged him from both
Raziel's pragmatism and Jabotinsky's abiding faith in Britain.[10]

Various attempts were undertaken by members of both Irgun factions
to effect some reconciliation. Then, in August, Jabotinsky suffered a massive coronary while inspecting a Betar training camp in upstate New York.
His death plunged the Irgun into further disarray. The group's members
were confronted with the painful choice of electing to stay with Raziel or
to leave with Stern.[11]

Raziel and his followers derisively referred to the splinter organization
as the Stern Group, although it called itself Irgun Zvai Le'umi B'Yisrael,
dismissing it as a "small isolated movement with no public backing, without a moral basis or a political plan." The British disdainfully called them
the Stern Gang. Stern, however, paid no attention to Jewish doubters and
defeatists and still less to Palestine's colonial masters. Instead, he set about
to create an appropriately grand "historical mission" for the fifty or so
fighters who gathered around him. In this, Stern was inspired as much by
the nineteenth-century revolutionary ethos of "propaganda of the deed"
as he was by the personal heroism and self-sacrifice of the Irish rebels
during the 1916 Easter Rising. He therefore looked to the nineteenth-
century Russian revolutionary organization Narodnaya Volya (People's
Will) and its struggle against the tsar. These idealistic young men and
women had understood that their comparatively small subversive movement could not hope to overcome the Russian monarchy's capacity for
repression. Accordingly, they attempted to draw attention to themselves
through heroic acts of violence designed to inform, educate, and ultimately rally the politically ignorant or indifferent masses behind their
revolution. Stern similarly saw terrorist attacks on the British in Palestine

as a means to teach the Yishuv that the liberation of their homeland would only be achieved through sacrifice and armed struggle.[12]

Stern and his followers were also convinced that Britain's preoccupation with the war presented the Jews with an ideal opportunity to seize control of their destiny either by driving a harder bargain with Britain in exchange for the Irgun's support or simply by continuing the revolt. In this, Stern had in mind the model of the 1916 Irish Easter Rising, which had been deliberately timed to occur when Britain was similarly distracted by World War I. He had studied P. S. O'Hegarty's book *The Victory of Sinn Féin*, translating parts of it into Hebrew, and was continually inspired by the Irish rebels' martyrdom and example. He thus consciously sought to replicate the Irish revolution in Palestine.[13]

It would be mistaken, however, to see the historical mission that Stern had ordained for his followers strictly in classical nineteenth- and twentieth-century secular-political-revolutionary terms. Indeed, unlike the assertive secularism of the labor-socialist-dominated mainstream Zionist political movement or the strident nationalist pride evidenced by the Revisionists, Stern placed his struggle in a religious and even messianic context. This is not entirely surprising given that Stern himself was a devout Jew who, according to his wife, prayed daily and "never went to sleep without first reading the bible." His melding of religion with revolution is revealed in one of his poems where he writes, "Like my father, who, on Shabbat, reverently carried his prayer shawl in his bag on the way to his house of prayer, I will carry in my bag holy pistols . . . Because there is a religion of redemption—a religion of the war of liberation. He who acknowledges this war—will be blessed; he who desecrates it—will be cursed."[14]

This was also the impression of Geula Cohen, the founder and leader of the extreme right-wing Tehiya Party and member of the Israeli Knesset from 1974 to 1992 who was a teenage member of the Irgun and followed Stern when he left the group. She describes how Stern imbued his followers with the conviction that the freedom they were fighting for "was not simply a freedom from foreign rule, but one that would enable us to create a new, distinctively Hebraic way of life." To Stern's mind this entailed resurrecting the Kingdom of Israel in a manner that conformed to the geographic dimensions of the biblical promised land along with the building of a Third Temple in Jerusalem to replace the Second Temple destroyed by the Romans two millennia before. He also called for the ingathering of Jews dispersed across the Diaspora and the complete restoration of the Jews' historical, cultural, and spiritual autonomy.[15]

Cohen in fact always refers to Stern by the underground nom de guerre he chose for himself: Yair—the Hebrew word for illuminator or "he who enlightens." This name was also clearly meant to evoke the heroism of Eliezer ben Yair—one of Jewish history's most famous revolutionary heroes. Following the Roman conquest of Jerusalem in 70 c.e., ben Yair and approximately a thousand Jews fled to the mountaintop fortress of Masada located on the eastern edge of the Judaean desert, overlooking the Dead Sea. There, they withstood a three-year siege by the emperor Titus's Roman legionnaires.[16]

Stern hoped his combination of revolutionary zeal and terrorism's didactic power would galvanize the masses behind his extravagant redemptive plans. His organizational and leadership styles, moreover, were just as unique as his hybrid ideology fusing secular, nationalist conceptions of insurrection with religious imperatives. Rather than the rigid, hierarchical, command-and-control structure typical of terrorist movements throughout history, Stern evolved a more networked, innovative structure decades before it became common among many contemporary terrorist movements. "We had no hierarchy, no GHQ [general headquarters], just a central committee," Shamir recalled. There was no distinction between officers and other fighters, no saluting or standing at attention on parade. There was no "follow the leader." But discipline, he states, was nonetheless very strict. Most important, Stern wanted his followers to be able to think for themselves and function on their own without having to constantly refer to orders or directives. "Study, train and think" was the guidance Stern regularly imparted to his followers. For all these reasons as well as his personal magnetism, Stern "was very highly thought of in the underground," Shamir claimed. "He was a mixture of statesman, philosopher, poet and also fighter." British intelligence, however, regarded him as little more than a "megalomaniac, fifth column gangster," while the mainstream Irgun regularly excoriated him for "leading a useless existence, supported by lies and promises."[17]

Stern's grandiose dreams and half-baked plans lacked at least one ingredient critical to their attainment: money. For an underground to survive, let alone pursue as ambitious an agenda as Stern had defined, it requires ample funds. Dwellings have to be rented or purchased for use as safe houses; food, clothing, and other necessities must be bought for outlaws unable to hold jobs or function openly in normal society; and resources are required to spread propaganda. The Stern Group, however, was bankrupt. Moreover, having issued its first communiqué on September 3, 1940—the one-year anniversary of Britain's declaration of war on Germany and the Irgun's truce—the fledgling organization now had to make good on its claim as the sole legitimate voice of the fighting Jewish nation. It therefore began robbing banks. On September 17, 1940, several gunmen grabbed £4,400 from the Tel Aviv branch of the Jewish-owned Anglo-Palestine Bank. Although everything went according to plan, with the loot quickly transferred from the getaway car to a motorcyclist who sped away in the opposite direction, police captured the hapless driver of the car. Information he provided led to the arrests of six other Sternists the following day. The group was consequently forced to eke out an existence derived from theft, extortion, and the kidnapping of wealthy Jews.[18]

Stern, however, sensed a potential turn in the group's fortunes when war suddenly intruded on Palestine. Over the course of several days in September, Italian aircraft bombed Haifa and Tel Aviv. More than a hundred people were killed and nearly 150 injured. Then, in the middle of the month, Italy's armies in Libya and East Africa began pushing east and north toward Britain's meager defenses in Egypt and the Sudan. The Battle of Britain meanwhile was being fought in the skies over England, coming hard on the heels of the setbacks suffered since the spring with Germany's conquest of France and the Low Countries and the evacuation of the British Expeditionary Force from Dunkirk. With British defeat in multiple theaters seemingly looming, Stern took the first fateful step toward an alliance with Italy and Germany.[19]

Stern's interest in pursuing such a partnership is not entirely surprising. He had lived in Florence between 1933 and 1934 and was steeped in Italian culture, and according to Joseph Heller, an Israeli academic, Stern himself was "enchanted by the Italian revolutionary movement, as expressed through the figures of Garibaldi, Mazzini, and in a different sense, Mussolini." He in fact had strong fascist leanings. "Stern's origins are in European fascism," Heller explains. "They're the most extreme group Zionism ever produced. They didn't just want a Jewish state, they wanted a Jewish kingdom. Nor did they fully grasp the portent of Hitler. They thought he was just another anti-Semite."[20]

Stern had already made contact with the Italian consul in Jerusalem before Italy entered the war in June 1940. But these feelers never went anywhere. They were resurrected three months later—supposedly after Stern learned from an Irgun double agent that Italy was interested in establishing a fascist Jewish state in Palestine under its protection. Bathed in the optimistic glow of an imminent Italian victory, Stern drew up the so-called Jerusalem Agreement to be concluded between his organization and Italy and eventually Germany. Its entire premise was based on the fatally erroneous assumption that for Hitler the crux of the Jewish problem in Europe could be solved by evacuation, not annihilation. Indeed, under its terms, Italy would facilitate the repatriation of European Jews to Palestine. Haifa would serve as the capital for a vast Italian-backed enterprise to organize, recruit, and build a Hebrew army and then a Hebrew state. This state would have a fixed 80 percent Jewish majority and be guaranteed the diplomatic recognition of, and enjoy economic cooperation with, the region's Arab states. Finally, the Vatican would assume responsibility for Jerusalem's governance—except for those sites in the Old City sacred to Jews. In return, Stern would turn his envisioned "Kingdom of Israel" into a German and Italian vassal. This patently implausible daydream went nowhere—whether from lack of Italian interest or sheer incredulity remains unclear. At the end of the year, Stern himself accepted its futility following Italy's dramatic battlefield reversals in the Western Desert and Greece. A secret British police intelligence report, however, claims that about this same time Stern was nonetheless successful in securing a monthly stipend of $2,000 from Italian intelligence officers based in Beirut.[21]

Undaunted by his failure to secure a modus vivendi with Italy, Stern shifted his attention to Germany. As preposterous as such an alliance now appears, there was an admittedly desperate logic behind Stern's overture. To his mind, Britain was the Jews' preeminent enemy because of its betrayal of the Balfour Declaration and throttling of the Jewish national home. Stern regarded Germany as only a "persecutor." His enmity against Britain had hardened when Stern learned that his father was trapped in Poland—barred from entering Palestine and therefore consigned to an uncertain fate in war-ravaged Eastern Europe.[22]

Even though the Nazi execution squads were already at work in Poland, Stern held out hope for a solution that would spare Europe's Jews annihilation. Given that the conference held in Wannsee, a Berlin suburb, where details of the Nazis' "final solution" of the Jewish problem were formally articulated, was still a year away, Stern's wretched gambit—however contemptible— is nonetheless barely comprehensible. It must also be kept in mind that he was absolutely certain that the Jews were now on the verge of a monumental historical turning point that could be exploited in their favor— provided that they were ruthlessly unsentimental and coldly calculating in parsing their few actual, remaining options.[23]

Although the precise chain of events remains obscure, it appears that the idea to approach the Nazis was Stern's alone. His two loyal deputies, Hanoch Kalay and Benjamin Zeroni, evidently offered no opposition. Toward the end of the year, Stern ordered Naftali Lubenchik to travel to Beirut bearing the alliance offer. Lubenchik arrived in early January 1941 and presented a memorandum proposing a formal alliance between the "new Germany" and the "renewed National Popular Hebrew Movement" (that is, the Stern Group). Its fundamental premise was that Nazi Germany wanted to rid Europe of its Jewish population and that this could be accomplished by their mass evacuation to Palestine.[24]

Precisely how Berlin greeted this unusual invitation remains unknown. However, there is some indication that the Nazis might indeed have taken it seriously. The Jerusalem Consular Files of the U.S. Department of State contain a memorandum of a conversation held on June 6, 1941, between President Franklin D. Roosevelt's secretary of state, Cordell Hull, and the Polish ambassador, Jan Ciechanowski. It states, "The Polish Ambassador . . . said that the Nazis were talking about the establishment of a Jewish state in Syria and Palestine where all Jews from central and eastern Europe would be located." Although both Hull and Ciechanowski regarded the report as Nazi disinformation, the ambassador's remarks suggest that Stern's entreaty might not have been dismissed completely out of hand.[25]

Stern could not of course have known this, because there is no evidence of any German reply and Lubenchik himself was never able to report back to him in person. British intelligence intercepted Stern's emissary in Syria and immediately transferred him to Palestine's Mazra detention camp. Lubenchik, along with other Stern Group and Irgun members, was eventually exiled to a prison in Eritrea, where he died in 1946.[26]

Meanwhile, as the war appeared to tilt even more decisively in the Axis's favor throughout the spring of 1941, Stern was becoming increasingly agitated by fears that the historic moment had passed. April 1941 alone saw Germany's conquest of Greece, the rout of British forces in North Africa by Lieutenant General Erwin Rommel, and a pro-Axis coup in Iraq that threatened British access to oil fields and its land bridge to India.[27]

Distraught over the prospect of a providential opportunity slipping from his hands, and powerless to effect any change given the paucity of men, weapons, and money at his disposal, Stern played the only card he had. For months the group had been preparing to inaugurate an underground radio station that purported to provide the Yishuv with the "correct news" about both Zionist and world events and would broadcast weekly on Saturday evenings. It went on the air in May with a scathing denunciation of the Jewish Agency, describing it as a "clique of ageing lobbyists . . . [whose] authority is less than that of a Jewish community in territories conquered by Germany." The reaction was swift and, for Stern, nearly catastrophic. Acting on information presumably provided by the Haganah's intelligence service, Shai (the acronym for Sherut Yediot—Information Service), police raids over the course of the following twenty-four hours netted several key Stern Group members. Stern's pathetic response was to offer his terms of an alliance to the British prime minister, Winston Churchill. Predictably, they demanded the white paper's immediate abrogation, the establishment of a Jewish army, and self-rule leading at the war's end to complete independence. Equally predictably, there was no response.[28]

Hence, by the summer of 1941, the grand historical mission that Stern had sought for his movement had run out of steam. Another major bank robbery, this time of the Ottoman Bank in Jaffa, was again bungled. A Saturday evening clandestine radio broadcast forlornly evoked the martyrdom of Ben-Yosef to a disinterested, if not actually hostile, audience. The Stern Group was also singularly bad at keeping secrets—the sine qua non for an underground movement's survival. All of Stern's overtures to the Italians and the Germans, for instance, were known to and closely monitored by British intelligence. The police, moreover, seemed able to apprehend group members almost at will.[29]

In these circumstances, the group turned on itself. Kalay was the first to challenge Stern and criticize his leadership skills. Others complained about Stern's failure to initiate any kind of a sustained terrorist campaign against the British. Zeroni in fact approached the mainstream Irgun to discuss the prospects of effecting a reunification. It thus was in desperation that Stern once more turned to Nazi Germany. In December 1941 he instructed the group's chief of staff, Nathan Friedman-Yellin (who later Hebraized his surname to Yalin-Mor), to go to Turkey and establish contact with the Nazis. But that mission also ended in abject failure. British intelligence intercepted Friedman-Yellin in Aleppo, Syria, the following month and arrested him. Meanwhile, back in Tel Aviv, Stern was scrambling to prevent his organization from falling into complete irrelevance. Stern himself now assumed direct operational command. In hopes that a quick infusion of cash would turn the situation around, he authorized a new series of bank robberies in late December. Although the first passed without incident, it only netted the group a few hundred pounds. A more ambitious plan was hatched early in the New Year to rob a bank courier. It, however, went tragically awry and set in motion a chain of events with catastrophic consequences.[30]

Shortly before 9:00 a.m. on January 9, 1942, a courier with a satchel under his arm stood waiting for a bus on Tel Aviv's Ahad Ha'am Street. He was approached from behind by two men, one of whom struck him in the head with a homemade truncheon while the other grabbed the case, which contained more than £1,000 in cash. Both men fled and as they ran down the street were joined by an accomplice who had been standing watch. The injured courier struggled to his feet, shouting "Robbery! Pursue them! Catch them!" as several bystanders gave chase. The thief with the satchel disappeared, but a passing police patrol, alerted by the commotion, followed and cornered the two other assailants. One man fired several warning shots in the air before dropping his revolver and raising his arms in surrender. His companion, however, opened fire at the police but instead shot dead two innocent bystanders.[31]

Stern was now presented with three new problems. First, the killings defied the group's lofty revolutionary aspirations as a self-proclaimed "covenant of freedom fighters." They were now condemned in the Hebrew-language press as common thieves and fifth columnists. Second, the continued hemorrhaging of personnel because of arrests was taking its toll as the group contracted from a high of fewer than a hundred men to only a few dozen. Moreover, this meant that more junior fighters, with considerably less experience and maturity, were increasingly thrust into command responsibilities. Finally, Stern was well known, in the words of a CID analysis, to "never desert a member of his group in trouble." Hence, in addition to engaging a lawyer for the two men, he instructed his followers to systematically intimidate any potential witnesses, threatening them and their families with death. This did little to improve Stern's or his organization's already negative reputation within the Yishuv. In frustration, he decided it was time for the group to take decisive action by targeting the heart of the British intelligence apparatus in Tel Aviv—the CID.[32]

Stern's plan was to decapitate police antiterrorist operations in the city by eliminating Assistant Superintendent Geoffrey Morton, the Lydda district CID commander, whose remit covered the country's major population hub—including Tel Aviv, Jaffa, Rehovot, Ramle, and Ramat Gan—and Inspector Tom Wilkin, his deputy. Wilkin was an especially high-priority target for Stern. Among the few British police officers fluent in both Hebrew and Yiddish, Wilkin was the PPF's leading expert on Jewish affairs, possessing "an awesome fund of information (including names and addresses) about the network of the Jewish undergrounds." The idea was to use a small explosion in a rooftop storage shed to lure Morton and Wilkin to investigate what would appear to be a Stern Group bomb factory. Upon their arrival, a spotter positioned on an adjacent, though slightly higher, rooftop overlooking the apartment would use a command wire to detonate a larger explosion—killing both police officers.

Still another explosive device would be secreted in a flower bed by the walkway to the apartment that would serve either as a backup in the event the second bomb did not detonate or to kill additional police arriving at the scene. Three years earlier the Irgun had successfully set a similar trap to kill Cairns and Barker, the Jerusalem CID's top antiterrorist officers.[33]

Around 9:00 a.m. on January 20, the police received an anonymous tip that there had been two explosions in a room on the roof of 8 Yael Street in Tel Aviv. Morton was busy and instructed another senior officer, Deputy Superintendent Solomon Schiff, to go immediately to the building. Morton said that he would follow as soon as his meeting ended. Schiff left with another Jewish police officer, Inspector Nahum Goldman. Both men were accompanied by a Jewish constable named Dichter and a British policeman, E. T. Turton, who had recently transferred to Tel Aviv from the Acre prison, where he had served as hangman and had been responsible for Ben-Yosef's execution four years earlier. The four men went up to the roof, where they found the door to the shed locked. They forced open the door, and just as Dichter entered, a tremendous explosion occurred. Schiff was blown through the wall and landed in the garden below, dying instantly. Turton and Goldman were trapped beneath the rubble, and Dichter was writhing in agony—the force of the blast having thrown him to the other side of the roof. Goldman died in the hospital early the following morning and Turton a week later. Only Dichter survived. The police discovered the third bomb, buried in the flower bed, containing twenty-nine sticks of gelignite, and safely defused it. The deaths were all the more cruel because Schiff and Goldman were popular and well liked both by their fellow officers and by the Jewish community as well.[34]

The Yishuv was horrified. Stern's followers had now murdered five persons within a week—four of whom were Jews. Within twenty-four hours, Shertok had written to Major Alan Saunders, the PPF's inspector general, to express the Jewish Agency's sorrow over the incident. Praising Schiff as one of the PPF's "bravest" and most "gallant" officers, Shertok pledged the agency's "wholehearted . . . support [for] whatever effective measures may be taken in order to track down the murderous gang and free Palestine and the Yishuv from this nightmare of holdups and assassinations." On January 26, the Vaad Le'umi passed a resolution condemning the attack and its perpetrators that also denounced Stern and his followers as a "lunatic band," a collection of "madmen," and a "gang of senseless criminals [who have] set out to create a reign of terror in this country." A delegation of the Yishuv's most senior leaders—including the Vaad Le'umi chairman, the mayor of Tel Aviv, and the chairman of the League of Local Councils—called on the chief secretary, Sir John MacPherson, to offer the Yishuv's unstinting cooperation in eliminating the terrorist group. According to Heller, the Haganah started to round up and detain Stern's followers. Interestingly, the official Zionist institutions also sought to use the murders as a pretext to goad the government to take action against their rivals in the Revisionist Party and the Irgun, falsely pointing the finger at their alleged responsibility for the recent violence.[35]

"For the first time," though, Morton observed, "the Government took Abraham Stern seriously." On January 27 the police offered £2,200 in reward money for information leading to Stern's arrest and the five members of his group believed to have been involved with the bombing. Stern alone had a £1,000 bounty on his head. Wanted posters appeared on walls and lampposts throughout Palestine, and quarter-page advertisements offering rewards for their arrest were prominently featured in major national newspapers like *The Palestine Post*. These outreach efforts quickly bore fruit. Tips began pouring into the police, and within the week four of the six persons wanted in connection with the Yael Street bombing were in police custody. Each had resisted arrest and was consequently shot; two of them died. One lead flowed from another as the roundup of Stern's followers continued. At the end of the month a police raid on the group's information office resulted in the seizure of a treasured duplicating machine and assorted literature.[36]

The police were now closing in on Stern himself. He was forced to adopt a furtive and peripatetic existence: never staying in the same place more than once, often sleeping in the rough in stairwells and alleys, carrying with him at all times a small suitcase containing a collapsible cot and a few clothes. But he also remained completely unapologetic for everything that had happened during those few weeks of heightened violence. Stern's propagandists explained in pamphlets and broadsheets pasted on walls as well as over their clandestine radio station that because of the group's small size the two members involved in the courier's robbery had no choice but to open fire and try to evade capture. They justified the Yael Street murders of the CID's Jewish "hirelings" on the grounds that the police routinely tortured arrested group members. One of the organization's Saturday evening radio broadcasts from its secret transmitter desperately sought to rally the Yishuv:

> Neither the kindness of other people nor the world's conscience will grant us the homeland. Hebrew weapons will conquer her from the hands of foreigners . . .
> Go to war for your great and persecuted people, be one of the anonymous soldiers.[37]

Meanwhile, the CID was keeping close watch on Moshe Svorai and Ya'acov Levstein, the two Stern Group members convalescing in a prison hospital after having been shot in a police raid on January 27. A British sergeant in charge of their guard detail happened to speak excellent Hebrew and had offered his services to the CID. A plan was concocted whereby the sergeant would solicit a bribe in return for acting as an intermediary between the two prisoners and their friends and families. On February 11 a note sent by Svorai to his wife via Mrs. Levstein made reference to an unnamed "guest." Then, the following morning, this sergeant overheard Svorai give Levstein's mother his address: "No. 8 Mizrahi B. Street—on the roof." Word was immediately passed to the CID, which rushed to the apartment—a small, two-room flat on the roof.[38]

Stern and Svorai's wife, Tova, were just finishing breakfast when they heard a light knock on the door. As always when a visitor called, Stern hid in the bedroom closet. Tova opened the door to find Wilkin and several policemen. Wilkin explained that they had come to collect some clothes for her husband, who was being moved that day from the hospital to prison. Tova went to gather the garments. Glancing around the room, Wilkin spotted a man's hat and some handwritten papers on a table in what appeared to be a man's penmanship. A search of the premises was therefore initiated. Morton breathlessly describes what happened next: "This tough gang leader, master-mind of terrorism, organizer of mass murder and of assassinations by the dozen, arch-enemy of Britain and the war effort, this would-be Quisling, was found hiding in the wardrobe under the petticoats of his hostess." Morton was summoned to the apartment and arrived soon after with several other detectives. Accounts of what happened next diverge. In his memoir, Morton recounts how Stern bent to tie a shoelace and then "suddenly dived under the gun of the policeman who was covering him and made a mad rush towards the open window leading to the flat roof." The CID commander explains that on numerous occasions Stern had reportedly boasted that he would never be taken alive—a point supported by American intelligence analysts in the Office of Strategic Services (OSS), the CIA's forerunner. Morton shot him dead. The official PPF report prepared by Saunders largely dovetails with Morton's recollection. Accounts from Jewish sources, however, paint a very different picture and have long argued that Stern was deliberately executed. Both in his memoir and in interviews with historians and journalists after, Morton always maintained that Stern's killing was entirely justified. Indeed, the coroner's inquest returned a judgment of justifiable homicide—"killed while attempting to escape." And, moreover, Morton won three libel suits against publishers of books claiming otherwise.[39]

Stern was buried that same afternoon at a local cemetery. His legacy to this day remains as mixed as it is controversial. For Friedman-Yellin, who would eventually succeed him as one of the group's leaders, Stern courageously charted the only possible course for Jewry on the eve of the Holocaust. But, according to Bernard Joseph, who was successively legal adviser to the Jewish Agency and head of its political department, Stern would likely have been forgotten if not for the mysterious circumstances surrounding his death. "Stern's ideas were totally crazy . . . If he'd been tried for murder and executed according to law, he wouldn't be commemorated now as a martyr." Efraim Dekel, who headed the Haganah's intelligence service, avers that Stern's death "was not a very good way for a leader of a guerrilla group to die, being dragged out of a cupboard . . . He was more of a poet than a fighter." Indeed, among the handwritten papers Stern had been working on in Svorai's apartment, the police found two poems he had composed—one praising those who "die for the fatherland."[40]

It had been only eighteen months since Raziel and Stern had parted company. Yet in that time the leadership and fortunes of both the Irgun and its more radical splinter had changed dramatically. In the weeks following Stern's death, the police arrested more than twenty of his most loyal followers, effectively neutralizing the organization. For very different reasons, the Irgun had similarly fallen into desuetude. Raziel's resumption of command following Stern's departure had failed to still the discontent welling within the organization. By December 1940, Raziel had had enough of the internecine squabbling and second-guessing of his leadership and resigned for the second time. But the remaining Irgun commanders could not agree on a successor. Hence, lacking both direction and a clear mission, the Irgun effectively ceased to function as an organized entity. Its activities, such as they were, appeared more in service to the CID than in pursuit of any demonstrable revolutionary ideal. The Irgun thus needed a mission to reclaim its purpose and focus. Just such an opportunity was presented to the group by British military intelligence in Cairo early in 1941.[41]

The war at this time was not going well for Britain, and its vital strategic position in the Middle East appeared threatened from all directions. In these dire circumstances, active British military cooperation with the Yishuv was resurrected. The Haganah created in May 1941 a new unit called the Palmach (the acronym for Plugot Mahatz, or Strike Force) that would soon undertake clandestine operations on behalf of Britain against

Vichy forces in Lebanon and Syria. In addition, covert British military organizations such as the Special Operations Executive (SOE)—charged by Churchill with setting "Europe ablaze"—turned to the Yishuv's population of recent European émigrés for agents who could be recruited and infiltrated back into their occupied homelands for intelligence gathering and subversive operations. SOE headquarters in London sent A. W. Lawrence (brother of the famous Lawrence of Arabia) to Palestine to assess the prospects for cooperation along these lines. His report painted a glowing picture of the possibilities. Working closely with the Jewish Agency to identify potential operatives, Lawrence approvingly described his encounters with "honourable fanatics who will stick at nothing. Physically and mentally tough, highly disciplined and used to guerilla warfare. No better human material could exist for our purpose."[42]

SOE, accordingly, established three secret facilities in Palestine: a special training school, known as STS 102, in a monastery on Mount Carmel in Haifa; a parachute training facility outside Nazareth; and a pre-deployment holding camp in a crusader fortress near Athlit. STS 102 was specifically charged with providing instruction in "unarmed combat, demolitions, pistol and knife fighting, map reading, etc., etc. and to instruct special parties of Allied troops in these subjects 'on sound English lines.' "[43]

It was into this new world of clandestine special operations that the Irgun and Raziel were drawn. In January 1941, British military intelligence headquarters for the Middle East summoned Yitzhak Berman, an Irgun liaison officer with British intelligence and future member of Israel's Knesset and a minister of energy and infrastructure, to a meeting in Cairo. An agreement was concluded, with Raziel's approval, whereby small teams of Irgunists would be infiltrated into North Africa, the Balkans, and southern Italy in support of British military operations. Soon after, the first Irgun operatives were given two months of training by their new mentors and were delivered via submarine to North Africa. For various reasons, none of the missions succeeded. Another opportunity for the Irgun to prove itself, however, arose in Iraq. Following the coup there, the Germans had deployed a Luftwaffe bomber wing at an airfield just outside Baghdad.[44]

On May 13, British intelligence headquarters in Cairo again approached Berman, asking whether the Irgun could, at short notice, mount a vital sabotage operation. Its mission would be to destroy the German bombers' fuel supply. Raziel enthusiastically agreed. "If we succeed in this activity," he confided to his deputy, Ya'acov Meridor, "additional appeals for bolder actions will come and then it might be possible to put on the British conditions which will coordinate our political views." Raziel added as a condition of the Irgun's acceptance of the mission that the team be allowed to kidnap the mufti, Haj Amin al-Husseini, as well. Ever since his arrival in Baghdad nearly two years before, Haj Amin had been a constant thorn in Britain's side. He had organized a secret committee of Arab leaders from Palestine, Syria, Iraq, and Trans-Jordan with himself at its head. Its purpose was to inflame popular opinion in those countries against Britain and thereby orchestrate a mass uprising that would ultimately produce a united Arab nation. Accordingly, for at least a year discussions at the highest levels of the British government and military had inconclusively considered whether the mufti should be abducted or assassinated. When presented with the Irgun's proposal, the British had offered neither their approval nor their discouragement. In short, Meridor recalled, "we understood that they would not resist the kidnapping plan."[45]

Raziel insisted on leading the operation himself. He selected Meridor and two young Irgunists named Ya'acov Aharoni and Ya'acov Tarzi to accompany him. They would depart for Iraq on Sunday, May 18. Raziel spent the Sabbath in Jerusalem with his wife, Shoshana. He left early the next morning, telling her that he had Irgun business in Tel Aviv to attend to and would return shortly. Raziel and the other men met in Tel Aviv and were driven to an RAF base in southern Palestine. There, they were given false documentation with assumed names and put on board a cargo flight to the besieged British air base at Habbaniyya, Iraq. They carried with them some forty kilograms of dynamite, along with detonators, fuses, and other equipment from the Irgun's stores. Upon landing in Habbaniyya, however, they learned that their mission had changed. Instead of sabotaging the Luftwaffe fuel depot outside Baghdad, they were ordered to assist in gathering intelligence behind the enemy lines encircling the British airfield. On May 20, the Irgun group split into two teams. Raziel and Tarzi—accompanied by a British army major and a noncommissioned officer as driver—left to conduct their reconnaissance, which passed without incident. They were heading back to the base when they heard a plane overhead. Raziel had just asked Tarzi for a cigarette. Before Tarzi had time to reach for the matches, however, the plane, a German fighter-bomber, was on top of them. "The whole world blew up," Tarzi recalled in an interview published in *Ma'ariv* twenty years later: "A bomb exploded on the roof of the car. I sat next to Raziel, and I saw his face dripping with blood. I was in shock. I didn't know if I was coming or going. Where the major had been sitting was a mound of flesh. His head was gone, and the sergeant's legs were removed. On the roof of the car was a big hole." Raziel was killed instantly.[46]

Two days later, the British attacked Baghdad and deposed Iraq's pro-Axis Rashid Ali al-Gaylani. Al-Husseini escaped to Turkey and thence made his way to Rome and Berlin, where he became an active Nazi collaborator and propagandist, helping to recruit Muslim volunteers from the Balkans to serve in Wehrmacht and Waffen SS units. Rashid Ali similarly sought sanctuary in Berlin, where he too availed himself to his Nazi hosts. Meanwhile, Meridor and the other two Irgunists returned to Palestine.[47]

Raziel was buried in the British military cemetery at Habbaniyya. A decade later, the Iraqi authorities gave permission for his coffin to be transferred to British-ruled Cyprus on condition that it not be brought to Israel. There, Raziel was reinterred in a Jewish cemetery outside Nicosia. Shortly after Cyprus obtained its independence from Britain in 1960, one of Raziel's successors as Irgun commander, Menachem Begin, then a member of the Knesset, persuaded Archbishop Makarios III, the new president of the Republic of Cyprus, to permit Raziel's remains to finally return to Israel. On March 16, 1961, Raziel was buried with full military honors at Israel's National and Military Cemetery on Jerusalem's Mount Herzl. The date of his death—the twenty-third of Iyar in the Jewish calendar—is annually commemorated as the date on which all Irgun members who fell in battle are honored.[48]

CHAPTER 7

The Revolt

E very other week the police force's intelligence department provided
the chief secretary and his staff with a numbered copy of a limited-
distribution, classified assessment of political trends in Palestine. The
CID's secret report for November 2, 1942, was unremarkable—except for
one item in the final paragraph. In what seems almost an afterthought,
the CID chief, Arthur Giles, concluded his biweekly report by noting
the arrival in Palestine of a lance corporal serving in General Władysław
Anders's Polish army in exile. "On more than one occasion recently Revisionists with a wide knowledge of Betar affairs in Palestine and abroad,"
Giles wrote, "have drawn attention to the arrival in this country of Mena-
kem Beigin [sic], a private soldier in the Polish Army, and ex-Betar leader
in Poland, and have hinted that he is an extremist who merits careful
supervision."[1]

The PPF of course had long been faulted for both its anemic intelligence and its perennial inability to anticipate trouble. But Giles's high-
lighting of Menachem Begin's importance was prescient. This lowly
noncommissioned officer in an army without a homeland would soon
become the most wanted man in Palestine. Physically at least, this future
prime minister of Israel and Nobel Peace Prize laureate was an unlikely
occupant of any country's most wanted list. Short, bespectacled, and slight
to the point of frailty, Begin, wearing his Polish army battle dress in photographs taken shortly after his arrival in Palestine, appears more rabbinical
and scholarly than soldierly and tough. It is perhaps because he so utterly
failed to fulfill the conventional image of a bloodthirsty terrorist that he
successfully evaded the manhunt for him throughout the final years of the
British mandate. His disguise for a time while underground between 1944
and 1947 was in fact that of a rabbi with the fictitious name of Israel Sass-
over. But despite Begin's innocuous, bookish outward appearance, he had
already been hardened by first having grown up with the anti-Semitism
endemic to Poland and then having experienced firsthand penal servitude
in the Soviet Gulag.[2]

The youngest of three children, Begin was born in 1913 in Brest-Litovsk, a backwater at the confluence of the borderlands of what then comprised Poland, Lithuania, and Russia. He and his family were devout, multilingual Zionists who believed fervently in the importance of education but who themselves remained consigned to the lower-middle or middle classes. Only Menachem and his sister survived World War II. Both his parents and a brother were among the estimated three million Polish Jews who perished in the Holocaust.[3]

From a young age, Begin showed an aptitude for both learning and public oratory. Life for the Begins, as for other Polish Jews, however, was not easy. Half a century later, Begin still remembered the hunger that he and his family endured during World War I. As a small child during the war, Begin watched as the tsarist secret police arrived at the family's front door to arrest his father, Ze'ev Dov, on suspicion of assisting the Bolsheviks. The elder Begin's comportment, dignity, and presence of mind made a lasting impression on the son. Some two decades later, when Soviet NKVD (the KGB's precursor) agents came for him, Begin drew on this memory. As his father had done, Begin politely inquired whether his visitors had a warrant for his arrest. They did not, but they told him he must come away with them anyway. The agents were taken aback when Begin then offered them some tea, which they politely declined. Begin then insisted on shining his shoes before departing, having secured permission to take two books with him: a biography of the great British statesman Benjamin Disraeli and the Bible.[4]

Ze'ev Dov's bravery in rushing to the aid of a rabbi being accosted in the street by an anti-Semitic Polish soldier who was threatening to cut off the cleric's beard with a knife was also something that the younger Begin never forgot. Heedless of the consequences, Ze'ev Dov struck the soldier with his walking stick. Both he and the rabbi were arrested and taken to a nearby fort where they were severely beaten. "I have never known a man braver than him," Begin explained many years later. "Throughout my life I have worked with courageous people. Yet I shall never forget how my father fought to defend Jewish honour . . . I remember two things from my childhood: Jews being persecuted and the courage of the Jews."[5]

It is not surprising therefore that Begin should inevitably be drawn to the aggressive, muscular Zionism espoused by Jabotinsky and Betar. He joined the youth movement at age fifteen and first heard Jabotinsky speak about two years later. Both were galvanizing, seminal experiences for the young Begin that left a lasting imprint on him. According to one of his biographers, Sasson Sofer, Betar was the "most significant milestone" of

Begin's youth and "served as the cradle of his astonishing career." Listening to Jabotinsky was no less of an epiphany. "My entire life has been influenced by him," Begin would later reflect. Jabotinsky's "willingness to fight for the liberation of the Homeland" and his "logical analysis of facts in political matters" deeply impressed Begin, who rose steadily within Betar, eventually becoming commander of the Brest-Litovsk chapter before leaving home in 1931 to attend Warsaw University Law School.[6]

Throughout his time in Warsaw, often at the expense of his studies, Begin familiarized himself with every aspect of Betar operations: recruitment and personnel management, training, propaganda, and even the illegal trafficking of weapons from Poland to Palestine. He thus acquired the fundamental skills essential to the successful operation of any political entity—not least one also engaged in illicit, clandestine activities. This led to Begin's promotion as head of the Betar organization in Poland and his subsequent advancement first to head of Betar's propaganda department and then, in 1936, as *natsiv* (commissioner) for Czechoslovakia—the movement's most senior national office. He finally managed to graduate with his law degree that same year.[7]

Begin was also becoming both more militant and stridently anti-British. In 1937, for instance, he was arrested for leading a demonstration at the British embassy in Warsaw protesting Britain's policy for Palestine. Inevitably, both inclinations brought him into conflict with his political mentor and idol, Jabotinsky. Indeed, in 1935 Begin had lamented the Revisionist Party's reinvention as yet another political entity rather than as a movement willing to use armed force.[8]

By 1938, Begin's growing stature within Betar afforded him the platform from which to amplify these views, thus setting the stage for his famous public challenge to Jabotinsky at Betar's Third World Conference, held in Warsaw in September 1938. Begin openly criticized his mentor's continued faith in Britain, the estrangement of Betar's leaders from their young followers, and Jabotinsky's clinging to an increasingly anachronistic vision of Zionism on a continent being inexorably pulled toward war. A stunned Jabotinsky repeatedly interrupted his disciple's speech, disputing his historical analogies and sarcastically questioning the practical implications of Begin's call to embrace a new phase of Zionism—predicated on armed struggle. But Begin's forceful oration had struck a chord among the delegates, who repeatedly erupted in thunderous applause. With the audience in his hands, Begin brazenly proposed that the Betar oath be changed so that instead of affirming to "use my strength for defence," new recruits would henceforth pledge themselves to "fight in defence of my people and to conquer the homeland." His proposal having been accepted, Begin confronted Jabotinsky again at the Sixth World Revisionist Conference that followed the Betar event. This time, he attacked Jabotinsky for trying to reconcile the Revisionists and the Labor Zionists and in turn the Irgun and the Haganah.[9]

Five months later Begin's ascendance within Betar was completed when, in February 1939, he became the movement's leader. His tenure, however, was brief. Germany invaded Poland seven months later, and Warsaw was attacked. Reluctantly, Begin fled the city with his bride of only a few months, the former Aliza Arnold, daughter of a Revisionist Party activist. In late October, after considerable difficulty and hardship, they arrived on foot in Vilna, Lithuania, where most of Betar's leadership had also congregated. The formerly independent Baltic state had just been annexed by the Soviet Union under the terms of the Molotov-Ribbentrop Pact, the agreement negotiated by Hitler's and Stalin's foreign ministers that allowed each country to devour all the territory between them. The following ten months passed mostly uneventfully for the Begins in their adopted home. However, news of Jabotinsky's death in August 1940 prompted various public memorial services among the Betarim in Lithuania that inevitably attracted the NKVD's attention. Begin's two eulogies brought him under increased surveillance, and on September 20, 1940, police arrived to take him to Vilna's Lukishki prison for questioning. After seven months of interrogation, which Begin frequently turned into a form of Socratic dialogue with his persecutors, he was informed of his conviction without trial on charges of being "an agent of British imperialism" and hence "an element dangerous to society." Begin was sentenced to eight years' imprisonment in a Soviet correctional labor camp.[10]

Hence, in June 1941, Begin found himself on a Russian ship carrying political prisoners to a Stalinist labor camp in Siberia when news of Germany's invasion of the Soviet Union interrupted the journey. With the collapse of the Molotov-Ribbentrop Pact, Stalin had concluded an agreement with the prime minister of the Polish government in exile, General Władysław Sikorski. Among other things, it authorized the establishment within Soviet territory of a Polish army in exile. Thus, in a sudden and dramatic turn of events, Begin was presented with the option to volunteer for service in the army then forming under General Anders's command or to continue his trek deeper into the Gulag. Begin chose the former, and for the next ten months he and the four thousand other Polish Jews who had also joined the exile army trained and marched.[11]

In a further stroke of good luck, Prime Minister Winston Churchill obtained Joseph Stalin's permission for General Anders's forces to be transferred to Palestine. On foot and by truck, Begin and his fellow soldiers slowly made their way southward—through Iran, Iraq, and Trans-Jordan. He recounts the convoy's arrival at the east bank of the Jordan River—the biblical boundary of Eretz Israel. "I left the automobile, waded a little way into the grass," Begin wrote, "and drank in the odour of the fields of my Homeland." It was May 1942.[12]

Once in Jerusalem, Begin was reunited with his wife, who had fled Europe shortly after his arrest. They settled into comfortable domesticity, though he led a double life, dividing his time between his duties as a soldier in the Polish army and his responsibilities as a senior Betar commander, alongside growing involvement in Irgun affairs. These extra-curricular activities brought Begin to the CID's attention when the British lodged a formal complaint with the Polish military command. Begin was forced to resign his Betar post as *natsiv* for Palestine. Although many of his friends urged him to desert, Begin's sense of personal honor forbade it. Accordingly, senior Revisionist Party officials, along with influential figures involved with the Irgun's aboveground political and fund-raising activities in the United States and other prominent friends, joined forces to lobby the Polish government in exile for Begin's release from service. Eventually, their efforts succeeded, and late in 1943 Begin was granted a year's leave that in practice amounted to an honorable discharge. That same day, Begin presented himself at a meeting of the Irgun high command in Tel Aviv. "I stand now before you," he declared, "in an Irgun soldier's uniform—in citizens' clothing."[13]

The organization that Begin immersed himself in had, however, fallen on hard times. The deaths of Jabotinsky and Raziel within a year of each other had deprived the Irgun of both leadership and vision at a critical moment when the group was already directionless and struggling. Meridor, Raziel's deputy, had proven incapable of reversing the drift and providing effective leadership. Whatever confidence remained in his leadership had largely dissipated.[14]

Although accounts vary whether Meridor himself proposed that Begin assume command of the Irgun or whether his fellow Irgunists forced the decision on Meridor, on December 1, 1943, at the age of thirty, Menachem Begin became the Irgun's sixth commander.[15]

Begin was not the most obvious choice, but there were few alternatives. His lack of military expertise generated the greatest concern within the group. The new Irgun leader was himself under no illusions about either the challenges before him or the steep learning curve he would need to surmount. Amichai Paglin, a senior Irgun officer, later explained, "We felt that someone had arrived who brought with him an awareness of [our] historic mission. He appeared confident of his authority and willing to accept the full responsibility."[16]

Few of his supporters, however, would have predicted either Begin's emergence as an underground strategist par excellence or his lasting influence on terrorism and revolutionary warfare to this day. His strategy was simple but made the most of the Irgun's limited resources and inherent weakness vis-à-vis the government's security forces. The handful of men and meager number of weapons that in 1943 constituted the Irgun could never hope to challenge the British army on the battlefield or confront the police force head-on and win. Instead, the group would function in the setting and operate in the manner that best afforded the terrorist the means of concealment and escape. Based in the city, its members would bury themselves within the surrounding community, indistinguishable from ordinary, law-abiding citizens. Then, after careful planning and preparation, they would emerge from the shadows to strike before disappearing back into the anonymity of Palestine's urban neighborhoods.[17]

Further, in contrast to other colonial rebellions that had either sought decisive military victories in actual battle or relied on protracted struggles of attrition, Begin's strategy involved the relentless targeting of those government institutions that symbolized Britain's oppressive rule of Palestine. His plan was not to defeat Britain militarily but to systemically undermine its authority. "History and our observation," Begin later wrote, "persuaded us that if we could succeed in destroying the government's prestige in Eretz Israel, the removal of its rule would follow automatically. Thenceforward, we gave no peace to this weak spot. Throughout all the years of our uprising, we hit at the British Government's prestige, deliberately, tirelessly, unceasingly." Accordingly, the Irgun sought to stage daring and dramatic acts of violence designed to attract international attention to Palestine and thereby publicize the Zionists' grievances against Britain and their claims for statehood. As with the mainstream Zionist movement, the United States and American Jewry would become a specific focus of the Irgun's propaganda and fund-raising efforts.[18]

Begin's most immediate priority, though, was to resume the Irgun's revolt. More than three years had passed since its suspension, and during that time the condition of European Jewry had become more desperate and the future of the Jewish national home in Palestine less certain. The white paper's continued immigration restrictions at once denied Europe's

Jews the prospects for salvation and the Yishuv the critical population mass needed to achieve statehood. The possibility of renewing hostilities against Britain had already preoccupied the Irgun during the months preceding Begin's appointment. But these discussions had stagnated because of internal divisions and inertia as well as from the vigorous interventions of the Yishuv's official leadership. According to British intelligence, the Jewish Agency and the Haganah had met with the Irgun and the Stern Group in June 1943 to persuade both dissident organizations that any unilateral, "premature action . . . would be worse than useless." This warning had achieved its intended effect within the Irgun, thereby prolonging its operational paralysis. But with the war's outcome now clear, even if its actual end remained uncertain, Begin was convinced that the time for talk and inaction had passed. In perhaps the most powerful passage in his memoir, Begin asks,

What use was there in writing memoranda? What value in speeches? . . . No, there was no other way. If we did not fight we should be destroyed. To fight was the only way to salvation.

When Descartes said: "I think, therefore, I am," he uttered a very profound thought. But there are times in the history of peoples when thought alone does not prove their existence . . . There are times when everything in you cries out: your very self-respect as a human being lies in your resistance to evil.

We fight, therefore we are![19]

His first move as the Irgun's new commander in chief was to reconfigure the group's high command. Begin asked Aryeh Ben-Eliezer to join a new leadership council, which in essence functioned as the Irgun general staff, and Eliahu Lankin and Shlomo Levi, who had both served under Meridor in a similar capacity, to remain. Meridor himself was granted leave with the understanding that upon his return to active duty he would become deputy commander. At the new high command's first meeting, Begin unveiled his plan to publish a proclamation of revolt followed by the recommencement of attacks on British government targets. His proposal was accepted, and the necessary steps were undertaken to prepare the Irgun for battle. Begin directed his subordinates to procure more arms for the Irgun's depleted armories, increase recruitment, improve training, and acquire additional finances. The organization's geographic command structure was also reorganized. New branches were established and existing ones revitalized in all of Palestine's main urban centers as well as at key rural settlements both in the southern half of the country and in the upper

Galilee. Within each of these commands, Irgun personnel were assigned to either assault teams, propaganda and information units, or logistics and recruitment duties.[20]

The number and geographic diversity of the Irgun's branches, however, belied the group's actual size and limited capabilities. Although both British and American intelligence reports from this period continued to insist that the Irgun's membership was in the four thousand to five thousand or even the six thousand to eight thousand range, the reality was quite different. According to the Irgun's official historian, David Niv, on the eve of the revolt the group numbered no more than a thousand members—of whom perhaps only about two hundred were trained, armed, and ready for combat. Further, despite Begin's concerted efforts to build up the Irgun's arsenal, its stores remained pathetically anemic, consisting at that time of little more than four submachine guns, sixty pistols, forty rifles, two thousand kilograms of explosive, and 150 hand grenades. Its finances were barely any better, amounting to a mere £800. The monthly base salary for unmarried Irgunists, whether a member of the high command or the rank and file, for example, was a paltry £25.[21]

It was against this singularly unpropitious backdrop, though, that the Irgun rose in revolt against the British Empire. The timing was especially critical to Begin. Like Stern, his strategy was shaped by the Irish exemplar of striking Britain when it was preoccupied with waging war elsewhere.

Begin's authorship of the Irgun's proclamation of revolt is noteworthy for its lawyerly, almost *ad seriatim* delineation of the dozen reasons for the uprising accompanied by the Irgun's ten core objectives. "We are now entering the final stage of the war," it begins, before delivering a searing indictment of British rule of Palestine:

> Our people's destiny shall be determined at this historic juncture. The British regime has violated the armistice agreement which was declared at the outset of the war . . . Instead they continue to work toward their goal—the eradication of Zionist efforts to achieve statehood . . . Let us fearlessly draw the proper conclusions. There can be no longer an armistice between the Jewish Nation and its youth and a British administration in the Land of Israel which has been delivering our brethren to Hitler. Our nation is at war with this regime and it is a fight to the finish.[22]

The proclamation was issued on February 1, 1944. Special teams of Irgun operatives pasted it on walls and affixed it to bulletin boards across the country. Eleven days later the Irgun initiated its battle plan and, in its first attacks on British targets since 1939, bombed the Immigration Department offices in Jerusalem, Tel Aviv, and Haifa. The blasts, which all occurred within two hours of one another, were calculated to publicize the group's struggle against Britain by striking at the organ of government responsible for implementing the white paper's restrictive immigration policy. Equally important was the Irgun's demonstration of its ability to mount coordinated operations in different parts of the country. The time of day that all the explosions occurred—between 9:40 p.m. and 11:00 p.m., when the offices were likely to be empty and there were few passersby on the streets—was also significant, according with Begin's strategy to undermine the government's prestige by asserting the Irgun's moral superiority. He believed this could be achieved by targeting the physical manifestations of British rule while deliberately avoiding the needless infliction of bloodshed. So long as Britain was at war with Germany, the Irgun had declared, it would not attack British military targets in Palestine but would concentrate instead on the civil administration and police.[23]

Two weeks later, the Irgun bombed the offices of the Department of Taxation and Finance—the arm of the Palestine government responsible for collecting the revenue used to fund its repressive policies—in those same three cities. Once again, the blasts occurred outside normal business hours—between 8:30 p.m. and 10:30 p.m.[24]

An early example of the Irgun's international outreach strategy, and particularly of its efforts to attract American attention to its cause, occurred the following day. A messenger arrived that morning at the home of the U.S. consul general in Jerusalem, Lowell Pinkerton. He delivered an envelope containing an Irgun press release about the attacks on the Immigration Department offices as well as a letter from the Irgun's "Adjutant"—written on behalf of the Irgun "Commander." It explained, "The Jewish fighting youth is convinced that the government and public opinion of your great country faithful to the best traditions of freedom and justice, will understand and appreciate our struggle for the life and future of an ancient nation—our people—suffering extermination by the Nazi Barbarians." In justifying the Irgun's revolt, Begin would claim inspiration from the great American patriots Thomas Jefferson and Thomas Paine in addition to the Marquis de Lafayette, the French nobleman who came to the aid of the American Revolution.[25]

But the Irgun's resurrection and renewal of its revolt now threatened to consign the moribund Stern Group to total irrelevance. Between the loss of its founder and leader and the apprehension of some forty of its most experienced operatives, the group all but ceased to exist. Since May 1942, it had been able to mount just three operations, only one of which succeeded—the murder of a lowly Jewish police informer.[26]

Before Stern died, he had secretly written to the imprisoned Yitzhak Yezernitzky, imploring him to work ceaselessly to orchestrate his and his comrades' escapes. The authorities, however, were determined to ensure that the Sternists remain in jail and had taken the precaution of moving Yezernitzky and the others to an isolated and heavily guarded, segregated compound at the Mazra detention facility. There, they were allowed no visitors and kept behind three rows of barbed-wire fence punctuated by watchtowers and illuminated at night by powerful searchlights.[27]

The British, however, became complacent about their own security arrangements. Astonishingly, between September 1942 and December 1943 more than thirty of the Stern Group detainees were able to escape. Yezernitzky, for example, crawled and cut his way through concentric rings of barbed wire; after the remaining prisoners were moved to Latrun, Nathan Friedman-Yellin and nineteen other Stern Group members spent five months digging an eighty-three-yard-long tunnel that enabled them to flee.[28]

Yezernitzky, Friedman-Yellin, and a fellow Stern Group officer named Israel Scheib, Begin's old friend from Vilna (who later changed his surname to Eldad), now formed a new quadripartite command structure that they referred to as Ha-mercaz (the Center). Yezernitzky assumed responsibility for operations and general administration; Friedman-Yellin for policy; Scheib for ideology and propaganda; and a fourth man, Shlomo Posner, for finances. This novel approach to running a terrorist group reflected Stern's flat leadership style and also amounted to a repudiation of the military trappings of Betar and the Irgun. Thereafter, this collegial entity—unique in the annals of terrorism and underground warfare—guided the Stern Group, which in August 1943 they had renamed the Lohamei Herut Yisrael (Fighters for the Freedom of Israel), known to Jews by its Hebrew acronym, Lehi.[29]

To signal its return to active service and dramatically commemorate the two-year anniversary of Stern's death, the Lehi high command formulated an ambitious plot to kill the highest echelon of the British administration in Palestine. They planned to detonate a bomb at Jerusalem's St. George's Cathedral on February 3, 1944, as the high commissioner and other senior government, police, and military officials attended Sunday services.[30]

Since 1941, the group that eventually became Lehi had its sights set on Harold MacMichael. More than any other British official in Palestine, the dour Scotsman had encapsulated for the Yishuv Britain's insensitivity to the plight of European Jewry. MacMichael's fluency in Arabic and long service in the Sudan were said to have biased him in favor of Palestine's Arabs. His aloofness and diffidence reinforced an impression among Palestine's Jews of arrogance and hauteur. MacMichael was especially loathed, however, for his role in the tragedy that ensued when the *Struma*, an ancient converted yacht packed with 769 Jews attempting to flee Europe, had been denied permission to proceed from Turkey to Palestine two years earlier. MacMichael had been instrumental in the British government's decision to bar their entry. Turkey was also unwilling to accept the refugees and had ordered the disabled vessel, which had been sitting in Istanbul for two months awaiting engine repairs, out to sea. It foundered and sank in mysterious circumstances. All but one person died. The Yishuv held the high commissioner personally responsible. Posters appeared throughout Palestine bearing MacMichael's photograph above the words "Wanted for murder of 800 refugees drowned in the Black Sea on the boat Struma."[31]

On the eve of the operation two Arab chauffeurs stumbled upon two members of the group planting the explosives and rigging up the command detonation wire. They alerted the police, and a shoot-out followed when two policemen attempted to arrest the Lehi team; one of the Arab drivers was also shot to death.[32]

Chastened by this latest failure, Lehi's commanders lowered their sights and shifted their focus from Jerusalem to Haifa. The latter city had already been reported by British intelligence to have become a "stronghold" of sorts for the group. On the evening of February 14, two officers stopped and searched two Lehi couriers. Both policemen were shot and mortally wounded. Ten days later, Lehi opened a new campaign of violence, targeting rank-and-file policemen in addition to senior officers and government officials. These efforts, however, fared no better than their predecessors.[33]

This resurgence of Jewish terrorism, now from two groups rather than one and on a more sustained basis than in the past, unnerved both the Yishuv and its political representatives. On March 1 the entire Hebrew-language press (except for *Ha-Mashkif*, the Revisionist Party newspaper) joined in publishing the following statement: "The assassinations and acts of sabotage which have been committed in recent weeks in various parts of the country under the cloak of high national slogans . . . endanger our national and political efforts at a time when Israel's fate is being decided." It concluded with a pledge that the entire community would "find the proper methods for stopping the irresponsible acts of sabotage, the threats and extortions, and defend the purity of the . . . Zionist enterprise. To this end the Hebrew press will exert all its influence and offer all its assistance."[34]

Various Zionist organizations and municipalities also passed resolutions and issued pronouncements condemning the violence and called on the Yishuv to assist the police in eradicating both terrorist organizations. But as the American consul general, Pinkerton, noted, "The police have, in the past, usually received little help from the local population which has been thoroughly intimidated by the terrorists." This was by no means a new problem. From the time of the Irgun's initial revolt in 1939, British officials in Palestine had complained about the Yishuv's lack of cooperation when it came to Jewish terrorism. Opposition to the white paper had hardened the Yishuv against the authorities, and the advent of war, coupled with the common goal of defeating Nazi Germany, had done little to temper such sentiments. "No help could be expected from the Jewish community in an attempt to destroy the Irgun," MacMichael had reported to London in 1941, "both because the community in general is not out of sympathy with much of the policy for which the Irgun stands, but also because of the Irgun's known ability to deal drastically with those who threaten its interests."[35]

MacMichael now made exactly the same point once again. "Jewish press and official bodies generally have strongly condemned [the] outrages," he told the colonial secretary, Oliver Stanley, but "both official bodies and public have made no effort to help in bringing the guilty to justice." British army intelligence agreed, presciently commenting that the Jewish Agency would "probably hesitate to take action until the Irgun . . . or the [Lehi] commit some act which is liable seriously to interfere with Agency policy. There is no doubt whatever that the Agency could if they so wished take effective action in the prevention of these outbreaks."[36]

The high commissioner also believed that the Biltmore Program was the source of all Britain's difficulties in Palestine. This was the resolution adopted by an extraordinary session of the Zionist Congress that had met in New York two years before and called for the establishment of a Jewish state in Palestine. "The carrying out of that programme," he explained to Stanley, "has become the central objective of the Agency, and the terrorists regard themselves as the chosen instruments whose task it is simultaneously to intimidate H.M.G. into further measures of appeasement." In conclusion, MacMichael again expressed the view prevalent among British officials in the country that the agency could, if it genuinely wished, stamp out the terrorist organizations. Instead, he groused, the Jewish leaders prefer to wring their hands and offer endless excuses for their continued inaction. U.S. intelligence analysts generally concurred with MacMichael's assessment of the Jewish Agency's role in exacerbating the situation—often using nearly identical language.[37]

These arguments, however, ignored the fundamental challenge of obtaining information on clandestine movements. An OSS analysis of Lehi, for instance, detailed how "each cell comprises four to six persons who do not necessarily know the members of other units. Liaison between two or more neighboring cells is reportedly maintained by the leaders. Operations are undertaken only upon the receipt of 'orders' from headquarters. The society's arms caches are likewise decentralized, so that the discovery of any one would not interrupt the terrorist activities."[38]

Nevertheless, the authorities had to obtain information from someone, somewhere, in Palestine if there was to be any progress in ending the violence. This was the subject of the first of many discussions that would be held between Jewish Agency and government officials. On February 28, 1944, Bernard Joseph, a member of the Jewish Agency Executive, met with MacPherson's successor as chief secretary, Sir John Shaw. Joseph explained that he was also distressed by the recent terrorist attacks, and the Jewish Agency had issued a statement that had unequivocally condemned the violence. Although Shaw had no reason to doubt the sincerity of these denunciations, he pointed out that "lip service was not enough." What was required instead was information, specifically the names of the members of the underground organizations. Joseph, however, took umbrage with any suggestion that he and his colleagues should "be expected to fill the role of a common informer. It was the job of the Police who were at the disposal of the Administration to discover who the perpetrators of the outrages were." Driving home this point, the Jewish Agency official warned the chief secretary that any attempts to coerce the Yishuv, such as through the wholesale arrest and interrogation of law-abiding Jewish citizens that had taken place some days before, would surely destroy any hope that the government had of obtaining the community's cooperation. The meeting concluded on that sour note.[39]

A similarly inconclusive meeting took place just a few days later between Captain John Rymer-Jones, the newly arrived inspector general of the PPF, and Harry Beilin, another Jewish Agency official. Rymer-Jones, however, was in no mood to listen to Beilin's list of grievances. "The only time you people come to see me," he thundered, "is when you have complaints to make. Terrorism is rampant in the country and none of you have thought fit to come in and talk to the I.G. about it."[40]

This unhappy meeting prompted a return visit, this time from Joseph, in hopes of smoothing relations with Rymer-Jones. The inspector general brusquely rebuffed Joseph's efforts to explain the Jewish Agency's position as he had Beilin's. When Joseph explained that the government's policies—specifically the white paper's restrictions on Jewish immigration—had alienated the Yishuv and undermined any inclination to cooperate with the authorities, Rymer-Jones replied that he was responsible not for determining government policy but for maintaining law and order in the country. The only thing that concerned him was the Yishuv's reluctance to assist the police. "If you don't want to give us the names of the people or help us directly," the inspector general suggested, then "why don't the Haganah stamp out these acts? If you agree that this is a bad thing why don't you stamp it out yourselves?" Joseph demurred, pointing out that this would lead to strife within the Yishuv. Although this explanation also failed to satisfy Rymer-Jones's demands, Joseph's enigmatic assurance that the agency would deal with the Irgun "in its 'own way'" was not insincere.[41]

Indeed, unbeknownst to the inspector general, the Jewish Agency had already begun to consider measures of its own against the terrorists. On February 29, OSS intelligence analysts reported that two members of the Histadrut's executive committee, Goldie Meyerson (who later changed her name to Golda Meir and served as Israel's fourth prime minister between 1969 and 1974) and David Remez, had called for "immediate action by the Histadrut to crush the terrorists by the creation of a corps of 'vigilantes' who would either take direct action against them or alternatively denounce them to the Government." Their argument that continued terrorism threatened all Zionism's political accomplishments in Palestine was of particular relevance given the expiration the following month of the five-year time frame within which the white paper had allowed continued Jewish immigration to Palestine. Although the cabinet had already indicated that it was inclined to extend this deadline until the seventy-five-thousand-person quota had been filled, Jewish Agency officials feared that unless the Yishuv took decisive action to bring the terrorists to heel, the government might renege on its commitment.[42]

As compelling as these arguments were, other Jewish officials strongly opposed any form of cooperation no matter what the cost. Eliahu Golomb, the Haganah's leader, for example, objected to Meyerson and Remez's proposal. The government, he argued, did not deserve the Yishuv's help given its refusal to recognize the Yishuv's right to possess arms for self-defense. Hence, it was abhorrent to him to even consider that Jewish arms should be used against fellow Jews—no matter how threatening or harmful their activities. Golomb also questioned whether the Yishuv itself would countenance an agency-sponsored counterterrorist campaign. Public opinion, he believed, would "react violently" against it, rendering any such effort impossible. Although Golomb's uncompromising opposition curtailed further discussion, the final word on this issue had not been heard.[43]

Thursday, March 23, appears to have been an ordinary day in Palestine. The news was mostly about the war in Europe. In the United States, twenty thousand people had gathered in New York City's Madison Square Garden to demand the white paper's termination as Jews both in Palestine and elsewhere observed a day of prayer and fasting in hope that Europe's Jews might yet be saved. The day had passed uneventfully for the police as well. The evening shift was taking over from the day one, and there was no indication that this night would be any different from any other despite the disparate terrorist attacks of the past few weeks.[44]

Around 6:30 p.m., however, a clerk working at the Jaffa district police headquarters was cut down in a hail of gunfire. About thirty minutes later, a British police constable was shot three times as he stood outside the magistrate's court in Tel Aviv. At 7:30 p.m. gunshots struck a British officer as he walked out of the central police station. Thus, in less than an hour, and in multiple locations across Jaffa and Tel Aviv, Lehi gunmen had killed three British policemen and seriously wounded another.[45]

Whatever sense of alert the shootings should have aroused among the police seems to have been neglected by their colleagues working late at CID headquarters in Jerusalem's Russian Compound. Just after 10:30 p.m., John Scott, an assistant superintendent, was disturbed by unusual sounds coming from outside his second-floor office. He went to investigate—and happened upon four men, all dressed in what appeared to be police uniforms, armed with Mauser submachine guns, who had just climbed onto a balcony and entered through an open window using a ladder propped alongside the building. They were in the process of hauling up satchels of explosives from other members of their Irgun assault team waiting below. "Suddenly a piercing whistle punctured the silent darkness," one of the raiders recalled. Reaching for his pistol while sounding the alarm with his police whistle, Scott was flung backward by successive bursts of submachine-gun fire. He died on the spot.

Under covering fire from the Irgun unit positioned below, the raiders now threw hand grenades and set their explosive charges before retreating. They scrambled down the ladder and fled. One of the Irgunists, the twenty-year-old son of a wealthy Jerusalem family, gasped that he was wounded and then collapsed and died. The remaining nineteen members of the assault team dispersed, discarding their khaki Polish army battle dress and military peaked caps, which had been dyed blue to resemble standard-issue PPF headgear.

An hour later, the first of two explosions rocked the building. The second followed about ten minutes later. Witnesses reported that the blast convulsed nearby buildings "like an earthquake" and broke glass windows in businesses and residences up and down Jaffa Road. *The Palestine Post* reported that the scene resembled a "'blitzed' London street."[46]

Meanwhile, in Haifa, the police were similarly oblivious to the violence occurring in other parts of the country. A fifteen-man Irgun team had entered the local CID headquarters compound in that city, placed eighty kilograms of explosives against the building's southern wall, and set the timer to detonate in twenty minutes. A call was placed to the telephone switchboard operator instructing the police to evacuate the building. But before the warning could be conveyed, a miscalculation caused the bombs to explode at 11:30 p.m.—sooner than the Irgun had intended. Three British police officers were killed and three others seriously wounded.

Upon learning of the simultaneous assaults on the CID in Jerusalem and Haifa, the CID chief in Jaffa ordered an immediate search of district headquarters there—the scene of the evening's first incident. Four rucksacks filled with explosives were discovered, and the building was quickly cleared of its occupants. There had not been a moment to spare: within minutes, it was demolished by successive explosions. Reportedly, a warning had been telephoned to the Jaffa headquarters as well. Nonetheless, from the Jerusalem operation, six British police lay dead, and seven were wounded—the first British casualties that the Irgun had inflicted since the assassination of Cairns and Barker five years before.[47]

The following morning, the government imposed a 5:00 p.m. to 5:00 a.m. curfew over Tel Aviv and the Jewish sections of Jerusalem and Haifa. Roadblocks and checkpoints were set up in each locale, and additional foot and motorized patrols of police, now accompanied by troops, roamed the streets of each city.[48]

The day's events, featuring two waves of multiple attacks by both the Irgun and Lehi acting independently of each other, convinced both government and police officials that the resurgence of Jewish terrorism would not be easily contained or controlled. Unlike the previous month's incidents, when the Irgun's targets had been largely unprotected and undefended government office buildings, these operations were directed at the heart of the British security apparatus in Palestine and had successfully targeted three well-defended and presumably secure police facilities.[49]

The Irgun's brazen show of force had particularly unnerved the British. Army intelligence experts now spoke of the Irgun's belief that it possessed a "Divine decree" to drive the British from Palestine, noting that this fanaticism "does not mean that they are careless in their methods, for they combine skill and cunning with reckless courage." An analysis of the Haifa assault similarly warned about the danger of "sudden attack by fanatical assassins." "The terrorists are free to walk about the street," U.S. military intelligence analysts agreed, "hide in Jewish communities and spring from ambush at any moment. It is only in the split second after an attack that the British Police have any chance to identify their assailants. This puts them at a terrific disadvantage."[50]

It must also be said that police complacency had contributed to the terrorists' success. At least this was the conclusion of the same American intelligence analysts quoted above. "Incompetence of a gross nature" and "gross negligence of proper precaution" was how the PPF's performance under fire was described. The attacks, these analysts acidly noted, were the direct result of the "scandalous series of prison escapes" during 1942 and 1943 that had allowed the Stern Group to reconstitute itself as Lehi. Further, despite more than a month of escalating terrorist violence, the American critique continued, the CID had seemed curiously unperturbed. On that same evening, the CID's chief, Giles, was dining at the U.S. consulate in Jerusalem and in the midst of a postprandial poker game when gunfire and explosions were first heard from the Russian Compound, just a short distance away.[51]

This overall lack of alarm is all the more perplexing considering that the British section of the police—the backbone of the PPF, accounting for half its manpower—was again well below its established strength at precisely the time when both the Irgun and Lehi had resumed their respective terrorist campaigns. It was short some five hundred men, having been poorly served by an apparently desperate recruitment campaign in the U.K. that had allowed members of the British Fascist Party and other highly undesirable individuals to enlist and receive priority transport to Palestine, only to be dismissed and sent home shortly after their arrival. Thus, as had been the case during the Arab Rebellion, the police found themselves unable to function effectively without the support of the army, which, unlike in the past, was now severely constrained by wartime priorities.[52]

It doubtless was this concatenation of circumstances that prompted the Palestine government on March 28 to reinstate the emergency regulations promulgated under the 1937 Palestine (Defence) Order in Council. As will be recalled, these draconian powers were originally promulgated at the start of the Arab Rebellion in June 1936 and had been suspended only in July 1940—nearly a year after major hostilities had finally ceased. Among other provisions, these regulations established as capital offenses the discharge of "fire-arms at persons, the throwing or depositing of bombs, explosives and incendiary substances with intention to cause death or injury or damage to property; the carrying of fire-arms, ammunition or bombs; interference with or damaging of transport services, or the water, electric or telephone services."[53]

It had taken two months of unrelenting violence and countrywide upheaval during the Arab Rebellion before the Palestine administration had felt compelled to embrace this extraordinary step. The far more modest and isolated Jewish urban terrorist campaigns had accomplished the same feat in basically the same amount of time—a fact that gave Begin and his lieutenants immense satisfaction.[54]

The government clearly hoped that the curfews and reinstatement of the 1937 Order in Council would not only blunt the Irgun and Lehi offensives but also compel the Yishuv to provide the police with the information they needed to eliminate both organizations. Senior PPF officers, however, scoffed at both measures, arguing both that they were woefully inadequate and that the Yishuv should be punished more harshly and thereby coerced to cooperate. Giles was apparently complaining to whoever would listen that no progress would be made against the terrorists so long as London continued to prohibit the sustained deployment of British military units in Palestine on internal security duties. "To get a change in attitude in London," he was quoted, "we've got to wait till the High Commissioner is murdered. Any number of Police Officers, doesn't count."[55]

Giles was not entirely wrong. As had been the case in February, the Yishuv's response amounted more to weighty words of condemnation than to any tangible act of cooperation. The statement issued by the Vaad Le'umi, however, went much further. For the first time, an official institution openly called on the Yishuv to cooperate with the authorities and "do all in [its] power to isolate the evildoers and those responsible for the insane acts so that they cease, once and for all." With each passing day that the curfew remained in force, the Vaad Le'umi's once-controversial line was becoming less a subject of debate and dissension. Although the curfews' continuance into April generated new complaints from the Jewish

Agency, editorials in the Jewish press were appearing that now endorsed the Vaad Le'umi's position. Typical of these statements was one in *Davar*: "Only now do we realize the extent of the madmen's cries on Thursday [that is, the Irgun attacks] to have been greater than thought first. Greater still is the misfortune caused to the Jewish Community. The Yishuv is under curfew regulations—imposed for a crime they have not committed. They have been blamed for deeds perpetrated by the saboteurs of the Jewish national effort and struggle." These first stirrings of compliance were exactly what the government was after. Shaw made no bones about this when he met with Joseph on March 27. He was forcefully blunt: warning the Jewish Agency official of the dire consequences that would befall the Yishuv if it did not start actively assisting the authorities.[56]

Six days later, the Palestine administration announced that the curfews would be lifted. Although it had secured no firm commitment from the Yishuv or its representatives, MacMichael and his advisers were convinced that the curfews' prolongation at this stage might well counteract a palpable inclination on the part of the community to cooperate with the police.[57]

The Jewish Agency was in fact edging closer toward initiating a serious counterterrorist program. It was propelled forward by a meeting held at the Colonial Office in London on March 30 between Moshe Shertok, the head of the Jewish Agency's political department; the distinguished Manchester University historian Lewis Namier, who was a political adviser to the Jewish Agency; and the colonial secretary. Stanley opened the meeting by saying that he had a personal message from Churchill to convey: "The Prime Minister, who had always been a sincere friend of the Jews, had been horrified by these outrages, which in his view could do nothing but harm to the Jewish cause." So unequivocal a warning, especially at a time when the cabinet was seriously considering a plan to scrap the white paper and partition Palestine into separate Arab and Jewish states, produced the desired effect. Three days later the Jewish Agency approved a program of "broad enlightenment" designed to counteract any sympathy or support from the Yishuv for the two terrorist organizations. Although the new initiative fell far short of the active cooperation sought by the authorities, the program contained a set of practical guidelines for the Yishuv to follow that, it was hoped, would effectively ostracize the terrorists from the community. In addition, the Haganah established a special, internal policing unit to put an end to the terrorists' intimidation and extortion of money from Jewish merchants and businessmen.[58]

Golomb unveiled the program to great fanfare at the Tel Aviv Press

Club on April 6. He described the recent spate of attacks as "insane crimes of misguided young men" that threatened to undermine the Yishuv's most important priority: the rescue of its European brethren. The situation, he continued, was different from Ireland in the 1920s and even the Arab Rebellion, where the rebels' constituents "gained political concessions through terrorism." In this case, the Jewish terrorists' "mad recklessness might be borne by the entire community." Accordingly, the Haganah commander made clear that if the terrorist attacks continued, the Yishuv's official representatives would be compelled to take matters into their own hands and themselves "punish the culprits." Golomb then launched into a devastating critique of the government and the police, blaming their incompetence for the current security problems. The problem, he said, was not the lack of assistance from the public but the police force's failure to act on information that the Jewish Agency had already given it along with the PPF's utter fecklessness in allowing the successive escapes of Lehi operatives from prison. Finally, Golomb lambasted the authorities for the "official" and "intimate" relations that they had entered into with the Irgun prior to Raziel's death, citing the confusion this had sown in the Yishuv's mind when now asked to actively assist in the same group's eradication. Chaim Weizmann, the president of the World Zionist Organization and therefore de facto leader of the Yishuv, took this same line in a letter he sent to Churchill's private secretary. "It is simply not true that we are not—or have not been—co-operating," the Zionist elder statesman wrote. A memorandum prepared by the Jewish Agency detailing specific instances where information it had given to the police had led to recent terrorist arrests was attached to Weizmann's letter. All the information in the memorandum was later verified by British army intelligence.[59]

By May, the Jewish Agency and the Haganah were ready to implement the new program. Golomb presented Shaw and Rymer-Jones with a list of conditions on which the agency was prepared to cooperate with the authorities:

> One. 25 to 50 men picked by the Agency to be issued with firearms permits. Permits to be given in blank so as not to disclose names to the police.
>
> Two. These men would endeavour to apprehend those whom Jewish Agency considered responsible for terrorist outrages.
>
> Three. Those suspects apprehended to be detained by Jewish Agency in various settlements.
>
> Four. The Jewish Agency would inform [the government secretariat]

of the names of persons so detained but not (repeat not) disclose place of detention.

Five. The Jewish Agency demanded assurances that (A) No punishment should be imposed on any settlement found harbouring a wanted person. (B) Should Police obtain information of where-abouts of fugitive [terrorists] they would not (repeat not) at the same time search for arms.

Six. The Jewish Agency insisted that these negotiations should be conducted direct with police.

The Haganah commander also sought assurances that the security forces would take no action against any terrorist or suspected terrorist without first consulting the Jewish Agency.[60]

Shaw and Rymer-Jones were taken aback by the far-reaching terms of Golomb's proposal. They were being asked, in essence, to issue the Jewish Agency and the Haganah a blank check with which to deal with the terrorists entirely in their own way, completely outside the law, and without any vestige of due process. Moreover, by agreeing to suspend searches of Jewish settlements for illegal arms, the government was being asked to condone one form of illegal behavior in return for the agency's cooperation in eradicating another. The proposed arrangement was therefore less one of cooperation than a delegation of governmental authority to a private body. It was rejected out of hand. The Jewish Agency interpreted the matter differently. During discussions with U.S. State Department officials in Washington the following November, agency representatives blamed the British for the collapse of the negotiations. "The authorities," the Jewish delegation claimed, "had deliberately played down the role of the Jewish community in combating terrorism" and thereby had themselves sabotaged any prospect of cooperation.[61]

With the breakdown of negotiations, a perceptible chill in the agency's relations with the government followed. On June 9, for example, Shertok delivered a public address in which he declared, "In the near future [we will] have to place our political fate in the hands of the Haganah. We shall not allow our work of construction to be destroyed by the Arabs and the 'Brits.' "[62]

These same attitudes permeated the Yishuv. For example, press commentary on the trial and convictions of a young Lehi terrorist named Matityahu Shmulevitz in July differed significantly from the robust denunciations of terrorism of February and March. Shmulevitz was found guilty of various capital offenses under the recently reimposed emergency regulations, including shooting at a police officer and being found in possession of a handgun, ammunition, and a bomb. He thus became the first person to receive the death penalty since the new regulations took effect three months earlier and the first Jew since Shlomo Ben-Yosef was sentenced to die. As a British army intelligence analysis reported, although "both press and institutions formerly denounced the terrorists in the strongest terms . . . there has of late been noticeable both in the press and among the public a strong tendency to condemn the death sentence as harsh and unjustified." Worse still, another intelligence assessment complained, the Yishuv demonstrably regarded Shmulevitz in particular not as a criminal, much less as a terrorist, but "as a misguided youth . . . whose actions can be understood when viewed in light of the present tragic circumstances of world Jewry." U.S. intelligence had noted the same developments in its reports to Washington.[63]

In any event, upon review the GOC Douglas McConnel commuted Shmulevitz's sentence to life imprisonment. According to American intelligence sources, he had been pressured to do so by a threat from Lehi that it would kidnap and execute by hanging four British policemen if Shmulevitz was put to death. Some CID officers had in fact confidentially expressed their hope that Shmulevitz's life would be spared, fearing that his execution would "probably be extremely disastrous" for Palestine's security. A pamphlet that Lehi subsequently circulated to the Yishuv crowed about the group's success in intimidating the British and thus saving Shmulevitz from execution.[64]

Nor was the Yishuv's sympathy confined to Shmulevitz's specific case. On July 14, the Irgun launched a new series of attacks, simultaneously bombing the Jerusalem district police headquarters, a nearby police barracks, and the Land Registry Office. MacMichael was incensed by the editorial that appeared in *The Palestine Post* explaining away the attacks on the grounds that the terrorists had been driven to such desperate measures because of British indifference to the plight of European Jewry.[65]

For Begin, the Irgun had achieved an important milestone. In less than six months it had elbowed its way into the narrative that would determine Palestine's future. The Irgun could not be ignored or dismissed—whether by the British, the Yishuv, or its political representatives. "Our numbers grew. Confidence rose. Most important: belief in our strength was awakened," Begin later wrote. "We were loved or hated—but no longer jeered at. Any underground that passes beyond the stage of inevitable ridicule has gone half way—to its goal. During that period, I wrote the pamphlet 'We Believe' in which I expressed our unshakeable belief that 'out of our blood will flourish the tree of freedom for our country and the tree of life for our people.'"[66]

CHAPTER 8

Conscripted for Life

Just as the war was ending in Europe, another was gathering momentum in Palestine. This was the gist of a message that the Irgun delivered to the U.S. consulate general in Jerusalem in late June 1944. The D-day landings in Normandy had taken place three weeks earlier, and Germany's defeat was now only a matter of time. The Irgun congratulated the Allies on this triumph while also taking the opportunity to lament that Jews serving in the Allied forces were neither under Hebrew command nor in a Jewish army with its own flag. The brief message then concluded with the group's pledge "to go on fighting against the oppressive [British] Government and administration without disturbing the war effort of the Allied Nations."[1]

The main purpose of this tightly choreographed piece of self-promoting propaganda was to create the perception in America that British policy was ultimately responsible for the violence that had erupted in Palestine since the New Year. There were encouraging signs that these efforts were already succeeding. Since 1939 a group of Jabotinsky's loyal followers had been active in the United States pressuring the Roosevelt administration and lobbying Congress. Under the aegis of a variegated collection of political action committees, they all constituted what was known as the Bergson Group—named after their indefatigable leader, Peter Bergson (the former Hillel Kook).[2]

In May 1944, Bergson and Jabotinsky's son, Eri, had organized the Hebrew Committee of National Liberation, which functioned as the Irgun's aboveground support group in the United States, raising money and attempting to generate political support for the group.[3]

Among the Bergson Group's most significant achievements was the recruitment of the U.S. senator Guy M. Gillette, a Democrat from Iowa, to its cause. Shortly after the Irgun's coordinated assaults on the CID headquarters in March, he had publicly declared that although such acts of violence could not be condoned, "these outbreaks were the inevitable consequences of Britain's deliberate and consistent policy of refusing to honor its pledge to facilitate the establishment of a Jewish homeland." Other, better-known American supporters of the Bergson Group included Will Rogers Jr., the son of the legendary American humorist; the newspaper and magazine publisher William Randolph Hearst; and the renowned Jewish American author, playwright, screenwriter, director, and producer Ben Hecht, who wrote the screenplays for many of the blockbuster films of the 1930s and 1940s, including *Scarface*, *The Front Page*, *Twentieth Century*, and *Gone with the Wind*.[4]

All these developments were monitored with increasing anxiety from London. Foreign Office officials were divided, however, over the best means to counter the Irgun's American propaganda efforts. One sensibly proposed soliciting the advice of Isaiah Berlin, the distinguished Oxford scholar who was himself Jewish and was then on secondment as an information officer to the British embassy in Washington. His superior, however, disagreed. "The best method is to use the huge publicity machine we have to blacken the faces of *all* Jews with these [terrorist] incidents," he argued, "then the Jews themselves will quickly stop them. Only the PM [Churchill] is unlikely to allow it for his own reasons." For the moment, however, these efforts went nowhere.[5]

The Irgun's message to the American consulate was also designed to distinguish itself from Lehi, just as the communiqué following the March attacks on the CID headquarters differentiated the Irgun's assault tactics from Lehi's use of individual assassination. "To our regret there are human victims," the March statement read, "both from among our lines and from the other side, but those victims fell upon fight and planned military attack; the soldiers of the I.Z.L. DO NOT FIRE FROM HIDDEN PLACES AT ACCIDENTAL OPPONENTS, for their arms are full of morality and their battle is with aim."[6]

Lehi was no less vehement in its denigration of the Irgun's tactics, which it disparaged as "romantic," if not "ineffectual." "The British don't mind your blowing up their buildings," Friedman-Yellin recalled arguing with Begin. "They'll simply rebuild them with the money of Palestine taxpayers." Yezernitzky actually maintained that Lehi's operations were "more humane" than the Irgun's. "Frontal attacks on army camps or a bomb hurled in a police station . . . kill men at random," he later explained. "The Sternists were selective in their targets, killing on an individual basis for a specific tactical reason." Yezernitzky criticized Begin for a misplaced and, in his view, fundamentally hypocritical altruism and hollow morality.[7]

The British, however, disdained both groups in equal measure and made little effort to distinguish between the two. American intelligence analyses were far more nuanced and appeared to carefully delineate the Irgun from Lehi in reports to Washington. As one dispatch sent by U.S. Army intelligence in Cairo noted,

> The distinguishing feature between the two organizations is the IRGUN ZVAI LEUMI is waging a general war against the government and at all times took special care not to cause damage or injury to persons, going so far as to post warnings on the mined places advising all to stay away, while the Stern Gang is responsible for the shootings and their acts are personally directed against individuals and are perpetrated without any care for human life.
>
> Apparently, while the object of the IRGUN ZVAI LEUMI was mainly in the form of a protest against the government and the White Paper policy, the principal aim of the Stern Gang seems to be one of revenge against the Police and the CID, meanwhile timing this revenge campaign with the topical interest of the public in the White Paper policy, thereby lending a note of glory and patriotism to a personal terrorist campaign.[8]

But what really preoccupied Lehi's high command was that the Irgun seemed to be monopolizing the Yishuv's attention. In contrast to Lehi's cold-blooded murder of policemen, its rival's brazen assaults on government offices and police stations dominated the headlines. Although both groups were decried in equal measure as dangerous "fanatics" and "criminals" by Palestine's mainstream Jewish press, Lehi was especially loathed. *Mishmar*, the leftist Zionist newspaper, for instance, described the group as evidencing all the most "hideous elements of Fascism" and reproached it for threatening to "cloak Zionism and all that is dear to us with a mantle of disgrace before the liberal, civilized world." *Ha'aretz*, the independent Hebrew daily with the largest circulation in Palestine, and the leading English-language newspaper, *The Palestine Post*, were equally condemnatory.[9]

Hence, scorned by their fellow Jews, condemned in the press, and denigrated by their enemies as crazed killers, Lehi languished during the summer of 1944 in the shadow of the larger and only somewhat better-armed Irgun. To a large extent, Lehi's second-rate status was a product not only of its inferior numbers and constrained logistical capabilities but also of the strategy and tactics dictated by its small size and limited firepower. Nonetheless, despite the adverse publicity and unfavorable opinions, the group clung ever more fervently to its tactics. Its inability to carry out the coordinated, commando-type assaults that the Irgun preferred had decreed that Lehi continue to rely on the lone pistol-wielding gunman whose acts of "individual terrorism," Yezernitzky hoped, would "render the government weak and ineffectual . . . and have powerful echoes everywhere." Indeed, at the very foundation of the strategy that the Lehi operations chief had defined for the group was his unalterable conviction that "a man who goes forth to take the life of another whom he does not know, must believe one thing only—that by his act he will change the course of history."[10]

However, it was becoming obvious to Yezernitzky and his fellow Lehi commanders that the campaign against the police was neither changing the course of history nor having any demonstrable impact on the British. It had also failed to impress the Yishuv. Accordingly, they concluded that something needed to be done that would not only thrust Lehi into the limelight but firmly place its struggle within the wider political context of the Yishuv's fundamental grievances against the government. The assassination of MacMichael—alleged architect of the hated white paper and the British official most directly charged with its implementation—was therefore pursued with a zeal born of desperation. Seven separate attempts had been made on his life. Yet, like the aforementioned plan to blow up St. George's Cathedral during Sunday services, each Lehi plot was thwarted by a combination of unforeseen circumstances and poor timing. Time was also running out. MacMichael's five-year term in office had already been extended once by six months, and he was now due to leave Palestine at the end of August. "We decided," Friedman-Yellin recalled, that "MacMichael will not return alive to England, no matter what!"[11]

The high commissioner knew that he was a marked man. Since March, intelligence reports had repeatedly warned of Lehi's determination to kill him before he left Palestine. He was thus now more heavily guarded than ever: police motorcycle outriders accompanied by a separate vehicle containing his personal protection detail along with a truckful of armed policemen traveled with MacMichael everywhere. A potential window of opportunity, however, presented itself when Joshua Cohen, already a senior Lehi operations officer at only age eighteen, read in a newspaper that MacMichael would travel to Jaffa on August 8 to attend a party in his honor. Two and a half miles from Jerusalem there was a sharp curve in the road necessitating that vehicles slow down. It was an ideal spot for an ambush with a hill on one side and a steep slope on the other.[12]

Plans were quickly made. As the convoy with the high commissioner approached, a team of Lehi operatives would place large stones on the road to force the vehicles to stop. They would then detonate land mines planted in the roadbed to destroy the convoy. Meanwhile, a second team of gunmen armed with submachine guns and hand grenades lying in wait would open fire and hurl their grenades at any survivors. A third team would be held in reserve in the event any vehicles attempted to back out of the ambush and drive off.[13]

On the appointed day, Lehi fighters, disguised as surveyors, positioned themselves along the bend in the road as planned. From the start, however, things again went wrong. The command detonation wire for the mines had become hopelessly entangled while in transit and could not be unraveled. Accordingly, that part of the attack plan was scrapped. Then the frequency of advance police patrols sweeping the area made it impossible for the ersatz survey team to roll the heavy stones onto the road and create a barrier. Cohen quickly came up with a new plan. No sooner had he done so than the convoy came into view. "Positions!" he shouted as the Lehi teams sprang into action.

The convoy, however, was traveling at a faster speed than anyone had anticipated. Attempting to compensate for this miscalculation, one of the Sternists hurled a smoke grenade in its path. A makeshift gasoline bomb followed, and a wall of flame engulfed the road in hopes of blocking the convoy. The Lehi gunmen opened fire and threw hand grenades at the passing vehicles. The bullet-riddled limousine carrying the high commissioner swerved out of control and crashed into a roadside embankment. A female voice cried out for help—it was Lady MacMichael.

Assuming that their mission had been accomplished, Cohen ordered the teams to retreat before more police arrived. They were seen fleeing up the hill in the direction of Givat Shaul. When the smoke had cleared, the high commissioner's aide-de-camp, Major K. I. Nicholl, and his police driver, had been seriously wounded. Miraculously, Lady MacMichael was uninjured. MacMichael had also survived, suffering only minor wounds to his arm and thigh.[14]

In the wake of the assassination attempt, the Palestine government found itself in the quandary that sooner or later all regimes confronted by terrorist campaigns encounter: Having already resorted to extreme measures as a result of some previous incident, what does it do in response to the latest provocation?

Although one might have expected a reaction commensurate with the gravity of the crime—as had happened in the wake of Lewis Andrews's assassination in 1937—or, at the very the least, on par with the curfews following the Irgun's attacks in March, this was surprisingly not the case.

Security was increased around likely government targets and the high commissioner himself. British army units returned to the city in force. Machine-gun emplacements reappeared for the first time since the Arab Rebellion on the roofs of government buildings, and additional police patrols fanned out across Jerusalem. Armored vehicles took up positions, and at key strategic points all police were armed with rifles—many with small submachine guns in addition to their service revolvers. The police were also instructed to carry out spot checks of both pedestrians and taxis—but only after 11:00 p.m.

When MacMichael left Government House a few days later to attend another farewell reception in Nablus, the entire route was lined with armed soldiers and British police. Additional armored scout cars packed with British police now shadowed the entourage—which U.S. intelligence reported gave the impression of a "small military expedition." But apart from a somewhat bland and by now routine plea to the Yishuv to assist the authorities in their investigation of the attack, "especially by giving information to the security forces," the Palestine government took no other action.[15]

This proved to be a grave miscalculation. What the government had failed to consider was the Arab reaction to the assassination attempt and the government's tepid response. Since the resumption of the Irgun's revolt, Arab concern and criticism had been mounting. From the start, the Palestine government was repeatedly assailed for its alleged preferential treatment of the Jews as compared with the severe punishment meted out to the Arabs only a few years before. More disquieting were threats of a resumption of Arab violence should the authorities prove unwilling or unable to suppress the Jewish terrorism. The possibility that Britain could be confronted simultaneously by both Arab and Jewish violence had been raised in a secret MI6 report only weeks before. The commutation of Shmulevitz's death sentence in June had provoked still more derision. Not for the first time, Arab complaints were heard of the perceived government's fundamental pro-Zionist bias.[16]

The attempt on MacMichael's life had also raised new Arab fears in both Palestine and surrounding countries about the Jews' ultimate intentions. If they were bold enough to try to kill the high commissioner, Palestinian Arabs believed that it was only a matter of time before the terrorists' weapons would again be turned on them. Both King Farouk of Egypt and King Abdullah of Trans-Jordan had separately expressed concern to British officials about the Palestine administration's inadequate reaction to the Jewish terrorist campaigns. But the attempt on the high commissioner's life created a snowball effect whereby negative opinion over Britain's handling of the incident had spread across the region.[17]

From his office in Cairo, Lord Moyne, the minister of state resident in the Middle East, watched these developments with profound unease. A decorated veteran of the Boer War and World War I, Walter Edward Guinness, 1st Baron Moyne, was a scion of the Dublin-based Anglo-Irish family who had established the world-famous brewery of the same name. On August 18, he sent a sharply worded telegram to London criticizing the Palestine government's handling of the attack on the high commissioner. Seven years earlier when Lewis Andrews—a mere acting district commissioner—was murdered, the government had responded forcefully and immediately, outlawing the Higher Arab Committee and deporting its executive board to the Seychelles. The contrast now, he warned, had not gone unnoticed by the Arabs and had harmed British standing in the region.[18]

Roused by the growing controversy now surrounding its response, the Palestine government belatedly took punitive action against the Yishuv. Police investigators had determined that the terrorists had used the nearby Jewish settlement at Givat Shaul as both a staging area and an escape route. In the course of their inquiries, however, they were stymied by the settlers' denial of any knowledge of Lehi's preparations for the attack and their general refusal to provide any information whatsoever. The administration decided to punish the settlement by levying a £500 fine on it. This means of collective punishment had of course often been used against Arab villages during the 1936–39 rebellion. Accordingly, it was precisely the type of action that should have pleased the Arabs and assuaged their complaints of prejudicial treatment of the Yishuv. However, it not only failed to mollify Arab discontent but opened the Palestine administration to a new round of recrimination. The gravity of the crime, Palestinian Arab leaders now argued, was unprecedented; they regarded the imposition of a fine on just one settlement as grossly insufficient and instead demanded that the entire Jewish community be punished.[19]

Moyne made the same point in a letter to Stanley. He implored the colonial secretary to consider the implications of the Palestine administration's lenient treatment of the Yishuv on Arab opinion across the region. The failure to punish the Yishuv, he warned, "can hardly pass unnoticed in the Middle East and opinion here may begin to wonder if H.M.G. are either impotent to redress such threats or even willing to condone them."[20]

Neither the Colonial Office nor the Palestine government, however, was prepared to reconsider punishing the Yishuv. Officials in London and Jerusalem maintained that the cabinet's long-standing restrictions on the use of British military forces in Palestine for internal security duties prevented the adoption of any harsher measures. Although this argument was perhaps technically correct, it failed to take into account the consequences of doing nothing more. In addition to the Arabs' continued anger, the administration's passive response set the stage for renewed confrontation with the Yishuv. Newspaper editorials, for instance, paid lip service in the brevity of their condemnations of the attack on MacMichael and instead emphasized the incompetence of the police and the ineptitude of the Palestine government for having allowed the terrorist organizations to take root. The Jewish Agency made precisely this argument while also seeking to advance its own political agenda at the expense of the Revisionists by blaming the Irgun for the incident. Although Lehi had taken credit for the attack in pamphlets and posters distributed in Palestine's major cities on the night of August 16, the following day Reuben Zaslani, the Jewish Agency's head of intelligence, claimed that the Irgun was responsible. During a discussion with the U.S. Army intelligence and liaison officer attached to the Jerusalem consulate, he explained that the agency had offered to organize a police unit of its own to deal with the terrorists, but the British had rejected it out of hand. Zaslani made the same argument to the American consul. Significantly, these meetings had their intended effect of establishing a formal liaison arrangement between the Jewish Agency and the OSS.[21]

Meanwhile, the Irgun regarded the Yishuv's evident indifference both to the attack and to the government's renewed pleas for assistance as a green light to continue its own offensive. Just before midnight on August 22, the group launched a new series of attacks, simultaneously assaulting three British police facilities in Jaffa and Tel Aviv. In a communiqué reporting the coordinated operation, the Irgun provided its analysis of recent developments in Palestine. "The fight for liberation," it proclaimed, "is growing even more fierce. The oppressing Government has approached the Yishuv and asked them to help its C.I.D. men to find and arrest the Soldiers of Israel—but in vain. That is our luck. We know that the Yishuv is split on many social and political questions, but stands united behind the armed fight for our last hope. We also know that in his heart, every Jew is with us."[22]

MacMichael left Palestine on August 30. The route from Government House to the Jerusalem railway station was lined with police and soldiers—

as much out of affection for the high commissioner as for security. His farewell address to the people of Palestine the previous evening had faithfully captured the essence of his rule: a profound affection and admiration for the Arabs alongside an equally deep distrust and suspicion of the Yishuv. Eschewing sentimentality, the departing high commissioner concentrated instead on what he termed the dangerous "fanaticism" gripping the country; he was clearly referring to the Yishuv—and not only to the two terrorist organizations but to the Jewish Agency as well.[23]

MacMichael's message was not lost on the police who were also complaining about the Jews' favorable treatment compared with the Arabs'. Police morale, which was always tenuous given the PPF's chronic manpower shortages, had deteriorated further as a result of the additional security demands created by the two terrorist campaigns. Giles, the CID's chief, made no effort to conceal his dislike of Jews and opposition to any kind of Jewish state in Palestine. Teddy Kollek, the indomitable mayor of Jerusalem from 1965 to 1993, who was then a young official in the Jewish Agency's political department responsible for official liaison with British, American, and other Allied countries' intelligence services, points out this does not mean that Giles was anti-Semitic. Rather, he was typical of long-serving British civil servants in the Middle East, Kollek believes, who understood the Arabs better and therefore preferred them to Jews.[24]

This combination of factors might have persuaded the Palestine government that some additional punishment of the Yishuv was required. The Irgun attacks on August 22, coming so closely on the heels of the attempt on MacMichael's life, appear to have been the deciding consideration. Accordingly, in what was intended to be a dramatic assertion of governmental authority, the army and the police were authorized to carry out a mass cordon-and-search operation of the Jewish-populated city of Petah Tiqva, outside Tel Aviv. The stated purpose of the operation was twofold: to seize hidden arms stockpiles and to apprehend terrorists believed to be hiding there.[25]

At 6:00 a.m. on September 5, troops and police supported by units of the newly established Police Mobile Force (PMF)—the rapid-intervention force composed entirely of British officers—descended on Petah Tiqva. Unlike ordinary police, the PMF was armed with machine guns, mortars, and other automatic weapons and deployed in armored vehicles. While the troops sealed off the city and blocked all entry and exit, the PMF and other army units commenced the searches. A curfew was imposed, and the entire population was ordered to remain in their homes. Each search party was handed a map of Petah Tiqva schematically divided into square grids and assigned a sector. While these teams methodically combed through every dwelling on every street in their assigned areas hunting for hidden arms caches, the city's residents were rounded up and paraded before teams of police specialists, who checked their identities against lists containing the names and photographs of known terrorists. Over half were subsequently released; among the remainder were reportedly several members of both the Irgun and Lehi. But the police dragnet missed perhaps the biggest catch: Begin himself. His cottage, located in the Hasidoff quarter at the edge of Petah Tiqva, for some reason was not included in the sweep and thus was never searched nor its residents screened and questioned.[26]

A total of over fifty known and suspected Irgun and Lehi members were now in police custody as a result of the Petah Tiqva operation and arrests separately carried out in Tel Aviv. Even so, British intelligence officers remained skeptical that any dent had been made either to the terrorist organizations themselves or in the sympathy and limited support they enjoyed from the community. Indeed, unlike the curfews in March and April, the more severe operation in Petah Tiqva estranged the community further from the government while seeming to goad the terrorists to still greater excesses.[27]

Begin was quick to realize that the Petah Tiqva operation had provided the group with an opening to promote its self-appointed role as defenders of the Jewish populace against the oppressive machinery of British rule. Within days its propagandists had distributed pamphlets throughout the country proclaiming its intention to retaliate for the search, warning the government that continued use of the army in this manner would force the group to reconsider its policy of "non-interference in the war effort."[28]

On September 27, the Irgun made good on that pledge. In a dramatic show of force, at least 150 terrorists simultaneously assaulted the police stations in Haifa, Qalqilya, Qatra, and Beit Dajan. The operation was unprecedented both for the large number of Irgun fighters involved and because three of the targets were located in purely Arab areas, which had not been the scene of any Irgun attacks since the Arab Rebellion. Indeed, for the first time since then as well, both Arabs and British service personnel were killed and injured. With this bold stroke, the Irgun shattered the Palestine government's hopes that the deteriorating situation in the country could be contained until the arrival in a few weeks' time of the new high commissioner, Lord Gort.[29]

More bad news followed two days later.

Tom Wilkin, now a police assistant superintendent, was widely regarded as among the CID's best intelligence officers. He "knew more about Jewish politics and organizations," his boss, Assistant Superintendent Geoffrey Morton, recalled, "than did the rest of the Palestine Police put together." Accordingly, Wilkin had long been at the top of Lehi's target list; his part in Stern's death two years before had intensified these efforts as both he and Morton (who had actually fired the fatal shots) were relentlessly stalked. This had taken a heavy toll on Morton, who, at Wilkin's urging, had obtained a transfer to Trinidad the previous May. Lehi now redoubled its efforts to kill Wilkin—a fact that he was increasingly aware of. On September 24 the CID office in Jaffa told Wilkin about a highly credible plot to kill him in the very near future. For the first time in his career, Wilkin requested a police escort. Although his request was not denied, it was not promptly acted upon. Hence, Wilkin was alone when he emerged from his Jerusalem living quarters on St. Paul's Road, just two hundred yards from his office in the Russian Compound, five days later. Two Lehi gunmen were waiting. The CID officer must have realized what was happening, because he was found with his pistol drawn halfway from its holster. But Wilkin never had a chance. He was shot eleven times as both assassins emptied the chambers of their revolvers into his lifeless body before jumping into a waiting car.[30]

This time, the Palestine government's response was immediate. By late afternoon a twenty-four-hour curfew had been thrown over the Jewish sections of Jerusalem. The curfew was lifted for daylight hours the next day but remained in force during hours of darkness until October 5.[31]

But this was only the beginning. So far as Sir John Shaw, the chief secretary, was concerned, some signal action was required both to bring the terrorists to heel and to impress upon the public the importance of its cooperation. As the officer administering government until Lord Gort arrived, Shaw was plainly worried by the deterioration of security. In short order, the high commissioner had nearly been killed; coordinated, en masse terrorist assaults had been simultaneously launched against multiple defended targets; and now a revered senior police officer had been shot to death just steps from headquarters. Even though Shaw himself regularly carried a .38-caliber pistol in a shoulder holster beneath his familiar gray seersucker suit coat, he was not by nature or disposition an alarmist. In fact, he was known—and respected—for his professional bearing, calm demeanor, and unimpeachable impartiality, the latter a particularly rare trait among British civil servants then in Palestine. "I am not pro-Arab or pro-Jewish," he liked to tell people. "I am pro-British."[32]

Shaw also had a long and intimate knowledge of Palestine, having first come there a quarter of a century earlier as a young lieutenant in General

Allenby's conquering army. Six feet seven inches tall, he towered over virtually everyone he met. He also exuded an air of utter imperturbability. As a matter of both defiance and prestige, for instance, Shaw had insisted that the King David Hotel remain open to guests and diners despite the government's and military's ever-expanding presence throughout the establishment. Rymer-Jones would later complain, " 'Normal conditions must be maintained' was the parrot cry [and] John Shaw was the high priest of the great god Normal and this was to lead to nothing but tragedy."[33]

Accordingly, the three-page, single-spaced top secret telegram that Shaw sent to Stanley late the same night of Wilkin's murder could have only had a galvanizing effect on the colonial secretary when it was deciphered and read the following morning. "It is sufficiently evident," he argued,

> that the crises of the last 6 months, culminating in widespread concerted attacks on police stations by armed Jews in force on Wednesday night, in which four Arabs were killed and the murder of Superintendent Wilkin this morning, are not attributable to an isolated small gang of terrorists, but are planned and executed by a formidable organization, which is able to command a considerable force of well armed men . . .
>
> The police, with all possible support and co-operation by the Army, have done fine work in very trying circumstances. They have been searching and patrolling unceasingly; they have indefatigably sought for information; large numbers of suspects have been arrested, interrogated and detained. The strain on manpower has been heavy.
>
> It has become clear, however, that these measures, essentially defensive as they must be, are not enough and that unquestionably something more positive is required if lives are to be protected, law and order maintained, and the authority of the Government upheld.[34]

Shaw therefore proposed that the 276 male and 26 female Jewish terrorist suspects currently incarcerated at the Latrun and Acre prisons be secretly removed from Palestine and relocated to "such country as His Majesty's Government may select." He justified this extraordinary measure—whereby people who had been detained merely on suspicion of participating in, or encouraging, terrorist acts but had not yet been formally charged, much less tried, for their alleged offenses would be transferred to military custody, summarily deported from the country, and imprisoned elsewhere—on the grounds that it was no longer possible to ensure the security of Palestine's prisons from terrorist attack. "The details of removal and embarkation," he assured Stanley, "will be worked out in secrecy and in consultation with the army and the whole business will be organised as a military operation." Although the possibility that this action might provoke still worse violence had to be considered, the chief secretary argued that this concern was outweighed by the beneficial effect he believed the deportations would have on "rightminded members of the community" and the deterrent it would have on "evil-doers." In any event, the army was confident that there were sufficient forces to meet any such contingency. The Colonial Office's legal advisers had already reviewed the plan and confirmed the legality of the proposed deportations.[35]

The cabinet discussed the request at its meeting on October 7. It was clear that the security situation in Palestine, Stanley began, was more serious than had previously been thought. In contrast to the small number of perpetrators involved in the mostly isolated terrorist incidents of the recent past, the attacks on the police stations had evidenced "all the characteristics of a carefully planned military operation." Moreover, intelligence reports continued to stress the combined strength of the terrorist organizations was in excess of five thousand people, while the British section of the police force, upon which the main security burden had fallen, had no more than three thousand personnel. The cabinet approved the decision two days later, and on October 19, 251 imprisoned Jewish terrorists whom the authorities deemed the most dangerous were secretly flown from Palestine to British-occupied Eritrea aboard eighteen DC-3 transport aircraft accompanied by fighter escort.[36]

With the detainee issue resolved, Shaw's attention shifted to renewed efforts to obtain the Jewish Agency's cooperation. As if to underscore the startling deterioration of security, the government communiqué that announced the detainees' deportation had contained information about a new security measure whereby air raid sirens would henceforth sound in any urban location where terrorist activity was occurring. "Upon the siren being sounded," the public was instructed, "all vehicular traffic within the town area will come to a complete stop." The siren was thus intended as a "call to increased vigilance," which the public was expected to regard as an opportunity to report to the police immediately "any suspicious movements or persons" that it either encountered or observed.[37]

But what Shaw still sought was the community's active cooperation and assistance in preventing and preempting terrorist activity—not just responding when it had already occurred. The problem, as he explained in a lengthy telegram to Stanley, was the growing "numbers of Jewish young men and women who are becoming infected with the gangster virus; these are providing recruits for the terrorist organization." This was the direct outcome of the Jewish Agency's "totalitarian organization and regimentation" of the Yishuv—which amounted to nothing less than the "negation of free thought and speech." Sedition was taught in the schools and fomented by the Jewish youth movement in a manner, the chief secretary continued, that was "unpleasantly reminiscent of Hitler Youth." The effect could be seen both in the recruits swelling the terrorists' ranks and in the dangerous number of passive sympathizers who, "even while they doubt the wisdom of [the terrorists'] methods, are multiplying."[38]

Shaw regarded "terrorism in Palestine . . . [as] an infectious disease, all the more so when it has the semblance of success and appears, on the whole, to be attended by not very serious consequences for the perpetrators." In the circumstances, he concluded, there was a "very real danger" that if the security situation was not brought under control soon, police morale would continue to be affected, thus further undermining the government's counterterrorism efforts. The chief secretary argued that if the government could somehow convince the Yishuv that the terrorists' activities were having a detrimental effect on the war against Germany as well as undermining the Zionist cause in both the United States and Britain, the Jewish Agency and in turn the Yishuv might become more inclined to cooperate with the authorities. Accordingly, he proposed that British military headquarters for the Middle East join with the Palestine government in issuing a proclamation along these lines. Finally, the chief secretary suggested that the Colonial Office undertake a public relations campaign in Britain to influence "responsible Jewish" opinion in that country. Its purpose would be to garner not "big headlines in popular papers so much as leading articles" in prominent broadsheets such as *The Times* of London and *The Manchester Guardian* favored by the most educated and influential stratum of Anglo-Jewry. This effort would be supported by a weekly newsletter detailing Jewish terrorist activities in Palestine that the secretariat in Jerusalem would provide to the Ministry of Information in London for distribution to the British press.[39]

Stanley supported these proposals, and on October 10 the joint communiqué was duly issued. The thrust of the message was Jewish ingratitude. Although the British army had saved Palestine from the "ravages of war" by defeating Rommel in the Western Desert, Jewish terrorism was now impeding the war effort. It was also preventing the training of combat units destined for Europe and interfering with the battle-wearied troops sent to Palestine to rest and recuperate. In all-too-familiar tones, the community was admonished that verbal condemnation was insufficient and that "actual collaboration" with the authorities was required.

This specifically entailed the provision of information on the terrorists as evidence of the Yishuv's determination to "eradicate this evil from their midst."[40]

No one was more distressed by the deterioration in Anglo-Zionist relations caused by the Irgun's and Lehi's terrorist campaigns than Weizmann. From London he had watched with increasing dismay the unimpeded escalation of violence in Palestine since the winter. Weizmann had already been warned by the prime minister some months before that "if such murders continued and the campaign of abuse of the British in the American papers did not stop, we might well lose interest in Jewish welfare." This was a very serious admonition indeed. Churchill was an old friend of Zionism who at nearly every critical juncture since the Balfour Declaration had stood by his commitment to Jewish nationhood. His unqualified opposition to the 1939 white paper was a matter of record—as were his continuous efforts to overturn that policy and embrace an alternative solution more amenable to Zionist interests. The prime minister had forcefully intervened in 1943, for example, when Lord Cranborne, the lord privy seal, had stated during a cabinet meeting that the white paper was "the firmly established policy" of the government. To the contrary, Churchill argued in a note he circulated afterward, "I do not feel that the fact that we make no new declaration in any way compromises or commits those who have opposed the White Paper of 1939. Faced with the emergencies of war, we have left the question where it stood. We are free as a new Government to review the entire field at the end of the war."[41]

Churchill had perhaps scored his greatest victory on behalf of Zionism at a critical meeting of the war cabinet held on July 2, 1943, when he declared his undiminished support of the Balfour Declaration and his unmitigated hostility to the white paper policy, which he regarded as "a breach of that solemn undertaking." It was at this meeting that the war cabinet had decided that Jewish immigration to Palestine should be permitted beyond the white paper's March 1944 expiration date and moreover that it should remain in force until the entire quota of seventy-five thousand entry certificates was filled. The war cabinet had also agreed that there should be no attempt to "disarm the Jews unless or until equal measures could be effectively enforced against the Arabs." The final outcome of the meeting was the most propitious so far as the Zionism movement was concerned. The war cabinet had approved the appointment of a ministerial committee on Palestine to consider a new, long-term policy for the country—with the specific remit to reassess the previous government's rejection of partition.[42]

The committee's members included many of Zionism's British friends, such as Herbert Morrison (home secretary) as chairman, Leopold Amery (secretary of state for India and Burma), Sir Archibald Sinclair (secretary of state for air), R. K. Law (parliamentary undersecretary for foreign affairs), and Stanley. "On the whole a great day for the Jews if they had known of it," Amery confided in his diary. "Perhaps some day they will include Winston with Balfour (and to some extent myself too) as one of their real friends."[43]

The ministerial committee had approved a plan to partition Palestine into separate Arab and Jewish states on December 10, 1943—which the cabinet's Committee on the Middle East endorsed the following month. But Churchill thought that the full cabinet should wait until after the American presidential election scheduled for November 7, 1944, before taking further action. Accordingly, a final decision on partition was left in abeyance for nearly a year, hence Weizmann's immense anxiety that the resumption of Jewish terrorism in Palestine would crush Zionism's most fervent hopes at precisely the moment of their realization. Throughout the intervening eleven months, moreover, Churchill had repeatedly hinted at this positive outcome. He had told Harold Laski, a Labour leader, in the summer of 1943, "I have never forgotten the terrible sufferings inflicted upon the Jews; and I am constantly thinking by what means it may lie in our power to alleviate them, both during the war and in the permanent settlement which must follow it." And, after the Allied Big Three conference in Tehran in late 1943, Churchill had publicly declared, "We shall, however slowly, fulfill our pledge to the Jews." The prime minister himself had also personally assured Weizmann in 1944 that when the cabinet soon took up the partition proposal, the outcome would be welcomed by the Jews. Churchill had promised he would "plunge into the pie and extract a real plum" for Weizmann—in other words, a Jewish state.[44]

For this reason, by the latter half of 1944, with the prospect of Jewish statehood imminent, Weizmann had unhesitatingly thrown his full weight behind an official Jewish Agency program of active cooperation against the terrorists. There were already signs that opinion in the Yishuv was moving increasingly in this direction. A reliable OSS source, referred to only as "Z," had reported in mid-October 1944 that the Jewish Agency was preparing to launch a concerted counterterrorist campaign that would involve the actual arrest and detention of members of the extremist organizations. British intelligence had detected that month for the first time an inclination among more moderate elements in the Yishuv to view terrorism as a threat to both Zionist political aims and the authority of its official representative institutions.[45]

Weizmann now acted to ensure that this momentum continued. Both Shertok, the head of the Jewish Agency's political department, and Golomb, the Haganah's leader, were then in London negotiating with the War Office over the formation of an independent Jewish brigade to fight alongside the Allies in the final push against Hitler. Weizmann impressed upon both men the disastrous effect that any failure to proceed with the antiterrorist program would have on the government's forthcoming decision on partition. A chastened Shertok and Golomb returned to Palestine shortly after. Abandoning his earlier objections, Golomb addressed the Yishuv on October 18. He briefly outlined the nature of his discussion with Weizmann and then declared,

> Through the conviction of my responsibility for the security of the Yishuv and the fate of the People, I hereby demand from you:
>
> Go out and fight those demolishers and destroyers, that irresponsible handful of lunatic boys, who play with our fate, and disobey our orders. *Be ready even for bloody sacrifices in this holy war . . .*
>
> We must immediately liquidate them, and maintain in our country the great peace which has so far given us all our achievements and all our victories . . . The English have already become angry, and they might become more angry.

Failure to do so would have catastrophic consequences not only for the Yishuv but for European Jewry as well. Immigration to Palestine would be prohibited, extinguishing the last hope of salvation for Jews trapped in Europe. Indeed, those refugees presently interned by Britain in other parts of the empire would be barred from entering Palestine. Furthermore, a new white paper would be issued reaffirming the 1939 policy statement and thereby ending any prospect of statehood. The result would be the establishment of a unitary state in Palestine with a fixed Arab majority/Jewish minority.[46]

The Jewish Agency Executive met four days later to discuss the practical dimensions of implementing the counterterrorist program. Shertok emerged as its foremost exponent. He argued that the time was past when mere words of condemnation could suffice in place of signal action. The agency's effort to isolate the terrorists through a campaign of public awareness had clearly failed. Not only had terrorist outrages continued, but they had escalated. The Yishuv was now at a critical juncture where further violence would jeopardize all that had been achieved—and, moreover, risked closing Palestine permanently to Jewish immigration. Accordingly, Shertok proposed that the Jewish Agency dedicate itself to the elimination of the terrorist organizations, instructing the community to provide information on known and suspected terrorists and ordering the Haganah to act on that information. Golomb supported Shertok, declaring, "We must endeavour to finish this business without victims, but if it is necessary we will finish it even if it means victims."[47]

Opinion among the executive was by no means unanimous. Three members in particular—Rabbi Yehuda Fishman, Itzhak Gruenbaum, and Emil Schmorak—objected to the proposed campaign on the grounds that the Yishuv was betraying itself by assisting the British. They argued that fighting terrorism was the responsibility of the government and police and not the Jewish community. They also maintained that by actively participating in such a campaign, the Yishuv would be cast in the role of common collaborators. As long as the white paper remained in force, Fishman said, it was the British who were the Jews' real enemy, not their terrorist brethren. As the debate grew more fractious, Ben-Gurion offered a compromise solution. No information collected by the operatives would be given to the British authorities, he proposed, without the express and unanimous consent of the Jewish Agency Executive. His idea was accepted and the program approved. The Vaad Le'umi endorsed it on October 23 and the Inner Zionist Council the day after that.[48]

Preparations for the implementation of the Saison (Season, as in the expression "open season" of hunting parlance), the code name for the counterterrorist operations, commenced immediately. The Haganah's Intelligence Service, Shai, would be responsible for collecting information on known and suspected terrorists. Haganah personnel or members of the Palmach, its elite "shock troops," would then be tasked with apprehending, detaining, and interrogating suspected Irgun members in special Haganah incarceration facilities. Nearly two hundred men were selected to spearhead the campaign. In addition to their counterterrorism responsibilities, these handpicked, specially trained operatives would serve as bodyguards for Jewish Agency and Haganah officials who might be targeted in retaliation. They would also be detailed to provide protection for ordinary Jewish businessmen and citizens who had long been victims of terrorist extortion rackets. Within days, the Jewish Agency had distributed pamphlets and handbills criticizing the Irgun and attempting to rally the Yishuv behind the counterterrorism program.[49]

That the campaign was to be directed solely against the Irgun at this stage was justified by the Jewish Agency on ostensibly tactical grounds: given that the Irgun was the numerically larger and better armed and financed of the two terrorist organizations, it was the greater menace to Palestine's security. There was also the concern that simultaneous action against both terrorist groups might drive them into an alliance against the Jewish Agency and the Haganah. These fears were not entirely unfounded. Since the end of 1943, the Irgun and Lehi had been engaged in exploratory talks about establishing a joint command. But other, more political considerations appear also to have been a major factor in the Jewish Agency's decision to focus exclusively on the Irgun. It doubtless recognized that by meeting the government's demands for an active counterterrorist program, the Jewish Agency—and in turn the Labor Zionists—had been provided with an ideal opportunity to eliminate the main threat to their own political power base in Palestine.[50]

The new high commissioner, Lord Gort, arrived in Palestine on October 31. He had not been Churchill's first choice for the post. The prime minister had initially hoped to appoint Weizmann, resurrecting the success of the first holder of that office, Sir Herbert Samuel, who, though himself a Jew, had "held the scales there evenly." But by April 1944 the worsening security situation in Palestine had effectively scotched the Zionist leader's candidacy. Churchill had also briefly entertained the idea of appointing another prominent English Jew, Lord Melchett, but poor health had eliminated him from contention. In June, American intelligence reported that Churchill was seeking a "military man" to replace MacMichael given the expectation that "serious troubles in Palestine" were expected as the war in Europe wound down. This was the reason that MacMichael's term had been extended by six months, the report opined: virtually all the most able British flag officers had been consumed with the planning and execution of the invasion of Europe and could not be spared. Hence, it was not until July that Gort's appointment was finalized. "Look after our [Jewish] friends and see that they are treated well" were Churchill's parting words to the new high commissioner. "The Jews have rendered us great service in this war."[51]

Gort proved to be an immensely popular high commissioner. And unlike his immediate predecessor, the U.S. military intelligence liaison officer in Jerusalem reported, the new high commissioner "has been mixing freely and informally and is frequently seen walking on the streets without ostensible escort." When he attended a play or went to the cinema, the entire audience—Jew and Arab alike—would rise to its feet and cheer as Gort took his seat. "They daren't shoot me," Gort liked to say. "They will get something much worse." Ben-Gurion judged Gort "a rare and good man" who was deeply moved by the suffering of the Jews under Nazi rule.[52]

In one of his first reports to Stanley, the new high commissioner sounded a cautiously optimistic note. There has been "no overt manifestation of terrorist activities since the murder of Wilkin a month ago and the counter-measures which were subsequently taken." A major cordon-and-search operation of Netanya a few days earlier had resulted in the arrests of some fifty terrorists and suspects. Moreover, in contrast to previous search operations, the mayor and the population had been especially cooperative and helpful. Accordingly, although the likelihood of further attacks could not be ruled out, Gort seemed hopeful that ongoing police efforts would produce more terrorist arrests and that the quiet prevalent since his arrival would continue. Other, more experienced Palestine hands, however, knew better than to construe the warm welcome that had greeted Gort and the calm that had settled over the country as anything but evanescent.[53]

This was certainly the message that the terrorists themselves were intent on communicating. The absence of any new incidents during October did not mean that the Irgun and Lehi were inactive. To the contrary, their respective propaganda arms had been especially energetic. For more than a year, the Irgun's clandestine radio station, re-branded the Voice of Fighting Zion, had been broadcasting intermittent messages publicizing the group's aims and objectives and attempting to generate popular support. The Jewish Agency's counterterrorism program gave new impetus to these efforts, prompting both the Irgun and Lehi to issue a joint statement calling on the Yishuv to ignore the entreaties "to collaborate with the secret police in passing information, denouncing and delivering the Jewish Fighting Youth to the oppressive authorities." For the first time the Irgun's propagandists had also begun to tailor their messages to British service personnel. Posters called upon the troops to think about why they had left home to fight in the war. "Does your duty consist [of] oppressing Jews in their homeland? Don't you realize the humiliation to which you are subjected by participating in such police-actions? Is THIS your task in this war, which is being called by Your politicians [a] 'war of liberation'?"[54]

More ominous was the October issue of Lehi's underground newspaper, *He-Hazit* (The front). Its lead article, titled "Cairo: The Centre of Plots," contained a detailed indictment of the minister of state resident in the Middle East, Lord Moyne. Moyne had long been a particular bête noire of the Jews. While colonial secretary between 1941 and 1942, he had been instrumental in opposing the formation of a Jewish division in the British army. He had also opposed admitting the ill-fated *Struma* refugees to Palestine. During a critical debate in the House of Lords in 1942, Moyne had described the prospect of allowing further Jewish immigration to Palestine as akin to "putting exactly three pints into a pint pot." To these familiar charges, Lehi now added a new one: that the minister had connived to dispatch secret agents from Cairo "who are touring the Arab villages in Palestine, and distributing modern weapons among its inhabitants . . . instigating robbery and murder [of Jews], and preparing a new phase of the 1936–1939 'disturbances.'"[55]

Coincidentally, Moyne's name had also come up in a conversation between Churchill and Weizmann over lunch on November 4. The previous day, per Churchill's instructions, the cabinet secretary had placed discussion of the ministerial committee's partition proposal on the cabinet's agenda. Weizmann, however, was concerned by reports that the proposed Jewish state's boundaries would be much smaller than the Zionists hoped. Was it true, he asked the prime minister, that the Yishuv would be allocated "little more than a beach-head—or a bathing beach—in Tel Aviv"? Churchill hastened to assure his old friend that these rumors were no more than a "pack of lies" and moreover that it was his conviction that the Negev desert should be included in any Jewish state. Indeed, if the Jews "could get the whole of Palestine," the prime minister stated, "it would be a good thing." But, he cautioned Weizmann, although the cabinet committee was composed of Zionism's closest friends, including all the leading pro-Zionist Labour Party ministers, there was little support for Churchill's views within his own party. Accordingly, if it came down to a choice between no state at all or partition, the prime minister advised Weizmann that the Jews should take whatever partition deal was offered.[56]

Churchill concluded the lunch by noting that "nothing would happen until after the war with Germany and perhaps not until the general election was held in 1945." Nevertheless, the prime minister also told Weizmann that he saw "no harm in making known what he had said about waiting till the end of the German war." Before parting, Churchill urged the Zionist leader to visit Lord Moyne in Cairo soon. The minister of state, he explained, "had changed and developed in the past two years."[57]

Weizmann left the meeting contented. He was convinced, as he subsequently wrote to the Jewish Agency's representative in Washington, that "in the next six months we can so prepare the ground as to ensure our success."[58]

CHAPTER 9

The Deed

Eliahu Hakim was a good boy. At least his parents thought so. When they asked him to quit smoking, he did. And when they asked him to abandon his budding career as a terrorist, he complied. But, like most teenagers, he promised his parents one thing but did another. In 1943, at the age of eighteen, Hakim reluctantly acceded to their demand that he enlist in the British army. His parents mistakenly breathed a sigh of relief when he departed for training in Egypt, hoping he would now be far away from Lehi's reach and influence. Hakim detested serving in the military of a country that deprived the Jews of their national home and occupied their land. He was already plotting to desert and rejoin Lehi when he received word from Yezernitzky to remain in place and render the group a critical service by smuggling arms from Egypt to Palestine. Hakim excelled at this task, defying the efforts of the British military police by coolly ferrying weapons-filled suitcases on the troop trains that regularly crisscrossed the Sinai desert.[1]

Hakim was an atypical Lehi fighter. Whereas most members of the group were Ashkenazi Jews who hailed from Central or Eastern Europe, Hakim was Sephardim and had emigrated with his family as a child from Beirut. Moreover, where most Lehi recruits were from working-class or at best middle-class backgrounds, Hakim's parents were rather well-off. An ardent adherent to Jabotinsky's assertive Zionist ideology, he first joined the Irgun in 1941 but subsequently gravitated to the more extremist Lehi the following year. His drifting from one organization to the other and then from soldier to deserter had aroused Yezernitzky's distrust and skepticism of this seemingly impetuous youth. But Hakim's success and sangfroid as a smuggler greatly impressed the Lehi operations chief. In December 1943, Hakim was ordered to leave the British army and devote himself completely to Lehi. His brother, Menachem, noticed something markedly different in his younger sibling. "He became serious; overnight he grew up."[2]

Hakim was assigned to an operational unit commanded by Joshua

Cohen, the group's similarly young but already highly accomplished field officer. Cohen's assessment of Hakim was uncharacteristically effusive. Yezernitzky agreed, and Hakim was soon actively involved in all manner of Lehi operations. He participated in two of the attempts on Mac-Michael's life, including the abortive attack outside Givat Shaul. He was ordered back to Cairo in early September—masquerading as a British soldier named Moshe Cohen, complete with the requisite false papers. Hakim was not told anything at all about his mission, but was instead given a piece of paper with a name and a Cairo phone number scribbled beneath it.[3]

Hakim arrived in Cairo on September 14, 1944. As instructed, he made contact with a young Jewish woman from Palestine serving in the ATS, the British army's Auxiliary Territorial Service—the World War II equivalent of the U.S. Army's Women's Army Corps. Her name was Nadja Hess. She in turn introduced him to Raphael Sadovsky, a twenty-nine-year-old Egyptian Jew from an established Cairo family. Although he earned his living as a mathematics and language teacher at a local school, he was in fact a key figure in a conspiratorial cell of seventeen persons that Lehi had established in Egypt. Eight were serving in various arms of the British military there, including four other women in the ATS. The cell's leader was a Polish Jew named Joseph Sitner. Sitner had entered Palestine illegally in 1938 and subsequently came to the CID's attention as a member of the Irgun. This resulted in his arrest and imprisonment under the emergency regulations invoked during the Arab Rebellion. After three months in detention, Sitner was released. He immediately reimmersed himself in Irgun, Betar, and Revisionist Party activities. Following the split with the Irgun, Sitner joined Lehi. Astonishingly, despite being well-known to British authorities as a troublemaker, in 1942 Sitner had been allowed to enlist in the RAF. He was posted to Alexandria, where he was assigned to RAF headquarters as a clerk. It was the perfect cover for Sitner's activities on behalf of Lehi. In early August 1944 he met with Yezernitzky and was told to commence preparations for an important operation—the assassination of the minister of state resident in the Middle East, Lord Moyne.[4]

The idea to target the apex of British officialdom for the entire region had originated with Stern. He had envisioned a stunning one-two punch that would eliminate first the high commissioner and then the minister responsible for the entire region and thus convey an unmistakable message of Jewish resistance and opprobrium. Stern had begun planning such an operation in 1941, but before Lehi could act, an Australian diplomat became the first minister of state resident in the Middle East. Because the group "had no quarrel with Australia," Yezernitzky said, the ambitious sequential assassination plan was shelved. It was revived shortly after Moyne arrived in Cairo in January 1944 and finalized that July. The intention remained to kill MacMichael and then Moyne. Lehi was "looking for an act to shock the world," Yezernitzky had told Sitner. But the group's long-standing rivalry and competition with the Irgun figured as prominently as its animus toward Britain in the decision to pursue these two targets. The failed attack on MacMichael had created additional pressure to succeed in murdering Moyne.[5]

On September 18, 1944, Hakim met with Sitner, Sadovsky, and two female members of the Lehi cell, Ruth Grossbard and Yaffa Greenberg, at the fashionable Astra Café located on what is today Tahrir Square. Over coffee, they discussed how Hakim—accompanied by one of the ATS women in order to appear as a love-struck couple exploring the city— would conduct a thorough reconnaissance of Moyne's residence and office, as well as the route his chauffeured car followed daily. They would focus special attention on the time between 12:30 and 1:30 p.m., when the minister of state returned to his residence for lunch.[6]

The plan that eventually emerged was to shoot Moyne and not use a bomb as originally intended. But this created two new problems. First, Hakim would require a weapon, and, second, another gunman would be needed both to cover him and to intervene in the event of trouble. At the end of September, a Lehi agent arrived in Palestine with two pistols— a revolver and an automatic. Hakim chose the revolver. It was a Russian-manufactured seven-shot Nagant 7.62-mm revolver—the standard sidearm of tsarist-era military and police and later of the Red Army and Soviet intelligence and law enforcement officers. Sadovsky would recall that he often saw Hakim meticulously cleaning and oiling the Nagant, which was renowned for firing a cleaner cartridge than most revolvers and, if well cared for and kept in good working order, would greatly reduce the chances of misfire because of any fouling of the handgun's mechanism.[7]

This same handgun had become something of a talisman for the terrorists who wielded it. The pistol had first come to the attention of the Palestine Police Force as the murder weapon used by the Irgun to gun down an Arab notable on a Jerusalem street in 1937. The same weapon had then passed into Lehi's hands, where it was implicated in the shootings of no fewer than five British police officers over the preceding eighteen months.

Among its victims was Tom Wilkin, who had been murdered only a day or two before Hakim himself took possession of the Nagant—thus accounting for its delayed arrival in Egypt.[8]

Hakim continued to monitor Moyne's daily movements, paying special attention to the route that the minister of state's limousine daily traveled just past noon across the Kasr El Nil Bridge to his Zamalek residence. Everything seemed to be falling nicely into place. However, unbeknownst to the cell, British intelligence was aware of Lehi's presence in Egypt and keeping tabs on suspected Jewish terrorists serving in HM Forces there. It suspected that Lehi was plotting another attempt on MacMichael's life while he and his family were passing through Cairo. Sitner's frequent trips between Ismailia, Alexandria, Cairo, Tel Aviv, and Haifa had accordingly aroused their suspicions, and on October 2 he was spotted being led away by British military police.[9]

Yaffa Greenberg happened to be returning to Ismailia from leave when she stopped at the Ha-Tikva canteen in Alexandria, a popular gathering spot for Jewish service personnel. There, she overheard a conversation about Sitner's arrest. Fearing the worst, Greenberg left immediately for Cairo. She stopped to collect Sadovsky at his house before proceeding to a café where Hakim was waiting. But when they arrived, Hakim insisted that they go instead to the famous Maison Groppi. Sadovsky protested. Hakim was under strict orders from Sitner to lie low and specifically to "eat at small, out-of-the-way Arab restaurants." Groppi's *salon de thé*, popular among the British military, was anything but that.[10]

Hakim, however, was set on Groppi's. Sadovsky argued that this was also the second time that Hakim had gone there—a clear violation of his security instructions. But Hakim was as intoxicated by Groppi's heady atmosphere as was the rest of Cairo and ignored Sadovsky's remonstrations. Hakim at least had the good sense to request a corner table. He calmly took in the news about Sitner's arrest and then told Sadovsky he should leave immediately for Alexandria to verify the story and, if possible, contact Sitner.[11]

Sadovsky headed for the Ha-Tikva canteen, where the manager confirmed that an airman fitting Sitner's description had indeed been arrested. The following morning, a distraught Sadovsky was standing on the platform waiting for the train back to Cairo when he was stunned to see Sitner himself. Neither said a word, but they went their separate ways and then made sure to find seats facing each other on the train. The two men appeared to strike up a casual conversation, which the sound of the rails, engine, and rush of air from the open windows rendered inaudible to anyone who might be listening. Three days earlier, Sitner explained, he had been relaxing on his base when a soldier found him and said that the military police were looking for him. Alarmed, Sitner rushed back to his tent, where he gathered all the incriminating documents he could quickly grab. He set fire to all but the most sensitive ones. These he tore into tiny pieces and swallowed. He then casually presented himself to the waiting policemen and was taken away to a detention facility for questioning.[12]

In the course of a thirteen-hour interrogation session, Sitner was accused of plotting to bomb a forthcoming meeting of the Arab League in Alexandria. He repeatedly denied the charges and was released three days later because of lack of evidence. What Sitner did not know was that the Jewish Agency had provided British intelligence with information about the alleged plot. He was then transferred to another base and placed under surveillance. Sitner also told Sadovsky that he was expecting an important letter from Lehi headquarters. Accordingly, he needed Sadovsky to communicate a coded message to Yezernitzky that simply said, "Fellah was sick, he was sent to another place for convalesance [sic]"—meaning that Sitner had been arrested, had been transferred from Alexandria, and was being watched. Upon arriving back in Cairo, Sadovsky approached a girlfriend serving in the ATS who was not a member of the Lehi cell and asked her to pass the message to Greenberg, who duly transmitted it to Lehi headquarters in Palestine. Hakim listened to Sadovsky's account later that evening with great satisfaction. His mission had not been compromised, and the authorities, though worrisomely aware of the cell's existence, clearly had no clue of its real target.[13]

Nothing further happened until October 20 with the arrival in Cairo of another young Lehi operative from Palestine: a twenty-three-year-old sabra (Jewish person born in Palestine and Israel) named Eliahu Bet-Zuri, who carried with him instructions and money.[14]

Bet-Zuri shared with Hakim an involvement with militant Zionism that stretched back to his childhood. Born in Tel Aviv shortly after the 1921 riots, he grew up listening to his parents' accounts of the disturbances. At age ten or eleven, Bet-Zuri was already serving as a runner for the local Haganah detachment, carrying food, ammunition, and messages between the defense forces' guard posts in that city. In 1937, at the height of the Arab Rebellion, and aged only fifteen, Bet-Zuri was formally inducted into the Irgun. He was assigned to an Irgun cell led by Yezernitzky and progressed rapidly into an adept fighter. On one occasion, however, he and Yezernitzky were badly burned when a bomb they were planting exploded before they could make their getaway. Bet-Zuri regarded the scars left on his legs from the explosion with immense pride.[15]

By 1943, Bet-Zuri had left the Irgun and with two friends had formed his own terrorist group. An ambitious plan to assassinate MacMichael went nowhere, and a chance encounter at the Tel Aviv bus station changed his life. Bet-Zuri was waiting to board a bus when he heard an Orthodox Jewish rabbi, wearing the typical long black coat and hat and full beard, calling his name. It took a startled Bet-Zuri a few seconds to realize that the rabbi was Yezernitzky in disguise. Yezernitzky had just escaped from prison and was methodically rebuilding Stern's organization. He persuaded Bet-Zuri to join the group, and Bet-Zuri, like Hakim, was assigned to a training unit under Joshua Cohen. Cohen had nothing but praise for Bet-Zuri too. Upon completion of the course, Bet-Zuri was ordered to Jerusalem, where he affected the mien of a foppish young Englishman as a cover for his new vocation as full-time terrorist. He subsequently helped facilitate the mass escape of Lehi prisoners from Latrun in November 1943 and was also the operative designated to detonate the explosives that would have killed MacMichael while the high commissioner attended Sunday services at St. George's Cathedral the following February. Bet-Zuri had begged Yezernitzky to be sent on the mission to assassinate Moyne. And, disguised as a British soldier, in late November he left for Cairo.[16]

On Friday evening, October 20, Hakim waited in Cairo's Carmel Oriental Wine Shop per the secret instructions he had previously received. At 7:00 p.m., he had been told, a man would enter the shop and go up to the counter. Hakim should approach this man and offer him a cigarette. If he accepted it and said, "Thank you. My name is Zebulum"—Bet-Zuri's underground name in Lehi—Hakim was to reply, "It is a pleasure. My name is Benny," his own Lehi nom de guerre. The two men spent the rest of the month planning the assassination and debating whether to strike by day or night, at which venue—office or residence—and how best to effect their escape. On this last point, Yezernitzky had been explicit. "This is not a suicide action," he stressed to Bet-Zuri. "You are to make a reasonable plan for retreat and escape."[17]

By the end of October, the two Eliahus had agreed to a plan whereby they would shoot Moyne as he arrived home for lunch. They would escape on rented bicycles—disappearing into busy downtown Cairo by riding across the Bulak Bridge. They had ruled out either stealing or renting a motorcycle or a car as too risky. Fleeing on foot from the sedate environs of Zamalek was completely impractical. On November 1, Bet-Zuri and Hakim asked Sadovsky to direct them to a nearby shop where they could hire two bicycles. Sadovsky later saw them riding down a Cairo street together.[18]

Back in Palestine, Yezernitzky had received a coded message from Bet-

Zuri that greatly troubled him. "We should be finished with Uncle Jacques within two weeks," the letter read. Yezernitzky worried that the two Eliahus' enthusiasm for their mission had gotten the better of them and that they were carelessly rushing ahead with the attack. But there was nothing at this stage Yezernitzky could do given the time lag in communications between the Egyptian cell and Lehi headquarters.[19]

Having finalized their plan, the two would-be assassins thereafter passed the time playing backgammon at various cafés. On Saturday evening, November 4, Bet-Zuri assured Sadovsky that the operation he and Hakim had devised was foolproof. He put the chance of being arrested at no more than 2 percent—the same odds, Bet-Zuri confidently observed, of "being killed through a flowers-vase falling on his head while walking in the street." They arranged to meet again the next night.[20]

When Sadovsky arrived at the Café Américain, Hakim and Bet-Zuri were again immersed in a game of backgammon. The three men then sat together chatting. Suddenly Bet-Zuri declared to Sadovsky that he and Hakim "will finish the job to-morrow and after to-morrow we will be home." As Sadovsky had to rush off to another engagement, the three men agreed to meet later that night at another café. Hakim and Bet-Zuri then explained that the assassination would take place between 1:00 and 2:00 p.m. the next day when Moyne returned to his residence. Special arrangements were in place to spirit both men out of Egypt disguised as British soldiers. Their schedule was very tight, Bet-Zuri explained, because they had to be at a rendezvous point outside the city within only a couple of hours of the killing.[21]

On Monday morning, November 6, 1944, Hakim and Bet-Zuri left the small apartment that they rented from an elderly, Yiddish-speaking Jewish couple and biked through Cairo's streets to Gezira Island. They arrived before noon at No. 4 Sharia Gabalaya—Moyne's residence—and lay in wait. Hakim was armed with the Nagant revolver, while Bet-Zuri carried a 1916 Parabellum 9-mm Luger automatic pistol—the second handgun in the consignment sent from Palestine at the end of September. It too had an infamous pedigree, having been used by a Lehi gunman in the shooting death of a Jewish police officer near Tel Aviv eight months before. In the event of any trouble, both men had also stuffed several hand grenades into their pockets.[22]

The minister of state's daily lunchtime ritual was on schedule. Moyne emerged from his office, accompanied by his aide-de-camp, Captain

A. G. Hughes-Onslow, and his personal secretary, Dorothy Osmond. Lance Corporal A. T. Fuller, Moyne's backup driver, held the rear door of the long black limousine open as they entered and seated themselves. Just after 1:00 p.m., the car turned in to the gravel drive leading up to Moyne's redbrick villa. Osmond paid little notice to the two young men— one blond in appearance, who, she thought, looked like an Englishman, and the other dark like an Egyptian—whom she saw standing by the gate as the car drove by.[23]

The limousine glided to a stop in front of the house, and Hughes-Onslow was walking briskly to unlock the front door when he heard someone say in English, "Don't move. Stay where you are. Don't move." The voice was Hakim's. Fuller was standing beside the limousine and opening its rear door when he looked up to find Bet-Zuri coming toward him. Bet-Zuri later stated that he twice ordered Fuller to lie on the ground, but the driver instead lunged for the pistol in Bet-Zuri's hand. Three shots rang out, and Fuller collapsed on the driveway, mortally wounded. Hakim, meanwhile, had approached the rear of the car from the other side. He looked in the window at Osmond and told her not to move as he opened the car door and pointed his revolver directly at Moyne. Hakim fired three times. The first bullet hit the minister of state in the neck and the second in the abdomen. Moyne raised his hand in a feeble effort to ward off the third shot, which sliced through his fingers before lodging in his chest. "Oh, they've shot us!" Moyne exclaimed, clutching his throat, before losing consciousness.[24]

Hakim and Bet-Zuri ran from the residence to the street, where they jumped on their bicycles and pedaled furiously away. Hughes-Onslow was running behind them at a distance of about forty yards shouting for help. The two assassins tried to evade him and ducked down a side street before rejoining the main road. They were fast approaching the Bulak Bridge and were on the verge of making good their escape when a motorcycle policeman caught up with them. Bet-Zuri stopped and wheeled around, firing several warning shots in the air. The motorcycle policeman also dismounted, drew his pistol, and ordered Bet-Zuri to drop his weapon or he would shoot. Instead, Bet-Zuri took aim and fired at the motorcycle's tires, attempting to deflate them. But the Luger's magazine was empty. He was struggling to reload when the Egyptian policeman returned fire. A bullet struck Bet-Zuri in the chest. Hearing the commotion behind, Hakim immediately circled back to help his fallen comrade. In minutes, another policeman who had been guarding the bridge was on the scene, and Hakim and Bet-Zuri were under arrest.[25]

By that time, an ambulance and a doctor had arrived at Moyne's residence and were en route to the hospital with the grievously wounded minister. He was admitted at 1:40 p.m. Multiple blood transfusions were administered, and Moyne briefly regained consciousness. But then doctors discovered that he was bleeding internally from the bullet that had punctured his colon and large intestine, and Moyne was rushed into surgery. As his condition grew grave, King Farouk himself visited the hospital. Despite the ministrations of the king's personal physician, Moyne died at 8:40 that evening.[26]

Barely an hour earlier, at 5:30 p.m. London time, Churchill had broken the news of the shooting to the war cabinet. Initial reports stated only that Moyne had been critically wounded by two unidentified gunmen, neither of whom was an Egyptian. Indeed, both Hakim and Bet-Zuri had refused to speak. "We are saying nothing. We are waiting for the Court," they declared in Hebrew, according to a terse statement issued by the Egyptian police. This at least provided one key lead—both men were Jews. It was for this reason perhaps that the prime minister told the cabinet that the Irgun was most likely responsible. Stanley provided a brief précis of the Irgun and its place in the constellation of Zionist organizations before expressing the opinion that if the Jewish Agency really wished to put an end to the violence, it could do so. Churchill then asked the colonial secretary to meet with Weizmann as soon as possible and impress upon him this point.[27]

Weizmann arrived at the Colonial Office a few hours later. Stanley informed him that "unless the Jews could rid themselves of this murderous tail, people like [Churchill] who had done so much for them in the past would feel relieved of any responsibility in the future." In the summary of the meeting that the colonial secretary gave to Churchill, he reported that Weizmann was "naturally horrified" by the news and realized "to the full that this sort of thing is fatal to his hopes." The Zionist leader was returning to Palestine on Saturday, following a five-year hiatus imposed by the war. He promised Stanley that he would do everything in his power to convince the Jewish Agency Executive that there "must now be war to the knife against these extremists. There must be no longer any reservation or hanging back but complete cooperation with the Government in crushing them."[28]

The next afternoon, Churchill rose in the House of Commons to pay tribute to his slain friend. He and Moyne had worked closely together for more than thirty years. A selfless public servant, Moyne had served with distinction in two wars and had survived the carnage at Gallipoli, in France, and in Flanders, only to die, the prime minister mournfully observed, "at the hands of foul assassins in Cairo last night." Britain's affairs in the region had suffered a profound setback with his death. Over the previous year Moyne had devoted himself to finding an equitable "solution to the Zionist problem," Churchill said. Then, echoing the same point he had made to Weizmann when they had parted only days before, the prime minister painted a picture of the minister of state that few in the Yishuv and no one in Lehi would have recognized: "I can assure the House that the Jews in Palestine have rarely lost a better or more well-informed friend."[29]

Weizmann had sent a handwritten note to Churchill that same day: "I can hardly find words adequate to express the deep moral indignation and horror which I feel at the murder of Lord Moyne." Carefully choosing his words, Weizmann also sought to shield the Yishuv from any retribution—and to salvage whatever he could of the prime minister's encouraging words from just a few days before. The depth of Weizmann's personal anguish is perhaps best evidenced by his observation that Moyne's death hurt him more than even his own son's. Michael Weizmann, age twenty-five, had been an aviator in the Royal Air Force Volunteer Reserve when his plane was shot down over the Bay of Biscay in 1942. "When my son was killed it was my personal tragedy," the Zionist leader later reflected. "Hashem natan, Hashem lackah [God gives, God takes]—but here [Moyne's murder] is the tragedy of the entire nation."[30]

The shock in Palestine was all the more profound because there had been no terrorist incidents since Wilkin's slaying in September. Although this brief respite from a year of escalating violence had deceived no one into thinking that the terrorist threat had passed, the impact of the assassination was that much greater given the unusual quiet that it shattered. Moreover, like Weizmann, both Ben-Gurion and Shertok feared the worst—that the retribution inflicted on the Yishuv would be of a severity that would destroy all that had been achieved politically and diplomatically over the previous eighteen months. Ben-Gurion opened an emergency joint session of the Jewish Agency and Vaad Le'umi Executives the following day. "The situation is getting worse and we are facing the future in which our name will be execrated," he declared. Shertok followed, criticizing both bodies for their previous failure to deal harshly with the dissidents. Dismissing arguments that cooperation with the authorities would lead to civil war, Shertok proclaimed that such a war "would be worth while, if it could save our future and salvage our chances, which are now clearly discernible on the political horizon."[31]

Itzhak Gruenbaum, however, again rebuffed these arguments. The Yishuv's cooperation on this matter, he reiterated, should be made conditional upon the government's abrogation of the white paper. Eliahu Golomb exploded. The danger confronting the Yishuv, he stated, was far too serious to risk attempting to extract concessions from the British. Although Rabbi Yehuda Fishman and Emil Schmorak, who shared Gruenbaum's views, were willing to countenance independent action by the Jewish Agency against the terrorists, they too remained staunchly opposed to any form of active cooperation with the government. After protracted debate, the matter was put to a vote: ten members supported full cooperation; five the Fishman-Schmorak course; with only Gruenbaum voting for his own option before resigning. The public statement that emerged from the joint session broke new ground in these official bodies' willingness to go to war against the terrorists. "This revolting crime," it declared,

> committed outside the boundaries of our country under circumstances not yet cleared up, raises anew the growing danger of the continued existence of a terrorist gang inside Palestine. Terrorism in Palestine is calculated to wreck the chances of our political struggle and destroy our internal peace. The Yishuv is called upon to cast out the members of this destructive band, to deprive them of all refuge and shelter, to resist their threats and to render all necessary assistance to the authorities in the prevention of terrorist acts, and in the eradication of the terrorist organisation. Our very existence is here at stake.[32]

In Cairo, both Hakim and Bet-Zuri had remained silent despite being subjected to intensive interrogation, no doubt hoping to give the rest of the Lehi organization in Egypt time to flee or destroy any incriminating documents or evidence.[33]

But on November 8 both men suddenly admitted their crime. In a brief statement Hakim and Bet-Zuri declared simply, "We are members of the Fighters for the Freedom of Israel movement and what we have done we have done on the instructions of this organization." The text was revealed in a dramatic press conference given that afternoon. It was distributed to the Egyptian and foreign journalists in attendance along with a second handout containing further statements made by Bet-Zuri to the effect that he was pleased that their trial would take place in Egypt. He believed that the Arabs were friendly to Lehi and that he and his accomplice would therefore be either acquitted or given light sentences. Bet-Zuri's fantastical views on Lehi's popularity outside Palestine were only matched by his inflated accounts of the widespread support that he claimed the group enjoyed from the Yishuv and his conviction that the assassination would both let loose a deluge of financial contributions that would revitalize Lehi and shortly prove to be the opening shot in a "universal uprising" against British rule. Upon further reflection, British censors intervened and belatedly sought to suppress the information revealed in the second handout.[34]

Not until the following evening, however, did the authorities finally learn Hakim's and Bet-Zuri's real names. In addition, Bet-Zuri more specifically disclosed their motive. "We are fighting the British Government because it is bad," he explained.

> No calculations were made as to whether Lord Moyne was a good man or a bad man. It was considered only that he was the key man for Britain in governing the Middle East and as such [he] is responsible for what is happening in Palestine . . .
> The reason for killing Lord Moyne is that it is a step towards forcing the British Government to leave Palestine.

Upon also being asked why the minister of state was singled out for attack, Hakim stated only, "I was sent by the organization expressly to kill Lord Moyne."[35]

Shortly afterward, police discovered the apartment that both men had rented. It contained a veritable cornucopia of all the essential accoutrements required for a terrorist operation: two British army uniforms, two counterfeit army pay books, a forged navy pay book, and six blank leave passes, along with six cases of TNT and 612 rounds of Luger ammunition.[36]

From London, meanwhile, pressure was building on the Palestine administration to take precisely the sort of punitive action against the Yishuv that Weizmann, Ben-Gurion, and Shertok so desperately feared. Stanley raised this on November 8, telling Gort that he wanted to be able to present to the war cabinet a menu of possible punitive courses of action. Britain's "immediate and spectacular" response twenty years before when an Egyptian nationalist assassinated Sir Lee Stack, the sirdar (person in command) and governor-general of the Sudan, and Egypt had been fined £500,000 and humiliatingly compelled to withdraw its military forces from neighboring Sudan was prominently in his thoughts. The colonial secretary accordingly fastened on two options in particular: implementing the long-delayed operations to seize all illegally held Jewish arms and temporarily suspending Jewish immigration to Palestine. He regarded the latter option as ancillary to the former and more as an insurance policy designed to ensure the Yishuv's active and continued cooperation beside the government against the Jewish terrorist organizations. It also had the virtue of being relatively straightforward to implement. Stanley recognized that the arms search option was far more problematic. "To be effective," he wrote, the searches "would have to be done on the largest scale and it would be essential that there should be an overwhelming military force available both for the actual searches and for maintaining order throughout the country." The colonial secretary concluded his message by emphasizing that any measures taken "should be immediate and that every effort should be made to dramatise them in the public eye. We have to consider the effect not merely upon Palestine but upon the Middle East and the world in general. Some striking display will be required in the interests of British prestige. Troop movements on an impressive scale would clearly be one of the best measures to achieve this end."[37]

Gort agreed with the logic behind the arms search option. It would clearly demonstrate British resolve and also eliminate a long-standing challenge to the government's authority. But, he cautioned Stanley, it ignored the consequences of failure. The high commissioner feared that should such an operation be less than an unqualified success, the damage to Britain's prestige would be even greater than that already wrought by Moyne's assassination. And with military forces in Palestine already understrength, he continued, success was far from certain. An operation along the lines envisioned by the colonial secretary would require the transfer of an additional infantry division to Palestine—which was unlikely given wartime priorities. In the circumstances, Gort suggested to Stanley that the arms search option be abandoned completely. Instead, he advocated a return to the policy that had been in force before the 1943 incident at Ramat Ha-Kovesh, when a search of that Jewish settlement provoked widespread rioting and had led to a prohibition on further such operations so as not to impede the war effort. Under those terms, the high commissioner would again be permitted to authorize limited operations against specific locations on a case-by-case basis—but with one new, critical proviso: that these searches would only be conducted in circumstances when there was sufficient likelihood of their unqualified success. Stanley accepted Gort's glum assessment and duly apprised the war cabinet.[38]

The war cabinet considered the issue of response and reprisal on November 13. Although there was broad agreement that the Yishuv should be punished, there were sharp divisions over what form this should take and against whom it should be directed. Ideally, the people and organization responsible for the crime should bear the full weight of any punitive action. But because Lehi was a small, enigmatic underground movement, it was impossible to single it out for retribution and avoid punishing the rest of the Yishuv. This is why Churchill opposed suspending immigration, arguing that it would "play into the hands of the extremists" and thereby prove entirely counterproductive by undermining "the efforts being made by the Jews themselves to suppress the terrorist organisations." The war cabinet generally concurred but was reluctant to take the immigration option completely off the table. Accordingly, it proposed that the Jewish Agency be warned that if the Yishuv's full and unstinting cooperation against terrorism was not forthcoming, the government would be forced to reconsider this particular punitive measure. With regard to arms searches, the war cabinet decided to postpone further consideration of this option until the Joint Planning Staff had time to complete its own analysis of the proposed operation and the forces required to implement it.[39]

Across the Middle East the initial shock over the assassination was giving way to widespread bewilderment and anger. Earlier that same day the first reports began to arrive in London from British legations across the region. They painted a disquieting picture of disbelief and astonishment that a week had elapsed since Moyne's killing and still the British government had done nothing. From Baghdad, the British ambassador to Iraq, Sir Kinahan Cornwallis, wrote of a country in shock. "General reaction," he reported to the foreign secretary, Anthony Eden,

> seems to be one of expectancy that Britain will do something drastic or dramatic against [the] Zionists comparable [to the] sanctions which followed the Stack murder with which this crime is inevitably compared . . .
> The assassination of Lord Moyne has brought murder to the fore as [a] political weapon, which in itself is bad enough in [a] country where violence is never far from men's minds. But ultimate effect of the crime will depend largely on what action is taken to punish the assassins, and—equally important in Iraqi eyes—their masters.[40]

From Cairo, Brigadier Sir Iltyd Clayton, Moyne's adviser on Arab affairs, wrote a lengthy memorandum laying out the dire consequences of continued inaction. After four single-spaced pages of typescript, which didactically recapitulated the government's previous spinelessness in the face of repeated Zionist terrorist provocation in Palestine, Clayton got to the point. "All well-informed authorities in the Middle East," he wrote, "agree that the murder of Lord Moyne is not the end of the terrorist campaign but only a stage in its development." Indeed, he spuriously noted, "there are some grounds for believing that a 'black list' of British officials and personalities marked down for assassination is in existence." British authority was being undermined and its prestige eroded, Clayton warned: "Already the Arabs in Palestine are reported to be saying that when the Sirdar [Stack] was shot in Egypt in 1924, the British turned the Egyptians out of the Sudan; when the District Commissioner of Galilee was shot by Arab gangsters in 1937, the British rounded up and deported to the Seychelles every important Arab leader in Palestine; but when the Jews shoot a member of the British Cabinet, nothing happens." Inevitably, the notion that violence and terrorism pay in pressuring Britain would gain further currency with the effect that Palestine's Arabs will "be driven and encouraged to adopt similar tactics, in the hope of a similar result." Clayton's message was clear. Failure to severely punish the Jews would have dire consequences. But, equally significantly, in his opinion, Britain had been presented with a timely opportunity to further circumscribe the Jewish national home and decisively claw back its nearly three-decades-old commitment to Zionism. "H.M.G. must publicly make it plain," he warned, "that they do *not* support the opening of Palestine to unrestricted Jewish immigration and the creation of a Jewish State, which it is the avowed aim of the terrorist organisations to achieve. This involves a clear understanding that H.M.G. regard any obligations towards the Jews contracted as a result of the Balfour Declaration as having been already more than adequately discharged."[41]

Sir Walter Smart, counselor at the British embassy in Cairo, was similarly convinced that only drastic measures would produce salutary results. In his view, far too little had been done after the attempt on MacMichael's life three months earlier. "Something in the nature of a thunderclap, like that which followed the Sirdar's murder," had been expected by the Arabs then. "If now nothing is done about the murder of Lord Moyne other than the execution of the two murderers, a stop will not be put to this dangerous movement." The situation, in his view, called for nothing less than the dissolution of the Jewish Agency—a punitive measure he found especially appealing given that it was precisely the punishment that the Palestine government had imposed on the Arabs after Andrews's assassination seven years before when the Supreme Muslim Council was dissolved.[42]

On November 16, Clayton and Smart met with Weizmann as the Zionist leader scrambled between Jerusalem and Cairo to assure British officials of the Yishuv's commitment to uproot the terrorist organizations. Weizmann's efforts in this respect had even included, according to a U.S. intelligence report, "begging" the editors of Jewish newspapers in Palestine to refrain from criticizing Churchill's speech so as not to further alienate the prime minister and enrage British officials across the region. Clayton was left unconvinced by Weizmann's entreaties. Smart was appalled. "Weissmann [*sic*]," he caustically observed, "has always posed as a moderate having great difficulties in controlling Jewish extremists. By this attitude he has managed to get a great deal across the British Government."[43]

All these cables, assessments, minutes, and notes, however, failed to budge Churchill from his position that suspending Jewish immigration would accomplish nothing except to "play into the hands of the Extremists." Unlike Smart and other officials, the prime minister believed that the Yishuv had been genuinely shocked by the assassination, and he told Stanley on November 17 that the community was now in fact more open than ever to Weizmann's "counsels of moderation." Accordingly, the prime minister opposed issuing even a warning to the Yishuv about suspending immigration. Churchill was equally against launching any major arms search operations because that too would strike at the section of the Yishuv that comprised neither the terrorists nor their accomplices.[44]

On both these points Churchill's position was prescient. The Chiefs of Staff Joint Planning Staff had completed its analysis of the arms search option's feasibility the previous day. To be effective, the chiefs believed, such an operation would need to raid simultaneously an estimated sixty Jewish settlements where significant arms caches were believed to be hidden. Accordingly, rather than the one additional division initially assumed, in excess of two more divisions would be required. None of these forces, the Joint Planning Staff emphasized, could be spared from other operational theaters. And even if they could, it was by no means certain that the searches would achieve their objective. There was also the danger that they would make matters worse by stirring the Haganah to rebellion.[45]

Churchill had also correctly anticipated the Yishuv's reaction to any threat regarding the suspension of immigration. Within the week, for example, editorials had appeared in Palestine's Jewish press attacking this punitive option on the grounds that it would punish innocent victims of Nazi aggression rather than the handful of people responsible for Moyne's murder.[46]

On November 17 the prime minister again addressed the House of Commons. "This shameful crime," he began, has shocked the world. It has affected none more strongly than those, like myself, who, in the past, have been consistent friends of the Jews and constant architects of their future.

If our dreams for Zionism are to end in the smoke of assassins' pistols and our labours for its future to produce only a new set of gangsters worthy of Nazi Germany, many like myself will have to reconsider the position we have maintained so consistently and so long in the past.

If there is to be any hope of a peaceful and successful future for Zionism, these wicked activities must cease, and those responsible for them must be destroyed root and branch.

Churchill accordingly demanded the "wholehearted cooperation of the entire Jewish community."[47]

The prime minister clearly intended his remarks to be the "thunderclap" that Smart had argued was needed to rouse the Yishuv. Yet, according to Gort, the community and its leaders were still dragging their feet. Indeed, despite having been in Palestine for only three weeks, his own patience was already wearing thin.[48]

In Tel Aviv, the proposed counterterrorism program was then the subject of an intense debate at the Histadrut's Sixth Plenary Conference. Although the Yishuv's two principal executive bodies—the Jewish Agency Executive and the Vaad Le'umi—had approved these measures two weeks before, the program had yet to be ratified by the rank-and-file membership of important representative institutions like the Histadrut. The conference thus provided an ideal opportunity for Ben-Gurion and the program's proponents to champion the proposed effort and ensure it the widest support possible. But from the start, the same profound differences of opinion over the extent and form that the cooperation should take surfaced at this gathering as well. Ben-Gurion vigorously lobbied for approval of the measures. The Yishuv, in his view, had no choice but to actively cooperate with the government against the terrorists or risk harsh reprisals, which he warned would likely include attempts to seize the Haganah's weapons. "We cannot fight terrorism by condemnation alone," Ben-Gurion declared. "For people whose only argument is dynamite, persuasion is useless. We need drastic action to wipe out terrorism." He further described Moyne's murder and its potential repercussions as a "dagger plunged at the heart" of the entire Zionist enterprise. In the end, his arguments prevailed, and on November 22 the conference approved the four-point program proposed by Ben-Gurion. It called on the community to terminate the employment of people suspected of belonging to either the Irgun or Lehi, expel them from the schools they attended, and evict them from rental property. Terrorist attempts at extortion were also to be "firmly resisted." Lastly, assistance was to be rendered to the authorities and the police. A similar program tailored specifically for Jewish schools was roundly endorsed by some sixteen Zionist youth groups, the classes of six secondary schools, and the Hebrew Teachers' College in Jerusalem. Four days later, posters began to appear in Tel Aviv outlining these steps and directing the public to shun the Irgun. Within twenty-four hours, Haganah agents had reportedly apprehended nearly sixty Irgun members. British army intelligence had essentially predicted exactly this outcome of the Haganah's targeting the Irgun and, remarkably, that an assassination of a leading British official would likely precipitate it—nine months before. "The culmination of these outrages," an assessment prepared by the MI5 station in Jerusalem had concluded in February 1944, "may take [the] form either of an attempt on the life of a person of importance in the Administration or of some kind [of] demonstration of force. This would not suit the book [of] the Jewish Agency in any way."[49]

The government, however, was clearly less adept at anticipating the firestorm of incredulity and rage that its handling of the reprisal issue continued to provoke among key British officials across the Middle East. On the morning following the prime minister's remarks in the Commons, an impassioned letter arrived on Eden's desk. Its author was Lord Killearn (né Sir Miles Lampson), Britain's long-serving ambassador to Egypt who also held the title of high commissioner for the Sudan. The Middle East Defence Committee, a smaller, regional variant of the war cabinet, which Moyne had chaired as minister of state and on which Killearn and his fellow ambassadors sat along with the region's military commanders in chief and most senior national police officers, weighed in the next day. In a lengthy telegram to Eden, the committee endorsed the points that Cornwallis had previously made. It then went on to argue that London had gravely underestimated the crisis that both Moyne's murder and the government's hitherto anemic reaction had sparked across the region. The situation was sufficiently serious, the committee believed, as to warrant the diversion of "necessary naval, land and air forces even at the expense of operations elsewhere" to Palestine in support of these punitive measures. In other words, Britain stood to lose more by allowing its authority to be challenged in this manner than by delaying the war effort in Italy.[50]

Not for the first time, a bureaucratic struggle now emerged between the Foreign Office and the Colonial Office to determine the government's policy for Palestine. The combined interventions of the Baghdad and Cairo plenipotentiaries, backed by the Middle East Defence Committee, had now become irresistible. Stanley was therefore compelled to revisit the entire reprisal question. Soliciting Gort's views, he discovered that the high commissioner was now at one with the ambassadors. Gort had become similarly alarmed about the adverse repercussions that any perception of "apparent undue leniency" would have on his ability to govern the country. He was also concerned about the possible impact on the morale of the Palestine police and civil service. The colonial secretary was now boxed in and had no choice but to place the matter before the war cabinet once more for discussion. He again proposed that consideration be given to the two previously discussed options, albeit with some minor amendments:

(1) Explicit warning should be given that unless outrages cease immigration to Palestine may have to be suspended; and

(2) If the necessary troops can be spared they should be moved into Palestine as soon as practicable but should not be used for wholesale arms searches unless further outrages occur.[51]

Killearn was furious, his anger doubtless stoked by a report the previous day that two British soldiers in Egypt had been shot at and one severely wounded. Suspicion had immediately fallen on Lehi, though it was later disproven. Nonetheless, there was a perception that Moyne's assassination had been not an isolated event but part of a Jewish terrorist campaign that had now spread to Egypt. Not content to let the matter rest, Killearn sent a second impassioned message to Eden. He beseeched the foreign secretary to do everything in his power "to overcome this shocking CO [Colonial Office] weakness" by pressing for "*immediate* effective action." Referring to Moyne by his forename, Killearn lamented, "Poor Walter's murder is surely a pretty high price to have had to pay for our previous inaction. Do I *really* understand that the CO are deliberately prepared to await another outrage (they in fact say so) before having the guts to do the needful. If so, one really begins to feel ashamed that one is an Englishman!"[52]

On November 23, Stanley submitted a memorandum explaining his own position to the war cabinet. He proposed a two-track middle course. First, the Foreign Office's objections notwithstanding, the Yishuv should indeed be publicly warned that if further terrorist outrages were to occur, the government would be forced to take what he termed "drastic action," including suspending immigration. Second, additional troops should be moved to Palestine as soon as possible, although they would be deployed for wholesale arms searches only in the event of renewed terrorist violence—again, in contrast to the Foreign Office position.[53]

The war cabinet considered the matter on November 24. It agreed that no wholesale searches for arms should at this time be undertaken. A new assessment prepared by the Chiefs of Staff had painted an even more dismal picture of the likelihood of success than the Joint Planning Staff had. The chiefs argued that the previous year's search of Ramat Ha-Kovesh had clearly demonstrated the difficulties and risks attending any effort to seize illegally held Jewish arms. They therefore concluded that the search option was impractical given the uncertainty of success coupled with the harm that would be done to the war effort in Europe. The war cabinet concurred, noting that "searches were rarely productive; secrecy as to the action contemplated was difficult to maintain; mistakes were made by the troops and bad feeling engendered." Such operations were thus best left to the police. At the same time, however, the war cabinet acknowledged that there were too few police in Palestine to execute this mission. Therefore the chiefs were instructed to reorganize military units already in-country into mobile columns with a strength of two hundred men each to better assist the police with such operations. The war cabinet further decided to notify the high commissioner that although he was free to carry out local, specific searches, "no systematic searches for arms should . . . at this stage be undertaken." The discussion then turned to the immigration suspension option. The war cabinet concluded that for the moment no *public* warning regarding the suspension of immigration would be issued. Instead, the high commissioner was authorized to approach Weizmann privately and inform him that in the event of any new outbreak of terrorism the government would not hesitate to take such action.[54]

CHAPTER 10

Tears of Bereaved Mothers

The war cabinet's meeting on November 24, 1944, had also resurrected long-standing concerns about the PPF's condition and performance. Not for the first time in its history, the police force was found to be well below its authorized strength and seriously handicapped by a shortage of British police. This was especially lamentable in Churchill's view given the constraints on military manpower imposed by operations in Italy. Drawing on his experiences as secretary for air and colonial secretary in the early 1920s, when he had direct responsibility for Ireland during the Irish War of Independence and then in the treaty negotiations that followed, Churchill averred that terrorism was always best "tackled as a police problem rather than by military forces in conventional formation." The war cabinet agreed and recommended that all possible steps immediately be taken to increase recruitment to the PPF and improve its intelligence capabilities through the addition "of carefully picked expert personnel."[1]

Only a few days before, the inspector general, Rymer-Jones, had lunched with Stanley and the deputy prime minister, Clement Attlee. He had assured both ministers that provided the Yishuv's cooperation was forthcoming, the police would have no trouble vanquishing the terrorists. Rymer-Jones made exactly the same point to Guy Liddell, MI5's head of counterintelligence and a future deputy director general of that service, when they met on November 25. However, the symbiotic deficiencies in manpower and intelligence grossly belied that claim. His visit to London in fact had been prompted not by the Moyne assassination but rather by Rymer-Jones's efforts to kick-start a long-promised Colonial Office recruitment drive. When he met with Stanley and Attlee, he bluntly told them he required at least fifteen hundred British police beyond the existing complement to cope with the Jewish terrorist threat. Without this allocation, he said, "it was like trying to make bricks without straw."[2]

Although an ambitious recruiting campaign was duly promised, the fact remained that the vast majority of young British men eligible for military service preferred to join one of the branches of the armed forces rather than enlist in the colonial police. Moreover, the overall shortage of man-power five years into the war, coupled with the exigencies of the fighting itself, made the military extremely reluctant to provide troops for internal security duties.[3]

The intelligence issue was perhaps even more problematic. At various critical moments in its history, poor intelligence had repeatedly under-mined the PPF's performance. The situation in 1944 was no different; until the war cabinet's discussion on November 24 there is little evidence that any serious attention had been paid to the quality of the CID's intel-ligence gathering and analysis. It might have been that the early successes against the Stern Group, including the killing of its founder and leader, had blinded nearly everyone to the more grievous threat now presented by the Irgun's revolt. In any case, it was not until Alexander Kellar of MI5 arrived in Palestine in late November as part of a two-month visit to the Middle East that the scope and depth of the CID's incompetence became apparent.[4]

Kellar was perhaps the archetypal twentieth-century British spymaster. Educated at Edinburgh, Yale, and Columbia Universities, he was a dandy, a snob, a homosexual, and what the postwar director general of MI5, Sir Percy Sillitoe, himself a policeman, disdainfully referred to as one of the "long-haired intellectuals" then populating the U.K. intelligence estab-lishment. According to the British historian of intelligence Christopher Andrew, the nefarious ministerial intelligence adviser named Maston in John le Carré's first novel, *Call for the Dead*, was modeled on Kellar.[5]

Kellar was the British intelligence community's preeminent expert on the Jewish terrorist organizations. His detailed knowledge and thorough understanding of Zionist politics and both its legitimate and its sub-rosa institutions had greatly impressed his boss, Liddell, the counterintelligence division's head. Kellar's expertise in these areas was greatly facilitated by his access to the fruits of the intelligence community's tightly guarded, and reluctantly shared, ability to secretly read and listen to both coded and open messages sent between London and Jerusalem by Jewish Agency officials.[6]

Since at least 1939, both the British Government Code and Cypher School (the forerunner to today's GCHQ, the Government Communica-tions Headquarters, which is the British counterpart of the U.S. National Security Agency) and the Radio Security Service, maintained by MI6, had been intercepting these communications. In addition, Home Office war-rants had authorized MI5 to tap the phones at the Jewish Agency's Lon-don offices at 77 Great Russell and open its mail. British intelligence had therefore been privy to the intense discussions held at the end of October between Shertok and Golomb in London with their colleagues in Jerusalem over the cooperation issue. All this information was duly provided to Stanley and Churchill. Kellar appears to have been the main conduit of this traffic. It was known by its top secret code name, ISPAL—presumably an acronym for "Intelligence Service—Palestine."[7]

ISPAL was highly confidential, but Gort seems to have become thoroughly acquainted with its intelligence products while he was in London prior to leaving for Palestine in late October. As ISPAL's principal guardian at MI5, Kellar became the incumbent high commissioner's personal guide through the intricacies of both this top secret treasure trove of information and the various Zionist institutions and officials. The two men, Liddell recorded in his diary, "established a complete bond of confidence"—to the extent that Gort was "popping in and out of [Kellar's] office every day . . . [and] even rehearses with Kellar what he is going to say to Shertok."[8]

By coincidence Kellar was scheduled to make his second tour in seven months of MI5's outstations in the Middle East in early 1945. He traveled to Egypt, Palestine, Lebanon, Iraq, and Iran. While in Jerusalem, Kellar stayed in Government House as Gort's guest, and at the high commissioner's explicit request he agreed to extend his stay in order to "look into certain security matters which had acquired urgent importance through the increasing tenseness of the political situation existing there." It was a measure of how critical the security situation in Palestine had become that Kellar spent most of his trip in Jerusalem and fully three-quarters of his report was devoted to Palestine.[9]

During his previous visit, Kellar had reported his concerns over the PPF British section's susceptibility to bribery and especially the insecure communications at Government House that rendered the high commissioner's telephone lines vulnerable to interception. But, reflecting the views of all the government officials with whom he had spoken, Kellar had been decidedly upbeat at the time about the police force's ability to handle any trouble. The tone and content of the report of his second visit, however, were considerably more troubled. Kellar was brutally critical of the police and especially the CID. Probing more deeply, he found fault with its feckless record keeping and the poor organization of its files—perhaps the most fundamental requirement of any effective police or intelligence apparatus. Kellar also criticized the quality of the CID's information and the incompetence of its interrogators.[10]

He was particularly taken aback by the lack of institutional knowledge pertaining to the terrorist organizations and their important figures. And Kellar despaired over the abject state of liaison between the CID and the Defence Security Office (DSO), the British Security Service (MI5) station in Jerusalem, and with army intelligence as well. He was especially perturbed by the cooperative arrangement that the CID had entered into with the Jewish Agency in order to gain information on the terrorists. To his mind, this created a dangerous dependency on the agency that both underscored the police force's own enfeebled intelligence capabilities and made it impossible to independently verify any of the information it was being fed. Kellar regarded this servile relationship as proof positive of the CID's ineptitude in penetrating the terrorist organizations. Worse still, it laid bare this failure before the Jewish authorities who would therefore draw their own conclusions about the abysmal state of British intelligence. None of this went unnoticed by the Irgun's leadership, according to the memoir of Mendel Malatzky, a senior commander in the group at that time.[11]

Kellar was also critical of the CID for its lax handling of intelligence. "The fact that the Police lack personnel and officers with proper and up-to-date C.I.D. experience has much to do with this state of affairs, but personal friction also plays a part." Kellar went on to detail how relations between the CID chief, Giles, and his DSO counterpart, Henry Hunloke, were strained to the extent that the sharing, collation, and analysis of intelligence were severely compromised. He described Giles as difficult to work with and suffering "from a noticeable inferiority complex [making him] unnecessarily sensitive to any suspected slight." The nub of the liaison problem lay in the fact that Giles resented Hunloke because the latter had been asked to Government House for consultations more than Giles.[12]

Richard Catling, then a deputy superintendent under Giles's command, admitted to Kellar that the CID resented the DSO station's activities. Giles and his men felt that DSO personnel had no business poking their noses in what they regarded as exclusively police business. Kellar had to assure Catling that "members of the Defence Security Organisation had no idea of stealing any kind of march on the Police and were only too anxious to pool their resources with the C.I.D., more particularly at a time when [Catling] himself felt, everything should be done to lessen the dependence of the Authorities on the Agency for the information they needed on the terrorists."[13]

But Kellar's sharpest indictment was of the CID's failure to properly interrogate *any* of the detained Jewish terrorists before they had

186 | ANONYMOUS SOLDIERS

been shipped off to Eritrea in October. He suggested to Catling that it might not be too late to glean some useful information from the exiled detainees. Catling agreed. Accordingly, arrangements were made to fly six terrorists—whom the CID regarded as "ring-leaders"—to the special MI6 interrogation facility at Maadi, on the outskirts of Cairo, for intensive questioning. The results, however, were disappointing. "The men concerned are cast in the fanatical mould," Kellar explained, "and, like the I.R.A. during the 'Black and Tan' period, they will probably prove difficult or perhaps impossible to break." But this did not absolve the CID from either its failure to thoroughly interrogate these men in the first place or its evident lack of competence to do so.[14]

The section of the report on Palestine concludes with Kellar's prescient observation that "much clearly needed to be done at Military Headquarters in the King David Hotel, Jerusalem." Security procedures were so lax that people summoned for interviews to the government and military offices in the southern wing of the building simply wandered the halls until they were called. In addition, local cleaners went about their business without oversight. Kellar was astonished to find a secret military transit order under a bush on the hotel's grounds. He did what he could to tighten controls on access by unauthorized people and hotel service personnel and also to improve the telephone system's vulnerability to interception— a problem he found pervasive on both his visits to Palestine.[15]

Kellar's grave reservations about intelligence cooperation with the Jewish Agency and the Haganah raised no eyebrows in either London or Jerusalem. Eden defended this cooperative arrangement to his Middle East ambassadors and their advisers, explaining that the only "really important thing is to round up the terrorists." To this end, he had assured Killearn in particular on November 30, 1944, that "drastic immediate and practical steps have been and are being taken to round up Stern Group and other terrorists . . . Numerous arrests have already been made, including some persons known to belong to Stern Group. Inspector General is confident that given a little time and a police force of sufficient strength [the] power of criminal gangs can be broken." Whether Eden's two explicit references to the Stern Group were deliberately misleading or simply based on inaccurate information given to him is unclear. What is clear, however, is that the Palestine administration still had serious concerns about the Jewish Agency's determination to press ahead with the counterterrorism campaign and moreover was fully cognizant of the fact that the agency's efforts were directed exclusively against the Irgun and not against Lehi.[16]

Only two days earlier, Gort had complained twice in two separate telegrams to Stanley about the meager results of the Haganah's counter-terrorist efforts. "Since the murder of Lord Moyne," he reported in the first communication, "there has been no cause to complain of the overt attitude of the Agency and Vaad Le'umi leaders, but no real proof has yet been displayed of the will and ability to regain control." But as the day wore on, the high commissioner's criticism shifted from that of effort to attitude. Although "Jewish opinion is belatedly aroused against terrorists," he complained, the "main emphasis is upon possible disastrous consequences of terrorism to Zionism, rather than moral or civic duty." Indeed, on the same day that Eden was sending the above message to Killearn, Gort was once again finding fault with the Jewish Agency and the Haganah's conduct. "After a short period of acute alarm," the high commissioner reported to London, "there are signs that they are beginning to believe that they have 'gotten away with it,' and that they will be able to preserve . . . their internal unity and armed strength intact against the day when the use of force to achieve their major aims is deemed appropriate." Contemporaneous American intelligence reports made the same point.[17]

British intelligence, however, took a very different—and surprisingly far more laudatory—view of the counterterrorist efforts' initial results. Liddell noted in his diary, for instance, how a highly placed agent in the Jewish Agency, code-named Snake, had passed to the PPF the names and addresses of more than five hundred terrorists. An additional tranche of information contained the locations of terrorist arms dumps. Nearly half the people on the list, Liddell noted, were already in custody. To his mind, this was ample proof that "the more moderate elements in the Zionist movement are afraid that the actions of the extremists may jeopardize the whole future of Zionism." According to the Canadian historian Steven Wagner, Snake was likely Kollek, the Jewish Agency's liaison officer to both British military intelligence and the police.[18]

On December 6, Gort lunched with Weizmann. As they strolled in the garden together before sitting down to eat, the high commissioner reminded Weizmann, per the war cabinet's directive from its November 24 meeting, that any hesitation in moving decisively against the terrorists would entail for the Yishuv the most dire consequences. Weizmann was shocked that there should still be any question of the Jewish Agency's determination to stamp out the terrorist organizations. Indeed, he assured the high commissioner that the Yishuv was doing everything in its power to fight terrorism. Shaken by the mere suggestion of any doubts about the agency's sincerity or determination concerning this matter, Weizmann asked Gort to please communicate the gist of his message to Churchill while hastening to add that he would himself be writing to Churchill shortly with a more expansive account of the agency's cooperation.[19]

That letter arrived within the fortnight. In it, Weizmann impressed upon Churchill that he was very much aware of the "gravity of the situation" and that in his opinion cooperation with the authorities "is proceeding satisfactorily." He described how "severe blows" had been dealt to the terrorists with more to follow until "decisive results" were achieved. In closing, the elderly Zionist leader's deepest fears that the Yishuv might yet have some terrible punishment visited upon it are plainly evident.[20]

But British officials in Palestine remained unconvinced of both the sincerity and the effectiveness of the Haganah's counterterrorism campaign. Shaw was especially dismissive of the inflated claim that five hundred terrorists were now off the streets thanks to the Jewish Agency and the Haganah. In point of fact, he explained to Sir Arthur Dawe, an assistant undersecretary at the Colonial Office, the police had been able to locate and arrest only slightly more than half that number. Of those, thirty-seven had been freed because of insufficient evidence, and another twenty-eight were released but kept under police surveillance. This meant that fewer than a hundred terrorist suspects remained in custody. The police attributed these anemic results to the stale information they were fed by the agency. Further, the few scraps that were accurate pertained mostly to "unimportant members of the illegal organisations" rather than the core leadership and senior operational commanders. When these complaints were brought to the agency liaison officer's attention, Shaw continued, he professed not to know whom the police were referring to. In response, the CID drew up its own list of fifty-six high-value targets complete with photographs and presented it to the Jewish Agency. The results, however, remained depressingly meager until mid-December, when the Saison—the counterterrorist operation's code name—finally netted its first big catch.[21]

The weather in Jerusalem that winter had been especially harsh. It had rained for what seemed weeks on end. Then, on Friday, December 15, the skies cleared and the temperature warmed. The streets were full of people enjoying the break in the clouds or hurrying to finish their last-minute pre-Sabbath shopping and errands. Having been kept behind closed doors in shuttered safe houses for days on end, Eliahu Lankin, the Irgun's Jerusalem detachment commander, decided to go out for a walk. He later recalled passing two men loitering on the staircase of the apartment building as he went out. Lankin squeezed past them and headed in the direction of Ben Yehuda Street. The two men followed. He now walked faster and then quickly crossed to the other side of the road. The two men also increased their pace and rapidly drew up behind Lankin as he approached the corner. It was there that they pounced. Lankin's arms were pinned behind him and bound tightly together. Almost immediately, several other men appeared on the scene to help bundle the still struggling Lankin into a waiting taxi. It sped off in the direction of the police station at the Mahane Yehuda outdoor market. From there, Lankin was transferred under heavy guard to police headquarters at the Russian Compound for interrogation. Later that day he was brought to the adjacent central prison facility and, deemed the most dangerous of the lot, quickly transferred to Acre prison and then exiled to the secret terrorist detention facility in Eritrea.[22]

But even this coup failed to mollify Shaw or assuage complaints from the police that the Jewish Agency and the Haganah were withholding the best information and simply feeding the CID unimportant snippets. The chief secretary believed politics lay behind the fact that the full weight of the Saison had been brought to bear only against the Irgun and *not* against Lehi, the organization actually responsible for Moyne's murder. The ostensible reason for this focus on the Irgun was the Jewish Agency's previously cited tactical argument that predated the Moyne assassination and held that the counterterrorist campaign should first be directed against the numerically larger and better armed Irgun before turning to the smaller and less powerful Lehi, lest they be driven into an alliance against the Jewish Agency. But tactical considerations alone cannot explain why Lehi was now excluded from the agency's counterterrorist efforts. Instead, the same political rivalries that had long divided internal Zionist politics, coupled with what some observers have argued was the Jewish Agency's determination to deal with its most serious rival, account for the Saison's exclusive focus on the Irgun.[23]

For Yehuda Bauer, a leading Israeli historian of this period, the explanation is both far simpler and much less conspiratorial. He argues that Lehi simply "read the writing on the wall and suspended operations for about six months." But the reality appears to be more complex. Following the Saison's kidnapping of a Sternist named Todi Peli in mid-December, the Haganah and Lehi supposedly made a deal. Such was the mistrust between the two organizations that when Friedman-Yellin met with Golomb to finalize its terms, the Lehi leader reportedly placed a loaded pistol next to him on the table where they sat. Lehi agreed to suspend all terrorist operations for the duration of Hakim and Bet-Zuri's trial in order to avoid potentially prejudicing their case. Friedman-Yellin also promised Golomb that Lehi would make no attempt to assassinate Churchill—even though it is not entirely clear that such an operation had been contemplated. The outcome, according to the Israeli historian Joseph Heller, was that only one Lehi member (Peli) was ever seized by the Haganah compared with the dozens of Irgunists. Moreover, neither the Jewish Agency nor the Haganah reportedly ever gave the name of even one Lehi member to the police. By comparison, the two organizations furnished the police with the names of more than seven hundred Irgun operatives and actively assisted in their apprehension.[24]

One such person was Ya'acov Meridor, the Irgun's former commander who was now Begin's deputy. He was arrested on February 13, 1945, at the house he shared with his wife, daughter, and young son. At 3:00 a.m. they were awakened by pounding on their front door. Meridor's wife went to investigate, and when she opened the door, British soldiers, uniformed police, and plainclothes CID officers forced their way inside. Meridor's false documentation in the name of Meyer Silverman was cursorily inspected and then dismissively tossed aside. The police already knew that they had their man. Meridor was handcuffed and frog-marched out the door. He recalled passing a man dressed in ordinary street clothes standing slightly to the side. In the brief exchange of glances between this person and one of the arresting officers, Meridor knew immediately that this man was a Jew, a member of the Haganah, and a Saison operative. A decade later, Meridor could barely contain the sense of rage and repugnance he felt staring into the eyes of his betrayer. "This man was one of my people, of my faith, of my flesh," he recalled in his memoir of life underground. "He had not been bribed to do this job. That was what hurt most. Every society has its degenerates, but this was the depths of degeneration. This was betrayal."[25]

The Irgun was now reeling from the combined blows rained down upon it from both the police and the Saison. Its officers and rank and file alike pressed Begin to strike back at the Jewish Agency and the Haganah. From the very outset of the Saison, however, Begin unequivocally forbade it. "Do not raise a hand and do not use a weapon," an Irgun order issued on November 13, 1944, had read. "They [the Saison operatives] are not guilty. They are our brothers . . . there will not be a civil war, but [we] will approach the big day, in which the nation will rise up—despite the will of those obstructing the way—as one fighting camp." This point was driven home repeatedly in subsequent directives. As Begin later reflected, the Irgun

decided to strike out along a road which no underground had ever chosen in similar circumstances. We decided not to suspend, nor promise to suspend, our struggle against British rule; yet at the same time we declined to retaliate for the kidnappings, the denunciations and the handing-over of our men . . .

This dreadful situation continued for many months. We said there would be no civil war but, in fact, throughout the whole country a one sided civil war raged.[26]

The Saison, just as Begin anticipated, sowed the seeds of its own destruction. It was not long before new cracks surfaced in the relationship between the authorities and the Jewish Agency and the Haganah. Repeated government complaints of agency foot-dragging were rebuffed with countercharges of unwarranted interference in, and willful hindrance of, Saison operations. By the middle of January 1945 the focus and tone of Jewish Agency public pronouncements about the counterterrorism program had also changed dramatically. No longer were the dissidents assailed for their transgressions. Instead, the government and the police were harangued respectively for pursuing policies that needlessly antagonized the Yishuv and for an incompetence that had allowed the terrorist organizations to flourish in the first place.[27]

In this vein, the Jewish Agency took full credit for the cessation of terrorism in Palestine. Its officials boasted that information they had supplied to the police accounted for 95 percent of all terrorist arrests, including that of Meridor. American intelligence analysts thought such claims wildly exaggerated, but with respect to the only metric that really mattered, British intelligence was forced to concede that since the Saison operation had commenced the previous November, there had not been a single terrorist incident.[28]

In late January the British suddenly realized that they had created a monster. The first intelligence reports had begun to trickle in that in addition to hunting down terrorists, the Jewish Agency was using the Saison to settle old scores and sideline political rivals, thereby eliminating any challenge to its authority. OSS analysts were reporting the same development. They noted that of seven persons recently arrested by Saison operatives, none had any connection whatsoever to the Irgun. Indeed, the police now confirmed that the Jewish Agency was routinely violating the terms of the November 1944 cooperation agreement. Suspected terrorists swept up in the Saison dragnet were no longer being handed over to the police and instead were being held in secret Haganah detention facilities. The Palestine administration attempted to intervene. Its demand that the agency surrender immediately to the police all people in its custody was ignored, and the kidnappings and detentions continued.[29]

Ironically, previous British complaints about Jewish Agency foot-dragging were now superseded by protests of overzealousness and even ruthlessness. Gort and Shaw met twice in February with Weizmann and Shertok, respectively, to reiterate the government's profound "disapprobation of these methods and . . . [its] determination to put a stop to them." These remonstrations proved no more successful than previous entreaties either in halting the kidnappings or in obtaining the detainees' release.[30]

Meanwhile, pressure had already been mounting within the Yishuv for the agency to abandon the Saison. At the end of January, the first accusations had appeared in the Jewish press of "illegal prisons" and "torture chambers" in which the Saison detainees were subjected to "Gestapo methods." The right-wing-leaning Jewish daily *Ha-Boker* (The morning) decried the counterterrorist campaign as a thinly veiled effort to "eliminate once and for all anyone who could interfere with the absolute domination of the Left over the Yishuv." *The Palestine Post* went so far as to call for the creation of citizens' self-defense units to resist the kidnapping squads. Finally, the Chief Rabbinate of Palestine issued a strongly worded condemnation of what it termed "this hateful and cruel action."[31]

Discontent over the Saison was also welling within the Haganah's ranks. Moshe Dayan, a future major general and chief of staff of the Israeli army and subsequently minister of defense and minister of foreign affairs, was then a young Haganah intelligence officer stationed in Tel Aviv who was tasked with the counterterrorist campaign's implementation. He accepted the logic behind it, saluted smartly, and followed orders but did so without enthusiasm. Others were less pliant and openly resented being cast in the role of common police informants and collaborators. Their disillusionment produced disdainful songs and jingles that circulated among the Haganah rank and file.[32]

By March 1945, the Saison had basically run out of steam, and the kidnappings, detentions, interrogations, and cooperation with the police halted. Not only had it failed in its principal mission to destroy the Irgun, but the Saison by some accounts had almost the opposite effect, earning the dissidents newfound respect and support. In any event, whatever lingering ardor remained for the campaign's continuance was overwhelmed by the news emerging from liberated Europe as the Soviet, British, and American militaries drove unrelentingly toward Berlin. The Yishuv was now consumed with helping its surviving brethren and getting them to Palestine and not with fighting fratricidal battles on Britain's behalf. Unable and unwilling to sustain the Saison, the Jewish Agency finally announced its disbandment in May 1945. The internal war against the terrorists was over.[33]

In retrospect, this time was a turning point in the history of British rule over Palestine and the establishment of the State of Israel. Among the hundreds of terrorist incidents both before and after the assassination of Lord Moyne, few can compare with that act in terms of significance, impact, and sheer drama. It swept away the possibility of an early solution to the Palestine problem, immersing Britain in an intractable struggle with the Yishuv that was not to be resolved until the State of Israel arose four years later. Its implications for internal Zionist politics were equally profound, propelling the Yishuv to the brink of civil war. The assassination's repercussions, moreover, were felt not only in Jerusalem and London but across the Middle East, intertwining the maintenance of order in Palestine with preserving British prestige in the Arab world—which some officials argued should take precedence over even the prosecution of the war in Europe.

In this respect, the most consequential repercussion of Hakim and Bet-Zuri's deed was to extinguish the prospect of resolving the Palestine problem before the war ended. The death of Moyne, a dear friend and steadfast political ally of Churchill's, had a profound and lasting effect on the prime minister's determination to press ahead with partition and overturn the hated white paper. The progress patiently achieved in this direction over the previous eighteen months under his quiet tutelage ground to an abrupt and irrevocable halt. Only days earlier, as we have seen, the cabinet secretary had placed discussion of the ministerial committee's report recommending partition on the war cabinet's agenda. It was dropped from the schedule when news of Moyne's murder broke— and never considered.[34]

It is impossible, of course, to determine whether Churchill's endeavors to establish a Jewish state in Palestine through partition with the British government's forthright endorsement would have succeeded. Given the formidable opposition from the Foreign Office, the Chiefs of Staff, and members of Churchill's own party, there can be no certainty that the war cabinet would in fact have approved the partition proposal plan. But at the same time it is clear that on the eve of Moyne's assassination the war cabinet had come to the threshold of a major redefinition of Britain's policy for Palestine. Hence, the Yishuv suffered a far greater penalty because of the assassination than its leaders had feared: the loss of what was likely to be an immediate and favorable decision on the mandate's future. Isaiah Berlin, the Oxford don then serving in the British embassy in Washington, thus rightly describes the killing as "a critical turning point" in the Jews' journey to statehood—alas, an ideal opportunity that was cruelly squandered. As Weizmann himself observed in his autobiography five years later, "The harm done our cause by the assassination of Lord Moyne, and by the whole terror—this apart from the profound moral deterioration involved—was not in changing the intentions of the British Government, but rather in providing our enemies with a convenient excuse, and in helping to justify their course before the bar of public opinion."[35]

Perhaps the most climacteric effect of the murder was that when Churchill arrived at the Big Three conference with Stalin and Roosevelt in Yalta in February 1945, he brought with him no British plan for Palestine's future. And throughout the discussions he remained conspicuously silent whenever the matter was raised by his Russian and American counterparts. Ironically, just days before Moyne's assassination, Churchill had discussed with Roosevelt the possibility of holding the meeting in Jerusalem. The prime minister had just finished lunching with Weizmann when he raised the idea. In Jerusalem, he had enthused, "there are first-class hotels, Government houses, etc. and every means can be taken to ensure security."[36]

No less profound were the consequences of the failed counterterrorist campaign on Anglo-Zionist relations and internal Zionist politics. In the wake of the assassination, the Jewish Agency embraced the Saison as a means both to head off the threatened government reprisals and to eliminate a long-standing threat to its own power. Although the agency succeeded in sparing the Yishuv from punishment—and, not incidentally, also saved its arms caches from seizure and preserved the monthly immigration quota, thus enabling fifteen hundred European Jews to enter Palestine legally—it failed to destroy the Irgun or please the British. So far as the Palestine government was concerned, the agency's prosecution of the Saison was either inadequate or overzealous.[37]

The Saison also imposed a moral dilemma on the Yishuv that further estranged the population from the government, arguably undercut the Jewish Agency's authority, and inadvertently generated sympathy for precisely the underground organization that it was meant to eliminate. As much as the Jewish community might have abhorred the terrorists' methods, it remained reluctant to betray individual members of either the Irgun or Lehi to the authorities—regardless of the agency's repeated entreaties. Moreover, the Irgun won newfound sympathy and support from the community that it might otherwise have never obtained by refusing to retaliate against either the Haganah or the Jewish Agency. Finally, the collapse of the Saison ended forever the prospects of further cooperation with the government against the terrorists. To the contrary, it laid the foundations for the alliance that would be concluded between the official Zionist institutions and both terrorist organizations less than six months later.[38]

"What kind of man was Lord Moyne?" the Jewish-American author Leo Budovsky, writing under the pseudonym Leo Benjamin, asked in his 1952 book, *Martyrs in Cairo*. "To the people of Israel this English nobleman was like some horrible, blood-drinking monster, a wretch vile and depraved. He was the scourge and bane of their nation . . . He was an implacable enemy of the Jewish nation. He knew that they yearned for freedom in their homeland. But they must never live to see it. They must forever be serfs, abject and groveling, of imperial England." In an interview two decades later, Yezernitzky (Shamir) similarly explained that Moyne "was an anti-Semite" and "there were good reasons for him being shot." The former Lehi commander justified the assassination not only because of the office Moyne held and the government he represented but also because "we had known about his hostile attitude towards Zionism, towards the idea of [the] ingathering of the Jewish people here. He was against any Jewish aliyah, any Jewish immigration. He didn't believe that there exists such a thing like a Jewish nation, or a Jewish people . . . and therefore, we decided to make this operation."[39]

These were the same arguments that Lehi used to justify and explain its killing of Moyne to the Yishuv. Ten days after the assassination, posters addressed to "Jews in the Homeland" appeared throughout Palestine. Moyne was described as "an arch enemy of the freedom aspirations of the Jewish people in their country." Although some of the accusations pertaining to what Lehi termed his "brutality, foulness, cynicism and humiliation" of the Jews were familiar from the October 13, 1944, issue of *He-Hazit*, many others were new. On top of all his other crimes, Moyne was assailed for interfering with debates in the U.S. Congress over Palestine, deliberately plunging the Yishuv into economic crisis and thereby taking "away the bread from the mouths of Jewish workers," and being "an ardent follower of the Nazi racial legislation" by seeking to deprive Jews of their historical claim to Palestine. Yet Churchill had fulsomely praised Moyne on the floor of the House of Commons as the Jews' best and best-informed friend. What can explain these two seemingly irreconcilable claims?[40]

It is indeed true that as colonial secretary, Moyne had been at the vortex of several crucial decisions that had not gone in the Yishuv's favor. In this capacity he of course was beholden to enforce the government's policy of not establishing a separate Jewish army on the ostensible grounds that Jews were able and welcome to enlist in HM Forces as private individuals, thus obviating the need for a special unit of their own. By denying the Jews an army, the government of course was intent on avoiding either needlessly antagonizing the Arabs or providing the Yishuv with a pretext that could later be contrived into justifying the establishment of a Jewish state. It is also accurate that Moyne was profoundly skeptical of Palestine's ability to absorb large numbers of new Jewish immigrants and on one occasion had told two Zionist leaders that "Palestine could not solve the whole Jewish problem." Moreover, it was his intervention in 1942 that consigned the doomed passengers on board the *Struma* to their horrific fate. But despite repeated claims to the contrary, Moyne was not in fact a racist with Nazi-like beliefs of racial purity. As a serious anthropologist and ethnographer, he made the point about "the Jewish race [having] been much mixed with Gentiles since the beginning of the Diaspora" during the same House of Lords debate cited above not to disparage or demean the Jews but to state the obvious: that all modern peoples are to an extent racially mixed.[41]

In fact, Moyne might have been more balanced on the question of the Jews and Palestine than Lehi maintained. His secretary, Dorothy Osmond, for instance, recalled in a letter to Moyne's son and heir to his title the story of a dinner party that Moyne was planning in Cairo just weeks before his death to honor Gort, who was then en route to Palestine to take up his post as high commissioner. According to the British author and biographer Christopher Sykes, who was given access to the letter, Moyne had instructed her to remove Brigadier Clayton from the guest list, explaining that he did not want Clayton's strong pro-Arab biases to unduly influence the new high commissioner. As Sykes explains, "Lord Moyne was not the sort of administrator whom Zionists could in the normal course of things regard as ideal. He had a typically British compromising mind, devoted to fairness as the supreme virtue which could cure every ill in the world . . . [but] fairness was of little avail in the affairs of post-Balfour Palestine."[42]

Perhaps the most searing indictment against Moyne is the long-standing canard that he callously blocked the entrance to Palestine of one million Hungarian Jews whose freedom the Nazis had offered in exchange for trucks, coffee, tea, cocoa, and soap. Moyne's alleged role in this scheme originated in an "as told to" biography written about Joel Brand, an emissary from the Hungarian Jewish community who in March 1944 had communicated this proposition to the British government. More than a decade after the event, the book relates a confused account of a conversation that Brand remembers having in the garden of Cairo's British-Egyptian Club with an unidentified British official who happened to be sitting next to Brand and his host, a British military officer. When asked by this official, who had not introduced himself or given his name, how many Jews Adolf Eichmann actually proposed to free in exchange for the trucks and other goods, Brand replied a million. According to Brand's recollection, this official then exclaimed, "A million! What on earth are you thinking of, Mr. Brand? What should we do with a million Jews? Where would we put them?" As Brand rose from his seat and left the club in disgust, his host caught up with him and asked, "Do you know whom you were speaking to? That was our Minister of State Lord Moyne." However, in the very next sentence of the book, Brand explains that his interlocutor was not Lord Moyne.

> I afterwards heard that the man with whom I spoke was not, in fact, Lord Moyne, but another British statesman . . .
>
>   I later learnt that Lord Moyne had often deplored the tragic fate of the Jews. The policy which he had to follow, however, was one dictated by a cold and impersonal administration in London. It may be that he paid with his life for the guilt of others.

Nonetheless, apologists for Lehi have never allowed the truth to get in the way of a good story and, seeking to further justify Moyne's murder, have persisted in perpetuating this fiction.[43]

   In the end, the main reason that Lehi targeted Moyne and MacMichael before him was the offices they held and the British rule they represented. Hakim, the assassin himself, is clear on this point. According to Sadovsky, Hakim had told Sitner that Lehi had marked Moyne for death primarily because he was "the official representative of the British General Policy in the Middle East." He then added that Moyne's complicity in the *Struma* disaster had also been a consideration. Significantly, Hakim said nothing about Moyne's alleged personal racist views or any other opinions he had about Jews or Zionism as justification for his having been targeted. Bet-Zuri had already told his Egyptian interrogators the same thing.[44]

   Even Yezernitzky, the assassination mission's architect, would later assert that Lehi turned its attention to Moyne after the failed attempt on MacMichael's life because the minister of state was vulnerable given that he did not have the same heavy personal protection detail that thereafter routinely accompanied Palestine's high commissioners everywhere.

Moreover, the explanation that Yezernitzky recalled giving to both Hakim and Bet-Zuri before they each departed for Cairo further belies the targeting of Moyne as a person as opposed to the office he held. "Our attack on Moyne," Yezernitzky remembered separately telling the two Eliahus, "will clarify exactly who the enemy is . . . We smash the dragon's head, not the tail . . . We believe Great Britain simply cannot carry out her promises to both Jews and Arabs . . . The deed against Moyne will bring the whole issue into the world forum where it will merit the attention of world opinion and world diplomacy."[45]

Almost from the time it became known that Moyne's killers were members of Lehi, British authorities in both London and Cairo were deeply concerned that when they were eventually tried in open court, Hakim and Bet-Zuri would use the proceedings, like other Lehi defendants who had been tried in Palestine, as a platform to amplify the group's seditious, Anglophobic propaganda, but it would now be broadcast to audiences in Egypt, elsewhere in the Middle East, and beyond—including America. Bet-Zuri had alluded to just such an intention, it will be recalled, when he was first interrogated. After being told that he would be tried in Egypt, Bet-Zuri said that this pleased him greatly because the "Arabs generally were in sympathy with the Stern Group" and he would therefore receive a fair trial. Indeed, a Lehi propaganda statement to that effect had been found in Bet-Zuri's pocket when he was arrested.[46]

As preposterous as this claim of Arab support for Lehi might have been, the British authorities were nonetheless alarmed and pressed the Egyptian government to exercise its complete powers of censorship when dealing with press reports concerning the trial. So acute was this concern that British and Egyptian authorities delayed the delivery of letters written by Bet-Zuri and Hakim to their parents in order to prevent their contents from being published. Journalists accredited to cover the trial were bluntly warned by the deputy chief censor, a British national named Mac-Donald, that "no attempt to 'make political capital' of the trial would be passed." A small army of Egyptian and British officials representing the various civilian, military, and intelligence censorship apparatuses in Egypt as well as from Palestine was deployed to enforce this edict.[47]

The trial began on January 10, 1945. Contemporary accounts describe a tumultuous scene of two to three hundred spectators packed into a small courtroom within a building ringed by hundreds of mounted and foot policemen standing guard shoulder to shoulder alongside Egyptian troops with fixed bayonets. At the center of this chaos, the two defendants—watched over by "six giant impassive Egyptian policemen"—were reported to have sat calmly, chatting with their guards. The court was called to order and the charges read. Both men readily admitted their guilt. "We both came in accordance with instructions we got from the secret organisation to which we belong," Bet-Zuri declared. "We met in Cairo and began acting in accordance with instructions—instructions to assassinate Lord Moyne." Bet-Zuri also explained how his orders to avoid injuring any Egyptians in the course of the operation had prevented him from shooting the motorcycle policeman who arrested them, thus foiling his and Hakim's escape. It was further revealed that Lehi had specifically selected Hakim for this mission because he was regarded as "one of the best shots in the gang and this would guarantee the accomplishment of the mission." Lehi had chosen Bet-Zuri for his "brilliant" oratorical skills under the assumption that he would be an effective "instrument of defense if the men were caught. Both men," a U.S. intelligence officer who attended the trial observed, "have well accomplished their mission."[48]

Throughout the proceedings neither man would evince any sign of contrition or regret for his act, and they repeatedly rejected their attorneys' suggestion that they save themselves by pleading temporary insanity. "What I did is right," stated a note that both defendants signed and gave to the London *Daily Express*'s Cairo correspondent. As Bet-Zuri later explained, in a statement that is perhaps the classic elucidation of the terrorist mind-set, "Our deed stemmed from our motives, and our motives stemmed from our ideals, and if we prove our ideals are right and just, then our deed was just!"[49]

The censors duly forbade the publication of such statements by the press. Just as the British authorities had dreaded, Bet-Zuri's impassioned but eloquent defense and Hakim's placid yet confident demeanor greatly impressed the court. The account published in *The Egyptian Gazette* remarked how "both prisoners looked uncommonly cheerful and talked and laughed together." Even one of the British military censors present at the trial was moved to admit in his report, "Both of the accused conducted themselves with extraordinary dignity. However wrong their crime may be, the majority felt that the two men are sincere and in many respects admirable. It is obvious that they are not common murderers or hired assassins."[50]

The trial ended on January 16. Two days later the court pronounced the defendants guilty and imposed the death penalty. The verdict accorded perfectly with the wishes of the British government, which saw in Hakim's and Bet-Zuri's executions a means finally to defuse continued Arab criticism over Britain's inadequate response to the assassination. From the outset, therefore, London had maneuvered to ensure that the assassins would receive the maximum penalty for their crime, insisting that they be tried by an Egyptian court and not a British tribunal. In this manner, Churchill was determined to avoid a repetition of the situation that had occurred in 1938, when the death sentence imposed by a British military court on another Palestinian Jew, Shlomo Ben-Yosef, had prompted an international campaign for clemency.[51]

With the sentence now passed, British efforts energetically shifted to ensuring that the Egyptian government would not succumb to any such appeals. Churchill personally impressed this point on Killearn. "I hope you will realize," the prime minister stated, "that unless the sentences duly passed upon the assassins of Lord Moyne are executed it will cause a marked breach between Great Britain and Egyptian Government. Such a gross interference with the course of justice will not be compatible with the friendly relations we have established. As they may be under pressure from Zionists and American Jewry I think it right to let you know my personal views on the matter."[52]

Churchill's concerns were not unjustified. Less than two weeks later, Killearn reported that the Egyptian procurer general had made an offer to Bet-Zuri whereby his sentence would be commuted if only he "would help to put an end to terrorism by denouncing members of the Stern Gang." Although Bet-Zuri rejected the deal out of hand, Killearn was furious that the Egyptian authorities should even have considered making such a proposal. "This is shocking," Churchill agreed in a handwritten note scrawled at the bottom of the ambassador's telegram. The prime minister's reply, which bore the foreign secretary's signature as well, was blunt and to the point. "It is of the utmost importance that both assassins should be executed."[53]

Hakim and Bet-Zuri were hanged on March 22. Neither had revealed to the authorities the names of their confederates either in Egypt or in Palestine or any other useful information. That night, Sadovsky visited Hakim's and Bet-Zuri's burial sites in Cairo's Jewish cemetery to pay his respects and recite Kaddish, the Jewish mourner's prayer for the deceased. The police, however, were waiting and promptly arrested him. Under interrogation, Sadovsky confessed to belonging to Lehi and revealed the names of eight group members serving in HM Forces in Egypt. They were also arrested, and together with five other suspected terrorists were discharged from the RAF and transferred to prisons in Palestine. Sitner, the ringleader of the cell, had already been deported to Palestine in January 1945 and, despite being kept under RAF police surveillance, somehow managed to disappear. The CID, however, finally tracked him down in July 1945, and with his imprisonment the final remaining member of the Cairo cell involved in the assassination was behind bars.[54]

Hakim and Bet-Zuri were reported to have gone to their deaths singing the Zionist national anthem, "Ha-Tikva," as well as religious hymns. It is said that Hakim told his executioner that the traditional condemned man's red shirt and trousers were "the finest suit I've ever worn."[55]

That both men accepted their fate without fear or remorse can be conjectured not only from their bearing in court and on the scaffold but from a letter Hakim wrote to his parents shortly after his arrest. "In the first minutes after my capture," he admitted, "I was a little depressed but now I am absolutely calm and my conscience is settled because I have the feeling that I have done my duty. I am glad to stand this test, because now, more than at any other moment of my life, I am certain of the justice of my ideal, because my ideal is the ideal of truth." Hakim then assured his mother and father, "I am prepared for everything . . . I beg you not to worry too much about me and I wish you all the best and that you should see in our days the liberated Jerusalem."[56]

In 1975, the bodies of Eliahu Bet-Zuri and Eliahu Hakim were disinterred from their simple graves in Cairo and brought back to Jerusalem. They were accorded a state burial, complete with full military honors, and reinterred on Mount Herzl, where Israel's warriors and heroes rest.[57]

CHAPTER 11

Wider Horizons

On May 7, 1945, Germany surrendered, and the war in Europe ended. Even more than in 1918, the Yishuv had cause to rejoice. Jewry's most demonic enemy had been vanquished, and the Zionist dream of a reconstituted Jewish national home in the Land of Israel had survived perhaps the gravest threat yet posed to its existence. But the Yishuv's jubilation was tempered by melancholy and uncertainty. Millions of Jews had perished as a result of Hitler's final solution, and at least a hundred thousand others were languishing across liberated Europe. An editorial in *Mishmar* published on V-E Day captured the community's mood: "The destruction of European Jewry demands from those concerned to hasten the rescue of the survivors and bring redemption nearer to the whole Jewish nation by permitting mass immigration into Palestine and by immediately fulfilling the aims of Zionism." Yet the prospect of independence and statehood, which only a few months earlier had seemed within reach, now appeared to have been irretrievably cast aside, if not completely forgotten.[1]

The assassination of Lord Moyne accounted for this cruel twist of fate. Not only had it derailed the government's progress toward adopting partition, but it had also profoundly alienated the prime minister. Churchill refused to reconsider the matter until he was satisfied that the Yishuv had extirpated terrorism from its midst. Thus a critical window of opportunity for Zionism closed as the prime minister became consumed by more pressing postwar issues and his attention and priorities shifted elsewhere. The white paper, with its severe limits on Jewish immigration and land purchase, remained as the government's policy for Palestine. This was particularly unfortunate for the Yishuv, because the guiding assumption behind the special cabinet committee's deliberations had been that the 1939 policy statement had outlived its relevance. Moreover, except for the implementation of its immigration and land settlement restrictions, none of the white paper's provisions—such as those intended to prepare Palestine for self-rule and eventual independence as a majority-Arab state— were ever enacted. But in the absence of a final decision on the mandate's political future, the government had also made no attempt nor signaled any inclination either to revise or to replace the white paper. In the tense and anticipatory atmosphere of postwar Palestine, however, this political vacuum breathed new life into the Irgun's struggle.[2]

"With the end of the war, the world had opened to us," Begin recalled in his memoir, "and we were enabled to draw attention to our small corner in it. Wider horizons had been opened for our military struggle as well. The oppressor had expected we should be drawn into a bloody civil war which would assure him of 'peace' and mastery. But we, the rebels, had determined to disappoint him in this, too. With the turning-point that came at the close of World War II we decided not only to continue our struggle but . . . to intensify it."[3]

As the German capitulation neared, the Irgun had brazenly announced that V-E Day for Britain "would be D-Day for [us]." The plan was to strike on the night of May 13 with coordinated attacks and dramatically announce the recommencement of its revolt the following morning. From the start, however, the operation went awry. The Irgun's armorers had devised a new type of time-controlled mortar that could fire remotely and thus afford the perpetrators ample time to escape. The three-foot-long, nine-inch-diameter weapon was accurate to about a half mile and could be mounted on the back of a truck and positioned within range of the intended target. An Irgun team was in the process of doing so a short distance from the Police Mobile Force camp in Sarona, outside Haifa, when watchmen from a nearby Jewish settlement came upon the scene. The police were summoned, and four Irgunists, including a senior officer, were arrested.[4]

Nonetheless, the following morning posters printed in Hebrew, Arabic, and English appeared on walls in Jaffa, Tel Aviv, and Jerusalem. Signed by "The Irgun Zvai Le'umi in the Land of Israel," they ominously read,

WARNING!
1) The Government of Oppression should WITHOUT ANY DELAY evacuate children, women, civilian persons and officials from all its offices, buildings, dwelling places etc. throughout the country.
2) The civilian population, Hebrews, Arabs, and others are asked, for their own sake, to abstain from now until the warning is recalled, from visiting or nearing Government offices, etc.
YOU HAVE BEEN WARNED![5]

The Irgun had better luck that same evening when small explosive charges affixed to more than two hundred telegraph poles outside Jerusalem, Lydda, Nablus, and Haifa temporarily disrupted countrywide communications. The next night mortars were fired on the internment camp at Sarona and the district police headquarters in Jaffa. Apart from some windows shattered by the projectiles, however, there was no significant damage, nor was anyone killed or injured. The Irgun's mixed fortunes continued for the remainder of the month. On the night of May 22, Irgun sappers damaged the Kirkuk–Haifa pipeline. But three nights later a second attempt to attack the Sarona PMF camp was foiled.[6]

British intelligence had accurately forecast the resumption of violence that would coincide with V-E Day, and therefore the security precautions undertaken by the authorities in Palestine at least a month before Germany's surrender may explain the Irgun's unusual string of failures. This had followed an intelligence assessment prepared for the Chiefs of Staff in December 1944 that had predicted that as the end of the war drew near, "Jewish extremists" would likely "become impatient and force the pace by intensifying their 'IRA' [Irish Republican Army] tactics." But the threat that the chiefs still feared most was a mass uprising spearheaded by the Haganah. "The Jews have an armed and organized strength of 54,000," a report on internal security in the Middle East that the chiefs submitted to the war cabinet that same month explained. "Their technique in guerilla warfare is likely to be good, and among their leaders will be British, German and Polish Army trained officers and a number of experienced terrorists from Eastern Europe." The current forces on hand in Palestine—an infantry division and a handful of support units—would likely be overwhelmed. Accordingly, a second infantry division supported by an armored brigade, three companies of Royal Engineers, and five RAF squadrons would need to be transferred to Palestine. Because these forces could not be spared from their wartime commitments, the chiefs recommended that the manpower and equipment deficiencies still plaguing the recently formed PMF should be redressed immediately.[7]

As always, the police were the weak link in Palestine's security. Rymer-Jones was literally watching the PPF melt before his eyes. His repeated pleas to the Colonial Office to prioritize recruitment had gone unanswered. By March 1945 the situation had become so dire that the British section, which included the PMF, was now nearly 2,000 men below its authorized strength of 5,445 persons. Moreover, the quality of recruits entering the PMF was so poor that Rymer-Jones was given no choice but to dismiss many of the new entrants—of whom no small number had been found to be functionally illiterate. He thought the training staff, which had also been recruited from the British military, was thoroughly inadequate as well.[8]

It was perhaps a reflection of the desperate straits that the enervated and overstretched British military found itself in at the close of World War II that General Sir Bernard Paget, the senior British military commander in the Middle East, requested permission in January 1945 to use heavy weapons—artillery, mortars, naval bombardment, and aircraft bombing and strafing—in the event of any new disturbances in Palestine. More astonishing is that this request to use indirect fire in built-up, urban areas against enigmatic irregular fighters concealed within the civilian populace aroused no great concern among the strategic and operational planning staffs in Whitehall. Indeed, within the week the Joint Planning Staff had produced a draft assessment. It cited as precedent the rules of engagement during the 1936–39 Arab Rebellion. There had then been no restrictions placed on the use of artillery, but air-delivered munitions and machine-gun fire were subject to strict regulation. Initially, only 20-pound bombs could be dropped—and only beyond a five-hundred-foot radius of any town, village, or even a single standing edifice. Machine-gun fire from aircraft could only be directed against armed rebel bands sighted in open country. However, after three RAF planes had been shot down in one day five months into the rebellion, use of 112-pound bombs was authorized. Toward the end of the rebellion, some restrictions were further loosened. The RAF, for instance, was now permitted to strafe houses or other buildings from which rebel fire was being directed. But at no time had the cabinet permitted bombing of rebel targets where civilians were present, as was now being proposed.[9]

The staff officer tasked with drafting this assessment, Colonel W. R. Rolleston, saw no reason that any of these restrictions should remain. Technological advances in precision bombing, he argued, had improved its accuracy. Furthermore, the bombing of populated civilian areas was now an accepted part of modern warfare. Accordingly, there were no tactical or moral reasons to limit these weapons' use in postwar Palestine, he argued. The only appropriate restriction to Rolleston's mind should pertain to designated holy places that, if damaged or destroyed, would likely cause international outcry. The Joint Planning Staff's response to the draft affirmed the extraordinary proposition that the "principle of the minimum force should not operate to hamper the operations of responsible commanders" in Palestine.[10]

Colonial Office officials were not nearly as sanguine about the propriety of attacking civilian targets by either artillery or air-delivered munitions, but the Joint Planning Staff saw little reason to demur from the initial assessment, noting only that technological advances in bombing accuracy notwithstanding, a certain margin of error had still to be taken into account. They conceded, however, that considerable discretion would need to be exercised by local commanders in the use of such weapons.[11]

It was only when the proposal reached the Chiefs of Staff that cooler heads prevailed. The chiefs instructed the Joint Planning Staff to redraft the proposed policy directive to require at a minimum the various Middle East commanders in chief explicitly consent to any use of such weapons. The commanders in chief were also asked to draw up a list of specific areas and buildings against which all forms of attack would be strictly prohibited—for example, religious sites and the entirety of Jerusalem's Old City.[12]

So far as officials in the Jewish Agency in Palestine were concerned, the Irgun's reemergence could not have come at a worse time. Immigration, not confrontation, was their foremost concern. Jews now constituted nearly a third of Palestine's population—more than four times the World War I figure. Muslims accounted for 61 percent and Christians for nearly 8 percent. The agency hoped that this reality, coupled with the Yishuv's unstinting support for the British war effort, would be rewarded by the loosening of immigration restrictions and eventual statehood. The dreadful condition of European Jewry had endowed this matter with grave urgency, not least because the quota of Jewish immigration certificates for the six months ending March 31, 1945, had still not been filled. Some nine thousand Jews were thus legally entitled to enter Palestine. The government, however, had not yet signaled whether it would in fact issue any certificates beyond the March expiry date.[13]

At this delicate moment in Anglo-Zionist relations, the renewal of the Irgun's revolt was at best an additional complication and at worst a potentially fatal blow to Zionist aspirations. It also inconveniently laid bare the Jewish Agency's claims about the Saison campaign's effectiveness.[14]

Alarmed by the renewed violence, Shertok had written to Shaw within hours of the appearance of the Irgun's warning posters to offer the agency's continued assistance. He proposed to put at the disposal of the police for counterterrorist purposes a contingent of handpicked Haganah fighters.[15]

Shertok called on Robert Scott, who was acting chief secretary in Shaw's absence, to discuss the offer two days later. The meeting did not go well. In what Scott doubtless imagined would be seen as a reciprocal gesture of goodwill, he told Shertok that the high commissioner was pleased to authorize the issuance of three thousand of the unused immigration certificates. The Jewish Agency leader responded with derision rather than gratitude, expressing his "utter disappointment" at such a "small figure."[16]

General Sir Edmund Allenby entering Jerusalem's Old City
on foot through the Jaffa Gate, December 1917

Colonial Secretary Winston Churchill
with Colonel T. E. Lawrence, the famed "Lawrence of Arabia,"
and Emir Abdullah, Jerusalem, March 1921

Government House, the official residence of the
high commissioner of Palestine and Trans-Jordan, in 2006

British troops manning a checkpoint in an unidentified
Jewish neighborhood, circa 1947

The Jewish Agency headquarters office building in Jerusalem surrounded by
British troops during Operation Agatha, June 1946

British constable serving in the
Palestine Police Force's Camel Corps, date unknown

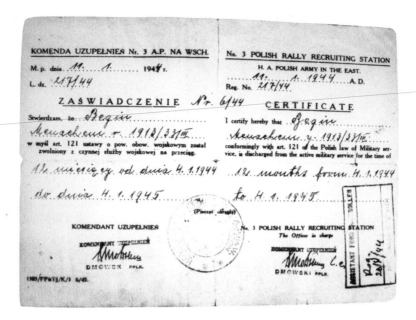

Certificate issued by the Polish army discharging
Menachem Begin, November 1944

Irgun commander Menachem Begin
reviewing Irgun forces, circa 1948

Polish passport issued to Menachem Begin, date unknown

Portrait of Major Roy Farran
from the painting by Denis
Fildes, Special Forces Club,
London, in 2013

Lieutenant General Sir Evelyn Barker, GOC,
Palestine and Trans-Jordan, greeted by
Major Richard Gale, GOC First Infantry
(left to right), with an unidentified staff
officer standing between them,
at Qalandia Airfield, Jerusalem,
November 1946

General Sir Alan Cunningham, high commissioner for Palestine and Trans-Jordan, 1945–48, photographed with General Sir Miles Dempsey, C-in-C, Middle East Land Forces, in the gardens of Government House, Jerusalem, November 1946

Field Marshal Sir Bernard Montgomery of Alamein arrives in Cairo en route to Palestine, June 1946.

Lord Moyne (Walter Edward Guinness), minister resident in the Middle East, January–November 1944

Sir Harold MacMichael, high commissioner for Palestine and Trans-Jordan, 1938–44

The discussion then moved on to counterterrorism. Scott accepted on Rymer-Jones's behalf the agency's offer and promised that appropriate arrangements would quickly be made to enroll thirty Haganah men as PPF "special constables" and immediately deploy them to Jerusalem, Tel Aviv, and Haifa. But any hope that Shertok had of sparing the Yishuv from blame or punishment for the Irgun's resumed campaign was shattered the next moment by Scott's blunt warning that "in the event of [any] new outbreak [of violence], public opinion in Great Britain from the Prime Minister downwards would not differentiate" between the Irgun and the Haganah and would blame the Yishuv as a whole. Shertok retorted that the government in fact was to blame for the failure to eliminate the Irgun, pointing out that the Saison's "unorthodox measures" had proven "highly effective" until their enforced discontinuance. He warned Scott that "any attempt to resort to wholesale anti-Jewish reprisals by way of curfew, mass arrests or other punitive action going beyond measures specifically directed against terrorists, would have disastrous effects generally and, as far as terrorism was concerned, would do infinitely more harm than good."[17]

Weizmann now intervened in hopes of averting a complete breakdown in relations. Within the week he had written to Churchill politely seeking clarification of the government's postwar intentions regarding Palestine. Churchill's reply was bluntly noncommittal. There could be "no possibility of the question being effectively considered," the prime minister tersely noted, "until the victorious Allies are definitely seated at the Peace Table." Weizmann was stunned. He again wrote to Churchill, bitterly recalling,

I had always understood from our various conversations that our problem would be considered as soon as the German war was over; but the phrase "until the victorious Allies are definitely seated at the Peace table" substitutes some indefinite date in the future. I am sure that it cannot have been your intention to postpone the matter indefinitely, because I believe you realise that this would involve very grave hardship to thousands of people at present still lingering in the camps of Buchenwald, Belsen-Bergen [*sic*] etc., who cannot find any place to go if the White Paper is to continue for an unspecified period.

The government had likely anticipated Weizmann's entreaty and had framed its response in advance because all Shertok's communications with Zionism's elder statesman were being intercepted by British intelligence and duly reported to the prime minister and the Colonial Office. In any event, there is no record whether Churchill ever replied.[18]

Meanwhile, the Irgun's ill-fated efforts to kick-start its terrorist campaign continued. On June 12, police discovered a battery of clockwork mortars in a vacant lot overlooking the government printing office. Then, the following day, acting on information provided by the Jewish Agency through its intelligence liaison, Teddy Kollek, police found an identical mortar battery behind the YMCA building on King George V Avenue pointing in the direction of the reviewing stand erected across the street from the King David Hotel. It was where less than twenty-four hours later the high commissioner and other senior government, police, and military officers and assorted dignitaries would be seated to take the salute on the king's birthday and watch the annual parade.[19]

Seeking to capitalize on the Jewish Agency's key role in foiling the assassination attempt, Shertok met with Gort a few days later. He requested that the high commissioner authorize on compassionate grounds the immediate issuance of an additional hundred thousand immigration certificates beyond the paltry six thousand remaining in the quota. Gort rejected it out of hand. The stage was thus set for a new confrontation between the British and the Yishuv when Ben-Gurion publicly announced on June 24 that the Jewish Agency would defy the government's restrictions on legal immigration to Palestine and would instead illegally bring as many Jews to the country as possible. "If the British Government really intends now to maintain and enforce the White Paper," he declared, "it will have to use constant and brutal force to do so."[20]

That same day, Gort left Palestine for the second time in a month. A persistent illness described to the press as a "feverish chill" had left him bedridden during his home visit earlier in June, but X-rays and a complete physical examination had found nothing wrong. The high commissioner had accordingly returned to Palestine. But he continued to feel unwell and decided to go back to London for more tests. Doctors again could find nothing wrong except for a mild stomach infection "as a result of a chill on the tummy" and prescribed rest. This seemed a reasonable diagnosis of illness brought on by stress, fatigue, and overwork. Accordingly, he remained in the U.K. throughout the summer to convalesce. Given the events unfolding in Palestine, it was an inauspicious time to be away.[21]

Zionism's opponents in the Foreign Office both at home and in Cairo saw their chance to bury partition once and for all. From Cairo, Sir Edward Grigg, Moyne's successor as minister of state, produced a memorandum that was extraordinary for its unrestrained condemnation of the Yishuv. "The self-imposed regimentation of Jewish life in Palestine," one excerpt reads, "and the rigid fanaticism of their system of education from infancy up, are evidence of the fact that a considerable majority hail from Russia or Eastern Europe. The methods of the Stern Group and still more the Irgun show that too many spring from an underworld of the lowest type. A system largely organized and controlled by men of that character is irreconcilable with the liberal ideals which we have fought to preserve. If tolerated much longer, it will produce war."[22]

Two weeks later, Grigg forwarded another, considerably more modulated memorandum on imperial security in the Middle East to the cabinet for consideration. It represented the views of the Middle East Defence Committee, which Grigg chaired, and described the region as having "life-and-death consequences for Britain and the British Empire." Accordingly, the Palestine issue, the region's ambassadors and military commanders argued, could not be considered in isolation from these wider imperial strategic and political implications. "I cannot indeed see," the minister of state explained, "how any conceivable system of British security in the Middle East can be reconciled with the partition of Palestine." Such a solution not only risked alienating the entire Arab world but would also imperil the imperial lines of communication, deprive Britain of key strategic ports and airfields in the country, and eliminate its control of the Kirkuk–Haifa oil pipeline. Palestine, he concluded, is "the core of our Middle East security and must be administered as an undivided whole."[23]

Grigg's analysis reflected the Chiefs of Staff's position. Indeed, despite the end of the European war, several new construction projects had already commenced, including a base near Haifa that U.S. intelligence observed "is reported to be the largest British military installation in the Near and Middle East . . . Obviously the military authorities plan for permanence in Palestine." Palestine's centrality to British postwar strategic thinking is perhaps best illustrated by the views of Harold Beeley, the Foreign Office's principal adviser on Palestine to the foreign secretary. "Abdication in Palestine," he minuted, "would be regarded in the ME [Middle East] as symptomatic of our abdication as a Great Power, and might set in motion a process which would result in the crumbling away of our influence throughout this region."[24]

As the ministry directly responsible for the day-to-day administration of Palestine, the Colonial Office had far more mundane concerns. Officials there thus regarded the risks involved in partition as no worse than those of any other alternative. When, for instance, in July, the idea was raised to simply transfer responsibility for the mandate to the United States and be done with Palestine, the chiefs predictably opposed it. Stanley, on the other hand, found merit in the proposal, noting to Churchill that he was hard-pressed to "see what advantage has ever accrued to Great Britain from the Palestine Mandate which has proved a continual drain on resources of material and manpower." All these arguments were depressingly familiar. The same points had been made by the same ministries and by the chiefs during Britain's previous search for a new Palestine policy nearly a decade before. This latest quest, however, was cut short by the outcome of the general election held in Britain on July 5—the first since 1935.[25]

On July 26 the results were announced. In a surprise, landslide victory, the Labour Party was swept into power. Only twice before in British history—in 1832 and 1906—had the country swung so decisively away from the ruling party. Pledging "a world of progress and peace," Labour's platform of full employment; the nationalization of utilities, transport, and key industries; the establishment of a national insurance system and nationalized health care; and an ambitious program of agricultural and housing reforms had catapulted the party to a commanding majority of 393 seats in the House of Commons—more than twice its preelection figure. The Tories' presence in the House was halved—with Churchill, despite being widely regarded as the war-wearied country's savior, shockingly turned out of office. That same evening he drove to Buckingham Palace to tender his resignation to King George VI and advised the monarch to send for Clement Attlee, who, as the victorious leader of the Opposition, would form the new government.[26]

It would be difficult to imagine two more contrasting personalities than those of the prime minister elect and his predecessor. Attlee was laconic where Churchill was voluble, unemotional where Churchill was stirring, and singularly lacking the charisma and star power that had made Churchill a household name around the globe. A survivor of Churchill's spectacularly failed Gallipoli campaign in Turkey during World War I, Attlee had nonetheless always deeply respected Churchill for his strategic boldness and vision, thus accounting perhaps for the extraordinarily effective relationship that both men established as deputy prime minister and premier in the government of national unity that ruled Britain for most of World War II. Indeed, Attlee and Churchill were the only members to serve in the coalition war cabinet from its first day in October 1940 until the last in May 1945.[27]

Attlee chose as his foreign secretary Ernest Bevin. Here, too, the contrast between two men in appearance, personality, and mien could not have been greater. Attlee was modest in stature, girth, inclination, and deportment. The same could not be said of Bevin, who was truly a larger-than-life figure in every way—in physique, temperament, and opinions, with an unbridled willingness to express them. Born of humble, working-class stock, Bevin was orphaned when he was eight years old. He started work as a common laborer at age eleven in order to help support his mostly illiterate family. Although Bevin never completed secondary school, Attlee described him as having "the most capacious mind of any man I ever knew." Churchill, who brought Bevin into the war cabinet, recognized these same qualities in him. His name was the first on a list of four men "whose services in high office were immediately required," Churchill had told Attlee as he set about building the coalition government in May 1940.[28]

Bevin was similarly indispensable to Attlee. At age sixty-four, however, he was also quite ill, suffering from advanced heart disease and often complete exhaustion. Bevin had recurrent, mild heart attacks and was also susceptible to fainting. As the Zionist historian Michael J. Cohen observes, "The great strains imposed on Bevin's infirm health go a long way to explain his frequent outbursts of pith and anger, especially, but not only, on the Zionist issue."[29]

Indeed, Palestine was to prove the Labour government's Achilles' heel—and perhaps the most problematic issue on Bevin's plate. Although day-to-day governance matters affecting the mandate remained within the remit of the Colonial Office, Attlee handed to Bevin the task of formulating the new government's policy for Palestine and determining the mandate's future.[30]

Initially, at least, this was not something that would have displeased Zionists and their supporters. Bevin was regarded as a friend. In 1930, for instance, his intervention had been pivotal in softening the terms of the Passfield White Paper, which was ultimately repudiated by Ramsay Mac-Donald in his "Black Letter." In 1940, Weizmann had described Bevin as one of the few Britons who understood the problems confronting Jewry and the Jewish Agency's efforts to ameliorate them. He was a man, the Zionist leader believed, who was willing not only to listen but more critically to take action on the Zionists' behalf. He was among the handful of ministers whom Ben-Gurion had found supportive of his efforts to raise a Jewish army early in the war and had backed Churchill's partition plan during the cabinet's discussions in 1944.[31]

Bevin's views reflected the Labour Party's position on Zionism. In December 1917, just weeks after the Balfour Declaration was issued, the party had enthusiastically endorsed the creation of a Jewish national home in Palestine. Ten successive party conferences, including the most recent one held in December 1944, had reaffirmed that pledge. That conference in fact had endorsed a geographically and politically expansive pro-Zionist platform that included monetary incentives to persuade Palestine's Arab population to relocate elsewhere. Such proposals went beyond what even Ben-Gurion and the Jewish Agency were advocating. The Labour Party had also staunchly opposed the 1939 white paper, which it had previously denounced as both a regrettable "breach of faith" and a "breach of British honour." Indeed, as the end of the war in Europe neared, its National Executive Committee had called for the gates of Palestine to be opened to the Jewish survivors of Hitler's death camps. "There is surely neither hope nor meaning in a 'Jewish National Home,'" a report of the executive's 1944 meeting had proclaimed, "unless we are prepared to let Jews, if they wish, enter this land in such numbers as to become a majority. There was a strong case for this before the War. There is an irresistible case now, after the unspeakable atrocities of the . . . Nazi plan to kill all Jews in Europe."[32]

Labour's election victory thus raised Zionist expectations to new heights. So prevalent was the belief that the change in government would soon be followed by a dramatic change in Britain's Palestine policy that even the Irgun felt obliged to give the new government the benefit of the doubt and, as a sign of goodwill, suspended operations. It was not long, however, before these heady expectations began to sour as anticipation turned into frustration. The first blow had arguably come with the composition of the new cabinet itself. Although, for all the reasons previously noted, Bevin was a not unpopular choice, Hugh Dalton—who was chiefly responsible for the party's pro-Zionist election platform—was the Zionists' preferred candidate and had been expected to receive that portfolio.[33]

Still more disconcerting was Attlee's selection of George Hall, an old friend and political crony, as colonial secretary. Although Hall had previously served as undersecretary of state for the colonies from 1940 to 1942 and as parliamentary undersecretary for foreign affairs until the war's end, he had neither a particular interest nor an expertise in Palestine or Zionist affairs. The same could be said about Bevin. "The truth is," his biographer Alan Bullock explains, "that until he became Foreign Secretary himself Bevin had never taken an interest in Palestine or the Middle East comparable with that which he had long had in Europe and that he was nothing like so well-informed about the issues."[34]

Attlee doubtless reasoned that the appointment of Arthur Creech Jones, a protégé of Bevin's with deep knowledge of colonial affairs, to the number two position in the Colonial Office as undersecretary would compensate for Bevin's and Hall's unfamiliarity with these issues. Zionists admittedly derived some solace from this news but remained concerned that the anti-Zionism prevalent among some permanent officials would unduly influence the ministers in both the Foreign and the Colonial Offices.[35]

They were right. Bevin had only been at the Foreign Office a few days when he requested a meeting with Attlee to discuss Palestine. "Clem, about Palestine. According to my lads in the office we've got it wrong. We've got to think again." Despite having been implacably against the 1939 white paper while in the Opposition, once in power the Labour government made it its de facto policy until a new one could be considered, agreed upon, and formally adopted. But with the fate of tens of thousands of European Jews hanging by a thread in the abject conditions of the war-torn continent, any delay was regarded by Zionists as intolerable and unacceptable. In Central Europe alone, for instance, some fifty-five thousand Jews had been crowded into displaced-persons camps awaiting exit permits for Palestine or elsewhere—anywhere, they hoped, so long as it was far from Europe.[36]

More disappointment followed. That summer, the World Zionist Congress was meeting in London. Despite Weizmann's counsels of moderation, Ben-Gurion led an impromptu delegation to confront the colonial secretary directly about the party's preelection promises by demanding the immediate admission of a hundred thousand Jews to Palestine. Hall was deliberately noncommittal, promising only to get back to Ben-Gurion and his colleagues in due course. He did so three weeks later. Jewish immigration could continue at the current rate of two thousand persons per month until the remaining white paper quota was filled. However, in view of the conditions in Europe, the colonial secretary offered to consult with Palestine's Arabs and hopefully obtain their consent to allow an additional fifteen hundred immigrants per month. "Either we stand on the threshold of a state . . . or we stand on the threshold of a grave," Ben-Gurion had declared to the conference just a few weeks before. He now had his answer.[37]

In a speech Bevin made the following year to a foreign policy gathering in New York, he explained, "We knew that at the end of the war the world would be very different from the world with which we had been familiar in the past . . . The guiding principle of the Labour Party has been to assist in the shaping of a new world." But the role that Britain could play in shaping that new world was greatly circumscribed by the country's postwar financial condition and declining position as a world power. The war fundamentally altered the old balance of power centered on Europe that Britain and Germany had dominated for the first half of the century. Instead, two non-European powers—the United States and the Soviet Union—were now the world's new superpowers. This occurrence was as much the result of American and Soviet strength as it was the eclipse of German and British power. But whereas defeat accounted for Germany's demise, victory paradoxically accounted for Britain's decline. Exhausted and financially enfeebled after six years of war, Britain now saw its control over the lines of communication to the empire, as well as parts of the empire itself, threatened by both external and internal forces. Its traditional domination of regions like the eastern Mediterranean and the Middle East was increasingly challenged by Soviet expansion and American influence, while indigenous nationalist movements and growing anti-colonial agitation in countries like India and Egypt, coupled with the emerging civil war in Greece, tested Britain's ability to reassert its authority in various corners of the globe that it had long ruled or controlled.[38]

At the heart of Britain's weakened postwar condition were its anemic finances. Indebtedness to other countries had increased almost tenfold between 1939 and 1945, and the country was spending approximately £2 billion abroad, while overseas income was only £800 million. The extent of Britain's parlous economic situation was underscored on August 21 when the new U.S. president, Harry S. Truman, abruptly canceled the prewar lend-lease agreement that had significantly eased Britain's terms of indebtedness to the United States.[39]

This unilateral move put Britain, Dalton said, in "an almost desperate plight." The famed British economist John Maynard Keynes, who even before news of the cancellation had warned of the country's severe economic problems and proposed negotiation of a new loan from the United States, now declared that Britain faced a "financial Dunkirk." Without an American loan of at least £1.5 billion, Britain could not afford to feed its citizens—let alone the war-ravaged people living in lands occupied by its army, repatriate its troops from abroad, restore its industries to peacetime production and the manufacture of consumer goods, or meet its manifold domestic and international financial obligations. An essential element of Britain's economic recovery was the need for an adequate workforce to get the country's industries back on their feet. But this would necessitate the expeditious mass demobilization of the three million men still in uniform.[40]

Against this backdrop of great-power rivalry and the emerging cold war along with financial cutbacks and strategic retrenchment, the Labour government began to consider its policy for Palestine. The Chiefs of Staff were quick to note their objections to any precipitous change of policy. "From the military point of view," they argued, "an announcement on PALESTINE at the present time would be most inconvenient, in view of our many other commitments." Because sufficient reinforcements would not be available for internal security duties in the region for at least another year, the chiefs judged it imperative that the status quo be maintained for as long as possible.[41]

Implicit in this assessment was the centrality that Palestine had come to assume in Britain's postwar strategic planning. "Apart from Cyprus, which has limited capacity, and the Sudan, which is unsuitable, Palestine is the only territory between Malta and Aden," a Joint Planning Staff assessment explained, "in which we can confidently expect to have facilities for the stationing of troops or the establishment of installations." This was the thrust of the amended orders that the War Office issued to Paget on August 9. Henceforth, Paget should consider the depots and installations in Egypt *and* Palestine as the foundation for British power projection across the region. Most important, the chiefs' position meshed perfectly with the views of Bevin, who was convinced that the Middle East would henceforth be the strategic center of gravity for Britain that India had once been.[42]

On August 22, Attlee made his first move with respect to determining the new government's policy for Palestine by appointing Bevin, Hall, and Dalton to serve with other cabinet members on a special ministerial committee. The committee was charged with advising the cabinet on an interim policy for Palestine until a final decision on the mandate's future could be made. It was agreed that the committee would report back to the full cabinet in two weeks.[43]

The complexity and challenges facing the new government in fashioning a new policy for Palestine were underscored by a lengthy assessment that Shaw, the officer administering government in Gort's absence, sent to Hall in late August. Running to twelve typed, single-spaced pages, the letter painted a disquieting picture of a volatile situation poised on the brink of explosion. The imminent expiration of the white paper's immigration quota was the driving force behind the confrontation that Shaw believed was imminent. He cited the relentless stream of tendentious public statements being issued by Zionist officials as clear evidence "that the Yishuv is being psychologically prepared for what will be in effect an armed rebellion." Material preparations for the coming struggle, Shaw continued, were also proceeding at a feverish pace. The Haganah, accordingly, "now considers itself equal to any task to which its leaders may assign it," while the Irgun's intensification of terrorist operations throughout June and July constituted "an openly proclaimed period of preparation for a final trial of strength." But perhaps the most troubling aspect of these developments was the cessation of Jewish counterterrorist cooperation, which, the chief secretary predicted, could produce an alliance of all three underground movements against Britain.[44]

The Arabs were quiescent. But this, Shaw emphasized, was less a product of any change in their attitudes toward Britain or Zionism than a reflection of the community's continued exhaustion and political paralysis. Although the Arabs constituted a less serious menace than the Jews, he warned that they too were "being worked into the frame of mind in which terrorism and gang-warfare will again become political weapons." In sum, Shaw concluded,

> the picture is a somber one. The young Jewish extremists, the product of a vicious education system, know neither toleration nor compromise; they regard themselves as morally justified in violence directed against any individual or institution that impedes the complete fulfillment of their demands . . .
>
> On the other side are the Arabs, for the most part backward and less politically alive. As far as Palestine is concerned there is probably nothing that has contributed so much to the growth of a sense of Arab nationalism as has the pressure of Zionism. Their political leadership may still be inept. Their daily life may still be hampered by mediaevalism and marred by ignorance and religious bias. But even in their poverty and ignorance . . . the mass of the Palestinian Arabs are still capable of resisting, savagely and tenaciously, what they may consider as an attempt to reduce them to a minority status in a land which they regard as theirs.

Paget had provided a similarly depressing assessment, which in turn prompted both Beeley and Charles William Baxter, the head of the Foreign Office Eastern Department, to note, "Trouble with the 2 terrorist organizations cannot be avoided, whatever policy is adopted. But the important thing is the big battalions of the Hagana."[45]

The ministerial committee delivered its report to Attlee on September 8. Until a new long-term policy could be decided, it proposed that the 1939 white paper policy remain in force, thus formally endorsing Hall's response to Ben-Gurion's demands from the previous month.

Jewish immigration should be allowed to continue until the white paper quota was exhausted but thereafter would be permitted—only with Arab consent—at a rate of fifteen hundred per month. In making this recommendation, the ministerial committee recognized that Britain ran the risk of provoking Jewish civil unrest in Palestine in addition to increased terrorism and illegal immigration. But it regarded these potentialities as less serious than the trouble that would erupt throughout the Muslim world, including India, if the white paper was abandoned. Although both options presented their own challenges, the latter would doubtless require a military commitment at least two or three times greater than the former. Moreover, there was the widespread perception among the ministers that no matter what option was chosen, Britain would be criticized by the United States. "If we adhere to the White Paper," the committee concluded, "we *may* escape without adverse repercussions; there is no hope of doing so under the alternative course."[46]

The memorandum on security conditions in Palestine that Hall submitted to the cabinet two days later, however, belied that hope. "In connection with the report of the Palestine Committee," he wrote, "I must draw the attention of my colleagues to the grave and threatening situation in Palestine." Citing Shaw's letter from the previous month and more recent discussions with Lord Gort, who was still in London, the colonial secretary explained that the Yishuv was poised on the brink of open revolt. "Extremists" had taken control of the Zionist movement and were "confidently and loudly" making demands for increased immigration and a Jewish state. There have been terrorist attacks on government buildings by the Irgun and "cold blooded murders by its off-shoot, the Stern Gang." And the police were still nearly two thousand men below their authorized strength. Recruitment continued to be a serious problem. Efforts to lower standards in terms of educational attainment and intellectual rigor to attract more volunteers to the PPF had proven fruitless. The army, accordingly, would have to compensate for this grave deficiency of police manpower. But this was problematic too. The First Infantry Division had returned to Palestine earlier in 1945 to rest and recuperate from the long campaign to liberate Italy. It would shortly be joined by the Sixth Airborne Division—veterans of the D-day parachute assault on Normandy, the Battle of the Bulge, and the victorious crossing of the Rhine into Germany. By November, there would be some thirty-five thousand combat-hardened troops in Palestine. Even so, the Chiefs of Staff still judged this number insufficient, estimating that another two divisions (that is, thirty-five thousand more soldiers), supported by an additional nine thousand administrative personnel, were required in Palestine to maintain order if the white paper was to remain in force. These additional troops were needed because the Sixth Airborne had been assigned to Palestine not for internal security reasons but for training purposes as part of the Imperial Strategic Reserve meant to support other British forces throughout the region and farther afield. As events would show, this proved to be a forlorn hope.[47]

To Menachem Begin, the war's end, coupled with the Saison's collapse, and the Labour Party's procrastination over Palestine provided the Irgun with a unique opportunity to place itself at the vanguard of the Yishuv's nationalist aspirations. Although its remote-control mortar campaign suffered a new setback at the end of July when police raided two workshops in Tel Aviv where the weapons were fabricated, the group adjusted and effectively shifted tactics. Irgun gunmen hijacked a truck carrying a large supply of gelignite, fuses, and detonators, killing its police escort. Twelve days later, the group used the same explosives in its first joint attack with Lehi—the destruction of a heavily used railway bridge. Then, in early August, Irgun gunmen robbed a Tel Aviv bank of several thousand pounds with which to fund future operations. Another theft in mid-August provided more gelignite, fuses, and detonators. The Irgun and Lehi also concluded a formal "working alliance" in August that mutually reinforced the capabilities of both organizations. It also marked Lehi's abandonment of its long-standing, self-described strategy of "individual terror"—as evidenced by the Moyne and Wilkin assassinations—and its adoption of the Irgun's paramilitary-style assault operations.[48]

As long as the police continued to be fed a stream of intelligence from the Jewish Agency despite the Saison's demise, they were confident that they could handle the joint terrorist campaign. The assistance from Teddy Kollek, the agency's liaison officer assigned to military and police headquarters, now led to the identification of a large Irgun training facility at Suneh, near Benyamina. Twenty-seven male and three female members of the group were arrested, and a variety of armaments, including Thompson submachine guns, rifles, pistols, hand grenades, and explosives, had been seized. In addition, Kollek's information was instrumental in frustrating a Lehi plot to blow up oil storage facilities in Jerusalem and Haifa.[49]

But the growing rift between the Zionists and the new government, coupled with Ben-Gurion's increasingly confrontational policies, now threatened to deprive the police of this critical source of knowledge about the terrorists' plans and intentions. Still more worrisome was the steady stream of intelligence reports that the Haganah had entered into negotiations with the Irgun and Lehi to coordinate antigovernment operations. What Begin described as the Yishuv's "Midsummer Night's Dream" was ending. "No Labour promise, no Blackpool resolution, no friendship. All that remained was the traditional British fist." And with this "disillusionment," he recalled, "ended the most difficult phase in the period of the anti-British revolt. The Agency leaders realised that they could no longer collaborate with such 'authorities' . . . And the first feelers were sent out to us for the establishment of a united front."[50]

As a complete rupture of Anglo-Zionist relations loomed, Weizmann appealed to Attlee. Rumors were circulating that the government was about to announce its interim policy for Palestine. "If what we hear is true," the Zionist leader wrote to the prime minister on September 21, "it would mean that nothing short of a tragedy faces the Jewish people, and a very serious conflict might ensue, which we would all deplore." Attlee's reply was brusquely dismissive: "If we thought that further consultation were required at this stage or that it would serve any useful purpose, we should certainly arrange it; but at the present juncture that is not so."[51]

The prime minister's gruff response likely reflected his anger upon learning from British intelligence of the contents of an encoded telegram that Moshe Sneh, who had succeeded Golomb as the Haganah's leader upon the latter's death, had sent to the Jewish Agency's London office on September 23. The intercepted communication revealed that the agency had already decided to *cause one serious incident* . . . [and] then publish a declaration to the effect that it is *only a warning and an indication of much more serious incidents* that would threaten the safety of all British interests in the country, should the Government decide against us." The message also confirmed the alliance negotiations under way between the Haganah and its two terrorist counterparts.[52]

The commanders of each underground movement in fact met earlier that same day to finalize the terms of their alliance. Although they all agreed that it would be useful to establish some joint command arrangement, Begin resisted a formal merger of the three organizations. Talks resumed on September 29, when a compromise was reached. While the Irgun and Lehi would retain their organizational independence, both groups agreed not to carry out any operation without first obtaining the Haganah's consent. The arrangement governing the Tenuat Ha-Meri Ha-Ivri, or Hebrew Resistance Movement, as the alliance was known, also called for the establishment of a joint command, known as X Committee. This coordinating body would meet to discuss, plan, and approve joint operations. Additional provisions gave the Haganah high command the authority to order either of its allies to undertake specific operations, but each group would retain complete independence over operations designed to procure arms, secure funding, and free imprisoned members from British custody.[53]

Two days later Ben-Gurion instructed Sneh to implement the campaign of active resistance. Within the week, the British were confronted with mass demonstrations and outbreaks of civil disobedience as well as outright attack. On October 6, for instance, Jewish settlers at Kfar Giladi violently clashed with a contingent of the Trans-Jordan Frontier Force attempting to search for illegal immigrants. Two days later, demonstrators took to the streets to protest the white paper's continued enforcement. Some sixty thousand people attended the Tel Aviv march. And on October 10, the Haganah carried out its first attack on a British government target. Before dawn a force of some fifty Palmach commandos raided the detention facility for Jewish illegal immigrants at Athlit, south of Haifa. A British constable was shot dead as police patrols attempted to round up the escapees. Later in the day, Jewish settlers armed with ax handles succeeded in releasing nine of the detainees whom the police had recaptured.[54]

The Jewish Agency made no secret that it had known about and approved the attack, warning—just as the intercepted telegram had stated it would—that this was only a hint of the trouble to come if the government rejected the Zionists' demands. This message was communicated by Kol Israel (Voice of Israel), the Haganah's clandestine radio station, which had commenced broadcasting the previous evening.[55]

Palestine's deteriorating security now prompted the U.S. military command to declare the country off-limits to American troops. These developments were also watched with mounting unease by the British. In letters to his mother, Robert Scott, the Palestine government's financial secretary, described how he had been assigned three bodyguards to accompany him wherever he went—a British constable and two Bedouin. "It is a very astringent thought that reversion to peacetime conditions means in Palestine a return of the pre-war conditions of gangsterism but this time it is the Jews and they are much more efficient."[56]

On October 11, Gort, who had recently returned to Palestine, requested an urgent meeting with Jewish Agency officials. Like Weizmann, the high commissioner regarded the strained relations between the government and the Yishuv as a personal setback. Both men had worked hard to establish a dialogue and thus avert precisely the violent confrontation that had now materialized. Since taking office eleven months earlier, the high commissioner had indeed shown himself to be a tireless and personable administrator, admired and respected by Arab and Jew alike. Writing to Churchill in January 1945, Grigg marveled, following a visit to Jerusalem, at the "great difference in the atmosphere" of Palestine that Gort had achieved "by being so human, cheerful, fearless and accessible, and by moving about so freely. (I can confirm this, for I walked with him in the jostling streets of Old Jerusalem, and found him greeted on all sides by hats off, salaams and smiles of welcome)." He was certainly far more popular with the Yishuv than his predecessor had been. Although Lehi had tried on several occasions to assassinate MacMichael, it never once attempted to kill Gort.[57]

But all these accomplishments were now threatened, not only by the emerging violence and outright rebellion, but by Gort's own mortality. Although he did not know it, and the doctors whom he had consulted in London were unable to diagnose his condition, at age fifty-nine Gort was dying of liver cancer. Despite being in great pain and discomfort, he resolved to carry on with his responsibilities and insisted on returning to Palestine at this time of acute crisis.[58]

With a purposefulness and determination driven by an awareness of his declining health, Gort desperately tried to reason with the three Jewish Agency officials—Bernard Joseph, Yitzhak Ben-Zvi, and Eliezer Kaplan—who arrived at his office that day. He got nowhere. Events had gone too far for either party to find common ground. The high commissioner's warning that the government would tolerate no further violence and disorder was rebuffed by the officials' proposal that the agency would suspend all resistance if the government promised henceforth not to deport any illegal immigrants from Palestine. Gort rejected the offer outright, beseeching the officials to consider the harm that would be done to the Zionist cause should the "impression get abroad that [the] Yishuv was trying to force the issue by a policy of lawlessness and violence." The meeting ended on that dour note.[59]

Two weeks later Sneh published an article in *Ha'aretz*. "To this day," it began,

> every political activity of the Zionist movement has relied on two forces—the distressing plight of Jewry in the Diaspora . . . and the creative genius of Jewish pioneering in this country . . . However, these two factors have not been strong enough to achieve in 1945 the materialisation of the Zionist solution by international agreement . . . In these circumstances, we cannot afford not to resort to the third force hidden

in Palestine Jewry—its power of resistance . . . Let the cost of sticking to the White Paper policy exceed that of scrapping it . . . We shall never acquiesce in the prohibition of immigration and settlement, and, if we prove that, no superiority of British force will be of avail.

Five days later the Hebrew Resistance Movement launched its first joint operation.[60]

In a dramatic show of force, the Haganah, the Irgun, and Lehi carried out a series of coordinated attacks throughout the country on the night of October 31. Explosive charges laid by Palmach sappers cut the rail line in more than 150 places, paralyzing rail service across Palestine for a full two days. Meanwhile, an Irgun raiding party destroyed three locomotives, a railway maintenance shed, and a signal box at Lydda. Palmach units sank two police launches in Haifa and a third in Jaffa that were used to intercept illegal immigrants on vessels at sea. And a Lehi assault team struck the Consolidated Oil Refinery in Haifa.[61]

The Jewish Agency deplored the attacks publicly while exulting in them privately. A telegram from Jerusalem to London intercepted by British intelligence clearly revealed the agency's duplicity. "The activities have made a great impression in the country," the cable read. "The authorities are bewildered and have proclaimed a curfew on the roads at night. They are waiting for instructions from London."[62]

For the new Labour government, the unrest was an unwelcome distraction at a time when it was maneuvering to chart a new course for Palestine. Since the summer, pressure had been building from the United States to loosen the restrictions on Jewish immigration to Palestine. In July, Attlee had found waiting for him a letter that Truman had written to Churchill anticipating the latter's election victory. Truman expressed the hope that the 1939 white paper's immigration restrictions would now be lifted, because they were the subject of "passionate protest from Americans." The new prime minister was about to depart for the final Big Three conference in Potsdam and had other things on his mind. He discussed it with Bevin, but neither gave the issue much thought as more pressing international and domestic matters were competing for their attention. After a few weeks had passed without a reply, in mid-August Truman disclosed the letter's contents at an impromptu press conference in Washington. But this was just an opening gambit.[63]

Armed with the report of a special emissary whom the president had sent to Europe at the end of June to investigate the condition of Jewish displaced persons, Truman called on Britain to issue a hundred thousand immigration certificates for the refugees to be resettled in Palestine. He further instructed the secretary of state, James Byrnes, who would soon be in London for a meeting of the Allied foreign ministers, to raise the matter with Attlee personally. Byrnes did so on September 10 and four days later communicated Truman's request to Bevin, adding that the president intended to publicize these demands that same evening. Bevin exploded. Should Truman issue such a statement, the foreign secretary warned, he would proclaim before the House of Commons that Britain expected the United States to deploy four divisions of troops to Palestine to assist in maintaining order there. A panicked Byrnes persuaded Truman to delay any new policy pronouncement on Palestine in the interests of Anglo-American harmony. A telegram from Attlee arrived that same day at the White House, driving home this point. Continued pressure from Truman on Palestine, the prime minister wrote, "could not fail to do grievous harm to relations between our two countries."[64]

The reality of the situation was captured by Arthur Creech Jones, the number two person at the Colonial Office, who later reflected that it was already clear that, like it or not, "no considerable diplomatic or practical changes in Palestine and the Arab countries could be made without American financial and strategic support." Hence, however much British officials resented American attempts to dictate policy while offering no assistance in its implementation, U.S. support for any solution to the Palestine problem would be critical, not least because the issue would eventually need to be considered by the new United Nations organization—the successor to the League of Nations that had awarded Britain the Palestine mandate more than twenty years earlier. Moreover, negotiations for a new American loan were then under way in Washington. Bevin, accordingly, began to formulate a plan to draw the United States directly into the Palestine problem by inviting the Americans to serve on a joint committee of inquiry. At the very least, Lord Halifax, the British ambassador in Washington, told Bevin, such a joint undertaking "would get us to some extent away from the uncomfortable position in which the Americans criticise us without sharing responsibility."[65]

The foreign secretary unveiled his idea for the Anglo-American Committee of Inquiry (AAC) at the cabinet meeting on October 4. Increasing "agitation in the U.S.A." over Palestine, he explained to his colleagues, "was poisoning our relations with the U.S. Government in other fields." The AAC thus offered the possibility of engaging the Americans constructively to reach a joint solution on Palestine's political future. The cabinet agreed and unanimously approved the foreign secretary's proposal. There now remained the dual challenge of persuading the Americans to go along with the scheme while avoiding a complete breakdown of security in Palestine that would doom the proposed commission from the start. An additional complication was the mounting apprehension among Arabs both inside Palestine and elsewhere over the increasing stridency of the Zionists' demands coupled with the latest outbreak of antigovernment violence.[66]

On November 3, Bevin met with Weizmann and Shertok. He was in no mood to listen to excuses. As a result of the intercepted telegrams, he knew precisely the extent of the Jewish Agency's involvement in the October 31 operations. Without revealing his source, the foreign secretary stated, "It is clear to me that the Jewish Agency can no longer be regarded as an innocent party in relation to these outbreaks in Palestine." Bevin concluded the meeting by cautioning the two Zionist officials that "we should have to re-examine our position in light of these [attacks], and that our future course would be determined to a very large extent by whether this kind of action was not only denounced but stopped."[67]

That same evening's Kol Israel broadcast answered Bevin's question whether the Jewish Agency intended to settle the Palestine question by violence or negotiation. "The nights of heroism since Athlit," the announcer proclaimed, "are an expression of our strength and decision. We lament the British, Arab and Jewish victims who fell in the attacks on the railways and ports of Palestine. They are all victims of the White Paper." Identically defiant editorials appeared in the Hebrew press the following day. "We are today fighting with our backs to the wall," *Hatzofeh*, the newspaper of the Orthodox Party, opined. "We have been systematically pushed to our final position."[68]

Evidence of this hardening of attitudes across the Yishuv was palpable. Earlier that day, a police tracking team following the trail of the railway line's attackers arrived at the Jewish settlement of Ramat Ha-Kovesh—the scene of violent disorders two years before. Nearly a thousand people from the settlement and the surrounding area hastily assembled to block the search, forcing the police to withdraw. The unrest shifted to a Tel Aviv suburb on November 3, when an angry mob freed an illegal immigrant being arrested by police and then stoned a police armored car attempting to extract the beleaguered arrest party.[69]

These events were to be the final repudiation of Gort's determined effort to avoid a violent confrontation between the government and the

Yishuv. The high commissioner's physical health had declined precipitously since his return to Palestine the previous month. He was now in constant, agonizing pain. On November 2, the Palestine government announced that Gort would relinquish his post and leave Palestine within the next few days. The unexpected announcement caught the country by surprise. An editorial in *The Palestine Post* reflected the mood of Jew and Arab alike. "No High Commissioner in the twenty-five years of British rule in Palestine enjoyed greater popular trust and none repaid it with greater personal kindness." The high commissioner's farewell message to his staff clearly evinced his own profound sense of regret. "The wheel of Fortune," he wrote, "has called me abruptly to lay down the task on which I embarked with such high hopes last year . . . To all of you I say good-bye with a heavy heart and a very real and deep sense of personal loss."[70]

On the morning of November 5, Shaw accompanied Gort on his final journey from Government House to an RAF air base near Tel Aviv. Given the high commissioner's condition, a stretcher team was waiting to carry him on board. Gort, however, refused their assistance and, attired in his field marshal's uniform, climbed the steps to the fuselage on his own. He paused for a moment, turned, and waved farewell to the small group assembled to see him off. In London, at Guy's Hospital, exploratory surgery revealed the extent of the cancer and the hopelessness of any cure. Gort died four months later.[71]

On November 13, the AAC was jointly announced by Bevin in London and Truman in Washington. The foreign secretary explained that Palestine's Arabs would be asked to permit the continuance of Jewish immigration at a rate of fifteen hundred persons per month once the remaining two thousand certificates allocated under the 1939 white paper were exhausted. Thereafter, Jewish immigration to Palestine would cease until the government had the opportunity to consider the AAC's interim report and proposed recommendations and consult with all concerned parties in Palestine. Following the release of the AAC's final report, Britain would then submit to the United Nations the terms of a final settlement that would provide for Palestine's independence—as a "Palestinian, not Jewish state."[72]

The Yishuv was furious. To its eyes, delay and more discussion had been adopted as the new government's policy rather than the decisive, positive action that the Labour Party had once promised. The Jewish Agency's statement in response angrily denounced the committee as "a cynical and treacherous device to postpone [a] decision on mass immigration until displaced Jews in Europe in despair accept rehabilitation in [the] Diaspora." Bevin's tactless remark during the press conference that followed his statement to the House that "if the Jews, with all their sufferings, want to get too much at the head of the queue, you have the danger of another anti-Semitic reaction" poured oil on a burning fire. At an emergency session of the Vaad Le'umi hours later, the national council declared a noon-to-midnight strike and called for countrywide protests to commence the next day. The depth of the Yishuv's despair was perhaps best illustrated by the Chief Rabbinate's response to the announcement. The Yishuv's supreme religious authority designated November 15 as a day of prayer and fasting. The rabbinate further decreed that the shofar, the sacramental ram's horn—whose plaintive tone, symbolizing the suffering of Jews through the ages, which is usually heard only on the High Holidays of Rosh Hashanah, the Jewish New Year, and Yom Kippur, the Day of Atonement—also be sounded throughout the country.[73]

CHAPTER 12

To Defend and to Guard Forever

The weather in Tel Aviv on November 14, 1945, was perfect for a protest. Work was suspended at noon, and by dusk a crowd of some fifty
thousand people had gathered at the Kiryat Meir parade ground in the city
center. The assembly stood with heads bowed in silence as a prayer was
recited in memory of Jews who had perished in the Holocaust. A series
of speeches followed denouncing the Labour government and Bevin in
particular. A proclamation was then read on behalf of the city rejecting
the proposed Anglo-American Committee and pledging that "no force
would deter the Jewish people in their struggle." The crowd dispersed,
and everyone headed home. As one group passed through the Carmel
Market, they were joined by what government and press reports termed a
bunch of "hooligans." The newcomers took control of the procession and
steered it in the direction of the cluster of government offices situated on
Levontin Street in downtown Tel Aviv. The once orderly parade had now
become a seething mob baying for broken glass and eager to mix it up
with the few police in their path.[1]

Arriving at the district offices, the marchers stormed the building,
smashing office furniture, destroying files, and tearing light fixtures
from the walls and ceilings that were hurled onto the street below. Police
attempting to control the crowd were pelted with stones and forced to
withdraw. Someone then set fire to the building, and the mob descended
in succession on the offices of the Income Tax Bureau, the Control of
Light Industries, and the local branch of the British-owned Barclays Bank.
Multiple fires now raged as the crowd headed toward the city's General
Post Office. There, they were met by a cordon of police reinforced by a
company of the Eighth Parachute Battalion that had been urgently summoned from their nearby base at Sarafand. Stones, bottles, other objects,
and at least two homemade hand grenades were thrown at the security
forces. Six baton charges by the police failed to scatter the rioters. The
paratroop company commander then gave the order to open fire. Two
persons fell dead, and the crowd withdrew.[2]

The government's imposition of a dusk-to-dawn curfew provided only a temporary respite as the disturbances began anew in the morning. Once more, buildings in Tel Aviv were sacked and set on fire, and the paratroops again had to fire upon the rioters to disperse them. The government now ordered the entire Third Paratroop Brigade—numbering four thousand men—into the city to restore order. The unrest finally abated with night-fall. The casualty toll after two days of disorders stood at three Jews killed and scores injured, forty of whom required hospitalization. All but eight of these were under the age of twenty—with the youngest eight years old. Thirty-seven policemen and soldiers had also been hurt, some seriously. Damage and cleanup costs exceeded £200,000.[3]

Midway through the unrest, the Palestine government had taken the extraordinary step of issuing a public proclamation. Posted on walls and spread across the front pages of the country's newspapers, it warned the Yishuv of the severe consequences that would befall it in the event of continued lawlessness. Not since the Arab Rebellion eight years before had the public needed to be reminded that the penalty for unlawful possession of firearms, bombs, grenades, or "other warlike stores" was life imprisonment and for their carriage or use it was death. As had also been the case during the Arab Rebellion, the government resorted to press censorship to control the dissemination of news of the disturbances. In addition, two Hebrew-language papers—*Davar*, the leftist-leaning mass-circulation Hebrew daily, and its Revisionist Party counterpart, *Hamashkif*—were charged with intent to "incite public opinion" and ordered to suspend publication for a week as punishment. A political cartoon in *Davar*, which the censor had in fact passed, had nonetheless drawn the ire of government officials. It depicted a surgeon in an operating theater remarking sarcastically on the accuracy of British marksmanship given the high number of children wounded. Gershon Agron, *The Palestine Post*'s founder and editor, met with Shaw later in the month to protest, on behalf of his fellow editors, both the censorship and the publication suspensions. During their discussion, Agron also showed the chief secretary a letter that had been sent to the *Post* by one of the paratroopers deployed to Tel Aviv. It expressed dismay that virtually three-quarters of the author's fellow soldiers had claimed they had enjoyed "shoot[ing] Jews." Shaw was visibly shaken by this assertion, Agron reported, but then dismissed it as patently untrue.[4]

The chief secretary's denial, however, ignored the accumulating evidence to the contrary. Only three days earlier, for example, Shaw had received from his staff a summary of a letter sent to Palestine's chief justice, Sir William Fitzgerald, by a Jewish resident of Tel Aviv. It provided a disturbing account of how "adults and children standing on the verandas of their houses as well as innocent passers-by were shot, wounded and killed by soldiers" during the Tel Aviv disturbances. The writer himself had observed this from the roof of his own apartment building, where he was nearly struck by bullets fired by troops below. Two persons standing beside him, however, were seriously wounded by the gunfire. This was only the latest manifestation of the entrenched hostility toward the Yishuv that was now prevalent among British security forces in Palestine.[5]

Only weeks before, a British officer with several years' service in Palestine had written to the Foreign Office. "Among the British in Palestine," he began, "suspicion and hatred of the Jew is being widely voiced with the bitterest venom. In some cases the crude surge of anti-semitic passion is worthy of a Nazi." Such attitudes were shared by both officers and enlisted men and in the police as well as the army, but they were especially prominent among officers of both. "I'm not for the Jews or against them," one major was quoted, "but I can't help feeling that Hitler was on the right lines." Identical opinions were reportedly regularly voiced by other officers. A sampling of comments included statements alleging that the Jews were deliberately exaggerating their persecution for sympathy, that Hitler could hardly be blamed for trying to exterminate European Jewry, and that the Holocaust was "a mere trick of [Jewish] political propaganda."[6]

Similarly anti-Semitic views could be heard from both civilian officials and other Britons resident in Palestine, the letter's author continued. "The atmosphere of the British community is poisoned by a constant stream of slander freely and vigorously expressed, so that each new entrant whether he knows it or not has his thoughts coloured for him against the Jews." Such repugnant views, this officer believed, arose from the lack of "deference" shown by the Yishuv to its colonial masters. The Jews refuse to be treated like the "natives" in other British possessions, he observed, and therefore "answer back [and] claim equality." Because the Arabs were superficially more obsequious and "obliging," and thus better conformed to the servile mold that these Britons expected, they were treated much better than Jews.[7]

But what this officer found most troubling was that these sentiments were progressing beyond mere verbal expressions of opprobrium into threats of physical violence. "Already 'responsible officers' are talking with vindictive relish of smashing the settlements to search for arms," he warned. "The swine must be squashed" had become something of a battle call, with the Yishuv widely described as "The Enemy." In this respect, the terrorist acts perpetrated by the Irgun and Lehi "played into the hands of the anti-semites, who were quick to blame the whole Jewish population for the political crimes of a few."[8]

Although this letter of course depicts the views and observations of one person only, the attitudes and prejudices described are clearly evident in orders issued by Palestine headquarters just a few weeks later. Under the subheading "Commercial Considerations" is the following statement: "Jews all over the world interest themselves in 'business.' Those in PALESTINE are no exception to the rule." The Yishuv, therefore, was deemed more susceptible to being influenced and manipulated by the disruptions to commerce caused by curfews, searches, and other security measures. A subsequent section, titled "The Jewish Character," also explains, "Although possessed of great agility of mind, they lack genuine wisdom. They have a strong material side, a love of business, and a love of preserving their property, on the other hand they have within them a very strong and unpredictable strain of emotionalism. They are often mystics. They still think of the prophets and their deeds as great things."[9]

Further evidence of how ingrained these attitudes had become among soldiers in Palestine may also be discerned from the annual report of Chaplaincy Services, Middle East Command, for 1945. It specifically calls attention to the poor quality of troops arriving in Palestine, expressing concern over their lack of education and generally undisciplined nature. Such men, the deputy chaplain general feared, were particularly receptive to facile racist and religious generalizations and prone to intemperate opinions, if not outright bigotry.[10]

The extent to which these anti-Semitic views were either preexisting or situational—or both—is not clear. Certainly, any claims of British bias against the Jews were repeatedly denied.

Nevertheless, a perceived sense of ingratitude figured in an animus felt by some British troops toward the Jews. It was beyond the comprehension of many to understand why the Yishuv, in the words of the Sixth Airborne's official historian, "were misguided enough to regard the British army as their oppressor." Similarly, Major Roy Farran, one of the most highly decorated British officers during World War II, who had fought as a tank commander and then a commando in the elite Special Air Service (SAS) and in 1945 was serving as second-in-command of his old regiment, the Third Hussars, then attached to the Sixth Airborne Division in Palestine, also writes of the "displaced personnel we had seen in Europe, humble in their gratitude to us, their saviours, but I could not identify them with these ungrateful, well-fed whiners. No, rather I thought of the boys who had been urged forward to their death by propaganda about German atrocities to the Jews. Where did these things fit in?" The best explanation perhaps is the ambiguous security conditions that prevailed in Palestine at this time. Brigadier R. N. Anderson, a combat engineer, explained the difficulties of coping in this perplexing environment. "Unlike the war, when one had one's period of rest (normally amongst liberated peoples who were friendly)," he wrote, "the soldier is always on duty [in Palestine] and alert to the fact that, at any time, he may expect a murderous attack. In conditions where the moderate Jew will not cooperate with the Security Forces it is impossible to know who is friend or who is enemy."[11]

"Of all burdens cast on soldiers by politicians," the British military historian Gregory Blaxland has written, "surely none ever chafed so painfully as that which grew out of the Balfour Declaration." Had the Palestine Police Force been capable of maintaining order, this burden would not have fallen on the army. Indeed, the conventional wisdom in British military circles at the time was that "one policeman is equal in value to six or seven soldiers for the kind of work which is required in Palestine." Shaw himself fully understood this and had again written to the Colonial Office on November 26 to urge a massive new recruiting effort across Britain and the empire in hopes of attracting through higher salaries and improved benefits a new generation of police whose military service during the war would put them in good stead for Palestine's unique security environment.[12]

The problem, however, was that having fought (and survived) one war, few suitable candidates were willing to volunteer for another—no matter how high the pay or excellent the benefits. And, in any event, the starting salary of a PPF constable, at just over £2 per week, was barely more than half that of the entry-level pay rate for police throughout the U.K. Accordingly, although a new drive at the end of November had generated a seemingly healthy number of applicants, only twenty-two had in fact been deemed fit for police service. This was by no means atypical, as the rejection rate generally hovered around 90 percent, prompting some frustrated Colonial Office officials to suggest that the bar for entering the PPF was set too high. But any lowering of standards had long been resisted by Rymer-Jones and emphatically opposed by Gort as well.[13]

In the circumstances, the War Office had no choice but to rush the Third Infantry Division from Germany to Palestine. Its arrival, however, provided only a short-lived fillip. The exodus of demobilized soldiers from the First Infantry Division had so enervated it that no sooner had the Third Infantry taken up positions in Jerusalem than the First departed for Egypt to rest and regroup.[14]

Playing policeman in Palestine was not a role for which these combat-hardened troops were either trained or prepared. Soldiers are taught to fight and to kill and to make war against an identifiable enemy under rules of engagement where the use of lethal force is axiomatic. Police, on the other hand, are trained in the rules of law and evidence and instructed in the use of lethal force as a last resort only. The operational environment that these troops encountered in Palestine—densely crowded urban areas within which the terrorists concealed themselves, indistinguishable from the surrounding population—was also vastly different from their formative experiences on the battlefields of Europe. There, they engaged a uniformed enemy in demarcated conflict zones, along fronts where the fighting occurred, and whatever civilians were present were noncombatants.

The restrictive rules of engagement imposed on security operations in Palestine's populated, built-up areas thus emerged as a major irritant among both soldiers and police in Palestine. Prevented from striking back in the manner they were trained, many soldiers channeled their frustration and anger toward the Yishuv. "We were never allowed to hit back at the terrorists," Farran groused. According to Major R. Dare Wilson, the Sixth Airborne's historian, the problem was as much strategic as it was tactical. "In 1945 the Division had reached a standard of training in offensive warfare of which it was justly proud," he writes. "But the requirements of Internal Security duties necessitate the application of minimum force; and, when the Division had to adapt its ideas from the previous doctrine of the use of maximum force, an entirely fresh approach was clearly needed."[15]

Britain, however, lacked not only a policy for postwar Palestine but also a strategy for containing Jewish unrest. Instead, the same stale ideas circulated with depressing regularity. The first Hebrew Resistance Movement attacks, for instance, prompted Attlee to request from the Chiefs of Staff an assessment of the available military options in response. Echoing the lengthy deliberations following Moyne's assassination, the tired arguments for and against arms searches of Jewish settlements were debated and discussed in a series of committee meetings that unfolded throughout November. Bereft of any new ideas, the committee invited the chiefs to "consider whether the time had not come to call for an appreciation from the Commanders-in-Chief in the Middle East of action required to achieve the surrender of illegal weapons in Palestine."[16]

Britain's Middle East commanders, however, had no new insights to offer either. Although they accepted as inevitable that sooner or later it would be necessary to disarm the entire population of Palestine—Jew and Arab alike—and also arrest senior Haganah and Palmach commanders, they firmly believed that now was not the time. Their reasoning had less to do with the anticipated scale of violence or the uncertainty of success than with the fear that such an operation would "lay [Britain] open to a charge of torpedoeing" the recently announced Anglo-American Commission of Inquiry before it even got started. The matter accordingly once again lapsed into abeyance. The only new wrinkle was the general staff's disconcerting observation that the difficulties of effectively conducting searches had now become "as great [as], if not greater" than, before, given the combination of precautions and countermeasures that the Haganah had implemented. "Caches of arms," its report explained, "are spread over a considerable area and buried at some depth, and even when likely areas in which the illegal arms are concealed are known, success in finding them depends on being able to pinpoint their location. Moreover, the use of mechanical means, such as mine detectors, is frustrated by the practice of scattering small pieces of metal in the vicinity of the hidden arms."[17]

Further evidence of the stagnation in British military thinking may be seen in the discussions that now resumed concerning the use of heavy weapons (for example, artillery fire and aircraft bombardment) in Palestine. With arms searches again ruled out, the Chiefs of Staff lobbied for permission to use "'appropriate weapons' once the responsibility for quelling any disturbances had passed from the Civil to the Military Authorities." The policy directive that ultimately emerged in December 1945 from these renewed discussions embraced the same three categories of geographically defined areas and structures and buildings that had first been proposed by the Joint Planning Staff the previous February. Accordingly, any use of such weapons was completely prohibited in Category A, which included the Old City of Jerusalem and important, historical religious shrines and sites elsewhere in Palestine. Category B listed significant cultural sites, like the Jerusalem Museum, that could only be targeted with the express consent of both the high commissioner and the Middle East commander in chief. Finally, Category C defined structures that should not be attacked unless the successful execution of military operations made it "unavoidably necessary" and included some ancient synagogues and crusader castles. Restrictions on attacking populated areas were not, as the staff officer charged with the first draft of the policy had initially feared, "watered down"—but in fact were eliminated completely. At the cabinet Defence Committee meeting that approved the directive, Bevin was quick to recognize the politically explosive repercussions should this policy become public. Hence, the committee agreed that the granting of this authority to the commanders in chief in the Middle East must remain a closely guarded secret.[18]

"Dead battles, like dead generals, hold the military mind in their dead grip, and Germans, no less than other peoples, prepare for the last war," the Pulitzer Prize–winning American historian Barbara Tuchman famously wrote in *The Guns of August*. Alas, this was no less true for British generals contemplating the Jewish rebellion in 1945. Conditioned by their experiences fighting rural Arab rebels and brigands a decade earlier, they assumed that the same weapons and tactics would succeed against the Jews as well. The Arab Rebellion, however, was very different from the escalating Jewish conflict. It had been both a guerrilla war and a popular uprising. Virtually all of the fighting had occurred in the countryside, where rebel bands had moved and fought in large, discernible formations. Accordingly, the methods that the army used to defeat the rebels were straightforward. The enemy had been easily sighted and engaged in open country well suited to aerial and artillery bombardment. Pitched battles were often fought with the security forces that lasted hours and in one instance an entire day. The Arab guerrillas, moreover, had been almost unanimously supported by the rural Arab populace. Therefore, villages guilty of assisting the rebels had been punished without difficulty: either the houses of specific people implicated in revolutionary activities were destroyed, or a collective fine was levied on the entire village. Artillery and air bombardment were also used against rebel firing positions in houses and other structures without much concern for collateral casualties among civilians close to the fighting.[19]

But unlike the Arab Rebellion, the Jewish revolt was predominantly urban. It was fought in the setting that best provided the terrorist with means of concealment and escape. In addition, the Jewish terrorists were organized into small, conspiratorial cells that buried themselves within the surrounding community. They did not fight en masse or in open spaces, but functioned in stealth, in small numbers, and in conditions where guile counted more than firepower. Indistinguishable from the ordinary, law-abiding citizen, these men and women remained anonymous and undetectable in the absence of informants or intelligence from agents who had been able to penetrate the groups, and they were hence beyond the reach of the army and the police. Moreover, only a small portion of the Yishuv actually belonged to or actively supported the Irgun or Lehi. Although a far larger number were involved in Haganah activities, actual membership in that organization was not universal. This meant that punishing Jewish communities either monetarily or with artillery or air bombardment was problematic. Only once was a Jewish settlement or neighborhood penalized: the government had imposed a £500 fine on Givat Shaul the previous year for having served as a staging area and escape venue in Lehi's attempted assassination of MacMichael. Indeed, despite the granting of the authorization for aerial bombardment, no Jewish settlement or neighborhood was ever bombed or strafed.

In addition to these key differences, the Arab Rebellion was a particularly poor model on which to base a strategy given that it had never actually been militarily defeated. Rather, communal exhaustion brought on by three years of warfare, unrelenting strikes, and internecine bloodletting, coupled with the dramatic reversal of British policy contained in the 1939 white paper, accounted for the insurrection's collapse. Regardless, Britain's most senior military commanders were intent on applying an anachronistic inheritance from a previous conflict to the present one. The Colonial Office appears to have been the only government entity attempting to make any distinction between the Arab Rebellion and the Jewish revolt and draw the appropriate lessons.[20]

At this critical juncture in Britain's rule of Palestine, with Anglo-Zionist relations having reached a nadir, on November 21 the new high commissioner, General Sir Alan Cunningham, arrived in Palestine. This was the first civilian job for the fifty-eight-year-old bachelor, a career soldier. In 1941, he had been among Britain's most celebrated wartime generals. Taking command of the East African army, Cunningham led seventy-seven thousand Commonwealth troops in a relentless advance from Kenya to Ethiopia. In less than ninety days he had achieved the impossible: vanquishing an enemy force four times larger; restoring the deposed Ethiopian emperor, Haile Selassie, to his throne; and destroying Italy's African colonial ambitions. Lauded for his military brilliance by a nation desperate for victory after the previous year's successive reversals in Norway and France, Cunningham was catapulted into command of the legendary Eighth Army in the Western Desert in August 1941.[21]

Cunningham, however, was an artillery officer who knew nothing of armored fighting, much less desert warfare. Moreover, he had been ordered to achieve a decisive victory in an impossibly unrealistic, compressed time frame. Arrayed against German and Italian forces commanded by Lieutenant General Erwin Rommel, Cunningham committed a series of tactical blunders that threatened to turn imminent victory into abject defeat, and he was removed from command. He returned to Britain depressed and disconsolate. Churchill was adamant that he never again be employed as a soldier and threatened to make a public example of Cunningham's alleged loss of nerve and lack of initiative—comparing him to the hapless admiral John Byng, who was shot by firing squad in 1757 for failing "to do his utmost" to engage the enemy. Only the repeated intercession of Cunningham's influential friend General Alan Brooke, who had recently become CIGS, rescued his military career, although Cunningham thereafter occupied a succession of unimportant command positions in Northern Ireland and England.[22]

Palestine thus provided Cunningham with a chance to reclaim a shattered career. Although he hated being out of uniform, like Gort, Cunningham did not dwell on his misfortune. Thomas Scrivenor, the Palestine government's principal assistant secretary, lived in Government House with Cunningham for five months and recalled the high commissioner as "charming . . . a delightful host and a very nice man." Ivan Lloyd Phillips, the district commissioner for Gaza and Beersheba, similarly found Cunningham a "pleasant rational individual . . . essentially honest, straightforward and direct; an English country gentleman."[23]

"It has always been said that the soldiers were by far the most successful of the British rulers of Palestine," wrote Professor Edward Ullendorff, who was a student at Hebrew University before the war and briefly afterward a junior civil servant in the Palestine government. This was exactly *The Palestine Post*'s reaction. "It is noteworthy," an editorial comment read, "that the Governors who have left behind the kindest memories, and taken with them the greatest measure of goodwill have all been professional soldiers." They were certainly the most popular with the Yishuv, and Cunningham was no exception. Ben-Gurion described Cunningham as "courteous and friendly"—if somewhat out of his depth. The Jewish community was thus generally pleased by the appointment. "Good—that means fairness and firmness," a shopkeeper told the London *Times*'s Palestine correspondent in a comment taken to reflect the prevailing sentiment. In his inaugural address to the country, Cunningham pledged to work impartially with all sides to achieve a just and lasting peace. "I am therefore as certain as I stand here that unless in the future we can cooperate, the one with the other, then this world is doomed indeed," he said. "I have come here with no preconceived ideas, no sense of partisanship . . . [and] I will never forget that those problems which are presented to me are human problems and ones to be dealt with in human sympathy and understanding." True to his word, Cunningham was lauded by the prominent American attorney and member of the Anglo-American Committee of Inquiry, Bartley Crum, as "one of the few British officials I met in whom I found a sympathetic understanding of both the Arab and Jewish positions."[24]

These hopeful words of conciliation notwithstanding, the enormity of the task before Cunningham must have seemed overwhelming. Only hours earlier, the curfew imposed on Tel Aviv had been lifted, and the last airborne troops had returned to their barracks. The goodwill and cheering crowds that greeted the new high commissioner along the route he traveled from Lydda Airport to his residence at Government House barely concealed the tensions permeating the country. "Appreciate my job at moment is to keep things as quiet as possible to let [the Anglo-American] Committee get to work," Cunningham wrote to Bevin shortly after his arrival. "But lid may blow off. Situation seems to have got past swaying by logic . . . [I]s it the Government's policy," the high commissioner asked, "to clean up the situation even if [it] means much bloodshed? i.e., a major military operation?" "If necessary yes" was the foreign secretary's laconic reply.[25]

It is significant that the high commissioner, who in fact reported to the colonial secretary, nonetheless took his instructions from Bevin as well. From the beginning, Cunningham thus found himself in an impossible situation: charged with fulfilling the dictates of two masters and perennially having to navigate between foreign policy priorities and internal governance exigencies. As Ben-Gurion later observed, "Cunningham must often have felt like a fireman sent to quell a blaze, standing with hose in hand while the stop-cock was being operated by the commander back at headquarters; and what the commander was sending through the pipe was not water but petrol." By "commander," Ben-Gurion meant Bevin.[26]

Cunningham hardly had time to settle in before he was presented with his first crisis less than thirty-six hours after his arrival. Under cover of darkness on November 22, a Greek schooner, the SS *Demetrius* (rechristened the *Berl Katznelson* in memory of a recently deceased Labor Zionist leader), lay at anchor off an empty stretch of beach about twelve miles north of Tel Aviv. On board were more than two hundred European refugees who had been transported from Europe by the Haganah as part of its clandestine immigration operation, Bricha (escape or flight). Two rowboats manned by Palmach fighters were methodically bringing the penultimate group of illegal immigrants ashore when a Royal Navy destroyer appeared. A boarding party arrested the remaining twenty refugees, who were transferred to the internment camp at Athlit, as well as the Palmach oarsmen, who were sent to the prison at Latrun. This was the government's first successful seizure of a ship illegally transporting Jewish survivors. The Haganah decided to retaliate by implementing an existing plan to destroy the lighthouses in the Coast Guard stations at Givat Olga and Sidna Ali—the two posts closest to the spot where the *Demetrius* was boarded. Two nights later, units of the Palmach's Fourth Battalion blew up both facilities. Fourteen police were wounded.[27]

The next morning, police tracker dogs picked up the trail that the raiders had used to attack the Givat Olga station and followed it to two nearby Jewish settlements. The officer in charge was Raymond Cafferata, the same police superintendent who two years before had overseen the raid at Ramat Ha-Kovesh and had been present in Hebron during the 1929 riots. He ordered the mukhtar (village head) at Givat Hayim to assemble the male inhabitants so that identification checks could be conducted. The mukhtar refused as settlers armed with sticks gathered menacingly at the front gates, forcing the police to withdraw. A siren was sounded inside the compound that could be heard as far away as the city of Netanya, some six miles down the coast. It was a prearranged signal to summon help from surrounding communities. Workers immediately commandeered city buses, instructing the drivers to head straight for Givat Hayim. A roadblock manned by paratroopers stopped them, but trucks coming from different directions were able to cut across the fields and reach the settlement. Additional police and paratroop units now also arrived and by nightfall had cordoned off the area.[28]

At daybreak police again attempted to enter Givat Hayim and were once more repulsed. Several baton charges failed to disperse the crowd, which fought back with bricks and clubs. Troops in full battle gear, backed by tanks, were now ordered into the compound. Just as a semblance of calm was returning, a mob of some five hundred people, armed with all manner of clubs and cudgels, was spotted advancing in a line about five hundred yards across toward the settlement. They were residents of Hadera, Pardess Hannah Karkur, and Ein Hahoresh who had come to join the settlers. The paratroopers quickly took up positions to block their path. According to Hall's statement in the House of Commons, the soldiers came under automatic weapons and rifle fire—a claim vigorously denied in a statement issued by the Vaad Le'umi. Only then had the unit's commander given the order to open fire. Five Jews were killed and more than fifty wounded before the mob dispersed and order could be restored.[29]

Events at Rishpon and Shefayim followed a similar pattern. In addition to multiple baton charges, the police had to use tear gas and the soldiers their rifle butts and bayonets to quell rioting in both locations. After some three thousand people from the surrounding area tried to break the cordon around Rishpon manned by First Infantry troops, RAF Spitfire fighter planes were called in to swoop down low and scatter the crowd. By the time the disturbances finally ended, eleven battalions of troops—

approximately eleven thousand men—had been deployed, in addition to the quick-reaction Police Mobile Force and regular uniformed officers. Eight Jews lay dead, seventy-five had suffered injuries of various kinds, and nearly four hundred had been detained for questioning.[30]

The country's major Jewish city and the heartland of its agricultural belt had now been rocked by violence within two weeks of each other. Each had necessitated massive military interventions before order could be restored, thus illustrating both the depth of popular despair and the Yishuv's intention to forcibly resist any policy line that did not accord with Zionist demands. The British military and the Zionist leadership respectively drew their own lessons. For the military, it was clear that the response to the searches was well planned and well executed: the product of a disciplined organization with formidable command-and-control capabilities. Henceforth, the manpower requirements for security operations that only a few weeks earlier would have been regarded as routine would have to be adjusted significantly upward.[31]

For Ben-Gurion, the lesson was as profound as it was depressing. To his mind, the heavy-handed military response was an unmistakable signal that the Foreign Office's entrenched anti-Zionism had triumphed over the pro-Zionist sensibilities of the British Labour Party. There was little doubt that more serious confrontations would follow. But for the moment Ben-Gurion remained unwilling to precipitate or authorize that clash, rejecting a Palmach plan to ambush British forces returning from search operations.[32]

British intelligence thus correctly interpreted these developments as defensive in nature and limited to facilitating illegal immigration. The DSO's analysis was also correct in dismissing the likelihood of any outright revolt involving both the Haganah and the Palmach. Although the police took the same position, army intelligence was more equivocal. Both the Irish War of Independence and the Arab Rebellion, its analysts argued, had established precedents of how armed struggle had changed British policy—which now figured prominently in the Yishuv's calculations.[33]

Palestine's civilian administrators were clearly even more pessimistic. Two weeks earlier, the Executive Council, on which all the country's most senior colonial administrators sat, had authorized the issuance of firearms to its members as well as to all district commissioners, assistant district commissioners, and other senior officers "considered to be in particular danger of attack." And within days of the dissemination of the above intelligence assessment, these same officials had presented Cunningham with a proposal to impose martial law over the entire country. The high commissioner was genuinely perplexed. The army had not requested such authority, he explained to Shaw, nor had the GOC, Lieutenant General John D'Arcy, expressed any particular concerns. For the moment at least, he saw no reason for so extreme and drastic a measure that would have placed Palestine under complete military control and rendered continued civilian governance irrelevant.[34]

But Cunningham was under no illusion about the volatility of the current situation. Ten days earlier, the Irgun had raided the Ras al-Ain RAF base and made off with two truckloads of armaments, including forty machine guns and two cases of hand grenades. "Jewish leaders are intransigent and intractable," he told Hall on December 4. Nearly half the Yishuv, moreover, is "definitely desirous of offensive armed action against us no matter how foolish or suicidal this policy may seem to be." Appeals to reason had gone nowhere, the high commissioner continued, because the entire Yishuv was in "a highly emotional and hysterical state." Cunningham was still hopeful that an outright confrontation could be avoided, but he believed that the best means to achieve this was "by influencing world opinion rather than by anything we can do here." Specifically, he thought that an aggressive public relations campaign needed to be undertaken in America to counter the increasing stridency of Zionist propaganda efforts there. Although Halifax, the ambassador in Washington, was skeptical, senior MI5 officials in London jumped at the opportunity. In addition to tapping the phone lines and intercepting all mail to and from the Jewish Agency's London, Jerusalem, and New York offices, they received permission to include its Washington, D.C., facility.[35]

As the New Year beckoned, Cunningham's overriding preoccupation was to quiet the country and thus smooth the way for the Anglo-American Committee's visit. To this end, he tried to think boldly and broadly, casting about for some modus vivendi with the mainstream Zionist leadership that would address the Yishuv's most immediate grievances and hopefully isolate the extremists and undermine their influence. The high commissioner outlined his thoughts in a two-page, handwritten letter to Shaw just before Christmas. The problem, Cunningham explained, could be divided into its "humanitarian" and its "political" dimensions. The plight of European Jewry understandably consumed the Yishuv, the high commissioner reasoned. And it was this issue that a minority extremist element had seized upon to further its own hard-line political agenda. The solution was obvious: because those Jews in Palestine with family members remaining in liberated Europe were likely to be the most aggrieved, it was this constituency whose concerns should be addressed first in order to begin to wean popular opinion away from the extremist camp. He therefore proposed that the government consider issuing immigration certificates to "proved destitute close relations" of Jews already resident in Palestine. This measure would have the multiple benefits of reuniting separated families and assuaging a salient source of discontent, calming an explosive situation, and thus permitting the committee to conduct its investigations in a "more rational and less disturbed" atmosphere. Alas, before Cunningham could present his idea to London, Palestine was once again plunged into crisis.[36]

Shortly after 7:00 p.m. on December 27, an Irgun team blew up an electrical substation in Jerusalem, blacking out the downtown commercial district. At that very moment, a combined force of Irgun and Lehi fighters positioned in the historic Assicurazioni Generali Insurance Building opened fire with automatic weapons on the CID headquarters across Jaffa Road in Jerusalem's Russian Compound. A Lehi demolition squad now stormed the CID offices and blew the door open. Rushing inside, they shot dead a police officer and, advancing deeper into the building, laid their explosive charges, lit the fuses, and withdrew. The ensuing explosion ripped the façade off the three-story building. The blast killed another police officer and four South African Basuto soldiers on guard duty. A gun battle erupted in the streets as other police gave chase. Three more British police were gunned down a couple of blocks away, outside the Orion Cinema off Ben Yehuda Street. One of the attackers was also mortally wounded before the rest of the team could make good their escape. A simultaneous assault was foiled at the CID district headquarters situated on the Tel Aviv–Jaffa border, as police and Sixth Airborne troops positioned on the surrounding rooftops were able to disrupt the attack. Explosive charges nonetheless damaged part of the building and claimed the life of an Arab telephone operator. Concurrently, an Irgun unit attacked the Royal Electrical and Mechanical Engineers workshop in Tel Aviv in search of weapons. The workshop's armory was less well stocked than had been anticipated, and under heavy fire the raiders withdrew after killing a British sergeant and losing one of their own men. The death toll of British security forces was ten dead and twelve wounded in the worst spate of terrorism in more than a year.[37]

The Palestine government responded swiftly, imposing a curfew on the Jewish sections of Jerusalem and on Tel Aviv and Ramat Gan early the following morning. At daybreak, police and soldiers commenced house-to-house searches and identification checks in all three locations. According to one account, as many as fifteen thousand people were screened in Jerusalem, of whom four thousand were detained for further questioning. In Tel Aviv and Ramat Gan, fifteen hundred people were similarly scrutinized and nearly sixty taken into custody. Although the curfews and searches were certainly undertaken in hopes of apprehending the people responsible for the attacks, they were also clearly meant to be punitive. An indignant government spokesman drove home this point, arguing that "only people like Hitler . . . have indulged in this sort of [wanton violence]—Hitler, the greatest enemy the Jews ever had. It was the British who had a very considerable part in eliminating Hitler and today here in Palestine they are being attacked by Jews."[38]

The personal tragedy suffered by nine-year-old Ann Turton only heightened the sense of outrage explicated by the above spokesman. She had now lost two fathers to Jewish terrorism. Her natural father had been one of the four CID officers who three years earlier had been lured by Lehi to a booby-trapped Tel Aviv apartment building where they all were killed. Her mother, who had just recently died, had subsequently married another British police officer, Assistant Superintendent George F. Smith. His body had been pulled from the rubble of the Jerusalem CID headquarters, and her designated guardian, Superintendent Howard Beard, had been wounded by the blast. In a 1973 interview, Beard, the longest continuously serving officer in the history of the PPF, having joined in 1920, bitterly recalled the incident: "It was cold blooded savagery and of all the nations of the world, the British deserved such treatment less than any. I wondered then, as I wonder now, what one has to do to convince Jews that they have no more and no less rights than anyone else."[39]

On the morning of December 28 both Ben-Gurion and Shertok were summoned to Government House. The high commissioner wanted answers to two questions: whether the Jewish Agency had been involved in the attacks and, if not, whether it was prepared to cooperate with the government in apprehending the people responsible for the previous night's "outrages"—the euphemism widely used by British authorities in both Jerusalem and London to describe acts of Jewish terrorism. Ben-Gurion glibly replied that the agency was no more responsible for the attacks than the government's policies that had provoked them. He then tried to change the subject, complaining that all requests for an official inquiry into killings of Jewish settlers by British soldiers at Givat Hayim the previous month had been ignored. Cunningham would have none of it, retorting that he had conducted his own investigation of the Givat

Hayim incident and was satisfied that the shootings were justified. Returning to the matter at hand, he asked if the Jewish Agency was prepared to
help bring the perpetrators of the violence to justice. Again Ben-Gurion
prevaricated. He could not commit to anything without first consulting
his colleagues. In any event, Ben-Gurion's own view was that cooperation
was no longer feasible; anti-British feeling within the Yishuv was now too
strong.[40]

The following day Ben-Gurion issued a detailed statement to the press
recounting almost word for word the discussion that he and Shertok had
with Cunningham. As Daphne Trevor observed in her contemporaneous chronicle of the final years of British rule over Palestine, the Jewish
Agency statement "was not a declaration of principle, but a statement of
political facts. The regime which had to come into existence to establish
and maintain the White Paper had at last created so general and so solid
a hostility to the Government that the Agency leaders judged it futile to
call for active opposition to terrorism. They believed that if they tried to
do so they would fail and would thus cease to represent Palestine Jewry in
any effective sense."[41]

To Cunningham, however, it was a declaration of war. Only hours earlier
he had recounted for Hall his discussions with D'Arcy about the options
at the government's disposal given Ben-Gurion's statement that the Jewish Agency could no longer control the Yishuv. Cunningham thought it
was still premature to implement the ultimate sanction of occupying the
Jewish Agency headquarters building (popularly known in Hebrew as the
Sochnut) in Jerusalem and interning its leadership. The potential disruptions that would attend the Anglo-American Committee's visit again figured prominently in his thinking. But after reading Ben-Gurion's account
of the meeting in the press, Cunningham changed his mind.[42]

The cabinet met on New Year's Day 1946 to consider the matter. The
arms search option was again raised, discussed, and dismissed. The proposal to detain the Jewish Agency leadership was also considered—but
deferred for the time being. However, Cunningham's suggestion to grant
immigration certificates to Jewish Holocaust survivors with close relations already in Palestine was approved, though pending the consent of
the region's Arab governments.[43]

In point of fact, the Haganah had neither approved nor authorized the
December 27 attacks. Its own statement, issued under the heading "This
Is Not the Path," termed the operation "irresponsible acts that facilitate
the government's war on the Zionist enterprise and hinder our crucial
struggle." At the same time, though, the Jewish Agency had known in

advance of the Irgun's plans, even providing the authorities with what British intelligence described as a "half hearted warning that . . . [the] targets might be police stations." But the information was judged too imprecise to be of any practical value and, as Paget explained to the CIGS, Field Marshal Alan Brooke, "probably had [the] object of covering" the agency's back. The reality of the situation as 1946 began was perhaps best summed up by Nathan Friedman-Yellin, a member of the Lehi high command, in an interview with the Jewish Telegraphic Agency. "We are at war with the British Empire now," he stated. "There is no other way. The British are determined that Palestine shall never become a Jewish State. We are equally determined that it will." Any hopes of resolving this dispute peacefully had been overtaken by events. "It is clear now," the Lehi commander declared, "that the aim of the Jewish people cannot be realized through conferences, commissions and the writing of memorandums."[44]

To a country wearied by six years of warfare, with its citizens still queuing because of food, gasoline, and other rationing, the advent of the New Year in Great Britain was a correspondingly somber affair. As a percentage of population, Britain had almost twice as many men still serving in its armed forces as the United States—a further burden on its depleted Treasury. Of this number, nearly fifty thousand were required in Palestine to maintain order. And a succession of bleak intelligence assessments throughout the fall and winter had repeatedly underscored the impossibility of a reduction in those troop levels anytime soon.[45]

Numbers alone painted a sufficiently depressing picture. Both American and British intelligence put the Haganah's strength at some 50,000 trained personnel, with the Palmach's "shock troops" comprising an additional 5,000 men. The Irgun was thought to have between 3,500 and 5,000 members, of whom 1,200 to 2,000 were estimated to be combatants. Lehi was reckoned by some reports to have no more than 250 members and upwards of 500 by others. If we adjust for imprecision or exaggeration, a parity of sorts thus existed in the number of government security forces and Jewish fighters—an unenviable balance in the best of circumstances. The rule of thumb for government success in counterinsurgency, for instance, has historically been set at a ratio of ten or even twenty soldiers and police to every irregular fighter. Even accepting five to one as the minimum ratio required for successful urban operations, the number of British forces positioned in Palestine at the start of 1946 was woefully inadequate.[46]

Worse, reports came that the Irgun's operational capacity had been further enhanced by the arrival of some three hundred illegal immigrants with prior experience as Jewish partisans fighting the Nazis in Poland, including six persons who had taken part in the Warsaw ghetto uprising. These men joined an estimated sixty Jews who had served in British army commando units during the war and had recently been organized as an elite strike force within the Irgun. Still more disquieting news followed at the end of the month, when British intelligence learned of the Haganah high command's decision to strengthen collaboration between the Palmach and the Irgun. To this end, some 460 Palmach fighters had been lent to the Irgun, and £300,000 of Haganah funds was allocated to its new ally to underwrite the joint operations. A first installment of this payment, amounting to £56,000, had reportedly already been paid to the Irgun, and the first Irgun mission involving the Palmach men had been successfully executed—the armed robbery of £35,000 from a train near Hadera. As a quid pro quo the Irgun had reportedly agreed to stop extorting money from wealthy Jews and stealing from Jewish merchants and to submit for Haganah review and approval all its attack plans.[47]

The increasing reach and growing sophistication of the Jewish underground's intelligence gathering was another source of profound worry. A CID assessment, for instance, described the formidable capabilities of the Irgun's intelligence unit and its penetration of both the Palestine government and the police. "They are in a position to tap telephones, open mail, and even to have access to official correspondence between Government Departments," the report explained, with the effect of obtaining advance knowledge of "exactly when and where searches are to be made, and make their arrangements accordingly." Another PPF analysis of the Irgun noted that "their 'Intelligence Branch' is excellent, with secret agents in all walks of life: employed in the main hotels, and even in police headquarters. A number of their rank and file—apart from their normal military training—must enlist for a year in the Palestine police: Inspector-General Rymer-Jones said 'We must have had a turn-over of thousands.' Finally their discipline is as strict as any army in the world."[48]

A document captured at a Lehi safe house in Tel Aviv early in January 1946 was similarly revelatory about that organization's intelligence capabilities. Lehi operatives routinely cultivated sources among police officers, government officials and employees, soldiers and seamen, personnel in Jewish organizations, journalists, radio and telephone operators, factory owners, and private security guards and watchmen. "In connection with the acquisition of equipment," the document recounted how "attention is paid to the prospects of acquiring arms by theft and purchase; tailors and launderers are to be contacted to obtain uniforms of all kinds; topographical instruments, maps, binoculars, military headgear, Government and Army forms, passes and documents, rubber stamps, radio and signaling equipment, military telephone directories and other military literature and the use of transport are wanted." The challenge of extracting information from captured Lehi fighters was cited in still another intelligence report. "I must warn you . . . that these terrorists are hard nuts to crack," Alexander Kellar advised Trafford Smith in the Colonial Office, "and it is by no means easy to get them to talk."[49]

At a meeting held in the Colonial Office on January 9, Rymer-Jones detailed for Hall the extent to which the Jewish police section of the PPF had been thoroughly suborned by all three underground organizations. Jewish police officers, accordingly, "could be relied upon only for routine duties not involving security," with the situation especially grave in Tel Aviv, where PPF operations had been the most negatively impacted.[50]

Rounding out this dismal picture was the terrorists' own growing popularity with the Yishuv and the mounting disquiet their activities were causing among Arabs both in Palestine and farther afield. "Admiration for the skill and the courage of the terrorists" was palpable across the entire Jewish community, Lieutenant Colonel Martin Charteris, the director of military intelligence at army headquarters in Jerusalem during 1945 and 1946, who later became private secretary to Queen Elizabeth II, wrote. "Actuated by a spirit of complete ruthlessness, which takes no account of human life, provided with an abundance of targets and the initiative enabled to make their reconnaissance on the spot, and, above all, protected by the local population who are at best too frightened to give them up and at the worst, entirely their supporters, they have an enormous advantage over the forces of law." Arab opinion in Palestine, meanwhile, was reportedly becoming more hostile to Britain, with complaints about the inadequacy of the government's response to both Jewish terrorism and illegal immigration increasingly expressed. These developments, the British legation in Baghdad reported, were unfavorably impacting Iraqi attitudes toward Britain.[51]

The challenges facing the army in Palestine at this time are perhaps best captured by Lieutenant General Richard "Windy" Gale's recollection of his first inspection visit to the country in January 1946. Gale had just been appointed to command the First Infantry Division, which was completing its retraining and reorganization in Egypt before returning to Palestine. This innovative, battle-hardened soldier was stunned by what he saw on a large wall map of Palestine at Jerusalem headquarters depicting with red pushpins the myriad installations, communications nodes, and other vital facilities deemed vulnerable to terrorist attack and thus requiring protection. "The map looked more like a child suffering from an attack of measles than a display of serious military dispositions," he recalled. His commanding officer, D'Arcy, also regarded the situation with grave dismay. "I can find no precedent and little help in our long history of Imperial policing," he wrote to his men in a directive dated January 11. "You will realise too," the GOC emphasized, "that the object of the opposition will be, very largely, to discredit us in the eyes of the world and that no occasion for propaganda to that end will be missed and that no sacrifice of their own innocent people will, for one moment, deter them."[52]

The uneasy quiet that had settled over Palestine with the start of the New Year ended on January 19, when the Irgun struck multiple targets in Jerusalem. The pattern was similar to the previous month. An Irgun team blew up the electric substation on St. Paul's Road shortly after eight in the evening, thus blacking out the area of the city where the main assaults would occur. Minutes later, under cover of darkness, separate Irgun teams simultaneously converged on the Russian Compound police headquarters, the central prison on the compound's eastern edge, and the nearby Palestine Broadcasting Service studios on St. Paul's Road. A series of explosive charges planted by Irgun sappers damaged parts of the police facility and the prison, and the attackers safely withdrew. A British army patrol intercepted the twin assault parties approaching the radio station. A fierce firefight erupted in which an army officer was mortally wounded and two of the terrorists were killed. A third was wounded and taken prisoner. As the raiders retreated, they planted land mines to slow any pursuit. An army truck detonated one of the mines, and then a police bomb disposal expert died while attempting to disarm another. Given the restrictions that the cabinet had recently imposed on security operations, Cunningham had few options. For the second time in a month, he ordered a curfew imposed on Jerusalem's Jewish neighborhoods, the previous one having been lifted only two weeks before. This curfew, however, was stricter. All movement was forbidden between the hours of four in the afternoon and ten in the morning. Police and army units also mounted house-to-house searches of several Jewish neighborhoods. Some 3,000 people were interrogated, of whom 150 were detained for further questioning. The network of ancient caves and cisterns beneath homes in the Old City's Jewish Quarter was subjected to especially intense searches for hidden arms by the PMF and a battalion of the Highland Light Infantry.[53]

The following evening brought more bad news. Earlier in the day, a Palmach demolition team disguised as painters had smuggled explosives concealed in paint cans into the Coast Guard station at Givat Olga, which was being rebuilt following the November attack. Shortly before 9:30 p.m. a phone call was made to the installation warning the British police and the anti-aircraft squad stationed at the facility to evacuate the area without delay. The warning was ignored, and seventeen men were injured, including a soldier who later died of his wounds. About the same time, the RAF radar installation on Mount Carmel in Haifa, which also tracked ships suspected of bringing illegal immigrants to the country, received a similar phone message. The caller explained that a time bomb was set to explode and hence the facility should be evacuated immediately. A soldier, however, was able to defuse the device. "We learnt a lesson from this incident," Yigal Alon, the group's commander, said later. "It is necessary to also use booby traps that cannot be defused and that will at the very most kill only the person attempting to dismantle" any bombs.[54]

At a loss of what else to do, Cunningham decided to strengthen the existing Defence (Emergency) Regulations in force over the country since September 1945 with additional amendments. These extraordinary legal powers, it will be recalled, had first been promulgated as the Palestine (Defence) Order in Council in 1936 shortly after the start of the Arab Rebellion. Subsequent amendments in 1937 had introduced increasingly severe penalties for people convicted of a variety of violent and seditious acts. Under its core provisions, people convicted of carrying, discharging, or possessing firearms and explosives faced either the death penalty or life imprisonment. With the end of the Arab Rebellion, however, life imprisonment was adopted as the most severe penalty that could be imposed on a person found guilty of these crimes.[55]

The Order in Council had been invoked again following the resumption of the Irgun's revolt in 1944 and then expanded under the Defence (Emergency) Regulations promulgated in September 1945 mostly so that the death penalty could be imposed on people convicted of carrying, discharging, or possessing firearms or explosives. Now, under the 1946 amendments, soldiers were given the right to arrest people without having to produce a warrant or court order and to detain them for up to seven days without having to justify this action before a court of law. Nor were warrants needed to conduct searches of any dwelling or building. Trial by military tribunals was also reinstated with the tribunals rendering summary judgment: that is, no pretrial inquiry was required, nor was there any disclosure requirement, so the prosecution did not have to furnish evidence of its case to the accused. Tribunal members did not require any prior legal training, and although the rules of evidence based on English law governed court proceedings, these could be relaxed at the court's discretion. Finally, there was no right of appeal: the GOC alone had the authority to confirm, pardon, or overturn convictions. Life imprisonment was mandated for people convicted of wearing uniforms, parts of uniforms, or any police or military insignia or headgear, and five years' imprisonment was specified for harboring or abetting any person suspected of violating the regulations. Stiff penalties were also imposed on the master, owner, and agent of any vessel transporting illegal immigrants to Palestine, whether knowingly or not. Lastly, the high commissioner was given the right to order the forfeiture of all the property of any person convicted of any offense.[56]

The revised regulations had no impact on the worsening security situation. The day after their promulgation, the Irgun brazenly launched the first of three operations to procure arms. Although each of the assaults was thwarted, it was clear that a watershed had been crossed in terms of the logistical sustainability of the Irgun's violent struggle. Equally obvious were the nugatory prospects of deterring further attacks. Indeed, during January alone nearly a hundred police antiterrorist operations had been mounted—to no tangible effect. "We have enough physical force to prevent Britain ruling Palestine peacefully," Begin boasted in a clandestine interview given to a reporter from the *News Chronicle*, a London tabloid. A CID intelligence assessment similarly called attention to the age-old terrorist conceit that one wins against a numerically superior, better-armed, and better-equipped government opponent simply by avoiding losing: "The I.Z.L. leaders are aware that they will never intimidate Britain nor be able to combat British forces in a straight fight, but they believe in the efficiency of their present tactics, for they are convinced—and this is a fundamental tenet of their creed—that violence is the only way of inducing the British Government to give political concessions." An MI5 report that same month reached an identical conclusion, citing its own well-placed, unnamed informant.[57]

Both the police and the Palestine administration increasingly mourned the cessation of Saison operations the previous May and the collapse of antiterrorist cooperation that followed. The consequent impoverishment of police intelligence was thus a further subject of lamentation. Inevitably, the repeated assaults on heavily guarded and well-protected government facilities raised serious concerns among British officials over the security of other key government buildings, particularly the government secretariat offices and military and intelligence headquarters located in the southern wing of Jerusalem's King David Hotel. At the end of December 1945, the CID's chief, Giles, had informed Rymer-Jones of a reliable report that the Irgun was planning to blow up the hotel, part of which was still open to the public, by planting a bomb beneath the government offices in La Regence nightclub. Rymer-Jones went to see Shaw, who dismissed the threat. "I have told you that we must retain as far as possible, normal conditions," he recalled the chief secretary's reply, "and you can't take a last place of amusement away from the people." In hopes of averting what he believed to be certain disaster, Rymer-Jones appealed to Cunningham. Together with Shaw they went to Government House, where the inspector general proposed closing La Regence, positioning a policeman or soldier at every entrance to check identification of anyone wishing to visit, and generally strengthening security both inside and around the perimeter. This was in addition to the platoon of heavily armed troops, manning machine-gun pits and other defensive positions, that had already been deployed to the site since the previous year. Cunningham agreed with Rymer-Jones that the measures currently in force might now have been rendered insufficient and promised to have another security review conducted. In the end, however, the high commissioner concluded that the existing arrangements were adequate and rejected almost all of Rymer-Jones's suggestions. "We are trying, in between outrages," Cunningham explained to Hall, "to carry on a normal administration under 'peace.' The conditions are however nearer those of war than of peace."[58]

The authorities had now to contend with the threat of Jewish terrorism spreading beyond Palestine's borders as well. On February 11, Hunloke's successor as DSO, an aristocratic Oxford University graduate and former Shakespearean and Hollywood actor named Gyles Isham, informed Kellar of a Lehi plot to kill senior government ministers in England. Sources judged reliable by the CID had reported that Lehi members were being trained for this purpose and that at the top of their target list was the foreign secretary. For nearly a year, similar reports had been circulating between Jerusalem, Cairo, and London. The sophisticated operation to assassinate Lord Moyne made it difficult for British intelligence to discount completely this fragmentary information. Moreover, the extent to which Lehi had already successfully penetrated HM Forces in Egypt had given rise to genuine concern that assassins under deep cover as service personnel could travel undetected between the Middle East and England.

Information gleaned from one of the central figures in the conspiracy to assassinate Moyne, Raphael Sadovsky, substantiated these fears.[59]

These reports all dovetailed with information passed by the Jewish Agency to British intelligence that the Irgun had also already seeded overseas agents among both military personnel and merchant seamen. Irgun pamphlets posted on the doors of government offices on Whitehall during the summer of 1944, criticizing Britain for refusing to create a Jewish army, gave credence to fears that terrorist operatives were already active in London. It was now reported that Lehi was working especially hard to ensure that it had operatives in all three services "in the hope that this will facilitate travel abroad in order to keep an eye on leading English personalities."[60]

By the spring of 1945 the corpus of accumulated information on this subject was sufficiently worrisome that the director general of MI5, Brigadier Sir David Petrie, thought it time to inform the Home Office. Within months, some forty additional terrorist suspects serving with British forces in Egypt had been identified. Military leave policy was amended so that only Anglo-Jewish service personnel would be permitted to travel back to the United Kingdom. Jews from all other countries were prohibited. Jewish merchant seamen drew special attention from the authorities, because they were not subject to normal visa control procedures. Accordingly, a process was initiated whereby the identity of any Jewish seamen at a British port was carefully checked with both SIME (Security Intelligence, Middle East) in Cairo and the DSO in Jerusalem. Home Office warrants allowing MI5 to intercept mail and tap phone lines were now applied to all the major Zionist organizations with offices in London.[61]

With the New Year new reports began to surface about plots to assassinate the foreign secretary. Additional intelligence reports around this same time also claimed that Lehi was intent on killing Cunningham and D'Arcy along with senior CID officers such as John J. O'Sullivan, Richard Catling, and Arthur Giles. Any lingering skepticism of the gravity of these threats was dispelled on February 15 when a Lehi gunman tried to assassinate Superintendent Raymond Cafferata in Haifa. Shortly afterward, Cafferata returned to England. According to British officials cited in the *Daily Express*, it had become too dangerous for him to remain in Palestine. In view of the continuing reports about possible Lehi operations in Britain, on February 20 Paget ordered that all Jews traveling to the U.K. from any Middle Eastern and North African port of embarkation, including Turkey, be subject to special, enhanced security screening procedures.[62]

It had taken only ninety days to disabuse Cunningham of the hopeful optimism that had attended his arrival in Palestine. The only consistent dimension of Jewish Agency policy, the high commissioner complained, was its refusal to cooperate with the authorities. The agency's position, he continued, had again been made clear in a particularly incendiary speech that Shertok had given to the Vaad Le'umi a few days earlier. In addition to the now-standard denunciation of the 1939 white paper's continuance, the Jewish leader had delivered a seditious critique of the newly strengthened Emergency Regulations, terming them "murderous and atrocious laws, which threaten the public as a whole."[63]

On March 6 the Anglo-American Committee of Inquiry arrived in Palestine. "We left Cairo at 9:30 p.m. by the Palestine high commissioner's special train, painted white and with an extra car—between the engine and our compartments—on which the terrorists' mines could blow up," Richard Crossman, a former Oxford University don and recently elected Labour MP, recalled. It was a needless precaution. Each of the three Jewish underground organizations had pledged to abjure from operations while the committee was in Palestine—a message reinforced in repeated broadcasts by Kol Israel. However, in the hour before the commissioner's train pulled in to Jerusalem, the Irgun seized the opportunity to launch one more attack on a Sixth Airborne arms dump both to impress the country's distinguished visitors and to acquire much-needed weaponry. Army intelligence subsequently concluded that the attack had been facilitated by information that Jewish service personnel stationed at Sarafand and other bases had provided to the Irgun, thus again demonstrating the reach and sophistication of the organization's intelligence capabilities. These same officers also marveled at the preparation and precautions that the Irgun had undertaken. A team of trained Jewish nurses, for instance, had been stationed nearby to provide immediate treatment to any casualties that might be sustained in the operation.[64]

Security was thus exceptionally tight as the twelve members of the joint commission alighted at Jerusalem's incongruously small train station and paused for a group photograph. Armored vehicles and armed guards ringed the station and surrounding roads. The committee members were then quickly whisked away to their accommodations at the King David Hotel—about a quarter of a mile away—in huge, brand-new Ford Mercury sedans. "It was immediately apparent that Jerusalem, at least, was an armed camp," Bartley Crum observed. "Barbed wire in great coils was everywhere, tanks could be seen at various intersections, special pill boxes had been put above the entrance of the hotel, and on the roofs and on the lawn of the imposing YMCA building across the street, soldiers manning machine guns surveyed all avenues of approach."[65]

These security precautions only heightened the tense atmosphere already gripping the country. Neither the Arabs nor the Jews had welcomed the committee's creation in the first place, and they had initially vowed to boycott it. The stakes, however, were too great to lose this opportunity to present their respective cases to the world via the AAC. On the one hand, the Arabs hoped to persuade the commissioners that Palestine should be granted its independence as a unitary state with a fixed Jewish minority; on the other hand, the Jews sought a favorable decision on partition that would remove the restrictions on Jewish immigration and result in the establishment of a separate Jewish state. The prevailing opinion was that this latest commission's chances of resolving the Palestine issue were no better than any of its predecessors'. In a letter to his father, Ivan Lloyd Phillips was unapologetically skeptical. "The prospect is gloomy," he wrote. "As I see it the attitude of both races is hardening and any chance of a compromise is fast vanishing."[66]

The committee's hearings commenced the following day in the auditorium at the YMCA, directly across the street from the King David Hotel. A huge, U-shaped mahogany conference table, last used nine years before by the Royal Commission, was brought out of storage and extended by two specially constructed sections to accommodate all the AAC membership.[67]

The first government witness to testify was the chief secretary, Shaw. Having twice served in the country over an eight-year time frame that spanned both the Arab Rebellion and the current Jewish uprising, Shaw arguably possessed a depth of experience and knowledge of Palestine shared by few British officials. The crux of the problem in his view was that a firm, consistent policy toward Palestine had never existed. "There have been commissions and commissions," he explained in a subsequent letter to the committee, "and they have recommended this and that and there have been debates in all the Parliaments of the world and everything else, and it has never been clear where we are heading . . . [T]he result is that both sides have always been encouraged to feel that by agitation, by terrorism and by propaganda . . . they can always swing the pendulum over to their side."[68]

Shaw's bleak assessment was echoed by D'Arcy, the GOC, whose testimony on internal security was heard in camera. He was accompanied by

Charteris, the senior army intelligence officer in Palestine, and Isham, his MI5 counterpart. "Since I have been here, since 1944, the whole threat and menace to security has come from one side," D'Arcy began. "It has come from the Jews. The Arabs have been completely quiescent." The GOC explained that although he had the equivalent of two and a half divisions of British troops in addition to the PPF, which was operationally under his command, these forces were hard-pressed to maintain order given the size and capabilities of the Jewish underground. Over the previous four months alone, terrorist attacks had claimed the lives of fifteen soldiers and police and injured more than 150 others. "As regards security generally," D'Arcy continued, "it is my firm opinion that a very large section of the Jewish community in this country is determined to get and to hold this country by force. It is a fact that large illegal Jewish armed organizations exist and it is my opinion that they exist for the purpose I have mentioned and none other." Of these, the Haganah was the largest. The GOC put its total strength now at some forty thousand people, including a well-equipped and well-trained "field army" of sixteen thousand fighters alongside an additional two thousand full-time members of the Palmach—backed by an additional four thousand trained reservists. Both groups were also well armed—mostly as a result of the extensive stocks of weaponry left behind, scrounged, or stolen from battlefields in both North Africa and Syria. "Sufficient small arms exist to give every combatant member a personal arm, rifle, submachine gun or pistol," and arms caches could be found in virtually every Jewish settlement throughout the country.[69]

D'Arcy described the Irgun as having between three thousand and five thousand members, though lacking arms. Lehi was dismissed as "nothing more than a gang" that used "assassination for the furtherance of political aims" and consisted of no more than two to three hundred members. The most serious threat was still posed by the Haganah. This same point had been made to Crossman in Cairo by a knowledgeable British source who had described the Haganah as "the most powerful military force in the Middle East, apart from the British Army," and had credited it with having "completely transformed the balance of power." The Haganah's arms were so dispersed and well hidden, the GOC declared, that it would never be possible to completely disarm the Yishuv. Even if the British could, it would accomplish nothing given the power and influence that the Jewish Agency leadership exercised over the community. "It would, in fact, be like disarming Germany after the 1914–18 war," D'Arcy commented, "and leaving the German High Command in its position to organize afresh."

His unambiguous assessment of Jewish martial prowess and preparations would have a powerful influence on the committee's thinking.[70]

The Anglo-American Committee spent a total of three weeks in Palestine. The commissioners visited Jewish kibbutzim and Arab villages, toured factories and inspected farm cooperatives, and either met with or heard testimony from a wide variety of Arab and Jewish notables along with British officials. On March 28 they departed for Lausanne, Switzerland, to write their report. Seeking to capitalize on the humanitarian plight of the Jewish displaced persons that the committee's investigations and hearings had focused on, the Jewish Agency launched a new propaganda campaign directed at British soldiers. Leaflets titled "Talk it over with your Pals" were distributed only hours after the committee left Palestine. They contained photographs of the mufti of Jerusalem, Haj Amin al Husseini, reviewing Croatian Nazi SS troops contrasted with images of soldiers from the Jewish Brigade who had fought in the British army and asked if the troops thought it was "fair or in Britain's interest to give Palestine to the Arabs." Additional photographs showed bodies of Jewish children and living survivors of Hitler's death camps with numbers tattooed on their arms side by side with happy immigrants arriving in Palestine and healthy children working and playing at a kibbutz. "Please soldier," the fly sheets implored, "don't let them make Nazis out of you."[71]

The Irgun's response to the conclusion of the Anglo-American Committee's visit unfolded on the night of April 3, when coordinated attacks were made on the Palestine railway system, causing some £16,000 of damage to track, station buildings, and rolling stock. The operation's success was vitiated, however, when a column of thirty armed Irgun fighters were spotted by an RAF reconnaissance plane near Rehovot and captured.[72]

One immediate result of these latest provocations was the recommencement of discussions in London about the military means that might be employed to bring the Yishuv to heel. The region's commanders in chief as well as Cunningham were in complete agreement with D'Arcy that seizing illegally held Jewish arms was no longer a viable option unless the entire Jewish Agency Executive and the Haganah's commanders were simultaneously arrested and indefinitely interned. This conclusion represented a major change in security policy—the first since the events at Ramat Ha-Kovesh in 1943—and one that would set the government and the Yishuv on a new collision course. Authorization for such a move, pending the cabinet's approval, was readily provided by the Chiefs of Staff. More striking still was the urgency attached to its implementation as soon as was practicable.[73]

On April 20 the Anglo-American Committee submitted its report to the British and American governments. The document itself was not publicly released for another ten days. The committee's most important recommendation was for the immediate admission of a hundred thousand Jewish displaced persons to Palestine. It also proposed that all restrictions on Jewish land purchase and transfer be terminated. The report, however, failed to endorse partition as a solution to Palestine's most fundamental political dilemma. Although the commissioners had exhaustively discussed and debated this solution, in the end they dismissed it on the grounds that "any attempt to establish either an independent Palestinian State or independent Palestinian States would result in civil strife such as might threaten the peace of the world." Accordingly, they recommended the continuation of the status quo: that British rule should continue pending review by the United Nations and the execution of a new trusteeship arrangement.[74]

The report paid particular attention to the militarized environment that the commissioners found in Palestine. "Palestine," it plainly stated, "is an armed camp." Addressing the state of public security, the commissioners recounted how "we became more and more aware of the tense atmosphere each day. Many buildings have barbed wire and other defences. We ourselves were closely guarded by armed police, and often escorted by armoured cars. It is obvious that very considerable military forces and large numbers of police are kept in Palestine." They termed the emergence of "large illegal armed forces" an especially "sinister" development and therefore recommended that if the British and U.S. governments adopted the report, "it should be made clear beyond all doubt to both Jews and Arabs that any attempt from either side, by threats of violence, by terrorism, or by the organisation or use of illegal armies . . . will be resolutely suppressed." The Jewish Agency was also directly prevailed upon to resume at once "active co-operation" with the authorities both in the suppression of Jewish terrorism and in the prevention of illegal Jewish immigration.[75]

The cabinet's Defence Committee began the British government's consideration of the report at its meeting on April 24. Bevin was alone in finding anything positive to say about it. Although he expressed profound concern about how the Arabs would react to the recommendation pertaining to the immediate admission of a hundred thousand new Jewish immigrants on top of the suspension of the land transfer restrictions, he felt that the prospect of America's support in the report's implementation and its active involvement in solving the Palestine problem outweighed any misgivings. On one point, however, the foreign secretary was emphatic: before Britain could agree to admit any more immigrants to Palestine, all illegally held arms in the country would have to be surrendered and all illegal Jewish paramilitary forces disbanded. Accordingly, he proposed asking the United States to contribute sufficient troops to assist in the enforcement of these key security provisions. Attlee, the minutes tersely record, "took a less rosy view of the report." In addition to his deep skepticism about obtaining the assistance from the United States that Bevin envisioned, the prime minister could not see how the report offered any sort of a satisfactory solution from the British point of view. To his mind, it instead "proposed a policy which would set both the Arabs and Jews against us and that we should have to go it alone . . . The burden of Palestine," he observed, "was a heavy one. It was time that others helped to share it with us"—implying that broader international involvement and support, beyond even the United States, was required.[76]

CHAPTER 13

Only Death Will Free Us

At half past eight on the evening of April 25 three vehicles pulled up to a house in a working-class district of Tel Aviv near Jaffa. Moments later its inhabitants were being held at gunpoint as one group of Lehi fighters quietly took up firing positions on the upper floor overlooking a parking lot across the street, while another group of some two dozen men crowded into the downstairs hallway. Directly opposite them was the entrance to a Sixth Airborne Division motor pool used to transport men on leave to and from the city. It was guarded by a section of six enlisted men from the Fifth Paratroop Brigade, commanded by two noncommissioned officers, all of whom were billeted in a handful of tents surrounded by a defensive perimeter consisting of a single coil of barbed wire.

The impending attack's purpose was to seize the stock of arms kept in the guard tent near the car park entrance. At 8:45 p.m. a bomb was thrown from the upstairs window toward the encampment—the signal for the assault to begin. The machine guns upstairs opened fire, raking the car park as the Lehi assault party rushed from the house—tommy guns blazing—into the encampment. Two soldiers were cut down in the guard tent as they dove for cover. Their sergeant miraculously escaped injury by lying on the floor and feigning death. He was the only survivor. The attackers hastily grabbed the weapons from the gun rack and withdrew. Meanwhile, another team of gunmen shot to death two unarmed paratroopers in an adjacent tent while they lay in bed. Three more soldiers were killed, two while coming to the aid of their fallen comrades, before the firing ceased and the Lehi team withdrew.[1]

The unbridled shock and anger that swept through the ranks both in Palestine and beyond was unprecedented. The account carried by the *Mid-East Mail*, the Cairo-based daily newspaper of British forces in the region, reported that the raid was "carried out with almost incredible barbarity," noting that one of the assailants had "callously shone a torch into the darkness so that his accomplices could riddle with automatic gun bullets British soldiers resting in their beds." Civilian British officials were equally condemnatory. Cunningham termed the massacre "nothing less than premeditated murder. There was no military objective whatsoever. This is gangsterdom in its worst form."[2]

The following morning, every major representative Jewish body in Palestine—the Jewish Agency, the Vaad Le'umi, the Histadrut, the Chief Rabbinate, and Weizmann himself—hastened to offer messages of condolence and assertions of their collective, unmitigated horror. Neither, however, could mollify the authorities nor spare the Yishuv retribution. Only hours later Cunningham met with the Palestine government's most senior officials. Nine options were considered:

- demolishing with explosives all the houses surrounding the car park—including those that had played no role whatsoever in the Lehi assault;
- seizing and having troops occupy those same structures for an indefinite period of time;
- seizing and occupying a block of buildings elsewhere in Tel Aviv for a similarly indefinite period;
- imposing a collective fine on the entire city;
- withholding government grants previously earmarked for the Tel Aviv municipality;
- delaying a £1 million government development loan to the municipality that had been approved but not yet paid;
- ordering the indefinite closure of all the city's cafés, bars, cinemas, and other places of entertainment;
- declaring Tel Aviv out-of-bounds to HM Forces; and
- imposing a curfew on the city's roads.

Two hours of exhaustive discussion followed, overshadowed throughout by the forthcoming publication of the Anglo-American Committee's report. In the end, accordingly, all the options save the general curfew and closing of all places of socializing and entertainment were rejected as either politically undesirable or impractical. Astonishingly, even declaring Tel Aviv out-of-bounds to British military personnel was dismissed because of the adverse effect on troop morale.[3]

That evening, the Sixth Airborne's commander, Major General James Cassels, summoned Tel Aviv's mayor, Israel Rokach, to his office. He explained that at 8:00 p.m. a dusk-to-dawn curfew would be imposed on all vehicular traffic in Tel Aviv and that all places of entertainment would remain closed from 8:00 p.m. until 5:00 a.m. daily for the next two weeks.[4]

But neither these measures nor a public statement conveying Cassels's opprobrium was sufficient to mitigate the anger and frustration welling inside officers and enlisted men alike. "For the first time the word outrage acquired true meaning," Blaxland writes of the attack and its aftermath. Only a week before a group of Sixth Airborne soldiers sitting in a café in Tel Aviv had been set upon by a crowd that, an official report stated, had "savagely chased . . . and kicked and injured them until they were exhausted." Jewish passersby had attempted to trip the soldiers rather than help them, and shopkeepers had denied them refuge. Rokach had also deplored that incident and had apologized to Cassels. But with this latest attack, the soldiers' pent-up rage and frustration could no longer be contained. On the night of April 26 a group of Sixth Airborne troops billeted at Qastina ran amok in Netanya and the nearby settlement of Beer Tuvya, ransacking homes and vandalizing property and beating any Jews that they happened upon. Although the miscreants were swiftly identified and punished, their actions, an intelligence assessment ominously reported, "were generally sympathised with or even applauded" by their comrades-in-arms.[5]

As Major Roy Farran, then serving in an armored unit assigned to a different part of Palestine, recalled in his memoir, "The first bitter, one sided blow was when the Stern gang murdered six [sic] parachutists in the Airborne car park in Tel Aviv . . . That was the beginning. The troops were all the more incensed that they were not allowed to retaliate. In the Arab Rebellion there had been no deep emotions. But here was the beginning of something very different." Shortly afterward a poem titled "A Soldier's Will" began to circulate among British troops in Palestine. It read,

> *A British soldier boy dying*
> *And on his bed he lay.*
> *To friends who around him sighing,*
> *These dying words he did say.*
>
> *A Jewish boy had got me at last lads,*
> *I haven't much longer to live,*
> *But before I hand my checks in,*
> *These last words of advice I do give.*
>
> *Put a bomb in the Agency building,*
> *Wipe the synagogues all off the earth,*
> *Make every damned son of Zion,*
> *Regret the day of his birth.*[6]

Lehi, on the other hand, wondered what all the fuss was about. Posters that appeared on the walls of various Jerusalem neighborhoods on the night of April 28 presented their version of the attack. It was a military operation carried out against a military target—plain and simple. "The enemy troops, being in perpetual alert position, put up armed resistance. Their resistance was broken down by our fighters," the posters explained. Lehi also specifically voiced its objections to the emotive language used by British authorities to describe the operation, now widely referred to by the military and the government alike as "the car park massacre." "This is an additional example of the record of disgusting British hypocrisy. Those who have murdered people in shackles are daring to complain about cold-blooded murder," Lehi's propagandists opined, before detailing a list of British depredations against Jewish women and children as well as those meted out to the terrorist detainees exiled to Eritrea. "The soldiers of the Airborne Division, killed during the action in Tel-Aviv, were no children, no women, no people in shackles, nor were they unarmed, they were soldiers of the 6th Airborne Division," the group unapologetically declared.[7]

It was against this backdrop of renewed tension and heightened Anglo-Zionist antipathy that the cabinet formally began its consideration of the Anglo-American Committee's report. Following the inconclusive results of the Defence Committee's meeting on April 24, Attlee had tasked a working group of senior ministerial officials to prepare in coordination with the Chiefs of Staff a more complete analysis of the report's recommendations. Its conclusions were somber. The Yishuv, they agreed, would not be satisfied with anything short of partition. "Widespread action by the Haganah is thus a possibility and continued outrages of the terrorist groups a certainty." The likely Arab reaction to the report was hardly more encouraging. Its adoption "would only provoke a general Arab rising in Palestine, which would be supported both materially and financially by the Arab states." Although sufficient troops were on hand in Palestine to cope with any immediate disturbances, implementing its recommendations would be an entirely different matter—requiring substantial reinforcements. This would further undermine the already slow pace of postwar demobilization. The working group could therefore find little in the committee's report favorable to Britain. It would have "disastrous effects on our position in the Middle East and might have unfortunate repercussions in India. It would not silence the Zionist clamour in the United States, where our administration of the policy would continue to be misrepresented and . . . provide a weapon for anti-British propaganda." The only circumstances under which the Anglo-American Committee's recommendations could be accepted, these officials and the Chiefs of Staff believed, were if the United States would agree to actively assist in their implementation. Specifically, American troops were required to enforce the provisions to ensure the surrender of illegal weapons and the dissolution of the Jewish paramilitary organizations. Both were deemed imperative given British fears that "these illegal armies would be swollen by recruits drawn from the new immigrants."[8]

At the full cabinet meeting on April 29, Bevin alone remained optimistic about both the report and the prospects of American assistance. He was also desperate to avoid having to submit the matter before the new United Nations organization. The foreign secretary wished especially to avoid the Security Council's involvement, which, he averred, would only "invite the Russians and others to get their fingers into the Palestine pie." "The essence of our policy," Bevin told the cabinet, "should be to retain the interest and participation of the U.S. Government." His colleagues disagreed. In their view, the committee's recommendations created more new problems rather than resolving existing ones. The economic burden that Britain alone would have to shoulder was a key point. According to Dalton's calculations, the cost of settling a hundred thousand Jewish immigrants in Palestine, coupled with the additional expenditures for Arab economic development that the joint inquiry recommended, would initially require some £100 million with recurrent expenses of between £5 million and £10 million annually. The cabinet therefore agreed that the report should be rejected unless the United States was willing to provide both financial and military assistance to implement it. Both those contributions, it noted, would be vital if the recommendations pertaining to the surrender of all illegal weapons and the disbanding of illegal organizations were to be enforced.[9]

Bevin's hopes of obtaining American assistance, however, were dealt a fatal blow the following day. Without first consulting or even informing Attlee, Truman announced his endorsement of the report's recommendations pertaining to Jewish immigration and land acquisition—while mostly ignoring those affecting Palestine's Arabs and Palestine's security requirements. Coming only days after the car park massacre, the president's remarks effectively doomed from the start Bevin's plan to enlist U.S. support. Grasping at straws, the foreign secretary made one last effort to win the Americans over. Appealing to his counterpart, Byrnes, Bevin wrote, "I must remind you that in Palestine British soldiers have been foully murdered by the armed forces of the Jews . . . This is a position which the British people will not be prepared to tolerate any longer, and I shall be bound to call attention to it in public . . . If the United States do not accept the implications regarding the need for disarming illegal armies before immigration, a situation which will endanger the security of the Middle East is likely to arise."[10]

Byrnes was completely unsympathetic—and in fact counseled Truman against making any military commitment whatsoever. Like Britain, the United States was intent on rapidly demobilizing its citizens still under arms as soon as possible. The British request that American forces on the order of two infantry divisions and at least one armored brigade be made immediately available for indefinite deployment to Palestine was a nonstarter. Moreover, Truman and his advisers were suspicious that British concerns about Palestine's internal security masked a grander scheme to lock the United States into a direct policing role that the United States both did not think necessary and wanted to avoid at all costs. The Pentagon's Joint Intelligence Committee concluded that there were already sufficient British troops on hand to handle any trouble that might arise.[11]

The Anglo-American Committee's report was publicly released on May 1. That day, Attlee informed the House of Commons that Britain would only accept the report's recommendations if the United States agreed to contribute military and financial assistance. On the matter of the admission of a hundred thousand Jewish immigrants to Palestine, the government's position was firm. There could be no question of allowing their entry until all illegal organizations in the country agreed to surrender their arms and disband. The prime minister specifically called upon the Jewish Agency to pledge itself to work closely with the authorities in Palestine to effect these two essential prerequisites. In that instant, the Yishuv's hopes for an immediate resolution of the displaced persons' plight vanished. Eleven days later Moshe Sneh instructed the Haganah's clandestine radio station, Kol Israel, to broadcast a warning to the British to expect a resumption of antigovernment violence.[12]

Cunningham was already anxious. On April 29 he had written to Hall to request permission to execute the internment operation. In his view, the car park attack had been a turning point in the government's efforts to avoid resorting to such an extreme measure. All other alternatives had been tried and found wanting. Cunningham worried that if the Yishuv was not brought to heel now, there would be more incidents like those that had occurred in Netanya and Beer Tuvya. "I am therefore clear that unless the Jews disband their armed forces by agreement," the high commissioner argued, "action should be taken against them as soon as possible." The Chiefs of Staff were fully behind him. They similarly believed that the security situation in Palestine was now critical: security force morale was low, anger and frustration were high, and the need to respond to the massacre of the seven paratroopers was urgent.[13]

The latest news from Palestine gave added weight to these arguments. Intelligence reports indicated that a new terrorist offensive was imminent. The Yishuv was also said to be in an especially truculent frame of mind as a result of the Anglo-American Committee's recommendations. There were also new reports that the Irgun was planning to attack the wing of the King David Hotel where the government secretariat and military and intelligence headquarters were located. And the Arabs were in a sour mood. Letters and petitions flooded the chief secretary's office denouncing the committee's proposals.[14]

"I agree the present situation is dangerous," Bevin had scribbled in the margin of a detailed letter sent to Attlee by General Hastings "Pug" Ismay, the cabinet's long-serving military secretary, whom the prime minister had sent to Palestine to assess the situation. Ismay related Cunningham's growing concern that the negotiations with the Americans had tied his hands by preventing military action against the illegal Jewish organizations. "From the military point of view," Ismay warned, "it is essential that there be no such restriction . . . Moreover if nothing is done there is [a] risk that troops will take [the] law into their own hands."[15]

This was at the forefront of D'Arcy's concerns when he met with the Chiefs of Staff on May 15. The troops had reached "the breaking point," D'Arcy argued, and should a new round of terrorist attacks occur, he did not think it would be possible to restrain them. The police were the main source of Britain's security difficulties in Palestine. The GOC described the situation as "catastrophic" given that the British section was deficient twenty-eight hundred men from its total authorized strength of fifty-five hundred personnel with recruitment efforts still foundering. As a result, duties previously performed by the police had fallen to the army, which, the GOC argued, "was utterly wrong" because it undercut the ability of the army and the police to coordinate operations and thus placed the onus for maintaining security in Palestine on the military. Replenishing the PPF's depleted ranks, the chiefs agreed, must be a priority.[16]

D'Arcy painted a similarly bleak picture when he met with Attlee and Hall at No. 10 Downing Street the following day. His emphasis, however, was more on the inherent disadvantages that confront conventional armies fighting enigmatic enemies who conceal themselves within the surrounding civilian population in urban environments. The terrorists, D'Arcy explained, always held the initiative against British forces. They had ample scope and time in choosing their objectives and carrying out any necessary reconnaissances. They could thus put in an attack when and where they pleased.

This initiative meant that British troops were always on the defensive, a role to which they were unaccustomed, and almost guaranteed that a certain success would be achieved initially.

The behavior of his troops in these difficult circumstances was "beyond praise," but the warning implicit in D'Arcy's message was clear. Unless the army was unshackled from the restrictions on offensive operations, morale and discipline would suffer. For the moment, though, Attlee's priority was to enlist U.S. support for the implementation of the AAC report's recommendation. And it was this consideration that overrode all others. Accordingly, despite the concerns repeatedly expressed by both Cunningham and D'Arcy, the restrictions on military operations in Palestine remained in place.[17]

The problem, however, was that the often febrile pace of events in Palestine rarely conformed to the ebb and flow of Whitehall's deliberative processes and still less when delicate bilateral negotiations further slowed decision making. So while the British and the Americans traded entreaty and innuendo and appointed new expert committees to reconsider their predecessors' recommendations, the Irgun and Lehi busily laid plans for renewed operations. Lehi struck first. On June 6, Dr. Israel Scheib, the group's chief ideologue and a member of its high command, known by his underground nom de guerre, Eldad, was scheduled to travel under armed escort from Latrun prison to a Jerusalem orthopedic clinic for treatment of a severe back injury sustained during his capture the previous year. The subject of a massive police manhunt, he had been cornered at the Tel Aviv high school where he taught under a pseudonym. Attempting to avoid capture, Scheib leaped from the school's roof—hence the reason he was sitting that day in the waiting room with his two-man police escort. There was a commotion as two stretcher bearers carrying a seriously injured patient rushed into the clinic. The injured man, however, suddenly jumped to his feet, pistol in hand. One of the policemen raised his tommy gun but was shot in the thigh by the Lehi gunman; the other promptly dropped his weapon. Scheib was hustled into a waiting taxi that sped off while under fire from an RAF guard detail positioned outside the clinic. The flawlessly executed operation, British intelligence subsequently noted, revealed the extent of the communication that the terrorist organizations maintained with their imprisoned comrades.[18]

It was now the Irgun's turn to embarrass the authorities. Around 6:30 on the evening of June 10, two passengers seated respectively on the Lydda–Haifa and the Lydda–Jaffa trains calmly stood up and pulled the emergency cord, forcing both trains to immediately come to a stop. Suddenly several passengers, men and women alike, were on their feet, brandishing guns. They ordered the passengers and the crew off both trains and then blew up the engines. A third attack against the Lydda–Jerusalem train instead involved a large party of some thirty armed Irgunists who boarded the train after it had stopped because of a red flag placed on the rails in front of it. Once again, the train was evacuated and rigged with explosives. The coordinated operation completely destroyed two engines and ten coaches and heavily damaged a third engine—at a cost of about £100,000. Cunningham repeated his request to put into effect the internment operation. He was again rebuffed.[19]

These events, however, were quickly overtaken by a series of developments that threatened to plunge Palestine more deeply into an abyss of mutual suspicion, recrimination, and ultimately bloodshed. On June 9, Haj Amin al-Husseini, the exiled mufti of Jerusalem and accused wartime Nazi collaborator, dramatically surfaced in Damascus. Three days of tumultuous celebration had followed across Arab Palestine, doing little to allay Jewish suspicions that Britain had somehow contrived the mufti's deliverance to the region as part of some grand conspiracy to put the Yishuv again at risk and thereby make it once more dependent on British protection. With tension thus already rife, on June 12 Bevin again stuck his foot in his mouth. Addressing the Labour Party conference in Bournemouth, the foreign secretary remarked that the only reason the United States was pressing Britain so hard to admit the hundred thousand Jewish displaced persons into Palestine was that it "did not want too many Jews in New York." Though less offensive, his further observation that Palestine's absorption of these immigrants would necessitate the deployment of at least another whole division of British troops on top of new expenditures totaling £22 million, neither of which Britain was willing or able to provide, was widely interpreted by Zionists and their American supporters as proof that despite the continuing Anglo-American discussions Bevin had already made up his mind to bar their entry into Palestine. In response, Kol Israel warned that in fact at least two or three more divisions of British troops would be required to suppress the violence that would erupt if the hundred thousand displaced persons were not admitted. This was by no means an idle threat as the Haganah and the Palmach laid plans to resume their own offensive.[20]

Into this volatile mix was added the outcome of a trial held in a Jerusalem military court on June 12 for two of the Irgun fighters apprehended following the raid on the Sarafand army base in March. Yosef Shimshon, aged nineteen, and Itzhak Ashbel, aged twenty-four, became the first two persons to receive death sentences under the recently amended Defence (Emergency) Regulations. A succession of prominent voices pleaded for mercy—among them leading editorialists and prominent religious and political figures, including Dr. Weizmann. They all condemned the crime but counseled against making martyrs of criminals and further poisoning Anglo-Zionist relations. Ashbel was in particular deemed worthy of clemency. He was described as a "poetic soul with literary ability," driven to violence by the tragedy that had been visited upon his family in wartime Poland. The Irgun, however, refused to scrape or bow on bended knee to beg for commutation. Its high command simply warned the government not to "hang the captive soldiers. If you do, we shall answer gallows with gallows."[21]

Then, in the midst of this already explosive situation, there was a development of seismic impact. On June 15, Kol Israel announced that the Haganah had obtained details of the long-standing, top secret plan, code-named Operation Broadside, to arrest and intern the Yishuv's political leadership. According to Israel Galili, the Haganah's chief of staff, this information had reached the group as a result of a casual conversation between a gentile British army officer stationed at Sarafand and his Jewish girlfriend. Like many of these officers' paramours at the time, she was a clandestine Haganah agent. Alerted to the planning document's existence, the Haganah mounted an operation to penetrate the Sarafand camp and surreptitiously gain access to the safe where the "blacklist" was kept. The document was reportedly removed, photographed, and returned without anyone in authority knowing. The radio broadcast described to its incredulous listeners every detail of the British plan before concluding, "It is perfectly clear from the order that this blacklist of candidates for imprisonment and deportation is aimed not only at the liquidation of the Hagana, but the liquidation of the entire leadership of the Yishuv . . . Let the Yishuv, the Diaspora and the whole world know what Bevin, Attlee and their henchmen are preparing for us, and let the world know that we shall fight."[22]

The Haganah moved swiftly to make good on this promise. In a brazen and unprecedented show of force, multiple Palmach commando units destroyed or damaged ten of the eleven road and rail bridges linking Palestine with Trans-Jordan, Syria, Lebanon, and Egypt the following night. Most of the targets, especially the Allenby Bridge spanning the Jordan River, were heavily guarded by British and Arab forces. Nonetheless, the meticulously executed assault—enshrined in Israel's pre-state history as "the Night of the Bridges"—caused the death of only one member of the security forces. As a message later broadcast over Kol Israel explained, the bridges had been attacked to demonstrate that if Palestine's borders were to be closed to Jewish immigrants, then they would be closed to everyone else as well.[23]

But this was just the beginning of a triad of attacks. Under cover of darkness on June 17, Lehi launched an uncharacteristic en masse assault on the Kishon railway workshops in Haifa. Some forty-five men and women attempted to bomb their way into the rail yard, having obtained details of its physical layout and defenses from an agent employed there. According to Scheib, the high command's decision to mount this operation was a reflection not only of the target's strategic importance but also of Lehi's desire to better compete with the Irgun for young recruits. At 9:15 p.m. a loud explosion was heard across Haifa as the Lehi fighters stormed the facility. Fourteen smaller blasts followed: one of which claimed the lives of two of the raiders. A locomotive was destroyed and some buildings were set on fire before the assault party withdrew. The assault took longer than had been anticipated, and the rapidity with which the army could blanket the surrounding area with roadblocks was gravely underestimated. Accordingly, a truck carrying the fleeing attackers blundered into one such checkpoint, manned by troops with heavy machine guns supported by tanks and other armored vehicles. Nine more raiders were killed, at least thirteen others were wounded, and everyone else was captured. "It is lamentable evidence," Cunningham told Hall of both the bridges and the railway workshop attacks, "of the moral and psychological degeneration caused by political extremism that this wanton destruction should have been carried out with the connivance, if not by the direction, of the Jewish authorities and that it has been greeted with no genuine expression of regret from the Jewish community."[24]

Then, the following afternoon, the Irgun put into motion its plan to blackmail the government into commuting the death sentences imposed on Shimson and Ashbel. At 1:15 p.m. a taxi carrying five armed Irgun men stopped in front of the British officers' club located in Tel Aviv's Hayarkon Hotel. That was the signal for one group of Irgunists waiting nearby to detonate a small diversionary explosion and thus distract the attention of the four-man guard detail positioned outside the hotel and for another group of Irgun gunmen to quickly surround the sentries and disarm them. The taxi's passengers now marched unimpeded straight into the hotel's dining room with pistols drawn. The roomful of officers, who just moments before had been enjoying a quiet lunch, found themselves herded into a corner where the most senior ones were pulled aside. Two who resisted were subdued with blows from a lead pipe, and the five captives (including three Sixth Airborne Division officers) were herded into two waiting cars that sped away. Shortly afterward, they were transferred to a truck that had been cleverly modified with secret coffin-like compartments concealed beneath the floorboards to prevent detection if the vehicle were stopped at a roadblock. Meanwhile, about an hour later in Jerusalem another Irgun team abducted a British army major as he strolled along King George V Avenue. A third kidnapping, however, was foiled shortly afterward when two other majors walking down the same street fought off their assailants but ended up getting shot in the process. The ease with which the Irgun seized the six men is all the more astonishing given the warning issued by the DSO's office three days before that the group had already told the Jewish Agency it was planning just such an operation.[25]

The government immediately ordered a dawn-to-dusk curfew in Tel Aviv and declared all Jewish premises out-of-bounds to British forces. Almost every Jewish newspaper and elected leader in the country pressed the Irgun to free the hostages. Fearing harsher government reprisals, the Haganah implored Begin to do the same. According to the Irgun leader, however, the Haganah's intervention was prompted less by concern over the impact that the kidnappings would have on the Yishuv than that its assaults on the bridges a few nights earlier would now be eclipsed by press coverage of the abductions. The Irgun ignored all these entreaties. Indeed, the fate of the Irgun's prisoners now became inextricably linked to that of Shimson and Ashbel—and whether or not their death sentences would, as the Emergency Regulations required, be confirmed by the GOC. That decision fell to Lieutenant General Sir Evelyn Barker, who had only recently arrived in Palestine to replace D'Arcy.[26]

Nicknamed Bubbles because of his effervescent personality, Barker had previously served in Palestine with the Tenth Infantry Brigade at the height of the Arab Rebellion in 1937. He later distinguished himself during World War II as one of Field Marshal Sir Bernard Montgomery's most competent corps commanders during the 1944–45 campaign in northwestern Europe. Barker had ended the war as the military governor of Schleswig-Holstein—an experience that likely gave the new GOC greater insight into managing military relations with the local civilian population than other senior officers in Palestine at the time arguably possessed. This is clearly reflected in his measured reply to a letter from Weizmann concerning the two Irgun terrorists awaiting confirmation of their death sentences. In prose suggesting perplexity more than petulance, Barker struggled to find some common ground with both Weizmann and the Yishuv. As a document reflecting the contradictory mix of emotions—ranging from compassion to frustration and from sympathy to enmity—that came to define the last years of British rule of Palestine, it is worth quoting in full. "You may rest assured," Barker informed Weizmann,

> that all the points that you mentioned are recognised, and will be fully considered when the case comes in front of me. It is naturally an unpleasant task for me, and one which will require full legal consideration.
>
> I feel it would help if the Yishuv would, without favour or affection, sometimes balance up the debt that they owe to the British, and realise that, firstly by defeating the Turks in the first world war we made the settlement of Jews in Palestine a reality, and secondly, in the second world war, by defeating the Germans, we made it possible for the settlement of Jews to continue.
>
> A visit to the British graveyards in this country and in North Africa would quite clearly show where the balance lies.
>
> This senseless violence and animosity only makes it more difficult for both our peoples, and with many of us who have deep sympathy for your people, merely makes one lose that sympathy.
>
> Having had the unpleasant task of visiting Belsen after my troops . . . liberated it, I am fully aware of what the Jewish people have suffered.[27]

Barker's conciliatory words are all the more extraordinary given the rumors then circulating in Palestine that the Irgun's actual plan had been to kidnap him, as well as the extraordinary pressure that the new GOC now found himself under from the equally newly appointed CIGS. Only a few days before, the now ennobled viscount Montgomery of Alamein, Britain's most celebrated wartime general and Barker's former commanding officer in Europe, had completed his second visit to Palestine in as many weeks. Selected by Attlee to succeed Field Marshal Alan Brooke as CIGS, Montgomery had embarked on an inspection tour of Britain's most important overseas bases in the Mediterranean, the Middle East, and India. He was so alarmed by the deteriorating security situation in Palestine that he rearranged his schedule to accommodate another stopover to meet with Paget and Barker while en route back to England from India. "I was much perturbed by what I heard and saw," Montgomery recalled in his memoir.

A political decision was, of course, needed in Palestine but the terms of it were not at the moment my concern. What was very definitely my concern was the action of the Army in aiding the civil power to maintain law and order, and in this respect the outlook was dismal. The High Commissioner seemed to me to be unable to make up his mind what to do. Indecision and hesitation were in evidence all down the line, beginning in Whitehall; a policy was required, and then decisions. The Palestine Police Force was 50 per cent below strength, and this at a time when the situation was clearly about to boil over; its morale was low and it was considered as a force to be no more than 25 per cent effective— through no fault of its own. All this had led to a state of affairs in which British rule existed only in name; the true rulers seemed to me to be the Jews, whose unspoken slogan was—"You dare not touch us."[28]

Montgomery's gloomy assessment had been shaped by the succession of briefings he had received from Paget in Cairo and Barker and his senior staff officers in Jerusalem. Individual discussions with Cunningham, Shaw, and Colonel William Nicol Gray, late of the Royal Marines, who had arrived in Palestine only two months before to succeed Rymer-Jones as the police force's inspector general, had done little to allay his growing concern. To the contrary, according to Montgomery's official diary, the CIGS designate had concluded that "General Cunningham was not the man to be High Commissioner in these troublous times. He appeared to be quite unable to make up his mind [about] what to do," the diary states, "and was pathetically anxious to avoid a showdown." Montgomery clearly considered Cunningham "a broken reed."[29]

So harsh a judgment does not square with Cunningham's repeated efforts to obtain cabinet approval for the internment of the Jewish Agency and Haganah leadership—an issue that he first raised, and had continually pressed, virtually since he arrived in Palestine the previous year. Whether Montgomery was actually aware of the high commissioner's persistent lobbying efforts for this measure but simply chose to ignore or dismiss them is not recorded. What is beyond doubt is that Montgomery clearly felt a profound, almost visceral animus toward Cunningham that would deeply affect his attitude toward the Palestine issue as well. The fact that the high commissioner had once commanded the same Eighth Army that Montgomery subsequently led to victory at El Alamein alone appears to have ensured him the latter's unmitigated enmity.[30]

Montgomery even took credit himself for the proposal to arrest and intern Jewish Agency and Haganah officials—when it had of course first been proposed by Cunningham months earlier. Indeed, so intense was Montgomery's dislike of Cunningham that among the former's personal papers may be found a document, written in Montgomery's hand, titled "The true story of how Auchinlek removed Alan Cunningham from command of the Eighth Army in November 1941," detailing the high commissioner's complete unsuitability for that previous position of command, too.[31]

Montgomery's vengeful mien and uncharitable behavior toward Cunningham were by no means atypical. The British military historian Ronald Lewin, for instance, has written of Montgomery's utter "ruthlessness, intolerance, and sheer lack of empathy." Rick Atkinson, author of the classic accounts of World War II's North African, Italian, and northern European campaigns, has similarly described the hero of Alamein as "puerile, petty and egocentric, bereft of irony, humility, and a sense of proportion. It would not suffice for him to succeed; others must fail."[32]

Montgomery's appointment as CIGS, the pinnacle of British military command, clearly did little to blunt his characteristic imperiousness and impatience. Although he had not yet officially assumed this post, Montgomery blithely ignored that technicality. As his official diary records, before returning to England and actually taking up his appointment, Montgomery made certain that both Paget and Barker had a "proper understanding of the task that lay ahead of them." Drawing upon his own experiences as the divisional commander for northern Palestine during 1938 and 1939, Montgomery laid out the elements of what he deemed would "form the basis of his doctrine when he became CIGS." Foremost among these was the need to overcome the lamentably defensive frame of mind that the army and the police had assumed in Palestine and embrace a decidedly more aggressive and offensive posture. "All ranks must understand that they were in for a very unpleasant job," Montgomery ordered. "The first task was a political one, namely to re-establish British authority; this would mean that the army would have to strike a real blow against the Jews by arresting the heads of the illegal Jewish armed organizations and those members of the Jewish agency known to be collaborating with the

Hagana." The CIGS designate acknowledged that this would "lead to war against the Jews" and all that it implied. Montgomery termed the Jews an especially "fanatical and cunning enemy who would use the weapons of kidnap, murder and sabotage; women would fight against us as well as men: no one would know who was friend and who was foe." Therefore, a total ban on all social activities and unofficial contact between HM Forces and the Yishuv must be enforced immediately. Stringent force protection measures would also have to be implemented. Accordingly, "all ranks would have to be 100% prepared to enter into this unpleasant task with the fullest determination to finish it off with 100% success in the shortest possible time." Finally, Montgomery pointedly instructed Barker that there should be no question of his commuting the two convicted Irgun fighters' death sentences. "This did a good deal to strengthen [Barker's] resolve," Montgomery reflected.[33]

To those more intimately familiar with Palestine like Shaw, Montgomery's pronouncements were but the latest in a long list of bold yet invariably ineffectual initiatives. "The great Monty is here at present and I have had a short talk with him," the chief secretary wrote to D'Arcy, who was now enjoying retirement back in England. "I have the impression that he thinks the situation is easier than it is and that we are somewhat spineless and alarmist. They all do at first (including General Barker, but I think he is learning!)."[34]

Montgomery, of course, cared not a fig for the shilly-shallying of colonial civil servants or the endless posturing and preening of their political masters back home. Hence, having grasped the essence of Britain's current travails in Palestine, he pressed his views with characteristic fervor on Whitehall, the War Office, and No. 10 Downing Street. "There is no doubt," Montgomery's official diary thus records, "that this greatly influenced the Cabinet to give their approval to the taking of strong measures in Palestine in order to restore the authority of British rule."[35]

That events in Palestine during the latter part of June 1946 were being pushed to their inevitable climax is certainly beyond doubt. But these fresh policy gambits were far more a product of Cunningham's persistence and dynamism than of Montgomery's carping and boasting. The fact that Montgomery's newfound bête noire was so forcefully behind them may explain why, even by the hero of Alamein's long-established track record of shameless self-promotion, his diaries purport to take full credit for the momentous decisions made between June 19 and June 20—a period, it should be noted, when the CIGS designate was mostly airborne, making his way from Cyprus to Greece and thence to Italy and back to England on the last legs of his inspection tour.[36]

Shortly before 2:00 a.m. on June 19, the cipher clerk at Government House was handed an urgent message marked MOST IMMEDIATE. TOP SECRET AND PERSONAL from Cunningham for transmission to Hall. As news had continued to trickle in throughout the previous afternoon about the succession of kidnappings and attempted abductions of British officers, Cunningham had spent the latter part of the day and the entire evening immersed in discussions over the fate of the kidnapped officers. It was well past midnight when he finally collected his thoughts and sat down to write to Hall. As things presently stood, Cunningham explained, the options to secure the officers' release were limited. Intelligence on both the Irgun and Lehi was woefully inadequate, thus ruling out any hope of a rescue operation. Moreover, both British and U.S. intelligence sources were reporting that the Irgun was planning to abduct more British personnel, including high-ranking civilian officials. Despite the heightened security measures in force and the intensive, round-the-clock searches that the army and the police were mounting, the high commissioner despaired at the prospects for success, explaining that most Jews now either sympathized with the terrorists or were unwilling to inform on them for fear of retribution. To his mind, the Haganah's attacks on the bridges marked a turning point in Anglo-Zionist relations: the extremist wing of the Jewish Agency, championed by Shertok in this instance, had decisively triumphed over the moderates, led by Weizmann. Confrontation, not conciliation, Cunningham had concluded, now ruled the day so far as Zionist policy toward Britain was concerned. Finally, there was the matter of the security force's morale to be considered. Earlier that same evening, after word of the kidnapping had spread throughout the ranks, a British officer had shot dead a middle-aged Jewish man walking down a Tel Aviv street who had refused to step aside for him. The possibility could no longer be disputed that the months of pent-up frustration over the defensive posture imposed on the army by the ongoing Anglo-American negotiations might explode into widespread violence.[37]

In the circumstances, Cunningham proposed to Hall a two-pronged course of action. First, Britain should break off negotiations with the Americans about admitting the hundred thousand Jewish displaced persons to Palestine and announce that they would not be resumed until the hostages were freed. Second, the time had come to move against the Jewish Agency and the Haganah. The high commissioner therefore requested permission to implement the standing plan to arrest the leaders and

occupy the Jewish Agency offices. He was not proposing to do this immediately, but rather to use the threat of its implementation for leverage in
a last-ditch round of negotiations with the Jewish Agency leadership. He
was scheduled to see Weizmann at 5:45 p.m., and the high commissioner
hoped for a reply before then.[38]

By mid-morning, Hall had prepared and circulated to both the cabinet
and the Chiefs of Staff a detailed brief. The colonial secretary's own view
was that the talks with the Americans had progressed to a point where
it would be politically inadvisable to disrupt or otherwise impede them.
Accordingly, Cunningham's proposal to link the hostages' release with the
immigrants' admittance to Palestine should be rejected. However, "in the
absence of any alternative means of dealing with the situation," and subject
to the approval of the Chiefs of Staff, he advocated that Cunningham be
granted the authority to execute the internment plan. The chiefs also met
that morning. They agreed with Hall's assessment and roundly endorsed
his recommendation that the restrictions on military operations in Palestine be removed. The necessity of maintaining troop morale in the face
of escalating violence figured prominently in their discussions—as did the
recurrent fears of a repeat of the incidents at Netanya and Beer Tuvya.
"The time has now come for the High Commissioner and Commanders-
in-Chief, Middle East to be given the full power to deal with any situation
that may arise." As Montgomery's formal ascension to the post of CIGS
was as yet nearly a week away, and he himself was still traveling abroad,
there is no evidence that the CIGS designate played any role in, or had
any input to, the chiefs' decision.[39]

The groundwork for this major policy change was completed later that
same afternoon when Averell Harriman, the U.S. ambassador to Britain,
was invited to call on Attlee at No. 10 Downing Street. The prime minister asked the ambassador to inform President Truman of the impending operation and to explain the rationale behind it. At about that same
time in Jerusalem, Cunningham was attempting to reason with Weizmann
and prevent a total breakdown of Anglo-Zionist relations. The crux of his
message, having been cleared by Hall, was that the escalation of violence
had imposed an intolerable strain on the security forces "which could
not be endured for much longer." Accordingly, the high commissioner
beseeched the aged Zionist leader to use all his powers of persuasion to
steer the Yishuv away from impending disaster.[40]

As Cunningham himself was doubtless already aware, the time had
already passed to avert this clash. Indeed, that was what Hall had also concluded from his meeting with Ben-Gurion, who was then in London, that

same day. Their discussions had gone reasonably well at first, with Ben-Gurion appearing "genuinely distressed" by the kidnappings and promising to issue a public statement deploring them. He had also provided his "categorical assurance" to the colonial secretary that there was no connection whatsoever between either the Irgun or Lehi and the Jewish Agency. But to Hall's consternation, Ben-Gurion was much less forthcoming when asked point-blank whether the Haganah maintained relations with either or both terrorist organizations. What Ben-Gurion did not of course know was that British intelligence had been monitoring the agency's communications for years and had accordingly amassed an incriminating dossier of both its duplicity and its involvement in all aspects of Haganah operations, including the latter's alliance with the Irgun and Lehi.[41]

Just before 10:00 a.m. on June 20, Attlee and his ministers took their seats in the cabinet room at No. 10 Downing Street. Palestine was the third and final item on that morning's brief agenda. The meeting's outcome must have seemed preordained given all that had transpired the previous thirty-six hours. Nonetheless, Hall began with a summation of recent events in Palestine. "The patience of the Administration and the military was being seriously tried," he argued, "and there was grave risk of the troops taking matters into their own hands"—a point that the outgoing CIGS, Alan Brooke, and the secretary of state for war, Jack Lawson, both reiterated. The cabinet agreed with Hall that it was a mistake to break off negotiations with the United States over the hundred thousand immigration certificates—not least because it would again appear as if the government had never intended to admit the Jewish displaced persons and were simply using the kidnappings as an excuse. Subsequent discussion revealed broad agreement that the "situation in Palestine called for firm action. We could not longer tolerate a position in which the authority of Government was set at nought." The proposal to initiate a countrywide search for all illegally held weapons was again raised, only to be rejected. "The important step at the moment ... was to break the illegal organizations," the minutes of the meeting record, "rather than to compel individuals to surrender their arms. The wholesale disarming of Jews and Arabs might follow later, but it would be a difficult operation and it was impossible to foresee its implications." The sustained and heavy commitment of additional troops once again outweighed all other considerations. Instead, the cabinet directed the high commissioner to "take such steps as he considered necessary to break up the illegal organisations in Palestine; that for this purpose the premises of the Jewish Agency might be searched and persons connected with it arrested; but that the Agency as such should not be closed or proscribed." Finally, notwithstanding the leaked operational order that Kol Israel had already broadcast, the cabinet believed that secrecy would be paramount to the forthcoming operation's success.[42]

The directive accorded perfectly with Cunningham's intentions. Earlier in the day he had reported to Hall that Barker was now "extremely doubtful" that a massive arms search would succeed, thus leaving internment as the only viable option. Indeed, both the high commissioner and the GOC were convinced that the illegal weapons issue could only be resolved as part of a broader, comprehensive political settlement between Britain and both the Jews and the Arabs and not as a result of military operations. On this final point, the new GOC was especially emphatic. In a general order issued to his command two days later, Barker did not mince words, explaining the need for firm action against the Jewish Agency and the Haganah leadership. But at the same time he was exceptionally careful both to condition expectations and to frame the operation within the context of the wider, long-term political and security challenges that Britain faced in Palestine. "To sum up," Barker concluded the order, "I could repeat that whatever the decisions of His Majesty's Government regarding the [Anglo-American] Commission report it is essential that we get rid of the extremists now, whether more outbreaks occur or not. However, I would point out that it is impossible perpetually to subjugate a country by force, especially a virile and intelligent people like the Jews. The ultimate solution must depend on a satisfactory political answer."[43]

That answer of course had been continually delayed since the Labour Party had come to power nearly a year before: first by Bevin's efforts to draw America into the effort to resolve Palestine's political future, then by the Anglo-American Committee's formation and its inquiries, subsequently by the drafting of its report, and now by the negotiations over the report's implementation. Pressed in the House of Commons for a timetable by Churchill, Attlee could only assure Parliament that a new government statement on Palestine would be forthcoming in early July. But this promise did little to blunt the tensions in Palestine that had been progressively sharpened both by these delays and by the recent spiral of violence.[44]

Arab opinion toward Britain was also hardening. "A Dark Age," read the headline of one editorial that appeared in *Al-Difa'*. "The Government is adopting weak defensive tactics against strong waves of organized sabotage," it stated. "It is the Government that encourages Jewish recklessness. So far this Government has completely failed in securing peace in the Holy Land." "Why Should We Bear the Expenses of Terrorist

Destruction?" was the title of an editorial in *Falastin* written in response to the Palestine government's announcement that the cost of replacing or repairing the trains damaged or destroyed by the string of Irgun and Lehi attacks would fall on all Palestinian taxpayers. The only explanation for the government's continued passivity in the face of continued Jewish violence and provocation, *Al-Ittihad* opined, is the "connection between Zionist terrorism and imperialism": "They cooperate with each other against our national movement and prospective independence."[45]

Motzei Shabbat, the end of the Jewish Sabbath, on the evening of June 22, however, brought some unexpected good news. In a gesture of good faith, Begin instructed his men to release two of the six kidnapped officers. They were blindfolded and then driven in circles around Tel Aviv for some twenty minutes before being dropped off near the Hayarkon Hotel from which they had been abducted—cleanly shaven and with a pound note each stuffed in their pockets, supposedly by Begin himself, as compensation for the "wear and tear" that their seizure might have caused to their uniforms. Another captive officer had managed to escape from custody two days earlier and flee the Jerusalem safe house where he had been confined. The sense of relief, though, was only temporary. New intelligence reports from American sources revealed that the Haganah and the Irgun had agreed to launch another series of attacks on the railways and that the Haganah had reorganized its defenses at rural settlements to better resist any organized search for arms.[46]

Word of the impending internment operation—now renamed Agatha—was passed by Barker to his divisional commanders on June 23. The following day individual officers cradling Thompson submachine guns in their laps and accompanied by armed escorts delivered the orders by hand to the units involved in the operation. The GOC set the target date for Saturday, June 29. The final list of people slated for arrest was approved by Cunningham on June 25. They included political leaders with any known or suspected connection to the "Jewish resistance movement," Cunningham explained to Hall, "and others who have been guilty of inflammatory incitement." The rationale was that anyone deemed by the authorities to "constitute a dangerous influence over the youth of the Yishuv after the operations have started should not remain in a position to do so." In one fell swoop, the army would simultaneously arrest the Jewish Agency's leaders, who, it was assumed, would most likely be asleep at their homes early on the Sabbath morning, and occupy the Jewish Agency headquarters in Jerusalem for as long as was necessary to seize the documents that the authorities were convinced would provide conclusive evidence linking it

to the Hebrew Resistance Movement. Special search teams of CID officers and government officials had already been organized to identify and
catalog the incriminating documents. Similar processes would take place
at the Haganah general headquarters and at the Palmach's command center in Tel Aviv. In addition, as many officers and lower-ranking personnel
as possible of both paramilitary organizations would be arrested. Searches
for arms, the order stressed, should be "incidental and only when it can be
done without interfering with the main objects of the operation."[47]

Meanwhile, Montgomery formally took up his appointment as CIGS
on June 26. The following day he sent a personal directive to Paget's successor as commander in chief, Middle East Land Forces, General Sir Miles
Dempsey. Montgomery's instructions were simple and straightforward:
Britain was at war with the Jews, and no effort should be spared to achieve
their defeat. "You will ensure that every officer and man in any way connected with this struggle realizes to the full, the fanatical and cunning
nature of his enemy, the un-English methods that this enemy will use, and
his personal responsibilities against kidnap and loss of arms and weapons,"
reads one paragraph. Another stipulates that all social contact with the
Jewish community must cease and that all ranks should be instilled with
the "vigour and determination to finish off the job in the shortest possible
time." Montgomery also decreed that there was to be no hesitation in the
confirmation of death sentences imposed on convicted Jews regardless of
threats of reprisal, including "murder of British officers or men held as
hostage." Montgomery's conception of the struggle as an entirely military
one with no reference to, or perception of, the wider political and humanitarian issues stands in marked contrast to Barker's more nuanced and per-
ceptive orders to his subordinates. Indeed, no distinction whatsoever was
made by Montgomery between the Jewish people and the Yishuv, between
the moderate and the extremist wings of the Jewish Agency, between the
Haganah and the two terrorist organizations, or between the community
and those directly responsible for the violence. Rather, there is a palpable
sense of profound umbrage toward a subject people who dare to challenge
British rule and resist governmental authority. "Finally, it must be clearly
realized by all ranks that, now that the Jews have flung the gauntlet in
our face," Montgomery concludes the directive, "they must be utterly and
completely defeated and their illegal organization smashed forever."[48]

By June 28 everything was in place for that process to begin. Throughout the preceding week, all meetings concerning the operation had been

held at a variety of secret locations so as not to alert anyone watching divisional and regimental headquarters by the unusually large number of officers coming and going. As an additional precaution staff officers had been instructed to temporarily remove the distinctive red headbands from their caps. Everyone otherwise involved had been instructed to behave normally. Indeed, the two-day annual Jerusalem Horse Show went ahead as scheduled on the twenty-eighth. H hour was fixed for 4:15 the following morning. Starting at about 3:45 a.m., teams of Sixth Airborne signals officers and their men, escorted by detachments of the Glider Pilot Regiment, began to fan out across the country to take control of the main telephone exchanges. Less than ninety minutes later Palestine was completely without telephone service, the lines manned by British troops with their civilian operators kept under close guard. Search parties now converged simultaneously on the Jewish Agency headquarters in Jerusalem and its offices in Tel Aviv as well as those of the Histadrut, the Loan and Savings Bank, the WIZO (Women's International Zionist Organization), and the command centers of the Haganah and the Palmach. Twenty rural settlements were also raided, and curfews were declared in the country's three major cities and in four additional districts as well.[49]

Meanwhile, an assortment of Zionist leaders found themselves abruptly awakened by loud pounding on their front doors. Awaiting them were soldiers and police who placed the bleary-eyed leaders under arrest and removed them to specially prepared detention facilities at the Latrun and Athlit camps. The dragnet indiscriminately swept up hard-liners and moderates. Some detainees cooperated and went quietly, while others had to be forcibly subdued. One officer, for instance, reported being offered a brandy and soda while waiting for the leader he was assigned to apprehend to dress and pack a bag. Soldiers had to resort to fisticuffs, however, to manhandle the seventy-year-old rabbi Yehuda Fishman into the car waiting to transport him to Latrun after his offer to walk to a nearby police station rather than violate the Sabbath by riding in a vehicle was rejected by the officer in charge of his arrest detail.[50]

By the time the operation concluded on July 1, some seventeen thousand troops and police had taken 2,718 Jews into custody, including 56 women. Among them were 4 members of the Jewish Agency Executive, 7 Haganah officers, and nearly half of the Palmach's fighters. The search teams carted away an estimated nine tons of documents from the various Jewish institutions that had been raided. Over the three preceding days, a total of twenty-seven settlements had also been searched, from which more than three hundred rifles, 425,000 rounds of ammunition, eight thousand hand grenades, fifty-two hundred mortar bombs, and a panoply of explosives were seized.[51]

The army hailed the operation as a success. "Palestine is a wasps nest. We dug it up on Saturday and captured a good many wasps," Dempsey told Montgomery. "The remainder are now buzzing about angry and bewildered." One British soldier lost his life, and one other was injured—both as a result of accidents. Despite the fierce resistance encountered by the search teams at many settlements, the Jewish casualty toll was similarly modest: three killed and three wounded by rifle fire with an additional fourteen persons requiring hospitalization for various injuries. That Agatha achieved its objective of surprise was indisputable. Despite the leaked planning document, the Haganah's otherwise highly efficient intelligence service and its effective penetration of the British government and military establishment in Palestine, and even the Jewish Agency's own anticipation of just such an operation at least six months earlier, the sheer scope and broad sweep of Agatha caught the Yishuv off guard. The loss of the vast quantity of weaponry discovered at Kibbutz Yagur alone, one of the Haganah's three central arms dumps, dealt the Yishuv a major setback in its efforts to prepare militarily for independence. Such a series of bold, concerted blows, Cunningham had hoped, would bring the community to its senses. "I call upon all those who have the true interests of Palestine at heart to co-operate with the Government," the high commissioner pleaded in his public announcement of the operation. "The door of negotiation and discussion is not shut."[52]

But it was. And Agatha, as even the army recognized, had slammed it closed. "What imbecility as well as what evil this Government is capable of!" an incensed Blanche "Baffy" Dugdale, the influential London-based adviser to the Jewish Agency, Weizmann's long-standing confidante, and a niece of Arthur Balfour's, wrote in her diary that day—henceforth referred to as the Black Saturday or Black Sabbath. Indeed, so far as the Yishuv and its leaders were concerned, Britain had declared war on the Jews. That was precisely how Weizmann described the operation's effects to Cunningham when they met at Government House within hours of the arrests' announcement. Moreover, although the operation's planners had anticipated trouble with the settlers, the depth of the hatred and the vitriol directed toward the troops conducting the searches still came as a shock. Soldiers were taunted with shouts of "Gestapo," "Hitler's Bastards," and worse. Children were marshaled into lines by their elders and directed to spit on troops conducting searches or making arrests. They also sang the popular Hebrew song "Kalaniot"—Hebrew for the red poppy "with the black heart"—which was also the Yishuv's nickname for the Sixth Air-borne Division because of the paratroops' distinctive maroon beret. The violent struggles that ensued with women settlers when the soldiers and police tried to effect arrests were also unexpected. At Kibbutz Yagur, the troops had to use tear gas to incapacitate the women and thus take into custody the male settlers on their arrest lists. Even so seasoned and sensitive an observer of events in Palestine like Martin Charteris, Barker's intelligence officer, could only shake his head in bewilderment. The Jews, he observed in a top secret intelligence appreciation of the operation, are "quite unbalanced, dangerously emotional and psychologically insecure. This," he posited, "may be the result of Centuries of pursecution [sic]."[53]

Provoked, goaded, spat upon, and subjected to all manner of physical and verbal abuse, the troops responded in kind. "Hitler didn't finish the job!" or "What we need is gas chambers!" they shouted back. Although there were only a few instances of looting, vandalism appears to have been rife. According to Vera Weizmann, the WIZO building in Jerusalem was completely wrecked by the search teams, with entire walls demolished and windows, furniture, and crockery wantonly smashed. In addition, large sums of cash and other monetary instruments had been removed from safes blown open by explosives. She also recounts how thirty electric irons had been seized by troops from the building's laundry along with rugs, embroidery, and other handiwork made by young women enrolled in WIZO's evening classes. Mrs. Weizmann recorded identical damage and cash and documents seized from other Jewish institutions where swastikas were found scrawled across what walls remained beneath declarations like "Death to the Jews."[54]

After touring the damaged WIZO building, Mrs. Weizmann asked her attorney to prepare a detailed report that she forwarded to Cunningham, Barker, Shaw, and Charteris. In reply, Charteris—who had personally warm relations with the Weizmanns and had often taken tea at their Rehovot home—attempted to smooth things over, admitting, "The British Army are NOT all angels; sometimes things are done thoughtlessly for which everyone is sorry, but I sincerely believe they are the best behaved Army in the world. They do NOT hate. They are NOT making war upon the Jewish people."[55]

Regardless, the harm done to Anglo-Zionist relations was irreparable. "This is the first time that the public cannot escape the feeling that the bridges between us and Britain have been blown up and that the action taken by the Government affected not only this or that political scheme but the very foundation of the idea of the National Home," *Ha'aretz* opined. Even the Sixth Airborne's after-action report of the operation had to concede this point. Struggling to put the best face on the Yishuv's unrestrained opprobrium, it noted, "The operation has temporarily lost us what friends amongst the Jews we still had." Such hopes, however, were little more than wishful thinking. That much was already clear to Colin Mitchell, a young subaltern serving in a Scottish regiment attached to the Sixth Airborne. "So far as we could see," he commented, "Operation 'Agatha' achieved little more than further inflaming Jewish opinion against the British."[56]

On June 30 the Vaad Le'umi convened to pass a set of resolutions that would tangibly communicate the Yishuv's indignation. All relations between Jewish municipalities and the authorities were severed. Jewish officials resigned from all but two of the thirty-nine government committees on which they served (the exceptions were those dealing with the citrus crop and demobilized soldiers). A tax strike was declared, and in essence a policy of deliberate noncooperation with all aspects of British rule was adopted. Weizmann's impassioned appeal, on the grounds that these measures would ruin the Yishuv's economy and might therefore put at risk the eventual hoped-for absorption of the hundred thousand new immigrants, resulted in an agreement to postpone their actual implementation and enforcement.[57]

On July 1, Attlee delivered the government's promised statement on Palestine to Parliament. Rather than the long-awaited explication of policy, the prime minister provided a lengthy defense of Agatha. The passages from the Anglo-American Committee's report that pertained to the "sinister" existence of illegal armed forces in Palestine were invoked to justify the operation, as was the Jewish Agency's refusal to cooperate with the government in their suppression. The AAC, he explained, had determined that "such private armies constituted a danger to the peace of the world and ought not to exist," hence the reasoning that had guided the government in approving the operation. Indeed, over the previous six months these underground movements had collectively been responsible for the deaths of twenty-one British soldiers and police as well as for material damages exceeding £4 million. The suffering experienced by European Jewry during the war, Attlee continued, "cannot condone the adoption by Jews in Palestine of some of the very worst of the methods of their oppressors in Europe." The accumulating evidence of the Jewish Agency's close connection with the Haganah had therefore compelled the government to take this unprecedented action. "The operations are not directed against the Jewish community as a whole," the prime minister assured the House, "but solely against those who have taken an active part in the campaign of violence and those responsible for instigating and directing it."[58]

An editorial in the usually pro-Labour *Manchester Guardian* that morning had offered a different explanation for Britain's travails in Palestine. The blame lay not with the terrorists or the Jewish Agency, it argued, but with the government for failing to articulate a clear policy for Palestine after months of repeated promises, raised expectations, and false hopes. Equally problematic, it averred, was the patent failure to take into account American sensibilities. "It would not seem, for instance, that this brusque action was the most tactful way to secure the help of the United States Government in Palestine to say nothing of the American loan," the editorial stated. "We must expect a hurricane of abuse from across the Atlantic." It came forty-eight hours later in the form of a joint statement released by President Truman and the American members of the Jewish Agency's executive committee that decried the operation and again called for the immediate admission of the hundred thousand immigrants to Palestine per the Anglo-American Committee's recommendation.[59]

The message was not lost on Hall. To his mind, the American Zionists were responsible not only for influencing Truman but also for encouraging terrorism in Palestine and creating sympathy for the terrorist organizations both in Palestine and in the United States. Tendentious and mostly inaccurate articles, for instance, had long been a feature of *The Answer*, the American League for a Free Palestine's weekly newspaper. The article describing Operation Agatha depicted scenes where "thousands of Jews were arrested and dragged off to detention camps" and said the "cries of the tortured" at Athlit could be heard miles away. This propaganda was indeed effective. U.S. intelligence reported that American donations to the Irgun increased dramatically, with large-denomination U.S. banknotes now circulating in Tel Aviv. An investigation commissioned by Mrs. Weizmann of conditions at the camps revealed no instances of torture, although some men had been taken into a room and beaten by police at Athlit for refusing to give their names. Nonetheless, as a result of Operation Agatha, the American League for the first time openly proclaimed its affiliation with the Irgun.[60]

But what the British feared most was that the Americans would now try to link the ongoing negotiations for the desperately needed loan with the Operation Agatha detainees' release. Indeed, it was not long before the undersecretary of state, Dean Acheson, raised this very matter. Cunningham was resolutely opposed to any such deal unless the Jewish Agency first agreed to the surrender of illegally held Jewish arms and to cooperate with the government against terrorism. The impact of such a deal on Arab opinion, he warned, would be catastrophic and might provoke a violent response, which the military had long argued it could not handle in tandem with Jewish unrest. The Agatha operation in fact had already failed either to impress the Arabs or to allay their suspicions of Britain's inherent pro-Zionist inclinations.[61]

On July 10 the occupation of the Jewish Agency buildings ended. The soldiers withdrew, and those officials and employees who had not been on the arrest lists returned to their offices to find them bereft of all manner of records and documents. Hall assured the House the following day that the damage caused by the searches had been minor—less than £150 in total. He was also very pleased to report that the influence of Weizmann and other moderates was growing. The Zionist leader had told Shaw only a few days earlier that his efforts to persuade the Jewish Agency to abandon its policy of armed confrontation had nearly succeeded. On July 14, Cunningham met with Weizmann, who confirmed this but cautioned the colonial secretary that it affected only the two underground groups under the Jewish Agency's control—the Haganah and the Palmach. Weizmann's commitment was completely irrelevant so far as the Irgun and Lehi were concerned. Indeed, British and American intelligence was reporting a significant upsurge in recruits to the Irgun, including experienced partisans who had fought against the Germans in occupied Central and Eastern Europe, as well as in the Warsaw ghetto uprising. Equally disquieting was renewed intelligence traffic concerning a Lehi plot to assassinate Barker as well as a joint effort with the Irgun to murder Bevin either in England or during the foreign secretary's forthcoming visit to Cairo.[62]

Meanwhile, CID and military translators were combing through the tens of thousands of documents seized from the Jewish Agency. Among the treasure trove of materials found were top secret documents prepared by the British embassy in Cairo on the recently concluded Anglo-Egyptian Treaty that Jewish sources had somehow managed to acquire. There was also a detailed account of the closed proceedings of a government subcommittee charged with studying the Anglo-American Committee report. And copies of important government dispatches sent between Jerusalem and London and between Cairo and Jerusalem as well as between Cairo and British legations across the Middle East and various embassies' communications with the Arab League were also discovered in the Jewish Agency files. "Documents found in the Jewish Agency," a CID report concluded, "leave no doubt as to the existence of an elaborate Jewish intelligence system operation both in Palestine and abroad."[63]

Leaving aside the further erosion of Anglo-Zionist relations that Agatha caused, the operation otherwise achieved its objective. "It is enough to say that the events of that day changed the policy of the Haganah," the Zionist historian Yehuda Bauer argues, "and, it may be added, had an important influence on British policy as well." Henceforth, the Haganah focused exclusively on transporting illegal Jewish immigrants to Palestine, and any violence between its forces and the British was incidental to that activity.[64]

Wielding the threat of resignation, Weizmann appealed successively to the Haganah, the Palmach, and the Jewish Agency to ensure that no acts of retaliation against the British would be attempted and that all cooperation with the Irgun and Lehi would cease. Despite being ill with a high fever, the frail, aging Zionist leader had summoned all his strength to attempt to avert what he feared was a still greater disaster should Anglo-Zionist relations be irreparably damaged. He sent an aide, Meyer Weisgal, to communicate this demand directly to Sneh, who, along with most of the Haganah's senior leadership, had been warned in advance of the impending operation and had thus avoided capture. The Haganah commander in turn had brought the matter before the so-called X Committee, the secret entity that oversaw the joint resistance movement. By a four-to-two vote, the committee accepted Weizmann's ultimatum. He next had his wife deliver a message to those members of the Jewish Agency Executive not in detention. "In every country in the world it is customary that the President is also the Commander in Chief of the military forces," Weizmann explained. "I have never before needed to use this authority and have never interfered. But now, for the first and only time, I must demand this right and demand that you cease all military activities." The executive fell into line and also authorized Weizmann to seek the release of their interned colleagues by offering in exchange to surrender all Jewish-held arms not required for the defense against possible Arab attacks. Cunningham himself later cited the cessation of Haganah involvement in the Hebrew Resistance Movement as Agatha's most important achievement.[65]

Finally, for the first time perhaps since the Arab Rebellion nearly a decade before, the British army was convinced that it had seized the initiative in the fight against terrorism and lawlessness. This may account for Cunningham's decision, announced on July 3, to commute the death sentences imposed on the two Irgun fighters, Shimson and Ashbel, to life imprisonment. The Irgun's remaining three British military hostages were released the next day. Believing the situation now sufficiently under control to permit his absence, Cunningham left Palestine on July 19 for consultations in London.[66]

In 1946, air travel between the eastern Mediterranean and England still consumed nearly an entire day. It was therefore not until late the following morning that Cunningham's plane touched down at London's Northolt Aerodrome. A car was waiting to bring him straight to the Colonial Office, where he was greeted by Hall and congratulated for the skill with which Operation Agatha had been executed. The two men spent the next hour and a half in discussion. The colonial secretary was unstinting in praising Cunningham, and the high commissioner was as modest as ever, giving all credit to the army, which, he averred, had done a "wonderful job." Cunningham then detailed for Hall the salutary effects that Agatha had engendered among both communities in Palestine. The Arabs as well as the Jews now realized that they "must behave themselves." The impact on the Yishuv was especially profound, producing what Cunningham described as a "considerable change of outlook." Indeed, it was even possible to envision an arrangement where the Haganah might agree to place itself completely under the command of either the GOC or the inspector general of police and fully integrate its units into the British security force structure in exchange for the release of the interned Jewish leaders. The possibility of renewed attacks by both the Irgun and Lehi could not of course be ruled out. But the high commissioner was confident that any recrudescence of violence would be limited in scope and certainly less significant than the previous month's string of alarming incidents.[67]

A very different picture, though, was emerging from both U.S. and British intelligence sources in Palestine. Criticism of Weizmann's calls for moderation was mounting, and members of all three Jewish underground organizations were said to be pressing their commanders for permission to retaliate for Agatha. More disquieting were reports that despite Sneh's pledge to withdraw the Haganah from the Hebrew Resistance Movement, cooperation with the Irgun had not only continued but intensified. OSS analysts believed that this development was likely the product of the Haganah leader's deepening pessimism over the ultimate outcome of the ongoing U.S.-U.K. negotiations over Palestine's future. His concerns were well-founded.[68]

Coincidentally, on the same day that Sneh was expressing these fears to a closed meeting of Haganah commanders in Tel Aviv, the Chiefs of Staff were discussing this very issue in London. Their conclusions were somber.

Adoption of the Anglo-American Committee report, the chiefs were convinced, would not satisfy the Yishuv's more militant elements, who would continue to resort to terrorism in pursuit of their declared goals. Not only would there be continued violence from the Jews, but it would be accompanied by renewed Arab unrest—"more serious and more widespread than in 1936 and 1938/39" and also more vigorously "supported with volunteers and arms from neighbouring Arab states" than before. The result would be a prolonged period of immense regional instability necessitating the commitment of additional British military forces. Demobilization of men drafted during the war would therefore have to be suspended, and personnel who had already been discharged would likely have to be called back into service. The cost of this remobilization alone would amount to at least £38 million above the existing £96 million allocated to Middle East Command—a figure that did not include the expenditures incurred by the actual operations required to suppress the anticipated lawlessness and restore order. Britain's supplies of oil and access to regional ports and bases would also be impacted and Soviet expansion into the region thus facilitated. Finally, the chiefs cited the very real challenge of "sustaining the morale of British troops called upon to take action against Arabs in support of Jews, whose terrorist activities have already inflicted upon them irritations, insults, hardships and casualties." The only viable option in their view was, as it had always been, to obtain American assistance, but this had long ago been taken off the table.[69]

The cabinet agreed with the chiefs' assessment when it met the following day. The Anglo-American Committee report's recommendations, Attlee and his ministers concluded, "offered no practical prospect of progress towards a solution to the constitutional problem in Palestine." Bevin's scheme to draw the United States into helping with Palestine was now dead and buried. Hereafter, Britain—just as Sneh had worried—would alone determine Palestine's future.[70]

According to Elizabeth Monroe, the British journalist and scholar of the Middle East, the Labour government's rejection of the report's recommendations was a grave miscalculation, reflecting a grievously misplaced "overconfidence in British power." Attlee and Hall, along with their fellow cabinet members, had doubtless been emboldened by Cunningham's unbridled optimism and the similarly upbeat assessments provided by Montgomery and Dempsey, who also argued that a decisive corner had been turned in the suppression of the Jewish rebellion. But, along with the Americans, British intelligence was warning of more trouble ahead. On July 10 the Irgun had advised the Yishuv to stockpile sufficient food

and water for a period of at least fourteen days in preparation for the com-
mencement of a major new terrorist offensive. Then, lest that message be
misconstrued or ignored, four days later Tel Aviv awoke to find the city's
walls plastered with Irgun posters calling upon the Yishuv "with weapon
in hand [to] be ready for the fight!" "The atmosphere is very electric at the
moment," Lloyd Phillips wrote to his father, "and we have to be prepared
for Jewish terrorist retaliation at any moment." Indeed, unbeknownst
to him or anyone outside a small circle of the most senior Haganah and
Irgun leadership, plans were being laid for an attack that would shake the
very foundation of British rule over Palestine.[71]

CHAPTER 14

Defense and Conquest

There was no other place in 1940s Palestine like Jerusalem's King David Hotel. The uncontested cynosure of the country's social life, it was also the nerve center of British rule, housing the government secretariat, army headquarters, and the local offices of Britain's military and civilian security and intelligence services. The hotel incongruously remained open to the public, even though it was ringed with barbed-wire defenses, searchlights, machine-gun pits, checkpoints, roadblocks, armored cars, radio police vans, and continuous foot patrols. Accordingly, Britons, Jews, and Arabs, along with a glittering array of visiting potentates, dignitaries, and the well-heeled, regularly congregated at its popular bar, dined and danced in its basement nightclub, La Regence, or took tea in the aptly named Grand Lobby.[1]

The famed Israeli novelist Amos Oz recalled how his comparatively impoverished parents venerated the King David as a place "where culture-seeking Jews and Arabs mixed with cultivated Englishmen with perfect manners, where dreamy, long-necked ladies floated in evening dresses, on the arms of gentlemen in dark suits, where broad-minded Britons dined with cultured Jews or educated Arabs, where there were recitals, balls, literary evenings, *thés dansants*, and exquisite, artistic conversations." A British army officer stationed in Palestine at the time vividly recalled the weekly Saturday evening dances that attracted "the youth and beauty of Jerusalem"; another fondly remembered the hotel as an island of comfort and serenity—what he described as a "never-never land" far removed from the horrors of the battlefield and discomfort of garrison life. Although the price of drinks was exorbitant, the spectacular surroundings were more than fair compensation.[2]

Built during the 1929 riots, the hotel was also specifically designed to withstand earthquakes and aerial and artillery bombardment. It occupied a coveted four-and-a-half-acre site overlooking the Old City and featured two hundred bedrooms (and a perennially long waiting list for accommodation), sixty bathrooms, central heating, a tennis court, two restaurants, the aforementioned bar, a banquet hall, and a lovely rose garden. Upon arriving at the King David in 1941, Sir Henry "Chips" Channon, the American-born, millionaire Tory MP and bon vivant, recorded in his diary how he immediately "fell in love with it: next to the Ritz in Paris, it surely is the world's best hotel."[3]

The King David, however, was unique in one other key respect: the government and military offices housed there. At the height of the Arab Rebellion, in October 1938, the British army had requisitioned the forty bedrooms and seventeen bathrooms on the hotel's fourth floor for use as its Palestine headquarters. Then, the following month, the Palestine government took over the ground floor, mezzanine, and the three remaining upper floors of the hotel's south wing for its secretariat. Less than a third of the grand hotel's rooms remained open to the public, and these were all located in the center and north wings of the hotel on the first two floors only. The secretariat, accommodated in the hotel's south wing, had its own entrance and staircases. But the military had to use the front entrance to access its space, resulting in a policy whereby only officers and guests were allowed to use the hotel's elevators; other ranks and hotel employees had to make do with the crowded, narrow service stairs in the main part of the building.[4]

The heavy foot traffic of both British officers coming in and out of headquarters and government officials popping over from the secretariat for a meal, a drink at the bar, or tea in the lobby created a frisson of importance and intrigue that attracted diplomats, spies, and journalists who mixed with the hotel's guests and other civilian visitors. For all these reasons the King David, despite the two hundred soldiers who worked there and the four hundred more bivouacked three hundred yards away, presented an irresistible target to the Irgun.[5]

Accordingly, sometime in April 1946 Begin put before the Hebrew Resistance Movement a plan to blow up the hotel. The group had developed a new weapon for this purpose—a time bomb that could be neither moved nor defused but that would also permit the issuance of a warning to evacuate the hotel and thereby avoid civilian casualties. Begin was confident that his fighters could penetrate the King David's formidable defenses, accomplish their mission, and effect their escape. Although he accepted the Haganah's initial veto of the operation, Begin wasn't prepared to abandon it completely and instructed his men to continue to refine the attack plan, now code-named Chick. Then the British launched Operation Agatha, and everything changed. Within seventy-two hours, Sneh and the five other Haganah commanders still at large approved a new series of attacks in retaliation for "Black Saturday." First, the Palmach would raid the British arms dump at Bat Galim and seize all the weapons removed from Kibbutz Yagur. Second, Lehi would attack the Palestine Information Office, located in the David Brothers building, at the intersection of Julian's Way and King George V Avenue. And, third, the Irgun would bomb the King David Hotel, located just a few hundred yards away.[6]

Begin always maintained that the Haganah had another, equally critical objective in targeting the hotel. Sneh reportedly intended that the Irgun's bomb would also destroy the highly sensitive documents directly implicating the Haganah in the resistance movement that had been taken from the Jewish Agency's offices during Operation Agatha. The Irgun commander maintains that he was told that these documents were kept in the military and intelligence offices on the hotel's upper floors.

But Israel Galili, who succeeded Sneh as the Haganah's chief of staff, contends that the documents' destruction had nothing to do with the attack: "It is nonsensical to imagine that the explosion would destroy specific documents. It is nonsensical to assume that these documents were kept in only one copy. The question of documents was raised only as a by-product." Nonetheless, according to British intelligence sources, the Haganah was convinced that these documents were stored at the King David. Accordingly, this consideration does in fact appear to have been behind Sneh's request.[7]

Whatever the Haganah's motives, it is equally clear that the Irgun had reasons of its own for undertaking the attack. Begin makes no secret of his conviction that such an operation was needed to restore the Yishuv's pride and, in Agatha's dispiriting aftermath, reignite its fighting spirit. "Defeatism raised its deathly head," he wrote, and the Irgun was "therefore greatly relieved by the request of the Haganah, and plunged with enthusiasm into a re-examination of every detail of the operation."[8]

Begin assigned Amichai Paglin, the group's operations chief and, at twenty-three, the youngest member of its high command, to oversee preparations for the attack. Paglin was perfectly suited to the task. Within months of graduating from high school in 1942, he and two friends had formed their own terrorist cell with the intention of assassinating the high commissioner, MacMichael. One Sunday night shortly afterward, they lay in wait outside Government House intending to climb into MacMichael's second-floor bedroom and slit his throat before it dawned on them that they lacked the courage required to murder someone in cold blood. Three years later, however, one of these same boys—Eliahu Bet-Zuri—would be hanged for assassinating Lord Moyne. Meanwhile, undeterred by this collective loss of nerve, Paglin next concocted a plan to kill MacMichael with a mine as the high commissioner traveled in his official car along the Jerusalem–Tel Aviv road. But after weeks of waiting, when the opportunity finally presented itself, the mine malfunctioned. Paglin then came up with an idea to dynamite Government House. To accomplish this, he needed hundreds of pounds of TNT, and this drew him to the Irgun. He met with Meridor in 1943 but was unimpressed with the Irgun leader and consequently abandoned the plot. When the Irgun resumed its revolt under Begin's command the following year, however, Paglin joined the organization and thereafter rose rapidly through its ranks.[9]

Paglin, who would later serve as Prime Minister Begin's adviser on combating Arab terrorism, decided that the King David operation would be carried out by the group's Jerusalem branch. He impressed upon its commander, Yitzhak Yagnes, the urgency that the Haganah high command attached to striking quickly. Yagnes, who went by the underground nom de guerre Avinoam and at age twenty-five was already a nine-year veteran of the Irgun, in turn selected twenty-year-old Yisrael Levi, whose code name was Gideon, to lead the attack. Levi, who had joined the Irgun at age fifteen and was considered among the bravest and most experienced of the organization's fighters, wasted no time. On the morning of July 2, surveillance teams began reconnoitering the hotel. And by midnight the following day, a plan had taken shape. The previous February, Gideon and another male Irgun operative had gone on a double date with two women to La Regence to undertake a very general, preliminary reconnaissance. As they danced and drank champagne, Gideon took note of the four massive columns at the center of the room, which he deduced supported the hotel's entire southern wing—and the four floors of government and military offices above it. Recalling that epiphany five months later, he dispatched another Irgun team to the nightclub to map the hotel's basement—and especially its entrances and exits. Hence, on the evening of July 3, two couples went to La Regence, ostensibly for a night out. Three were members of the Irgun; the fourth was a well-known Jerusalem prostitute who, though not aware of the revelers' intelligence-gathering mission, provided additional cover. While pretending to look for the men's lavatory, one of the operatives walked into the kitchen. There, at the end of the room, a set of swinging doors had been propped open. Beyond it, he could see the green walls of the basement corridor, and with that crucial observation the plan fell into place.[10]

A few days later Paglin briefed Sneh and the Haganah's operations officer, Yitzhak Sadeh. Without going into detail, he explained how the Irgun planned to bring down the hotel's southern wing. Approximately eight hundred pounds of explosives would be placed in the basement and set to detonate forty-five minutes after a warning to evacuate the hotel was given. According to both David Niv, the Irgun's historian, and Begin himself, Sadeh interjected that this duration was too long as the British might still be able to remove the documents before the explosion. He suggested no more than a fifteen-minute delay. In the end, they compromised on a half hour. But just as all the preparations were in the process of being finalized, a new problem arose: Weizmann's demand that the Haganah cease attacks on Britain and abandon all cooperation with the Irgun and Lehi. The X Committee's vote to accede to the Zionist leader's ultimatum—despite Sneh's strenuous objection—resulted in the immediate cancellation of the coordinated operations Sneh had assigned to each resistance movement partner. The Haganah commander resigned in protest and prepared to leave for Paris to confer with Ben-Gurion. But rather than call off the Irgun and Lehi attacks, he allegedly decided not to inform them of the X Committee's decision and instead on July 17 simply communicated a request to Begin and the Lehi high command that they postpone their respective operations for the time being. Sneh supposedly hoped to string both leaders along until he could meet with Ben-Gurion and persuade him to override the X Committee's decision.[11]

The smaller, more logistically challenged Lehi was already having difficulties synchronizing its attack on the Palestine Information Office with the Irgun's on the hotel and readily acceded to Sneh's request. Begin, however, did so reluctantly and rescheduled the operation for the week of July 19. Every delay, he believed, incurred the risk of someone's being captured or leaking information. The nineteenth arrived, and so did another request from Sneh. Begin again agreed to postpone the attack, as did Lehi. It was now decided that the joint operation would take place without fail at eleven on the morning of Monday, July 22. The Irgun had intentionally selected that time of day in order to maximize the likelihood that La Regence nightclub would be deserted and few hotel staff would be present in the basement. At the last moment, however, Lehi dropped out. Undaunted, the Irgun resolved to act alone. A final adjustment, though, was made to the attack plan: it would commence around noon instead of eleven because that was the time of the hotel's regularly scheduled milk delivery.[12]

At approximately 11:45 a.m. on July 22, a stolen delivery truck pulled up to the basement service entrance at the front of the King David Hotel.

An Irgun operative disguised as an Arab laborer alighted and approached the clerk sitting at the door, who asked to see his delivery order. The Arab instead produced a pistol and ordered the clerk into a nearby office where he and his fellow employees were held at gunpoint. Meanwhile, a second laborer strode from the truck into the basement and began gathering up whatever other hotel staff he could find, who were then herded into the kitchen and similarly kept under guard. The remaining four Irgun fighters now began to unload seven large milk churns that they carried into La Regence. Each contained over one hundred pounds of high explosive. Gideon supervised their placement alongside the columns supporting the six floors above. When he was satisfied that they were properly positioned, he wrapped detonating cord around the churns, set the timing devices, and activated the booby-trap mechanisms that the Irgun had designed to prevent the bombs from being tampered with. Signs printed in English, Arabic, and Hebrew warning MINES — DO NOT TOUCH were then attached to each milk churn. It was just a few minutes before noon, and everything was going exactly according to plan.[13]

The Irgun team left La Regence and was proceeding back down the corridor toward the basement exit when they were confronted by a British army Royal Signals Corps captain. What the group's February and July reconnaissance visits to the nightclub had failed to discern was the existence of a basement room located between the service entrance and La Regence that housed the hotel's telephone exchange. Because of this oversight, Gideon and his men could not have known that it was the switchboard for the military headquarters offices upstairs and was therefore staffed not by civilian operators but by six women serving in the Auxiliary Territorial Service. It was their commanding officer who, curious about the unusual noise and commotion he heard outside the room, had stumbled upon the assault unit.

A fierce struggle ensued as two of the intruders grappled with the Signals Corps captain, who was dragged flailing and kicking toward the kitchen. Alerted by sounds of the scuffle, one of the ATS operators went to investigate and saw a pair of pistol-wielding Arabs pummeling her boss. She immediately rang the military police post in the hotel's annex to report the incident. At that same moment, the bloodied officer broke free from his assailants and tried to escape up the service staircase to the hotel lobby. One of the Irgun men raised his revolver and fired at point-blank range: the young captain staggered up a few more steps and then collapsed, mortally wounded. And with that, the Irgun's plan unraveled.[14]

A hotel porter coming down the stairs from the lobby saw everything and raced back upstairs to another military police post on the hotel's third floor, where he breathlessly recounted what had happened. Meanwhile, the Irgun fighter guarding the hotel staff in the kitchen, distracted by the sounds of the hallway scuffle and gunfire, failed to notice that one of the clerks had inched his way over to an alarm button set in the wall, which he was frantically pressing. The distress signal was received at 12:15 p.m. in the Jerusalem district police's wireless transmission room, on the Mamillah Road, about a quarter of a mile down the street from the King David, and a police radio van was duly dispatched to the hotel. By this time, the duty officer from the third-floor military police post, accompanied by a soldier, had come to the fallen officer's aid. They were followed by a sergeant who raced past them into the basement, where he encountered the retreating Irgunists. More shots rang out as the sergeant and one of the Irgun fighters exchanged fire.

Military police were now rushing out of the hotel's main entrance toward the sunken driveway leading to the service entrance. They arrived just as Gideon and his men emerged from the basement. A gun battle erupted in which one of the assault team was fatally wounded. Forced to abandon the truck as bullets rained down upon them, the men fled on foot through the hotel's garden in the direction of the Old City. Running down King David Road, just north of the hotel, they were joined by a second Irgun team that had been positioned outside the hotel as a blocking force in the event that any of the ubiquitous police radio vans were summoned. Everyone piled into a waiting taxi parked in front of the French consulate as a backup escape vehicle, and it headed toward the Old City.

Just about the same time that the taxi with the assault team was speeding away from the French consulate at 12:20, the small bomb left by another Irgun unit exploded outside an Arab-owned souvenir shop located next to the YMCA, directly across Julian's Way from the King David's southern wing. Its purpose, Begin later explained, was to "make a big noise and disperse the people. We achieved this goal, to disperse the passers-by without anyone being hurt." The device, however, was considerably more powerful than the Irgun commander recalled and perhaps had even been intended. It not only damaged the shop but also shattered the windows of a passing No. 4 bus, injuring several of its Arab passengers, who were taken into the secretariat to be treated for their wounds. The explosion also automatically triggered the police municipal alarm system operated by the Jerusalem district police's control room. Accordingly, sirens now blared the warning that a terrorist attack had occurred. All vehicular traffic in the city immediately came to a stop, and all government and military facilities went into lockdown mode.[15]

The CID's report of its investigation into the bombing clearly depicts the confusion that reigned. The police unit that had originally been summoned by the alarm call from the King David's kitchen instead now rushed to investigate the presumed bombing of George Salameh's popular store. Only two days before, the CID's chief, Giles, had informed Salameh of a threat from Arab terrorists that if Salameh did not observe the commercial boycott declared the previous month of Jewish businesses and, moreover, if he continued to allow Jews to patronize his shop, he would be punished. Having satisfied themselves that this was the cause of the bomb blast, the police reported this information back to Jerusalem headquarters, and at 12:31 the municipal sirens sounded the all clear—the signal that the terrorist threat had passed and normal activity could resume. What the police had failed to realize was that the events unfolding around them were not individual, isolated occurrences but all part of a coordinated terrorist operation that had been compromised by the alarm issued from the hotel's basement sixteen minutes before.[16]

Meanwhile, a young woman had been waiting patiently by a public telephone in an Armenian-owned pharmacy just down the road. Upon hearing the sound of the explosion outside Salameh's shop, she immediately dialed the King David's number. Obeying the instructions given to her, Adina Hay-Nissan, a member of the Irgun's Jerusalem branch, spoke quickly in English, telling the switchboard operator who answered her call, "This is the Jewish Resistance Movement, we have planted bombs in the hotel. Please vacate it immediately. You have been warned." She repeated the message in Hebrew and hung up. Hay-Nissan then ran through the side streets linking Julian's Way to King George V Avenue, where she entered a telephone booth and rang the French consulate. Speaking only in English this time, Hay-Nissan told the person on the other end of the line to open all the windows in the building so that they would not be shattered by an explosion. Finally, she ran to a telephone booth across the street from the central bus station on Jaffa Road and called *The Palestine Post*'s office. Speaking in Hebrew, she repeated her warning about an impending explosion at the King David and told the operator to inform the hotel that it should be evacuated immediately. Hay-Nissan believes that she placed the last call no more than ten minutes after the diversionary bomb had exploded.[17]

At 12:37 the bombs concealed inside the seven milk churns detonated—ripping the stone façade from the building and slicing through the six floors of government and military offices that then collapsed in a massive heap of shattered glass, broken masonry, and crushed, lifeless bodies. It was as if a thousand-pound aerial bomb had been dropped on the King David. "The chandelier fell down on my desk and the room filled with dust and smoke," Shaw recalled of the explosion's force. "I went out into the corridor and it was black as soot. You couldn't see your hand in front of your face. I walked long [sic] the corridor, with one hand to guide me, when suddenly I saw a yawning chasm under my feet, almost the whole depth of the building, from the fourth floor to the ground."[18]

The carnage was appalling. Ninety-one persons had been killed—forty-one Arabs, twenty-eight Britons, and seventeen Jews, as well as two Armenians, a Russian, an Egyptian, and a Greek national—and nearly seventy others injured. The overwhelming majority of the dead were civilians: low-level clerks and typists, junior government officials and hotel employees, canteen workers, and five members of the public who happened to be in the hotel or on the street outside at the time of the explosion. More than two-thirds of the secretariat's staff was either killed or wounded. Among the dead were some of its most senior officers: nine assistant secretaries, two undersecretaries, one principal assistant secretary, an economic adviser, and the postmaster general. The departments of finance, economics, and personnel had suffered especially grievously. Only a quarter of their employees had escaped death or injury, and the files and records maintained by each were completely destroyed. Almost as many women (twelve) as military personnel had perished (thirteen). Three police officers were also among the dead. The physical damage caused to the hotel was substantial. The compensation that would eventually be paid by the government and the army to the King David's owners amounted to over triple the initial estimate—a sum of £350,000.[19]

"Even the centuries-old turbulent annals of the Holy Land record few crimes worse than the outrage perpetrated by the Irgun Zvai Leumi on the 22nd of July," Cunningham told Hall. Indeed, for decades to come, the Irgun's bombing of the King David Hotel would hold the infamous distinction as the most lethal terrorist attack in history, surpassed only in 1983 with the suicide bomb attack on the U.S. Marines barracks in Beirut, Lebanon, by a fanatical Shia terrorist organization. It is for this reason, perhaps, that the bombing of the King David Hotel has always been shrouded in controversy. Blame for the horrific loss of life and catastrophic injuries has been variously laid on the Irgun, the Haganah, the Palestine government, and indeed Shaw himself. It has been voiced by Briton, Jew, and Arab alike as well as by those intent on proving that Jewish terrorism has historically been no less sanguinary or abominable than its modern-day Islamic counterpart.[20]

Begin, however, always denied that the Irgun's intention in attacking the King David was to harm anyone. This was why, he maintains, the Irgun had affixed timers to the bombs so that the hotel could be evacuated and had also set off a small, diversionary explosion across the street to clear the area before telephoning three separate warnings to the hotel, the French consulate next door, and *The Palestine Post*. Yet, despite all these precautions, tragedy ensued. A careful reconstruction of the chain of events that transpired from the time that the Irgun assault team shot their way out of the King David to the moment that the bombs exploded reveals why.[21]

In his tiny, ramshackle house on Yeoshua Bin-Nun Street, a nondescript, run-down Tel Aviv neighborhood, Begin awaited word of the attack. Together with Chaim Landau, the Irgun's chief of staff who would later co-found with Begin the Herut Party and himself be elected to the Knesset and go on to serve as a cabinet minister in successive Israeli governments, and Yitzhak Yagnes, a.k.a. Avinoam, Hay-Nissan's commander, they sat listening to the hourly news bulletins. Each successive one painted an increasingly grim picture of the slaughter that had occurred at the King David. According to Landau, the color drained from the Irgun leader's face as the death toll mounted. "Begin was shocked," his chief of staff recalled. "It could be seen that the broadcasts produced shame in him. He continuously muttered as if to himself: 'What happened there?'" When Paglin arrived later, the Irgun leader did not blame or chastise him. Instead, he simply remarked, "I don't know what mishap occurred there, but know you are not personally responsible; we are all equally responsible." Paglin took this to mean that Begin "believed that the warning was not given for some reason."[22]

"Why was the King David Hotel not evacuated?" Begin asked five years later in his memoir of the Irgun's struggle, *The Revolt*. "In this tragic chapter," he claims, "there are certain facts which are beyond all doubt": first, that the Irgun's warnings were inexplicably ignored; and, second, that the hotel's evacuation was specifically prevented. "There is reason to believe," the Irgun leader wrote, "that a specific order was given, by someone in authority, that the warning to leave the hotel should be ignored. Why was this stupid order given? Who was responsible for it?" Although Begin provides no answers, his version of events has assumed almost totemic importance in the mythology of both the Irgun's struggle and the history of pre-state Israel. It is today enshrined, albeit in redacted form, on a large tablet affixed to the wrought-iron fence outside the hotel's southern wing. In white letters against a blue background, the colors of the Israeli flag, the plaque reads,

King David Hotel

The hotel housed the British Mandate Secretariat as well as the Army Headquarters. On July 22, 1946, Irgun fighters, at the order of the Hebrew Resistance Movement, planted explosives in the basement. Warning phone calls has [*sic*] been made, to the hotel's dispatch, the "Palestine Post" and the French Consulate, urging the hotel's occupants to leave immediately. The hotel was not evacuated, and after 25 minutes, the bombs exploded. The entire western wing was destroyed and to the Irgun's regret 92 persons were killed.*

The problem is that, like Begin's account of the bombing, which claims that "twenty-five or twenty-seven minutes . . . elapsed from the receipt of the warnings to the moment of the explosion," this purported statement of fact not only is inaccurate but also perpetuates an image of British malfeasance that is as false as it is self-serving.[23]

Its provenance can be traced directly to the Irgun's own acknowledgment of responsibility for the bombing in the form of a brief statement distributed to newspaper offices in Jerusalem the following night. The communiqué asserts that "the tragedy which occurred in the civil offices was not caused by Jewish soldiers who carried out their duty with soldierly courage and self-sacrifice, but by the British oppressors who disregarded the warning." In support of this claim, the Irgun stated that it had given ample warning to the authorities via three telephone calls made between 12:10 and 12:15 as well as from the small bomb that exploded outside George Salameh's shop, which was intended "to notify the guests so that they may leave the hotel and to passers-by in the neighbourhood." Accordingly, the document concludes, "if the announcement of the British liars is correct, the big explosion occurred at 12.37, meaning that they still had twenty minutes to clear the building. The responsibility for the loss of life among the civil population [therefore] falls entirely on them."[24]

Even in the pyretic atmosphere engendered by Operation Agatha, with suspicion and hatred of Britain rampant, the Irgun's shameless effort to absolve itself by in effect blaming the victim fell on deaf ears. Both the

---

* The ninety-two persons cited on the plaque include one of the Irgun men who was killed at the King David Hotel in the course of the operation.

Vaad Le'umi and the Jewish Agency Executive held a special joint session for the express purpose of declaring their "utter horror at the outrage" and calling upon all Jews to "help stamp out the desperadoes," while the chief rabbi, Ben Zion Uziel, called upon "all who have had a hand in this sin [to] cease from this dangerous path which is forbidden by the law of Israel." The Hebrew press was particularly unsparing in the opprobrium heaped on the Irgun.[25]

None of this, however, mattered to Begin, who brushed off the criticism as "journalistic hysteria and self-abasement." What did wound him profoundly was the totally unexpected, searing rebuke from the Haganah. Ignoring its own role in the operation, the Haganah broadcast a statement over Kol Israel on July 23 denouncing the "heavy loss of life caused by the dissidents' operation at the King David Hotel." The Irgun commander was dumbstruck. It was not so long ago that the Haganah had used the same language to justify its cooperation with the authorities during the Saison campaign. As Begin pondered the matter, a courier sent by Galili arrived at his door bearing an urgent message requesting they meet at 9:00 that same evening.[26]

"What does this mean?" Begin recalled asking his Haganah counterpart. "Don't you know what and who caused the 'heavy toll'? Why do you denounce us? The plan was agreed between us, our men carried out their instructions precisely, the warning was given—why don't you tell the truth?" According to the Irgun leader, Galili prevaricated. He presumably did not wish to reveal that the operation had been vetoed weeks earlier by the X Committee, which in addition had forbade continued cooperation with the Irgun and Lehi. Instead, Begin recalled, Galili regaled him with a story about a member of the Haganah's Information Service who had learned of a conversation that had supposedly taken place between a senior British police officer and a senior British official shortly before the bombing. Upon being informed of the Irgun's warning, this official—whom Galili's mysterious informant believed was the chief secretary—had replied that he was not here to take orders from Jews but to give them, thus preventing the hotel's evacuation.[27]

Begin demanded that this information be publicized. Galili complied and ordered Kol Israel to broadcast a statement to this effect that was heard throughout Palestine on August 6. The same tale had been fed to U.S. intelligence officers in Palestine the previous week, and the day before the broadcast it had been related to the MI5 station chief by Zeev Sharif, Kollek's successor as Haganah liaison officer. Sharif's account was dismissed as a craven effort "both to discredit Sir John Shaw, and to place on British heads guilt for the deaths at the King David Hotel. The Agency are, in other words," the MI5 report to the Colonial Office correctly intuited, "attempting in some measure to find excuses for the Irgun Zvai Leumi." The American historian and journalist Thurston Clarke reached precisely this conclusion in his exhaustively researched 1981 account of the bombing. "In fact, the story was a baseless rumor promoted by the Haganah in order to mollify the Irgun and fix responsibility for the carnage on Shaw."[28]

Begin and his followers, however, swallowed the story whole. Desperate to cleanse their bloodstained hands and deflect blame onto any plausible target, the Irgun wrapped their arms around this secondhand bit of tittle-tattle and embraced it with a fervor that belied both its questionable pedigree and the motive of the person who originally conveyed it. When the Irgun issued a pamphlet titled "The Truth About the King David" to mark the bombing's first anniversary, this canard was prominently featured. Like all the best propaganda, which is built upon a kernel of truth but surrounded by lies, the document's first four paragraphs accurately describe the operation. But it then diverges into fantasy, blaming "the criminal Shaw" for "the many casualties" caused by the Irgun's bombs. "A representative of the 'Resistance Movement' told us privately," the pamphlet continues, "that Shaw replied to the British Police Officer who informed him of our last telephonic warning, 'I do not take orders from Jews—I give them orders.'" The remaining paragraphs are devoted to burnishing the Irgun's image and sullying the Haganah's—an indication of the depths to which their relations had sunk in the year that had followed the King David operation and the Hebrew Resistance Movement's cessation. These same points were reiterated in a separate Irgun pamphlet, titled, "Background of the Struggle for Liberation of Eretz Israel: Facts on the Relations between the Irgun Zvai Leumi and the Haganah," that was distributed in the United States by the American League for a Free Palestine around the same time.[29]

Nor did it take long for the allegation to appear in print. In 1947, a book was published in New York titled *Palestine Underground: The Story of the Jewish Resistance* by J. Borisov, the pseudonym of an Irgun propagandist who, the book's introduction explains, "was in a position to secure first-hand information about the resistance." In the text, Borisov cites "abundant evidence" that British officials ignored the Irgun's warnings but provides no evidence to support his claim beyond a vague reference to some "documentary proof" in the Haganah's possession that confirms the story of Shaw's alleged statement. On that basis alone, Borisov concludes that "the heavy loss of life was caused exclusively by Sir John's vain pride and obstinacy." This charge was repeated in Britain the following year with the publication of a revised edition of the 1938 book *The Rape of Palestine*, written by William B. Ziff. A prominent Jewish-American publisher, Ziff was a loyal follower of Jabotinsky's as well as a former president of the Revisionist movement's U.S. branch and a militant opponent of British rule of Palestine.[30]

Although there is no evidence that Shaw was aware of the Borisov book, when *The Rape of Palestine* appeared, he sued Ziff and his British publisher for libel. The case was heard in the High Court of Justice, one of Britain's most senior courts. Among those called to testify was Marjorie King, Shaw's personal assistant in the secretariat at the time. She confirmed under oath that the chief secretary had received "no unusual [telephone] calls [from] outside the building" about a bomb or warning of any other kind of attack on the King David that fateful afternoon. Investigators hired by the defense in Israel were unable to discover any evidence to support Ziff's allegation. The court decided the case in Shaw's favor, ordering the author and his publisher to withdraw the book from publication, "unreservedly" correct "all imputations" of Shaw's character, and apologize to the former chief secretary for slandering him.[31]

Perhaps for this reason, Begin was careful not to cite Shaw by name when *The Revolt* appeared in British bookstores two years later. Among Shaw's personal papers, however, is a letter to the Colonial Office's Legal Department, detailing how he had consulted with his personal attorney about suing the former Irgun commander and Begin's British publisher, W. H. Allen. Shaw, however, was advised against it on the grounds that Begin's reference to "a high official" was insufficient to justify a claim of personal defamation. He did nonetheless write to the publisher in order to set the record straight. "The statement that any such warning reached me, that I made any comment on it, or gave any orders as the result of it, are lies and I categorically deny them," Shaw declared. "No such warning reached me in any shape or form, or my Secretary through whom all telephone calls to me had to be made."[32]

None of this, however, deterred Begin and his apologists from continuing to peddle this canard—as the plaque outside the King David Hotel today attests. For example, volume 4 of the Irgun's official history, *Ma'archot Ha-Irgun Ha-Zvai Ha-Le'umi* (Battle for freedom: The Irgun Zvai Le'umi), published in 1975, not only repeats the story along with Shaw's alleged reply—citing Galili as the source—but also grafts onto it the additional allegation that the chief secretary deliberately prevented the evacuation by ordering British soldiers to open fire "in the direction of those trying to leave" the hotel. The author, David Niv, does not explain how, if Shaw had refused to communicate the warning to the rest of the secretariat, as is alleged, any of the staff would have known of the warning and therefore attempted to leave the hotel. As Shaw himself observed in a letter to Isham in 1972, "It is interesting that every time this story is revived some new detail embellishes it. This, if nothing else, is sufficient to indicate that it is untrue."[33]

Thirty years after the event, Begin, then Israel's prime minister, stubbornly clung to this version of events in an interview with the British historian Nicholas Bethell. And, when pressed by Clarke in 1977, Galili, who had gone on to serve as a cabinet minister in several Israeli governments, was unable to provide any proof that the warnings ever reached Shaw or that the chief secretary had acted to prevent the hotel's evacuation.[34]

All of the above, however, should not be taken to imply that the official British accounts of the warning issue were any more accurate. In particular, the British army's version of events must be treated with caution. The Quarterly Historical Report of the Third Parachute Brigade, for example, dismissed the Irgun's initial statement that it had provided ample warning as "grossly untrue and issued as an attempt to justify . . . [the] outrage." The official historical record maintained by Palestine headquarters concedes that warnings were issued but that they were so minuscule in timing as to have been rendered useless. "The telephone warning to the civilian operator on the Hotel exchange," it states, "was received one minute before the explosion." The hotel manager, the historical record continues, was informed of the warning "only a second before the explosion took place." Moreover, this version claims that the Irgun's calls to the French consulate and *The Palestine Post* were not made until "*after* the main explosion occurred," concluding that the "myth of humanitarianism which [the] Irgun attempted to create was thus exploded and the cold-blooded nature of the attack revealed."[35]

The truth of the matter, however, is both more complex and more complicated than any of the preceding explanations allow. Although it is true that warning calls to evacuate the King David were received by both the hotel switchboard and an operator at *The Palestine Post*—a fact confirmed at the time by U.S. intelligence officers in Jerusalem—and were in turn communicated to the hotel's assistant manager, Emile Soutter, the jumble of events and noise and confusion simultaneously occurring inside and outside the hotel—including the shoot-out in the basement between the Irgun assault team and the British soldiers as well as the running gun battle across the hotel's garden that followed; the diversionary explosion out-side George Salameh's shop; and the sirens sounding the terrorist alarm, only to shortly afterward issue the all clear—together conspired to ensure that word was never passed to Shaw or any other person of authority in time. Indeed, the British army's own historical account of the attack sub-scribes to this explanation of events to describe the failure to evacuate the King David. "The 'success' of the Jewish terrorists," it states, "was aided by the confusion their disguise created and the terror their entry caused among the hotel employees in the basement. When the British officer was shot and fatally wounded, events moved with such rapidity that it was still impossible to elucidate from hotel employees that Jewish terrorists had been in the building for over half an hour. When it did become apparent that the Jewish raiders had conveyed milk churns and bulky packages in the direction of La Regence restaurant, it was too late to avert disaster."[36]

This final sentence is key to understanding why the warnings did not have their intended effect. The Irgun's and Begin's various claims both at the time and since to have provided twenty-two-, twenty-five-, twenty-seven-, and thirty-minute windows of time between the first call to the hotel and the bombs' explosion have never been proven. Nor has the Brit-ish army's official histories' assertion that the warnings were not received until either a minute or even a second before the blast. Rather, Clarke established that the first warning call was made to the hotel at 12:27—ten minutes before the blast—and the second was conveyed by *The Pales-tine Post*'s operator to the King David's switchboard at 12:32, five minutes before the explosion. Soutter was in fact made aware of both calls but chose to take no further action for two reasons. The first was that British government offices in Jerusalem had long been subjected to bomb threats that had proven to be nothing more than disruptive hoaxes. Hence, the assistant hotel manager was not overly alarmed by the calls and, in any event, did not wish to cause potential panic by ordering the building's evacuation. Soutter and his wife had themselves experienced two false alarms the previous month while waiting in line at a nearby Barclays Bank branch and then at the main post office. Both incidents had turned sham-bolic as patrons and employees alike had rushed for the exits. "He did not want to be responsible for a similar fiasco at the King David," Clarke explains. "Furthermore, there had just been shootings and a bombing in the streets outside. Was it wise to send hundreds of people rushing into Julian's Way?" It must also be said that because so many Jews either worked in the King David or regularly visited it, there was a false sense of security among the British and everyone else frequenting the hotel that terrorists would never dare to attack a target that might in any way cause Jewish casualties.[37]

Ironically, the sad truth of the matter is that even if the King David had been evacuated, as the Irgun intended, the casualty toll would likely have been even greater. Those passersby and personnel who had already gathered in front of George Salameh's shop before the main explosion were mercilessly cut down by flying shards of glass and bits of masonry hurled in their direction by the force of the blast. Accordingly, had everyone in the building been standing on the pavement in front of the YMCA across the street from the King David, still more people would doubtless have been killed or hurt.[38]

Begin and the Irgun had apparently neglected to consider this possibility in planning the attack. Therefore, arguments that the Irgun gave warning of the impending explosion—albeit with insufficient time to permit the hotel's evacuation—and that the group's proclaimed policy was to avoid harming civilians cannot in the final analysis absolve Begin and his organization from responsibility for the loss of life and harm that their bombs inflicted.

The attack evoked horror and umbrage back in London. Addressing the House of Commons, Attlee termed it an "insane act of terrorism." Daniel Lipson, a Jewish member of the opposition Conservative Party, declared that the bombing brought "dishonour and shame to the name of Jew"; his fellow Tory, the Earl of Winterton, described the Irgun "as vile and treacherous a foe as the Nazis." Comment in the press was identically condemnatory in tone but significantly different in substance. For the first time, just as Begin had intended, doubt began to creep into the calculus of whether Britain should persevere in its stoic quest to achieve a just settlement of the Palestine problem. "Hopes that the teeth of terrorism had been drawn by recent arrests and discoveries of hidden arms dumps have been disappointed," *The Daily Telegraph* lamented. *The Manchester Guardian* likewise observed that the bombing "will be a shock to those who imagined that the Government's firmness had put a stop to Jewish terrorism and had brought about an easier situation in Palestine. In fact, the opposite is the truth . . . Yesterday was their answer and it would be foolish to hope that it will be the last." Partition, the editorial concluded, "more than ever seems to be the best answer, and it is to be hoped that the British and American representatives will not reject it without far more careful consideration than the Anglo-American Committee gave it."[39]

Both the high commissioner and the chief secretary had independently come to the same conclusion. A month before the bombing, Cunningham had warned Hall that "the sands are running out. I am definitely of the opinion that the only hope is to introduce a plan of partition." Based on his discussions with other senior officials in the Palestine administration as well as with Barker, Shaw was convinced that the government realistically had only two choices. It could either institute the perennially postponed countrywide arms searches as a necessary first step to the forcible disbandment of the illegal Jewish paramilitary movements, in hopes of creating a more favorable climate for negotiations, or simply cut to the chase and impose a political solution of its own devising on Palestine. The first option, Shaw cautioned, would likely "create conditions tantamount to a state of war . . . make a bad situation worse and final success . . . problematical." For that reason, the second was infinitely more preferable, not least because Shaw was convinced that "in view of this latest outrage, further negotiations with the Jews seemed impossible."[40]

However, although Montgomery agreed with the chief secretary in principle that a political solution was needed, he thought that the King David bombing demanded an immediate military response commensurate with the outrage. "It is difficult to reconcile the recommendation of the Chief Secretary," he told Dempsey, "with the fact that during the past six months some 20 . . . outrages have been committed by the Jews with practically no action by us . . . Are we to remain on the defensive waiting for the next blow and be dictated to by the terrorists? I agree that a political settlement is what we want but it must take time to get it and meanwhile we are doing nothing." The CIGS, with Bevin's support, therefore pressed for the disarming of the Yishuv through searches of all its settlements.[41]

Attlee, however, was unconvinced. When the cabinet met on July 23 to discuss the government's response to the hotel bombing, the prime minister argued that arms searches would further alienate the Yishuv and counteract the positive effect that he believed Operation Agatha had achieved in strengthening the community's "more moderate" leadership. Attlee was also concerned that any unilateral declaration of a policy would compromise the discussions then under way in London with the United States—which, according to Bevin, were "going very well," with the American delegation hopeful of obtaining Truman's approval of a new plan for Palestine's future by the end of the week. The cabinet therefore agreed that nothing should be done for the moment that might adversely affect the outcome of these negotiations. It did, however, approve publication of a white paper detailing the Jewish Agency's complicity in the previous year's acts of violence.[42]

Titled *Palestine: Statement of Information Relating to Acts of Violence*, the white paper was publicly released the following evening. It presented overwhelming evidence of the Haganah's alliance with the Irgun and Lehi; its active participation in the series of coordinated Hebrew Resistance Movement attacks that occurred between November 1, 1945, and June 18, 1946; and the Jewish Agency's political control and oversight of these activities. Telegrams passed between agency officials in London and Jerusalem, which had been intercepted and decoded by British intelligence, were quoted in full, detailing the nature and scope of these relations. The list of people sending and receiving these communications or cited in them comprised a veritable who's who of the Yishuv's senior political leadership, including Ben-Gurion, Sneh, Bernard Joseph, and Eliezer Kaplan. Although a Jewish Agency spokesman dismissed the white paper as a "jumble of alleged telegrams," suggesting that they had all been faked, the implications of the government's intimate knowledge of both the Jewish Agency's and the Haganah's involvement in the resistance movement must have been devastating to the leaders of both organizations. Hitherto, the agency and the Haganah had assumed that the only incriminating evidence against either was to be found in the documents seized on "Black Saturday"—now supposedly destroyed in the King David bombing. The white paper, however, laid bare the mendacity of these Zionist institutions and revealed the extent to which the authorities were fully aware of the joint operations and close relations that existed between the Haganah and the Palmach, on the one hand, and the two terrorist organizations, on the other.[43]

The cabinet's optimism over the progress of the latest round of Anglo-American talks was initially rewarded on July 25, when agreement was reached on a provincial autonomy scheme for Palestine. Under the terms of what was dubbed the Morrison-Grady Plan—in reference to the heads of the two delegations, Herbert Morrison, the deputy prime minister and leader of the House of Commons, and Henry Grady, a U.S. diplomat—Palestine would be divided into semiautonomous Arab and Jewish provinces under British trusteeship. The British high commissioner, accordingly, would retain control over all matters pertaining to the country's defense, foreign relations, customs and excise, and immigration. Subject to Arab and Jewish acceptance of the entire plan, a twelve-month quota was to be established whereby a hundred thousand Jewish refugees would be allowed to settle in Palestine. Thereafter, the high commissioner would be responsible for setting annual quotas. But five days later the Labour government's high hopes that the plan could form the basis of a lasting political settlement overseen by both the United States and Britain were dashed when Truman caved in to pressure from the American Zionist lobby. Because the plan did not provide for the unconditional admission of a hundred thousand Jewish displaced persons to Palestine, the president refused to support it.[44]

Although this effectively marked the end of Bevin's efforts to draw the United States into cooperation over Palestine, the Labour government was determined to resolve the Palestine issue along the lines that the joint plan had proposed. The cabinet therefore decided to go ahead with plans to invite representatives from Palestine's Jewish and Arab communities, as well as from neighboring Arab states, to a conference in London to discuss the provincial autonomy scheme. Events had gone too far—with the King David bombing adding to the pressure on Britain—to turn back now. The government had in fact already painted itself into a corner by having informed the Arab states of its intention to hold the conference.[45]

The continued uncertainty over Palestine's political future had a predictably pernicious impact on the deliberations concerning the appropriate military response to the King David bombing. By the time the cabinet resumed its discussions on July 25, pressure had risen appreciably in Palestine for some signal measure. Indeed, this was one of those rare instances when the CIGS and the high commissioner appeared to be in almost complete agreement. "It is essential that some immediate and striking action should be taken to avoid the Arabs taking the law into their own hands and to maintain the morale of [the] British community and soldiers in Palestine," Cunningham had written to Hall the previous day. He was especially concerned that the large number of Arab casualties, which included members of some of Palestine's most prominent families, had created an even more incendiary situation than usual. Accordingly, he advocated a three-pronged approach. In lieu of countrywide arms searches, whose success Cunningham believed was far from assured, the high commissioner supported Barker's plan to cordon off Tel Aviv and search the entire city. Given that army intelligence had reported (albeit, erroneously) that some, if not all, of the bombers had come to Jerusalem from Tel Aviv, this measure made more sense and was "more politically appropriate," Cunningham argued, than searches for illegally held arms in rural Haganah settlements. He also recommended that the Palestine administration be allowed to impose a fine of £500,000 on the Yishuv—freezing its bank assets and sequestering the funds of selected Zionist institutions such as the Jewish National Fund and the Palestine Foundation Fund. Finally, the high commissioner proposed the immediate suspension of all legal Jewish immigration as well as a change in policy whereby illegal immigrants would be interned somewhere other than in Palestine—rather than continue to be deducted from the standing monthly quota, as was the current practice.[46]

The cabinet considered each and, at Montgomery's urging, also revisited the countrywide arms search option. Although the ministers agreed that sooner or later it would be necessary to seize all illegal arms in Jewish hands, they also concluded that now was not the time. The minutes record a consensus that "the Jewish community were in a pathological state of mind and we did not wish to provoke a general conflagration." Cunningham's proposals about fining the community through the sequestration of funds and suspending immigration were also rejected for fear of undermining the planned conference on the provincial autonomy scheme. The proposed Tel Aviv operation alone was approved.[47]

That same morning, David Courtney had lamented in his front-page column in *The Palestine Post*, "It is difficult for the harassed citizen to make head or tail of what is happening or is likely to happen. Monday's outrage had shocked him and may shock many people of the habit of cool judgment." Courtney (whose real name was Roy Elston) was that rare species in Palestine: a British gentile who had formerly worked for the Palestine government yet retained a lifelong affection for the Yishuv and remained a loyal friend of the Zionist cause. His words turned out to be more prophetic than he could perhaps have imagined given the general order issued later that day by Barker.[48]

Under the heading "Terrorist Activities in PALESTINE," the GOC explained, "The Jewish population of PALESTINE cannot be absolved from responsibility for the long series of outrages culminating on Monday with the blowing up of a large part of the government offices in the King David Hotel, causing grievous loss of life." Their support, both active and passive, had created a climate where terrorism thrived and "terrorist gangs" operated with impunity. "I am determined that they shall suffer punishment," Barker continued, "and be made aware of the contempt and loathing with which we regard their conduct." Effective immediately, all Jewish places of entertainment—including cafés, restaurants, shops, and private dwellings—were declared out-of-bounds to all ranks. "No British soldier is to have any social intercourse with any Jews and any intercourse in the way of duty should be as brief as possible, and kept strictly to the business in hand." Then, in harsh language that stands in marked contrast to the expressions of sympathy and conciliation evident in Barker's letter to Weizmann only a few weeks before, the GOC launched into what subsequently was widely regarded as an odious anti-Semitic tirade. "I appreciate that these orders will inflict a measure of hardship upon the troops," he declared, "but I am confident that if my reasons are fully explained to them they will understand their propriety and that they will be punishing the Jews in a way the race dislikes as much as any, namely by striking them at their pockets and showing our contempt for them."[49]

Although the order was marked "Restricted," it was leaked to the press a few days later. In his 1977 memoir, the Israeli diplomat and politician Abba Eban explained how in July 1946 as a British army officer he came upon Barker's order displayed on a notice board. "It was a vulgar, anti-Semitic tract," Eban recalled. "It seemed to me that the public interest demanded that the style as well as the contents of the document become widely known." So as not to draw attention to himself, Eban casually strolled past the notice board at least half a dozen times in order to memorize the order's contents, retiring to the lavatory after each pass to write down what he had absorbed. He then headed straight for the Eden Hotel, off King George V Avenue, where he knew the Anglo-Jewish journalist Jon Kimche was staying. "Within a few minutes Kimche had cabled the [order] out of Jerusalem to the international press," Eban writes, "where it reverberated with full force."[50]

The New York Times broke the story on July 28, publishing an essentially verbatim text of Barker's order. It hit the British papers the following morning and was raised at the cabinet meeting a few hours later. The secretary of state for war, Lawson, promised to provide a full report the next day. His first inclination appears to have been to sack Barker. Only Montgomery's threat to resign if Lawson did saved Barker his job.[51]

The CIGS presented a similarly vigorous defense of his subordinate when the cabinet met on July 30. "British forces were conducting very difficult and delicate operations," he argued, "and . . . it was established that any information which reached a Jew was liable to be conveyed to the terrorist organisations." Montgomery's assumption of full responsibility for the order, and his assurance that he himself would handle the matter, thwarted calls for both the order's immediate retraction and Barker to be either censured or disciplined. The cabinet agreed instead that when Morrison addressed the House of Commons in Attlee's absence on July 31, he would simply dissociate the government from the order's language, assure the House that the CIGS had the matter in hand, and leave it at that. Montgomery's reprimand in fact amounted to little more than a mild slap on the wrist. Delivered via Dempsey, the rebuke admonished

Barker, saying, "The spoken word is better than the written and is far safer." The matter was closed completely when, for reasons that neither were publicized at the time nor have ever been sufficiently explained, the BBC announced on August 8 that the nonfraternization order had been revoked.[52]

"The episode may have been small in itself," Eban later reflected, "but it did much to illustrate how untenable British rule in Palestine had become." Its timing—coinciding with the long-anticipated debate in the House of Commons on July 31 over the Labour government's protracted efforts to formulate a new Palestine policy—only exacerbated the frustration welling within the House over the continued absence of a declared government policy for Palestine and the escalating violence. Speaking for the Opposition, Oliver Stanley recounted the escalation of violence that had taken place in Palestine over the previous four years and the government's failure to halt it. To his mind, these developments raised serious doubts about the viability of continued British rule and, accordingly, the practicality of any solution other than partition. "I and many others have, over the last two or three years," the former colonial secretary argued,

> been forced to consider whether the dreams with which people started this great experiment in Palestine—it is now nearly 30 years ago since the Balfour Declaration—may not have been proven capable of attainment. The dream which everyone had . . . was of a Palestine in which Jew and Arab would settle down together, would be members together of a Palestinian State, where they would be able to rule themselves, and not desire to rule each other . . . I wonder whether the time has not come to say that we are deluding ourselves if we really believe there is any prospect . . . of an outcome of that kind in Palestine.[53]

The government, however, had to contend with criticism not only from the Tories but from its own party as well. Labour backbenchers like the Reverend Gordon Lang complained that the entire episode involving Barker's order had been "passed over much too lightly," noting that one of the banes of Labour's tenure in power had been the presence of "reactionary people in key positions" who, whether knowingly or not, were undermining its policies. Describing the order as "just vulgar anti-Semitism," Lang wondered whether in fact it was part of a broader pattern that had included deliberately scheduling Operation Agatha on the Jewish Sabbath. His point was taken up by Richard Crossman, a member of the Anglo-American Committee, who was troubled by the growing anti-Semitic attitudes evident within both the military and British society. His concerns were well justified. A report provided to army intelligence by an officer who had just returned to Palestine from leave in the U.K. evidenced precisely the same intemperate attitudes toward Jews that the Labour MP stated had taken hold in Britain. The pervasiveness of such views in the wake of the King David bombing is borne out by the Mass Observation research project, which documented the popular views of ordinary Britons from 1937 until the 1950s. "Leave them there to scrap it out," one respondent commented, reflecting the prevailing mood. "It's one of those dead end problems with no possible way out."[54]

When debate resumed on August 1 in the House of Commons over Palestine's future, many Conservative and Liberal MPs had evidently reached the same conclusion. Although Churchill agreed with them that Britain's assumption of the League of Nations mandate had proven to be a "thankless, painful, costly, laborious, inconvenient task," he disagreed with those who precipitously embraced a cut-and-run solution, cautioning the House, "We must not be in a hurry to turn aside from large causes which we have carried far." American help, Churchill believed, was essential to the success of any lasting settlement, but if it could not be obtained, Britain should "resign our Mandate, as we have, of course, a perfect right to do."[55]

While these debates and discussions continued in London, pressure was intensifying in Palestine for what Cunningham had the previous week described as an urgent need for "some immediate and striking action" in response to the bombing. Within twenty-four hours of the incident, Jamal al-Husseini, the acting chairman of the Higher Arab Committee, had written to Bevin to protest the "death of tens of innocent Arabs" that he maintained were the result of the government's previous inadequate response to repeated acts of Zionist terrorism and provocation. Unless stern measures were taken immediately to "terminate [Jewish] terrorism," al-Husseini warned, the Arabs would do so themselves—"holding our Government responsible for all consequences."[56]

Although it was easy for the administration to dismiss such threats as bluster given the weakened condition of the Palestinian Arab polity, the familiar fear that Britain could again be confronted simultaneously with violence from both communities was quickly rekindled. Indeed, a succession of communications from Cunningham depicted a seething Arab population. The high commissioner described how large crowds had attended the funerals of the King David's Arab victims, hailing them as martyrs and pledging revenge. Contemporaneous U.S. intelligence reports similarly noted the potential for renewed Arab unrest, as did Dempsey in his general overview and assessment of trends in the region.[57]

The morale of the security forces was another consideration prominent in the thoughts of everyone involved in formulating a response to the bombing. "There is no necessity for me to tell you what the soldiers feel about this business," Dempsey had already apprised Montgomery on July 24. "They will accept being murdered in cold blood up to a point. I repeat up to a point. They will want to use their strength and weapons and so will I." That the situation in Palestine was one that prized guile over firepower had not yet occurred to officers and men whose formative combat experiences had been on the conventional battlefields of Europe and North Africa. Hence, the cordon-and-search operation had become the default option upon which the army depended when some dramatic show of force was required. The problem was that it was also a singularly blunt instrument, driven by catharsis more than intelligence and thus calculated to further alienate the same population whose assistance was so ardently sought and urgently required.[58]

The experience of one Jerusalem resident shows how, far from being intelligence-driven, such operations were coercive exercises designed to upend daily life and, through inconvenience and discomfort, compel cooperation. Chronicling his experiences in a letter to the editor of *The Palestine Post*, the writer explained how he had been among the four hundred people detained when the army descended on the city's Rehavia neighborhood early one morning the previous January. "The first intimation one has of these things," he wrote, "are loud bangs with rifle-butts on one's door . . . From then and until your happy return from detention you had best forget that the English language boasts such expressions as 'please,' 'thank you,' 'sorry,' 'if you don't mind.'" Thus awoken, all males—regardless of health or infirmity—were escorted outside by troops who hustled them aboard waiting military vehicles. They were then taken to a local military detention facility and placed in a large basement area with barbed-wire windows. There, "chairs, benches, boxes or other articles which might be used as seating facilities are conspicuous by their absence." Hours passed. Finally, at 1:00 p.m., groups of five were summoned for interrogation. Exhausted and stiff from having been made to stand for five hours, the younger men were separated from those over age forty and taken elsewhere for questioning under the supervision of a plainclothes police officer—presumably a CID detective. A major then appeared who seemingly at random ordered some of the men to produce their identity papers, asked others what their occupation was, and mostly ignored everyone else. After another forty-five minutes, he announced that they were free to go—without explanation or apology.[59]

"If it is accepted that the problem of defeating the enemy consists very largely of finding him," General Sir Frank Kitson, arguably Britain's pre-eminent expert on counterterrorism and counterinsurgency, has written, "it is easy to recognize the paramount importance of good information." Such intelligence, as the above vignette illustrates, was in woefully short supply in Palestine. For example, although as recently as May the CID had warned of an Irgun plot to blow up the secretariat, the vagueness of the information, coupled with the fact that since December 1945 several other such threats had failed to materialize, led to the threats' repeated dismissal not only by Shaw, as Rymer-Jones repeatedly complained, but also by Cunningham and Barker. Accordingly, the lack of more specific intelligence, the repeated false alarms about impending attacks, and the widespread belief that the Irgun would never undertake an operation that risked harming Jews all led to tragedy.[60]

Moreover, in the days preceding the bombing, British intelligence might have been the victim of a colossally successful Irgun deception operation. On July 9, H. A. R. "Kim" Philby, a senior officer in the Secret Intelligence Service who would later be unmasked as a Soviet spy, had written to the Foreign Office with information about an Irgun plot to attack British diplomatic personnel and facilities in Beirut. British intelligence was already aware of the existence of Irgun operatives in that city. Accordingly, the threat was judged sufficiently serious to warrant sending both Isham, the DSO, and Giles, the head of the CID, to Lebanon. The threatened attacks never materialized, and nothing more was ever heard of the alleged plot. Isham was convinced that it was a deliberate Irgun ploy to ensure that the country's two most senior intelligence officers would not be present in Palestine when the attack on the King David occurred.[61]

In the bombing's aftermath it was bad intelligence again—that the attackers had come from Tel Aviv—which accounted for the decision to undertake the massive cordon-and-search operation, code-named Shark, in that city rather than in Jerusalem, where the assault unit in fact was based. Military intelligence had identified Tel Aviv as the attack's origin based on the fact that one of the vehicles used in the bombing had been stolen in Tel Aviv, hence the conclusion that the "inhabitants of Tel Aviv were involved."[62]

Operation Shark began shortly before dawn on July 30. It involved four infantry and parachute brigades, three independent battalions, and three cavalry regiments drawn from the Sixth Airborne and the First Infantry Division—amounting to fifteen thousand troops. Together with additional uniformed police and CID personnel, these units cordoned off and searched the entirety of Tel Aviv. "At last the Lion was roused," Dare Wilson approvingly wrote in his official history of the Sixth Airborne's time in Palestine.[63]

The city's 170,000 inhabitants were placed under curfew and allowed to leave their homes for only two hours each day to obtain food and medicine. According to the official history prepared by army headquarters in Jerusalem, "Every house, attic and cellar in TEL AVIV was thoroughly searched and every inhabitant old or young, healthy or infirm, was screened by the Police." A total of 102,000 people—including every male between the ages of fifteen and fifty and female between fifteen and thirty years of age (excluding those who were pregnant or with small children)—passed through a basic screening process carried out by each company. Approximately one in ten of this number were detained and passed to brigade headquarters for more intensive screening by teams of CID officers. Employing special, top secret directories complete with photographs and descriptions of known terrorists, along with their own intimate familiarity with the two organizations and their members, the detectives meticulously examined every suspect paraded before them. To keep track of everyone screened, the police painted a different-color dye on the foreheads of those selected for additional investigation from that used on those either awaiting questioning or who had been cleared for release.[64]

Although the Irgun boasted that Begin himself was screened but escaped detection because of the quality of his false papers, Lehi's operations chief, Yezernitzky, was not as fortunate. In his usual disguise as a learned rabbi, with long black coat and hat, full beard, and false eyeglasses, he had nearly escaped detection until an alert detective sergeant named Thomas Martin first noticed his recent beard growth and then, upon closer scrutiny, the distinctive kink in one of Yezernitzky's eyebrows. As Yezernitzky left the screening queue, Martin called out to him, "Shalom, Yitzhak." As soon as Yezernitzky turned around, Martin knew that he had his man.[65]

The Lehi leader was brought to Jerusalem for in-depth interrogation at the Russian Compound's central prison. Following several weeks of solitary confinement, Yezernitzky was taken from his cell, manacled, and driven to an RAF base. There, he was placed aboard a British Halifax bomber and flown to exile at the prison camp in Asmara, Eritrea, where some 250 other Jewish terrorists were confined. Two months later Martin was gunned down by a Lehi hit team, disguised as tennis players, in retaliation. When interviewed by Bethell thirty years later, Yezernitzky—now Yitzhak Shamir and Speaker of the Knesset—denied that he had been consulted about the murder but said that he nonetheless applauded it. "Martin was one of the most active men of the CID, emotionally involved in the fight against us," the former Lehi leader explained. "It was even published in the newspapers that Martin had recognized me. So it was like a challenge. It was very important from the morale point of view for us to do something about it, to make a demonstration to the Jewish people. You could say he signed his own death warrant."[66]

Operation Shark concluded on August 3. Lauded by its commander, Cassels, as "more ambitious than any similar operation ever staged" and "one of the most difficult" that he personally had ever undertaken, it was judged an unequivocal success. The army had shown itself capable of mounting at very short notice a large, complicated operation with especially complex logistical requirements—such as assuring the cordoned-off city's population access to food, water, and medical attention. Nearly eight hundred people had been detained and five major arms dumps discovered, including one that was found in Tel Aviv's Great Synagogue. Some two hundred rifles, twenty-three mortars, four machine guns, over 100,000 rounds of ammunition, and a large quantity of explosives were seized.[67]

In trumpeting its prowess, the army did not conceal that the operation had been undertaken mostly to assuage Arab criticism and attendant accusations of British "weakness, leniency and unpreparedness" in the face of Jewish terrorism. If that was indeed the case, the impossibility of achieving that result had already been acknowledged. The day before Shark commenced, Cunningham had advised the cabinet that by itself the operation "would not . . . be enough to reduce tension among the Arabs." Further, given the faulty intelligence that underpinned the entire exercise, it is not surprising that an internal CID report on the investigation of the King David bombing groused that after five months "not one of the criminals" responsible for the attack had been apprehended.[68]

Meanwhile, Jerusalem's Jewish neighborhoods were subjected to a dusk-to-dawn curfew that lasted sixteen days. When it was finally lifted on August 7, the city's residents found the downtown municipal district completely transformed. Army engineers had driven six-foot-long iron posts into the roads and sidewalks bounding the Russian Compound to which they attached two layers of steel fencing. Three concentric rings of barbed-wire coils radiated outward from the fence, encircling the police headquarters, the law courts, the government hospital, and the central prison as well as all the buildings to the east along Jaffa Road—including the Assicurazioni Generali Insurance Building, the General Post Office, the Anglo-Palestine Company building (now the Bank Leumi's main office), and all shops, business offices, and residential apartments as far as the historic Barclays Bank building on Allenby Square, at the end of Jaffa Road, facing the Old City. An identical security zone encircled the area surrounding the King David Hotel, the YMCA, and the other government and municipal buildings on Mamillah Road and Julian's Way. The authorities promised to find alternative accommodation for the evicted residents and businesses in vacated government facilities that had been relocated inside the security ring.[69]

Even the world-renowned German-Jewish physician Julius Kleeberg, who had counted King George V and Churchill, among other leading British personalities, as his patients, was forced to move out of his own home because it abutted the villa occupied by Barker. "Probably never in the history of this old city has there been constructed so much that looks like war preparations," an OSS informant observed. "Since the King David episode, both Indian and British troops are feverishly, as it were, preparing for a siege, and even to a novice a sort of system of much disconcerting activity seems to be emerging."[70]

The city's Jewish populace derisively called these special security zones "Bevingrads"—in reference to the besieged Russian cities of Leningrad and Stalingrad during World War II. They were similarly derided by the Arabs, and even the British in Palestine mourned the city's ugly transformation. "Jerusalem never forgot it," Richard Gale recalled, "and this beautiful city from now on knew barbed wire, protective dispositions and military patrols."[71]

The new security measures had been implemented partly in response to the grave concerns expressed by the association representing British civil servants in Palestine over their continued vulnerability following the King David bombing. But the main reason behind the "Bevingrads" was the government's own fears about the Yishuv's likely reaction to the new policy adopted on July 30 governing the disposition of illegal Jewish arrivals to Palestine—and the increased violence that it would cause. From the start of the cabinet's consideration of the government's response to the bombing, Cunningham had been quick to fasten on the immigration issue as a potential trump card to obtain the Yishuv's renewed cooperation against terrorism. Although the cabinet had rebuffed his proposal to suspend the legal quota, the high commissioner rightly sensed that a proposal to intensify existing efforts to stanch the rising influx of illegal immigrants might be greeted more favorably. This issue had already emerged as a flash point in Anglo-Arab relations, and Cunningham now worried that as a result of the bombing's Arab victims, any further arrivals might provoke widespread antigovernment violence.[72]

The recent pogrom in Kielce, Poland, where some forty Jews were set upon by mobs and brutally murdered, could not have been far from the high commissioner's thoughts. It had been front-page news in Palestine for five days and the subject of multiple dispatches from British legations across Europe predicting increased Jewish emigration as a result. The probability that this development would also produce a new surge of illegal immigrants seeking to reach Palestine thus figured prominently in the cabinet's deliberations concerning Palestine's security. Further, information gleaned from Palmach documents seized at Kibbutz Yagur during Operation Agatha revealed that all three Jewish underground organizations were giving seasoned guerrilla fighters and former anti-Nazi partisans from Europe priority for passage to Palestine. They were regarded as having already strengthened the attack capabilities of both the Irgun and Lehi. One such group of men, for example, had been quickly pressed into service for Lehi's assault on the Haifa railway workshops the previous month—even though none of them could yet speak or understand Hebrew.[73]

Shaw was invited to brief the cabinet at its meeting on July 30. The situation in Palestine, he reported, was dire. The Arabs were in a state of acute agitation and the Yishuv mostly uncooperative. "It was therefore of vital importance," he argued, "to prevent any more illegal immigrants arriving in Palestine." The current legal quota provided for the admission of only 350 immigrants per month. Yet several thousand illegal immigrants were already detained at Athlit camp, and nearly 3,000 more had arrived in Palestine over the previous forty-eight hours. Accordingly, the current practice of deducting their number from the legal monthly quota would consume all the available certificates through at least November. The Chiefs of Staff also favored taking decisive action to end this traffic. Indeed, the previous day they had prepared a detailed assessment proposing that illegal arrivals in Palestine be henceforth brought to Haifa and then transshipped to specially prepared camps on Cyprus.[74]

Although Cunningham had taken a hard line on stopping illegal immigration, he began to have second thoughts about the transshipment solution that the chiefs proposed. He felt so drastic a move would completely alienate the Yishuv, prompt even more widespread disturbances, and thereby undermine the prospects of achieving a lasting political settlement through continued negotiations with the Zionists. But having flagged this concern for the cabinet's attention, the high commissioner then waffled, stating that he did not oppose the deportation option outright. Montgomery was furious. In a sharply worded rejoinder addressed to Attlee, the CIGS conceded that there would "undoubtedly be strong Jewish reaction." But he assured the prime minister, this *"can and will be dealt with;* the necessary forces are available and I will ensure that at all times we keep one step ahead of the Haganah and other Jewish illegal armed forces." The cabinet was persuaded, and it approved the chiefs' proposal on August 7. The army in turn undertook arrangements to accommodate the detained illegal immigrants under armed guard in barbed-wire encampments.[75]

But Montgomery would not let the matter rest. Seizing on this opportunity to further tarnish Cunningham's reputation, he wrote to Dempsey, instructing the commander in chief to "see that CUNNINGHAM does not begin to wobble or try to sit on the fence. Once we begin the business it must be got on with firmly and with great energy and there must be NO repeat NO question of looking over our shoulder." The CIGS asked to be informed immediately if Cunningham or anyone else in the Palestine administration "shows any signs of not wanting to face up to its responsibilities or to shirk the issue."[76]

Montgomery then telephoned Hall with the intention, his diary records, of telling the colonial secretary that "Cunningham was useless and that he should be sacked." Unable to reach Hall over the August bank holiday weekend, the CIGS instead vented his spleen to the colonial secretary's private secretary. He followed up this telephone conversation the next day in a letter to Hall. Montgomery wrote that Cunningham "is NOT the right man to govern Palestine at the present time. We require there a man who has a firm and robust mentality, who knows what he wants, who will stand no nonsense, and who has the character to inspire confidence in others. Cunningham has none of these qualities." The CIGS then inquired whether Hall was aware that Cunningham had been removed from command of the Eighth Army "in the middle of a battle because he was quite unable to make up his mind what to do. That is not the sort of man we want in Palestine today." The CIGS thought that a "good civilian" would be much better as high commissioner—but, of course, Montgomery hastened to add, "that is not my business."[77]

Finally, the King David bombing raised anew fears of Jewish terrorist attacks outside Palestine. MI5 had received new information about a Jewish terrorist plot on Bevin's life. On July 24, accordingly, representatives from the Security Service and Scotland Yard's Special Branch met with Foreign Office officials and members of the foreign secretary's staff to discuss additional security measures for Bevin, who was then attending the peace conference talks in Paris. Their concerns for his safety were heightened by the fact that for more than two years British intelligence had been aware of the active assistance being provided by France's external military intelligence agency—the fabled Second Bureau of the General Staff, colloquially known as the Deuxième Bureau—to all three Jewish underground organizations. The Deuxième Bureau had reportedly not only turned a blind eye to Lehi and Irgun operations in Lebanon but also been providing funds to Lehi and selling arms to the Haganah. France's motive, MI5 believed, was to stir up trouble in Palestine in retaliation for the support British intelligence had given to Lebanese and Syrian nationalist movements demanding independence from French rule as well as to distract Britain's attention from the Levant by, Alexander Kellar surmised, "embarrassing our position in the Mandate."[78]

It was therefore decided that the French Foreign Ministry should be approached and asked to clear the luxurious George V hotel, where the British delegation was staying, of all guests; close its restaurants and bars; place armed guards on each floor and at each entrance; and assign plainclothes police officers to pose as waiters and bellmen and thus mingle with the hotel staff. From Palestine, Cunningham authorized the dispatch of a Palestine Police Force CID officer to Paris to serve on the joint MI5–Scotland Yard security detail protecting the foreign minister. The French, to everyone's surprise, readily agreed to these demands, and by early afternoon on July 28 they all were in place. News of the threat, and the precautions undertaken, appeared in the British press on August 29, only to be strenuously denied by a Foreign Office spokesman.[79]

Similar concerns had also been raised at the July 24 meeting about Bevin's security during a likely forthcoming trip to Egypt. There, the danger was equally from Arab and Jewish terrorists. But whereas the Egyptian authorities were confident that they could neutralize any Arab threat, they were unable to make any such guarantee regarding Jewish terrorism. Accordingly, the Foreign Office and the Security Service agreed that the foreign secretary should stay at the British embassy in Cairo during his visit—which would not be announced ahead of time and would be restricted to two or three days at most. It was also decided that the level of security at the embassy should be commensurate with that in force when Prime Minister Churchill had hosted both President Roosevelt and the Chinese leader, Generalissimo Chiang Kai-shek, at Mena House hotel, just outside Cairo, in 1943. Furthermore, the foreign secretary's route of travel would always be lined with Egyptian troops and police facing the crowd and his personal vehicle escorted fore and aft by British troops in jeeps armed with automatic weapons.[80]

These fears intensified the following month after Lehi announced that it would kill one hundred Britons if the death sentences imposed on eighteen of its fighters who had attacked the Haifa railway works in June were implemented. Both the Cairo- and the Jerusalem-based Jewish Agency liaison officers to British intelligence were emphatic that the threat was genuine, explaining that the Irgun had joined forces with Lehi for this purpose. These attacks, they emphasized, could conceivably occur in Palestine, elsewhere in the Middle East, or in Britain. To this end, an MI5 source had also reported that five cells of Lehi and Irgun terrorists had been dispatched to London to "operate in a manner similar to the I.R.A." and assassinate British VIPs. Their intention—the informant had quoted the terrorists planning the operation as saying—was to "beat the dog in his own kennel."[81]

CHAPTER 15

Beating the Dog in His Own Kennel

Amid great fanfare the theatrical production of *A Flag Is Born* debuted on September 5, 1946, at Broadway's Alvin Theatre. Written by the Jewish-American screenwriter, director, producer, playwright, journalist, and novelist Ben Hecht, with music composed by the renowned German-Jewish refugee Kurt Weill, the play featured the Academy Award–winning actor Paul Muni in the role of Tevya, with Celia Adler, the "first lady of the Yiddish theater," as his wife, Zelda. They portray an elderly couple who, having survived the Holocaust, are intent on reaching Palestine. In one of the play's most poignant scenes Tevya asks the character in the role of the anonymous English Statesman, "Why did you fight the Germans, so you could take over their work of killing the rest of the Jews?" An up-and-coming twenty-two-year-old actor named Marlon Brando had the role of David, a young Holocaust survivor who accompanies Tevya and Zelda on their journey. Tragedy befalls the couple as, exhausted and shorn of hope, first Zelda and then Tevya die. A distraught David is on the verge of suicide when suddenly the stirring sounds of the Zionist anthem, "Ha-Tikva," fill the theater. Three soldiers emerge onstage, representing the Irgun, the Haganah, and Lehi. "Don't you hear our guns, David?" one asks. "We speak to [our enemies] in a new Jewish language, the language of guns. We fling no more prayers, or tears at the world. We fling bullets . . . We promise to wrest our homeland out of British claws as the Americans once did . . . Come, David, and fight for Palestine." The play repeatedly drew such parallels between the Hebrew struggle for national liberation and the American Revolutionary War.[1]

The production was staged for a mere $40,000—with Brando, Muni, and Adler accepting the minimum Actors' Equity fee and the rest of the cast and crew forgoing their usual wages. Lauded by mass-market news-and-photo weeklies as well as by *The Hollywood Reporter* and the famed newspaper and radio gossip columnist Walter Winchell, *A Flag Is Born* was nonetheless panned by the highbrow media. *The New Yorker*, for instance, termed it "a combination of dubious poetry and political oversimplification," and the doyen of Broadway critics, *The New York Times*'s Brooks Atkinson, described it as a "turgid stage polemic urging the Jews of the world to unite and concluding with an episode of flag waving, that from the point of view of stage craftsmanship, comes straight out of the rummage basket." But even he had to concede that Weill's score was "one of the finest" he'd ever written and praised Muni for giving "one of the great performances of his career."[2]

Earning rave reviews was not the play's purpose. Raising money was. And its beneficiary was one of the various U.S.-based Irgun front organizations, the American League for a Free Palestine, that Peter Bergson had established. As an article in *The New York Times* heralding the production's opening night noted, "Proceeds from the limited engagement . . . will be used by the American League for a Free Palestine, sponsor of the offering, to defray the expense of transporting Hebrews from Europe to Palestine." In describing the play, Hecht, the first screenwriter to receive an Academy Award for best original screenplay, explained, "It is pure and unabashed propaganda for a race that I feel has been disenfranchised." Indeed, on opening night he was up onstage immediately after the actors took their final bows, beseeching the audience, "Give us your money and we will turn it into history."[3]

To promote the play and its fund-raising mission, Bergson had put together a sponsoring committee that included such luminaries as Eleanor Roosevelt, the composer Leonard Bernstein, the German-Jewish refugee novelist Lion Feuchtwanger, and Mayor William O'Dwyer of New York City. Rabbi Judah Magnes, the president of Jerusalem's Hebrew University and a prominent Jewish-American pacifist who clung to the ideal of a binational state in Palestine, wrote an open letter to Mrs. Roosevelt that appeared in *The New York Times*. It implored her to resign from the committee and dissociate herself from the play on the grounds that the revenue it generated would be used to fund Irgun violence. Mrs. Roosevelt, however, ignored the plea and remained a committee member.[4]

A Flag Is Born's original four-week run in New York was extended twice for a total of fourteen weeks before it went on the road to Detroit, Philadelphia, Chicago, Boston, and Baltimore. Congressmen, government officials, and other dignitaries were taken by a special train from Washington, D.C., to attend the Baltimore performance. Hecht would later claim that *A Flag Is Born* raised nearly $1 million for the Irgun—enough to warrant a vessel transporting illegal immigrants to Palestine the following year to be named in his honor (the Zionist historian Judith Tydor Baumel claims it raised only a modest $166,000, though more was raised through ancillary events, such as a fund-raising dinner honoring Muni on September 30, which alone reportedly netted the Irgun an additional $74,000).[5]

Fund-raising advertisements placed in mass-market daily tabloids such as the *New York Post* in conjunction with the play so alarmed London that a formal protest was delivered to the State Department questioning the legality of openly raising money for illicit activities in a territory governed by "a friendly power." Such activities by "extreme American Zionist groups," Hall groused to Cunningham, "bear heavy responsibility for the increasing tendency of the Jews in Palestine to resort to terrorism. At the very least they have helped to create an atmosphere of sympathy for terrorism, both in Palestine and in the United States."[6]

The Irgun's American support entities helped the group in other ways as well. While the Colonial Office parried the American League for a Free Palestine's attempts to obtain information on the nearly three hundred Irgun and Lehi fighters interned at a British detention facility in Eritrea, its sister organization, the Hebrew Committee of National Liberation, succeeded in persuading the International Committee of the Red Cross to intervene on the detainees' behalf. Unable to rebuff a request from an esteemed nongovernmental organization like the Red Cross, the Colonial Office granted permission for a representative to visit the facility in June 1946. His report was released at the end of September. Although it presented a mostly satisfactory assessment of conditions at the camp, the Red Cross official came away very concerned about both the circumstances of the detainees' imprisonment and the deterioration of their physical and mental health. A combination of the dry climate and high altitude had perpetuated a cycle of insomnia and anxiety among some detainees that had in turn bred chronic heart and pulmonary problems. He was also disturbed by the deterioration of the mental health of other prisoners who had never been charged with any crime; having spent five and six years in indefinite captivity, they despaired of ever regaining their freedom and hence were suffering from acute anxiety and even hysteria. Their British jailers, the Red Cross official reported, were completely unsympathetic, maintaining that terrorism's inherently conspiratorial nature meant that evidence could rarely be obtained with which to secure convictions and therefore these men could never be tried in a court of law. Hence, deportation and exile were the government's only recourse. In a revealing observation the Red Cross delegate observed, "Although the British Authorities are unable to furnish peremptory evidence of the guilt of each detainee, they feel convinced that every Palestinian Jew plays the part of accomplice in Palestine."[7]

This was also the view of British soldiers and police in Palestine. It was vividly illustrated at the trial of a British officer accused of shooting to death a Jewish passerby on a Tel Aviv street the previous June. Lieutenant B. Woodworth testified that he had been among the diners at the British officers' club in the Hayarkon Hotel on June 18 when Irgun gunmen had burst into the room. Although he was not taken captive because of his comparatively low rank, the entire experience had so rankled Woodworth that when he and a fellow officer were jostled while out walking the following evening, he feared that they were being attacked. He therefore drew his pistol and fired—killing a young Czech immigrant whose parents had perished in the Holocaust. In his defense, Woodworth claimed that "the people of Tel Aviv were 98 per cent anti-British" and that "it was very difficult to differentiate between peaceful and terrorist Jews." Although he was acquitted of the murder charge, Woodworth was convicted of manslaughter and dishonorably discharged from the army. Nonetheless, the trial highlighted the suspicion and antipathy toward the Yishuv that, in the aftermath of the King David Hotel bombing, had resulted in a marked increase in the number of scuffles between British troops and Jewish passersby as well as acts of vandalism directed against Jewish-owned property. The problem had become sufficiently alarming that additional military police patrols had to be mounted in Jerusalem. The Sixth Airborne's simultaneous searches of two Jewish settlements in the Gaza district, Dorot and Ruhama, in August provided further proof of the depth of this animus.[8]

At dawn on August 28 both kibbutzim, with populations of 235 and 170 persons, respectively, were surrounded by at least ten times that number of troops, backed by police. The two settlements had ostensibly been targeted, according to Wilson, because they were "known . . . centres of illegal armed training" and were therefore believed to have large stockpiles of hidden arms. But the operation's real intention, the division's historian admits, was to pressure the Haganah into abandoning its efforts to transport illegal immigrants to Palestine or risk the continued confiscation of its arsenal. The searches, which lasted nearly a week, were unparalleled in terms of the damage and destruction of property that the troops caused. This perhaps explains why the operations' commander barred a group of journalists, including a newsreel camera team, from entering either Dorot or Ruhama—despite an invitation from the army's public relations officer and Sixth Airborne headquarters to observe the searches.[9]

When *The Palestine Post*'s correspondent finally gained access to both settlements on September 2, he reported, "Not a single room was intact.

All floors had been ripped up, and there were holes in some places to a depth of more than two metres. Holes were also knocked in walls and ceilings." Although such extensive damage could be attributed to the search parties' determination to discover caches of weapons hidden behind false walls, in ceilings, and beneath floors, less explicable were the smashed typewriters and duplicating machines in the settlements' administrative offices, the deliberate sabotaging of farm vehicles and industrial equipment, the broken furniture, shattered windows, torn-up clothing, and destroyed kitchen utensils—in addition to the many swastikas scrawled across walls and doors. According to Daphne Trevor, when settlers pleaded with the officers directing the searches to intervene and halt the vandalism, they were reportedly told, "We'll stop the trouble if you tell us where the arms are."[10]

Although army investigators breezily dismissed the accusations of vandalism as "a deliberate campaign of propaganda," Cunningham privately told Hall that "a certain amount of unnecessary and willful damage" had in fact occurred. The high commissioner, however, attributed this "in part at least, to the fact that the troops were provoked by shouts of 'Gestapo' etc." Wilson himself also concedes that the wreckage done by the paratroopers was a product of the taunting that they were subjected to. "It was certainly not in the interest of the soldiers deliberately to stir up hatred," he explains. "But expressions such as 'Gestapo' and 'English bastards' spat out with such venom could hardly be ignored indefinitely, and without doubt were sometimes answered in kind." A Ruhama settler, however, recalled how the troops responded to shouts of "Nazi! Nazi!" with chants of "Heil Hitler! Heil Hitler!" with "both sides spitting at each other." In a public address he gave shortly before returning to England the following month, Martin Charteris implied that there was another reason behind the aggressiveness shown at Dorot and Ruhama: British forces simply no longer saw any difference between the community and the terrorists. Indeed, the army's own historical account for that period noted the "growth of anti-Jewish feeling amongst all ranks." Accordingly, it is perhaps not surprising that the first report of British deserters selling arms and explosives to Palestinian Arabs surfaced at this time.[11]

Thomas Scrivenor had not been back to Palestine for three years. As assistant district commissioner for Tel Aviv from 1937 to 1943, he had gotten to know the country and the Yishuv well before promotions took him first to Malta and then to a policy-making position at the Colonial Office in

London. He was thus surprised by what he found when he returned that fall as the newly appointed principal assistant secretary of the Palestine government—his predecessor having perished in the King David Hotel bombing. "Oh yes, we were on our way out then, there is no doubt about it," he recalled in a 1969 interview, "and we were in the—to my mind—invidious position of putting ourselves behind barbed wire in all the major centres of government and leaving the terrorists very largely in command. In spite of the fact that we had I think two divisions of troops and 15,000 armed police. It was a wholly unsatisfactory, frustrating set-up."[12]

Perpetuating and exacerbating this "unsatisfactory, frustrating set-up" was precisely Begin's strategy. As he explained in *The Revolt*,

> Eretz Israel was a centre of world interest. The revolt had made it so. It is a fact that no partisan struggle had been so publicized throughout the world as was ours . . . The reports on our operations, under screaming headlines, covered the front pages of newspapers everywhere, particularly in the United States . . . The interest of the newspapers is the measure of the interest of the public. And the public—not only Jews but non-Jews too—were manifestly interested in the blows we were striking in Eretz Israel.[13]

The opening of the Attlee government's long-awaited conference on Palestine's political future in early September thus presented Begin with the opportunity to divert the attention focused on the proceedings in London to the Irgun and its struggle in Palestine. The conference had already gotten off to a bad start when the Jewish Agency and Palestine's Arab leaders had announced that they would boycott the meeting. It would therefore be attended only by representatives of the seven member states in the Arab League and its secretary-general along with senior British officials. Begin was determined to ensure that the news from Palestine would further erode the conference's chances for success.[14]

The Irgun's offensive commenced just after midnight on September 9 with a series of widespread sabotage attacks across the country, specifically targeting Palestine's railways and the Shell Oil facility in Haifa. Accordingly, when the London Conference convened that morning, newspaper coverage of the terrorist incidents had superseded commentary on the talks. But that was only the beginning. As the day wore on, the violence escalated. The most serious incident occurred in Tel Aviv when cars transporting at least ten armed Irgun fighters pulled up in front of the Public Information Office. While one team raked the building with submachine-gun fire, killing an Arab constable, another ran across the street, where they placed a large bomb on the ground floor of an apartment block. Above them, Major Desmond Doran was dining with his wife on their balcony. The ensuing explosion collapsed the building, killing Doran and seriously injuring his wife. His death was not coincidental. As the MI6 area security officer for Tel Aviv, Doran was in charge of British intelligence for the city. That alone would have earned him a prominent place on the Irgun's hit list. But his previous position in the intelligence service's Cairo-based Inter-services Liaison Department, where he had acquired the reputation as a "skilled interrogator" of captured Jewish terrorists, had singled him out for assassination. There were additional assaults on railway targets as well. Three railway bridges were damaged, and one line was cut in thirty places. Mines buried beneath major thoroughfares with warnings posted at bus stations in Hebrew warning Jews to avoid travel that day also disrupted bus and private vehicular traffic. The final spasm of violence occurred later, when Lehi gunned down the CID detective responsible for Yezernitzky's arrest the previous month.[15]

Within twenty-four hours, security conditions in Palestine had yet again crossed a new threshold. The requisite curfews were thrown over Jerusalem, Tel Aviv, neighboring Ramat Gan, and farther up the coast in the seaside town of Netanya. The predictable panoply of roadblocks and checkpoints were also erected along the country's major roads. But far more significant were the thousands of additional troops rushed from Egypt to guard the railways and help keep the country quiet while the London Conference continued. With these reinforcements, British military forces in Palestine peaked at a hundred thousand personnel. This meant that government forces now outnumbered the Irgun and Lehi by a ratio of approximately twenty to one. There was now "one armed soldier to each adult male Jew in Palestine"—a staggering numerical advantage for any government seeking to maintain order in a rebellious country and decisively defeat a terrorist challenge to its authority. But, without intelligence, even these numbers could not cope with the threat presented by the Irgun and Lehi, even though the underground's collective power had been deflated by the collapse of the Hebrew Resistance Movement and the loss of the Haganah and its elite Palmach force as allies.[16]

The alliance's demise had also adversely impacted the Irgun's finances—having deprived it of the Haganah's regular subventions. Given that the Irgun paid each of its approximately one thousand members individual stipends of between £30 and £60 per month, the termination of the Haganah's largesse had forced the Irgun to focus its efforts as much on robbing and blackmailing ordinary Jews as on attacking government targets. But the amount of money gleaned from these activities was as piecemeal as it was unpredictable, varying from as little as £50 to as much as £1,000, and was insufficient to sustain the group's operations. Therefore, on September 13, the Irgun put into motion an ambitious plan to simultaneously rob three banks in Tel Aviv and Jaffa. The operation, however, went wrong from the start. The police responded far more quickly to the holdups than the Irgun had anticipated, disrupting the robberies in progress at branches of the Ottoman Bank and the Arab Bank in Jaffa. Gun battles ensued at both, resulting in the capture of thirteen Irgunists, the death of one policeman, and injuries to ten others. Only the assault on the Ottoman Bank in Tel Aviv succeeded. But it netted the group less than £5,000, a fraction of what it had hoped to obtain. Nonetheless, on September 20 the Irgun resumed its attacks on Palestine's railways, blowing up the Haifa station and causing some £23,000 in damage, and three days later its fighters wrecked a train transporting oil between Hadera and Benyamina.[17]

The inevitable curfews, roadblocks, searches, and identity checks that followed had by now become a fixture of daily life in Palestine. "After every major incident and after most minor ones," Trevor observed in her contemporaneous account of the last years of British rule over Palestine, "there would be a curfew, searches, identity-checks and arrests. It is perhaps difficult to know what else the military could have done, but their methods never seemed to prevent further incidents and some—road curfews, for instance—seemed to facilitate them, while they looked as if they were designed for the sole purpose of harassing as many people as possible." The minutes of the high commissioner's daily evening conference on September 30 appear to substantiate this claim. They reveal that the army was wont to impose curfews on Jewish neighborhoods not because of any specific intelligence in its possession but rather for vaguely referenced "preventative" reasons.[18]

The frequency with which these measures occurred had created an impression both in London and within the Yishuv that the army and not the Palestine administration was now in charge. This view had become so prevalent by September that Cunningham was forced to defend himself and his administration against accusations emanating from Whitehall as well as Palestine. He assured Hall that military action was never undertaken for punitive reasons, was always based on solid intelligence, and was specifically designed to impact the community as little as possible. The high commissioner flatly denied that the army had taken over.[19]

The Yishuv saw things differently, as the meeting of Weizmann and other Jewish Agency officials with Hall and Bevin on October 1 evidenced. Weizmann and his colleagues had been invited to the Foreign Office not to discuss security matters or administrative arrangements in Palestine but to address the conditions under which the Jewish Agency might agree to attend the London Conference. This session, billed as the first in a series of "informal talks," quickly degenerated into an indictment of British security policy in Palestine and General Barker's role in its implementation. The septuagenarian Zionist leader was still a commanding figure despite being hobbled by an array of maladies, including partial blindness, cardiopulmonary problems, and recurrent, enervating fever. He persisted, despite these myriad health woes, because—as he had told his trusted adviser and confidante Blanche Dugdale—"only his presence has so far restrained 'rivers of blood,' for the Army were longing for an excuse to wipe out the Yishuv, and on the Yishuv's side the hatred and anger against Britain will never be wiped out except by partition and a Jewish State."[20]

After a perfunctory welcome by Bevin, Weizmann laid out the Jewish Agency's demands. First, the hundred or so agency officials detained since "Black Saturday" must be freed. Second, Palestine's governance must be readjusted because, Weizmann believed, the "administration was virtually under the Army, which in turn was under the command of a man who had made his feelings clear." Third, the government must agree that partition represents the only viable, permanent settlement of Palestine's political future. Rabbi Fishman then spoke, echoing Weizmann. "A man like General Barker," he contended, "did no honor to the name of Britain. The Jewish people had tried for sixty years to convert the desert of Palestine into a paradise; General Barker was now making it a hell for Jews. As long as this situation remained, there could be no peace in Palestine."[21]

Bevin was characteristically blunt in his reply. "The British Government had not taken the initiative in blowing people up," he told his guests. The foreign secretary described how a year earlier he had warned Weizmann and Shertok that "this terrorism was a dangerous thing to play with." Britain, he continued, had long been the Jews' "best friend . . . and now seemed to be almost their last friend." Anti-Semitism was growing in Britain because of terrorism in Palestine. Bevin had never known it to be as blatant or rampant as it had become; indeed, the "destruction of the King David Hotel had burned deeply into the heart of the British people." Bevin then warned that if agreement on Palestine could not be reached through negotiation between Britain and the Arabs and the Jews, it "should be handed back to the United Nations with a confession that we could not solve it."[22]

This was a stunning volte-face for the foreign secretary. Only a few months before, he had taken the opposite position during internal discussions on British strategic priorities in the Mediterranean, North Africa, and the Middle East. Countering Attlee's suggestion, supported by Hugh Dalton, that these commitments had become financially untenable, Bevin had forcefully argued that Britain's stature as a great power was inextricably linked to the maintenance of its Middle Eastern strategic and economic interests. The foreign secretary thus had clearly envisioned Britain remaining in Palestine for at least another decade—and retaining military basing rights beyond even that time frame. His position accorded completely with that of the Chiefs of Staff.[23]

The meeting with the Zionist leaders ended on a sour note when Bevin commented that Truman's "repeated insistence" on admitting a hundred thousand Jewish refugees to Palestine had been singularly unhelpful. The foreign secretary was unambiguous that "if the Arabs refused partition he was not prepared to force it on them at the point of British bayonets." For the moment, however, everyone agreed that the Zionist leaders should meet with Hall to continue their discussions on both security issues and the attendant administrative arrangements in Palestine and, once these were clarified, that discussions with the foreign secretary regarding the Jewish Agency's attendance at the London Conference would resume.[24]

Over tea at the Dorchester hotel later that afternoon, Berl Locker, a political adviser to the Jewish Agency Board in London, briefed Dugdale on the meeting. She was skeptical about everything she heard. "I do not think there is much hope of good coming out of these talks," Dugdale recorded in her diary. "Bevin is obviously full of good will, but as far as ever from understanding the elements of the Jewish case." Nonetheless, both she and the Jewish leadership were pleasantly surprised three days later when, in a cabinet shake-up, Attlee replaced Hall with the latter's deputy, Arthur Creech Jones—a staunch, lifelong pro-Zionist. Still more good news came later that same day when, just before the start of Yom Kippur, President Truman again called on Britain to admit a hundred thousand Jewish immigrants to Palestine immediately. The president also, for the first time, appeared to endorse the Jewish Agency's demand for partition and the establishment of an independent Jewish state. As the Zionist historian Michael J. Cohen notes, this was the "last straw" for Bevin in his increasingly futile attempt to draw the United States into a common effort to resolve Palestine's future political status. The foreign secretary now realized that not only were the Zionists unwilling to compromise but they had no reason to, given the influence they were able to exert over both the president and Congress.[25]

History would show that the Zionist delegation's profound concern over Barker's bias against the Yishuv and, in turn, his ability to act impartially as GOC was well-founded. Indeed, decades after the October 1 meeting evidence has come to light detailing both the depth of Barker's enmity toward Zionism and his anti-Semitic attitude toward the Jewish people. The evidence is in the form of about a hundred letters written in hand by Barker, on official army stationery, to his paramour, Katy Antonius, the widow of the famed Arab nationalist George Antonius. Of most relevance is Barker's letter to her of October 11, 1946, where the GOC poetically describes themselves as "only birds of passage" on this earth before venting his frustrations with the Jews. "Balfour has made this uncomfortable bed on which we are all lying," he wrote, "and my sympathies are with the Arabs who are in no way responsible for it. I often think if I ever become a bachelor I shall return to the Middle East to help fight for their rights." He reiterates the same desire two weeks later, reflecting, "I would give a lot to be able to contribute in some way to the peace and happiness of the country. To think that a few hundred terrorists force us to react as we do makes me furious. As you know my sympathies are so much with the Arabs and I hate to see their country mucked up by us."[26]

As the conflict with the Jewish terrorist organizations wore on, Barker's letters to Antonius become increasingly more vitriolic. Echoing his infamous nonfraternization order of the previous year, Barker expressed the view in April 1947 that the Jews "do hate having their pockets touched as I [have] said in my letters." Later that month he more caustically observed, "Yes I loathe the lot—whether they be Zionists or not. Why should we be afraid of saying we hate them—it's time this damned race knew what we think of them—loathesome [*sic*] people."[27]

"It wasn't so much our actions that I objected to, it was our attitude," Charteris later told Nicholas Bethell about relations between the army and the Yishuv. John Kenneally, a half-Jewish noncommissioned officer who served with the First Guards Parachute Battalion in Palestine and had previously been awarded the Victoria Cross (Britain's equivalent of the U.S. Medal of Honor) for valor during World War II, similarly recalled how the British officer corps in Palestine was demonstrably hostile to the Yishuv. Indeed, the Quarterly Historical Reports for units stationed in Palestine during this period describe the nadir to which Anglo-Jewish relations had sunk.[28]

The strain imposed on British forces by the Irgun's renewed offensive had been further exacerbated by Lehi's resumption of its practice of randomly assassinating individual soldiers and police. On October 7, two enlisted men were shot down on a Jerusalem street; one died, and the other was seriously wounded. A week later a CID inspector was assassinated. Irgun road mines had meanwhile killed two British soldiers and injured five others. Then, seeking once again to distinguish itself from the Irgun, Lehi announced on October 21 that it was adopting a shoot-to-kill policy with respect to British members of the security forces in retaliation for such alleged transgressions as firing on unarmed Jewish demonstrators, using "burning gasses" against Hebrew fighters, "molesting and terror- izing" people during searches, and generally "playing havoc in the streets of our homeland." Henceforth, Lehi therefore proclaimed, "all British soldiers and policemen . . . where appearing armed in the streets and on the roads of our country, [are] liable to be hit by a Hebrew fighter."[29]

Tensions were thus already high when the Irgun bombed four check- points manned by the First Battalion of the Argyll and Sutherland High- landers to enforce the nighttime curfew that had been in force over Jerusalem for nearly a week. Eleven soldiers were wounded, one fatally. Their commander, Lieutenant Colonel Richard Webb, was a legendary figure in the regiment, a "soldier's soldier," whose leadership and hero- ism during the war inspired respect and awe in equal measure. Enraged by the attack and the casualties inflicted on his men, "the Squire," as he was called by his men, ordered ten domestic and overseas journalists, who together represented a dozen or so newspapers, press agencies, and broadcast services, to be brought from the scene of one of the bomb- ings to his headquarters at the fortresslike Hospice de Notre-Dame de France, opposite the Old City's New Gate. Meeting individually with each reporter in succession, Webb told one that "the Jews are a despicable race"—repeating that same phrase three times in the span of six sentences. "These bloody Jews—we saved their skins in Alamein and other places and then they do this to us," he remarked before summoning another journalist into his office. Webb complained to him that the Jewish women he had encountered during searches "bulged all in the wrong places" but then abruptly changed subject, observing that "his boys are pretty hot- tempered" and, by way of explanation, admitting that they "sometimes use the butts of their rifles and do a spot of looting." Each reporter was harangued in a similar manner. Webb then assembled the reporters and addressed them as a group. He stated that the army's counterterrorism strategy was indeed to harass the Yishuv. "By making a nuisance of our- selves," he asserted, "we shall turn the people against the terrorists." One correspondent, an American, asked, "Isn't it having the opposite effect?

A British soldier and a Palestine policeman stand guard following
the Irgun's bombing of the Ramle train station, May 1947

Damage caused to the façade of the British embassy in Rome
by two Irgun suitcase bombs, October 1946

The Yarmuk Bridge in the Jezreel Valley, northern Palestine,
destroyed by the Haganah, June 1946

Damage caused to the Farran family home in Codsall, Wolverhampton,
by a Lehi bomb concealed in a package that killed Roy Farran's
brother Rex, May 1948

Wreckage is hurled through the air by the explosion at Jerusalem's
King David Hotel as police and civilians flee the blast scene, July 1946

A wounded soldier on a stretcher is carried from the rubble of
Jerusalem's King David Hotel, July 1946

A British army officer and troops outside the destroyed southwest corner
of Jerusalem's King David Hotel, July 1946

Plaque affixed to the wrought-iron fence outside the King David Hotel commemorating the sixtieth anniversary of the bombing, in July 2006

Palestine police examining the identity papers of Jewish males being screened during Operation Shark, Tel Aviv, August 1946

Jewish males awaiting interrogation by the Palestine police
during Operation Shark, Tel Aviv, August 1946

British soldiers search an unidentified Jewish settlement for the
two sergeants kidnapped by the Irgun, July 1947.

Wanted poster of Irgun and Lehi terrorists sought
by the Palestine police, date unknown

Brigadier Johnson, commander of Operation Polly (the evacuation of all
nonessential personnel from Palestine), speaking with one of the wives
at the Lydda railway station as the evacuees begin their long trip back
to the United Kingdom via Egypt, February 1947

Damage done to the Palestine Police Criminal Investigation Department's
offices in Jaffa after an Irgun assault, December 1945

Isn't it turning them against the British?" Webb had no answer except to inquire rhetorically what that reporter thought the U.S. military would do in the same circumstances. When pressed whether everything he had told them both individually and collectively was for attribution, Webb replied, "Print everything I've said. Use my name. I don't care if I'm out of the Army tomorrow."[30]

Described by one of his admiring subalterns as a "brave officer of the old school" and by another as the "epitome of an Edwardian gentleman: a great soldier, good at games, a great shot, and very knowledgeable about game birds," Webb was also completely ignorant of the emerging power of mid-twentieth-century communications—and the reach and impact that impulsively uttered, intemperate comments would now have. His words were transmitted to audiences far beyond Palestine, especially in the United States, where Webb's unsavory views served only to reinforce the pejorative impression of British rule in Palestine that Bergson and his ilk had so tirelessly cultivated.[31]

The resulting scandal cost Webb his job. He was swiftly relieved of command on grounds of publicly expressing "unauthorized and unofficial" opinions and given twenty-four hours to pack his kit and leave Palestine. Furthermore, Webb's comment acknowledging, indeed condoning, looting by his soldiers also proved singularly unhelpful, vitiating the repeated claims made by Cassels and other commanders that such accusations were baseless products of Zionist "propaganda."[32]

The international attention given to Webb's remarks accorded perfectly with Begin's strategy of transforming Palestine into a "glass house," where any misstep by the British would be broadcast to the world. "We knew that Eretz Israel, in consequence of the revolt, resembled a glass house," the Irgun commander explains in *The Revolt*. "The world was looking into it with ever-increasing interest and could see most of what was happening inside. That is very largely why we were able to pursue our struggle until we brought it to its successful climax in 1946–47. Arms were our weapons of attack; the transparency of the 'glass' was our shield of defence. Served by these two instruments we continued to deliver our blows at the structure of the Mandatory's prestige." At this strategy's foundation was Begin's conviction that the British, unlike the Nazis, were incapable of visiting barbaric reprisals on a civilian populace—an observation reflected in Kenneally's reminiscence that "the British soldier is not of the stuff the SS troops were made from."[33]

Accordingly, the Irgun commander correctly assessed that the British army would respond to terrorist provocation with a predictably self-limiting repertoire of set-piece countermeasures—including curfews, roadblocks, snap checks, and massive cordon-and-search operations—that were conceived to inconvenience and harass rather than slaughter and destroy. Begin further banked on the fact that the disruption to daily life and commerce that these activities caused would inevitably create new frictions between the populace and the government, thus further alienating the Yishuv and thwarting British attempts to obtain its cooperation. In other words, the Irgun was intentionally provoking precisely the strategy that Webb admitted the army was pursuing. Moreover, by forcing the army and the police to impose this unrelenting security regimen on the Yishuv, Begin hoped that blame would be focused on the highly visible, almost omnipresent government forces rather than on his unseen and elusive fighters. In this respect, the Irgun commander sought to exploit the elevated security presence to portray the British as the Jewish community's oppressors and the Irgun as its true defenders. Finally, Begin deliberately fostered and exploited the fundamental paradox inherent in counterterrorist operations: the more pervasive and extensive the deployment of government security forces, the more powerful and threatening the numerically inferior terrorist organization appears. In the case of Palestine, the army's increasingly dominant role in internal security because of the manifestly understrength police inadvertently created an image of terrorist strength and ubiquity divorced from reality.

A key element in Begin's strategy was to take the struggle against British rule beyond Palestine—to "beat the dog in his own kennel," as the aforementioned MI5 informant had reported following the King David Hotel bombing. To do so, however, the Irgun first had to establish the conspiratorial infrastructure necessary to support such overseas operations. As we have seen, repeated alerts of possible terrorist attacks in the U.K. had already led to the tightening of border controls and closer monitoring of the movements of Jews attempting to enter the country from the Middle East and Europe. Intensified scrutiny had also been applied to domestic right-wing Zionist organizations, such as Betar's British affiliate, which the authorities feared would be used to provide logistical support to Irgun operatives dispatched from Palestine to Britain or whose members themselves might feel emboldened to carry out attacks on the Irgun's behalf. The threat to the U.K. was judged serious enough and the countermeasures proposed to thwart it so extensive as to warrant the recently appointed director general of MI5, Sir Percy Sillitoe, to personally brief Attlee.[34]

Sensing that the environment in the U.K. was for the moment less propitious to infiltration and operational planning and execution, the Irgun changed gears and focused its propaganda and recruitment efforts outside Britain, concentrating on the vast pool of young Holocaust survivors and displaced persons arrayed across eastern, central, and southern Europe. Irgun emissaries were thus actively engaged in such activities in countries as varied as Austria, Bulgaria, Czechoslovakia, Italy, Germany, and Cyprus. Italy in particular, the British historian David Cesarani explains, "was a perfect base for Irgun activity. The country was awash with survivors of the ghettos and the concentration camps. Many were young and had been radicalised by their experiences. More than a few had acquired military training in the Jewish underground or various national resistance movements during the war. They were conveniently gathered together in Jewish Displaced Persons camps run by the United Nations Relief and Rehabilitation Administration (UNRRA) or were clustered in ports waiting to board ships intending to run the British blockade of Palestine."[35]

The priority that the Irgun attached to Italy is demonstrated by Begin's selection of one of his top lieutenants, Eliahu Tavin, to take command of the group's operations there. Tavin had been a high-priority target for the Haganah when the counterterrorist Saison campaign commenced in November 1944. He was walking along a Tel Aviv street three months later when a car carrying Saison agents pulled up beside him. The Irgun intelligence chief was bundled into the backseat and taken to a makeshift jail at a kibbutz near Ein Harod. Tavin was chained to a bed and roughly interrogated. Despite the increasing severity of his treatment and harsh conditions of his imprisonment, Tavin refused to divulge the names of the Irgun's sources within the Haganah. At one point, he was ceremoniously taken to an isolated orange grove, told that he had been sentenced to death, placed in front of a mock firing squad, and given a final chance to talk and escape execution. Tavin still refused to speak. His treatment again worsened. He was threatened with hanging and had his teeth forcibly extracted with pliers. In August 1945, Tavin was living in his own excrement, confined to a cave at the Mishmar Ha-Emek settlement, when word came that he was to be freed under the terms of a truce concluded between the Haganah and the Irgun. Begin had made Tavin's release an ineluctable condition of the agreement.[36]

Tavin was spirited out of the country on Begin's orders to Italy. The Irgun commander tasked him with building an infrastructure that would both support illegal immigration activities and facilitate terrorist attacks. Tavin trawled the UNRRA camps for recruits, seeking former Revisionist

Party members, battle-hardened partisans, and radicalized young refugees eager to fight for a Jewish state. He set up training camps and also oversaw the group's increasingly active information operations—all the while awaiting word from Begin for the attacks to begin. It finally came early that fall—concealed in the heel of a shoe belonging to Samuel Katz, a longtime Jabotinsky acolyte who had immigrated to Palestine from South Africa in 1936 and was now in charge of Irgun external relations.[37]

Tavin selected the British embassy in Rome as the Italian cell's target. Two thousand years earlier the Roman Empire had conquered the Kingdom of Israel. The rich symbolism of executing the Irgun's inaugural overseas attack in that empire's former capital figured prominently in his thinking. And the embassy—later described by the Irgun's newspaper as "a centre of anti-Jewish intrigue," responsible for coordinating regional efforts to stanch the flow of illegal immigrants from southern Europe and the Balkans to Palestine—loomed equally large as the embodiment of the modern-day foreign occupation and repression of Eretz Israel.[38]

The plan that Tavin devised entailed the placement of two suitcase bombs at the embassy's main entrance under cover of darkness that would be timed to explode sometime in the early hours of the morning. Accordingly, on October 31, an Irgun team deposited the devices on the embassy's front steps. A notice was attached to the suitcases that read, in a combination of Italian and Polish, "Attenzione—Miny" (Attention—Mines). Identical signs, complete with red flags—the universal symbol for explosives—were placed at either end of the street where the embassy was located. The ambassador's Italian chauffeur, however, happened upon the mysterious suitcases when he returned to the embassy at 2:30 a.m. He alerted a guard who in turn was able to rouse the embassy staff asleep inside and evacuate the building. Fifteen minutes later the bombs exploded. The damage was extensive: the building's ornate entrance and grand staircase were completely destroyed, its elegant façade reduced to a pile of rubble, and a large part of its roof blown away. The only person injured was an Italian man who happened to be bicycling past just as the blasts occurred. Police specialists sent from Palestine to assist in the investigation assessed the force of each explosion as approximating that of a thousand-pound bomb.[39]

The Irgun's temerity, coupled with the threat of further attacks in both Europe and Britain—made explicit in the Irgun claim of responsibility for the attack—prompted the Palestine government to dispatch two of its most senior and experienced intelligence officers to Rome. Richard Catling, the head of the CID's Jewish Affairs section, arrived on November 3. He was accompanied by John J. O'Sullivan. Although officially gazetted as an assistant superintendent of police, O'Sullivan was Isham's replacement as MI5 station chief in Palestine. The morning after they arrived, letters posted by the Irgun claiming responsibility for the attack were delivered to American journalists stationed in Rome. The attack, they warned in stilted English, "marked opening of Jewish military front in the Diaspora. Armed might of eternal people will reply with war everywhere until our fatherland is freed and people redeemed." Catling and O'Sullivan quickly confirmed the letters' authenticity.[40]

The first big break in the case followed soon after. Not far from the scene of the explosions, Italian police had detained a suspicious-looking man. Upon further investigation, they concluded that he was responsible for a third suitcase found abandoned nearby that contained explosives and detonators wired to an electric fuse. The arrest subsequently led Italian authorities to a Jewish-owned boardinghouse frequented by Polish Jews. There, they found a discarded warning sign identical to those left at the embassy. Further inquiries led to a Jewish displaced-persons camp outside the city, where police learned six Jews had arrived on October 25, only to vanish without explanation on November 1.[41]

Catling had to leave for a previously scheduled high-level meeting in London. O'Sullivan, accordingly, continued the investigation on his own, combing through immigration records at the camps for suspicious recent arrivals and departures. In this manner, he identified a known Irgun operative named Moshe Krivoshein, who had fled Rome on November 13 and was believed to be hiding in Athens. When O'Sullivan went to search Krivoshein's hotel room, he was surprised to find someone else staying there—another Jew named Israel Epstein. Although Epstein had no role in the embassy bombing, he was an old and trusted friend of Begin's from their days in the Polish Betar. The Irgun leader had sent Epstein to Italy to strengthen the group's operational capacity. He had now been inadvertently swept into the bombing investigation's widening dragnet. For the moment, O'Sullivan remained unaware of just how important a catch he had. Nonetheless, his hunch that Epstein was somehow involved in the embassy bombing was sufficient to ensure that the Italian police detained him. Demands for Epstein's release sent by the American League for a Free Palestine to the Colonial Office, to the British ambassador in Rome, and to the commander of British military forces in Italy served only to confirm O'Sullivan's suspicions.[42]

Two other breaks came over the succeeding weeks when both Krivoshein and Tavin were apprehended. The British now presented the Italian authorities with extradition requests to return all three men to Palestine for trial. Epstein panicked and, having made contact with members of the Irgun still at large, persuaded them to help him escape. The plan, however, went disastrously wrong. While attempting to scale the prison's walls, Epstein was shot dead by guards. Krivoshein and Tavin, however, kept quiet and were eventually released for lack of evidence.[43]

The investigation, in any event, had started to unravel once O'Sullivan returned to Palestine on November 14. "The Italians are not a persistent race and soon get bored with difficult subjects, particularly anything to do with the Jews, about whom their policy is to forget as far as possible," an after-action report prepared by the Rome embassy in October 1947 complained. No one in fact was ever charged with the bombing, much less brought to trial and convicted. And, except for a series of Irgun pamphlet bombs that exploded harmlessly in eight Italian cities in January 1947, as well as a series of hoax telephone calls warning of attacks on a Rome hotel used by RAF personnel and their families and on a building where both American and British intelligence agencies had offices, no further Irgun attacks ever occurred in that country.[44]

Nonetheless, the bombing instantly reignited British fears that the long-anticipated international Jewish terrorism campaign had begun. The Foreign Office urgently instructed legations across Europe and the Middle East to tighten security. Attlee himself wrote to Bevin to express his concern for the foreign secretary's safety during his upcoming visit to New York. The prime minister assured him that the State Department had been asked to ensure that "extra precautions for yourself and staff" would be taken "in view of [the] Rome outrage." The British consul general in New York was also directed to bring the matter of the foreign secretary's security to the attention of both the local FBI field office and the New York Police Department. Although demonstrators pelted Bevin with eggs, his visit to New York otherwise passed without incident.[45]

London meanwhile braced for an anticipated terrorist onslaught. An anonymous call placed to the War Office on November 6 only heightened the anxiety already gripping both Whitehall and its intelligence and security services. "Listen carefully my friend. If another drop of blood is shed in Palestine, retribution will follow to the War Office and to military officers. This will begin tomorrow. Tell Field Marshal Montgomery. You have been warned," the caller instructed the CIGS's military assistant in a voice described as that of a "typical screen villain." Although the caller did not identify himself or the organization behind the threat, the call had indeed been made at the Irgun's behest.[46]

The London press soon got hold of the story. On November 11, headline stories warning of impending Jewish terrorist attacks appeared both in sensation-prone tabloids like the *Daily Mail* and *The Evening News* and even in more sober broadsheets like *The Daily Telegraph*. "Stern Gang Here," screamed the *Daily Mail*. *The Evening News* breathlessly recounted how "emissaries of Jewish terrorist organisations have arrived in Britain from France in spite of the measures taken to prevent them. Terrorist chiefs have drawn up a 'death list' and 'operational instructions,'" it reported, "have been issued by the secret combined general staff of the two terrorist organizations to the terrorist agents now being infiltrated into Britain." Adding to the frenzy was the new session of Parliament scheduled to begin the following day, which was thought to be an especially inviting terrorist target as it would be formally opened by the king and attended by the queen and various other dignitaries. The army was called out and every police officer in London mobilized for duty. In addition to the strong uniformed police presence along the route that the king and queen traveled from Buckingham Palace to the Houses of Parliament, armed plainclothes detectives circulated throughout the crowds lining the Mall and in front of Parliament. The usually straitlaced *Times* was also carried away by the prospect of terrorist attack. It reported that "two-way radio telephone patrol cars ready to receive instructions from and supply information to the operations room at Scotland Yard" were prowling the city on heightened alert. The number of guards at government buildings was also doubled, and they were instructed to carefully scrutinize the identity documents of all visitors.[47]

Both John Rymer-Jones, now back with the Metropolitan Police, and the director of military intelligence, Major General Sir Gerald Templer, were inclined to regard the threats as inflated and the precautions as excessive. Nonetheless, they also readily conceded that the possibility of a terrorist attack could be neither confidently nor completely dismissed. The arrest in Glasgow only a few weeks earlier of a suspected Lehi operative, posing as a Polish soldier attached to General Anders's army, had lent greater credibility to fears of impending terrorist attack, as did the appearance of an important Irgun defector, who claimed to have knowledge of definite plans by the group to "carry out acts of sabotage" in Britain. Brought to London for further questioning by Special Branch officers at Scotland Yard, the man professed to be unaware of any decision to attack specific targets but insisted "that if they attempt anything they will try to sabotage buildings."[48]

The acute anxiety that reports from a variety of shadowy informants claiming access to the masterminds behind these plots generated within the British intelligence and security establishment is perhaps best illustrated by the seriousness with which a contemporaneous account of the Irgun's alleged interest in "atomic fission" was taken. According to the MI5 Haifa office, information had been received from a trustworthy source that the terrorist organization was running a "Canadian spy-ring" that, in tandem with American and Canadian sympathizers and "Jewish scientists and others connected with research work on atomic energy and atomic bomb production," was providing the Irgun with a steady stream of documents pertaining to atomic weapon research and development. The group reportedly hoped to barter its access to such information with the Soviet Union in exchange for its assistance in transporting illegal Jewish immigrants to Palestine. Although nothing more apparently was heard of any Irgun efforts along these lines, the sense of genuine alarm pervading both the intelligence community and its political masters had given rise to a remarkable situation where, on the eve of the cold war and just six months since Churchill's famous "iron curtain" speech at Westminster College in Fulton, Missouri, the prospect of Jewish terrorist attacks in the U.K. was regarded as a more serious threat than that of Soviet spying and subversion. "For the only time before the closing years of the Cold War," the renowned historian Christopher Andrew has observed, "counter-terrorism thus became a higher Secret Service priority than counter-espionage."[49]

While British intelligence struggled to contain the spread of Jewish terrorism beyond Palestine, the army was dealing with a sharp escalation of attacks inside the country. The heady optimism that had attended Operation Agatha back in June, a month when a record twenty-four significant terrorist incidents had taken place, seemed to have been validated by the precipitous decline in activity during July and August, when a total of just three attacks occurred. But this new surge in confidence was short-lived as nearly as many terrorist incidents were recorded in October as in June and six times the number for July and August combined.[50]

There had admittedly been some good news at the end of October when, acting on a tip, police thwarted an Irgun plot to bomb Jerusalem's central train station. One terrorist was killed and five others captured—although a police officer died while removing an explosives-filled suitcase left behind by the attackers. But by November the upward spiral of attacks was raising new doubts about the army's ability, despite its overwhelming numerical superiority and firepower, to sustain the momentum from Operation Agatha, much less effectively counter the threat presented by two small terrorist organizations. This was also adversely impacting morale, fostering an impression across the ranks of an army cast on the defensive—reacting and responding to an opponent who had brazenly seized the initiative. The government, however, had yet to propose a clear policy for Palestine—with little progress evident since Labour's accession to power and every prospect for the existent stasis to continue.[51]

The London Conference had indeed proven to be a frustratingly inchoate exercise, adjourning the day after it had begun—undermined by the fact that neither of the two key parties to the negotiations would attend. The entire effort had been rescued from oblivion only by the government's face-saving announcement promising a resumption of the talks following the conclusion of the Zionist Congress and the United Nations General Assembly session, both slated for December.[52]

The new colonial secretary, Creech Jones, recognized that an essential step in divining that plan entailed persuading the Zionists to join the next round of talks. He also knew that the ineluctable quid pro quo to obtain their participation required the release of the seven remaining Jewish Agency leaders detained at Latrun since June (116 other persons detained during Operation Agatha remained imprisoned along with 423 suspected members of the Irgun, Lehi, and the Palmach). Despite Cunningham's grave reservations, the colonial secretary was prepared to make this concession. In fact, the Labour government was so desperate for a breakthrough that as a further sign of good faith it agreed to transfer Barker from Palestine. Accordingly, on October 22 the War Office announced that because of the unexpected early retirement of General Sir Oliver Leese, the GOC, Eastern Command in England, Barker was being promoted to full general and appointed Leese's successor. The Jewish Agency immediately issued a statement applauding Barker's reassignment, terming it "a step in the right direction." And the Inner Zionist Council, the senior most executive body within the World Zionist Organization, quickly followed suit by issuing a declaration denouncing terrorism and calling upon the Yishuv to deny all assistance and support to the terrorist organizations. The Arab community unsurprisingly decried Barker's transfer as a craven British surrender to "America, Truman and the Jews."[53]

Creech Jones made no secret either to his colleagues in the cabinet or to the high commissioner that the declaration was not "as satisfactory as could have been wished." But, putting the best face on the situation, he argued that "in this particular resolution the Council had taken a courageous stand against terrorism which had been reinforced in public speeches subsequently by senior members of the Jewish Agency. There were signs that representative Jewish institutions in Palestine were now anxious to re-educate the Jewish Community towards a disavowal of violence." The continued detention of the leaders without trial, he explained to Cunningham, would in any event "be quite unacceptable to large sections of public opinion" both at home and abroad. Accordingly, the Inner Zionist Council statement presented an ideal opportunity to resolve that dilemma before it became still more acute. The high commissioner remained unconvinced. Two Irgun attacks earlier that morning, including the attempt to blow up the Jerusalem train station, had only affirmed Cunningham's misgivings. A policeman and two British soldiers lay dead with another thirteen persons injured, among them six Arabs. Coming less than twenty-four hours after the Inner Zionist Council's resolution, the incidents further underscored its irrelevance to the reality of Palestine's deteriorating security.[54]

Both the army general staff in London and British military intelligence in Palestine shared Cunningham's skepticism. The general staff's assessment was that the resolution would indeed have no effect on either the Irgun or Lehi and moreover would anger the Arabs while further undermining troop morale. The Sixth Airborne Division's intelligence officer similarly dismissed the resolution as meaningless given the plethora of caveats that ensured the Yishuv's new measures would fall far short of the kind of active cooperation and offensive action that had been undertaken during the Saison campaign. The Irgun, he noted, remained as defiant as it was unrepentant, not only pledging to continue to fight against the British, but also declaring that it was prepared to take on the Arabs as well as the Jewish Agency and the Haganah, if necessary.[55]

All these developments greatly perturbed Harold Beeley, Bevin's principal adviser on Palestine in the Foreign Office, who saw dark, increasingly malevolent forces at play. "Zionism has become more and more nationalistic and has, by a strange irony, inherited much of the panoply of the original persecutors of the Jews, the Nazis," he wrote in a memorandum to the foreign secretary. "The Jewish subversive organizations," to Beeley's mind, "have much in common with the Nazi S.S. and S.A."[56]

But the Jews were not the only restive community in Palestine that the government had to worry about. It had hoped to mute the inevitable chorus of Arab complaint about the Jewish leaders' release by simultaneously announcing that five Palestinian Arab leaders who had been exiled to the Seychelles during the Arab Rebellion would also be freed and allowed to return to Palestine. But even this concession could not overcome the profound sense of umbrage and injustice felt by a people still traumatized by the large number of their brethren killed and wounded when the Irgun had bombed the King David Hotel. The group's attempted robbery of the Arab Bank's Jaffa branch in September had prompted anew fears within the Arab community that it would not be long before the violence was directed against them as well. "The release of the Jewish leaders has, of course, been received with bitterness by the Arabs and the fact that their own exiles have been allowed to return does little to console them," army intelligence reported. "They contrast the ten years' detention endured by the Arabs with the four months of the Jews, and feel that it is another concession on the part of H.M.G. to Zionist pressure."[57]

The perception among Palestinian Arabs was that the government could put a stop to Jewish terrorism if it wished but instead was so completely under the Zionists' influence that it was unwilling or unable to do so. An alternative explanation that was then also gaining currency held that the government was deliberately encouraging the violence as an excuse to prolong British rule in Palestine. Whichever the case, British officials in Palestine were plainly alarmed by the hardening of Arab opinion against the government and concerned about a powerful Zionist lobby that now seemed to have London as well as Washington firmly under its omnipotent thumb.[58]

The Irgun's all-out assault on Palestine's railway system, which had commenced with the attack on the Jerusalem station and continued throughout November, appeared to vindicate the pessimistic assessments by British military intelligence and senior administration officials in response to the Inner Zionist Council's antiterrorism declaration. Seven incidents in as many days were enough to prompt Dempsey to make an unscheduled visit to Palestine on November 7 to meet with Cassels, the Sixth Airborne commander. No sooner had he returned to Cairo, however, than the Palestine Railways authority announced that because of the security forces' inability to guarantee the safety of nighttime travel, all passenger services from dusk to dawn had been indefinitely suspended. The weekend brought still more bad news when three police officers, acting on a tip about a hidden Irgun arms cache, were lured into an abandoned house in Jerusalem and killed by a remote-control-detonated bomb.[59]

Cunningham flew to London to consult with Creech Jones. Little, however, came of their discussions. The perennial default option of countrywide arms searches was once again raised, only to be dismissed for fear of creating a worse security problem that would necessitate the transfer of still more forces to Palestine to cope with the anticipated unrest. Accordingly, the only palliative that either the colonial secretary or the high commissioner could identify was the equally familiar desideratum of bringing the chronically undermanned police force up to strength as soon as possible.[60]

Meanwhile, as London dithered, the Irgun offensive continued, targeting rails and rail beds, engines and rolling stock, and stations and signal boxes. By the middle of November, it had also claimed the lives of thirteen soldiers and policemen and resulted in injuries to sixty others. In addition, at least £30,000 in damages had been caused—against terrorist losses of only one death and ten injuries. The single worst night of violence to date occurred on November 13, when widespread road and rail mining killed six policemen, injured ten others, and wounded a dozen troops. Then, two nights later, three more soldiers were injured, two seriously, when an Irgun mine exploded beneath an army trolley patrolling the railway line near Benyamina.[61]

This was the last straw for Dempsey. The following afternoon he sent an urgent, top secret cable to Montgomery. "The situation in Palestine is steadily getting worse," he explained. "There are murders and acts of sabotage each day and not a terrorist is caught." Security conditions had deteriorated to the point where "all trains have stopped running at night and there are no passenger trains at all between Lydda and Jerusalem." Although the Yishuv was to blame for its noncooperation, it was the Palestine government's "policy of appeasement" toward the community, Dempsey believed, that accounted for the escalating violence. He accused Creech Jones and Cunningham of conniving to release the remaining Jewish Agency detainees and barring the army from conducting arms searches without obtaining any kind of quid pro quo "that Terrorism would be fought." According to the Middle East commander in chief, the government had two means at its disposal to ensure the Yishuv's compliance: political pressure and coercive physical measures. Implicit in Dempsey's analysis was that the political approach had utterly failed. Therefore physical coercion was the only option. The seventy-three casualties sustained by British security forces over the preceding six weeks, he argued, "surely gives us the right" to execute the long debated—and delayed—massive arms search operations. "We soldiers had the initiative in Palestine in July and August and things were satisfactory," Dempsey concluded. "Then we stopped and handed over to the Civil Government. We are getting mighty near now to the time when the soldier takes over again."[62]

Before Montgomery could respond, the situation in Palestine took yet another turn for the worse. On November 17 an Irgun mine derailed a freight train traveling between Lydda and Gaza. Then, a few hours later, a police vehicle struck another mine planted on the Sarona–Tel Aviv Road. Three policemen and an RAF sergeant were killed and four other police constables and two airmen wounded. Incensed by the mounting casualty toll inflicted on their comrades, a group of about fifteen British police descended on Tel Aviv's Hayarkon Street. There, they vandalized three cafés—wrecking the premises and beating patrons. They also stole six cars, all of which were later found burned out or damaged. The following day brought another round of railway sabotage. An army sapper died while attempting to defuse an explosive device left on the tracks, and four others were injured. Once again, British police ran amok in Tel Aviv, attacking Jewish passersby and damaging Jewish-owned property. More than fifty cases of vandalism were reported along with thirty-two instances of assault, requiring the hospitalization of five Jewish citizens. Although Dempsey told Montgomery there was no indication that any troops were involved, *The Palestine Post* carried an eyewitness account the next day of soldiers cruising around Tel Aviv who had opened fire on a passing Jewish police patrol. None of the police were injured.[63]

Dempsey returned to Palestine on November 19—this time to confer with Barker. The breakdown of discipline that had produced the violent outbursts in Tel Aviv was clearly on his mind, as was the prospect of vigilantism spreading from the police to the army. He had come in search of answers, and the day of meetings and briefings had convinced him that the problem lay in the Palestine administration's policy of restraining the army while appeasing the Jewish Agency in the vain hope that it would revive the moribund Saison campaign. Dempsey thought this was as wrong as it was forlorn. Like Montgomery, he made no distinction between the Haganah and the Irgun or Lehi. They were all illegal organizations that had to be stamped out. Later that day he again wrote to Montgomery. "Since my last signal we have lost in killed and wounded nine British soldiers and seven British police," the commander in chief reported.

We have caught no terrorists.

The time has now come when we must take action. Mere defensive tactics such as increasing guards on railways are purely negative and can always be outwitted by our cunning adversary.

We must make the people of the country realise that their tacit acceptance of terrorism does not pay. I see no better way of doing this than finding and thoroughly searching for arms and explosives in the locality of each outrage directly [after] it occurs.[64]

Montgomery presented Dempsey's views to the cabinet's Defence Committee the next day. The progress attained against terrorism with Operations Agatha and Shark, he explained, had been reversed by the restrictions that the Palestine administration had since placed on army operations. Morale had suffered—not least because of the growing burden imposed on the military by the persistent shortage of British police. The British section was 50 percent below strength and required at least three thousand recruits to erase this shortfall. "The whole situation was rapidly deteriorating," the CIGS continued, "and it would be impossible for the Army to play an effective part unless authority could be given to use the Army fully as an aid to the civil power for the purposes of maintaining law and order in Palestine. The only means of stamping out this type of warfare," he claimed, "was to allow the Army to take the offensive against it." Although Creech Jones agreed with Montgomery's bleak assessment, he could not accept that either he or Cunningham was responsible as neither had ever interfered or otherwise inhibited any military operation. To the contrary, the colonial secretary understood that the "recent cessation of searches for arms had been agreed by the High Commissioner and the G.O.C. as being unlikely to produce any further material results." Attlee then intervened. Had not Montgomery only recently assured the cabinet that Operation Agatha had "seriously crippled" the illegal Jewish organizations? Yet the CIGS's depiction of the current situation now belied that claim. Accordingly, the prime minister directed both Creech Jones and Montgomery to provide him with a detailed explanation in the form of a report concerning the use of the armed forces in Palestine to be prepared by the Colonial Office in consultation with the military. Both the colonial secretary and the CIGS hastened to contact their respective subordinates in Jerusalem and Cairo to obtain this information.[65]

Montgomery received Dempsey's reply less than twenty-four hours later. The news from Palestine, meanwhile, was again bad. The previous day the Irgun had blown up the Income Tax Office in Jerusalem. A Jewish police officer had been killed and a British army officer and a police sergeant seriously injured. The army was now suffering casualties at a rate of two per day. In addition, all rail traffic in the country had come to a halt because of renewed terrorist attacks. The Irgun's offensive had resulted in an estimated £325,000 in damages to the railway and daily revenue losses of some £3,000. Half of the citrus crop earmarked for export now had to be trucked to ports at an additional cost of £10,000. If this continued, the agriculture industry faced paying up to £100,000 more in transit fees than usual. Oil transport by rail had been reduced by a third and potash by 75 percent. As a consequence, twelve battalions of troops—over eight thousand men—had been permanently diverted to static railway guard duties. Henceforth, the railway authority announced, every train would be preceded by soldiers traveling in armored trolley cars. Sentry posts were also being established at one-kilometer intervals along the entire line. And the PPF command had decided that it was no longer safe for unarmored police vehicles to operate at night and had therefore removed them from patrol duties during hours of darkness—with the army expected to compensate for this additional diminution of police operations as well.[66]

These developments perhaps explain why Dempsey now emphasized to Montgomery the inherent challenges of fighting an enigmatic enemy who wore no uniform nor displayed any distinctive badge or identifying insignia. "They are of the people, and the people will give us no clue as to who they are," he lamented. Unless caught in flagrante, the terrorists simply vanished into the surrounding community, blending in with, and indistinguishable from, ordinary folk. The only solution, the Middle East commander in chief believed, was to come down hard on the Yishuv. "We must therefore comb the homes of the people in the hope that we may find the terrorists or at any rate their weapons and explosives," Dempsey argued. "And by doing so we must try to bring home to the people their responsibility for these murders and outrages." But the Palestine administration, he explained, prohibited such operations. No action could be undertaken without the high commissioner's express authorization, and even then the army had to be "one hundred percent sure" that there was a direct connection between the locality where the attack occurred and the surrounding populace. Moreover, Cunningham routinely vetoed any operation that could in any way be interpreted as retaliatory or punitive. Accordingly, unlike with the Arab Rebellion, the army was barred from imposing monetary fines on communities deemed responsible for facilitating terrorist attacks. "It is a matter of deciding how much longer we wait for Jewish Agency to take action against terrorism," Dempsey grumbled. "Meanwhile our casualties continue to mount."[67]

Cunningham's response, predictably, provided a completely diametrical view. He stressed, however, that his rebuttal had been crafted in close consultation with Barker, who, the high commissioner hastened to add, "agrees with all the answers I have given." Operation Agatha, Cunningham pointed out, had not gained the initiative against the terrorist organizations for the simple reason that it was directed not against them but against the Jewish Agency and the Haganah. In this respect, it had achieved its objective by engineering the resultant collapse of the Hebrew Resistance Movement and what now appeared to be the permanent breach in the Haganah and the Palmach's relations with the Irgun and Lehi. Moreover, there was evidence of growing agency and Haganah counterterrorist activities. Although most of these initiatives remained confined to public denunciations and attendant information operations meant to undermine popular support for the two terrorist organizations, he was sufficiently encouraged by these reports and others of a Haganah ultimatum issued to both groups that they suspend operations to believe that this approach should be allowed to run its course. But what troubled the high commissioner most was the "outrageous suggestions that I have prevented action being taken if intelligence is received previous to incidents occurring"—which Barker also confirmed was inaccurate. Cunningham also scoffed at any suggestion that there was not the fullest and most effective cooperation between the Palestine government and the army. Indeed, the GOC, Cunningham asserted, "is perfectly satisfied with arrangements as they stand." Nor had Dempsey ever previously complained to him about them. "It must be realized," the high commissioner pointed out,

> that the whole situation regarding terrorist activities has changed. The outrages are now carried out by 2 or 3 men as opposed to formed bodies of the past and operations against them are really a police rather than a military matter. I, at present, strongly object in principle to reprisals or punishments carried out against the people, numbers of whom are opposed to terrorism, unless some connection with an incident can be shown and feel in fact that by alienating further the populace we would break our only feasible weapon for controlling the terrorists.

Barker agreed with him that punitive measures alone would "not end terrorism" but thought them desirable to strengthen troop morale. "It is my immediate policy, therefore," Cunningham concluded, "to encourage to the greatest possible extent the growing tendency amongst the Jews to deal with the matter themselves."[68]

The high commissioner, however, could not let the matter rest. In a second dispatch to Creech Jones later that day, he reiterated his opposition to punitive measures. Citing Ireland during the 1920s and Palestine during the 1930s, Cunningham argued that the "results of such action only serve to alienate if not to send over to the terrorists those elements of the population who are now showing signs, if not of co-operation, yet of taking action themselves with a view to the same end as ourselves." Although he was sensitive to the issue of troop morale, the high commissioner believed that reprisals would do more harm than good, not only alienating the Yishuv, but imperiling the "imminent political solution to this thorny problem." Searches of localities in which terrorist attacks occurred were pointless, because the terrorists now regularly traveled great distances by car to carry out their operations. "I am having police methods examined by an expert at this time," the high commissioner ended his second communication of the day, "to see whether we cannot get some improvement in our hunting of these men and in catching them when on the job. I have always been clear that the best method of dealing with terrorists is to kill them."[69]

Montgomery, however, was intent on blaming Creech Jones and Cunningham for the army's failure to contain terrorism and maintain order in Palestine. "My view is that the lawless elements or terrorists or whatever one likes to call them have almost complete liberty to do what they like," Montgomery complained to his deputy. Cunningham, he continued,

> seems to think that provided we take no excessive action against lawlessness the Jewish Agency and the Hagana will suppress it and restore the peace. He also seems to think that we could not stop lawlessness by offensive action and that any such offensive action on our part would merely make matters worse and would annoy the Jews. I cannot follow such reasoning. It is tantamount to admitting that we can no longer govern Palestine except on sufferance of the Jews which is in fact exactly what is happening in the country today.[70]

Had Montgomery and Dempsey paused to consider Barker's perspective on these issues, they might have drawn a different conclusion. Demonstrating an astuteness and political sophistication that his personal communications to Katy Antonius and the crass wording of his nonfraternization order following the King David Hotel bombing belie, the GOC cut immediately to the heart of the matter in his November 21 message to Dempsey. "It is true," he wrote, "that militarily we are now on defensive and have not got initiative. On [the] other hand we are not at war with Jews as a whole but only with terrorists." Barker stressed that Cunningham had never stopped him from carrying out searches when a direct connection to a terrorist incident had been established. Although it was true that the high commissioner prohibited army operations of a purely punitive or retaliatory nature, this restriction was justified, the GOC believed, because of the acute difficulty of targeting only that section of the Yishuv responsible for the violence. "As military are not at war with

Jews we consequently have hands very much tied for fear of antagonizing the innocent . . . we cannot therefore exploit our full military potential." To Barker, the ineluctable center of gravity in any counterterrorism campaign was the political dimension. "Answer to terrorist problem lies largely in political sphere," he perceptively argued. "No action that can be taken by the military acting [alone] can stop terrorism. It must be in support of some political policy which is not existent at present." The only reason that the GOC had advocated intensified searches and the levying of fines was indeed, as Cunningham noted, to maintain troop morale.[71]

This was a remarkable admission on Barker's part: that military operations in Palestine were designed less to impact the terrorists and prevent attack than to fortify morale. But Montgomery, as well as Dempsey, ignored the GOC's assessment. Blinded by his personal animus to Cunningham and wedded to the outmoded, heavy-handed tactics that had succeeded during the Arab Rebellion—but were largely irrelevant to the current conflict—Montgomery persisted in blaming Cunningham rather than realizing that the army's strategy in Palestine was wrong. On November 28 the CIGS left for Palestine intent on confronting Cunningham and resolving the matter of who would prevail in directing the struggle against terrorism in that country—the army or the Palestine administration.[72]

Montgomery, Dempsey, and Barker met with Cunningham at Government House the following day. A terse, page-and-a-half memorandum records the salient points discussed—and the absence of any agreement. Among the former was a list of five restrictions that the CIGS was convinced the Palestine administration had placed on the army:

(a) No action to be taken to disarm the population. *Note.* Possession of arms is illegal and is punishable by death.
(b) No offensive action to be undertaken except as a direct result of intelligence information.
(c) No offensive action to be taken after an outrage unless it is considered that there is a definite connection between the perpetrators and the locality concerned.
(d) No major offensive operation to be undertaken without the permission of the High Commissioner.
(e) The immense defensive task laid on the Army, e.g., twelve battalions guarding the railway.

Under the "Final conclusions" section was a statement declaring that the restrictions placed on the army were so profound as to completely undermine military operations in Palestine and render impossible the formulation of a viable plan to crush the illegal Jewish organizations. The army, it read, was therefore cast irrevocably on the "defensive waiting for the next blow."[73]

Cunningham insisted that even if the army was granted the freedom of action that Montgomery sought, its actions "would still be ineffective against the type of terrorism that we are experiencing." Further, massive arms search and cordon-and-search operations would antagonize a "major section of the population who are in agreement with us on the question of terrorism." The meeting adjourned with the CIGS's having the last word. Above Montgomery's signature appears the statement "It must be clearly understood that at present strong military action is not repeat not being taken to maintain law and order in Palestine."[74]

The chasm separating Cunningham and Montgomery boiled down to one critical issue: whether war was to be indiscriminately waged on the Yishuv or specifically directed against the terrorists. Drawing on his experiences during the final years of the Arab Rebellion, the CIGS clung to a strategy of coercion, whereby the military would in essence function as an army of occupation policing a hostile population. The Jewish community would be compelled through hardship, upheaval, and disruption to divulge information on all three of the illegal organizations, with no distinction made between the Haganah, the Irgun, and Lehi. But, as Cunningham repeatedly argued, this was an apples and oranges comparison. The Arab Rebellion was a mass uprising that enjoyed the widespread support of a large majority of that community. The struggle involving the Jewish terrorists was more nuanced. They were a minority element of the Jewish community with limited popular support. Moreover, the best way to defeat them, he believed, was to secure the Yishuv's support and the Haganah's assistance—as had been the case with the Saison. The high commissioner also judged the Irgun and Lehi to be far more sophisticated than the Arab rebels of the 1930s; hence they posed a more complex threat. As he later wrote in an article published in *International Affairs*,

These were true underground movements which had learnt much and indeed had recruited members from the underground movements which had achieved success in Europe during the war. Their murderous attacks were of the tip and run variety carried out after much reconnaissance and preparation; after them, the perpetrators sank back into the population under whose cover they were dispersed. Here was no formation for the soldiers to attack, but furtive individuals probably widely separated and unknown to each other. It seemed to me, therefore, except that soldiers when attacked should inflict the maximum casualties on the attackers, that it was a police rather than a military affair to deal with these movements; moreover, that the only sure method of stamping out this evil was in co-operation with the local population.[75]

For Cunningham, the fundamental lesson from Britain's experiences in Ireland and other dependencies beset with violent insurrection was that terrorism could not be defeated without the public's help. For Montgomery, the problem was that the army had lost the initiative in Palestine because of the civil administration's interference. To regain it, the army required a free hand to bring to bear the full weight of its coercive powers against the Yishuv.[76]

With this impasse, the battle for bureaucratic supremacy in Palestine and the clash of individual wills shifted back to London, where, Montgomery wrote in his diary, "all this will be discussed soon by the Defence Committee; the lines will really be whether His Majesty's Government is to continue to appease the Jews in the hope of reaching a solution or whether it will decide to impose its authority by force."[77]

CHAPTER 16

Blunted Bayonets

Looking out across the Valley of Hinnom from Government House to the demolished wing of the King David Hotel, Cunningham pondered why the government was losing its war against terrorism. There were a hundred thousand troops in Palestine, yet the number of terrorist incidents had quadrupled over the past year. Although the high commissioner was unwavering in his conviction that terrorism was best fought by police and not soldiers, like most of his predecessors he had been frustrated by the PPF's recurrent manpower deficiencies, anemic intelligence capabilities, and uneven performance. Bodies were still being pulled from the rubble at the King David when Cunningham wrote to Hall on August 1 to propose that an outside expert be brought to Palestine to conduct a thorough evaluation of the police force. The person he had in mind was revered as "one of the Empire's most experienced policemen." His name was Sir Charles Wickham.[1]

A decorated veteran of the Boer War, World War I, and the postwar military intervention in Siberia, Wickham had joined the Royal Irish Constabulary in 1920. He served two years as a divisional commander in Ulster before being appointed the first inspector general of the newly created Royal Ulster Constabulary (RUC). Wickham retired in 1945 at age sixty-six and departed for Athens to oversee the training of Greek police as director of the British Police Mission to that country—a post he held until 1952.[2]

Wickham's vast experience of policing violently contentious sectarian communities and countering popularly supported subversive terrorist organizations was thus particularly relevant to Palestine. He arrived on November 16. A colleague named William Moffat, the former head of the RUC's detective branch, preceded Wickham by three weeks so that he could get an early start on the CID assessment.[3]

Wickham and Moffat submitted their joint report on December 2. It presented a depressing account of incompetence, inefficiency, and a misconstrued mission. As with the Dowbiggin inquiry following the 1929 riots, and Tegart's at the height of the Arab Rebellion, the most searing criticism was leveled at the CID.

The report also provided a bleak assessment of Palestine's current security. In this respect, Wickham's views corresponded exactly with Montgomery's—whom he had met with in Jerusalem on November 30. Two small Jewish terrorist organizations, Wickham stated, had single-handedly undermined the government's prestige, caused untold damage to property and considerable injury and loss of life, thrown the security forces on the defensive, and, perhaps most corrosively, resulted in the withdrawal of police from many of their normal duties. No counterterrorist operation or initiative, he observed, had yet succeeded. In fairness to the police, Wickham noted the immense challenges such situations present. He went so far as to argue that "it is impossible completely to suppress [terrorism] unless perhaps 100 percent of [the terrorists'] demands [are] conceded." The best that could be expected was to contain the violence, which the police in Palestine had proven manifestly unable to do. According to Wickham, this was because the PPF had lost sight of its core mission and had allowed itself to become militarized to the point where it was neither a fully functioning police force nor an army—but a problematic combination of the two. "If it is agreed that the police should do the policing and the army the fighting," he argued, "then the role of the police is clear." Here again, Wickham and Montgomery were in complete accord.[4]

The problem, as the CIGS had also intuited, was that in direct contravention of the most fundamental tenets of policing, the PPF had distanced itself from the public. This, in turn, had deprived the force of the principal information source upon which all effective police work depends—and especially the intelligence needed to successfully fight terrorism. "Present police methods," Wickham explained, "are confined in most places to armoured car patrols and a reserve of mobile companies on military lines. An armoured car performs no useful police duty and is no substitute for a foot patrol. Its crew have no contact with the public and cannot use their powers of observation." Moreover, police prowling the streets concealed in menacing-looking vehicles invariably alienate the public and, in Wickham's view, bore a profoundly disquieting resemblance to the Gestapo and Nazi model of policing, hence ignoring "the first lesson of a policeman—civility to the public." The Yishuv's hostile attitude was of course an enormously complicating factor but no excuse for the PPF to have abandoned the cultivation of good relations with the community. The temptation to resort to retaliatory or punitive measures, Wickham also cautioned—in contrast to Montgomery's view—would only make a bad situation worse.[5]

Although Wickham deliberately avoided any direct criticism of the PPF's leadership, the message implicit in his assessment was that the Colonial Office had gravely erred in appointing Lieutenant Colonel William Nicol Gray to succeed Rymer-Jones as inspector general. Gray, a distinguished veteran of the Royal Marines Commandos and an expert in training methods, had seemed an ideal choice. Although Cunningham strongly favored the selection of another experienced policeman at the PPF's helm, senior Colonial Office officials were convinced that a seasoned military officer would be better. The situation in Palestine, they argued, was unique so far as policing was concerned. The military had already assumed the dominant role in maintaining security, and as long as the new man's deputy was a long-serving PPF senior officer, a soldier was thought to be the better fit given the need for close coordination and cooperation between the army and the police. Moreover, several recent commissioners of Scotland Yard had proven successful despite having no previous experience in law enforcement. Accordingly, the Colonial Office selected Gray, who had arrived in Palestine in April 1946 and assumed command from Rymer-Jones the following month.[6]

Although Wickham might have been reluctant to criticize the new inspector general, Montgomery showed no such hesitation. The thirty-seven-year-old former farmer and surveyor was not even a professional soldier, the CIGS sneered, let alone an experienced policeman. As events would shortly prove, Montgomery's reservations were well-founded.[7]

Wickham identified the PPF's continuing personnel shortages and the poor quality of recruits entering the force as having utterly compromised its effectiveness. With the end of the war, young men in Britain reporting to fulfill their National Service obligation had the option of enlisting in the PPF. Although by July 1946 this change had resulted in an impressive surge of 13,500 requests for more information about service in the PPF, for one reason or another the majority of prospective candidates were found unsuitable. This proved to be a mixed blessing in another key respect: although the pool of potential recruits certainly was expanded, they were younger, less mature, and considerably less experienced than the types of men who had joined the force in the past. Further, whatever compensation might have been provided by a rigorous training regimen had been negated by the manpower shortage that in turn resulted in a reduction of the time allocated to training and instruction from six months to just one.[8]

The British section nonetheless remained woefully undermanned—functioning with half as many police as were authorized. Moreover, from January to October 1946, nearly 500 British policemen had returned home upon the expiration of their contracts, with an additional 518 men having simply resigned and left the force of their own accord.[9]

The dearth of experienced policemen had, in turn, created two more problems. One was the lack of knowledgeable, seasoned instructors, thus accounting for the poor training that Wickham thought recruits received. Instruction was so cursory, Wickham reported, that everyone who had passed through the training depot in the past year or so would need to be brought back and properly trained. The second problem was that there were too few veteran police left in the PPF to guide and mentor their younger, inexperienced colleagues once they had completed training. In fact, nearly half of the British section had served in the PPF for less than a year, and no more than a quarter had been in uniform for more than five years. Morale had suffered commensurately.[10]

Wickham was unreservedly critical of the Police Mobile Force. It epitomized to him precisely what was wrong with the PPF. The brainchild of the previous inspector general, Rymer-Jones, the PMF had been conceived two years earlier as an elite, rapid-reaction, counterterrorist force that would also be available to support other police operations when additional manpower was required. It received an initial infusion of £2 million to facilitate both recruitment and construction of special depots at Jenin and Sarona. The PMF had also been given priority in the allocation of weapons, equipment, and vehicles from military stocks.

The elite force's authorized strength was fixed at two thousand men, and volunteers were solicited from serving officers and enlisted men in the regular army. At the PMF training depot, they were provided with detailed instruction in the handling of heavier weapons than the revolvers ordinarily carried by police in Palestine and also in commando tactics not normally associated with police operations. Wearing army khaki battle dress and with nearly fifty armored vehicles at its disposal, the PMF resembled a military armored formation more than a British colonial constabulary. According to U.S. intelligence, the PMF was conceived by Rymer-Jones to be "capable of coping with any situation that might arise." In this respect, he hoped that the mobile force would eliminate the understrength PPF's dependence on the army and thus pass the initiative back to the police.[11]

But in reality the PMF neither fulfilled any of the lofty goals set for it nor did it eradicate the PPF's reliance on the army. Like the mainstream force's British section, the PMF was also chronically undermanned. Rather than the nearly two-thousand-man force organized into eight companies originally envisaged, it possessed fewer than a thousand men divided into four companies—each of which was deficient some forty personnel. Moreover, its standard of training, so far as Montgomery could tell, was pitiful. The PMF, he believed, "could never be any better than third class soldiers." In fact, by 1946 the paucity of suitable volunteers for the PMF had necessitated a lowering of the minimum age requirement to join. Hence, 75 percent of recruits that year were between the ages of eighteen and nineteen with a commensurate lack of both maturity and experience of prior police or military service. Nearly a decade earlier, while in command of the Eighth Division in Haifa at the end of the Arab Rebellion, the future CIGS had expressed similar concerns about the police. He had warned that if these problems were not corrected, troops in Palestine would inevitably remain saddled with internal security duties—which is exactly what had happened.[12]

Because the PMF had clearly failed its primary mission of reversing the PPF's dependence on the military, Wickham questioned both its entire raison d'être and the value it brought to the police force as a whole. The tasks routinely assigned to the PMF—static guard duties, convoy escorts, armored car patrols, and manning roadblocks—he believed could be better performed by regular police. In perhaps his most damning critique of the PMF, Wickham explained that "the personnel would make a better contribution to the common cause if employed as police proper in stations when at least each man would perform daily some active and useful police function."

Implementing this change would thus free personnel to perform proper police work, such as walking a beat. This meshed with the thinking of the CIGS, who similarly argued that the PPF required a complete overhaul and reorganization to transform it back into "a proper civil police force doing its proper job" as opposed to the "quite ineffective" force it had become.[13]

The remedial measures that Wickham advocated, he readily conceded, "amount to a reversal of the role of the force from a military to a police conception." This could be quickly accomplished, he argued, simply by abolishing the PMF and transferring its personnel to the regular police. Given the continued difficulties in attracting qualified recruits, Wickham saw no other option to compensate for the British section's acute manpower shortage. The restructured police establishment, he believed, would effectively ameliorate the conditions that had contributed to the force's operational and morale problems. In conclusion Wickham reiterated, "Police are civilians and are extremely jealous of their civilian status. They resent a military atmosphere, military discipline or military units where their efficiency inevitably must be judged as soldiers and not as police. They joined to do police duty and not to be soldiers." Pursuant to Wickham's recommendations, the PMF was gradually disbanded and its personnel eventually transferred to regular police duties. The target date set for the completion of this process was February 1, 1947.[14]

Moffat's evaluation of the CID was nearly as long as Wickham's report on the entire PPF. The problems that afflicted the uniformed branch also plagued its plainclothes division: a scarcity of experienced, properly trained detectives; thoroughly inadequate training; and the heavy burden shouldered by its British personnel. The main problem was that terrorism, surprisingly, did not appear to be a priority for the CID as a whole and was instead considered to be solely the provenance of its political department. Moffat thought this was wrong because, in his experience, the entire police intelligence apparatus needed to be mobilized to effectively contend with any terrorist threat. Moffat also urged that the salaries of CID detectives be increased to ensure the retention of these highly trained personnel. These changes were absolutely imperative, he argued, if the CID were to have even "a reasonable chance of handling the terrorism problem effectively."[15]

Moffat also found the British CID officers' lack of knowledge of the Hebrew language appalling. Only three senior British detectives, for instance, could speak and understand Hebrew, and less than 6 percent of the entire force had achieved even the most basic competency in the language (by comparison, well over a quarter had obtained the basic Arabic qualification). Perhaps the most damning aspect of Moffat's critique was his recommendation that CID personnel be sent back to England for training at Scotland Yard or the headquarters of another experienced metropolitan British police force. "In London, at any rate," he caustically noted, "there would also be opportunities for acquiring a knowledge of Hebrew and Arabic."[16]

All these problems led Moffat to conclude that greater reliance must be placed on the department's Palestinian personnel. But this recommendation in particular was anathema to British CID officers in the Jewish Affairs section. Because the loyalty of Jews serving in the PPF was suspect, the CID's policy was to bar Jewish detectives from serving in the unit. Nonetheless, Moffat stressed that in the course of his inquiries he had yet to encounter any British officers who believed that the police force could function effectively without the contributions made by Jewish police and detectives; in fact, he said, many had praised the work of their Jewish colleagues. Wickham made the same point about the uniform branch in his report.[17]

Moffat was similarly astonished by the antiquated and thoroughly inadequate condition of the CID's forensic capabilities, especially the police force's laboratory. Both required prompt attention, including the provision of suitable facilities and much-needed upgrades to state-of-the-art technologies. By themselves, all these changes would not significantly improve the CID's intelligence capability, Moffat believed, unless they were accompanied by a drastic reordering of the department's priorities. He thought that the CID was not aggressive enough in going out into the field to obtain intelligence and was especially troubled by the department's poor handling of informants. Moffat specifically urged that more money be allocated to this crucial aspect of intelligence acquisition. Out of a total budget of £6 million for the 1946–47 fiscal year, for instance, only a paltry £50,000 had been allocated to informant payments.[18]

Finally, both Moffat and Wickham commented on the low wages paid to British and Palestinian officers alike, the absence of sufficient incentives given the dangers that service in the PPF entailed, and the equally miserly pay scales for officers with specialized skills.[19]

The Colonial Office had already successfully appealed to the Treasury to redress the wide variation in salary between the PPF and the metropolitan police forces. But even so, the crown agents responsible for police recruitment reported in December 1946 that they were able to enlist just over seven hundred men—a figure nearly two hundred short of their target quota. This was despite significantly increased outreach efforts, including the production of a glossy brochure titled *Palestine Police as a Career* and a nineteen-minute film, *Palestine Police*, that the Palestine government had commissioned army filmmakers to produce; the film was widely shown throughout the U.K. during 1946, especially at secondary schools and boys' clubs. The situation was sufficiently desperate that the inspector general was prepared, if necessary, to send up to twenty British officers—whom he could hardly spare—back to the U.K. to take charge of recruitment.[20]

The 1946 holiday season brought to Palestine little bonhomie, peace, or goodwill toward men. December had begun badly when, twice in two days, army vehicles struck Irgun road mines. One incident had claimed the lives of four soldiers. This brought the total number of military casualties for 1946 to forty-five killed and ninety-three wounded in addition to the deaths of twenty-eight policemen and injuries to thirty-five others. To the beleaguered Palestine government, it was also becoming clear that, reflexive expressions of reproach apart, the Jewish Agency was unwilling to do anything more against terrorism. As Cunningham himself understood, nothing short of a "radical gesture on immigration" by the government would secure the Jewish Agency's cooperation.[21]

Nonetheless, on the afternoon following the latest land mine incident, Cunningham summoned Yitzhak Ben-Zvi, a member of the Histadrut Executive, to Government House to plead again for the Yishuv's assistance. Since Arthur Creech Jones had taken office nearly two months earlier, the government had freed the remaining Operation Agatha detainees, lifted the order banning Ben-Gurion and Sneh from returning to Palestine, and allowed Jewish illegal immigrants who had been deported to Cyprus back into Palestine so long as their number did not exceed the legal monthly immigration quota of fifteen hundred persons. Yet the killings of soldiers and police continued without respite—undercutting Creech Jones's attempts to accommodate the Yishuv's various demands and Cunningham's efforts to restrain the army from instituting the harsh measures that Montgomery and other senior commanders demanded. The meeting ended inconclusively, however, with Ben-Zvi only promising to convey to his colleagues the high commissioner's concerns.[22]

Ben-Zvi was back at Government House two days later. A terrorist attack had occurred the morning after he and Cunningham had met when an Irgun truck bomb exploded inside the massive Sarafand army camp, killing two soldiers and wounding thirty others. This had been followed that same evening by a series of Irgun attacks on military targets throughout Jerusalem. Alarmed by this escalation of terrorist activity, both the Jewish Agency Executive and the Vaad Le'umi had quickly issued yet another statement denouncing terrorism. But such measures, Cunningham complained to Ben-Zvi, had no impact on the terrorists, and actions as well as words were therefore required. The Jewish Agency leader was again noncommittal. However, in his report to Creech Jones of the meeting, Cunningham expressed satisfaction that both the Irgun and Lehi had succumbed to Jewish Agency pressure and agreed to suspend operations for the duration of the Zionist Congress, which was to begin four days hence in Basel, Switzerland. He even hazarded a cautious prediction that this demonstration of the agency's ability to influence both groups might yet translate into something more tangible than its current ineffectual policy of "re-education and ostracism."[23]

No such optimism, however, remained in Britain. The past several months of heightened violence and bloodshed in Palestine had exhausted the patience of the British public. Constituent letters asked MPs why, more than a year after World War II had ended, British boys were still in uniform, dying and suffering for what was already a lost cause. "So Monty leaves Palestine," one diarist, enlisted as part of the nationwide Mass Observation project to record the contemporaneous views of ordinary Britons, wrote on December 3. "I had hoped he'd stay a bit and do something definite," this forty-four-year-old Sheffield housewife continued,

> as it seems we just go on and on there without doing a thing to get matters straight.
>
> As more and more lads are killed there, I begin to wish we had started the war a bit later, so that Hitler would have exterminated a few more Jews. All very well for good Jews to write to the papers saying ALL Jews aren't bad—oh yeah? Why don't the good Jews, then, use their influence with the bad Jews? Our benevolent attitude doesn't seem to stop their murderous deeds.

Though offensive even as a diary entry, such views were not isolated. Morale reports of units serving in Palestine that December evidence similar sentiments. "The feeling of all ranks in Palestine," a typical entry relates, "was one of loathing and contempt for all Jews."[24]

Dempsey's patience had also been sapped. The lesson he drew was that only outright coercion of the Yishuv would succeed. Montgomery agreed completely; it was also the Foreign Office's position. "I do not agree that stronger action would 'further alienate the populace,'" Harold Beeley, Bevin's adviser on Palestine, noted with respect to Wickham's report. "There is no hope that the Jewish population, or any part of it, will actively cooperate with the Administration against terrorism until they are convinced that the Administration itself means business. Sooner or later a strong police becomes unavoidable, unless we are to evacuate Palestine altogether."[25]

A military court sitting in Jerusalem had recently provided exactly the type of stern measure that Beeley believed was required to bring the Yishuv to heel. On December 11 it had convicted Abraham Kimchin, a sixteen-year-old Irgun fighter who had been arrested during the botched robbery of the Jaffa branch of the Ottoman Bank in September, of illegally discharging a firearm and possessing both that weapon and five rounds of ammunition; all three charges were capital offenses. In view of Kimchin's age, however, the court instead imposed sentences for the first offense of eighteen years' imprisonment and eighteen strokes of the cane with an additional twelve years in jail for the second and third.[26]

With the indelible image of whips wielded by Nazi storm troopers and snarling concentration camp guards still fresh in the minds of Jews everywhere, the British had inadvertently handed the Irgun a public relations gift—an issue that elicited widespread condemnation among even those who had no time for the organization and abhorred its tactics. Although flogging had not been part of the Ottoman penal code, it had been adopted for politically related offenses in the final months of the Arab Rebellion, when another British military court had imposed a similar penalty on a fourteen-year-old Arab boy found in possession of a handgun. A Jewish youth convicted in 1940 of charges stemming from a disorderly protest march in Tel Aviv appears to have been the last person to have received this punishment for a politically motivated offense. The caning sentence imposed on Kimchin was therefore meant to send a powerful and unmistakable message to the restive Yishuv.[27]

Begin instinctively understood this. Using the basic knowledge of English that he had acquired during the previous three years by listening to the BBC World Service while in hiding, he composed the text of a communiqué that would be distributed throughout the country. In his haste and perhaps also confusion of English usage, the Irgun leader—like others in the Yishuv—equated caning with flagellation and strokes with lashes. "WARNING!" posters declared in Hebrew as well as English.

> A Hebrew soldier taken prisoner by the enemy was sentenced by an illegal British Military "Court" to the humiliating punishment of flogging.
>
> We warn the occupation Government not to carry out this punishment, wich [sic] is contrary to the laws of soldiers honour. If it is put into effect—every officer of the British occupation army in Eretz-Israel will be liable to be punished in the same way: to get 18 whips.[28]

The warning was not taken seriously. Less than a week later, the same military court found Aaron Cohen, a seventeen-year-old, guilty of distributing Irgun pamphlets and sentenced him to twelve strokes of the cane—in addition to a lengthy jail term. Under the Emergency Regulations, it now only remained for Barker, as GOC, to confirm the sentences. The Vaad Le'umi, the Palestine rabbinate, and the Jewish Bar Association, among others, beseeched Barker to remit the caning sentences—

maintaining that rather than imparting a harsh lesson, each stroke would create new wellsprings of sympathy and support for the Irgun. The GOC, however, ignored their plea, and on December 27, Kimchin was caned. That night the Irgun issued a second warning:

> For centuries you have been whipping "natives" in your colonies—with impunity. In your foolish pride you dared to consider the Sons of Israel in Eretz-Yisrael as "natives" too.
>
> You are mistaken. Zion is not Exile. The Hebrews are not Zulus. You will not whip Hebrews in their Homeland. And if you do—then "His Majesty's Officers" will be whipped in full public view.[29]

The following evening Major Paddy Brett of the Second Parachute Brigade was enjoying a quiet dinner with his wife at Netanya's waterfront Metropole Hotel when several men approached their table. A revolver was produced, and the major agreed to accompany them outside. He was bundled into a waiting car and driven to a deserted spot on the outskirts of town where he was given eighteen lashes from a rawhide whip. Police and troops in armored cars had immediately sealed off the area, and search parties were about to be dispatched when, less than an hour later, Major Brett reappeared at the hotel—naked from the waist up, the skin on his back lacerated. Shortly afterward a car carrying five men was stopped at a roadblock between Petah Tiqva and Kfar Saba. A gunfight ensued, and the men were arrested. When troops searched the trunk, they found a variety of weapons—as well as two rawhide whips. Meanwhile, four other armed Irgunists seized a British noncommissioned officer in Rishon-le-Zion, who was subjected to the same treatment as Major Brett. About the same time ten Irgun fighters abducted two British staff sergeants in Tel Aviv and, after whipping them with a length of rope, left them tied to a tree in the Hadassah Gardens.[30]

Montgomery was livid. "I am particularly anxious to know," he told Dempsey, "if the Army is to be forced to accept this insult or if it is to be allowed to take the offensive against such terrorist acts." Preeminent among his concerns was the effect on troop morale, which, as Cunningham also knew, was at the breaking point. Only days before, Ben-Zvi had complained to the new chief secretary, Sir Henry Gurney, about the increasing number of random assaults on Jewish citizens by often inebriated troops. The potential for more widespread violence against the Yishuv was thus taken seriously by the army. Accordingly, all troops were immediately confined to barracks as preparations were made for a massive show of force. Countrywide antiterrorist operations commenced early on December 30 when troops from the Sixth Airborne Division cordoned off and searched Petah Tiqva and Netanya and then the next day moved on to Rishon-le-Zion and thereafter on consecutive days to Tel Aviv and Rehovot. More than six thousand people were screened, of whom just over a hundred were detained for further questioning. The amount of arms seized was frustratingly meager, amounting to only a pistol, some spare rifle barrels, and a handful of ammunition.[31]

The Yishuv saw these operations for what they were: punitive instruments of coercion meant to impact the community regardless of whether the terrorists themselves were affected. For the Irgun, however, they provided yet another opportunity for the group to taunt the security forces and embarrass the government. On the night of January 2, 1947, while the army was preoccupied with searching Rehovot, Irgun fighters struck in a dozen places throughout the country. As dusk fell, multiple teams simultaneously assaulted the Syrian Orphanage complex in Jerusalem, now an army billet known as the Schneller Barracks, and a military camp in Hadera, south of Haifa. For the first time, homemade flamethrowers produced in Irgun workshops were used in some of the attacks. Within the hour, additional incidents had been reported in both cities as well as in Tiberias, Lydda, and along the Haifa–Tel Aviv road. Although security force casualties were surprisingly light (one killed and twenty wounded), the psychological blow dealt to the government and its security forces was significant.[32]

"Palestine: Full Scale Terror; Irgun Attacks with All Resources," blared the headline on The Daily Telegraph's front page the following morning. Successive editorials both in that paper and in The Times blamed the Labour government for the policy vacuum that had given rise to the renewed violence. According to The Daily Telegraph, this had also critically deprived the security forces of direction and purpose, thus casting them on the defensive and rendering them vulnerable to attack. "The finest troops in the world," it warned, "will not put up indefinitely with being allotted the passive role of bomb-fodder." The Times was equally blunt: Continued inaction, it opined, was unacceptable. The time had come to impose increasingly more "onerous regulations" on the Yishuv until the terrorist organizations were eliminated and the attacks on British forces ceased.[33]

The coverage and the editorial commentary provided renewed validation of the Irgun's strategy. "In many cases the British Sunday papers report terrorist incidents in so sensational a manner," Gurney complained

to Creech Jones, "as to constitute what is, in fact, advertisement for terrorist organisations." This was precisely Begin's intention.[34]

Indeed, there was also no denying that the January 2 operations had
achieved all their objectives. Not only had they focused attention on the
Irgun's growing martial capabilities, but they had clearly revealed the
increasingly repressive nature of British rule. Following the assault on
the British military headquarters at Citrus House in Tel Aviv, for instance,
troops belonging to the Sixth Airborne Division had rounded up approximately seventy Jewish males, including a cripple and an invalid dragged
from his bed. They were then taken to the Sarona army base, Gurney
confirmed to Creech Jones, and forced to run a gauntlet of troops as well
as British and Arab police who tripped and beat them with fists and rifle
butts. Four men lost consciousness during the ordeal, and six required
hospitalization for their injuries.[35]

None of this was welcome news for the Labour government, which, with
the advent of the New Year, faced a series of hard decisions on Palestine.
To date, every one of its initiatives to formulate a policy—whether in concert with the United States or in negotiation with Palestine's Arab and
Jewish communities—had failed. The latest blow had come just before
Christmas, when the Zionist Congress meeting in Basel voted to boycott
the London Conference, scheduled to resume in late January 1947. The
decision dealt a crushing setback both to Bevin's hopes of restarting the
talks and to Creech Jones's futile attempts to placate the Zionist movement's moderate wing through the concessions he had dispensed throughout the fall. It was also a stunning repudiation of Weizmann's leadership
and a rejection of his judiciousness, patience, and abiding faith in Britain.
Half-blind and enfeebled by age and illness, Weizmann had delivered an
impassioned speech to the assembly decrying both terrorism and extremism. Drafted in part by the Oxford political philosopher Isaiah Berlin,
it was hailed by Weizmann's confidante Baffy Dugdale as "perhaps the
greatest I have ever heard." But it could neither turn back the tide of anti-
British sentiment that dominated the proceedings nor counter the influence of the decidedly confrontational, mostly American hard-liners, who
rallied around Ben-Gurion and pressed for a program of active resistance,
including the renewal of armed struggle. Arguments from leading figures
like Golda Meyerson, the acting head of the Jewish Agency's political
department, that the terrorists' popularity was growing in direct proportion to official Zionism's perceived passivity had proven irresistible. These

concerns were by no means unfounded. According to British intelligence, the Irgun had bragged of having attracted so many recruits at the expense of the Haganah that it did not have enough officers to train them all.[36]

It was not only the Yishuv that had soured on Britain. Palestine's Arabs were just as unyielding and similarly ill-disposed to negotiations unless their own ineluctable demand that Palestine remain a unitary state was accepted. In addition to their long-standing fears of Zionist conquest and displacement, the recent intensification of Jewish terrorism had produced fantastical notions of British perfidy and collusion. Conspiracy theories abounded to explain all manner of government decisions and policies, including the release of the remaining Operation Agatha detainees, the fact that no collective punishment measures were levied against the Yishuv, the perceived tolerance of repeated disruptions to rail traffic across the country, and the announcement in late December that the cost of maintaining the Jewish illegal immigrants in camps on Cyprus—at an estimated £2 million per year—would be borne by all of Palestine's taxpayers.[37]

The most immediate problem facing the Labour government, however, was getting the Colonial and War Offices to agree on a security policy for Palestine. The divergence in assessments that had followed the previous spike of terrorist activity back in November had resulted in Attlee's directing Creech Jones and Montgomery to produce a joint memorandum on the subject. But the document that had emerged a few weeks later was notable less for any apparent modus vivendi than for the wide chasm that continued to separate the Palestine administration and the military. The sharp uptick in terrorism at the end of 1946, coupled with the ignominy of the flogging incidents, had endowed this issue with even greater urgency. Regardless of whatever policy for Palestine's future the government might decide, it was absolutely imperative that order be maintained in the country to facilitate its implementation.[38]

With this in mind, the cabinet's Defence Committee, which comprised all the relevant principal ministers, including the prime minister, and the CIGS, met on New Year's Day to try to resolve this impasse. Creech Jones spoke first. In his view, political considerations had to take precedence over security concerns, especially if the London Conference was to be revived and given any prospect of success. The colonial secretary claimed that great strides had been made in strengthening the Yishuv's moderate leadership and had produced a discernible inclination toward cooperation. Bevin followed. It was impossible, he believed, to separate Palestine's immediate security needs from the government's ultimate determination of the mandate's future. In the meantime, however, British prestige across the region was crumbling. This was very dangerous, he warned, because Britain's prosperity and stature as a world power depended on its continued access to Middle Eastern oil. Palestine was thus "strategically essential" to British interests in the region, and any settlement of Arab and Jewish claims must take account of this. Montgomery spoke next. He proclaimed his complete and utter disbelief in the Colonial Office's assertion in its section of the joint memorandum that the Jewish Agency "had the extremists under control." According to all the intelligence he had seen, nothing could be further from the truth. Instead, the "whole country was in the grip of lawlessness." Harking back to his experiences in Palestine during the Arab Rebellion, Montgomery urged that the entire country be flooded with mobile columns of troops.[39]

Attlee spoke last. The current status quo in Palestine was completely unacceptable, the prime minister declared. The military had been placed "in an impossible position" by the operational restraints imposed on it. He therefore again instructed the Colonial and War Offices, this time in direct consultation with Cunningham, to draft a completely new directive that would clearly define the rules of engagement under which the military's power could be brought to bear to restore and maintain order in Palestine. "The Prime Minister came down heavily on my side," Montgomery records in his memoir, "and the Colonial Secretary was routed." This perhaps explains why, as the Defence Committee members left the meeting room, Creech Jones surprised Montgomery by asking him to prepare the draft of the directive for discussion at a meeting to be held in two days' time, with the high commissioner attending, at the Colonial Office.[40]

Cunningham arrived in London via Malta on the afternoon of January 3. The meeting began testily that evening with the high commissioner once more rebutting the CIGS's accusations that he had prevented the army from taking offensive action against terrorism. The crux of the matter, Cunningham reiterated, was that counterterrorism was primarily a police responsibility, because success depended on information provided willingly by the civilian populace—a point that Wickham had also emphasized in his recent report. The CIGS strongly disagreed. The problem as he saw it was that the army "was not allowed to act unless there was evidence of terrorist activity: it must wait for the terrorists to act and was always on the defensive." Citing the success achieved by the army during the Arab Rebellion, Montgomery outlined his plan of "turning the place upside down" through countrywide searches without waiting for either evidence or provocation. He conceded that this would likely inconvenience innocent people and upset daily life, but that was precisely the point. The Yishuv, he predicted, would then "tire of being upset and would co-operate in putting an end to terrorism." So fervent was his faith in this outcome that the CIGS was prepared to stake "the whole strength of the British Army" on it and if necessary to relocate sufficient forces to Palestine from either Germany or Egypt for these operations. After further discussion, agreement was reached on the four-point directive that Montgomery had drafted. In a concession to Cunningham, a carefully worded proviso was inserted prohibiting purely punitive operations that would needlessly impact law-abiding communities. As the meeting concluded, the CIGS inquired whether Cunningham was now prepared to give military commanders a free hand in Palestine to carry out the directive. An appalled Cunningham replied that he most certainly was not because his job was to take into account the political as well as the security aspects of governing Palestine. Creech Jones then intervened, suggesting that this was an issue best left for the cabinet to decide. Montgomery was clearly perturbed, and on that note the meeting adjourned.[41]

The cabinet considered the matter at its January 15 meeting. The minutes record a consensus that "more vigorous action" was required in Palestine and that "leniency towards the terrorists would not strengthen the influence of the Jewish Agency." The directive, as drafted by Montgomery, was approved and the army given the green light to take the offensive. In anticipation of just this outcome, the CIGS had already written to Dempsey with instructions that once authorization for these more aggressive operations was obtained, the army must be ready to act with alacrity. This, Montgomery had advised, would also entail "that the whole life of the armed forces in Palestine be at once adjusted to the new policy" so that terrorist opportunities to kidnap soldiers were minimized, if not eliminated completely. Accordingly, new orders were issued declaring out-of-bounds all but a handful of cinemas, restaurants, cafés, and bars in Palestine that the military authorities judged to be secure. Troops were also instructed to walk or travel armed in pairs when venturing outside military facilities or encampments.[42]

Similar restrictions were now imposed on civilian officials as well. The newly appointed undersecretary of finance, John Fletcher-Cooke, arrived that winter to replace his deceased predecessor, Julius Jacobs, one of the King David Hotel bombing's Jewish victims. He described the grim existence that he and his fellow civil servants endured. "My life and work in Jerusalem, like those of every other Government officer," Fletcher-Cooke recalled, "was severely circumscribed. Armed guards accompanied me to my Jewish dentist for treatment; armed guards patrolled the main shopping area for an hour or two on certain days, which were the only times we could visit the shops and the banks; and travelling outside Jerusalem was only permitted with armed escorts." Their dependents were subject to the same strict precautions. As a young boy, David Tomlinson remembered going with his family in early 1947 to Jerusalem, where his father commanded an army transport company. He initially traveled to school by bus with other British children. But then intelligence surfaced of a Lehi plot to blow it up. Thereafter, Tomlinson rode to and from school in the backseat of an army staff car—accompanied by armed escorts sitting on either side of him.[43]

Despite all these security measures, the terrorist attacks continued. On January 12, Lehi carried out its first major operation in months, using a stolen staff car, packed with explosives, to demolish the Haifa district police headquarters. Four policemen were killed and more than sixty people injured; the cost of rebuilding the facility was estimated to be well over £200,000. Then, two days later, a military court convicted another seventeen-year-old Irgun fighter implicated in the attempted robbery of the Jaffa Ottoman Bank to life imprisonment and eighteen strokes of the cane. With tension already running high, the Palestine administration sought a face-saving solution to avert a complete breakdown of relations with the Yishuv. It found one in the form of a government doctor who was sent to examine the boy in his cell at Jerusalem's central prison. The doctor duly concluded that the young man was not healthy enough to tolerate corporal punishment, and the administration, citing medical reasons, revoked the caning sentence. This still left Aaron Cohen, the Irgunist convicted in December, whose sentence of a dozen strokes from the cane Barker had already confirmed. However, citing the incongruity of penalties stipulated in the Emergency Regulations and the Palestine Juvenile Offenders Ordinance, where the latter limited caning only to people aged sixteen or younger and took legal precedence over the Emergency Regulations, the Palestine government announced that this component of Cohen's sentence was being nullified. At age seventeen, the press release explained, Cohen had not in fact been eligible for this punishment in the first place.[44]

Montgomery was incandescent at this craven surrender to terrorist threats and had made his feelings clear on this subject at the cabinet meeting on January 15. Since 1938, he complained, no Jewish terrorist convicted of a capital offense had yet to be executed. In 1946 alone, eighty-three such offenders had escaped the gallows for one reason or another. More appalling, even cases of corporal punishment were now being remitted. "It is a weak and thoroughly bad policy," the CIGS maintained. "It is merely laying up great trouble for ourselves if we remit sentences because we are afraid of possible Jewish reaction. We are afraid of nothing and it is high time we made this clear to all illegal armed organisations in Palestine." He had the cabinet's full backing—with Attlee noting the adverse impact that this serial commutation of sentences was also having on Arab opinion. Montgomery personally apprised Cunningham of the cabinet's decision the following day, just hours before the high commissioner was due to return to Palestine. Henceforth, terrorists convicted of capital offenses would be put to death without either delay or demurral.[45]

Imperial history is littered with examples of decisions to embrace the death penalty for convicted terrorists as a means of imparting a stern deterrent message and thereby demonstrating governmental resolve and steadfastness. In reality, the results more often than not have been counterproductive, turning popular opprobrium into sympathy and terrorists into freedom fighters. Martyrs thereby arise where none had previously existed. Both Jabotinsky and Ben-Gurion, who agreed on little else, clearly understood this a decade before, when a young member of Betar named Shlomo Ben-Yosef became the first and only Jew to be hanged in Palestine for a political crime. The Revisionist Zionist leader had then presciently warned the British that "martyrs become prophets and bombs become altars." Within weeks of Ben-Yosef's execution a thoroughly revitalized and further radicalized Irgun had unleashed a renewed campaign of violence that greatly complicated British efforts to restore order in Palestine at an especially critical time. Looking back on these events, Ben-Gurion had bitterly observed that Ben-Yosef's death, more than any other contemporary event, had galvanized popular support within the Yishuv behind the Irgun. Addressing the House of Commons on January 31, 1947, the Labour MP Richard Crossman, a member of the Anglo-American Committee, had made the same point within the context of current developments in Palestine. A recently convicted Irgun fighter named Dov Gruner would provide the first test of both the government's determination to enforce the Emergency Regulations' death penalty statutes and the utility of capital punishment as a coercive instrument with which to defeat terrorism.[46]

As a test case demonstrating British resolve, however, Gruner was a particularly poor choice. It is easy to see why the authorities would have thought otherwise. At the time of his arrest the previous April, Gruner was thirty-four years old and had been caught in flagrante during an Irgun raid on a police armory in Ramat Gan shooting at members of HM Forces and planting explosives. Shot in the face and his jaw shattered, Gruner had spent more than eight months recovering in the hospital before he was judged fit to stand trial. But however much the British saw him as epitomizing the cold-blooded Jewish terrorist, to other eyes Gruner's life story evoked simultaneously the suffering of European Jewry, the courage and tenacity of a new generation of Palestinian Jews willing to take control of their own destiny, and an ethos of self-sacrifice and personal integrity that reflected positively on the Irgun.

Born in Hungary before World War I to a religiously observant family, Gruner had studied engineering before illegally immigrating to Palestine in 1938, at age twenty-six. In 1941 he enlisted in the British army. A twice-wounded combat veteran of the Italian campaign, Gruner learned at the end of the war that most of his family had perished in the Holocaust. He joined the Irgun shortly after being demobilized in 1946, only to be arrested during the abortive arms raid a few months later. Articulate and intelligent, Gruner had delivered a searing indictment of British rule when offered the opportunity to make a final statement before being sentenced, eloquently denying the military officers who sat in judgment their authority and right to do so. Even Churchill had been moved to call attention in Parliament to Gruner's bearing and demeanor, observing that the "fortitude of this man, criminal though he be, must not escape the notice of this House." On January 24, Barker confirmed Gruner's death sentence, and the execution date was fixed for the twenty-eighth. The chief rabbi, citing the Irgun fighter's exemplary military record while serving in the British army and tragic family circumstances, unsuccessfully beseeched Cunningham to spare the condemned man's life. The Irgun's appeal came predictably as a threat. "Execution of prisoners of war is premeditated murder," it stated. "We warn the British regime of blood against the commission of this crime."[47]

Nonetheless, fortified by the new operational directive and the recent arrival in Palestine of the Third Infantry Division, military commanders there remained supremely confident of their ability to meet any challenge. Indeed, when questions had been raised in Parliament whether the army now had all the powers it required in Palestine, Creech Jones had hastened to assure the House that it did. But what the army still lacked was the intelligence necessary to begin, much less sustain, a genuinely effective counterterrorism effort. At a meeting held at Government House with

Cunningham, Gurney, and Dempsey, for instance, Barker had disclosed that the major searches then under way in various parts of the country were being conducted without any hard information or even suspicion of terrorist activity in those areas. The Irgun thus retained the initiative—as Begin proved on January 25, when the group put into motion its plan to thwart Gruner's impending execution.[48]

Shortly past 5:00 that evening, a retired British army major named H. A. I. Collins was serving tea to a Jewish lady friend in his downtown Jerusalem apartment when there was a knock at the front door. After leaving the military in 1945, Collins had served for a year in the Palestine government as deputy controller of light industries before striking out on his own. Unique among the British expatriate community, he was widely known for his many connections with Jewish businesses and more so, as *The Times* observed, for being "especially well disposed towards Jews." Accordingly, Collins doubtless thought nothing of the woman waiting on his doorstep who said there was someone with her who wished to speak with him. As Collins opened the door, three Irgun men armed with Sten guns barged in and ordered him to face the wall. A fourth Irgun man came up behind Collins and covered his face with a rag doused in chloroform. Collins collapsed and was carried outside into a waiting car. His female companion was held in the apartment for nearly an hour and then freed. She immediately called the police. Terrorism alarm sirens sounded as hastily erected roadblocks brought all traffic in the city center to a standstill. Soldiers erected barricades on every corner, forcing pedestrians to pass through a series of checkpoints arrayed along each street. A curfew was imposed over Jerusalem's Jewish neighborhoods the following morning as police and army units conducted house-to-house searches. Roving armored police vehicles and army foot patrols also swept the city—all to no avail.[49]

While the hunt for Collins continued in Jerusalem, Judge Ralph Windham, scion of the aristocratic Bowyer-Smyth baronetcy and newly promoted president of the district court, was presiding over a Tel Aviv courtroom. Resplendent in traditional British judicial wig and gown, Windham was hearing what he later recalled as a "rather boring succession case," when about half past noon six armed men arrived at the building on Yehuda Halevy Street. While three kept watch outside, the other three burst into the courtroom and seized Windham. He was hustled into a waiting car and driven away. Roadblocks were quickly established, but they were again too late, and Palestine once more was plunged into crisis.[50]

The Irgun had successfully maneuvered the government into a corner. To proceed with Gruner's execution risked condemning a distinguished jurist from a renowned family and a former officer of the British army to certain death. But to succumb to this brazen act of blackmail undermined the rule of law that the execution was designed to uphold and risked the continued erosion of British prestige both inside Palestine and beyond. The fact that this new imbroglio had occurred on the same day that the London Conference reconvened only made matters worse. In desperation, the Palestine administration seized upon yet another face-saving solution. With less than twenty-four hours remaining before Gruner would hang, Barker was prevailed upon to sign a respite order granting him a two-day stay of execution so that Gruner might consult with his attorney about filing an appeal with the Privy Council in London—the king's most senior, standing advisory body. Having bought some time with which to continue the search for Collins and Windham, Cunningham now turned his attention to obtaining the Yishuv's assistance. That same afternoon, the Jewish Agency's Golda Meyerson and Eliezer Kaplan together with Israel Rokach, the mayor of Tel Aviv, were summoned to Government House. Cunningham delivered a blunt ultimatum: either Windham and Collins were freed, unharmed, within forty-eight hours, or martial law would be imposed over Tel Aviv, Petah Tiqva, and Ramat Gan. This measure, which was unprecedented even in the Palestine mandate's long and violent history, would entail, the high commissioner explained, the withdrawal of all civil administration from the affected areas, which would be cordoned off and placed under military rule and hence subject to the orders of the local military commander. In essence, the entire populations of those communities would be confined to their homes under strict curfew, and all commerce and social interaction would cease.[51]

The threat of martial law had been raised by Gurney earlier in the month when he had met with two other senior Jewish Agency officers following the flogging incidents. At the time, Colonial Office officials had judged it to have been effective in pressuring the agency to persuade the terrorists to accept a temporary, self-imposed truce. When again wielded now, it produced similarly salutary results. The Jewish Agency Executive promptly passed a resolution unequivocally condemning the kidnappings and calling upon the "demented desperadoes" responsible for this outrage to release their captives. Rokach issued a similar plea. At just past nine o'clock that same evening, a telephone call was made from a factory at Ramat Gan to the Jaffa police station. It was Windham informing them that he had been freed—minus his wig, which the kidnappers had kept as a souvenir. Collins was released the following night. Although Windham had been treated well, Collins suffered serious injury from the chloroform, which burned his eyes, nose, and mouth and prevented him from eating. He had also been kept at the bottom of an abandoned well just outside Jerusalem, whereas Windham was held in the comparatively more comfortable confines of a simple shack, where he was given fresh fruits and other food to eat as well as copies of *The Palestine Post* and Arthur Koestler's novel about militant Zionism, *Thieves in the Night*, to read. Windham would go on to lead a full and vibrant life, eventually becoming chief justice of Tanganyika, whereas Collins would thereafter be burdened with recurrent respiratory problems believed to have been caused by the chloroform before dying of emphysema in 1960.[52]

The kidnappings of Collins and Windham had laid bare the government's inability to protect Britons living and working in Palestine. In the abductions' aftermath, troops were now ordered to walk or travel everywhere in groups of at least four armed persons. But all the Palestine administration could do with respect to the country's expatriate community was to advise them to remain indoors. Accordingly, on January 27, Cunningham proposed to Creech Jones that all British women, children, and nonessential personnel be evacuated from Palestine and the remaining civil servants all be concentrated behind the aforementioned special, barbed-wire security zones popularly known as Bevingrads. He still believed that security conditions had not deteriorated to a point requiring the imposition of martial law over the entire country. But the high commissioner was convinced that the evacuation should proceed without delay given the Irgun's threat to "turn Palestine into a blood bath" if Gruner hanged. Barker agreed. In a letter to an irate Katy Antonius, who regarded the decision as yet another capitulation to the Jews, the GOC defended the decision. "We cannot go on having a pistol held at our hearts by these terrorists," he patiently explained, "and we must make kidnapping almost impossible." Dempsey also supported Cunningham's proposal, telling Montgomery that the high commissioner would now be able to "adopt a firm policy without fear of unpleasant reprisals."[53]

The CIGS, however, was again appalled. He wrote immediately to Creech Jones and then to Dempsey. "It is quite monstrous," he fumed to his Middle East commander, "to negotiate with illegal organisations and to say that unless they do this then we will do that." Montgomery had no objections to Cunningham's plan to evacuate British wives and children but instructed Dempsey that once this was accomplished, "you must set about the illegal armed organisations properly and go into battle with a bang." He then vented his frustrations in a manner that could as easily be interpreted as criticism of the Labour government as of his perennial bête noire, Cunningham.[54]

The letter that Montgomery had sent to Creech Jones on January 28 was unrestrained in the opprobrium that it heaped on Cunningham for pressing Barker to grant Gruner's stay of execution and for providing forty-eight hours' notice of the imposition of martial law if Collins and Windham were not freed. Although the colonial secretary's reply to the CIGS was polite and even conciliatory, it is clear that he regarded the repetition of Montgomery's intemperate views as both impertinent and inappropriate. Creech Jones brought the matter before the prime minister, who then summoned Montgomery to No. 10 Downing Street. Attlee explained to the CIGS that if the contents of either communication ever became public, it would cause grave embarrassment to the government—especially while the London Conference was meeting and a critical debate on Palestine was to take place shortly in Parliament. The prime minister therefore told the CIGS that he would be obliged if Montgomery would retract both missives. Montgomery readily agreed to do so.[55]

The CIGS was not alone in his acute distaste for what was happening in Palestine. On January 27 an editorial published in *The Times* had come out unequivocally in favor of partition—citing the danger and abuse that British troops and police had continually been subjected to because of the government's delay in announcing a long-term policy. And four days later, the much-anticipated debate on Palestine clearly displayed the depths of parliamentary despair and disgruntlement over the Labour government's prolonged procrastination. Speaking for the Opposition, the former colonial secretary Oliver Stanley argued that it was no longer possible to carry on ruling Palestine given the events of the past few weeks. "No authority can stand up against such blows," he declared. "No troops, no police can carry out their duties in circumstances such as these. We cannot have a situation where the administration of justice and the punishment of offenders is being dictated by the criminals themselves. Frankly, so far as I am concerned, sooner than this country should have to endure further humiliations of this kind, I would prefer that we should clear out of Palestine and tell the peoples of the world that we are unable to carry out our Mandate there." Both Reginald Manningham-Buller, a fellow Tory, and the Labour backbencher Richard Crossman agreed that the mandate in its present form was no longer tenable. Churchill, the leader of the Opposition, had come to the same conclusion. He saw "absolutely no reason" that "poor overburdened heavily injured" Britain should have to continue to bear the responsibility of Palestine alone. The only practicable alternative, the former prime minister suggested, was if the United States was willing to cooperate with Britain on a fifty-fifty basis in implementing an agreed-upon policy for Palestine. In the absence of such a partnership, Churchill argued that the London Conference should be allowed to run its course, but if it failed to produce a solution, Britain should within six months turn the entire question of Palestine's future over to the United Nations. "It is quite certain that what is going on now in Palestine is doing us a great deal of harm in every way," he declared. "This is the road of abject defeat, and though I hate this quarrel with the Jews, and I hate their methods of outrage, if you are engaged in the matter, at least bear yourselves like men."[56]

It was now the government's turn. Creech Jones paid tribute to the security forces and Palestine administration but deflected questions about a long-term policy while the London Conference and other, unspecified consultations continued. It was what he did not say, however, that was important. Earlier that afternoon, in fact only minutes after the debate commenced, the Palestine Broadcasting Service had announced that evacuation orders were being issued to every British household in the country. No appeal was permitted, and everyone to whom this order had been served was instructed to be ready to leave Palestine at forty-eight hours' notice. Operation Polly—the transfer of all the evacuees by rail to Egypt and eventually home to Britain—was fixed for February 5. In the interim the evacuees would be housed at facilities throughout Palestine. The baggage allowance for each household was limited to only one suitcase, two blankets, one day's rations, and a baby carriage, if needed. Troops would be posted at vacated residences until the belongings left behind could be packed and removed for shipment. The announcement of Polly also contained news of Operation Cantonment. This entailed the required relocation of all remaining British civilian personnel to special security zones in each of Palestine's major cities. That same afternoon, troops had already begun to unroll coils of barbed wire around residential areas in Jerusalem, Tel Aviv, and Haifa in order to expand and reinforce existing zones or create new ones. All dwellings within these newly established perimeters that were not owned by British nationals were requisitioned from their owners, who were forced to find accommodation elsewhere. "The object of CANTONMENT," an operational order explained to the troops, "is to enable the Government to operate and to give the military freedom of action whilst NOT hampered by terrorist blackmail and kidnapping."[57]

The twin operations immediately rekindled Jewish fears that the government was preparing to impose martial law. On February 2, Meyerson told a press conference, "There is no doubt whatever that a regime of this kind will probably result in very little harm to the small number of persons in the two terrorist groups, but it will strike at the vast majority who have no connection whatever with them." An editorial in *The Palestine Post* similarly described the new measures as "ominous and depressing" and designed "less . . . to pacify this country than to appease the 'strong hand' advocates in Britain." Palestine's Arabs remained unimpressed. To their mind, these developments provided further evidence of British perfidy and of a grand scheme to deprive the country's rightful inhabitants of their homeland. "Can you conceive of such a state of affairs in a country ruled by Britain," *Falastin* asked, "and where she has mustered 100,000 soldiers, that is, one fully-equipped soldier to every five Jews! By Allah, if we were asked what was the greatest lie ever told, we would say that it is the reason for the evacuation."[58]

In the Yishuv's case, its suspicions were indeed well-founded. Less than twenty-four hours before the first British evacuees were due to depart Palestine, Creech Jones had informed Attlee of Cunningham's intention to impose martial law on select Jewish neighborhoods in the event of some new terrorist incident. The high commissioner unveiled his plan the following day at the weekly top secret security meeting held at Government House. British military commanders made no effort to conceal the punitive-cum-coercive dimensions of Operation Cantonment and an ancillary operation code-named Fantail. On February 5, Sixth Airborne headquarters instructed its officers to tell any Jew who complained that it was the terrorists, and not the army, who were to blame for the seizure of their homes and that they should expect to be further inconvenienced if they did not begin to actively assist the authorities in ending the violence.[59]

Operation Polly concluded successfully on February 8. Although thought to have been named for Barker's spouse, the evacuees joked that "Polly" really was an acronym for "Panic Over Lots of Lousy Yids"—as much an unseemly retreat in the face of terrorism as it was unnecessary. Robert W. Hamilton, the government's director of antiquities, excoriated the policy "of scuttle" in a letter to his wife. It "can only bring the British government and British people into contempt," he fumed.[60]

Some seventeen hundred British civilians were evacuated from Palestine without incident. The original plan had been to fly the families to Egypt in Halifax bombers. But after one crashed in a sandstorm while en route to Palestine to collect the evacuees, the military decided to transport them by train instead. The journey took a full day on board what one young participant recalled as the longest passenger train ever assembled by the Palestine Railways authority. As he and his mother departed Jerusalem's Allenby Barracks with the other evacuees in an armed convoy for the train station just down the road, the pipers of the Black Watch serenaded them with "The Skye Boat Song." Although the first group of evacuees would be back in Britain by the beginning of March, it was not until July that this young boy and his mother finally made it home.[61]

Because so few military wives and dependents were still in Palestine by 1947, Operation Polly inevitably affected the troops less directly than it did the British civil servants who remained behind after their families had departed. Their morale, already shattered by the King David tragedy, now sank to a new low. "Yes, we are in an upset here!" Lloyd Phillips complained to his father, describing his new living conditions "behind simply masses of barbed wire and Bren guns" at the Gaza police headquarters as "pretty dreadful." The situation in Jerusalem, he reported the following week, was hardly any better. "I hope to be left undisturbed in St. George's [Cathedral compound] where a number of women and clergy are residing, protected by the odour of sanctity—a more efficient agent, I trust," Hamilton told his wife, "than the blunted bayonets and misdirected bullets of the British army."[62]

That the morale of remaining officials stayed afloat at all was credited to the tireless efforts and immense popularity of Gurney. An old Africa hand who had spent his career in the Colonial Service, the chief secretary had quickly won the praise and admiration of the entire secretariat for his superb managerial skills, remarkable efficiency, "complete imperturbability" (in Fletcher-Cooke's words), and sincere concern for the welfare and careers of his subordinates. An accomplished golfer, he could be found most afternoons on the course outside Jerusalem popular with the expatriate community—playing while surrounded by armed guards. In the new, heavily circumscribed and austere existence imposed on civil servants following Polly, Cantonment, and Fantail, Gurney indefatigably arranged picnics, games, dinners, and bathing parties for the secretariat officers in hopes of enlivening their otherwise drab lives. The Jerusalem Sports Club also strove to continue its various sports and recreational programs. Indeed, the only activity that appeared to suffer was field hockey, as it was not possible to field a team that year because of both security conditions and a lack of time to properly train. Even the annual Ramle Vale Hunt went ahead as planned—despite a few days' postponement until Operation Polly was completed.[63]

Daily life for soldiers, though, had become even more exacting and demoralizing than for civilians. All Jewish areas, including the entirety of Tel Aviv, were declared out-of-bounds. This meant that the troops had no social life or opportunities for relaxation outside their heavily guarded bases and encampments. Thus the inherent monotony of garrison life was further exacerbated by the lack of amenities and poor condition of the eighteen facilities throughout Palestine where British military forces were domiciled. This was a constant concern of Montgomery's as most housing consisted only of tented accommodation, which was insufferably hot during the summer and brutally cold in the winter. Living quarters also often lacked electricity and "all those things which go towards making life even bearable for a soldier," the CIGS complained in his diary.[64]

Barker acknowledged these hardships in a special order of the day issued to British troops on February 12—his last in Palestine. The GOC paid tribute to their discipline and comportment despite immense suffering and provocation. He cited the "considerable odium and abuse from sections of the Jewish community" and the lack of amenities that had made a difficult situation worse. "The future," Barker concluded the farewell message, "is still not clear; it does not, however, appear that peace will come to this unhappy country immediately." Just before boarding the plane that would carry him back to England later that day, Barker reportedly paused and, in a symbolic gesture of contempt, urinated on the ground.[65]

The prospects for peace, which, as Barker noted, were already slim, suffered a further blow on February 10, when both the Arab delegation to the London talks and the Jewish Agency rejected the government's latest proposals on Palestine's future. Called the Bevin Plan, the new scheme had been presented to the cabinet the previous week by both the foreign secretary and Creech Jones. It represented a stunning reversal of the colonial secretary's thinking. Until then, he had remained convinced that partition was the best of several problematic options. But a combination of entrenched Arab opposition and the prospect that an economically viable Jewish state would inevitably contain a large and implacable Arab populace, coupled with the uncertainty of obtaining the UN's approval and, most of all, the large number of British troops that would be needed to implement partition, had conspired to convince Creech Jones of its impracticality. Accordingly, he agreed to support Bevin's proposal that Palestine become a unitary, binational state following a five-year period of continued British rule under UN trusteeship. The provincial autonomy scheme that the cabinet had found so promising only a few months before was swept aside. Instead, a joint Arab and Jewish central government would administer a series of not necessarily geographically contiguous Arab- and Jewish-majority "cantons." Up to a hundred thousand Jewish immigrants would be allowed to settle in Palestine over the next two years, with future immigration left to both communities to determine or, failing agreement, for a UN arbitration tribunal to decide.[66]

"*Quite* unacceptable" is how Shertok described the plan to Dugdale on February 10 over a dim, candlelit lunch imposed by nationwide power cuts at London's popular Carlton Grill. It was "worse in most respects" than the provincial autonomy scheme, he explained, and anathema in terms of immigration both in stretching over two years a process that the Zionists demanded be immediate and in putting a cap on the total number. A Jewish Agency delegation, led by Ben-Gurion, was meeting with Bevin and Creech Jones that afternoon to formally convey its rejection. At what would prove to be the London Conference's final substantive meeting the following day, Palestine's Arabs restated their unalterable position that any proposal ceding any form of Jewish sovereignty in Palestine or allowing any further Jewish immigration was completely unacceptable.[67]

With all hope of a negotiated settlement now lost, the cabinet met on February 14 to determine Palestine's fate. Nearly a decade before, as the Arab Rebellion had approached its third anniversary, the Palestine government's treasurer, William Joseph Johnson, had predicted that the time would come "when the British taxpayer will not be prepared or able to make large grants in reimbursement of the cost" of internal security operations for that country. In February 1947 that time had arrived. An unrelenting succession of record snowfalls had paralyzed most of Britain as the harshest winter in nearly a century wreaked havoc on the nation's faltering economy. Growing fuel shortages had set in motion the first sporadic, local power cuts on January 28. Two weeks later widespread, nationwide outages were being reported. Factories and industries lay idle as some ten million workers were sent home, where they huddled in the dark with their families, trying to keep warm. Few would therefore have disagreed with George Taylor, a Sheffield accountant who two days earlier had noted in his diary, "We seem infinitely worse off than at any time during the war."[68]

Accordingly, the drag on the economy imposed by Britain's still vast overseas military commitments and attendant expenditure, alongside the continued slow pace of postwar demobilization, could not, as Bevin and Creech Jones reminded colleagues in a joint paper, be separated from the discussion about Palestine. Churchill had made the same point in his peroration before the House of Commons the previous month. The cost of maintaining British military forces in Palestine was about £35 million annually—approximately 3 percent of the 1947 defense budget. Although this proportion was small, its implications were huge. Four times as many troops were now in Palestine as had been there even at the height of the Arab Rebellion. As the government was eager eighteen months after the war had ended to demobilize at least 800,000 of the nearly 2 million people still in military service, the continuing commitment of so large a garrison to Palestine had become untenable. At a cabinet meeting the previous week, the Chancellor of the Exchequer, Dr. Hugh Dalton, had questioned Britain's ability to afford a military establishment even a quarter of its size on V-E Day and urged greater economies.[69]

Indeed, the rise of world commodity prices combined with a stronger than anticipated U.S. dollar had almost completely eroded the three-year $3.75 billion loan that America had made to Britain in December 1945. The war might have ended, but rationing of bread and most other foodstuffs continued. With defense spending still consuming 40 percent of the budget, the cabinet faced a stark choice: either drastically pare back military expenditure or reduce "the standard of home consumption"—a politically treacherous move that the government recognized would cause "crippling dislocations in our national economy."[70]

In these economically grim circumstances, a sweeping reevaluation of Britain's overseas commitments had become as inevitable as it was unavoidable. Indeed, by the end of that same week, the Labour government would announce in rapid succession its intention to place the question of Palestine's future before the United Nations, withdraw its military forces from Greece and have the United States assume responsibility for defending both that country and Turkey against communist subversion, and grant independence to India. Surprisingly little debate or discourse attended the meeting on Palestine. The minutes simply record, "Further discussion showed that it was the general view of the Cabinet that the right course was now to submit the whole problem to the United Nations." A series of important caveats, however, followed. Referring the issue of Palestine's future to the UN entailed neither an outright surrender of the mandate nor an irrevocable, final step. Britain would remain responsible for the administration and security of Palestine until such time as the UN reached a decision on the mandate's future. Moreover, it was under no obligation to implement or enforce whatever solution the UN might eventually propose. "If the settlement suggested by the United Nations were not acceptable to us," the cabinet noted, "we should be at liberty then to surrender the Mandate and leave the United Nations to make other arrangements for the future administration of Palestine." In addition, there was nothing to preclude Britain from continuing to work with both Arabs and Jews to reach some mutually agreed-upon solution. Neither community, Bevin pointed out, seemed inclined to have the UN decide Palestine's future. Accordingly, he was hopeful that the government's decision might bring both parties to "a more reasonable frame of mind." Should negotiations resume and a breakthrough occur, Britain would be free to withdraw the matter from UN consideration and proceed with the implementation of whatever solution was found. Perhaps most important was the fact that the next session of the UN General Assembly was not scheduled until September, and convening an extraordinary meeting for this purpose was deemed impractical. Accordingly, for the next seven months there would be no change in the status quo, and British rule over Palestine would continue along the same frustrating lines that it had since Labour had come to power eighteen months earlier.[71]

CHAPTER 17

An Instrument of Death

Nineteen long months of procrastination and prevarication had deprived the Labour government of any credibility on Palestine. The decision to involve the fledgling United Nations had thus been greeted with suspicion in Palestine, skepticism in Parliament, and criticism in the press. Neither the Yishuv nor the Arabs were persuaded of the government's sincerity, regarding this latest development as a cynical ploy to perpetuate British influence and deny both communities their respective claim to the country. In the House of Commons, Opposition and Labour backbench MPs alike expressed incredulity that the government remained incapable of producing either a clear policy or a coherent vision for Palestine while bemoaning the paretic stasis that had consigned an already demoralized civil administration and military there to at least seven more months of muddled uncertainty. Neither *The Times* nor *The Economist* nor the *New Statesman* was persuaded that Palestine's referral to the UN would result in any outcome other than partition and similarly lamented the British lives and treasure that would be expended before the UN would meet in September.[1]

A critical component of the government's thinking had been the hope that the referral decision might bring both communities to their senses and, in turn, restrain the extremists within their ranks. The cabinet based this faulty premise on the belief that the two sides would not wish to "prejudice[e] the case which they would have to present to the General Assembly." Bevin had specifically cited this rationale when he addressed the House on February 18. The fact that there had been no terrorist incidents since the beginning of the New Year contributed to the illusion that this overly optimistic scenario might actually materialize. But it was dashed within hours of the foreign secretary's statement when, that same evening, the Irgun resumed offensive operations with the first in a string of attacks against military convoys traveling in Jerusalem, along the Haifa–Jaffa Road, and the following day in Haifa itself.[2]

Each involved what had now become a favored Irgun tactic of either burying an improvised explosive device (IED) in the road or disguising it to resemble some innocent roadside object. These mines were quickly and easily laid and had proven devastatingly effective by both day and night. An Irgun team would lie in wait and then, just as a vehicle or convoy came into view, electrically detonate the device via a concealed wire. This means of attack had become so pervasive that in December 1946 army head-quarters issued a meticulously detailed thirty-five-page pamphlet, complete with photographs and diagrams, describing these weapons and their emplacement and effects. Even so, as both the Palestine government and the army acknowledged, these IEDs were virtually impossible to defend against.[3]

The night of February 20 brought a fresh round of incidents. Irgun bombs damaged the Iraq Petroleum Company pipeline in two places near Afula. Shortly afterward the group launched a coordinated, mortar-backed assault on an RAF base outside Hadera that was repulsed by its defenders after a twenty-minute gun battle.[4]

Only a few weeks before, British forces in Palestine had welcomed the announcement of the enforced evacuation of British women and children, according to the Sixth Airborne Division's historian, as a "sign of the firm measures which appeared at last to be on the way, and of the decks being cleared for action." But to their immense frustration, the latest attacks evoked no such response. Instead, the War Office issued a directive specifying that the word "terrorist" would no longer be used in any military communication to describe "members of the Stern and Irgun and other Jews involved in outrage and sabotage." The logic behind this change in terminology, the War Office explained, was to deprive the perpetrators of the "glamour" and publicity they received in press accounts of their operations. An ancillary intention was to counter a tendency among law-abiding Jews to "dissociate" themselves from these acts much the same as Germans now dissociated themselves from the Nazis. The invidious rationale used was that "everything was blamed against the Nazis, yet no one professed to be a Nazi or to hold Nazi views," while, in Palestine, "everyone blamed the terrorists as if they were a race apart" and provided no help to the authorities. "The so-called terrorists are in fact members of the Jewish community in Palestine. [The] word 'terrorist,'" the order concluded, "will therefore not be used; when referring to such persons terms such as armed Jews, Jews, thugs, murderers will be used." The troops applauded the decision, but it was completely ineffective as both the BBC and other news outlets continued to use the term.[5]

Regardless of this change in nomenclature, the attacks continued. On

February 28, Lehi bombed a building in Haifa from which the Admiralty made arrangements to expel illegal immigrants and where a military pay office was also located. Then, on Saturday, March 1, the Irgun struck in the supposedly impregnable security zone that the army had recently expanded in downtown Jerusalem.[6]

The Jewish Sabbath was arguably the only day of the week when everyone in Palestine could relax. Terrorist attacks seemed never to occur on Saturdays, and only once in recent memory had there been such an incident, and even then it was not clear whether the bomb had been timed to explode on a certain day. Hence, a fatally false sense of security pervaded the country at least once every weekend, and March 1 was no exception. The weather that day was magnificent. It was sunny and unseasonably warm. Jerusalem's streets were crowded with pedestrians taking advantage of the first sign of the end of winter and of an early spring.[7]

About 3:15 p.m., however, the tranquil repose of the Sabbath was broken by the sound of machine-gun fire coming from the stretch of King George V Avenue that bounded the eastern part of Rehavia. An Irgun squad had positioned itself on the roof of a building adjacent to the landmark Yeshurun Central Synagogue and was firing on a sentry post outside the four-story structure directly across the street. Known as Goldschmidt House, it housed the city's British army officers' club. Although the property was surrounded by successive layers of barbed wire and heavily guarded by British soldiers and police, the attack's planners had spotted a gap in the facility's defenses where the entrance to a military parking lot abutted the club. It was at this spot that the machine gun was concentrating its fire as a stolen army truck suddenly came into view. Accelerating past the dead and wounded sentries, it barreled into the parking lot before braking to a stop alongside Goldschmidt House. Three terrorists wearing British army battle dress jumped from the truck and hurled satchel charges into the building before quickly withdrawing. The ensuing explosions tore through the facility, collapsing its façade, killing thirteen persons, and wounding more than a dozen others. Among the dead were two officers and an enlisted man, a police officer, and nine civilian NAAFI (Navy, Army, Air Force Institutes) employees, including a female Polish switchboard operator and the club's Italian general manager. A number of passersby caught in the cross fire were also injured.[8]

The attack on Goldschmidt House was only the opening salvo in a sustained, daylong Irgun assault on military targets across Palestine that did not abate until midnight. Additional incidents were reported in Tel Aviv, Haifa, Hadera, Rehovot, Petah Tiqva, and Rishon-le-Zion. In all, fifteen attacks claimed the lives of eighteen persons and resulted in injuries to twenty-five others. Among the casualties were thirteen civilians, including eight Arabs. The Palestine administration had reacted immediately to the bombing of the officers' club by imposing a curfew over Jerusalem's Jewish neighborhoods that evening. As the violence spread, Tel Aviv, Ramat Gan, and Petah Tiqva were placed under curfew as well.[9]

Sunday morning brought the realization in both London and Jerusalem that a threshold had been crossed the previous day that now required some dramatic, signal response to avert a complete breakdown of security and also shake the Yishuv. For weeks the Palestine administration had been threatening to impose martial law in the event of any new terrorist outrage. The forty-eight separate incidents recorded over the previous dozen or so days had clearly demonstrated the futility of this exercise and the abject failure of all other attempts to secure the Jewish community's cooperation. In anticipation of this eventuality, Barker had instructed his officers back in January to formulate plans for the imposition of martial law. Skeleton orders as well as detailed maps had thus already been issued to the units charged with its implementation. In early February, Cunningham had obtained permission from London to impose this measure at whatever time he deemed appropriate. Accordingly, at 1:15 p.m. on March 2 the Palestine administration announced that statutory martial law was being declared in those areas already under curfew—with the addition of Bnei Brak.[10]

The government justified this extraordinary step on the grounds that since the New Year the Jewish Agency and the Vaad Le'umi had spurned repeated entreaties to actively assist in the suppression of terrorism. "The severe measures now necessary," the communiqué explained, "are the result of the lack of cooperation against bloodshed and terrorism which [the official Jewish] Institutions have themselves condemned." The localities placed under military rule, it explained, had been selected because of "direct evidence" linking the terrorists to each of those places.[11]

In actual fact, economic considerations and the number of available troops had dictated the operation's geographic reach and dimensions. Although Haifa, for instance, was cited in the communiqué as one of the venues of terrorist activity warranting martial law, it was exempted because any disruption of the port's commercial activities would adversely affect the collection of taxes and customs duty and therefore harm Palestine's economy. Further, despite a garrison of a hundred thousand men, there were still not enough forces to extend martial law beyond the five affected municipalities.[12]

Nonetheless, even this limited application of martial law to select areas affected some 300,000 people; its draconian provisions impacted almost every aspect of their daily lives. All commerce stopped. Bus, train, taxi, and delivery services were suspended. Banks closed. The operation of private cars and commercial vehicles was prohibited. Postal, telegraph, customs, tax collection, courts, and all other government services ceased. Telephone exchanges in the affected locales were shut, and calls could be neither made nor received. People were confined to their residences for all but three hours a day when grocery stores and some pharmacies were permitted to open between 10:00 a.m. and 1:00 p.m. No more than six persons, however, were allowed to gather in any one place, and no one was allowed to either enter or leave the cordoned-off areas within which soldiers and police conducted house-to-house searches for arms and terrorists.[13]

Although army headquarters in Jerusalem and the military commander responsible for martial law in Tel Aviv, Richard Gale, publicly denied any punitive motive, in reality that was exactly its purpose—as both his memoir and various contemporaneous government communications attest. This was also evident from the discussion held between Cunningham and Barker on February 5. They had then agreed that because "economic pressure [was] the crux of the matter," martial law must be applied to Tel Aviv—as the hub of Jewish commercial life in Palestine—regardless of whether that municipality was directly implicated or not in whatever future terrorist incident might prompt its imposition. An assessment prepared by the director of plans at the War Office specifically cites this objective as well. "Such measures by striking at the liberty and pockets of the private citizens," it argued, "may induce them to co-operate by laying information against and refusing to shelter the terrorists."[14]

This rationale is vital to understanding why the government and the military were so convinced that martial law would succeed where all previous measures and attempts to obtain the Yishuv's assistance against terrorism had failed. On February 13, for instance, Cunningham had explained to Creech Jones that "in martial law the Jewish community sees economic disaster as well as widespread hardship" and therefore was "paranoiac" with fear of its imposition. As Barker's infamous nonfraternization order following the King David Hotel bombing showed, senior military commanders were already convinced that money was the Yishuv's pressure point. This was also the conclusion reached by the Sixth Airborne's intelligence officer, who, on March 7, observed in relation to the supposed salutary effects that martial law was having on the Yishuv, "Making of money is almost a second religion with the Jewish race." A subsequent assessment by this same officer confidently predicted that the Jews would be forced to "go on a manhunt to save themselves and their pockets."[15]

The Yishuv's leadership never doubted martial law's real purpose. Within hours of its imposition, the Jewish Agency and the Vaad Le'umi issued a joint statement deploring the measure as an act of retaliation directed against the entire community "for the crimes of a few desperate young men." The government was also assailed for pursuing policies with respect to Jewish immigration and statehood that had long ago eliminated any prospect of cooperation. Nevertheless, both institutions vaguely promised that "the disciplined force of the Yishuv will intensify their action against terrorism so as to bring to an end all murder and bloodshed in this country."[16]

As for the Irgun, the government's resort to martial law accorded perfectly with its own objectives. Begin's preeminent goal had long been to make Palestine ungovernable. With the Goldschmidt House and subsequent countrywide attacks he had now nearly achieved that aim, with half of Palestine's Jewish population and two of the country's three major metropolitan areas under military rule. "Posterity will know that on that bright Saturday, March the First, 1947," Begin boasted, "we brought about a turning-point in the history of our country and our people. We deprived the enemy of time for secret preparations; we speeded up events by a full year. And whoever can appreciate what that year might have meant to us, can realise that the Jewish people owe a debt of gratitude to its sons in the Assault Force of the Irgun Zvai Leumi."[17]

Although Begin's claim is staked out in typically grandiloquent prose, his fundamental argument cannot be dismissed as mere hyperbole. The intent of the March 1 attacks appears to have been threefold: first, to demonstrate the group's ability to strike wherever and whenever it pleased—against even heavily defended and well-protected military targets; second, to underscore the Irgun's long-standing cri de coeur that there would be no peace for the British in Palestine until they acceded to Jewish demands on both statehood and unrestricted immigration; third, to deprive Britain of the time that the Labour government sought to arrange a settlement of the Palestine question favorable to its regional diplomatic and strategic interests. According to Samuel Katz, the group's chief propagandist, the Irgun high command regarded the UN referral decision as nothing more than a plot by Bevin to buy "sufficient time to demonstrate that Britain was indeed in effective and undisputed control" of Palestine in order to perpetuate its rule once, it anticipated, the UN had also proven unsuccessful in divining a lasting solution.[18]

Judging from the reaction of the British press, it would appear Begin achieved his first two aims and, at the very least, prepared the groundwork for the third. "Govern or Get Out," read the headline plastered across the front page of the following morning's *Sunday Express*. On Tuesday the title of *The Manchester Guardian's* lead editorial was "How Long?," and the author argued that the "renewed outbreak of terrorism in Palestine is a reminder that the Government's decision to submit the case to the United Nations has in itself changed nothing. The wanton savagery of the terrorists, the inability of the Jewish majority to stop them, the inevitable but futile reprisals, the general atmosphere of hate and fear which is making life intolerable for soldiers and civilians: all these things continue and will continue until a settlement is reached."[19]

The government was again assailed in the House of Commons by both Opposition and backbench MPs. "Why," Churchill inquired of the colonial secretary, "is it that measures now proposed to be taken are likely to be more effective than other measures which have been taken at various times in the last 12 months following on similar outrages?" With martial law having been in force for only a day, Creech Jones was understandably vague and evasive in his reply, but there were already disquieting signs that the Opposition leader's skepticism was well-founded.[20]

Indeed, within hours of martial law's declaration, the Irgun had already retaliated. Though the first two incidents were minor—involving an explosion outside an army encampment in Rehovot and a road mine that injured two paratroopers near Hadera—they were harbingers of more to come. Each day brought some fresh act of violence, so that by the end of the first week a total of fifteen terrorist attacks had occurred, resulting in the death of one soldier and injuries to seventeen others, in addition to the six policemen and nearly two dozen civilians (including five Arabs) who were wounded. Although most had occurred in areas not under martial law, Tel Aviv and the parts of Jerusalem that the military controlled accounted remarkably for more than a third of the incidents. The perpetrators belonged to either Lehi or the Irgun and appeared to have struck with impunity regardless of the restrictions on movement and relentless security sweeps.[21]

The following week showed only a marginal improvement in security. Fourteen terrorist incidents were reported between March 10 and March 17. One soldier died, while fifteen others sustained injuries. The most serious had occurred in the early hours of March 12, when, for the second time in as many months, the Irgun assaulted Jerusalem's Schneller Barracks, despite its location inside the martial law zone governing Jerusalem's Mea Shearim neighborhood. A Lehi attack two nights later on a freight train north of Petah Tiqva wrecked nineteen oil tank cars and left one Arab railway worker dead and another wounded—the week's only civilian casualties.[22]

Cunningham was rapidly coming to the conclusion that martial law was not the panacea to Palestine's security problems that Barker and other senior officers had touted it to be. In fact, only two dozen known terrorists had been arrested—none of whom had been caught inside any of the affected areas. Moreover, the vast majority of people detained for further questioning had subsequently been released when no evidence linking them to terrorism was found. And although some Jews had come forward to provide information to the authorities, this was only on a very limited and ad hoc basis. The more organized campaign, championed by the official Jewish institutions, that Cunningham had sought never materialized. It was also proving economically costly to the Palestine administration because of the loss of tax and other revenue.[23]

Most problematically, the longer martial law remained in force, the more concerned its military commanders were becoming about its effects. In a surprising twist, they now worried that should "the shoe pinch too hard for too long," all hope of ever obtaining the Yishuv's cooperation would be lost. Indeed, the previously cited War Office planning document had specifically cautioned, "Severe restrictions of public services . . . , owing to the dislocation they cause, cannot be continued for prolonged periods and if maintained for too long lose their value by antagonizing public opinion." Less than two weeks after martial law was declared, this was already occurring. Fearing outright defiance of the curfew as well as the outbreak of rioting and similar disorders if martial law were maintained, Gale, the Tel Aviv zone's commander, now lobbied for its removal. "I therefore preferred to lift the curfew myself rather than have it broken under my nose as a result of having insufficient forces to guarantee its proper imposition" is how he explained his rationale in the operation's after-action report. Cunningham concurred, and on March 14 he informed Creech Jones of his decision. "I wish to repeat that we shall not stop terrorism by any military or other repressive action alone," the high commissioner emphasized. In anticipation of the criticism that lifting martial law would provoke in London, Cunningham pointedly suggested that "those who advocate stronger measures and 'turning the country upside down'" would do well to read the section of Gale's assessment where the First Infantry Division commander stresses that martial law's continuation "would spell disaster and drive recruits into the I.Z.L. and Stern."[24]

On March 16 the Palestine administration announced that effective noon the following day martial law would be withdrawn. It sought to put the best face on a dismal outcome by explaining that the community's encouraging, albeit limited, inclination to cooperate with the authorities, coupled with the potentially dire effect that the measure's continuance would have on Palestine's economy, had prompted the high commissioner to suspend martial law. "It is hoped that it will not be necessary to resort to these severe measures again," the communiqué ineffectually fulminated. "It is clearly in the interests of both the Government and the Jewish community that such action should be avoided if possible."[25]

The Irgun and Lehi separately responded to the news with a new round of attacks that same night. Irgun bombs cut the Iraq Petroleum Company's pipeline in three places near Haifa, Kfar Hasidim, and Afula, while a roadside Lehi IED wounded four British soldiers. A new army intelligence assessment reported that the two groups had no "intention of easing up with their attacks against the security forces . . . and will listen to no amount of reasonable argument that they should do so. They are rabid and beyond reasoning," it forlornly concluded. The Yishuv, for its part, did not buy for one second the government's explanation for martial law's removal. The entire operation was decried by editorials in *Davar*, *Ha-Boker*, and *The Palestine Post* as an ineffectual and counterproductive exercise that left the terrorist organizations unscathed while adversely affecting law-abiding citizens. As Ben-Gurion explained in a terse telegram to Attlee, martial law had neither "affected terrorists nor stopped their outrages but instead ha[d] increased resentment of hard-hit population, created fertile soil for terrorist propaganda, frustrating community's attempts to combat terrorism by itself. Martial law absolutely futile and senseless unless really meant to punish whole community, ruin its economy and destroy the foundations of the Jewish National Home."[26]

No sooner had the announcement to lift martial law been issued than Cunningham became aware of pressure in London to extend it throughout the entire country. He immediately wrote to Creech Jones both to defend his decision and to preempt the arguments favoring its expanded reimposition. "Beneath the suggestion presumably lies the implication, which seems to die hard, that the administration or myself in some way hamper the military in their operations against terrorists, and that if martial law were imposed [throughout the country] the Army would be more successful in its campaign against them." Apart from the practical impediments, whereby the Arab community would be impacted as much as the Jews, there were simply too few troops in Palestine to guard the railway network, let alone enforce martial law over the entire country. Moreover, because only one-fifth of the Yishuv lived in the countryside, extending martial law beyond Palestine's urban centers made no sense. For all these reasons, Cunningham continued, "the Army themselves tell me that the imposition of martial law throughout the country is the last thing they want." As for his decision to suspend martial law, Cunningham emphasized that the recommendation to do so had come from Barker's replacement as GOC, Lieutenant General Gordon Holmes Alexander MacMillan, in consultation with his senior commanders, and had Dempsey's blessing, and not from pressure emanating from either himself or the Palestine administration.[27]

The cabinet reviewed the situation at its meeting on March 20. There was broad agreement that martial law had produced mixed results, and the consensus was that this was because Cunningham had lifted it too soon. The cabinet further concluded that martial law's hasty removal had imparted an "impression of weakness and must have encouraged the Jewish community and the terrorists to think that they had successfully resisted it." Discussion then focused on the possibility of imposing martial law over the entirety of Palestine—but without some of the more severe restrictions that had proven difficult for the army to enforce during its most recent iteration. In a remarkable admission, the minutes go on to record that "the Cabinet considered that a more definite plan should have been made for handling the situation in Palestine during the next few months" to maintain order in the country until the UN session in September. Accordingly, the Chiefs of Staff were belatedly instructed to prepare such an assessment, and both Cunningham and MacMillan were recalled to London for consultation.[28]

The idea of applying martial law throughout Palestine appears to have originated some weeks earlier with the Conservative politician Viscount Cranborne. Addressing the House of Lords on March 3, he had wondered how its selective geographic application to a handful of urban locales would prevent terrorist attacks elsewhere—which is exactly what happened. With precious few security options left that had not already been tried, the cabinet understandably fastened on some new variant of martial law as one of the few remaining viable measures with which to restore order in Palestine. It was doubtless encouraged by the enthusiastic assessments offered by the defense minister, Albert Victor Alexander, and Vice Chief of the Imperial General Staff General Sir Frank "Simbo" Simpson (substituting for Montgomery), who had both extolled martial law's virtues at the March 20 meeting. They maintained that the greater "freedom of action" granted to the army not only had produced an unprecedented number of terrorist arrests but had "shocked" the Yishuv into providing the information that made this possible. Although both assertions were baseless, neither was challenged by wearied government ministers desperate to find a solution to Palestine's deteriorating security.[29]

Arab opinion both in Palestine and across the region must also have played a part in the cabinet's continued faith in martial law despite evidence to the contrary. Reporting the reaction in the Middle East to news of martial law's suspension, Sir Ronald Campbell, Britain's ambassador to Egypt, warned of "wide spread feeling that the British Empire is going downhill." Accordingly, he advised that Britain "should as far as possible abstain from concessions [to the Yishuv] which might tend to confirm . . . that we are unable to offer unswerving resistance to violence."[30]

But if there was a novel military answer to Palestine's continued slide into lawlessness, the War Office didn't have it. Tasked by the chiefs to prepare an assessment of security options, including countrywide martial law, all that the Joint Planning Staff could come up with was a recommendation to maintain the status quo:

(a) The continuance of civil government, including the wide exercise of the powers already held by the High Commissioner.
(b) The application of intensified continuous military pressure against terrorists throughout the country.
(c) The re-imposition for limited period, when and where necessary, of statutory martial law in appropriate areas.

The only new idea they proffered involved the establishment of special summary military tribunals to deal more speedily and efficiently with terrorist offenses than the current system of courts-martial. Under the proposed scheme, individuals convicted of capital crimes under the Emergency Regulations would face far more limited rights of appeal, thus ensuring the swift execution of sentences. The chiefs endorsed the report virtually without amendment and sent it to the cabinet on March 26.[31]

The cabinet accepted the Chiefs of Staff recommendations without demurral, including the creation of summary courts empowered to impose the death penalty. The issue of imposing martial law throughout Palestine was momentarily laid to rest. The meeting, however, was more interesting for what was left unsaid. The Chiefs of Staff's verbatim incorporation of the Joint Planning Staff's report had contained a remarkably revealing assessment of the success of Begin's strategy. "The Irgun and Stern are still violently anti-British and will always be so," both reports explained. "They wish to force us to employ sterner measures which can be represented as punitive against [the] community, thereby swinging moderate opinion against us and obtaining more recruits for themselves." The chiefs' conclusion that British military strategy in Palestine was playing right into the terrorists' hands was by itself an astonishing admission. That it prompted no further reaction from either the chiefs or the cabinet and that neither apparently did anything about it border on the incomprehensible.[32]

The failure of martial law weighed especially heavily on those charged with either administering Palestine or maintaining order there. Having been unanimously heralded as the ultimate trump card with which to wrest the Yishuv's active assistance against terrorism, it had now been played to a nugatory result. For civil servant and soldier alike, the game no longer seemed worth the candle. Rex Keating, the assistant director of the Palestine Broadcasting Service, and his colleagues somewhat contemptuously referred to their enforced domicile, which was surrounded by coils upon coils of barbed wire and guarded night and day, as the "British Concentration Camp." "Never before, surely, has a group of Englishmen been placed in such a degrading position," Keating complained. Even Cunningham was completely disheartened. Other than lifting the restrictions on Jewish immigration, he had warned Creech Jones on March 13, "there is little prospect of stopping terrorism by any military or other action short of war with the Jews."[33]

Renewed fears for one's safety now compounded these officials' accreting despondency. The week after martial law ended, the Haifa chapter of the Palestine Civil Servants' Association petitioned the chief secretary to provide armed police escorts when curfews were in effect and at other times of acute "disturbances or unrest." The request was denied on the grounds that no police could be spared from more essential duties. Even in Jerusalem, the country's administrative capital, there were apparently insufficient armored vehicles and security personnel to accommodate the transportation needs of senior officials. Many, accordingly, resorted to a 1940s variant of telecommuting, managing their offices around the country by telephone rather than in person. "Under such conditions life assumes an unreality that is better imagined than experienced," Keating observed. It is no wonder that the administration was finding it increasingly difficult to fill vacancies and recruit new officers. "Apart from the considerations of continual loss of life and property caused by terrorist activities," Cunningham advised Creech Jones, "it is a matter of constant concern to me as to how long it will be possible to keep the civil administration in being under conditions which security demands have imposed on the civilian element in this country."[34]

Although troop morale and discipline in Palestine were widely reported to have remained high throughout March, when Abba Eban, now the Jewish Agency's political information officer based in London, addressed the Imperial Defence College that same month, he found that senior officers were seriously concerned about how long it could be maintained. An anonymous brigadier expressed the prevailing view when he asked, "What vision could be set before [the troops] as a worthy object of their sacrifice and hardship?" That the façade of British imperturbability was already crumbling may be inferred by the increase in the number of unprovoked assaults by soldiers on Jewish passersby.[35]

The Irgun of course sought to exploit these frustrations in order to further erode troop morale and sow doubt and dissension within the ranks. Although its propagandists had been crafting specific messages to British soldiers and police since 1939, their efforts appear to have intensified immediately following martial law. One poster that appeared on walls and lampposts was addressed from "The Soldiers of the Underground to the Soldiers of the Occupation Army." It asked Britons to imagine how they would react if their homeland had been invaded and inquired whether it was "worth dying for . . . Bevin's stupidity? Oil? Their Lordship's income?" Another was titled "It's Worth Thinking About" and explained how doing one's duty and obediently following orders were "the best way for you to stay in this country forever . . . Risk your life every day so that the Government may have ten more years to make up its mind: to clear out of Palestine."[36]

Creech Jones could argue in Parliament that martial law was never intended "in and of itself to put an end to terrorism," but it was a claim that fell mostly on deaf ears. Admittedly, the pace of terrorist attacks had slackened noticeably in the weeks that followed, but whatever optimism this might have encouraged was shattered in the early morning hours of March 31 when Lehi bombed the Shell Oil refinery in Haifa. A series of explosions destroyed a third of the site's seventeen storage tanks, causing the loss of sixteen thousand tons of oil and £400,000 in damages. The entire city briefly lost power as a result of the attack, and the following day visibility was almost completely obscured by smoke and flames that at times shot a hundred feet in the air. Fuel distribution and sales throughout the country were also affected.[37]

With security expenditure now nearly double the 1945 figure of £4.5 million and thus consuming a third of the Palestine government's budget—for a projected net deficit of some half a million pounds sterling that fiscal year—the administration announced the following day that the costs of the attack would again have to be borne by the Palestinian taxpayer. Precisely how these funds would be raised, however, was left unsaid—mainly because London had apparently not yet been consulted. In the weeks that followed, Cunningham scrambled to construct an equitable taxation scheme that, in the words of one Treasury official, would "soak the Jews" but somehow blunt the impact on the country's Arab population. The idea that eventually emerged involved a very modest surcharge of a few pennies added to commercial sales of benzene and heating fuel. A sum equivalent to the estimated expenditure by Arabs on both items was, however, to be earmarked for the development and improvement of particularly impoverished Arab communities that would otherwise receive no such financial assistance. Cunningham also resurrected a proposal dating from the King David Hotel bombing's aftermath the previous July to sequester the sum of some £5 million from the assets of the Jewish Agency and various other Zionist philanthropic entities. With this money, he proposed to create a fund that would both pay compensation to business in Palestine for losses caused by terrorism and cover the costs of transshipping and accommodating the 14,500 illegal immigrants then being kept in the detention camps on Cyprus. Although the cabinet subsequently rejected the sequestration proposal, the fuel surcharge was enacted and took effect on July 1, 1947. It underscored the dire financial straits that the Palestine administration was facing given the rising security expenditure and mounting revenue losses caused by Jewish terrorism.[38]

Perhaps more significant was the growing unease felt by some Colonial Office officials over the harsh policy choices being forced upon the government as a result of the escalating violence. "For my part, I dislike this proposal intensely," Trafford Smith, a young assistant secretary, had commented about the sequestration proposal on April 25 before going on to explain,

Under the present defence regulation regime under which any person may be imprisoned without trial more or less indefinitely on suspicion only, the liberty of the subject has been almost completely withdrawn in Palestine. It is now proposed to complete this odious process by taking power to seize the assets of any individual or organization—again on suspicion only—in a purely arbitrary manner. All this is quite wrong in principle, and is a measure of the extent to which we have sunk in Palestine in adopting the pernicious doctrine that the end justifies the means, the justification being, of course, that since the terrorists have adopted these methods, the only way the Government can counter them is in kind.[39]

This was not the first time that Smith had raised ethical questions about British counterterrorism policy in Palestine. Four months earlier his had been the lone voice of protest about the casual dispensation of habeas corpus and secretive removal of Jewish terrorists to indefinite detention in Eritrea. The response at that time had been a sharp rebuke from his superior, Assistant Undersecretary Sir John Martin, but by the spring of 1947 such misgivings were no longer confined to idealistic junior officers. "Quite frankly, I share Mr. Trafford Smith's dislike of the High Commissioner's proposal" to sequester Jewish funds, Sir Thomas Lloyd, the permanent undersecretary, wrote in a minute intended for Creech Jones's attention.[40]

Yet three years of nearly unremitting violence had left both London and Jerusalem bereft of any new ideas or novel thoughts on how best to restore order to Palestine. Martial law's meager results and pitiable impact on the terrorists nonetheless demanded that something be done to reassert British authority and check the country's continued slide into lawlessness, especially in the run-up to the UN session in September. Almost by default, attention returned to what appeared to be one of the only viable options left: the hangman's noose.[41]

A curious feature of the final decade of British rule over Palestine was, as we have seen, the infrequency with which Jews convicted of terrorist offenses were actually put to death. Although the three-man military tribunals that sat in judgment of violations arising from the amended Emergency Regulations were remarkably efficient in securing convictions—only 2 of the 127 Jewish terrorists tried between January 1, 1946, and March 8, 1947, were acquitted—to date none of the 25 defendants convicted of a capital crime had been executed. And of this group, the sentences of all but 4 had been commuted to life imprisonment. By comparison, 108 Arabs convicted of the same terrorist crimes were duly hanged between 1938 and 1939—without any of the delay or demurral that seemed to attend the Jewish cases. Although the British historian David French suggests that this was because of a tacit policy whereby the government actively discouraged awarding the death penalty to Jewish terrorists in hopes of avoiding "international embarrassments"—and perhaps further inflaming anti-British sentiment in the United States—such considerations were now swept aside by the more pressing exigency of curbing the escalating terrorist violence.[42]

Shortly after the withdrawal of martial law, an Army Council Secretariat memorandum declared, "Death sentences should be carried out irrespective of the possible repercussions from the Jews. Failure to do so would only encourage more terrorism, adversely affect troop morale, and further alienate the Arabs." Montgomery had in effect been making the same arguments since at least the previous November. The cabinet's decision on March 27 to accord military tribunals the authority to impose capital punishment and thereby reduce the opportunities for delay and postponement of execution thus sought to achieve through juridical fiat what the army and the Palestine administration had manifestly failed to accomplish with martial law.[43]

In April 1947, four Irgun fighters awaited execution. They were Dov Gruner, whose sentence Barker had confirmed in January, Yehiel Drezner (a.k.a. Dov Rosenbaum), Eliezer Kashani, and Mordechai Alkachi (a.k.a. Alkoshi). The last three were arrested on the night of December 29, 1946, after they tried to shoot their way past a military roadblock. Found in possession of two rawhide whips on the same evening that other Irgun units had kidnapped and flogged British soldiers, they had been condemned to death by a military court in Jerusalem on February 10. Two days later, in one of his final acts as GOC, Barker had confirmed their sentences. However, they remained on death row in Jerusalem's central prison, forlornly awaiting what was hoped would be the Privy Council's precedent-setting commutation of Gruner's sentence.[44]

Gruner neither encouraged nor supported any of the efforts undertaken in his name. Instead, as he reportedly wrote in a letter to Begin that was smuggled out of prison, he willingly accepted his fate. "It is a law of history that only with blood shall a country be redeemed. I am writing this while awaiting the hangman. This is not a moment at which I can lie, and I swear that if I had to begin my life anew I would have chosen the exact same path, regardless of the consequences for myself. Your faithful soldier, Dov."[45]

As further appeals were lodged in London and Jerusalem, all four condemned prisoners were secretly moved to Acre jail. Nearly three months had now elapsed since the date originally set for Gruner's execution—January 28. At the time, the cabinet had made clear its desire that it should proceed without any delay. The transfer of the men from the geographically vulnerable central prison in the heart of downtown Jerusalem to the forbidding crusader fortress in Acre had been the penultimate step in a process designed to fulfill the cabinet's wish.[46]

Smoke was still coming from smoldering fires at the Haifa oil refinery across the bay when at 4:00 a.m. on Wednesday, April 16, Gruner was abruptly awakened by his jailers. They crowded into his cell and ordered him to stand while the execution order was recited. Gruner refused, and a scuffle ensued during which he was pummeled before being forced onto his feet. As Gruner made his way toward the gallows, he sang Zionism's (and subsequently Israel's) plaintive national anthem, "Ha-Tikva." "As long as the Jewish spirit is yearning deep in the heart," his voice intoned,

> *With eyes turned toward the East, looking toward Zion,*
> *Then our hope—the two-thousand-year-old hope—will not be lost:*
> *To be a free people in our land,*
> *The land of Zion and Jerusalem.*[47]

At roughly twenty- to thirty-minute intervals, Drezner, Kashani, and Alkachi followed. Both a British liaison officer from the Sixth Airborne Division who was present at the prison that morning and the condemned men's fellow Jewish prisoners reported that each man went to his death singing "Ha-Tikva." Each had made the same final request: that he be buried at Rosh Pinna, the site of the grave of Shlomo Ben-Yosef, whom the British had hanged at Acre nine years before.[48]

At 7:00 a.m. the Palestine Broadcasting Service announced the four executions. Those listening to the radio that morning—including Begin himself—were shocked. Tuesday, not Wednesday, was the traditional hanging day in Palestine. Moreover, four persons had never been put to death in British-ruled Palestine on the same date. The condemned had also been deprived of the traditional rite of a last meal and the final ministrations of a clergyman—much less any warning of their imminent execution. Their families were apprised of their deaths only after the fact. Indeed, Gruner's sister, Helen Friedman, who had traveled to Palestine from America, had come downstairs to the lobby of the Tel Aviv hotel where she was staying to meet her military escort and proceed to Acre to see her brother one last time before returning home, when she was informed of the executions that had just taken place.[49]

The Jewish Agency issued a statement expressing its "profound shock and pain," and several Hebrew newspapers published the names of the deceased framed by thick black borders. Protest in the Yishuv, however, was muted because, as a precaution, curfews had been thrown over Tel Aviv, Petah Tiqva, and the Jewish sections of both Haifa and Jerusalem. Later that day, the Palestine administration announced the enactment twenty-four hours earlier of a new provision to the Emergency Regulations eliminating the right to appeal sentences passed by military tribunals. This amendment was declared retroactive and therefore took precedence over all previous statutes. "I believe there is no precedent in history," Begin observed, "of a Government carrying out a death sentence in such fear and in such secrecy"—a view apparently shared by the prison's warden, George Charlton, who was among the longest continuously serving officers in the PPF. Appalled by the shameful treatment accorded Gruner during his final hours, Charlton, "to his eternal credit," Rymer-Jones writes, refused to attend the execution, despite his legal obligation to do so. His principled stand cost him his job.[50]

The Irgun had previously warned that "if the British continue to disregard the elementary rights of prisoner[s] of war, if they arrogate for themselves the rights which in recent wars only Hitler and the Jap arrogated to themselves—if they 'hit below the belt' and call it fair play, we shall have to consider adopting the same 'rules.'" Hence, in anticipation of reprisals, including the abduction of military personnel, army commanders ordered increased security at bases and other facilities and imposed new restrictions on troop movement. Army vehicles were now directed to travel only in pairs. For the first time army patrols apparently left the main roads and organized ambush points on smaller dirt tracks and in orange groves. This was seen as a pioneering attempt by the army to adopt small-unit tactics in countering the terrorists. But even these redoubled measures were ineffective in halting a new round of terrorist attacks. The Irgun struck twice in Netanya alone, bombing an army medical facility and a military cinema. Additional incidents targeting security force personnel in Rehovot, Haifa, Jerusalem, and Jaffa left two persons dead and more than thirty others wounded.[51]

Just as the Yishuv was absorbing the shock of the multiple executions at Acre, a new death row incident occurred in Jerusalem that would forever be enshrined in the hagiography of the *Oley Ha-Gardom*—the ones who rose to the gallows.[52]

Fate and circumstance had conspired to intertwine the parallel lives of Meir Feinstein and Moshe Barazani. Feinstein, the younger of the two, was a sabra—born in Jerusalem's Old City in 1927 to religious parents who had recently emigrated from Poland. He had been forced to grow up quickly and start work to support the family at a young age after his father died. Strikingly handsome with a head full of thick, straight jet-black hair that he neatly combed swept back from his forehead, Feinstein looked older than he was and, combined with his exceptional maturity, was able to bluff his way into the British army in 1944 at age sixteen. A longtime member of the Irgun, he used his position serving with the Royal Engineers in the Middle East to smuggle stolen arms and ammunition to the group. He was discharged in 1946 and immediately joined the Irgun's Jerusalem cell. Feinstein was the driver of the stolen taxi used in the attack on that city's rail station in October 1946. A severe wound sustained during the operation had necessitated the amputation of his left arm. On April 3 a military court had sentenced Feinstein to death. Mac-Millan confirmed the sentence two weeks later—just twenty-four hours after Gruner and his three Irgun colleagues had been hanged. That same day, the GOC also upheld the death sentence that a Tel Aviv military court the previous month had imposed on Barazani.[53]

A native of the Kurdish region of northern Iraq, Barazani had immigrated with his family to Palestine in 1933. The son of an impoverished rabbi who devoted his life to the study of Kabbalah, as a young boy Barazani too had to work to help support his perennially destitute parents and five brothers, who lived in a cramped one-bedroom Jerusalem apartment. An ardent Zionist, Barazani eventually joined Lehi and was assigned to its local youth unit, which was responsible for disseminating the group's clandestine newspaper and affixing posters to the city's walls. After a year, the wavy-haired teenager with a captivating smile graduated to operational status, participating in an attack on a train. Barazani was arrested near the Schneller Barracks while Jerusalem was under martial law on March 9. A hand grenade was found in his pocket by a police patrol that had stopped and searched him.[54]

Feinstein and Barazani were remanded to Jerusalem's central prison, where, dressed in the red burlap attire of the condemned, they were kept in cells adjacent to Gruner, Drezner, Kashani, and Alkachi. Their execution was fixed for Tuesday, April 22. The British authorities were completely oblivious to the perfect martyrs they had inadvertently created for the terrorist organizations that both men served. One was aged nineteen and the other twenty. One was an Ashkenazic Jew of European heritage and the other a Sephardic Jew of Middle Eastern descent. Both were religiously devout as well as passionate Zionists. And both had resolved that rather than perish by the hangman's noose, they would take their own lives as they stood atop the gallows—and those of the entire execution party with them.

A plan was resurrected from the preceding weeks when Gruner and his comrades had plotted a "Samson death"—in reference to the biblical hero who kills both himself and his Philistine captors in a dramatic, final feat of strength and determination. But before the Irgun could smuggle hand grenades into the central prison for this purpose, the four Irgun men were unexpectedly transferred to Acre. On the eve of Feinstein's and Barazani's executions, the Irgun delivered two hand grenades concealed within hollowed-out oranges to the two condemned men. An unexpected complication arose, however, when the rabbi comforting them insisted on being present on the scaffold the following morning. Adjusting their plan, the two men embraced each other. Barazani held one of the hand grenades between them while Feinstein detonated it. The ensuing explosion killed them both instantly.[55]

"Man created and sanctified you as an instrument of death," a contemporaneous poem honoring Feinstein and Barazani relates, "and you will exact your revenge from him." Throughout the following week both the Irgun and Lehi struck almost daily. Six attacks against a variety of police and military targets claimed the lives of a dozen Britons and wounded more than twice that number. Among the victims was A. E. Conquest, an eighteen-year veteran of the PPF who was widely acknowledged as the force's best detective. His killing profoundly affected Barker, who, in a letter to Antonius, wondered whether "this senseless killing [will] ever stop." Then, in intemperate language, even by the former GOC's standard of anti-Semitic vitriol, he exclaimed, "Just to think all this life and money being wasted for these f—ing Jews."[56]

The Irgun had not forgotten Barker either. "He behaved like a Nazi Gauleiter in our country," Begin argued. "He tried to crush our resistance with hangings." The security surrounding Barker during his final weeks in Palestine had been extraordinarily tight, so the Irgun planned to kill him once he had returned to England. The person recruited to undertake this mission in the spring of 1947 was Ezer Weizman, the Zionist leader Chaim Weizmann's nephew (Ezer spelled his surname with one *n*). The younger Weizman had gone to London the previous June to study aeronautics. His family pedigree and wartime service as an RAF pilot doubtless made him appear to the authorities an unlikely terrorist. But even as a boy Weizman had begun to question the official Zionist policy of restraint during the Arab Rebellion, and more recently, albeit in the privacy of his famous uncle's London hotel suite, he had lauded the Irgun for blowing up the King David Hotel. A student friend at the London School of Economics approached Weizman about joining the Irgun, and shortly afterward he found himself in France being trained in sabotage and subversion.[57]

Back in England, Weizman discovered the location of Barker's residence and was in the process of planning the assassination when one day a detective from Scotland Yard's Special Branch appeared on his doorstep. Acting on a tip possibly provided by the Jewish Agency, the detective advised the future defense minister and subsequently president of Israel to "be so kind as to return to Palestine"; Weizman complied and shortly afterward left the country. Almost exactly a year later, the Irgun lost another opportunity to assassinate Barker when a parcel bomb sent to his home failed to explode.[58]

Intelligence concerning Jewish terrorist operations in Britain was rarely as good as the lead that brought the Special Branch directly to Weizman's front door. Repeated reports of Irgun and Lehi agents allegedly en route to or already present in the U.K. throughout 1946 consistently failed to materialize in the form of either hard evidence or actual arrests. Although relations between MI5 and Scotland Yard and between the Special Branch and the PPF were deemed excellent by all, the accuracy of the information they exchanged appears mostly to have been at the level of the multiple accounts of Begin's supposed presence in Paris during November and December 1946 and the plastic surgery he had reputedly undergone to alter his facial features and thus make his travel to and presence in the French capital possible.[59]

In hopes of getting a better grip on the threat, in December 1946 Rymer-Jones, now back at Scotland Yard, had enlisted the assistance of some of the same Jewish Agency intelligence officers with whom he had worked in Palestine. But more often than not, tragedy was averted less by the authorities' interdicting plots (such as in the first attempt on Barker's life) than by the malfunctioning of the terrorists' improvised explosive devices (as in the second). A lone exception, however, was the successful bombing that Lehi carried out in the heart of London in March 1947. The person responsible for the attack was Ya'acov Eliav, a.k.a. Ya'acov Levstein, the group's master bomb maker, known to his comrades as the Dynamite Man because of his expertise with explosives, and the self-described inventor of the letter bomb.[60]

Born in Russia in 1917, Eliav had immigrated to Palestine with his parents eight years later. He joined the Irgun in 1935 and within three years was directing the group's Jerusalem operations. In this capacity, Eliav had orchestrated the series of bombings of Arab targets that culminated in the infamous Black Sunday on November 14, 1937. He was subsequently one of a select group of twenty-six Irgun officers sent to Poland for training in conventional and guerrilla warfare tactics at a special camp run by the Polish army in the Carpathian Mountains. Returning to Palestine, Eliav was responsible for the bombing of Jerusalem's Rex Cinema in May 1939 that had injured eighteen persons and also for the assassinations of two senior CID officers, Ralph Cairns and Ronald Barker, three months later. Eliav was arrested shortly afterward. Upon his release from prison in June 1940, he left the Irgun with Abraham Stern, becoming commander of the dissident faction's Jerusalem cell, its first operational unit. Known by his nom de guerre, Yashka, Eliav built the bomb that killed several police officers at 8 Yael Street in Tel Aviv in January 1942. He was apprehended shortly afterward and spent nearly two years in Jerusalem's central prison before escaping at the end of 1943. In late 1945, Eliav persuaded Lehi's high command to allow him to open a second front in Europe. He traveled via Egypt to France, where he set about implementing his ambitious plan.[61]

Arriving in Paris, Eliav obtained the assistance of Alexander Aaronsohn—the brother of Aaron, the famed head of the World War I Jewish intelligence service NILI (an anagram derived from a biblical passage), which had assisted Britain's conquest of Palestine from the Turks. For his first attack, Eliav recruited a decorated veteran of the French Resistance named Jacques Martinsky who had lost a leg during the war. The plan involved sending Martinsky to London with explosives concealed in his artificial limb that he would then use to construct a parcel bomb to be sent to the Colonial Office. Although Eliav claims in his memoir that the plan in fact targeted the War Office and was indeed successful, it appears that Martinsky never made it out of London Airport when he arrived on a flight from Paris on March 6. Suspicious immigration officials, perhaps acting on information provided by MI5, refused to issue the Resistance veteran an entry permit, and Martinsky was immediately sent back to France.[62]

Eliav had better luck the following evening, when one of his devices wrecked part of the British Colonial Club, just off Trafalgar Square, injuring three persons. The bomber was another French member of Lehi, Robert Misrahi, a philosophy student at the Sorbonne and protégé of Jean-Paul Sartre's. He had successfully smuggled into Britain the explosives to be used for the attack ingeniously concealed in the shoulder pads of his topcoat. Although Eliav described the club as an "exclusive" facility frequented by "senior officials" where "several officials were killed and dozens wounded," it was in fact a recreational center for service personnel and students from the West Indies and Africa visiting or living in London. Accordingly, rather than paragons of the British imperial establishment, the three victims were lowly enlisted men from among the poorest corners of the British Empire. Eliav nonetheless issued a communiqué claiming credit for the attack, fatuously portraying the target as "the centre of British power in London" and "one of the centres of imperialist intrigue." In hopes of actually targeting such a power center, Eliav next set his sights on the Colonial Office itself.[63]

Security at likely Jewish terrorist targets in London had already been tightened following the Colonial Club bombing. It was increased further as a result of the executions of Gruner and the three other Irgunists on April 16. But the Dynamite Man was undaunted. "I learned an important lesson" from the Colonial Club operation, he recalled. "No security measures can stop sophisticated, imaginative planning. In any solid wall one could find a crack through which one could slip in and carry out an attack." To find that crack, he turned to Betty Knout-Lazarus—an attractive young woman with impeccable underground credentials. Her stepfather, the Jewish writer, poet, and prominent anti-Nazi partisan leader David Knout, had been one of Eliav's key contacts when he first arrived in France. Knout was too busy with other projects to become involved with Lehi, so he had referred Eliav to Knout-Lazarus. She was in every respect an ideal terrorist recruit. At age fourteen, she had become a courier for L'Armée Juive, the wartime Jewish partisan organization that the elder Knout helped found, and subsequently a war correspondent, before being injured by a land mine. Sharing her stepfather's militant Zionist ideology, Knout-Lazarus worked closely with Eliav, helping him to build a terrorist infrastructure in France by recruiting members for Lehi's fledgling overseas branch, organizing safe houses, acquiring weapons, planning operations, and crafting propaganda for the group's French newsletter, *L'Indépendance: Organe des Combattants pour la Liberté d'Israël.*[64]

Knout-Lazarus left for London in mid-April and checked into a nondescript hotel near Paddington Station. An initial reconnaissance of

Whitehall drew her attention to Dover House, a Colonial Office annex situated at one end of Horse Guards Parade. On the morning of the sixteenth, Knout-Lazarus assembled the time bomb in her hotel room according to Eliav's instructions. It consisted of a pocket watch attached to twenty-four sticks of dynamite wrapped in copies of the *Evening Standard* and *The Daily Telegraph* disguised to appear as an ordinary parcel. She checked out of the hotel, deposited her luggage in a locker at Victoria Station, and made her way to Whitehall. Immaculately attired in a smart suit with a blue leather handbag and carrying an expensive coat on her arm beneath which was the small parcel, she failed to arouse the suspicions of the guard at Dover House's front door when she innocently inquired if she might use the ladies' room to adjust one of her stockings. The unwitting guard asked a cleaning lady to escort Knout-Lazarus downstairs; she deposited the parcel in a toilet stall and departed, thanking the guard before stopping to collect her luggage at Victoria Station and boarding a train for the south coast and thereafter a ferry for Belgium. The bomb was discovered—unexploded—later that day. The hands of the pocket watch's timing mechanism had jammed, thus preventing the completion of the electrical circuit that would have detonated the explosives. According to Commander Leonard Burt, the head of Scotland Yard's Special Branch, had the device exploded, "it would have blown the sort of hole in the Colonial Office that was blown in the King David Hotel"—inflicting a similar number of casualties.[65]

Eliav's communiqué taking responsibility for the incident tried to put the best face on another botched operation. "The bomb laid by our fighters in the Colonial Office," his message stated, "was accidentally discovered before it exploded." Nonetheless, this was indeed "the second time within a month that the hand of the fighting Underground ha[d] reached the heart of the British Empire."[66]

The Dynamite Man understandably decided to change tactics for his next round of attacks, posting twenty-three letter bombs from Italy to Attlee, Bevin, Churchill, Stanley, Cunningham, Shaw, Sir Harold Mac-Michael, Sir Stafford Cripps, and Anthony Eden, among others. Several in fact reached their intended recipients but also failed to explode. The post office was alerted to the plot, and all the remaining explosive missives were intercepted and safely defused. Both Eliav and Knout-Lazarus were arrested that June at the Belgian border trying to return to France. Customs officials discovered a cache of additional letter bombs addressed to more British officials in the false bottom of Knout-Lazarus's suitcase. She was reported to be dressed in the same expensive suit and carrying the same distinctive blue leather handbag that she had at Dover House two months earlier. A thumbprint lifted by police from the pocket watch affixed to the Colonial Office device clearly matched Eliav's. Because no extradition treaty then existed between Britain and Belgium, Eliav and Knout-Lazarus were tried in Mons and sentenced respectively to just eight months and a year in prison. At a party in Tel Aviv celebrating Knout-Lazarus's release fourteen months later, she was totally unrepentant. "I'm sorry none of them was delivered," Knout-Lazarus told reporters, before announcing that her "terrorist days are over and done with now."[67]

That the terrorists' intelligence was generally superior to that of the security forces was again demonstrated on April 30 when a routine police sweep of the route along which MacMillan would shortly travel uncovered a land mine that the Irgun had buried. Thereafter, however, an ominous quiet descended on Palestine. Despite Begin's threat to hang four British officers for every Jew executed, the sustained onslaught of terrorist attacks that had followed Feinstein's and Barazani's deaths suddenly ceased—as did any further abduction attempts. British military intelligence nonetheless remained concerned that the Irgun was planning something spectacular. The fact that the United Nations was then meeting in a special session, called at Britain's request, to appoint a committee to study the Palestine question in advance of the General Assembly's consideration of the matter in September was cited by Sixth Airborne intelligence as providing a likely rationale for some new, dramatic act of terrorist violence. Indeed, Begin himself later admitted that the Irgun for this very reason "wanted to show to the whole world that the British could not control and rule this country." And it did so in suitably spectacular fashion on May 4.[68]

Of Palestine's two central prisons, the fortress at Acre functioned as the mandate's maximum security facility. It stood on the foundations of the bastion that the Knights of the Hospital of St. John, the Hospitallers, had erected in 1104. It was captured in 1187 by Saladin, the famed first sultan of Egypt and Syria and founder of the Ayyubid dynasty, only to be brutally retaken six years later by Richard the Lionheart. Acre returned to Muslim rule a century later, and this proved critical in withstanding Napoleon's months-long siege of Acre in 1799.[69]

When Allenby's forces captured the city in September 1918, Palestine's new British rulers were quick to grasp the fortress's potential as a high-security prison. With three-foot-thick, seventy-foot-high walls and a succession of internal iron gates and portcullises through which entry was gained only after crossing a forty-foot-deep and fifteen-foot-wide moat, the Acre fortress appeared to be impregnable. By 1947, it held a total of 671 male prisoners, including 163 Jews (including 60 Irgun and 22 Lehi fighters), 58 mentally deranged common criminals, and 450 Arab convicts.[70]

Begin and the Irgun's high command were neither impressed nor daunted by Acre's formidable defenses and impenetrable image. Virtually from the moment that Gruner and the three other death row Irgunists had been transferred there, the group's efforts to devise a means to free them were unceasing. Begin assigned Amichai Paglin, the Irgun's operations chief and architect of the King David Hotel bombing, to this high-priority mission. The direct line of communication that the Irgun had already established with its fighters imprisoned in Acre enabled Paglin to maintain regular contact with his predecessor as Irgun operations officer, Eitan Livni. The father of the future Israeli political leader and foreign minister, Tzipi Livni, the elder Livni was the Irgun's prison commander. Using coded scraps of paper concealed in bars of soap, cake, fruit, and clothing or information passed orally through the Jewish doctors, lawyers, and clergymen permitted access to the prisoners, he explained to Paglin that Lehi prisoners had been digging an escape tunnel that was nearing completion. But the chance discovery of a room within the fortress that abutted the Arab souk (market) outside changed everything. After careful reconnaissance undertaken by Paglin himself of the warren of alleyways bisecting the market and leading to the external walls of the prison fortress, he came up with a daring plan that would entail a simultaneous break-in *and* breakout.[71]

Sunday was the start of the workweek in mandate Palestine, and that morning a work crew arrived to cut back tree branches overhanging the power lines around the Acre fortress. Having subsequently learned from the Palestine Electric Corporation that it had no record of any maintenance being done in the prison's vicinity, British army intelligence concluded that the maintenance team was in fact an Irgun unit performing last-minute surveillance. The workers deliberately left behind two of the tall ladders that they had used to access the overhanging branches.

Around 4:15 p.m., a British military truck pulled up alongside the old Turkish baths, adjacent to the prison. An army telephone repair crew, attired in full battle kit—including webbing, anklets, belts, and pouches—and bearing the shoulder flashes of the Royal Engineers, alighted and, placing the work crew's ladders against the prison's exterior wall, began to hoist two heavy cases of telephone equipment that together contained the equivalent of 250 pounds of high explosive. A jeep soon arrived carrying more troops and a captain, who took charge of the detail. His name was Dov Cohen, a.k.a. Shimshon (Samson), and he was in fact the commander of the thirty-four-man Irgun assault team that Paglin had assembled for the operation. Cohen, aged thirty-one, was a decorated combat veteran of a British army commando unit during World War II who had fought with distinction in the Abyssinian, North African, and Italian campaigns, rising to the rank of staff sergeant. Short but powerfully built, with blond hair and piercing blue eyes, the former Hebrew University philosophy student made a perfect British army officer, complete with the appropriate English accent despite his Polish origins.[72]

Ascending to one of the barred prison windows high above the baths, the bogus telephone repairman positioned the two explosive charges just inside the wall and quickly scrambled down the ladder. A few minutes later a deafening blast filled the souk with smoke, rubble, and shattered chunks of masonry. This was the signal for the Irgun prisoners inside to implement the previously agreed-upon diversions that would facilitate their escape. The explosion had been deliberately timed to coincide with the moment when all the cells—including those of the condemned—were open and all prisoners, Arab and Jew alike, were exercising in the prison yard. Just as the mostly Arab guards were recovering from the shock of the blasts, three Irgun prisoners tossed hand grenades into the lunatic section of the prison to further sow confusion and disorder. Other Irgun detainees wielding sticks with rags soaked in paraffin immediately set fires in hopes of scattering the Arab prisoners and forcing them away from the south side of the fortress, where the blast had occurred. Meanwhile, the forty-one Irgun and Lehi prisoners preselected to take part in the escape quickly changed into the civilian clothes that had previously been brought into the facility and made their way toward the breach in the outer wall. Their path through two iron gates was cleared by inmates using smuggled explosives that had been hidden inside tins of a Glasgow-manufactured jam. Upon emerging from the huge, gaping hole in the fortress, some of the prisoners were handed spare weapons by the Irgun attack force. They piled into the waiting military vehicles that began to snake their way out of the market.[73]

In order to impede any pursuit, additional Irgun teams had mined all the roads north and south of Acre, especially at potential bottlenecks such as bridges. Only the eastern road out of the city had been kept clear as an escape route. Meanwhile, a third Irgun unit was positioned elsewhere outside the city, waiting in the vicinity of an encampment of the Second

Parachute Battalion. Just as the explosions breached the wall at the prison, it fired six mortar rounds into the camp to prevent the nearest available military from pursuing the Irgun force.

Paglin's plan, however, went disastrously awry when a bathing party of Sixth Airborne troops, alerted by the explosions and gunfire, hastily organized an impromptu roadblock about a half mile outside the city. A fierce firefight ensued as two of the fleeing vehicles careened to a halt. One of the soldiers was seriously wounded, and half a dozen others sustained minor injuries. The Irgun's losses, however, were substantial. Three members of the assault team, including Cohen, were killed, and five others had been captured. Six of the freed prisoners had also perished in the gun battle, and two others had been recaptured. Moreover, only twenty-three of the forty-one detainees selected for the escape had survived. In the confusion, more than two hundred Arab prisoners had inadvertently been freed as well, including nine persons serving long sentences for terrorist offenses committed during the 1936–39 Arab Rebellion.[74]

Hailed by Begin as "amongst the most daring attacks of the Hebrew underground and possibly of any underground," the raid—like the King David Hotel bombing ten months before—was incontestably audacious in planning but seriously flawed in execution. The high Irgun casualty toll, including the death of the operation's commander along with several of the freed prisoners, in addition to the fact that far fewer of the hand-picked escapees actually got away while far more of their Arab counterparts did, deprived the group of the unalloyed military triumph that the Irgun leader clearly desired. But although its results were decidedly mixed militarily, they were unequivocally triumphant in both psychological and propagandistic terms.[75]

The raid was featured in all the major American and British newspapers and, according to *The Palestine Post*, "temporarily overshadowed" the discussions on Palestine taking place at the United Nations. Much to Britain's consternation, it also provided a huge boost to the Irgun's image in the United States. Seeking to capitalize on the spectacular prison assault, a delegation from the American League for a Free Palestine was waiting at Ben Hecht's bedside when he awoke from surgery in a New York City hospital. "We need more money," one of them told him. "Millions." And they had someone willing to pay for full-page newspaper advertisements to solicit contributions. "I emerged from my [oxygen] tent," Hecht reminisced, "and called for stationery." The ad that he penned appeared under the memorable title "Letter to the Terrorists of Palestine." It boasted, the former advertising copywriter turned award-winning screenwriter and playwright recalled, a "full and honest report of our Committee's fiduciary and spiritual accomplishment." The best-known excerpt controversially read, "Every time you blow up a British arsenal, or wreck a British jail, or send a British railroad train sky-high, or rob a British bank, or let go with your guns and bombs at British betrayers and invaders of your homeland, the Jews of America make a little holiday in their hearts." The ad went on to credit the Irgun with compelling the British to submit the Palestine issue to the United Nations "because they were frightened of you. They were afraid your gallant fight for your homeland would gather to you the sympathy of the world," before promising, "Hang on, brave friends, our money is on its way."[76]

Hecht claimed that hundreds of newspapers in the United States, Mexico, South America, and France ran the advertisement gratis with only a dozen or so American papers charging their usual rates. The timing could not have been worse for Britain. For months the Foreign Office had lodged successive complaints with the State Department about the regularity with which tendentious advertisements extolling terrorism appeared in U.S. newspapers. British officials had taken particular umbrage at the blatant raising of funds with which to purchase weapons for use against America's closest ally. They had also repeatedly complained about the legal tax-exempt status enjoyed by registered charities, such as the American League for a Free Palestine, behind these allegedly philanthropic activities.[77]

This advertisement in particular had an especially chilling effect on Anglo-American relations. Sir Orme Sargent, the permanent under-secretary of state for foreign affairs, scolded Lewis Douglas, the U.S. ambassador to the U.K., for giving the New York press free rein to incite violence and bloodshed in Palestine. He pointedly asked, "What would be the feeling of the United States Government if, for instance, British Communists were to publish in the British press an advertisement to the effect that 'every time you blow up an American arsenal or wreck an American gaol or send an American railroad train sky high . . . British Communists make a little holiday in their hearts'[?] Mr. Douglas said that the indignation of his Government would know no bounds and they would not be slow to show it."[78]

The official U.S. government response was unhelpful. State Department lawyers had determined that nothing could legally be done to prevent the advertisements and fund-raising nor deprive these organizations of their tax-exempt status. It was therefore of little consolation to the British when the new U.S. secretary of state, George C. Marshall, voiced his opinion that such donations were clearly not charitable.[79]

Begin's assessment of the Acre raid as a milestone in the Irgun's struggle and a major propaganda victory is thus not without merit. The assault did indeed dramatically underscore the decline of the Palestine administration's capacity to maintain order by depicting its inability to secure even the country's maximum security prison. Indeed, so far as Cunningham was concerned, it was evidence that relations with the Yishuv had become completely irreparable. "The first and most important element in the situation," he dejectedly told Creech Jones,

> is that, because of political differences with the mandatory administration on account of the inability of His Majesty's Government to accede to Jewish demands, the Jewish community, whose dissident members are responsible for these outrages, have declined and still decline to give any assistance to the police and military forces in the maintenance of law and order . . . It is a situation in which a policeman is shot and lies wounded in the street beside a bus queue, no member of which will lift a hand to help him.[80]

CHAPTER 18

Buried Quietly in the Night

While the Irgun licked its wounds and quietly exulted in the attention and publicity reaped by the Acre raid, the authorities in Palestine pondered their next move. It was a depressing exercise. As the renowned historian of the British Empire William (Wm.) Roger Louis notes, "One-tenth of the armed forces of the entire British Empire now occupied a territory the size of Wales. There was one soldier for every eighteen inhabitants in the country, or, as one observer calculated, one for every city block." Indeed, the security forces enjoyed a twenty-to-one numerical superiority over the approximately five thousand terrorists that British military intelligence believed to make up the combined ranks of the Irgun and Lehi. Yet, despite this overwhelming numerical advantage, it remained an environment where "Jewish terrorism thrived as never before," according to the OSS's former chief Middle East analyst.[1]

The situation was regarded as so dire that a week after the prison attack William Nicol Gray ordered six of the CID's top intelligence officers to relocate immediately to the heavily defended PPF headquarters complex in the Russian Compound. The inspector general apologized for the inconvenience and overcrowding, implying that they might wish to emulate the example of two of their colleagues who had already made arrangements to sleep in their offices. As the U.S. consul general in Jerusalem, Robert Macatee, observed in a report to Washington on May 22, "One cannot escape the conclusion that the Government of Palestine is a hunted organization with little hope of ever being able to cope with conditions in this country as they exist today."[2]

In the circumstances, both Cunningham's and Gray's attention returned to what had historically been the Achilles' heel of governance and policing in Palestine: the lack of intelligence. The paucity of Hebrew linguists and skilled detectives had almost completely undermined the CID's effectiveness; its military counterparts were little better. The "intelligence section" at army headquarters, for instance, in the spring of 1947 consisted of only five young and inexperienced officers. Moreover, even at this late stage in the conflict, intelligence was relegated to a distinctly secondary priority by the headquarters' general staff.[3]

The Acre operation provided a stunning illustration of the poor intelligence capabilities and inadequate security procedures that characterized the Palestine garrison—and were ruthlessly exploited by the terrorists. The Irgun, for example, had assembled from around the country an array of stolen or disguised military vehicles without attracting any notice. According to Gyles Isham, army trucks that went missing were regarded as a sure indication that some major terrorist operation was in the works. Yet, in this instance, it apparently failed to arouse any alarm. The Irgun had also perfectly attired the raiding party in correct British military kit and battle dress and had provided them with the requisite bona fide identity documents and movement orders, thereby enabling the terrorists to travel unhindered along the length of Palestine's coastal highway.[4]

Accordingly, if the army and the police were to make any headway against the terrorists, they required actionable intelligence—timely information whose immediate exploitation can rob one's opponent of the initiative and decisively turn the tide of battle. Gray intuitively understood this from his wartime service leading 45 Commando Royal Marines. This elite special operations unit came ashore at Normandy and then fought its way across northwestern Europe into the heart of Nazi Germany. While visiting London in October 1946 to discuss with Colonial Office officials the PPF's chronic recruitment difficulties, the inspector general therefore sought the advice and assistance of members of the intelligence and security services. He needed their help to identify veterans of elite, specialized units who had operated behind enemy lines during World War II, such as the Special Air Service and the Special Operations Executive, who might be interested in serving in the PPF as undercover counterterrorist operatives. One of the first people he approached was Colonel Bernard Fergusson.[5]

"It could be said that Fergusson once seen was never forgotten," his obituarist wrote. Charming, literate, tall, and powerfully built with a posh accent, clipped mustache, and monocle jammed into his right eye socket, he cut a memorable figure. Descended from a long line of distinguished Scots soldier-statesmen, the younger Fergusson had attended Eton before graduating from the Royal Military College at Sandhurst in 1930. He joined the Black Watch the following year. In 1937, at the height of the Arab Rebellion, Fergusson was sent with his battalion to Palestine.

Assigned brigade intelligence officer, he worked closely with the police and also made the acquaintance at military headquarters in Jerusalem of a "grim, unsmiling" major named Orde Wingate, whose unconventional ideas about countering terrorism and insurgency dovetailed with Fergusson's own. He then taught at Sandhurst, and shortly after World War II began, the future Lord Ballantrae was assigned to the Middle East Command's headquarters in Cairo and subsequently to the Joint Planning Staff's general headquarters in Delhi. He was reunited in 1942 with Wingate, now a major general commanding the Chindits special operations force in Burma, renowned for employing guerrilla warfare tactics to disrupt the Japanese army's lines of communication. Like Gray, Fergusson had earned a Distinguished Service Order, second only to the Victoria Cross, Britain's highest honor for bravery in battle, while leading a Chindit column. Later, he became director of a jungle warfare training school beneath the Himalayan Mountains and subsequently was put in charge of military operations at Combined Operations Headquarters in London. He unsuccessfully stood for Parliament as a Conservative candidate in the July 1945 general election and thereafter produced in quick succession two books recounting his wartime experiences.[6]

In the fall of 1946, Fergusson was thirty-five years old and at loose ends. An offer earlier in the year to succeed Rymer-Jones as PPF inspector general had fallen through when the War Office refused to allow him to take a leave of absence. Fergusson was about to return to command a Black Watch battalion in India when Gray offered him the post of assistant inspector general in charge of the Police Mobile Force. Although Fergusson was initially reluctant to accept a position two steps down from the top one he had previously been offered, Gray presented him with an irresistible option. "I understood that although my nominal job would be to run the P.M.F.," Fergusson recalled in his autobiography, "I would in fact have a specific responsibility for all anti-terrorist activities. Now this as a job," he enthused, "did sound extremely interesting." The intervention of Lieutenant General Frederick "Boy" Browning, an old friend and colleague, who was now military secretary at the War Office, granted Fergusson the secondment to the police that earlier eluded him. "I was under no illusion: I knew I was going to a thankless and tricky job," the newly minted assistant inspector general of police recalled, "but it was to be a problem which constituted a challenge, in a country I loved, and with a Force that I admired." His appointment took effect on December 10, 1946, and following two weeks' embarkation leave Fergusson departed by air for Palestine.[7]

Upon landing at Lydda, Fergusson went straight to police headquarters, where Gray was waiting with some embarrassing news. Only a few weeks earlier, Wickham had submitted his report recommending the PMF's disbandment. Bereft of the job he had come to Palestine for, Fergusson was tempted to cable Browning and head off to India, but Gray was insistent that he stay and promised to create a new position for him. They agreed that Fergusson would now become assistant inspector general for operations and training—with the same counterterrorism remit as before.[8]

At Gray's request, his first task was to conduct a thorough study of current police counterterrorism operations and methods. Fergusson was profoundly troubled by what he found. "The Palestine Police had changed considerably, and not for the better, since I had first known it nine years earlier." The force had been denuded of manpower and was also far less competent than Fergusson had recalled. Moreover, unlike the Arab Rebellion, the Jewish uprising was an urban, not a rural, phenomenon. "The terrorists' planning was much more subtle," he noted, "and their techniques more sophisticated." The army and the police were thoroughly unsuited to the complicated task of discovering the terrorists' urban lairs and forcing them from hiding. Intelligence was less plentiful than it had been during the Arab Rebellion. "Now we got very few tips indeed, and from what little we got it was difficult to make deductions," Fergusson explained.[9]

Some three months of inquiry and observation had failed to inspire any new or novel thoughts on how to tackle the problem, and meanwhile terrorist attacks were increasing both in skill and in number. "I seemed to lack and my colleagues seemed to lack," Fergusson later reflected, "the sort of intuitive thinking that was inspiring our opponents. I tried to translate into the urban and suburban areas of Jerusalem, Haifa and Tel Aviv the kind of ideas that my subordinates had dreamed up for me in the jungles of Burma; but all I got was the sort of echo you might expect in an empty squash-court."[10]

Normal policing and existing countermeasures, Fergusson believed, had not succeeded in containing, much less eliminating, terrorism—and never would. Something new was required—a conclusion now shared by Cunningham and Montgomery as well as Gray. "I have always been clear that the best method of dealing with terrorists is to kill them," the high commissioner had told Creech Jones as Palestine had drifted deeper into lawlessness the previous November. Montgomery had similarly despaired of conventional military approaches applied to counterterrorism and instead argued that it was no longer possible to eliminate terrorism in Palestine "without employing very ruthless measures."[11]

According to the PPF's official history, Gray was also convinced that "the terrorists must be flushed from their cellars in Tel Aviv and elsewhere; then . . . harassed, pursued and given no rest until arrested or shot in action against the security forces." Mulling over the various options, Fergusson had an epiphany. "It seemed to me, baffled as I was," he recounts in his memoir, "that we needed people with experience of terrorism or something closely allied to it: people who would foresee the sort of plan that might occur to the imagination of terrorists: people, in short, who had been something like terrorists themselves: not to terrorise or to repay in kind, but to anticipate and to give would-be raiders a bloody nose as they came in to raid."[12]

Fergusson's idea was essentially to revive the PPF's mixed British and Arab Search and Seek squads, also known as Q Patrols, that had effectively fought Arab terrorists during the 1936–39 rebellion. These units' mission had been to force the Arab rebels into the open, where they would be more easily engaged in battle and killed or arrested. This time, however, these units would comprise Britons only: drawn from the PPF's British section and led by officers skilled in unconventional warfare who had served with elite special forces units during the war. The fact that these units would lack the social, cultural, and linguistic knowledge provided by local police officers that was critical to the Q Patrols' success does not appear to have been regarded by Fergusson as a serious impediment. Indeed, according to the PPF's official historian, Edward Horne, their mission remained the same: to "disappear into the Jewish areas, as previous squads had disappeared into Arab areas a decade earlier."[13]

With Gray's blessing and Cunningham's backing, Fergusson returned to London in February 1947. The ostensible reason for his visit was to oversee the purchase of new police cars. But his real purpose was to obtain permission from the Colonial and War Offices to recruit up to four regular army officers for the new police unit. He was specifically hoping to recruit officers who had served with distinction in elite wartime units such as the SAS or the SOE that had fought alongside indigenous European resistance movements against the Nazis. "There is in the Army a small number of officers who have both technical and psychological knowledge of terrorism," Fergusson's memorandum to the War Office explained, "having themselves been engaged in similar operations on what may be termed the terrorist side in countries occupied by the enemy in the late war." The men whom Fergusson had in mind were "exceptionally qualified; and rather than accept officers with inferior qualifications," he declared, "I will accept none. In this event, the project will fall to the ground, since it will be of no value unless the standard of training and operation is really high."[14]

Both the Colonial Office and the War Office responded with alacrity. Fergusson was able to obtain the services of three of the four men he requested. The first two arrived in Palestine on March 17, 1947. They were Alastair "Angus" McGregor, an SAS and MI6 veteran who had previously served in Palestine, and Roy Farran, among the most highly decorated soldiers of the war, who had fought in Egypt, Crete, Sicily, Italy, France, and Greece as both a conventional soldier and a special operator behind enemy lines with the SAS. Farran also had firsthand experience of conditions in Palestine as a result of his tour of duty as second-in-command of the Third Hussars during 1945 and 1946. Both men had served together during the war in the Second SAS. They had also been students of Fergusson's at Sandhurst, and each was trained and thoroughly versed in close-quarters battle. "Alastair and Roy had operated behind enemy lines with great success," Fergusson later explained, "and I thought that their minds would work like terrorists' minds." They were each given wide latitude both geographically and operationally to accomplish their mission. McGregor was assigned the northern half of Palestine, with responsibility for Haifa, and Farran was given the south, which included Jerusalem, Tel Aviv, and the coastal plain.[15]

"In Jerusalem Police HQ the brief was explained to us," Farran recalled in his memoir. "We would each have full power to operate as we pleased within our specific areas. We were to advise on defence against the terrorists and to take an active part in hunting the dissidents . . . It was to all intents and purposes a *carte blanche.*" He and McGregor had two weeks to recruit ten men each from the British police in their respective areas of operations and another two weeks to train them. There was no shortage of former SAS operators already serving in the PPF or military in postwar Palestine, and Farran was able to find five SAS veterans and two former commandos for his unit. Farran and McGregor trained their respective squads at a special, secret, cordoned-off area of the PMF depot at Jenin that Fergusson had allocated for their exclusive use. Although both units would be deployed primarily in Palestine's cities, no special training or attention was devoted to the unique operational and intelligence requirements of urban counterterrorism. As Fergusson himself admits, this was a mistake. "If I had been just a trifle more ruthless, I could have done that, by commandeering a length of street in Jenin; but I didn't," he later regretted.[16]

Farran took special care to ensure that his men could "put six rounds in a playing-card at fifteen yards" and that they were skilled in close-quarters combat. After two weeks, he was satisfied and thought them ready for action.

But so myopic and cursory a period of instruction was clearly inadequate—
as would shortly become all too tragically evident.[17]

Frank Kitson, whose own extensive experience of counterterrorist special
operations spanned the gamut of Britain's subsequent postwar campaigns
in Malaya, Kenya, Cyprus, Muscat and Oman, and Northern Ireland,
has written of the importance of extensive training if special operations
units are to function effectively. He cites the necessity of "attuning men's
minds to cope with the environment of this sort of war." Kitson argues, "It
involves explaining the fundamental nature of subversion and insurgency
with particular reference to the way in which force can be employed to
achieve political ends, and the way in which political considerations affect
the use of force." In this respect, Farran's preoccupation with his men's
marksmanship was clearly at the expense of familiarizing them with their
operational environment and providing the additional training needed
for them to execute the intelligence-gathering dimension of their mission. Indeed, Farran's wartime experience in the SAS had never involved
these types of covert operations. As M. R. D. Foot, the renowned historian of British special operations during World War II, observed of Farran's exploits in France, "Though romantic, [they] were more cavalry than
clandestine warfare."[18]

Although Farran could boast that his unit so closely resembled "any
party of Jewish youths from a kibbutz" that when they drove through Arab
villages they were "hissed," the truth of the matter was that their charade
could only go so far given the severe limitation on their ability to gather
intelligence. This particular shortcoming was exacerbated further by the
fact that both Farran's and McGregor's squads were entirely outside the
normal police channels of command and communication. Hence, they
were unable to benefit from any intelligence, advice, or assistance provided
by the CID or the uniformed police. Fergusson recognized this problem
and, accordingly, emphasized the squads' independent counterterrorist/
commando strike force function. Even so, this still ignored the squads'
main weakness: that of obtaining the intelligence necessary for them to
carry out their mission.[19]

Farran, however, remained completely aloof to any of these concerns
and smugly complacent about his and his unit's unique capabilities—
especially in comparison to the regular police and their plainclothes
counterparts in the CID. The former he derided for cowering behind
heavily sandbagged fortresses and the latter for possessing "about as much

information as would fill a thimble." To his mind, "police methods were so amateurish that even to a non-policeman they were wince-making." Worse still, Farran believed, this was all part and parcel of the Palestine government's weak-kneed, casualty-averse policy that was designed "to avoid 'provoking' the Jews." Indeed, in *Winged Dagger*, Farran depicts the approach to dealing with terrorism before his arrival as "Don't let's be cruel to the Jews . . . Only a few are naughty, and in the end, provided that we are nice to them, they will all forget how much they hate us and come forward with information." Farran, however, had a different approach to obtaining such information, as the incident that occurred on the evening of May 6, 1947, vividly demonstrates.[20]

Tension was running high throughout the country as a result of the raid on Acre prison that had taken place just forty-eight hours earlier. The pressure on the security forces for a breakthrough in the war against terrorism as well as on those tasked with acquiring the intelligence to facilitate it was doubtless intense as Farran and three subordinates set out on patrol in Jerusalem that evening. Driving a battered but specially outfitted six-seater sedan complete with souped-up engine, they hoped to come across a member of either the Irgun or Lehi, who would then be searched and interrogated and thereby persuaded to reveal information vital to the counterterrorist effort.[21]

Some time before 8:00 p.m., they spotted a teenage boy named Alexander Rubowitz. It is not known what specifically attracted their attention to the tall, lanky sixteen-year-old. Described as "quiet, delicate and shy" by his family, he was the antithesis of the hardened and cunning, streetwise terrorist that the British authorities usually associated with the Irgun and even more so with Lehi. Because they aroused less suspicion, Lehi regularly turned to its more youthful enthusiasts for a variety of low-level, yet undeniably risky, underground tasks such as distributing propaganda, pasting posters and announcements to walls, carrying messages, and on occasion transferring weapons from one location to another. Not only were these youths more expendable to the organization than the small number of seasoned fighters in its ranks, but as minors they faced less severe punishment—and could not be charged with capital offenses—if they were caught. Whatever the reason, Farran and his men's instincts that night were correct. Rubowitz was in fact a devoted Lehi activist known by the nom de guerre Chaim who had already been expelled from two schools for his extremism and, moreover, was a graduate of Lehi's commanders and firearms training courses. He was sufficiently well thought of by his superiors to have been appointed leader of a ten-person cell responsible for affixing Lehi posters to the walls of the city's Jewish neighborhoods.[22]

According to eyewitness accounts, a boy, later identified as Rubowitz, was seen running down Haran (now Aharon) Street chased by a burly, fair-haired man. In a desperate effort to elude his pursuer, Rubowitz darted onto Ussishkin Street, but at the corner of Keren Kayemet L'Yisrael Street the man caught him. A dark sedan quickly pulled over from which a second man emerged to help bundle the still-struggling Rubowitz into the backseat. The scene was observed by two schoolboys playing nearby. A third boy, fifteen-year-old Meir Cohen, brazenly approached one of the men and asked what was going on. He was brusquely told "in perfect English" to mind his own business by the man who claimed to be a police officer. Cohen, however, persisted and asked to see some identification. The man produced an identity card, stamped in bold letters "Palestine Police," and then, waving a revolver in the youth's face, told him to leave or risk being shot. At that moment he heard a cry in Hebrew from the back of the car. "I'm from the Rubowitz family," the abducted boy shouted, as he was struck repeatedly in the head in order to silence him. The car then sped away, but not before several onlookers recorded its license plate—number 993. The two schoolboys returned to their game and only then noticed a gray felt trilby hat that had been knocked from the head of one of the men during the scuffle and inadvertently left behind. The boys picked it up and brought it with them to their lesson at a nearby synagogue, where it was placed on top of a cupboard by another student and, for the moment, forgotten.[23]

The following morning, Rubowitz's brothers reported Alexander's disappearance to the police. The desk officer at the Mustashfa police station, near the family's home in the Mea Shearim district, told them that there was no record of anyone by that name having been arrested. With their parents now sick with worry, the brothers returned to the station daily, where further inquiries directed to the CID similarly failed to produce any new information on Alexander's disappearance. On May 8 the family placed missing-person notices in Palestine's Hebrew-language newspapers that included Alexander's description. And the next day *Ha'aretz* published a brief article under the headline "Abducted or Arrested?" However, it was not until May 12, when a photograph of Alexander appeared in *Yediot Ahronot*, that both Meir Cohen and the two boys who had found the gray trilby hat realized that the missing teenager was the same person they saw being shoved into a dark sedan. The two boys presented themselves in person at the Rubowitzes' home, while Cohen appears to have delivered an unsigned, typed letter to the family relating his version of the previous week's events. Upon hearing the two boys' account of the incident, Alexander's brothers hurried to the synagogue, where a caretaker gave them the hat. Inspecting it, they were able to discern a name embossed on the soiled sweatband that appeared to read "FAR-AN" or "FARKAN." The brothers brought the hat to the Mustashfa police station, where it was sent to the notoriously incompetent CID laboratory for analysis. Chemical tests failed to shed any new light on the identity of its owner, concluding only that it belonged to someone named either "FAR?AN" or "FARSAN." When questioned by an attorney whom the family had hired, the police denied that anyone named "FARAN," "FARKHAN," or "FARSAN" was on the PPF's rolls. Inquiries made to the army via the military chaplain on the family's behalf similarly failed to produce anyone with those names serving in Palestine.[24]

On May 22, however, *The Palestine Post* published an account of Alexander's unexplained disappearance that directly implicated the police. Citing three eyewitness reports of the abduction and details about the gray hat left behind with the name "Farkan" or "Farrkan" on the sweatband, it reported, "The C.I.D. are stated to have told the boy's family that they think his abductors were British, but also state that he is not held in any police prison or lock-up." The following day, the newspaper received a letter for Mrs. Rubowitz from someone who claimed to have had a passing acquaintance with the family some years before. The anonymous writer, who signed the letter with an *X*, wrote,

> that ink spreads, blotches, etc., and that the name is not FARKAN or FARRKAN, but after the first "R" there is a further "R" which should read "FARRAN" . . .
>
> The C.I.D. are right to have stated that the abductors were British, but are not right in saying that they do not know who the person is or do not know the person.
>
> I would frankly tell you, this man is a Deputy Superintendent of Police, in the Criminal Investigation Department, and is often seen wearing civilian clothes . . .
>
> Believe me what I say is true.[25]

More than half a century later, the release of declassified documents by the British National Archives conclusively establishes Farran's role in Rubowitz's disappearance. These materials substantiate the allegations leveled at the time by the Jewish Agency on the family's behalf. Working from fragmentary information and an unnamed "reliable source," the agency was able to piece together a remarkably accurate depiction of what occurred.

A letter sent by Golda Meyerson to Cunningham on June 23, 1947, correctly asserts that Rubowitz "was taken down the deserted Jericho Road, 'grilled' and tortured for about an hour. Finally Rubowitz succumbed to the torture and died on the spot. The policemen tried to get rid of the body, and finally handed it to some Bedouin in the neighbourhood and asked them to dispose of it. The men returned to their duties in Jerusalem." The agency's account, however, is on less solid ground with respect to certain details. For example, the gray trilby is incorrectly described as a police beret "on which the letters F R A N were legible." And the claim that Farran waited a week before informing Fergusson of the incident is also inaccurate. He had in fact done so the following morning.[26]

All the sordid details of the Rubowitz case are contained in the official police investigation conducted by Superintendent K. P. Hadingham, among the PPF's most highly regarded officers. On June 2, Arthur Giles, the acting inspector general while Gray was back in the U.K., had ordered Hadingham to take charge of the investigation—and to begin by interviewing Fergusson, whose statement essentially corresponds with the Jewish Agency's version of the abduction and alleged murder. According to Hadingham's report, Fergusson stated

that on the 7th May, 1947, Mr. R. A. Farran, D.S.P. [District Superintendent Police], had come to him and told him that on the previous evening British Police members of his squad who had been on special duty in Jerusalem watching for illegal pamphleteers came to him and told him that they had arrested a youth in possession of illegal pamphlets. That he (Farran) had, with others of his squad, taken the youth by car down the Jericho road for further questioning and had gone further than he should in trying to make the youth talk. That he (Farran) had killed the youth by bashing his head in with a stone and that knife wounds had been added to the body after death. That the dead youth's clothing had been removed and burned and that the body had been left unburied somewhere in the open country off the Jericho Road.[27]

Armed with this information, Hadingham was able to confirm that at 9:20 p.m. on May 6 an unmarked police sedan with the license plate M. 491 passed through a military checkpoint on the Jericho Road, east of Jerusalem, headed toward the Dead Sea. The same vehicle was stopped returning to Jerusalem at a minute before midnight. On both occasions, the name of the driver listed in the checkpoint's log was "FARRAND." It is believed that the previously reported license plate, denoting a civilian vehicle, was a fake and had been swapped with the proper police tags once Farran and his men left Rehavia.[28]

The PPF's "Notes for Interrogating Officers" provided explicit guidance for how interrogations were to be conducted. The expectation implicit throughout the document is that a suspect was to be brought immediately to either a police station or some other designated government facility. In addition to performing such routine tasks as photographing the suspect, taking his or her fingerprints, and properly recording various personal details, the arresting officer was required to complete a specific form documenting each interrogation session—"correctly and in detail"—as well as provide a specific recommendation whether to release or hold the suspect.[29]

Amassing such data is at the foundation of both good police investigatory work and established intelligence collection procedures. According to Hadingham's report, it is clear that none of these prescribed steps were followed nor were any details concerning Rubowitz recorded. Instead, a young boy was spirited out of the city and brought in the dark of night to an isolated olive grove in the Judaean desert near Wadi Kelt. There, his four captors tied him to a tree and tortured him for at least an hour. Throughout the ordeal, Rubowitz remained silent, refusing to divulge any information about either his confederates or the organization to which they belonged. Whether the blow that Farran allegedly struck to the boy's head with a rock was a coup de grâce or a futile attempt at further intimidation is not known. No autopsy was ever performed because Rubowitz's body to this day has never been found.[30]

Farran, alas, was not alone in failing to follow proper police procedure. Although Fergusson reported the matter to Richard Catling—the head of the CID's Jewish section and one of his few friends on the force—only hours after hearing Farran's account of the previous night's incident, Catling did nothing. Any illusion that Rubowitz's continued disappearance would go unnoticed was shattered less than seventy-two hours later when, on May 10, *Ha'aretz* carried a story about the boy's abduction. Fergusson now decided to inform Gray. Rather than calling on him at PPF headquarters during normal office hours, Fergusson turned up at the inspector general's living quarters late that same night. Despite having presumably been informed of a murder confession made by an officer under his command, as well as of serial violations of standard police procedure, Gray also did nothing. "I merely expressed my displeasure," he wrote in a letter of explanation sent to Gurney some six weeks later, "and informed Col. Fergusson that I would consider the matter and discuss it with [Catling]." The inspector general justified this decision on the grounds that documents found on Rubowitz contained the names of some forty-five Lehi operatives. This information, Gray was convinced, "might well have caused a break up of the Stern Gang in Jerusalem"—a claim Farran also repeats in his memoir. Accordingly, arresting or even suspending Farran from duty, he told the chief secretary, might have alerted the terrorists and thus compromised a potential major intelligence coup.[31]

On May 11, Gray told Catling to focus on the documents and forget about the missing-person report filed by Rubowitz's brothers. Two days later, however, Catling came to the inspector general with news of both the Rubowitz family's persistent inquiries and the missing-person notices that had begun to appear in the Hebrew-language press. Gray repeated his previous instructions, fully aware that the police were still telling the increasingly distraught family that they had no knowledge of Alexander's disappearance.[32]

Desperation thus rode roughshod over legality, much less common decency. The PPF knew that they were already losing their war on terrorism and were now threatened by a scandal of their own making. "I instructed [Catling] that normal police position was to be taken in respect of any evidence from this or other sources," Gray explained to Gurney. In other words, he ordered the acting head of the CID to stonewall the family and anyone else inquiring about the missing teenager. The inspector general justified his decision on the grounds that two British constables had been killed in Jerusalem the previous evening. "The arrest of a British Police officer following this incident," he argued, "would have had, in my opinion, a disastrous effect on the morale of the Force . . . In these circumstances, I felt that I was justified in delaying formal criminal proceedings."[33]

The affair took a new turn on May 14, when Farran informed Fergusson that he had lent a gray trilby with his name in it to one of his men who had only just informed him that the hat had been lost in the scuffle to subdue Rubowitz. The same hat was of course then being examined by forensic experts at the CID laboratory. But because the laboratory personnel remained clueless about the existence of someone named Farran on the PPF's roster given the Special Squads' clandestine nature, no connection was made. Repeated chemical tests on the sweatband, Hadingham subsequently reported, had failed to discern the missing middle letter or shed any light on the owner's name. But the article that appeared the following week in *The Palestine Post*, coupled with the anonymous letter to the Rubowitz family that it had prompted, ensured that Farran's name would eventually be linked to the youth's abduction. Accordingly, that same day Gray washed his hands of the case. The inspector general later informed Gurney that he had instructed his deputy, Arthur Giles, to "go into it in detail and to take such action as he considered correct."[34]

Giles had until recently been in charge of the CID. Popular and highly respected throughout the force, he had been the favored internal candidate to succeed Rymer-Jones as inspector general—until the Colonial Office had decided that it wanted a military officer running the police. Both this snub and the attendant ascendance of the commando element and mind-set to the PPF's most senior ranks weighed heavily on Giles and his fellow officers. This was why Catling was one of the few people in the PPF whom Fergusson could approach about the Rubowitz incident.[35]

Shortly after Gray departed for London on May 28, Giles went to Gurney and described what had transpired on the night of May 6—and everything that had occurred since. It took the chief secretary less than a day to order the acting inspector general "to proceed with the case as an ordinary criminal offence with the object of bringing Farran and any other accused to trial." It was at this point that Giles asked Hadingham to undertake the investigation—and to start by interviewing Fergusson. Within hours, the weeks of prevarication and foot-dragging ended. After reading Hadingham's report, Giles went straight to the acting attorney general for Palestine and the permanent undersecretary for police and judicial affairs, who agreed that Farran should be placed under arrest the following day and charged with murder.[36]

"On the evening of the 2nd June a friend tipped me off about certain decisions reached at a Government conference. They had decided to try me for murder," Farran wrote in his memoir. He was shocked. A "person could not be brought to trial on such slender evidence," Farran recalled thinking at the time. "Everything I had ever done had been reported to the Government, who had chosen to allow me to continue my activities against the terrorists without pause until the beginning of June. So far as I knew there was no change in my mandate, which was a *carte blanche*, as before." As Farran saw it, he was the victim of a Zionist conspiracy to discredit Britain on the eve of the arrival of the special United Nations fact-finding committee in Palestine. The spineless Palestine government, he was convinced, would gleefully seize this opportunity to sacrifice him, "thus demonstrating British impartiality to the world." And he, one of the most decorated British soldiers of the recent war, would be thrown to the wolves despite having an "unshakable alibi" of dining, while in disguise as an Arab, with three other Arabs in a completely different part of Jerusalem when the "alleged kidnapping" (Farran's words) had taken place. In the circumstances, Farran concluded that he had no option but to flee Palestine and seek refuge in Syria, where he could defend himself at a safe distance using the local British consul as intermediary.[37]

Farran had indeed left nothing to chance. "As soon as this foul wind had begun to blow," his memoir recounts, he had taken the precaution of obtaining £100 cash. An unmarked CID car with a powerful V-8 engine was conveniently sitting outside Fergusson's quarters, where Farran was staying. Without a second thought, he swapped out the vehicle's license plates for a pair of fake ones he happened to have with him and then drove as fast as he could away from Jerusalem. A quick detour brought him to the Special Squads' base in Jenin, where Farran explained to his men what was happening. Two of the squad agreed to accompany him, and within an hour they had crossed into Jordan and by nightfall were in Damascus.[38]

Meanwhile, all hell had broken loose in Jerusalem. Earlier that day, Fergusson had gone to Haifa to personally brief McGregor and explain why all Special Squads operations were being suspended. When he returned, Fergusson found Farran gone and an urgent summons from Giles waiting. The acting inspector general was in no mood for Fergusson's explanations or excuses. It rapidly became clear that Giles would not allow him to travel to Syria to try to persuade Farran to return to Palestine. Fergusson now considered his options. He had been invited to dine with the Weizmanns in Rehovot that evening but decided instead to bypass the police chain of command and appeal directly to the chief secretary. A small dinner party was just finishing at Gurney's residence in the nearby Jerusalem neighborhood of Qatamon when Fergusson arrived. "I know you've come to talk shop, and I can guess what it's about," the imperturbable chief secretary told him, "but there's no hurry." He and his guests were about to watch a film; whatever Fergusson wished to discuss could wait until after. His mind preoccupied with other matters, Fergusson sat in silence until the film ended, Gurney's guests departed, and the two men could finally talk. The chief secretary consented to Fergusson's scheme and gave him forty-eight hours to retrieve Farran, who was now in Aleppo and threatening to cross into Turkey, which did not have an extradition treaty with Britain. Presented the following morning with this fait accompli, Giles had no choice but to agree—but bluntly informed Fergusson that the Special Squads' experiment was over and that the units were to be immediately disbanded.[39]

Fergusson's mission got off to an unpromising start when he couldn't locate Farran in Aleppo. Then, if we are to believe it, strictly by chance Fergusson spotted his errant subordinate on the street and followed him down an alley to a seedy hotel. Farran was extremely drunk and singularly displeased to see his commanding officer, whom he threatened to shoot. Several more drinks and hours later, Fergusson thought he had persuaded Farran to return to Palestine. But in the morning Farran changed his mind when the small plane they were traveling in was forced to land at Damascus because of a sandstorm. The Syrian authorities were delighted to welcome so distinguished a fugitive as their honored guest and set about trying to persuade Farran to accept a commission in their armed forces given his excellent work against the Jews. "Although I was prepared to fight the menace of aggressive Zionism," he recalled, "I was not ready to train Arabs in terrorist methods, which might be directed at British troops" in Palestine. Farran thus declined the offer but happily hung about in Damascus in expectation that his request for political asylum would soon be granted.[40]

On June 9, with the Palestine government's patience exhausted, the Chief Magistrate's Court in Jerusalem issued a warrant for Farran's arrest, and soon after an extradition request was duly submitted to the Syrian government. The British legation in Damascus, however, was skeptical that the Syrians would accede to the request. Accordingly, Fergusson returned to Syria yet again but was once more unsuccessful in luring Farran back to Palestine. Indeed, in the company of Syrian officials, whom Farran had insisted be present at their meeting, he berated Fergusson for being "pro-Jewish." On June 13, Giles himself traveled to Damascus accompanied by Farran's former commander in the Third Hussars, Lieutenant Colonel Philip Labouchere, who succeeded where everyone else had failed. "My duty as a regular soldier, who had taken an oath of allegiance to the King, was to return to face my accusers," Farran recalled. "My very absence would be a tacit admission of guilt. Furthermore, [Labouchere] promised that many personal friends would help me to raise money for a proper defence."[41]

Farran thus was back in Jerusalem in time for lunch on June 17. He was taken to the Allenby Barracks, a sprawling military cantonment south of the Old City along the Bethlehem Road, where two CID officers were waiting. Hadingham arrived a few hours later to formally charge Farran with premeditated murder and offer him the opportunity to provide a statement and also to sign the charge sheet. Farran declined to do either. The next day, he submitted his resignation from the Colonial Service and reverted to military status. This appears to have been a critical element in Farran's decision to return to Palestine for trial because he would now be tried by court-martial rather than in a civilian court.[42]

The exercise yard at Acre prison in 2006

Acre prison in 2006

Exercise yard at the central prison,
Russian Compound, Jerusalem, 2006

Restored communal cell, central prison,
Russian Compound, Jerusalem, 2006

Gallows, central prison,
Russian Compound,
Jerusalem, 2006

Restored warden's office, central prison, Russian Compound, Jerusalem, 2006

A 1930s-era Tegart fort–cum–police station, built for the Palestine police. Many, like this one, are still used by the Israeli National Police (date unknown).

A soldier of the Sixth Airborne Division hands a Bren machine gun found in an underground arms cache at the Jewish settlement of Dorot to fellow troops, September 1946.

Mortars seized by British troops during the search of the
Jewish settlement of Yagur, June 1946

The vast quantity of arms and ammunition, including a mortar and machine
guns, discovered during a search of the Jewish settlement of Dorot by troops
of the Sixth Airborne Division, September 1946

Package containing a bomb wrapped in magazines sent by the Irgun to the home of Lieutenant General Sir Evelyn Barker, Cobham, Surrey, May 1948

Address label of a package containing the bomb sent by the Irgun to the home of Lieutenant General Sir Evelyn Barker, Cobham, Surrey, May 1948

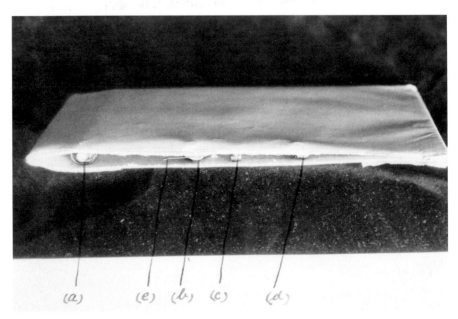

Letter bomb invented by Ya'acov Eliav, a.k.a. Ya'acov Levstein, Lehi's master bomb maker, known to his comrades as the Dynamite Man because of his expertise with explosives, April 1947

Headstones of fallen World War I servicemen who served in British
Commonwealth forces, Jerusalem British War Cemetery, Mount Scopus, 2006

Jerusalem British War Cemetery, for fallen servicemen of the British
Commonwealth from World War I, overlooking the city, Mount Scopus, 2006

Flag-lowering ceremony and honor guard,
British troops, Palestine, circa 1948

Farran had also insisted on assuming complete responsibility for the incident; hence the three members of his squad who were present when Rubowitz was seized and then tortured and murdered were never indicted. Farran then retired to the small apartment he had been assigned in the married officers' quarters to put in writing his version of the events of May 6 that would form part of the "summary of sworn evidence" to be presented at the court-martial. That same evening, he was escorted to the Kishle, the Turkish central police barracks just inside the Old City, facing David's Citadel, where he was to undergo a police lineup before witnesses who had been present at Rubowitz's abduction. Three witnesses identified Farran as the person who had seized the youth, while two others failed to do so. In any event, the three were later shown to be mistaken and the exercise was thus inconclusive.[43]

The gravity of his predicament was now beginning to sink in, and as a result the next day Farran was in a dark mood when Lieutenant Colonel Hugh Niven, the assistant adjutant general at Palestine headquarters, visited him. As Farran recalled in his memoir, "I was appalled by the relentlessness with which the Police were pursuing my case (a new feature in Palestine) and by the unwarranted accusations in some of the Jewish newspapers, which amounted to nothing less than libellous prejudgment." Indeed, news accounts of Rubowitz's disappearance and the Special Squads' existence were now also appearing in British and American newspapers. A story published in the *New York Herald Tribune* by the acclaimed reporter Homer Bigart, for instance, alleged that followers of the British fascist leader Sir Oswald Mosley had infiltrated the PPF and might also have been involved in Rubowitz's disappearance.[44]

An internal Jewish Agency memorandum suggests that it was behind the interest suddenly showed by the U.S. press in the case. The Bigart story in particular appears to have attracted the attention of No. 10 Downing Street—as a barbed inquiry sent by Attlee to Creech Jones the following day concerning the Farran case reveals. Although the high commissioner hastened to assure London that there was no truth to the accusation, neither the prime minister nor the colonial secretary was pleased with the way that the entire matter had been handled. Attlee was especially perturbed that the Palestine government had yet to issue an official statement rebutting some of the more lurid accusations circulating in the press about the incident.[45]

That same day, Creech Jones sent a stinging rebuke to Cunningham, but before the Palestine government had time to issue the statement that the prime minister had requested, the "good name of British administration" was cast into disrepute again when that same evening Farran once more escaped from custody.[46]

The ease with which Farran was again able to flee Palestine has never been satisfactorily explained. His account in *Winged Dagger* is deliberately glib to the point of evasiveness, suggesting nothing more than the timely exploitation of a serendipitous opportunity in the best commando tradition. This was also the conclusion reached by the police court of inquiry, which found Farran's two CID minders guilty of negligence rather than of any willful malfeasance. Nonetheless, both versions strain credulity since, at the height of the Jewish terrorist campaign the Allenby Barracks, given its critical location midway between the Jerusalem rail station and Government House, would almost certainly have been among the most secure military facilities in Palestine with all means of access and exit closely watched and tightly guarded.[47]

At the same time, the anomaly of the police having responsibility for an army officer, detained essentially under house arrest at a military facility, inevitably created a confusing situation that Farran was able to take advantage of. The police, for instance, had initially planned to imprison him at the police depot on Mount Scopus, as Farran was then a serving member of the PPF. But the deal that facilitated his return from Syria had stipulated that Farran would be tried in a military court as an army, not a police, officer. Accordingly, army headquarters in Jerusalem assumed responsibility for his confinement and arranged to have Farran brought to the Allenby Barracks, although his guard detail would consist of two plainclothes policemen. It was in the presence of one of these officers that Farran left his apartment at 8:15 on the evening of June 19, ostensibly to go for a stroll. They had only gone a few steps, when Farran suggested that they have a drink instead at the nearby officers' mess. Both men were finishing their beers when a Royal Artillery lieutenant colonel came in and struck up a conversation. Assuming that Farran and his minder were both police officers given their civilian attire, this lieutenant colonel suggested that they all have supper together in the dining hall just down the corridor. The detective replied that sandwiches were waiting for them back at the apartment, but after chatting some more, the artillery officer repeated his invitation and left. Farran followed him, but not wishing to intrude, the detective remained behind. About twenty minutes later he went to check on Farran, who was now nowhere to be found. It was later surmised that he had stopped at the lavatory en route to the dining hall and had fled through a small window.[48]

In his memoir, Farran astonishingly claims that he then climbed a tree with a branch overhanging the well-defended camp's barbed-wire perimeter fence, jumped to his freedom, and simply "wandered over the hills until I found friends" before wading across the Jordan River and crossing into Trans-Jordan. "I cannot go into more details about my ten days' freedom, during which time I walked most of the way to the Hejaz and back," Farran explained, "because it would mean that many kind Arab friends would be involved." He decided to return to Palestine and surrender after hearing of reprisal attacks being carried out by Lehi against British troops. The group had taken credit—and specifically cited the Rubowitz case and Farran's disappearance—for the simultaneous attacks carried out in Haifa and Tel Aviv on the night of June 28. An old friend of Farran's had been killed and another seriously wounded in one of the incidents. "It was not worth it," he wrote. So, the morning following the twin attacks, Farran presented himself to a sentry at the Allenby Barracks' main gate and turned himself in.[49]

The preliminary hearing to consider the evidence against Farran was held at the Allenby Barracks on July 17. The presiding military officer heard testimony from five witnesses, including one of Rubowitz's brothers and three persons who claimed to have seen the boy's abduction. Farran appeared to pay only fleeting attention to the proceedings, preferring instead to ostentatiously consult the copy of the Bible that he had brought with him. His feigned disinterest was an indulgence purchased with some of the best legal representation that money could buy. A solicitor had been sent from the high-powered London law firm of Laurence Collins and Fearnley-Whittingstall to defend Farran. True to his word, Labouchere had established a fund to cover Farran's legal fees. Word of the fund had spread quickly to England, where Farran's wartime commanders had rallied to his support. Such SAS luminaries as Colonel Bill Stirling, brother of the SAS's founder, David, and Major General Robert Laycock, chief of combined operations, had reached out to their vast network of friends and comrades-in-arms on Farran's behalf. Palestine policemen also contributed, responding enthusiastically to the appeal organized by Raymond Cafferata, the hero of Hebron and later target of a Lehi assassination attempt, who was now in London running the PPF recruitment depot there.[50]

Throughout the hearing, Farran's lawyer had been especially insistent that the prosecution's "Exhibit B" be suppressed on grounds of attorney-client privilege. This was the notebook that Gray had told Gurney contained Farran's "confession" and that Cunningham had described to Creech Jones as the "written statement found in Farran's quarters at Allenby Barracks, Jerusalem, after his escape on 19th June, unsigned, but believed to be in Farran's handwriting, [which] stated that he had killed Rubowitz."[51]

Given its incendiary content, his lawyer's vigorous effort to have the notebook declared inadmissible is not surprising. Indeed, as these and various other behind-the-scenes legal maneuvers continued throughout the summer, the Jewish Agency was becoming increasingly agitated about both the delay and the secretive adjudication process surrounding the case. Writing to Gurney, the president of the Vaad Le'umi, Yitzhak Ben-Zvi, drew the chief secretary's attention to the uncomfortable fact that, had a crime of this nature and in these circumstances been committed in the U.K., it would have been tried not in a military but in a civil court—a point that the judge advocate general at the War Office had coincidentally made just days before. But both Cunningham and MacMillan strongly opposed transferring Farran's case to a civil court, whether in Britain or Palestine, and their view ultimately prevailed.[52]

Amid extraordinary security, Farran's court-martial convened on October 1 at the military court for the district of Talbiya, not far from the street corner in Rehavia where Rubowitz had been abducted. The small courtroom, ringed by armed guards, could barely accommodate a crowd that included some thirty journalists, assorted military and police officers seated in the public gallery, members of the Rubowitz family, counsels for the prosecution and the defense, a judge advocate general sent by the War Office to advise the six army officers who sat in judgment on points of military law, and the defendant himself. When the court asked how he wished to plead, Farran answered, "Not guilty."[53]

Because Rubowitz's body had never been found, the case against Farran hinged on two pieces of circumstantial evidence: Fergusson's recollection of what Farran had told him on the morning of May 7 and the notebook containing Farran's alleged confession. The prosecution suffered an initial blow early the first day when the police officer who had taken possession of the gray trilby as evidence from one of Rubowitz's brothers in May admitted that he could no longer discern the letters "F-A-R-A-N" on the sweatband, as in their place was now a large smudge mark. Additional blows followed in rapid succession. The officer responsible for the identification parade held at the Kishle in June testified that none of the witnesses had been able to identify Farran as having been present at the Rehavia street corner the night that Rubowitz disappeared. Then Fergusson was called to the stand. Invoking the right against self-incrimination, he refused to testify about his conversation with Farran on May 7 and was excused without further questioning. The day concluded with Farran's lawyer arguing for the notebook's exclusion as admissible evidence. Astonishingly, the prosecution never called Hadingham, the person who had actually conducted the murder investigation, to testify.[54]

The trial got off to another bad start the following morning when the court ruled that Farran's confession was indeed privileged client-attorney communication and could not be introduced as evidence. With that, the prosecution's case collapsed. In the words of Farran's attorney, there was now not "a shred of evidence" against his client—a point conceded by the judge advocate general in his final instructions to the six-man tribunal. After a brief recess, the court reconvened shortly after 3:00 p.m. Its president, Brigadier Richard Maxwell, the commander of Jerusalem's southern district, announced the acquittal verdict. The room burst into applause amid shouts of "Good show" from the soldiers and police officers attending. Farran was immediately whisked away in an armored car sandwiched between jeeps mounted with heavy machine guns manned by the Highland Light Infantry. He spent the night at a military base in Gaza under heavy guard before being flown the next morning to the Canal Zone to board a troopship bound for Liverpool.[55]

"When I landed at Liverpool on October 13th, a bewildering surprise awaited me," Farran recalled. "I had imagined that my friends would never speak to me again, and here I was being received like a popular hero." He lay low for two weeks in the Scottish countryside as a guest of Colonel Stirling before resurfacing in London at the American ambassador's residence to receive the U.S. Legion of Merit for his wartime service in northern Italy. In February 1948, accompanied by his mother, Farran attended an investiture at Buckingham Palace, where King George decorated him with his Distinguished Service Order. "The King told me he was very glad the whole business was over," Farran boasted to reporters afterward.[56]

For the rest of his life, Farran stuck to his story. He and his squad were "on the verge of dealing a crippling blow to the Stern Gang [when] the 'Rubovitz Case' burst." In hopes of sabotaging this breakthrough and undermining the successes that Farran and his team were having, a shadowy Zionist conspiracy fed *The Palestine Post* stories about Rubowitz's disappearance and a hat in which there was a name supposedly like Farran's. "There was no evidence," Farran always maintained, "but the ugly finger of suspicion was pointed at me."[57]

In point of fact, the documents that he had found on Rubowitz—and that Gray had deemed sufficiently vital to delay the investigation into the youth's disappearance—proved to be of little value. By the middle of June, the CID had identified everyone on the lists. It determined that only one of the forty-five persons was an active terrorist, and he was arrested. No charges were ever brought against any of the others, who were judged simply to have given some money to Lehi at one time or another.[58]

Regardless, Farran's version of events persisted—effectively propagated by his best-selling memoir, which was published in April 1948, went through seven editions in two years, and by 1956 had sold some 300,000 copies. It gained new currency in the 1960s as a result of the publication of both a prizewinning essay in a British military journal and the memoirs of another prominent British soldier. The essay, written by Lieutenant Colonel Richard Clutterbuck, who would eventually rise to the rank of major general and subsequently become a respected academic and well-published authority on counterterrorism, claimed that Farran's squad killed more terrorists in six weeks than an entire army battalion employed in more traditional cordon-and-search operations. Similarly, in his 1969 book, Colin Mitchell argued that "Roy Farran's actions terrified the terrorists. But eventually they began to understand what was happening, identified Roy and were determined to put an end to his activities. To do this by force would have been difficult if not impossible, because the Farran team were as tough and experienced as any Jewish terrorists. They therefore snatched eagerly at what seemed like a scrap of evidence [that is, the gray trilby]."[59]

Neither source, however, can be considered completely unbiased, because both men became personally acquainted with Farran as his jailers. Clutterbuck had guarded him at the Allenby Barracks during the few weeks preceding Farran's preliminary hearing on July 17, while Mitchell was actually locked into his cell with him for extended periods of time as part of the "elaborate arrangements" in force while Farran was imprisoned at Sarafand awaiting court-martial. He and his unit had also previously been deployed to support some of Farran's counterterrorist operations in Jerusalem. It is therefore not entirely implausible that these two young officers were in thrall of this battle-hardened, much-decorated warrior-hero. Farran, in fact, is far more modest about his accomplishments in Palestine than either Clutterbuck or Mitchell. *Winged Dagger* is quite explicit about the operational frustrations and lack of progress Farran and his squad encountered. "For two months we worked night and day—watching, following, listening and occasionally making an arrest. We had limited successes, but nothing really big"—until the Rubowitz incident, he maintained, spoiled everything.[60]

Farran, however, remained forever unrepentant. In 1978, for instance, he told Nicholas Bethell that "Fergusson was right in the basic principle that an underground war can only be fought by counter-terrorist forces who are prepared to mix with the enemy in its own environment. Small groups can counter other small groups." These tactics are of course at the very heart of established counterinsurgency and counterterrorism practice. In one of the seminal books on the subject, Julian Paget, a British army officer who fought in many of these post–World War II campaigns (and whose father was the commander in chief of Middle East Command between 1944 and 1946), explains,

> Insurgents cannot be defeated by conventional warfare techniques, and a completely fresh approach is required . . .
>
> The task of the insurgents is made far easier if they are allowed to retain the initiative and to attack on their own terms. The Security Forces must therefore make every effort to move from the defensive . . . and to gain the initiative for themselves.[61]

In Palestine, however, its application was seriously flawed. The squads' fundamental weakness was that their experience and knowledge of irregular warfare were derived from fighting an entirely different type of underground warfare in a completely different setting—a fact noted by Montgomery himself when he visited Palestine in June 1947. In occupied Europe and Asia, these veterans of special units like the Commandos and the Chindits and the SAS and the SOE had fought against an unpopular, traditionally deployed military force that was regarded by the local population as a repressive army of occupation. In Palestine, however, the situation was reversed. British forces, including the Special Squads, were by this time widely regarded by the Yishuv as an unpopular, repressive occupation force. Further, they were arrayed against an amorphous body of underground fighters and not against traditionally organized and deployed armies.[62]

In the haste to implement Fergusson's scheme, these problems in the squads' organization, training, and mission were ignored or dismissed or simply not considered to be serious enough to warrant concern. In this respect, the most important failure was both Fergusson's and Farran's inability to grasp the implications of special operations that have the potential to go awry. As the Canadian historian David Charters has cogently argued,

The legitimacy of government rests upon rule of law, and the intention to restore and maintain law and order is the core of a proper counter-insurgency programme. The security forces, for their part, are bound to uphold the law. But special operations by their very nature are conducted in a legal and moral twilight zone; if control or discipline fails, they become merely a guise for counter-terror which reduces the government and the security forces to the status of criminals. Secret police methods make bad propaganda—if the cover is "blown," and tactical victories may be squandered by a strategic defeat.[63]

The Special Squads were a desperate, eleventh-hour attempt to turn the tide of battle in Palestine in the security force's favor. They brought only controversy and ignominy to the Palestine government, which found itself in the invidious position of having to lie. "No authority," the administration disingenuously declared in the public statement demanded by Attlee, "has ever been given for the employing of unorthodox methods against terrorists. No authority has ever been given for the use by any member of the police force of other than ordinary police methods in dealing with apprehending persons." MacMillan in fact specifically cited "The Farran Case" in his overview of the final year of British rule, noting that it further poisoned relations with the Yishuv at an especially critical juncture of the mandate's history.[64]

But none of this seemed to harm either Fergusson or Farran, who each went on to distinguished careers in government and public service. The same afternoon that Farran was acquitted, Fergusson recounts that he was "invited to resign" from the police and told to leave Palestine within thirty-six hours for his own safety. He was gone the next morning. "I was turning my back on a disastrous episode," Fergusson recounts in his memoir, "one on which I had embarked with high hopes of being effective. Far from doing any good, I had inadvertently done positive harm." No matter. He subsequently fulfilled his ambition to command a battalion of his old regiment, then headed up intelligence at Supreme Headquarters Allied Powers Europe under General Dwight Eisenhower, and was director of psychological warfare during the abortive Suez Expedition of 1956. Fergusson retired from the army two years later, and shortly afterward he was able to carry on a family tradition by serving as governor-general of New Zealand. Upon his return to Scotland, he was successively chancellor of the University of St. Andrews, lord high commissioner of the Church of Scotland, and chairman of the British Council. Fergusson was ennobled by the queen in 1972 and styled himself Lord Ballantrae. He died in 1980.[65]

Farran left the army in 1948 and worked briefly as a quarry master in Scotland and then in construction in Kenya and subsequently Rhodesia. During the 1950 general election he stood for Parliament as a Conservative candidate for a seat in England's West Midlands but lost. Farran then accepted an offer from one of his wartime SAS commanders to serve in the Malayan Scouts, a special operations unit then being formed to fight communist terrorists in Malaya. The offer, however, was withdrawn a week later on orders from the commander in chief, Far East, given the potential embarrassment to Gurney as high commissioner for Malaya and Gray as the inspector general of the Malayan Police Service—posts both men had assumed immediately upon leaving Palestine. Farran married that year and then immigrated to Alberta, Canada, where he took up dairy farming. Farran also worked as a journalist and in 1954 founded a successful weekly newspaper. In 1961, he was elected to municipal government and a decade later to the provincial legislative assembly, eventually being appointed minister of telephones and utilities and, after that, solicitor general for Alberta. A lifelong, devout Catholic, Farran died in 2006.[66]

That Farran could prosper unencumbered by the shadow of having been indicted for murder was largely because of the unstinting efforts of his lawyers to ensure that every copy of the notebook containing his alleged confession was promptly destroyed. Within days of his acquittal, Laurence Collins and Fearnley-Whittingstall had written to both the GOC and the judge advocate general on this matter and had obtained sworn affidavits of compliance. By December 1947 only two copies remained—much to the law firm's immense consternation. One was in the custody of the chief secretary, and the other had been retained by the police. Gurney was especially resistant to the demand that the notebook be surrendered for destruction, arguing that regardless of the fact that the document had been ruled privileged, it remained part of a criminal investigation that had yet to be resolved. Incensed by the chief secretary's response, Farran's lawyers had written to Creech Jones, threatening to bring it up in Parliament and to sue the Colonial Office. Following months of legal wrangling and increasing pressure from Farran's lawyers, the Colonial Office finally relented, and on April 24, 1948, in one of his last acts as high commissioner for Palestine, Cunningham provided a "Certificate of Destruction," signed by a senior CID officer, attesting that there were no remaining copies of the notebook.[67]

Indeed, the only misfortune that Farran seems to have subsequently suffered from the case was the death of his brother. From the time of Farran's acquittal, Lehi had vowed to avenge Rubowitz's death. In mid-October 1947 posters had begun to appear throughout Palestine warning that "Captain Farran's time will come. We shall go after him to the end of the world." About that same time Farran received two threatening letters at his family home in Wolverhampton on which was written the Hebrew word for revenge. "I'm not a bit scared of them," Farran had bragged to reporters covering the award ceremony at the U.S. embassy at the end of that same month. Six months passed without incident until a parcel arrived with the morning mail addressed to "R. Farran." Farran's twenty-six-year-old brother, Rex, a draftsman employed by an aircraft manufacturer, opened the package, which contained a book of Shakespeare's plays. Concealed within its hollowed-out pages was a bomb that exploded, eviscerating Rex's pelvis and groin and peppering his face and body with deadly shrapnel. The bomb had been constructed by Ya'acov Heruti, a twenty-year-old Lehi operative sent by Nathan Friedman-Yellin to London in October 1947 to assassinate Bevin and Barker. Farran was subsequently added to his target list. Lehi took credit for the bombing forty-eight hours later on May 5, vowing that next time it would get Roy. However, the following July, two members of the group told a *New York Times* reporter that Rex had actually been the target of the May attack. "We knew it would hurt Roy Farran more if we killed his brother. It would force him to live with his memory always. We meant to torture him." Although Heruti disavowed this claim in a 2005 interview, the effect on Farran was doubtless the same.[68]

The scandal surrounding Rubowitz's disappearance was only one of the vexatious issues that the Palestine government and the Colonial Office had to contend with that spring. The other involved a request from the International Red Cross (IRC) to pay a second visit to a secret detention facility known as Camp 119 in Sambal, Eritrea, where some 250 Jewish terrorists were held. It will be recalled that in 1944 the Palestine administration had again invoked the Palestine (Defence) Order in Council to deport people without trial on mere suspicion of "complicity in terrorism" to a special prison camp in Eritrea. This intentional denial of habeas corpus was justified on the grounds that the information leading to these people's arrests was so sensitive—derived from either human intelligence sources or signals intercepts—that it could not be divulged in court. Not wishing to risk acquittal on insufficient evidence, the Palestine administration, with the Colonial Office's consent, had embraced the imprisonment-in-exile solution—and justified it by blaming the Yishuv, who, as one official explained, "in many cases *could* give evidence sufficient for a conviction, [but] won't give it." Evidentiary issues apart, the CID had found this legal provision to be an extraordinarily effective interrogation tool. Simply implying to a detainee suspected of involvement in terrorism that he would be sent "on a long trip by air" was often sufficient, one skilled interrogator claimed, to produce the desired flow of information.[69]

As a result of intensive lobbying by Peter Bergson's Hebrew Committee of National Liberation, in 1946 the Colonial Office had granted the IRC access to the camp. It was less keen to do so again. The main reason was that following an escape in January 1947 the British army had decided to move the remaining prisoners to a more secure facility in Gilgil, Kenya. Operation Malvolio, as the relocation was code-named, was secretly completed between February and March 1947. The authorities were thus reluctant both to reveal this to the IRC and especially to allow its inspectors to visit the new camp. The Colonial Office accordingly had solicited the advice of the Foreign Office, which gladly provided a justification to reject the visit request. Because the 1929 Geneva Convention applied only to prisoners of war and the detainees in Kenya were not POWs, the IRC had no jurisdiction over them or their treatment. Indeed, the Foreign Office concluded, the camp's military jailers and the Palestine administration "were free to treat [the] suspected Jewish terrorists as they saw fit."[70]

Then, in May, a new problem had arisen over Kenya's capacity to accommodate any additional detainees. A message from the governor, Sir Philip Mitchell, that only eight more suspects could be accepted at Gilgil had sent a frisson of alarm through both Government House and the Colonial Office given the high expectations that both had attached to Fergusson's Special Squads. As events turned out, the anticipated surfeit of new terrorist suspects never materialized. But the discussions on this issue threw light on a troubling policy contradiction. "It is obviously necessary to deport those suspects from Palestine especially after the Acre jail attack," a Colonial Office official named E. M. Fitzgerald had written to his colleague in the Middle East Department, William Allan Mathieson, on May 8. But, he asked, was it not "rather inconsistent to keep *condemned* terrorists still here but to move mere suspects 3,000 miles away"? No other official, however, appeared troubled by this incongruity, and in any event within days it was eclipsed by the unfolding scandal regarding Rubowitz's disappearance and then the following month by a new set of death sentences imposed on three of the Irgun fighters captured following the Acre prison raid.[71]

On June 16 a Jerusalem military court condemned Avshalom Habib, Meir Nakar, and Ya'acov Weiss to die by hanging. Amnon Mikhaloff and

Nahman Zitterbaum escaped execution because they were minors and instead received sentences of fifteen years' imprisonment each. The three defendants facing execution once more presented a demographic cross section of the Yishuv that captivated the press and was grist for the Irgun's propagandists. They included two Sephardic Jews who had both been born in Palestine and an Ashkenazic immigrant. Habib and Nakar had lived in Jerusalem their entire lives, while Weiss hailed from Czechoslovakia and was a Holocaust survivor. Weiss's parents and six brothers and sisters had all perished at Auschwitz. Only he and a sister survived. As the president of the court, a British army colonel, read the sentences, the defendants burst into song, joined by their families and other spectators, as the mournful sounds of "Ha-Tikva" filled the small courtroom. They continued to sing as the guards shackled their wrists and legs and led them away.[72]

"We knew that if we did not save them, nobody would," Begin later explained. The British had already been warned what to expect should the executions continue. After Gruner and his three comrades-in-arms were put to death, the Voice of Fighting Zion had announced that henceforth the Irgun would

> no longer be bound by the rules of war, which we imposed on ourselves as the liberation army of a civilized people.
>
> The law of retribution, of reprisals which is also the law of war, will be applied at every opportunity.
>
> Every battle unit of ours will be accompanied by a field court-martial, which will try every Briton who is part of the Occupation Army or the Occupation regime . . .
>
> There will be no appeal from the sentences passed. They will be executed on the spot, either by shooting or by hanging.
>
> Tremble, you murderers of prisoners.

That this threat was taken seriously is evident in the new orders that the British military issued in anticipation of the trial's outcome. All vehicles were now required to have an armed soldier riding shotgun, and officers and men on foot were instructed to be armed at all times and to walk in parties of no fewer than four persons.[73] These precautions proved necessary as the Irgun was already hunting for hostages. A plan was hatched to kidnap three military officers who regularly swam at a public pool in Ramat Gan and, while doing so, would be unarmed. On June 9, half a dozen Irgunists, brandishing revolvers and tommy guns, arrived at the appointed time to find no army officers present. Instead, they seized two British policemen. The authorities immediately demanded their release and called upon the mayors of Tel Aviv, Ramat Gan, and Petah Tiqva to mobilize their respective communities' assistance in locating the captives. Fearing the adverse repercussions to the Zionist cause given the impending arrival of yet another commission to examine Palestine's political options, this one convened by the United Nations, the Haganah also publicly called upon the Yishuv to help find the two men. They were discovered unharmed twenty-four hours later when troops, acting on information obtained from their own sources, searched a Jewish settlement just up the coast from Ramat Gan.[74]

The happy resolution of the latest Irgun hostage-taking episode nonetheless provided a fresh reminder of how vulnerable Britons were to abduction despite the plethora of security measures already in place. In the circumstances, the Palestine administration could only respond by adding a new layer of prohibitions to the restrictions previously imposed on the expatriate community's daily existence. Henceforth, British civilians were forbidden to venture beyond the special security zones without military escort or, in exceptional circumstances, provided at least three persons in any group were armed. The extent of these additional security measures imposed on civilians and military personnel alike was immediately evident to Montgomery when he landed at Lydda Airport on June 21. The CIGS later described the route he took to Sarafand as "the most heavily guarded road [he] has ever seen."[75]

For the British authorities, the only bright spot in this increasingly melancholy picture was the Haganah's growing inclination to take independent action against the terrorists. Shortly after the Acre raid, the Jewish Agency had finally caved in to government pressure and ordered the Haganah once more to commence operations against the Irgun. A special two-hundred-man task force had been created for this purpose, drawn entirely from regular Haganah units. This was because, unlike with the original Saison, members of the elite Palmach had refused to participate in the new campaign—which was generally far less popular than the previous iteration had been. Dubbed the Little Saison by the Irgun, it scored its first success on June 18 by foiling a potentially catastrophic attack on the local British military headquarters in Tel Aviv.[76]

Situated within the special security zone adjacent to the Tel Aviv rail station, Citrus House—as the headquarters building was known—stood surrounded by concentric rings of barbed wire, pillboxes, high walls, and a heavily armed guard force. But the specialty of the Irgun's operations chief was overcoming precisely such daunting obstacles. In this case, Paglin concluded, if a ground attack wasn't possible, an alternative means of assault would have to be devised. His plan was brilliant in its simplicity. An Irgun operative posing as a potato merchant was sent to the neighborhood to inquire about leasing a cellar in which to store his produce. The ersatz merchant found exactly the place he was looking for in the basement of a building across the street from Citrus House. Thereafter, every morning a truck arrived to transport the sacks of potatoes stored in the basement to market. The sacks, however, contained not potatoes but dirt excavated from the forty-five-foot-long tunnel being dug by Irgun sappers toward Citrus House. Paglin's intention was to pack the end of the tunnel with explosives once it was beneath the headquarters building and then blow it up. The publicity that would attend the Irgun's ability to successfully target yet another bastion of British rule especially during the visit by the United Nations Special Committee on Palestine (UNSCOP) would be enormous. But it was foiled when the Haganah learned of the plan and sent its own men to seal the tunnel with cement. An explosives expert was killed when he attempted to enter the booby-trapped passage. British troops immediately converged on the blast site. There, they found a message to the Irgun that had been written in chalk on the basement wall. "The Haganah was here. We want you by force not to carry out your evil intention. Signed Haganah." Outside the building troops also found a truck loaded with bags of cement.[77]

These developments, along with reports that the Haganah had wrecked another Irgun plot—this time to blow up a section of railway track between Haifa and Acre—and had also taken to beating up teenage members of the Irgun in Tel Aviv and Haifa in hopes of intimidating them to leave the organization, accorded perfectly with the recurrent fantasies of senior British military commanders that a decisive corner had been turned in the three months since martial law. When Montgomery dined with Gale during his brief visit in late June, for instance, the CIGS was treated to an ebullient disquisition about the vast improvement of security conditions in Palestine. Kidnapping, the First Infantry Division commander confidently asserted, was now "out of favour." The Yishuv, moreover, was "fed up with terrorism and . . . heartily in favor of the restoration of law and order." Informants, accordingly, were coming forward to a greater extent than at any time in recent memory. And the estimated £2 million in economic losses that the Jews had suffered as a result of martial law, Gale opined, meant that the threat of its reimposition "was undoubtedly a very fine weapon for putting the heat" on them again should the need arise.

His optimism had clearly infected the otherwise dour Montgomery, who gushed in a letter to Frederick John Bellenger, the war secretary, "There seems to be no doubt that the hanging of Dov Gruner had a very salutary effect all round; equally, it is generally accepted now that a big mistake was made in reprieving those Jews whose death sentences had been confirmed."[78]

Such rosy assessments, however, were completely divorced from reality—as Montgomery would likely have been among the first to concede. The CIGS's running diary for February–June 1947, for example, directly contradicts his comments to Bellenger. Summing up events in Palestine during that same time period, Montgomery observed that although it "might have been expected that the referring of the [Palestine] case to the United Nations Organisation would have brought about at least a temporary lull in terrorist activities . . . this has not been the case. Hardly a day goes by without some further incident causing loss of life and injury to British soldiers and civilians, Jews and Arabs alike." Similarly, in his overview of the final year of British rule, MacMillan commented how both the Irgun and Lehi had actually "intensified their attacks on British persons and British interests" throughout that spring.[79]

By July, in fact, the Little Saison was losing momentum. Undaunted by Irgun threats of retaliation, the Haganah had initially persevered, thwarting a Lehi attempt to assassinate MacMillan on June 30, an attack on the Jerusalem–Tel Aviv road a few days later, and a planned Irgun assault on a British military base at Rehovot. But these were the new counterterrorist campaign's final accomplishments. Thereafter it degenerated into a disorganized series of kidnappings and beatings of one another's members that apparently never enjoyed any significant popular support.[80]

Hence, a more accurate portrayal of the Yishuv's continued hostility to the government may be found in the text of a radio address made by the Eighth Infantry Brigade commander to Jerusalem's Jewish populace pleading for better relations. The commander had specifically asked the community to keep in mind that many of his soldiers were now young conscripts completing their national service who "have no concern with politics" and are simply doing their duty. A letter sent by the intelligence staff officer at army headquarters in Jerusalem to a Jewish Agency official in late June, concerning a traffic accident that involved an army vehicle, depicts even more starkly the mutual antipathy that was now commonplace. A soldier had been killed in the collision and horribly burned and mutilated. Jewish passersby had acted gleefully, the officer recounted, evidently "pleased such a thing had happened to a British soldier." Some had also laughed when the "odd pieces of the soldier's body" were being extricated from the wreck. "I don't much like sending you the enclosed report," he apologized, "because I know that there are plenty of Jews in Palestine who do not regard the Army as the successors to the Nazis, but it does explain the occasional anti-semitic attitude of some of our troops."[81]

Coincidentally, only a few days later Barker had written a letter to Antonius in which he had expressed bewilderment over precisely what Britain had done to bring "all this anti-British feeling upon us." Surely, the existence of secret prisons in Africa where people were detained indefinitely without trial, simply on suspicion of terrorism, and even more so the fact that a sixteen-year-old boy had been abducted, cruelly tortured, and brutally executed, with evidence of the deed willfully destroyed by those same police officers and subsequent investigations into his disappearance deliberately stymied, accounted if only in part for the rise of "anti-British feeling" that senior officers like Barker, the Jerusalem brigade commander, and the intelligence staff officer seemed so utterly incapable of understanding. Barker's remark to Antonius some months later—"I am very pleased that Farran got off, though I never thought it could be otherwise"—perhaps best epitomized the hauteur and insensitivity that the Yishuv believed had come to dominate Anglo-Zionist relations following World War II.[82]

For the moment, however, the Palestine administration had more pressing problems to contend with. News of the Rubowitz abduction, Farran's involvement in it, and his unexplained sojourn to Syria, as we have seen, were all over the papers in June 1947. "There could scarcely be a worse time to disclose this murder (as it appears to be)," Cunningham had complained to Creech Jones, "but I am afraid it must come to light very shortly"—and it would just as the UN special committee's visit to Palestine was about to begin.[83]

CHAPTER 19

Drunk with the Hangman's Blood

A ny illusion that Britain was still in control of Palestine was shattered as soon as UNSCOP arrived in Jerusalem. The "armed camp" that Bartley Crum had observed fifteen months earlier, when he had visited the city with the Anglo-American Committee, was now even more pervasive and forbidding than it had been in March 1946. "As we came nearer the center of town," the Guatemalan member of the delegation, Jorge García-Granados, recalled, "we had our first glimpse of armored cars and barbed wire. The barbed wire, in tremendous confusion of huge coils higher than a man, was thrown about entire blocks of buildings." Ralph Bunche, the UN secretary-general's representative to the committee, was similarly unnerved by the intense security. The "British are everywhere and they all carry guns," he reported to New York. "As you go [through] the streets you're constantly stopped by sentries and control centers and required to show your pass. Buildings are surrounded by barbed wire, [and] pillboxes and roadblocks are abundant."[1]

UNSCOP was the twenty-second such committee or commission convened to study the Palestine problem since Britain was awarded the mandate a quarter of a century earlier. The UN General Assembly had charged UNSCOP with preparing a report and making recommendations in advance of the September session, when the assembly would decide Palestine's future. It was the first truly international group impaneled to look into the Palestine problem, with its members hailing from Australia, Canada, Czechoslovakia, Guatemala, India, Iran, the Netherlands, Peru, Sweden, Uruguay, and Yugoslavia. Judge Emil Sandström, the Swedish representative, was chosen chairman.[2]

Its first formal day of hearings had begun inauspiciously on the afternoon of June 16. Only a few hours before, a military court in Jerusalem had sentenced the three Irgun terrorists responsible for the Acre prison raid to hang. The prospect of another round of executions, coupled with the Irgun's inevitable response, thus fed an already combustible atmosphere. In addition, the Higher Arab Committee had declared a fifteen-hour strike to protest the committee's arrival. And even before the committee members had taken their seats in the ornate auditorium of the YMCA building, just opposite the King David Hotel, a dispute had broken out between UNSCOP and the Palestine administration. Citing security concerns, the administration had insisted that its officials would only testify in camera. This sudden imposition of secrecy threatened the committee's commitment to holding an open, public inquiry. It also provoked the ire and suspicion of some committee members. A compromise was reached whereby UNSCOP reaffirmed its intention to hold as many open sessions as possible but agreed to respect the wishes of, and in this instance grant an exception to, the Palestine administration. With the impasse resolved, the hearings commenced. The first witness was Gurney.[3]

García-Granados found the chief secretary evasive and uncommunicative—despite having been granted permission to testify in secret. His Indian counterpart, Sir Abdur Rahman, quickly became exasperated and resorted to interrogating Gurney as if he were a hostile witness rather than a servant of the crown freely and frankly providing evidence in a closed setting to a distinguished international body. The Guatemalan diplomat was able to elicit from the chief secretary the admission that the Palestine government was spending nearly $30 million a year on the police alone. Upon learning this, García-Granados thought to himself, *"Could anyone deny that this was a police state?"*[4]

Proudly embracing the mantle of "the Latin American revolutionary tradition," García-Granados quickly revealed himself to be the committee's sternest critic of Britain's Palestine policy. It was he who took the greatest umbrage at the timing of the military court's verdict, regarding it as a deliberate insult both to the committee and to the fledgling UN. García-Granados also actively championed the case of the families of the three Irgun men after they beseeched the committee to intervene with the Palestine government on their condemned relations' behalf. "Some of you say these men are criminals," he had lobbied his fellow delegates. "I don't know. Only history can pass judgment on the Palestine underground. History alone will state the last word on the French, the Dutch, the Polish, the German, the Yugoslav, and the British underground. These men fought Hitler in defense of their country and their principles. We applauded them because we thought they were right. These men are fighting now for similar beliefs. How, then, can you condemn what they are doing?"[5]

García-Granados was instrumental in UNSCOP's issuing an appeal to spare the lives of the three Irgun fighters, which was delivered to the British government via Trygve Lie, the UN secretary-general. The Palestine administration's reaction, he recalled, was "swift and sharp," consisting of a stern rebuke conveyed by Gurney. Not only had UNSCOP overstepped its remit, the chief secretary scolded the committee, but its appeal was irrelevant because the cases of Habib, Nakar, and Weiss were still sub judice given that the GOC had not yet confirmed the sentences. The government's message, García-Granados writes, was clear: no interference in this matter would be tolerated.[6]

The impression Gurney helped perpetuate of an omniscient, seigneurial administration presiding over a country desperate for its freedom profoundly colored García-Granados's thinking about the mandate. Reflecting on the nature of British rule, following dinner with Cunningham on the committee's final evening in Palestine, the Guatemalan had emphasized to the high commissioner that he was not anti-British. Indeed, García-Granados profoundly admired Britain for its culture and courage and steadfastness when it had stood alone during World War II. He was also an enthusiastic supporter of the Labour government's ambitious postwar social welfare program. But García-Granados had now come to realize that the British "really have no conception of their own rigidity and cruelty in the Palestine matter . . . One might say that the British are really cursed by their possession of the world's largest empire; in their desire to keep it intact they apply methods which their ethical principles certainly would prohibit them from using in private dealings."[7]

This was in essence the message that Begin also sought to impart to UNSCOP at the two meetings he had with some of its members. The first took place in late June and was facilitated by the Associated Press correspondent in Palestine. It was held in secret at the Tel Aviv home of the Hebrew poet Ya'acov Cohen, whose wife was an Irgun operative. The Irgun leader described his group's core aims as "the liberation of the country from the foreign yoke, the attainment of freedom for the Jewish people and the restoration of Jewish rule in Eretz Israel." Precisely what this entailed, he explained, could be summarized as follows:

1. The Irgun considers that Eretz Israel (Land of Israel) is the homeland of the Jewish people.
2. Eretz Israel means both East and West of the Jordan, including Trans-Jordan . . .
3. Immediate repatriation of all Jews wishing to be repatriated to Palestine . . . The right of option should be given to all Jews who wish to return to Palestine. Their return is prevented only by British illegal rule and by British armed force, which should be removed . . .

4. We reject any statement made by the Labour Party as to the transfer of any Arabs from the country. There is enough room in Palestine for all, both Jews and Arabs.

5. Since Britain has decided to keep the country under her own control by force of arms there is no other way to accomplish our aims than to meet force with force.[8]

Sandström naturally pressed Begin especially hard about his claims regarding Jewish coexistence with the Arabs, to which the Irgun leader fatuously replied that there was no such "phenomenon as independent Arab opposition to Jewish repatriation." It was all a plot manufactured by Britain to divide Palestine's inhabitants and thereby perpetuate its rule, he explained, a theme that the group had consistently peddled—predictably, without any success—since the resumption of its revolt in 1944. Lehi coincidentally had recently stepped up its own appeals to the Arabs using these same arguments, and this might have figured in Begin's own propagation of these fantastical claims. "To our brothers the Arabs," a Lehi pamphlet found in Nazareth the previous month had proclaimed, "we are fighting for your liberation and for your and our independence." It also invited the Arabs to join the Jewish fight against British rule as part of a united, anticolonial war of national liberation.[9]

The second meeting was also held in secret. It took place toward the end of July, just before the committee left Palestine, in the house of the fictional potato merchant from the Citrus House operation. Both García-Granados's and Begin's accounts describe the session as a meeting of kindred spirits. Accordingly, their discussions were less forced and more informal than the June meeting had been. "We too believe that the Mandate should come to an end," the Guatemalan diplomat had assured Begin. "I don't know if all our colleagues will support that thesis but I think we can obtain a clear majority on it." The Irgun leader and Enrico Fabregat, the Uruguayan delegate who had accompanied García-Granados, warmly embraced as they parted. "We are brothers in arms," Begin stammered, his voice choked with emotion. "All the world's fighters for freedom are one family."[10]

UNSCOP spent a total of five weeks in Palestine, before visiting Lebanon, Syria, and Trans-Jordan as well as touring displaced-persons camps in Germany and Austria. It held thirteen public hearings in which thirty-seven persons representing six Arab states and seventeen Jewish organizations testified in addition to four private hearings and thirty-nine private meetings. The Jewish Agency and the Haganah both provided evidence, and the Irgun and Lehi each submitted formal memorandums. The absence of any substantive input from Palestine's Arabs was palpable, as they had refused to meet with or testify before the committee. "The leaders of the Jewish Agency presented their case skilfully and indefatigably," William Roger Louis writes, "while the case of the Arabs went mainly by default."[11]

Meanwhile, the summer of 1947 brought Britain no respite from its economic travails. Abrupt global price increases for food and raw materials had drained the country's dollar reserves and deepened its balance-of-payments deficit. On June 30, Hugh Dalton announced in the House of Commons a series of austerity measures that one Tory backbencher described as "the most depressing piece of news given to the British public for several years." Substantial reductions in the import of tobacco, gasoline, and newsprint would be necessary to close the gap with Britain's exports. These steps were essential if Britain was to be able to pay for the food it required from overseas markets and thereby avoid further rationing—a possibility that the Chancellor of the Exchequer told the House he could not rule out.[12]

Dalton also cited the imperative of further cuts in defense spending. Accelerating the pace of demobilization figured prominently in these efforts both as a cost-saving measure and as a way to provide the manpower that British industry desperately required. That there were still men in uniform who had been conscripted prior to January 1, 1944, underscores the urgency attached to achieving this particular reduction. The large garrison required in Palestine to maintain security in the face of escalating terrorist attacks had emerged as a liability that Britain could no longer afford. Only a few weeks earlier, Gurney had complained to David Horowitz, the director of the Jewish Agency's economic department, "Our sterling balances are being reduced by [Zionist] terror. That is the core of the whole matter that we have a tremendous expenditure owing to terror."[13]

During the first six months of 1947, there had been nearly as many terrorist incidents as in the entirety of 1946. One week of attacks in April had alone cost the Palestine government some £60,000. Indeed, as of May, almost its entire reserve budget had been consumed by the escalating violence. Although the postwar Jewish unrest in Palestine was far less pervasive and intense than the Arab Rebellion had been, it was proving significantly more expensive to suppress. Over the course of some forty months a decade earlier, Arab violence had claimed the lives of four thousand people and caused at least £1 million in property damages. By comparison, in just two years Jewish violence had killed fewer than three hundred people but had already inflicted £1.5 million in damages (the equivalent of some $86 million today). In view of Britain's parlous economic condition, Dalton had already warned the cabinet in May that "the British taxpayer could not be expected to assume further burdens in respect of Palestine."[14]

July also brought more bad news from the United States. First was the announcement just in time for July 4 of the founding of Americans for Haganah. The new organization, whose fund-raising efforts were to be dedicated to facilitating the immigration of European Jews to Palestine—whether legally or otherwise—now joined the various Irgun front groups that Peter Bergson had organized alongside Lehi's more modest U.S. philanthropic arm, the American Friends of the Fighters for the Freedom of Israel. Then there was the joint resolution condemning British rule of Palestine introduced in Congress a week later. Although it never came to a vote, the strident language and censorious tone—roundly decrying the oppression of the "Hebrew population of Palestine . . . by a British Army of Occupation"—did little to ameliorate Anglo-American tensions.[15]

The resolution had followed by less than seventy-two hours Mac-Millan's confirmation of Habib's, Nakar's, and Weiss's death sentences. His decision had never been in doubt. "You don't understand the situation here nor the psychology of the terrorists," MacMillan had lectured García-Granados at a Government House dinner party the previous month when the Guatemalan had inquired about the fate of the three condemned Irgunists. "They would interpret a generous gesture as a sign of weakness."[16]

Indeed, the rationale behind the evacuation of the wives and children and the creation of the special security zones earlier in the year had been to accord the GOC and the high commissioner the freedom both to implement tougher security measures and to uphold capital punishment sentences without fear of terrorist retribution. It had nonetheless proven impossible to completely deprive the terrorists of hostage-taking opportunities. In addition to the swimming pool incident at the beginning of June, the Irgun had attempted to seize a police officer on June 22 while he was shopping in Jerusalem and more brazenly to abduct five soldiers bathing in the sea near Herzliya three days later. Lehi had also gotten into the act. Hoping to acquire a high-ranking British hostage to exchange for the missing Rubowitz, it had tried to kidnap the Palestine government's liaison to UNSCOP on June 26. The Irgun, however, had persuaded its rival to postpone any further kidnappings, according to Samuel Katz, so as not "to frighten British personnel away from Jewish areas and [harm] our chances of capturing British officers." With this agreement in place, the Irgun's hunt for potential captives intensified.[17]

Sergeants Clifford Martin and Mervyn Paice were attached to the 252nd Field Security Section of British army intelligence. Their mission was to circulate among the Jewish community in order to obtain information on the terrorist organizations and their local supporters. Accordingly, both men often operated in plain clothes and were not subject to the movement restrictions imposed on other British soldiers—that is, they did not have to walk in groups of four, nor were they necessarily always armed. On the evening of July 10, Martin and Paice were sitting at Café Pinati in Netanya with one of their informants, a Haganah intelligence officer named Aharon Weinberg who worked as a clerk at a nearby army camp. The three men made plans to meet there the following evening and departed. Whether they were overheard at the café or identified and followed by an Irgun surveillance team has never been established. What the police investigation subsequently determined was that the next day Weinberg asked his roommate, who worked at another café, the Gan Vered, to reserve a table there for him and two companions later that evening.[18]

At 7:30 p.m. on July 11, Weinberg took a seat at the Café Pinati and waited for the two sergeants. After an hour passed and they had failed to appear, the Haganah officer left. However, while walking down Herbert Samuel Street, he encountered Martin and Paice and the three proceeded to the Gan Vered. The men talked and drank beer for the next four hours or so and were the last to leave the café at 12:30 a.m.[19]

As the two sergeants walked Weinberg toward his home, a dark sedan pulled over. Five masked men armed with pistols and submachine guns alighted from the car and ordered the three men inside. One of the sergeants resisted and was struck in the head with a pistol and forced into the car. The other was subdued with chloroform. Weinberg pleaded that he suffered from asthma and was instead blindfolded and gagged. The car sped off. About twenty minutes later it pulled over and left Weinberg and two of his captors by the road. Another twenty minutes passed before the vehicle returned—without the two sergeants. Weinberg was taken to an orange grove, where he was left bound hand and foot and instructed to remain there until at least 4:30 a.m. At daybreak, he managed to free his feet and walked to a nearby pump house, where a night watchman untied his hands. Weinberg immediately reported the incident to an officer at the army camp where he worked, and at 5:45 a.m. police from the nearby Tulkarm station were alerted. Five minutes later the first roadblocks were thrown around Netanya, and the search for the two missing sergeants began.

At 9:00 a.m., the area military commander summoned Oved Ben Ami, Netanya's mayor, to his headquarters and obtained Ben Ami's assurance that both the town council and the city's residents would do everything possible to help locate the two captives. By midday the army had established a ten-by-three-mile cordon surrounding the entire area as parties of local youths also searched orange groves and other potential hiding places throughout the afternoon. A second meeting between Ben Ami and the commander occurred later that afternoon, during which a warning from General Gale was communicated to the mayor. If the two sergeants were not quickly found or released, Netanya and the surrounding environs would be declared a "controlled area," the First Infantry commander explained—the new nomenclature for martial law decreed by the cabinet the previous March.[20]

Massive security force sweeps of the city and its environs commenced just before dawn on July 13. Army units, accompanied by police, combed through Netanya and the surrounding area, searching dwellings, storage areas, places of business, settlements, fields, and fruit groves. The Jewish Agency instructed the Haganah to join in the hunt for the two sergeants. All told, five thousand First Infantry Division troops searched some twenty different settlements and communities in addition to Netanya that long day. Nearly fifteen hundred people were detained for further questioning, of whom all but nineteen were subsequently released.[21]

All these efforts, however, came to naught. In preparation for the kidnapping, Paglin had constructed an underground bunker beneath a disused diamond factory near the city limits. It comprised an airless three-meter cube separated from the factory floor by three feet of sand designed to muffle any sounds coming from below. He stocked it with bottles of oxygen so the captives could breathe, a mattress, some food, and a canvas bucket for use as a toilet. Both Martin and Paice had been brought there immediately after their abduction. The Irgun officer in charge of the kidnapping detail told them the reason why they had been seized and the consequences if the lives of the three condemned Irgun fighters were not spared. He had also advised the two sergeants that the entrance to the bunker was mined to discourage any thoughts of escape. The dungeon had been so carefully constructed that twice army patrols searched the factory above without discovering it.[22]

Netanya was placed under martial law that evening. Operation Tiger, as this military action was code-named, established at the high commissioner's direction a "controlled area" affecting fifteen thousand people and encompassing some thirteen square miles, from which no one was allowed to enter or depart. Telephone and postal communications were suspended and a twenty-four-hour curfew imposed. It remained in force for the next forty-five hours but was briefly lifted at 4:00 p.m. on July 16—before reverting to a dawn-to-dusk curfew, which, along with the searches, continued for another two weeks.[23]

The Irgun, meanwhile, struck repeatedly that same evening with a series of road mine attacks near Petah Tiqva and Hadera, killing one soldier and wounding twenty-five others. More significant, however, was the message broadcast by the Voice of Fighting Zion earlier in the day. "If the criminal hand is raised against our captive comrades," the announcement warned, "we shall make our arrows drunk with the hangman's blood."[24]

True to its word, the Irgun as well as Lehi unleashed a deliberately intimidating campaign of unrelenting road mining, mortar attacks, railway sabotage, shootings, and bombings. Not since the Arab Rebellion had the country been subjected to such a sustained onslaught. Over the succeeding twelve days nearly seventy separate incidents claimed the lives of eight soldiers and police and injured eighty others. Almost as many terrorist attacks occurred in that short space of time as in the previous three months combined. But neither this dramatic show of force nor the Irgun's continued possession of its two hostages was sufficient to shake the government's resolve to carry out the scheduled executions.[25]

Shortly after midnight on July 29, Haifa's chief rabbi, Nissim Ohana, was awakened by police and brought to Acre prison. There, he administered the last prayers to Habib, Nakar, and Weiss. Once again the plaintive melody of "Ha-Tikva" echoed throughout the prison as the three condemned men joined one another in song. Starting at 4:00 a.m., each man was delivered to the hangman at twenty-minute intervals. Although their families had also been summoned to Haifa in the middle of the night, they were not permitted to meet with the condemned men. Instead, the three Irgunists had asked Rabbi Ohana to pass along a final message. "Do not grieve too much," they consoled their bereft relations, "what we have done we did out of conviction." The rabbi reported that despite the imminence of death, each man was "composed and steadfast."[26]

The army's search for the two sergeants now expanded. More than a dozen locales in an ever-widening arc beyond Netanya were cordoned off and placed under curfew. On July 30 the hunt for the missing men was extended to Tel Aviv. Later that afternoon, telephone calls were received at the offices of various Jewish newspapers as well as some army and police installations. Claiming to speak for the Irgun, the callers stated that the two sergeants had been executed and explained where their bodies could be found. Police searches of the purported venues, however, proved fruitless. Rumors now swept the city that the Irgun was planning to sneak into Netanya under cover of darkness and string the sergeants' bodies up in front of Weiss's former home. The Haganah mobilized more than fifteen hundred people to blockade the city and prevent the Irgun from doing so. It was already late in the evening when Mayor Ben Ami received a telephone call from another person representing the Irgun. The bodies of Martin and Paice, he was told, could be found the following morning at map coordinate 13751895—a Palestine government forest preserve located a mile and a half southeast of Netanya.[27]

At 5:30 a.m. on July 31 two members of the Jewish Settlement Police on patrol reported that they had come across two corpses hanging from a pair of eucalyptus trees in the preserve but had neither approached nor actually examined them. About three hours later, police accompanied by a unit of the Welsh Guards, some civilian officials, and a handful of journalists arrived on the scene. An unimaginably barbaric tableau awaited them. Suspended only a few inches above the ground were the two corpses bound hand and foot. Each man was attired in the khaki trousers that he was wearing the night of July 12. They were shoeless and their khaki shirts had been tied around their faces as blindfolds. Pinned through their flesh and blood-soaked white undershirts was a copy of an execution order signed by a specially convened Irgun tribunal. "The two British spies, MARTIN and PAICE, who were under arrest by the Underground since 12 July 1947," it read, "have been put to trial, following the enquiry into their criminal anti-Hebrew activities." They had been charged with the following crimes:

1. Illegal entry into our homeland.
2. Membership in the British criminal-terrorist organization know[n] as "British Army of Occupation" which is responsible:
   for depriving our people from the right to live;
   for cruel, oppressive acts;
   for tortures;
   for the murder of men, women and children;

for the murder of prisoners of war;
and for the deportation of Hebrew citizens from their country
and homeland.
3. Illegal possession of arms, intended for the enforcement of oppression and despotism.
4. Anti-Jewish spying, disguised in civilian clothes.
5. Conspiracy against the Hebrew Underground, its soldiers, bases and arms—the arms of freedom.

The Irgun court had found the two men guilty as charged and sentenced them to hang "until their soul would leave them." Both sergeants' appeals for clemency had been denied and the executions carried out. This was not, the Irgun hastened to add, "a retaliatory act for the murder of Hebrew prisoners of war." Rather, it was claimed to be "an *ordinary legal action* of the court of the Underground which has sentenced and will sentence the criminals who belong to the criminal Nazi-British Army of Occupation."[28]

Despite the Irgun's insistence that the sergeants' execution was an act of justice and not blind retribution, Begin never denied its real motive. "We repaid our enemies in kind," he later asserted. "We had warned him again and again and again. He callously disregarded our warnings. He forced us to answer gallows with gallows." Indeed, immediately upon hearing the news from Acre, Begin instructed Paglin to carry out the Irgun's sentence. The Irgun operations chief went immediately to the diamond factory, where he pulled one of the sergeants from the stifling oubliette. Dazed and confused by the light and weeks of oxygen deprivation, the condemned man was quickly bound, hooded, and placed on a chair. A noose was then flung across a roof beam and fastened around his neck. A final request to leave a message behind was denied, and the chair was kicked from beneath him. The same procedure was repeated on the other sergeant. Both bodies were loaded into a jeep and taken to the eucalyptus grove on the outskirts of Netanya, which today is a park where there is a section known as the Sergeants' Grove.[29]

As a Royal Engineers captain proceeded to cut down Martin, the corpse fell to the ground, detonating a small mine that the sappers had missed in their initial sweep of the area. The ensuing explosion completely obliterated Martin's body and hurled Paice's some distance from the splintered trees. The captain also suffered serious wounds to his face and arms. This gratuitous act of vengeance was the last straw.[30]

The fear and alarm already pervading the Yishuv were virtually without precedent. A profound sense of mortification combined with a dark foreboding of the government's intended response to the hangings created a state of anxiety equaled perhaps only by the King David Hotel bombing twelve months earlier. The community's leaders were desperate to avoid the reimposition of martial law or of any security measure that would again adversely impact the Yishuv's economy and upset daily life. But to do so meant finding a way to navigate between collaborating with the same government that denied Holocaust survivors the right to enter Palestine and still meeting the Palestine administration's demands for the resumption of a counterterrorism campaign along the lines of the original Saison.[31]

The Haganah was deeply divided over this issue. Although one faction supported resurrecting the Saison, another opposed it on the grounds that this time civil war would result. A third, even more militant, but smaller element had completely lost faith in Britain's commitment to Zionism and therefore pressed for the return to armed resistance in concert with both terrorist organizations.[32]

The Jewish Agency tried to steer a middle course. The Haganah issued a public plea for any information on either the Irgun or Lehi—and most especially if it pertained to plans to kidnap British soldiers or attack military or police targets. In addition, the agency announced that a meeting had been called for the following day that would be attended by members of the Vaad Le'umi, the Histadrut, Agudath Israel, the Manufacturers' Association, and the rabbinical councils and by the mayors of Jewish townships and the heads of local councils. Its purpose was to agree to a new counterterrorism program. On successive days, Golda Meyerson, the acting head of the Jewish Agency's political department, met with Vivian Fox-Strangways, the acting chief secretary while Gurney was away, and then with Cunningham, in hopes of making a deal that would both satisfy the government and spare the Yishuv. She was not successful. The high commissioner expected nothing less than the agency's full cooperation. He was angered to learn that Meyerson's proposal fell far short of that. The "strong and definite campaign" she promised was one that would be undertaken completely independently of the government's own counterterrorism efforts. The high commissioner did not conceal his frustration. For the past six months the Jewish Agency had repeatedly assured him of various campaigns and initiatives that had either never materialized or proven halfhearted and therefore largely ineffectual. Moreover, the last time that the Zionist institutions had issued a resolution decrying terrorism, it had also included an attack on the government's immigration policy, thus thoroughly undermining its intent. The Jewish Agency,

Meyerson replied, fully understood that "terrorism was a cancer and was alienating sympathy for the Jewish cause in the outside world." It was therefore willing to risk provoking a civil war, but she nonetheless said that "the Agency should carry out this campaign in their own way." That was unacceptable to Cunningham, who admonished the Jewish Agency leader that "the patience of the British people had gone." Events later that same evening would show just how prescient the high commissioner's warning had been.[33]

"The feeling of revulsion which affected every member of the Government and Security Forces in Palestine cannot be adequately described," Dare Wilson recalled of the day when the discovery of the two sergeants' bloodstained bodies was announced. At 8:30 that evening a police armored car on patrol in Tel Aviv suddenly opened fire on a passing Jewish-owned bus. Although none of the passengers were injured, the incident was sufficient to trigger a two-hour-long shooting spree during which other police armored vehicles indiscriminately fired upon a taxi, two other buses, and two crowded sidewalk cafés. Police officers then descended upon one of the cafés to rob and beat its patrons. And for good measure, a hand grenade was tossed into the other—completely destroying the premises. All told, five Jews were killed and sixteen others wounded. Extensive damage was caused to at least twenty-five Jewish-owned shops.[34]

Although such instances of naked vigilantism were comparatively rare in Palestine, both the incident itself and the subsequent efforts of sworn police officers to shield the perpetrators from prosecution illustrate the profound frustration and unmitigated anger that the sergeants' deaths unleashed. A court of inquiry ordered by Gray, for instance, ran up against a conspiratorial wall of silence that prevented it from charging seven policemen with murder, assault, theft, vandalism, and other illegal acts because crucial evidence had also been willfully destroyed or tampered with.[35]

The Irgun's brazen attack on an RAF billet at the edge of the Jerusalem security zone the following afternoon lent new urgency to the increasingly fraught discussions still under way between Jerusalem and London concerning an appropriate response to the hangings. Gray reported that the security forces were angry and tense, anxiously awaiting word of the government's decision. Army intelligence similarly called attention to the "cold fury" suffusing the Palestine garrison. Even so, Gray and MacMillan were confident that there would be no further acts of indiscipline such as had occurred in Tel Aviv the previous night. Cunningham agreed, but he nonetheless was fully cognizant of the urgency to implement some singularly dramatic measure—not least because of the intense pressure from London to do so. Accordingly, both he and his Executive Council had concluded that in the absence of a commitment from the Jewish Agency to cooperate fully "in rooting out the terrorists," the only viable option was to impose martial law on the entire country.[36]

The counterterrorism declaration that emerged from the August 1 conference of Jewish leaders confirmed the high commissioner's worst fears. Although it called upon the Yishuv to "intensify its efforts with all its organized strength to eradicate terrorism," the statement specifically stipulated that its assistance be given to the "security forces of the Yishuv," not to the government. With this, Cunningham's hopes that martial law could be averted dissolved. "The two terrorist groups have grown perceptibly in actual strength during recent months," he wrote in his monthly report to Creech Jones, "but more significant perhaps is the growing sympathy with which they have come to be regarded (at least until the murder of the kidnapped sergeants) by large elements of the Yishuv."[37]

The high commissioner's options, however, were far more limited than he realized. Later that same day MacMillan had informed him that despite a ratio of one British soldier for each adult male Jew in Palestine, there were not enough troops to maintain martial law over Tel Aviv, let alone the rest of the country. Moreover, the additional troop reductions currently under review in London might render even this impossible. Cunningham was incredulous. He immediately sought the assurances of both the new Middle Eastern commander, General Sir John Crocker, and Creech Jones that sufficient troops would be kept in Palestine to maintain order and, should a major terrorist outrage or other contingency require them, additional forces would be made available.[38]

Neither man, however, had the authority to make that commitment. With the demobilization timetable already fifteen months behind schedule, the Labour government was determined to avoid any further delay in the planned release of troops from service. Britain's precarious economic condition simply would not allow it. The cabinet, Creech Jones informed Cunningham, would therefore strongly oppose any proposal that might necessitate the dispatch of additional forces to Palestine—especially in view of the fact that only hours before, it had set a deadline of March 1948 to shrink Britain's overseas military commitments by a further 200,000 men. With the Royal Navy's budget having been "already cut almost to the bone," *The Daily Telegraph* observed, the only remaining cost savings were to be found in reducing army and RAF expenditure. "Palestine remains the great question mark," its columnist Lieutenant General H. C. Martin opined. "It is here, above all, that economies are desirable."[39]

Cunningham and Creech Jones now considered all the possible alternatives to martial law. The high commissioner had just acceded to the military's long-standing request to be granted the authority to punitively demolish any structure from which a terrorist act was committed or where the families of a suspected terrorist dwelled. But neither he nor MacMillan nor Gurney nor anyone else in authority had any fresh ideas, other than martial law throughout the country.[40]

This was the option that Crocker favored. He was convinced that martial law was the only practicable means to blunt the terrorist offensive and demonstrate to the Yishuv "the wisdom of their assisting the Government." During the preceding seventy-two hours a new round of terrorist attacks had struck Palestine's railways, among other targets, thus increasing the pressure on both the Palestine administration and the army to take decisive action.[41]

While the Palestine administration and its military counterparts dithered and debated, the Irgun's propagandists were busy trying to demoralize the security forces and undermine confidence in both their political masters and their commanders. "You did not expect it—dirty oppressors?" a Voice of Fighting Zion broadcast crowed on August 3. "But we warned you. We warned you day in and day out, that just as we smashed your whips so would we uproot your gallows—or, if we did not succeed in uprooting them, we would set up next to your gallows, gallows *for* you . . . And," it ominously concluded, "we have not yet settled our hanging accounts with you, Nazo-British enslavers." A pamphlet distributed shortly afterward took a slightly different tack. Addressed to enlisted men, it sought to sow dissension between them and their officers by comparing the commutation of the flogging sentences the previous December, when British officers had been seized, with the decision to proceed with the death sentences on the Acre raiders when the lives of two mere noncommissioned officers were at stake.[42]

All these developments inevitably raised new concerns about the safety of British military and civilian personnel in Palestine. "I am disturbed at the comparative ease with which Jewish terrorists 'pick up' our people," the secretary of state for war, Frederick Bellenger, wrote to the VCIGS on August 4. But Simpson replied that there was nothing more that could reasonably be done beyond the stringent personal security procedures already in place. This was also the message that Cunningham conveyed to Creech Jones hours earlier. "Short of a withdrawal of branches of the Administration, or a reduction of Military and Police activities which would themselves endanger the security position generally, I do not see how the safety of British subjects could be enhanced under present conditions." Even placing the entire country under martial law, he admitted, would not completely eliminate the threat of terrorists again seizing British soldiers and civilians as hostages.[43]

Stymied at every turn and desperate to do something to assert the government's authority, Cunningham decided to invoke the Emergency Regulations and order the detention without trial of people merely suspected of terrorist sympathies. A long-standing plan to arrest leading Revisionist Party figures and outlaw its youth wing, Betar, was hastily put into effect. Among the thirty-five names on the lists drawn up by the CID were Israel Rokach and Oved Ben Ami, the mayors of Tel Aviv and Netanya, respectively, who, Cunningham explained to Creech Jones, were to be interned on the grounds that they "are known to be able to contact the terrorists."[44]

Shortly after 3:00 a.m. on August 5 the roundups began. Awakened in the dead of night, bleary-eyed officials and party functionaries were dragged off to indefinite imprisonment at Latrun. Many of them had only days earlier lent their support to the Jewish Agency's antiterrorism manifesto. Gale in fact had recently praised Ben Ami both publicly and in his classified after-action report for the assistance that the mayor had provided to the First Infantry during the search for the two sergeants. "Search all you please," Ben Ami remarked as he was taken from his home, "all that you will find is 20 years of close cooperation with the British." The government announced an additional security measure later that day. Henceforth, all Palestinian Jews were forbidden to leave the country until further notice.[45]

Whatever hopes that Cunningham might have harbored of sending a powerful deterrent message to the terrorists, however, were dashed that same afternoon when an Irgun bomb wrecked the Labour Department office in downtown Jerusalem, killing three British constables. A new series of attacks followed the next day. Six separate incidents, some perpetrated by Lehi, occurred on August 7. In the period leading up to the release of the UNSCOP report at the end of the month, the Irgun and Lehi were clearly intent on depicting Britain's inability to maintain order in Palestine through a dramatic show of the terrorist organizations' strength.[46]

Cunningham once more pleaded with Creech Jones to ensure that nothing was done to decrease troop strength in Palestine so that martial law would remain a viable option. "This measure now seems the only shot left in our locker," he explained. "I cannot guarantee that the situation will not deteriorate to such a degree that Civil Government will break down and as you know it is by no means clear how much longer I can keep the Civil Service working under conditions such as exist at present."[47]

Montgomery now flew to Cairo to confer with Crocker and MacMillan about the worsening situation. The consensus that they came to was disheartening. Despite a hundred-thousand-man garrison, there were simply too few troops in Palestine to impose martial law over the entire country. Even a far more modest operation applied to only a geographically limited area, Crocker concluded, was beyond the capacity of the existing forces in Palestine. Accordingly, he now reversed himself and argued that martial law should be avoided if at all possible. Its application even to one location only, the Middle East commander had concluded, would dangerously impact ongoing antiterrorist operations and impinge on routine security duties in addition to diverting units from their main priority—the defense of military installations, the guarding of the rail lines, and the protection of convoys. "Embarking on a line of action which we had not the military strength to see through," MacMillan agreed, "would be fatal."[48]

It was of course not so long ago that senior commanders in London, Cairo, and Jerusalem had all touted martial law as the ultimate panacea to Britain's security problems in Palestine. That it was now dismissed and disparaged in equal measure represented nothing less than a stunning volte-face in the military's thinking. Indeed, for all intents and purposes, martial law was now completely off the table—a point that Trafford Smith reiterated to his colleagues in the Colonial Office on August 12. "The imposition of 'martial law proper,'" he minuted,

> would be tantamount to throwing in our administrative hand in Palestine just at the moment when the United Nations were about to take a decision. Our prestige would suffer, and in particular, that administrative machine, which is now still running, with whatever difficulties and dangers, would probably suffer irremediable damage.
>
> Thus the political objections seem to me very strong . . . The definite view now expressed by the War Office is that the imposition of martial law is not practicable [which] rules out any threat of it.[49]

Events in Britain, however, had both superseded and rendered irrelevant these discussions about martial law—much less any other attempt to stabilize Palestine's worsening security. The reaction back home to the hangings had been pyretic and violent.

Emblazoned across the front pages of newspapers were photographs of the gruesome death scene, leaving little to the imagination. Describing the lynching as an act of "medieval barbarism," the *Daily Express* fumed that "not in the black annals of Nazi wickedness is there a tale of outrage more vile." The more staid *Times* was equally unrestrained, commenting that "the bestialities practised by the Nazis themselves could go no farther." The damage done to the Zionist cause, it lamented, was incalculable. Anglo-American relations over Palestine suffered as well, with the *Daily Mail* pointing an accusatory finger at the "American women whose dollars helped to buy the rope" used to execute Martin and Paice. "The Palestine situation was poisoning relations between the United States and Britain," Bevin warned Lewis Douglas, the American ambassador to Britain, a few days later.[50]

Demonstrations protesting the sergeants' deaths quickly turned violent in both Liverpool and Glasgow on Friday, August 1. The windows of Jewish homes and shops were broken, and in Liverpool a synagogue was vandalized with slogans proclaiming "Death to all Jews" painted on its walls. The disturbances resumed the following evening when arsonists torched a Jewish-owned furniture factory. A Jewish cemetery was also vandalized, and the windows of more Jewish shops were broken. Following the arrest of four men on vandalism charges, a mob gathered outside the Liverpool police headquarters and hurled stones at the building. Police reinforcements had to be summoned from around the city, and multiple baton charges were required to disperse the crowd. Meanwhile, the unrest had spread to London, Manchester, Birmingham, Hull, and Brighton. Vandals damaged a synagogue in south London and pillaged a Jewish-owned millinery shop in Brighton, while police in Manchester had to contend with menacing crowds in three separate parts of that city.[51]

It was unfortunate that Monday, August 4, was a bank holiday as trouble again flared in Liverpool—for the first time during daylight hours. Police recorded over a hundred acts of vandalism in addition to two more arson cases, including a second fire that completely destroyed the damaged furniture factory set alight on Saturday. There was more violence in Manchester again, where troublemakers brought traffic in the city center to a standstill. The sound of shattered glass could again be heard throughout the evening both there and in neighboring Salford.[52]

Army intelligence in Palestine now feared that the "rising wave of anti-Semitism in England" might incite renewed attacks on the Yishuv by disgruntled soldiers and police in Palestine. Their concern was not unfounded. On the night of August 29, a Jewish settlement in the Shomron bloc was once again subjected to sustained indiscriminate gunfire from a nearby army camp—this time killing a nine-year-old child.[53]

As inured to the almost daily reports of the death and deprivation suffered by the security forces in Palestine as the British public was, the sergeants' brutal execution had made a profound impression on the nation's psyche. "All home comment on that deed," the renowned British Middle East expert Elizabeth Monroe explained, "is different in tone from that on earlier terrorist acts, many of which caused greater loss of life—for instance, the blowing up of the officers' club or of the King David Hotel." This was precisely the point that Gurney, who was then in London, had sought to impress on Creech Jones. "I have tried to get it across to the Secretary of State," he told Cunningham, "that the two hangings, though more spectacular, are really no worse than the murders that go on every day or will go on, so long as Jewish denunciations stop short of calling for help to the Police."[54]

But this was not how either the public or the press in Britain regarded the slayings. For both, the murders seemed to demonstrate the futility of the situation Britain faced in Palestine by attempting to satisfy the nationalist demands of both Arab and Jew while reaping only the ingratitude and opprobrium of each. "It is time the Government made up its mind to leave Palestine," an editorial in the left-leaning *Manchester Guardian* declared on August 1, "not only because we have utterly failed to find a solution but because we cannot afford to stay there. Palestine is already a Jewish tragedy; it must not become also a British disaster." Nothing short of the immediate abrogation and surrender of the League of Nations mandate was therefore required. "These latest murders are too much," the conservative *Daily Telegraph* agreed. "Both assassination and atrophy must be stopped in Palestine, and stopped quickly." For *The Economist*, partition was the only solution—"not primarily because it is in the best interests of the Jews or the Arabs, or of the international community in general, it is simply because it is in the best interests of the British."[55]

The opposition Conservative Party now insisted that Palestine be placed on the House of Commons' agenda before it recessed until autumn. A visibly angry Anthony Eden successfully forced the issue, and a short debate was scheduled for the last day that the House would sit, on August 12. As it happened, the debate took place a day earlier—and lasted for nearly five hours. The Labour government was assailed by backbenchers and Tories alike. Creech Jones attempted to dampen the furor by pointing out that when Britain had in February solicited the UN's assistance, "we were all conscious, I think, that a very difficult period lay ahead of us before we could expect a decision or recommendation from the United Nations." Nevertheless, he conceded, the sharp rise in violence that followed had exceeded every expectation. The effect, the colonial secretary was forced to admit, is that "among the British public there is fierce questioning as to the burden and cost to Britain, and the tragedy involved by Britain continuing to shoulder this international liability."[56]

Speaking for the Opposition, Oliver Stanley, Creech Jones's predecessor in the wartime coalition government, described the "complete and irrevocable change in the whole situation in Palestine" since February. In his view the only solution had long been partition. Because the Labour government had consistently rejected this option, the only alternative now was evacuation. "I do not believe," the former colonial secretary declared, "that this country can continue to carry alone a burden in blood, in treasure, in work and labour in Palestine, on anything like the same lines as for the last 20 years."[57]

But it was the denunciation of the government's policy by its own members that cut deepest. Labour's Harold Lever spoke scathingly of "two years of planless, gutless and witless behaviour which has not only cost us treasure in terms of money but uncountable treasure in manpower and loss of life, all in order to prove that we are master of a situation of which we obviously are not master, and all for some obscure reason made plain not to our troops, not to the people of Palestine, and certainly not to us." Britain, he fulminated, had lost all moral or legal grounds for governing Palestine. Decrying the altruism supposedly guiding government policy, he derided British rule as "this military dictatorship in Palestine, this police State, this State of the flogging block and the gallows" and accused the colonial secretary of having drenched "his hands with more purposelessly shed blood than any other Minister of the Crown in this generation." The Mancunian MP concluded by stating unequivocally, "We must go, and the sooner we go the better it will be for the people of Palestine and the people of this country." His fellow backbencher Michael Foot agreed that Britain had morally isolated itself in the world because of its present policy in Palestine, urging the government "to make an act of policy for the first time in two years" by proclaiming its intention to surrender the mandate and leave Palestine no matter what the UN might decide in September.[58]

The strong reaction to the hangings from both the public and Parliament had convinced officials in the Colonial and Foreign Offices that the pressure on the government to end Britain's involvement in Palestine regardless of the UN's decision had become difficult, if not impossible, to resist. The Colonial Office was eager to extricate itself from its responsibilities in Palestine before conditions became worse. Its officials were convinced that even if the situation in Palestine were suddenly stabilized, the government would not be able to overcome opposition at home for Britain to remain there.[59]

The Foreign Office concurred, fretting endlessly over the harm that Palestine was having on Anglo-Arab relations. Michael Wright, an under-secretary, summed up the Foreign Office position in a paper that extolled the salutary effect that withdrawal from Palestine would have on Muslim attitudes toward Britain. By washing its hands of the mandate, Britain could avoid the prospect of further alienating the Arabs should the UN attempt to impose a solution that involved any measure of Jewish autonomy, as was now thought likely. Although Britain clearly had strategic interests in Palestine, Wright argued, "the political advantages of withdrawal outweigh the strategic advantages" of continued access to the port at Haifa and the oil refinery, pipeline terminus, and storage facilities there. "The Mandate," he concluded, "has proved unworkable. It has caused antagonism towards H.M.G. on the part of the Arab states, the Jews, and in America. British withdrawal from Palestine would remove this particular cause for antagonism."[60]

Opinion was also crystallizing within the cabinet that the government had no alternative but to announce its intention to withdraw from Palestine. "I am quite sure that the time has almost come when we must bring our troops out of Palestine altogether," Dalton told Attlee on August 11. "The present state of affairs is not only costly to us in man-power and money but is, as you and I agree, of no real value from the strategic point of view—you cannot in any case have a secure base on top of a wasps' nest—and it is exposing our young men, for no good purpose, to most abominable experiences, and is breeding anti-Semites at a most shocking speed."[61]

A few days later Creech Jones duly advised the British delegation attending the September meeting of the UN General Assembly, "Account should be taken of the strong feeling now apparent in the country and the House of Commons in favour of British withdrawal from Palestine."[62]

As the British government was pushed inexorably toward a final decision on Palestine that summer, an imbroglio of epic proportions was unfolding on the Mediterranean Sea. On July 11—the same day that the Irgun had kidnapped the two sergeants—the *Exodus 1947*, a Haganah ship illegally transporting more than forty-five hundred Jewish Holocaust survivors, had set sail from Sète, France, for Palestine. It was being tracked by Royal Navy ships and a special team of MI6 operatives aboard a civilian yacht. Trained in sabotage, they planned to plant a limpet mine on the *Exodus*'s hull with a three- to four-day time delay in hopes of disabling it. The Foreign Office, however, intervened and thwarted the intelligence service's operation, aptly code-named Embarrass. As the vessel neared Palestine on July 18, heavily armed British sailors boarded it. A desperate struggle ensued as the crew and the refugees attempted to prevent the boarding party from gaining access to the ship's wheelhouse. One crew member and two passengers were killed and many others injured—along with several sailors. With the *Exodus* now under British control, it was escorted to Haifa, where Sixth Airborne Division troops were waiting on the dock to facilitate the transfer of its passengers and crew to three other vessels that would return them to France. Judge Sandström, the UNSCOP chairman, and the Yugoslav delegate, Vladimir Simic, were on hand to observe the heartrending spectacle of the refugees' forced re-embarkation.[63]

Bevin's decision to deport the refugees to France rather than intern them on Cyprus, where previous ships carrying illegal immigrants had been diverted, quickly proved to be a colossal public relations blunder. When the three ships transporting the *Exodus* passengers arrived in Port-de-Bouc on July 29, they simply refused to disembark. The French declined to intervene and a three-week standoff followed. Then, on August 22, the British government announced that if the refugees did not voluntarily leave the ships, they would be taken to the British occupation zone in Germany and interned there. Only thirty-one of the *Exodus*'s original passengers accepted the offer to remain in France, and the three ships set sail that evening for Hamburg. They arrived on September 8, and after fierce resistance from some and resigned cooperation from others the refugees were disembarked and transported by rail to the former Nazi detention camps at Poppendorf and Am Stau.[64]

The image of Jewish concentration camp survivors struggling to reach Palestine, only to be dragged back and imprisoned in the country responsible for their torment and travail in the first place, caused irreparable damage to Britain's moral standing and credibility. The outcome of Bevin's petulant response was the extensive press coverage focused on the prolonged plight of the *Exodus* refugees. This in turn completely vitiated his intention "to teach the Jews a lesson" and marshal international support to help end the illegal immigration of Jews from Europe to Palestine. Instead, it generated immense sympathy for the Zionist cause and, with respect to UNSCOP, solidified the prevailing sentiment in favor of partition.[65]

On September 1 the 117-page UNSCOP report was released. The committee unanimously concluded that the British mandate should be terminated and Palestine should be granted its independence as soon as was practicable. A majority of the committee's members recommended that Palestine be partitioned into separate Arab and Jewish states with

Jerusalem set aside as an international enclave under UN auspices. A two-year transitional period was proposed during which Palestine would be governed by Britain but overseen by the UN. Independence would be granted at the end of that period provided that the constitutions adopted by the proposed Arab and Jewish states satisfied the UN and a treaty of economic union between the two states was concluded.[66]

A minority report submitted by the Indian, Iranian, and Yugoslavian delegates instead recommended the establishment of an independent, binational, federal state. Little attention, however, was paid to its proposals.[67]

The Labour government was not pleased. If, as appeared likely, the General Assembly approved partition, Britain would be saddled with the responsibility of enforcing that solution during the two-year transitional period. This was unacceptable, as editorials in *The Times* and *The Economist* similarly concluded. "Whatever solution was propounded for the problem," Creech Jones later reflected, "it called for the use of force which the British Government did not have and a use which the British public felt to be intolerable."[68]

The military's position on the UNSCOP recommendations was contained in an assessment prepared by the Chiefs of Staff that Albert Victor Alexander, the minister of defense, transmitted in his memorandum to the cabinet on September 18. The chiefs warned that adoption of the majority recommendations would trigger an Arab uprising in Palestine abetted by "irregulars and volunteers" from surrounding states that would lead to anti-British disorders across the Middle East. This would inevitably entail the deployment of British military reinforcements to the region and therefore require "a drastic revision" of Britain's defense policy. Even if the UN accepted the minority report, it was unlikely to receive the approval of both communities in Palestine—which was a prerequisite of the plan's implementation. Although the current strength of the Palestine garrison was sufficient to handle any Jewish unrest, it would be unable to cope simultaneously with Arab violence. But the targeted reduction in overseas personnel would render this existent capability evanescent. The cardinal principle of British policy, the assessment concluded, must in any event remain the "retention of Arab goodwill."[69]

In a memorandum submitted to the cabinet that same day, Bevin bluntly described the majority proposal as "so manifestly unjust to the Arabs that it is difficult to see how . . . we could reconcile it with our conscience." The foreign secretary also spoke of the likelihood of Arab disturbances in Palestine that would be vigorously supported by its neighbors and therefore necessitate the deployment of at least one additional army division to the Middle East. "The present situation in Palestine," he therefore believed, "is intolerable and cannot be allowed to continue. His Majesty's Government have themselves failed to devise any settlement which would enable them to transfer their authority to a Government representing the inhabitants of the country. If the [UN General] Assembly should fail, or if it were to propose a settlement for which His Majesty's Government could not accept responsibility, the only remaining course would be to withdraw from Palestine, in the last resort, unconditionally."[70]

Although Bevin conceded that by withdrawing unilaterally from Palestine, Britain might be criticized by both Jews and Arabs for failing to fulfill its obligations under the mandate, the foreign secretary argued, "We cannot permit ourselves to be kept in Palestine indefinitely by fear of this accusation." In any case, the advantages of withdrawal—primarily the preservation of good relations with the Muslim world and in turn the maintenance of British strategic interests in the Middle East along with an end to the bloodshed and hardship endured by British forces in Palestine—obviated the disadvantages of remaining there. "British lives," he explained, "would not be lost, nor British forces expended, in suppressing one Palestinian community to the advantage of the other, and we should not be pursuing a policy destructive of our own interests in the Middle East." Bevin hoped that such a decision might also have a positive effect on Palestine's Arab and Jewish populations and thus "induce a sense of realism and offer a prospect of a settlement. With this end in view," the foreign secretary concluded, "it should be made clear at an early stage in the Assembly that our minds are made up."[71]

The cabinet met on September 20 to discuss the government's options in view of the UNSCOP report and the forthcoming General Assembly session. Bevin reiterated his view that Britain should decline "to enforce a settlement which was unacceptable" to either the Arabs or the Jews. To his mind, "the right course was for His Majesty's Government to announce their intention to surrender the Mandate and . . . plan for an early withdrawal of the British forces and British administration from Palestine." Creech Jones spoke next and stated his agreement with Bevin's assessment, as did the rest of the cabinet. Emanuel Shinwell, the minister of fuel and power, stressed the importance of an orderly withdrawal so that Britain's relinquishment of its responsibilities in Palestine would not be seen as a sign of weakness. Dalton strongly opposed the deployment of any more service personnel and said "that a date for the withdrawal of the British administration and British forces should be announced as soon as possible."[72]

The prime minister concurred. The time had come, he said, for Britain to disencumber itself of the responsibility for Palestine. Attlee drew attention to the "close parallel between the position in Palestine and the recent situation in India," where independence had been proclaimed on August 15, as an example of how Britain had stated its intention to withdraw, fixed a definite time limit for the cessation of British rule, and had then left the two rival communities there to resolve their differences on their own.

The cabinet, accordingly, agreed to inform the UN that Britain "would not be able to give effect to any scheme unacceptable to both the Arabs and the Jews and that in any other event, the United Nations Organisation would have to find another implementing authority. The prime responsibility for the implementation would in any event be transferred to the United Nations Organisation."[73]

Creech Jones communicated the government's decision to the UN on September 26. "In order that there may be no misunderstanding of the attitude and policy of Britain," he stated, "I have been instructed by His Majesty's Government to announce with all solemnity that they have consequently decided that in the absence of a settlement they must plan for an early withdrawal of British forces and of the British administration from Palestine."[74]

Indeed, less than eight weeks after the cabinet had decided to surrender the mandate, it approved the evacuation timetable proposed by the Chiefs of Staff. "In order to dispel any remaining uncertainty of Britain's intention to withdraw," the British delegation at the UN was instructed to inform the General Assembly that all British forces and administrative services would be withdrawn from Palestine by August 1, 1948. This date was subsequently moved forward to May 15. And on that day British rule in Palestine ceased.[75]

Only Thus

Nearly a decade and a half after the events that brought Britain to its knees in Palestine, Creech Jones described the thinking behind the Labour government's fateful decision to surrender the mandate in two revealing letters written within five weeks of each other to Elizabeth Monroe and the Labour MP and future prime minister James Callaghan.

The first letter, dated October 23, 1961, and addressed to Monroe, identified four pivotal concerns that had driven the cabinet in September 1947 to conclude that the mandate was no longer tenable. First were the political differences separating Palestine's Arab and Jewish communities that the government had despaired of resolving. "Jews and Arabs had rejected every possible solution," the former colonial secretary lamented, "and each was so inflexible in their views as to make them irreconcilable." Second was the unrelenting pressure on Britain's already depleted economy imposed by the large garrison maintained in Palestine because of ongoing Jewish terrorism and the threats of more widespread Zionist resistance as well as renewed Arab violence. Third was the mounting criticism over the Labour government's inability to replace the 1939 white paper with a new policy acceptable to both Arabs and Jews. Lastly, he called attention to the "deadly blow against British patience and pride" that the hanging of the two sergeants had caused. Hence, with "accelerating speed," Creech Jones concluded his account of these seminal developments, "the Cabinet was pushed to the conclusion that they could [no] longer support the Mandate."[1]

In the second letter, sent to Callaghan on November 30, 1961, Creech Jones began by recounting his advocacy for partition from the time he became colonial secretary in October 1946. "It was too late and an impracticable policy at that stage in every respect," he explained. Bevin, moreover, had already "influenced the Cabinet along his line of policy and in the broad it was the inevitable one. Things were in crisis and steadily mounting to a climax" throughout the summer of 1947. The Labour government was under immense pressure from Parliament, from America, and from the British people to end its paralytic reign over Palestine and reach a decision about the mandate's political future that had eluded every other premiership for the past decade. "Meanwhile outrages were common in Palestine," he recalled.

> Terrorism was at its worst and the British public seemed unable to stand much more of it. For my part, I could only work within the confines of the Labour Government's Middle East policy and try to get order into Palestine and any acceptable interpretation of the Mandate . . . this was an impossibility and I knew it. Bevin was thoroughly co-operative but the situation was hopeless and intolerable. The Cabinet determined that the Mandate could not be worked and felt the only possible alternative was to leave it to the responsible International Authority in the world . . . and ask them to find a solution. That we did.[2]

Although the dramatic spike in Jewish terrorist incidents throughout July slowed in August, a series of terrorist attacks that month had claimed the lives of an additional twenty-three persons and caused injuries to forty-one others. Moreover, in a harbinger of greater trouble to come, for the first time in nearly a decade some of the operations had been specifically directed against Arab as well as government targets—with Arab civilians accounting for the majority of deaths and nearly a third of casualties.[3]

That Jewish terrorism played a salient role in helping to create and foster the sense of hopelessness and despair that Creech Jones refers to—and hence influenced the Labour government's decision to leave Palestine—is clear. History, however, is rarely mono-causal, and an overwhelming concatenation of other developments—including Britain's postwar economic travails, the granting of independence to India, the deterioration of relations with the United States over Palestine, the intense pressure of Jewish illegal immigration, the force of international and domestic opinion, the plight of the Holocaust's survivors and Jewish displaced persons languishing in Europe, and the UNSCOP report recommending the mandate's termination—all converged to push the Labour government toward this momentous climacteric.

The role of Jewish terrorism in this process is perhaps best understood in the context of British policy and decision making for Palestine throughout its three-decade-long rule. Britain never really had a firm or consistent policy for Palestine. This, in turn, rendered successive British governments susceptible to terrorist pressure. The impression shared by Arab and Jew alike was that London could be influenced, intimidated, or otherwise persuaded by violence. Shaw specifically cited this lacuna, and the pernicious perception it encouraged, to the Anglo-American Committee of Inquiry in March 1946 as the source of Britain's problems in Palestine. And Gurney, who succeeded Shaw as chief secretary, made exactly the same point to Montgomery two years later.[4]

In these circumstances, terrorism thrived. The prevailing belief in Palestine, Cunningham complained to Meyerson, was "that England always gives in to force." There was abundant evidence to support that claim. The Arab rioting that swept through Palestine in 1921, for instance, produced the restrictions on Jewish immigration and redefinition of British policy based on the new criterion of Palestine's "economic absorptive capacity." The 1929 riots in turn resulted in the clawing back of Britain's commitment to Zionism contained in the 1930 Passfield White Paper, which imposed additional restrictions on Jewish immigration, though these were subsequently overturned by the MacDonald "Black Letter." Finally, the massive countrywide uprising that erupted six years later with the Arab Rebellion prompted the most drastic reformulation of Britain's policy for Palestine to date. The 1939 white paper severely curtailed Jewish immigration and, after a five-year transitional period, made it completely dependent upon Arab consent. Similarly draconian limits had also been applied to Jewish land purchase in Palestine the following year.[5]

The Jewish terrorists who had initially created the Irgun to counter Arab violence drew their own conclusions from the Arab Rebellion and the reversal of British policy that followed. "Arabs use terror as a means in their political fight—and they are winning," the Irgun explained in launching its own revolt against British rule in May 1939. But the Irgun's inchoate uprising was short-lived. Less than three months later, Britain was at war with Germany. Confronted by the prospect of the greater menace of a victorious Nazi Germany, the Irgun declared a truce and announced the suspension of all anti-British operations for the war's duration. Like the rest of the Jewish community in Palestine, who had pledged to support the British war effort, the Irgun hoped that this loyalty would be rewarded by Britain after the war with the realization of the Zionists' dream of statehood.[6]

The hated white paper, though, remained in force. Accordingly, in 1944, as the terrible fate that had befallen European Jewry became known and the tide of battle turned decisively in Britain and the Allies' favor, the Irgun—under its new commander, Menachem Begin—decided to resume the struggle against British rule. Three preeminent considerations were behind that historic decision. First and foremost were the continued restrictions on Jewish immigration to Palestine. Reversing or removing this policy had now acquired greater urgency given the news from Nazi-occupied Europe and the impending expiration of the white paper's five-year immigration quota. Second was the consensus that had emerged within the Irgun that the reasoning behind the self-imposed truce it had declared nearly five years before—of potentially helping Germany by harming Britain—was no longer relevant. And, third, by renewing the revolt, the Irgun hoped to position itself at the vanguard of the active realization of the Jews' political and nationalist aspirations.

Begin's strategy, accordingly, was not to defeat Britain militarily but to use terrorist violence to undermine the government's prestige and control of Palestine by striking at symbols of British rule. "The very existence of an underground . . . must in the end undermine the prestige of a colonial regime that lives by the legend of its omnipotence," he later explained. "Every attack which it fails to prevent is a blow at its standing. Even if the attack does not succeed, it makes a dent in that prestige, and that dent widens into a crack which is extended with every succeeding attack." Hence, in contrast to previous colonial rebellions that either had sought decisive military victories in actual battle or had relied on a prolonged strategy of attrition, the Irgun adopted a strategy that involved the relentless targeting of those institutions of government that unmistakably represented Britain's oppressive rule of Palestine. This was why, when the group resumed its revolt in February 1944, Begin selected the Immigration Department's offices in Palestine's three major cities for attack. Subsequent Irgun operations targeted the government Land Registry Office, from which the white paper's provisions restricting Jewish land purchase were administered; the Department of Taxation and Finance, which collected the revenue used to fund the government's repressive policies; and, of course, the policemen and soldiers responsible for the white paper's enforcement.[7]

There was a dissident faction within the Irgun, however, that had never stopped fighting Britain. In 1940, Abraham Stern and a handful of followers left to found their own terrorist group, which eventually evolved into Lehi. It chose a different means from the Irgun to end British rule over Palestine. Steeped in the Russian revolutionary ethos of "propaganda by the deed," Lehi—in Yezernitzky's evocative words—aspired to "change the course of history" by assassinating senior British government officials. But lacking men, arms, and resources, Lehi never posed a serious challenge to British rule until, on November 6, 1944, two of its gunmen murdered Lord Moyne. But the outcome of the policy change for Palestine it sought turned out to be inimical to Zionist interests. Rather than cowing Britain into submission or intimidating the wartime coalition government to acquiesce to Lehi's fantastical nationalist schemes, Moyne's assassination effectively scuttled Churchill's bold plan to partition Palestine and thus achieve an early resolution of the country's political future before the war ended. Instead, absent a new policy or credible replacement, the white paper remained indefinitely in force. Thereafter, Lehi returned to irrelevance—feared by the British in Palestine as dangerous fanatics but militarily inconsequential and politically incapable of realizing its founding leader's grandiose ambitions.[8]

The Labour government that took power in 1945 thus inherited a policy for Palestine that its own party leadership had long ago repudiated and that had now been rendered obsolete by the war's end. Inundated with pressing domestic and international problems, the new government was also challenged to invent a new policy for Palestine. Bevin embarked first on a determined but fruitless quest to actively involve the United States in helping to determine Palestine's future via the Anglo-American Committee and then, after that failed, with Creech Jones on a desperate bid to obtain some kind of negotiated settlement between Arab and Jew at the ill-fated February 1947 London Conference.

"During the whole of this period when the political future of Palestine was being debated outside of the country itself," Cunningham recalled, "sabotage and terrorism by Jews was increasing and, so far as the dissident groups were concerned, in ever more violent and brutal forms." In these difficult circumstances, with Palestine suspended in a state of political limbo, all that he could do was "to try to keep the country quiet." This was an impossible task, Cunningham apprised Hall in July 1946, when both the Jews and the Arabs were "saying force pays . . . and interpreting lack of action as weakness . . . I can do little—[without a] policy."[9]

The vacuum created by the Labour government's vacillation and indecision therefore deprived the army of the explicitly stated mission and objective that are at the foundation of sound strategy. "The first essential in any counter-insurgency [or counterterrorist] campaign," the British soldier and author Julian Paget maintains, "is that both the political and military aims should be agreed upon by all concerned from the very start and should be clearly stated in a directive." Lieutenant General D. B. Lang, a specialist on military training and doctrine who also served in the British army, similarly argues that "the soldier expects to be given and is entitled to demand, a clear political directive, which must include, and in fact be built around, the object which the Civil Government wishes to be attained."[10]

Bereft of this guidance, the British army adopted a strategy that was an inheritance from its successful suppression of the Arab Rebellion a decade before. Senior commanders like Montgomery, who had fought in Palestine during the late 1930s, were convinced that terrorism was best defeated through the naked application of military force alone. Coercion and punishment had worked against the Arabs; hence, he and his subordinates reasoned, both would work equally well against the Jews. But this assumption ignored the fundamental differences between the two uprisings. The Arab Rebellion was essentially a popularly supported rural guerrilla war. Most of the fighting had occurred in the countryside, where the rebel bands moved and often fought in discernible—and at times numerically large formations, supported and abetted by the local population. Accordingly, the means and methods involved in that insurrection's suppression were both straightforward and unconstrained. Guerrilla units were harried and harassed by British infantry and armored units and, wherever possible, subjected to aerial and artillery bombardment. The homes of individual Arabs implicated in the violence were punitively blown up, and entire villages judged guilty of assisting the rebels were wantonly bombed or shelled.[11]

The army assumed that this strategy would be successful against the Jews as well. But that assumption willfully ignored three key differences between the Arab Rebellion and the Jewish terrorist campaigns. First, unlike the Arab uprising, this was a struggle fought almost entirely in Palestine's cities. Second, only a small portion of the Yishuv belonged to or actively supported the Irgun and still fewer Lehi. This meant that punishing the guilty by collective fine or by aerial or artillery bombardment was virtually impossible. And, third, the Zionist movement's ability to mobilize public opinion outside Palestine, especially in the United States, was an advantage that the Arab rebels conspicuously lacked. Accordingly, only once was a Jewish settlement fined—Givat Shaul in 1944 following Lehi's attempt on MacMichael's life—and it was not until August 1947 that the army, having exhausted all other countermeasures, sought permission to punitively destroy Jewish-owned dwellings and property. Within a week of having obtained Cunningham's authorization, army sappers blew up a Jewish house (coincidentally also in Givat Shaul) in which arms and ammunition had been found during a routine search. But, leaving aside whether this tactic would have proven any more effective than those previously tried, it was far too late in the day to have made any difference.[12]

In any event, the army already had for the previous two years permission to summon RAF aircraft to bomb so-called terrorist enclaves. But it had proven impossible for the authorities to discern and segregate those "enclaves" from the surrounding civilian populace. Hence, rather than risk killing or injuring innocent people and damaging or destroying their property, the army never utilized this measure. Citing the precedent of the Arab Rebellion, Creech Jones raised it again in August 1947 in hopes of finding some means of exacting retribution on the Yishuv following the hanging of the two sergeants. But, as Cunningham patiently explained, unlike the Arab rebel strongholds dotting the countryside in the 1930s, the Jewish terrorists were dispersed throughout Palestine's cities. This effectively rendered aerial bombardment not only irrelevant but ineffectual, "unless," the high commissioner added, "it is intended purely punitively against the whole Jewish population." As eager as the cabinet was to undertake some signal action in respect to the sergeants' execution, there was neither the will nor the stomach to brook the international criticism and opprobrium—especially from the United States—that would surely have followed.[13]

The army therefore clung to large-scale cordon-and-search operations in the cities and searches of Jewish settlements in the countryside for illegally held arms as its preferred terrorist countermeasures. Both Montgomery and Dempsey persisted in believing that the army's lack of success was not the result of an anachronistic strategy or failed tactics but the product of the political restraints they claimed had been imposed on military action by Cunningham. The CIGS repeatedly promised that once these restraints were removed and the full weight of the military was brought to bear on the Yishuv, the community's cooperation would follow. But harsh measures such as the imposition of martial law over Tel Aviv in March 1947 failed to anticipate that the hardship and inconvenience caused would so alienate the Jewish populace that all prospects of obtaining the community's assistance were lost. It was only very late in the struggle that the army recognized this mistake and began to employ the small-unit tactics better suited to—and more effective in—counterterrorism. But their use was sporadic and uneven and mostly confined to the First Infantry, whose commander, Gale, had been in charge of elite special operations units during the final thrust across Germany during World War II and thus understood the nature of irregular warfare. In fact, of the 177 search operations that the army conducted in Palestine between 1945 and 1947, more than half were battalion size or larger (that is, involving at least seven hundred soldiers). Two operations entailed entire divisions (approximately fourteen thousand men), and thirty-eight others were brigade size or more (that is, deploying some three to five battalions).[14]

Opinion across the entire spectrum of British officials responsible for

Palestine was that countering terrorism was a police, not a military, matter and that if the government were to defeat the terrorists, the cooperation of the Jewish community was essential. The basic tenet of British
doctrine governing imperial internal security had long been that the
police would "be a colony's first line of defense, as well as the provid-
ers of law and order." This principle, derived from Britain's experience
ruling Ireland, had been applied throughout the empire from the late
nineteenth century. The problem throughout the British Empire was
that these imperial constabularies were underfunded and understaffed.
Despite recurrent recruitment campaigns, service in violence-prone territories with harsh climates, in spartan conditions, for extended periods
of time far from home, and at pay scales considerably lower than those
for constables in Britain, made colonial policing a relatively unappealing
vocation with the result that, at times of crisis or grave trouble, the army
was called upon to assume responsibilities for which it was untrained and
unprepared and that would otherwise have been performed by the police
had they sufficient personnel.[15]

This was precisely what occurred in Palestine after World War II.
When Montgomery arrived on an inspection tour in June 1946, he was
appalled to discover that "at a time when the situation was clearly about to
boil over," the police force was nearly 50 percent below strength and considered to be "no more than 25 percent effective." The army, accordingly,
was forced to intervene. As Barker had to explain to his men, "In normal
peace times, the police would carry out their duties without assistance
from the military. As it is, the situation in the country is not normal and
furthermore the Police Force is much below establishment. As a result the
police, more often than not, will require help from the military."[16]

In his study of the counterterrorist campaigns conducted by British
colonial police forces from the 1930s to the 1950s, David Clark observes,
"The arrival of the army to support the police has tended to attract more
attention than the less spectacular, but no less essential police role. The
arrival of the army seemed to indicate that the police had failed." This was
certainly the case in Palestine. There, an understrength and intelligence-
starved police force had continually failed to anticipate and contain, much
less defeat, the succession of violent uprisings mounted by the Arabs and
then by the Jews.[17]

Like other colonial constabularies across the empire, the PPF was
always short of personnel. This deficiency was especially critical among
its British contingent—the only section of the mixed Arab and Jewish
force deemed reliable and trustworthy enough to be assigned to counter-

terrorism duties. Unsuitable British officers were therefore retained who would otherwise have been dismissed, and recruits were rushed into service through truncated training courses to compensate for the chronic manpower shortage. Rymer-Jones had hoped that the creation of the Police Mobile Force in 1944 would redress these problems and serve as the PPF's premier counterterrorism strike force. But it too was perpetually below strength and moreover contributed to the damaging "militarization" of the force cited by Wickham in his 1946 report. The effect of stressing the PPF's paramilitary capabilities at the expense of normal policing duties, this expert on colonial policing concluded, had turned it into neither a proper police force nor an army but an ineffective mixture of the two.

Bureaucratic parsimony had also denuded many colonial police forces of the robust intelligence-gathering and analysis capabilities essential for counterterrorism. Here, too, the Palestine Police Force's CID was an abject case in point. When Alexander Kellar, the London-based MI5 desk officer responsible for the Middle East, visited Palestine in late 1944 and early 1945, he was shocked by the CID's anemic condition and unprofessional demeanor. Its record keeping and files—the most fundamental requirement of a professional intelligence operation—were shambolic. The CID, he also reported, had thoroughly failed to penetrate either the Irgun or Lehi and was therefore completely and ill-advisedly dependent on the Haganah for information on both. Kellar was especially critical of the CID's interrogators, who, he argued, lacked the necessary training and detailed knowledge of the terrorist organizations to do their jobs properly. William Moffat, the police intelligence expert who accompanied Wickham to Palestine nearly two years later, was similarly unimpressed with the CID. He thought that its officers were insufficiently aggressive in going out into the field to obtain intelligence and was profoundly troubled by the poor handling of informants. Moffat had therefore urged that additional, specialized training be provided without delay to all CID officers and that sufficient funds be made available for the cultivation of well-placed informants.[18]

The integration of intelligence and operations, Sir Michael Carver, the chief of the Defence Staff between 1973 and 1976 and, as such, the commander of Britain's armed forces, has argued, is absolutely vital to the successful prosecution of a counterterrorist campaign. Yet, because of the CID's intelligence-gathering and processing inadequacies, this was never achieved in Palestine. Instead, the PPF was driven to try to compensate for these deficiencies by the adoption of ill-conceived and ultimately bungled initiatives such as Fergusson's Special Squads. Rather than gaining the initiative against the Jewish terrorist organizations, their operations resulted in scandal, thus further alienating the Yishuv from the authorities while heaping calumny and disgrace on the police and underscoring the bankruptcy of Britain's governance of Palestine.[19]

The army's clumsy operations and counterproductive interactions with the Yishuv, coupled with the enervated police force's incompetence and harmful militarization, thus helped to breathe life into the Irgun's struggle. Through terrorist violence, the group sought to foment a climate of fear and alarm in Palestine by demonstrating the security force's weakness and inability to maintain order. The inherent clandestine nature of terrorist warfare was therefore used by the Irgun to confuse the government and force it to treat the entire Jewish community as the enemy, harboring or protecting or otherwise refusing to divulge information on the terrorists within its midst. That Begin's strategy succeeded is evident in Gale's after-action report on Operation Tiger, the massive cordon-and-search operation that the First Infantry conducted in and around Netanya as part of the frantic hunt for the kidnapped sergeants. The "whole Jewish society in Palestine is riddled with underground and illegal organisations," the First Infantry commander had written. "Now that certain of the underground societies have gone beyond the pale, Jewish society is unable to cope with the situation . . . This is a people dogged by fear of their own underground organisations and worse, because in some cases the fear results from their own fingers being too dirty to enable them to come out in the open."[20]

In these circumstances the Palestine administration could respond only by imposing on the country a harsh regimen of security measures encompassing a daily routine of curfews, roadblocks, snap checks, cordon-and-search operations, and, for brief periods, the imposition of martial law on select locations. Although major counterterrorist operations such as Agatha and Shark were heralded by the authorities as decisive successes, they in fact proved to be counterproductive: ephemeral victories bought at the cost of further alienating the community. Begin banked on the fact that the upheaval and inconvenience caused by these operations would alienate the community from the government, thwart efforts to obtain the Yishuv's cooperation against the terrorists, and create an impression in the minds of the Jews of the army and the police as oppressive occupation forces. Further, the more aggressive and conspicuous the security forces were and the more pervasive the physical barriers and other visible defenses against terrorist attack became, the stronger and more powerful and threatening the terrorists appeared.

At the foundation of the Irgun's strategy was Begin's belief that the British, unlike the Germans, who during the war had carried out wholesale reprisals against civilians, were incapable of such barbarity. By pushing a liberal democracy like Britain to mount increasingly repressive measures against the Yishuv, the terrorists sought to push Britain to the limits of endurance.[21]

Finally, an integral and innovative part of the Irgun's strategy was Begin's use of daring and dramatic acts of violence to attract international attention to Palestine and thereby publicize simultaneously the Zionists' grievances against Britain and their claims for statehood. In an era long before the advent of 24/7 global news coverage and instantaneous satellite-transmitted broadcasts, the Irgun deliberately attempted to appeal to a worldwide audience far beyond the immediate confines of its local struggle—and beyond even the ruling regime's own homeland. The success of this strategy, Begin claimed, may be seen in the paucity of global coverage afforded to the civil war that had erupted in Greece after World War II, for example, compared with that devoted to events in Palestine.[22]

The Irgun's political front organizations in the United States—organized and directed by Peter Bergson—were particularly successful in this respect, generating publicity and raising funds for the Irgun, gaining access for an official of the International Red Cross to the special British prison for Jewish terrorists in Eritrea, and securing the passage of resolutions by Congress condemning "British oppression" in Palestine and reaffirming American support for the establishment of a Jewish state. These activities presaged the efforts subsequently undertaken by Irish American activists on behalf of Sinn Féin and the Provisional Irish Republican Army, which had similarly corrosive effects on Anglo-American relations.[23]

By September 1947 the Irgun had achieved its objective. Each successive terrorist outrage illuminated the government's inability to curb, much less defeat, the terrorists. Already sapped by World War II, Britain's limited economic resources were further strained by the cost of deploying so large a military force to Palestine to cope with the tide of violence submerging the country. Parliamentary sentiment and public opinion in Britain, already ill-disposed to the continued loss of life and expenditure of treasure and effort in an unwinnable situation, were further inflamed by the hanging of the two sergeants.

This was not a war of numbers. Winning was measured not in terms of enemy losses or assets destroyed but by psychological impact. The Irgun undertook innovative and spectacular attacks such as the bombings of the King David Hotel and the British embassy in Rome, the assault on the officers' club in Jerusalem's special security zone, the raid on Acre prison, and the hangings of the two sergeants specifically to demoralize the British and undermine the Labour government's resolve to remain in Palestine. Indeed, the butcher's bill was remarkably modest compared with the horrific standards of terrorism today. Between August 1945 and August 1947, a total of 141 British soldiers and police and 40 terrorists died, including those executed or who committed suicide while awaiting execution. Civilian fatalities during the same period were also remarkably low. Fewer than one hundred Arab and Jewish noncombatants perished as a result of terrorism between August 1945 and August 1947, and just over four hundred were injured. The overwhelming majority of these casualties were inflicted in one incident alone—the Irgun's bombing of the King David Hotel, which perhaps explains why that attack has never been forgotten and remains a source of perpetual controversy.[24]

In the final analysis, Britain's commitment in Palestine exceeded not only its financial resources but, most important, its will to remain there whether for reasons of prestige or strategic considerations. Without a firm policy it was impossible for Britain to define precisely what its interests in Palestine were. The absence of this policy also violated one of the basic principles of the use of military force: that of having a clear political objective.

The rise of Israel was the product of many powerful forces in addition to terrorism. At the same time, however, it is indisputable that at the very least the Irgun's success in attracting attention to itself and its cause and most significantly both hastening and profoundly affecting government decision making demonstrates that—notwithstanding the repeated denials of governments—terrorism can, in the right conditions and with the appropriate strategy and tactics, succeed in attaining at least some of its practitioners' fundamental aims. Even if the Irgun's accomplishments were not immediately reflected in terms of the actual acquisition of power in government—Begin and his Herut Party, for instance, remained in opposition for some thirty years—it is a measure of the recognition that the group achieved that Begin was twice granted audiences with members of UNSCOP, including its chairman, to explain the group's aims, motivations, and vision of a Jewish state in Palestine.

The Irgun's terrorism campaign in fact is critical to understanding the evolution and development of contemporary terrorism. The group effectively directed its message to audiences far beyond the immediate geographic locus of its struggle—in New York and Washington and Paris and

Moscow as much as in London and Jerusalem. This taught a powerful lesson to similarly aggrieved peoples elsewhere, who now saw in terrorism an effective means of transforming hitherto local conflicts into international issues. Less than a decade later, the leader of the anti-British guerrilla campaign in Cyprus, General George Grivas, adopted an identical strategy. Although there is no evidence that he ever read Begin's book (an English-language translation of *The Revolt* had been published in London and New York in 1951) or had studied the Irgun's campaign, the parallels between the two are unmistakable. The internationalization of Palestinian Arab terrorism that occurred in the 1960s and 1970s would also appear to owe something to the quest for international attention and recognition that the Irgun's own terrorist campaign pioneered a quarter of a century earlier. And the Brazilian revolutionary theorist Carlos Marighella's famous *Minimanual of the Urban Guerrilla*, which was essential reading for the various left-wing terrorist organizations that arose both in Latin America and in Western Europe during the 1960s and 1970s, embodies Begin's strategy of provoking the security forces in hopes of alienating the population from the authorities.[25]

Thus the foundations were laid for the transformation of terrorism in the late 1960s from a primarily localized phenomenon into the security problem of global proportions that it remains today. Indeed, when U.S. military forces invaded Afghanistan in 2001, they found a copy of Begin's seminal work, *The Revolt*, along with other books about the Jewish terrorist struggle, in the well-stocked library that al-Qaeda maintained at one of its training facilities in that country.[26]

Acknowledgments

I never thought that the hardest part of completing this manuscript would entail writing the acknowledgments. The writer's block that it induced was not for lack of gratitude, but because of the vastness of the debt I owe to the many institutions and individuals who variously assisted, supported, encouraged, and inspired me to undertake this project—and then to see it to completion.

First and foremost, I must thank the national and official archives as well as the museums and university libraries in Britain, the United States, and Israel that made the research for *Anonymous Soldiers* possible.

The National Archives (formerly the Public Record Office) in Kew, London, is unique in combining the efficiency and enthusiasm of archivists and staff with impressive technological innovation; the result of which is unparalleled ease of access to documents and other research materials. I am thus immensely grateful for permission to quote from the voluminous documentary material that I consulted both at Kew and online in the course of researching this book.

I found a similarly amenable environment at the U.S. National Archives—the original National Archives Building in downtown Washington, D.C.; the Washington National Records Center in Suitland, Maryland; and the bucolic "Archives II" facility in College Park, Maryland. I would be remiss not to acknowledge specifically the invaluable assistance I received from the legendary John Taylor in mining the extensive archives of the Office of Strategic Services.

In Israel, I was greatly assisted by the dedicated archivists and staff at the Central Zionist Archives, the Israel State Archives, and the Menachem Begin Heritage Center in Jerusalem; at the Haganah Archives and the Jabotinsky Institute in Tel Aviv; and at the Weizmann Archives in Rehovot (from whom material cited and quoted appears courtesy of Yad Chaim Weizmann).

The splendid collection of documents, personal papers, and photographs maintained since 1961 by the Middle East Centre Archive at St. Antony's College, Oxford, was indispensable to my research. The center's archivist, Debbie Usher, was especially accommodating and helpful, as was Eugene Rogan, the center's director at the time.

The Bodleian Library of Commonwealth and African Studies at Rhodes House, Oxford, is another important repository of personal papers used in this book. I am grateful to the archivists who assisted me there and in particular to Lucy McCann, who very kindly arranged for me to read the papers of John J. O'Sullivan.

The collections held at the Imperial War Museum, London, were also vital to my research. John MacMillan, the son of Lieutenant General Sir G. H. A. MacMillan, graciously allowed me to quote from his father's papers, as did Elizabeth Keating from the papers of her late husband, Rex Keating. The Head of Documents and Sound, Anthony Richards, very kindly granted me permission to publish extracts from the

Montgomery papers. In the case of the Clarke and Rymer-Jones collections held by the museum, every reasonable effort was made to obtain the necessary permission from the copyright holders who, unfortunately, could not be located.

The Lamport Hall Trustees graciously accorded me access to the papers of Sir Gyles Isham, housed at the Northamptonshire Record Office, and both the trust's executive director, G. P. S. Drye, and Scott Pettitt made my visit to the record office possible. I thank the trustees for permission to quote from Sir Gyles's letters and other documents.

I also acknowledge with gratitude Taylor and Francis, publishers of *Small Wars and Insurgencies*, for permission to use excerpts from two articles that previously appeared in that scholarly journal. In addition, through the efforts of the volunteers in Project Ben-Yehuda, the poetry of Abraham Stern has been made accessible online to the general public.

Several institutions materially supported the research and writing of *Anonymous Soldiers*. I was extremely fortunate to have been elected to a visiting fellowship at All Souls College, Oxford, for Michaelmas Term, 2009. Enveloped by the college's convivial and supportive atmosphere, I swiftly completed the first three chapters of the book. I therefore remain profoundly grateful to the warden and fellows for the privilege of briefly living and working among them. Sir John Vickers was a welcoming and engaging host and I benefitted enormously from the many discussions with Alexis Sanderson, James Adams, Sir Noel Malcolm, and Simon Quinn, as well as the Reverend John Drury. The other visiting fellows that term proved to be delightful colleagues as well, especially Norman Baxter, Anthony Corbeill, Marie-Therese Flanagan, and Katherine Warner.

Alia Brahimi, of Oxford University's Changing Character of War Program, first suggested that I apply for a visiting fellowship at All Souls, and Sir Hew Strachan, the program's director and the Chichele Professor of the History of War and fellow of All Souls, was pivotal in making it possible. It was a pleasure as well to have been appointed a visiting research fellow in the Changing Character of War Program and to participate in its vibrant seminar and lecture series.

I continued writing *Anonymous Soldiers* as a Public Policy Scholar from January to August 2010 at the Woodrow Wilson International Center for Scholars in Washington, D.C. This living tribute to America's twenty-eighth president is a reminder of the wisdom and vision that resides within the U.S. Congress in having created and continued to support this remarkable institution. It was at an absolutely critical juncture in my work on this book when the Wilson Center again gave me the opportunity to return less than two years later—this time as one of its first Distinguished Scholars. I am thus beholden to the center's president during my initial time there, the Hon. Lee Hamilton, and to his successor, the Hon. Jane Harman, for the wonderful opportunity to benefit twice from the center's intellectually stimulating and collegial environment. Janet Spikes, the center's librarian, and her assistant, Dagne Gizaw, were extraordinarily helpful in locating often obscure books from the Library of Congress. During my first stint at the Wilson Center I was also remarkably lucky to have Carrie Glassner as a research assistant—one of the best I've ever worked with. My greatest debt, however, is to the center's long-standing vice president for scholars, Robert Litwak, whose unflagging support, constant encouragement, and generous friendship helped make the completion of *Anonymous Soldiers* possible.

I actually finished writing a complete draft of the book between September 2012 and October 2013 while a senior fellow at the RAND Corporation—where I first started work as a terrorism analyst more than thirty years before. My boss at the time and subsequent friend and mentor, Michael Rich, now RAND's president and CEO, very kindly arranged for me to have an office at RAND's Washington, D.C., facility; and its director, Lynn Davis, another former boss, and a mentor and friend, provided the warmest of welcomes. As in the past, RAND's exceptionally talented IT team, headed by Todd McCombs, along with two of its consummate professionals, John Osuna and Reed Stoner, were tremendously helpful in resolving all manner of computing and printing problems.

For more than a decade, I have had the honor of being associated with the U.S. Military Academy's Center for Combating Terrorism. Lieutenant Colonel Reid Sawyer, a previous executive director of the center, was an enthusiastic advocate of this project. I am grateful to him and to his successors, Colonel Kip McCormick, Lieutenant Colonel Joe Felter (Ret.), Lieutenant Colonel Liam Collins, and Major Bryan Price, for their constant support, and to their commanders, both past and present, Brigadier Generals Russ Howard (Ret.) and Michael Meese (Ret.), and Colonel Cindy Jebb, for allowing me to contribute to their mission of educating a new generation of officers thoroughly versed in the intricacies of counterterrorism and counterinsurgency.

I am very pleased as well to acknowledge the financial assistance provided by Georgetown University's George T. Kalaris Intelligence Studies Fund and the School of Foreign Service's Center for Security Studies in the preparation of this manuscript.

As a professor at Georgetown, I was able to recruit my graduate students in the Security Studies Program as research assistants to help with a variety of both mundane and more specialized research tasks. It is a pleasure finally to be able to pay tribute in this manner to the dedication and hard work of Erin Brennan, Zeke Fraint, Anna-Britt Kasupski McCabe, David King, Alexandra Knatchbull, Rebecca Lindgren, Gideon Sher, Amy Buenning Sturm, Caitlyn Turgeon, Jessica Unthank, Christopher Wall, and Martin Wolberg-Stok. Sapir Yarden, an undergraduate in the School of Foreign Service, also helped with some translations of material from Hebrew to English.

At Georgetown, I must also thank the former dean of the School of Foreign Service, Carol Lancaster, and the current interim dean, James Reardon-Anderson, for their unstinting support and friendship. Similarly, the previous and current associate directors of the Security Studies Program, Ellen McHugh and Colonel David Maxwell (Ret.), both generously took on additional responsibilities in order for me to be able to devote my attention to writing and finishing this book. Both my faculty colleagues in the program and its superlative staff were remarkably understanding and supportive as well.

Many friends played an instrumental role in any number of dimensions of this book. My deepest thanks therefore go to Christopher Andrew, Peter Bergen, David Brannan, Tim Clifford, Mark Cochrane, Hannah Cotton, David Eisenberg, Richard English, Alon Kadish, the late Peter Lipton, Sean Magee, Ari Paltiel, Ami Pedahzur, Arie Perliger, Fernando Reinares, Anders Stephanson, Calder Walton, and Ali Watson among others. Walter Laqueur deserves special mention as a dear friend and esteemed mentor who was also fascinatingly right across the street when the King David Hotel was bombed, attended Roy Farran's trial, and met many of the dramatis personae described in *Anonymous Soldiers*.

When this project was at a very embryonic stage, one of my oldest friends, Carol

Ann Bernheim, together with Benjamin Pogrund, the founder and director of Jerusalem's Yakar Centre for Social Concern, arranged to host a seminar at which I presented a paper that eventually became the book's preface. This remarkable event, which was attended by Palestinian activists and Israeli government officials, including a future ambassador to the United States, underscored for me the utility of using Britain's unhappy rule of Palestine as a case study through which to better understand how governments respond to, and are influenced by, terrorism.

On another visit to Jerusalem, Julian Barnett very kindly arranged for me to be given a private tour of Government House by Francesco Manca, an official with the United Nations Truce Supervision Organization, whose headquarters are now located there.

In an entirely different category, I remain eternally grateful to Alan Dackiw, Andrew Umhau, Assil Saleh, Vincent Desiderio, Bruce Kressel, Samuel Potolicchio, and John Gualtieri for reasons of which they each are well aware.

My old friend and colleague Daniel Byman of Georgetown University read an earlier version of this manuscript, which was nearly double the book's current length, and provided a raft of useful comments and observations. Benny Morris of Ben-Gurion University read the final version and was also extremely helpful in pointing out various minor factual errors.

Eric Lupfer of William Morris Endeavor Entertainment was an early, enthusiastic, and long-standing proponent of this project and was tireless in his efforts to find the right publisher for it. That he succeeded is evidenced by the superb editing done by Knopf's Andrew Miller; the excellent assistance with maps, photographs, and securing copyright permissions provided by Will Heyward; and the outstanding support furnished by Maria M. Massey, the book's production editor. Ingrid Sterner did a truly amazing job copyediting a long and unwieldy manuscript that had gone through three rounds of significant cuts—and the numerous inconsistencies that inevitably creates.

As is almost always the case, an author's greatest debt is to his family. The first months of writing *Anonymous Soldiers* saw the successive deaths of my father, father-in-law, and a favorite uncle. I miss them all terribly and most especially my father, who would have been very pleased to read this book.

At the end of the day, whatever I have done and whatever I might still achieve is due entirely to my wife and children, to whom *Anonymous Soldiers* is dedicated with both love and the profoundest appreciation.

Appendix

Who Was Who

The brief biographical notes below pertain to people who played a leading role in the events described in this book. The information provided is mostly relevant to the period 1917–47, although in the case of some of the leading Zionist figures, their subsequent public roles in the State of Israel are also noted.

Allenby, General Sir Edmund Henry Hynman (1861–1936). Commander in chief, Egyptian Expeditionary Force, 1917–19; promoted to field marshal, 1919.

Andrews, Lewis Yelland (1896–1937). Military service, Australian Imperial Force, 1914–20; district officer and assistant district commissioner, 1920–32; development officer, 1932–36; liaison officer, Royal (Peel) Commission on Palestine, 1936; acting district commissioner, the Galilee, 1937.

Attlee, Clement (1883–1967). Member, Parliament, 1922–50; leader, Labour Party, 1935–55; lord privy seal, 1940–42; secretary of state for the dominions, 1942–43; lord president of the council, 1943–45; deputy prime minister, 1942–45; prime minister, 1945–51.

Balfour, Sir Arthur James (1848–1930). Member, Parliament, 1874–1922; secretary of state for foreign affairs, 1916–19.

Barker, Lieutenant General Sir Evelyn (1894–1983). General officer commanding British forces, Palestine and Trans-Jordan, 1946.

Battershill, Sir William Denis (1896–1959). Chief secretary, Palestine government, 1937–39.

Baxter, Charles William (1895–1969). Head, Eastern Department, Foreign Office, 1940–47.

Beeley, Sir Harold (1909–2001). Adviser to the foreign secretary on Palestine, 1945–48; secretary, Anglo-American Committee of Inquiry on Palestine, 1946.

Begin, Menachem (1913–92). Member, Betar, 1927–39; leader, Betar, 1939; incarcerated, 1940–41; military service, Polish army in exile, 1941–43; commander in chief, Irgun Zvai Le'umi, 1943–48; founder and leader, Herut Party, 1948–77; member, Knesset, Israel, 1949–83; prime minister, Israel, 1977–83.

Ben-Gurion, David (1886–1973). Secretary-general, Histadrut, 1920; chairman, Jewish Agency Executive, 1935–48; prime minister and minister of defense, Israel, 1948–53; prime minister, Israel, 1955–63.

Ben-Yosef, Shlomo (1913–38). Member, Betar, 1937–38.

Ben-Zvi, Yitzhak (1884–1963). Chairman, Vaad Le'umi, 1931–44; president, Vaad Le'umi, 1944–49; president, Israel, 1952–63.

Bergson, Peter (Hillel Kook) (1915–2001). Member, Irgun Zvai Le'umi, 1931–39; U.S.-based emissary, Irgun Zvai Le'umi, 1940–48; member, Knesset, 1949–51.

Berlin, Sir Isaiah (1909–97). British Ministry of Information, New York, 1941–42, Washington, D.C., 1942–45, Moscow, 1945–46.

Bevin, Ernest (1881–1951). General secretary, Transport and General Workers' Union, 1922–40; member, Parliament, 1940–51; minister of labor and national service, 1940–45; foreign secretary, 1945–51.

Cassels, Major General Archibald James Halkett (1907–96). Commander, Sixth Airborne Division, Palestine, 1946.

Chancellor, Sir John Robert (1870–1952). High commissioner, Palestine and Trans-Jordan, 1928–31.

Charteris, Lieutenant Colonel Martin Michael Charles (1913–99). Director of military intelligence, Palestine, 1944–45.

Churchill, Winston Leonard Spencer (1874–1965). Member, Parliament, 1900–1922, 1924–45; secretary of state for the colonies, 1921–22; first lord of the Admiralty, 1939–40; prime minister and minister of defense, 1940–45; prime minister, 1951–55; minister of defense, 1951–52.

Creech Jones, Arthur (1891–1964). Member, Parliament, 1935–50; parliamentary undersecretary, Colonial Office, 1945–46; colonial secretary, 1946–50.

Crocker, Sir John Tredinnick (1896–1963). Commander in chief, Middle East Land Forces, Cairo, 1947–50.

Crossman, Richard Howard Stafford (1907–74). Member, Parliament, 1945–74; British delegate to the Anglo-American Committee of Inquiry on Palestine, 1946.

Crum, Bartley (1900–1959). U.S. delegate to the Anglo-American Committee of Inquiry on Palestine, 1946.

Cunningham, General Sir Alan Gordon (1887–1983). General officer commanding, East Africa Forces, 1940–41; general officer commanding in chief, Eighth Army, Middle East, 1941; commandant, Staff College, 1942; lieutenant general and general officer commanding, Northern Ireland, 1943; general officer commanding in chief, Eastern Command, 1944; general and high commissioner, Palestine and Trans-Jordan, 1945–48.

Dalton, Hugh John Neale (1887–1962). Member, Parliament, 1924–31, 1935–59; minister of economic warfare, 1940–42; president, Board of Trade, 1942–45; Chancellor of the Exchequer, 1945–47.

D'Arcy, Lieutenant General John Conyers (1894–1966). General officer commanding British forces, Palestine and Trans-Jordan, 1944–46.

Dempsey, General Sir Miles (1896–1969). Commander in chief, Middle East Land Forces, Cairo, 1946–47.

Dill, Field Marshal Sir John Greer (1881–1944). General officer commanding British forces, Palestine and Tran-Jordan, 1936–37.

Dowbiggin, Herbert (1880–1966). Inspector general of police, British Ceylon, 1913–37; adviser on police, Palestine, 1930.

Dugdale, Blanche "Baffy" Elizabeth (1890–1948). Niece of Arthur James Balfour; British Zionist; Jewish Agency political department, London, 1940–48.

Eastwood, Christopher Gilbert (1905–83). Private secretary to successive colonial secretaries, 1940–41; principal assistant secretary, Cabinet Office, 1945–47; assistant undersecretary, Colonial Office, 1947–52.

Eden, Robert Anthony (1897–1977). Member, Parliament, 1923–57; foreign secretary, 1935–38, 1940–45, 1951–55; deputy prime minister, 1951–55; prime minister, 1955–57.

Eyres, Harry Maurice (1898–1962). Consul, Eastern Department, Foreign Office, 1938–44.

Farran, Major Roy (1921–2006). Military service, World War II, Third Hussars,

Crete and Greece, 1940–41; Second Special Air Service, North Africa, Sicily, Italy, France, Norway, 1942–46; Third Hussars, Syria and Palestine, 1946; seconded to Palestine Police Force, 1947.

Fergusson, Colonel Bernard (Lord Ballantrae) (1911–80). Military service, Black Watch, 1930–35; aide-de-camp to General Wavell, 1935–37; military service, Arab Rebellion; battalion intelligence officer, Jerusalem, 1937–38; instructor, Royal Military College, 1939; military service, World War II; General Staff, Middle East Command, Cairo, 1939–41; General Headquarters Joint Planning Staff, Delhi, India, 1942; Chindits, Burma, 1942–43; director, Jungle Warfare Training School, 1944; director, Combined Operations (Military), 1945–46; assistant inspector general of training, Palestine Police Force, 1946–47.

Friedman-Yellin (Yalin-Mor), Nathan (1913–80). Member, Irgun Zvai Le'umi B'Yisrael, 1940–43; member, Lohamei Herut Yisrael high command, 1943–48; member, Knesset, 1949–51.

Gale, General Sir Richard Nelson (1896–1982). Commander, First Infantry Division, Haifa, 1946–47.

Galili, Israel (1911–86). Head, Haganah National Staff, 1946–48; member, Knesset, 1949–51, 1955–77.

García-Granados, Jorge (1900–1961). Guatemalan delegate to the United Nations Special Committee on Palestine (UNSCOP), 1947.

Gater, Sir George Henry (1886–1963). Permanent undersecretary, Colonial Office, 1942–47.

Golomb, Eliahu (1883–1945). Founding member and leader, Haganah, 1920–45.

Gort, Lord Field Marshal John Standish Surtees Prendergast Vereker (1886–1946). Chief of the Imperial General Staff, 1937–39; commander in chief, British field force, 1939–40; inspector general to forces for training, 1940–41; governor, Gibraltar, 1941–42; governor, Malta, 1942–44; high commissioner, Palestine and Trans-Jordan, 1944–45.

Gray, Colonel William Nicol (1908–88). Military service, World War II; Royal Marines, 1939–46; inspector general, Palestine Police Force, 1946–48; commissioner of police, Malayan Federation, 1948–52.

Gruner, Dov (1912–47). Member, Betar, 1938–40; military service, World War II, British army, 1941–46; member, Irgun Zvai Le'umi, 1946–47.

Gurney, Sir Henry (1898–1951). Chief secretary, Palestine government, 1946–48; high commissioner, Malayan Federation, 1948–51.

Haining, General Sir Robert Hadden (1882–1959). General officer commanding British forces, Palestine and Trans-Jordan, 1938–39.

Hall, George Henry (1881–1965). Member, Parliament, 1922–46; parliamentary undersecretary, Colonial Office, 1940–42; financial secretary, Admiralty, 1942–43; parliamentary undersecretary, Foreign Office, 1943–45; colonial secretary, 1945–46.

Hunloke, Colonel Henry Philip (1906–78). Defense security officer, Palestine, 1944–45.

Husseini, Haj Amin al- (1897–1974). Mufti of Jerusalem, 1921; president, Supreme Muslim Council, 1922–37; grand mufti of Jerusalem, 1922–48.

Isham, Lieutenant Colonel Sir Gyles (1903–76). Defense security officer, Palestine, 1945–46.

Jabotinsky, Vladimir "Ze'ev" (1880–1940). Military service, World War I, British army, 1917–19; elected representative, Zionist Organization, 1920–23; head, Betar, 1923–40; president, Revisionist Party, 1923–35; president, New Zionist Organization, 1935–40.

Katz, Samuel (1914–2008). Member, Irgun Zvai Le'umi, 1936–48; spokesman and member of high command, Irgun Zvai Le'umi, 1946–48; member, Knesset, 1949–51; adviser to the prime minister of information abroad, 1977–78.

Keith-Roach, Edward (1885–1954). Public custodian of enemy property, Palestine, 1919; first assistant secretary, Palestine government, 1920–24; assistant district commissioner, northern Palestine, 1931–37; district commissioner, Jerusalem, 1937–43.

Killearn, Lord (Sir Miles Wedderburn Lampson) (1880–1964). British ambassador to Egypt and high commissioner, Sudan, 1936–46.

Kollek, Teddy (1911–2007). Deputy head of intelligence, Jewish Agency, 1942–45; chief liaison officer to British intelligence, 1945–46; Haganah representative in Washington, D.C., 1947–48; mayor, Jerusalem, 1965–93.

Lloyd, Lord (Sir George Ambrose) (1879–1941). Colonial secretary and leader of the House of Lords, 1940–41.

Lloyd Phillips, Ivan (1910–84). Colonial administrative service, Palestine, 1938–47; district commissioner, Gaza-Beersheba, 1946–47.

MacDonald, James Ramsay (1866–1937). Member, Parliament, 1906–35; prime minister, 1924, 1929–35.

MacDonald, Malcolm John (1901–81). Son of Ramsay MacDonald; member, Parliament, 1929–35, 1936–45; colonial secretary, 1935, 1938–40.

MacMichael, Sir Harold (1882–1969). High commissioner, Palestine and Trans-Jordan, 1938–44.

MacMillan, General Sir Gordon Holmes Alexander (1897–1986). General officer commanding British forces, Palestine and Trans-Jordan, 1947–48.

MacPherson, Sir John Stuart (1898–1971). Chief secretary, Palestine government, 1939–43.

Martin, Sir John Miller (1904–91). Secretary, Royal (Peel) Commission on Palestine, 1936; private (later principal private) secretary to prime minister, 1940–45; assistant (later deputy) undersecretary, Colonial Office, 1945–65.

McConnel, Major General Douglas Fitzgerald (1893–1961). General officer commanding British forces, Palestine and Trans-Jordan, 1941–44.

Meridor, Ya'acov (1913–95). Commander in chief, Irgun Zvai Le'umi, 1941–43; deputy commander in chief, Irgun Zvai Le'umi, 1943–45; incarceration, 1945–48; member, Knesset, 1949–69, 1981–84; minister of economics and inter-ministry coordination, Israel, 1981–84.

Meyerson (Meir), Golda (1898–1978). Secretary, Women's Labour Council of the Histadrut (General Federation of Jewish Workers), 1924–28; member, Histadrut Executive Committee, 1934–46; head, Histadrut political department, 1936–46; acting head, Jewish Agency political department, 1946; head, Jewish Agency political department, 1946–48; member, Knesset, 1949–74; minister of labor, Israel, 1949–56; foreign minister, Israel, 1956–66; prime minister, Israel, 1969–74.

Monroe, Elizabeth (1905–86). Director, Middle East Division, British Ministry of Information, 1940; diplomatic correspondent, *The Observer*, 1944; British representative, United Nations Sub-commission on Prevention of Discrimination and Protection of Minorities, 1947–51; staff, *The Economist*, 1945–58.

Montgomery, 1st Viscount (Field Marshal Sir Bernard Law) (1887–1976). Commander, Eighth Infantry Division, Haifa, 1938–39; chief of the Imperial General Staff, 1946–48.

Morrison, Herbert Stanley (1888–1965). Member, Parliament, 1923–24, 1929–31,

1935–59; home secretary, 1940–45; leader, House of Commons, 1945–51; lord president of the council, 1945–51; deputy prime minister, 1945–51.

Moyne, Lord (Walter Edward Guinness) (1880–1944). Member, Parliament, 1907–31; secretary of state for the colonies and leader of the House of Lords, 1941–42; deputy minister of state, Middle East, 1942–44; minister of state in the Middle East, 1942–44.

Ormsby-Gore, William (1885–1964). Member, Parliament, 1910–38; colonial secretary, 1936–38.

Paget, General Sir Bernard Charles Tolver (1887–1961). Commander in chief, Middle East Command (later renamed Middle East Land Forces), Cairo, 1944–46.

Paglin, Amichai (1922–78). Member, Irgun Zvai Le'umi, 1939–48; chief of operations, Irgun Zvai Le'umi, 1946–48; adviser to the prime minister on counterterrorism, 1977–78.

Qassam, Sheikh 'Izz al-Din Abd al Qadir al- (1870s/1880s?–1935). Imam, al-Istiqlal Mosque, Haifa, 1921–35; marriage registrar, northern Palestine, 1929–35; rebel, 1930–35.

Raziel, David (1910–41). Member, Irgun Zvai Le'umi, 1931–41; commander of Jerusalem district, Irgun Zvai Le'umi, 1937; commander in chief, Irgun Zvai Le'umi, 1938–41.

Rymer-Jones, Brigadier John Murray (1897–1993). Inspector general, Palestine Police Force, 1943–46; commander, Scotland Yard, 1946–50.

Samuel, Sir Herbert Louis (1870–1963). Member, Parliament, 1902–18, 1929–35; Liberal Party leader, 1931–35; president, Local Government Board, 1914–15; home secretary, 1916, 1931–32; high commissioner, Palestine, 1920–21; high commissioner, Palestine and Trans-Jordan, 1921–25.

Sandström, Emil (1886–1962). Swedish delegate to, and chairman of, the United Nations Special Committee on Palestine (UNSCOP), 1947.

Saunders, Major Alan (1886–1964). Inspector general, Palestine Police Force, 1937–43.

Scheib (Eldad), Israel (1910–96). Member, Lohamei Herut Yisrael, 1942–48; member, Lohamei Herut Yisrael high command, 1943–48.

Shaw, Sir John Valentine Wistar (1894–1982). Assistant secretary, Palestine government, 1935–38; senior assistant secretary, Palestine government, 1938; departmental chief secretary, Palestine government, 1939; colonial secretary, Cyprus, 1940–43; chief secretary, Palestine government, 1943–46.

Shertok (Sharett), Moshe (1894–1965). Head, Jewish Agency political department, 1933–48; member, Knesset, 1949–65; foreign minister, Israel, 1948–56; prime minister, Israel, 1954–55.

Shuckburgh, Sir John Evelyn (1877–1953). Deputy undersecretary of state, Colonial Office, 1931–42.

Smart, Sir Walter Alexander (1883–1962). Oriental secretary (later counselor), British embassy, Cairo, 1926–45; oriental minister, British embassy, Cairo, 1945.

Smith, Trafford (1912–75). Assistant secretary, Colonial Office, 1945–48.

Stanley, Sir Oliver Frederick George (1896–1950). Member, Parliament, 1924–50; secretary of state for the colonies, 1942–45.

Stern, Abraham (1907–42). Member, Irgun Zvai Le'umi, 1931–40; founder and leader, Irgun Zvai Le'umi B'Yisrael (later renamed the Lohamei Herut Yisrael), 1940–42.

Storrs, Sir Ronald (1881–1955). Military governor, Jerusalem, 1917–20; governor, Jerusalem, 1920–26.

Tegart, Sir Charles Augustus (1881–1946). Indian Police Service, 1901–31; adviser on police, Palestine, 1938.

Wauchope, Lieutenant General Sir Arthur Grenfell (1874–1947). High commissioner, Palestine and Trans-Jordan, 1931–38.

Wavell, Field Marshal Sir Archibald Percival (1883–1950). General officer commanding British forces, Palestine and Trans-Jordan, 1937–38; commander in chief, Middle East Command, Cairo, 1939–41.

Weizmann, Chaim Azriel (1874–1952). President, British Zionist Federation, 1917–20; president, World Zionist Organization, 1920–31, 1935–46; president of Israel, 1949–52.

Wickham, Sir Charles (1879–1971). Inspector general, Royal Ulster Constabulary, 1922–45; director, British Police Mission to Greece, 1945–52.

Yezernitzky (Jeziernicky, later Shamir), Yitzhak (1915–2012). Member, Irgun Zvai Le'umi, 1937–40; member, Irgun Zvai Le'umi B'Yisrael, 1940–43; member of high command and director of operations, Lohamei Herut Yisrael, 1943–46, 1947–48; Mossad operative, 1955–65; member, Knesset, 1974–96; Speaker, Knesset, 1977–80; minister of foreign affairs, Israel, 1980–86; prime minister, Israel, 1983–84, 1986–92.

Notes

PREFACE

1. "PM: Terrorists 'Will Never Win,'" Tony Blair Archive, http://www.number10
.gov.uk/output/Page7896.asp; "Prime Minister's Address to the Nation on Terrorist Attacks on the United States, Embassy of India: Prime Minister, 14 September
2001," http://www.indianembassy.org/special/cabinet/Primeminister/pm_september
_14_2001.htm; "David Cameron on 7/7," *ConservativeHome's ToryDiary*, July 7,
2006, http:// conservativehome.blogs.com/torydiary/2006/07/david_cameron_o
.html; Hoffman (2006), 1–42.
2. *Time*, March 7, 1977; *New York Times*, Nov. 8, 1983; "Speech to Conservative
Party Conference," Margaret Thatcher Foundation, Oct. 12, 1984, http://www
.margaretthatcher.org/speeches/displaydocument.as?docid=105763; *Ha'aretz*,
June 30, 2008.
3. Quoted in Abrahms (2006), 75, 45, 76; Carr (2002), 11.
4. Fanon (1990); Hacker (1976), 10.
5. Reich (1992), 7; Hoffman (2003), 40–47; Hoffman and McCormick (2004), 243–81;
Kydd and Walter (2006), 49–80; Lake (2002), 15–29; Pape (2003), 343–61; Pape
(2005); Crenshaw (1981), 385.
6. Hyams (1974), 9.
7. Christopher Clark (2012), 367–403; Oren (2002), xiii, 1–2.
8. Andrew (1986), xvi.

CHAPTER 1: TO DIE FOR OUR NATION

1. *Daily Telegraph*, May 14, 1948; *Manchester Guardian, New York Times*, and *Washington Post*, May 15, 1948; *Palestine Post*, May 16, 1948; Collins and Lapierre
(1973), xx; Golani (2009), 210; Kurzman (1970), 237.
2. "Final Message to Palestine" (n.d.), box 6, file 1, Cunningham Papers; Sherman
(1997), 243; Collins and Lapierre (1973), xx; "A History of Government House"
(1983), 1; Keith-Roach (1994), 102–3; Goldhill (2008), 298; Kroyanker (1994),
148; Segev (2000), 342; Shepherd (1999), 1–2; *Washington Post*, May 15, 1948.
3. *Daily Telegraph*, May 14, 1948; *Manchester Guardian, New York Times, Washington
Post*, and *Scotsman*, May 15, 1948; Collins and Lapierre (1973), xx, 395; Kurzman
(1970), 237; Sherman (1997), 243; "Final Message to Palestine."
4. Hughes (2004), 6.
5. Ibid., 10–11; Fromkin (2001), 308.
6. Hughes (2004), 8–9; Fromkin (2001), 308–9; Shepherd (1999), 23; Wavell (1941),
232.

7. Hughes (2004), 11, 92–93, 105–6; author's possession; *Independent*, Dec. 10, 1992; Monroe (1963); Krämer (2008), 152; Keith-Roach (1944), 69; Wasserstein (1978), 1.

8. Fromkin (2001), 312; *Independent*, Dec. 10, 1992; Wavell (1941), 230; Hughes (2004), 107; Segev (2000), 5.

9. Morris (2001), 77; Hughes (2004), 7.

10. Krämer (2008), 155–56; Segev (2000), 22; Pappe (2004), 73; Wasserstein (1978), 1–2; Wasserstein (2003), 9–10.

11. Wasserstein (1978), 18.

12. Krämer (2008), 157; Stein (1961), frontispiece; Morris (2001), 73; Fromkin (2001), 269, 298.

13. Fromkin (2001), 297; Morris (2001), 76.

14. Antonius (1971), 164–83; Kedourie (1976), 3–4; Hurewitz (1976), 19–20; Morris (2008); Hadawi (1967), 59; Krämer (2008), 158; Segev (2000), 6.

15. Krämer (2008), 157; Sherman (1997), 42; Storrs (1939), 312; Fromkin (2001), 445; Pappe (2004), 72, 269; Morris (2001), 89; Wasserstein (1978), 24, 26–27, 58–59, 244.

16. Morris (2008), 4, 7–8; Morris (2001), 25, 40, 47–49, 52–54; Borisov (1947), 9; Dinur (1954–72), 1:113–312; Luttwak and Horowitz (1975), 6; OSS R&A Report 1014, Sept. 30, 1943, RG 226 097.3 21092, NARA; Pedahzur and Perliger (2009), 10; Schiff (1974), 2–4.

17. Perlmutter (1969), 7; Segev (2000), 130; Wasserstein (1978), 63.

18. Schechtman (1956), 293; Mitchell Cohen (1987), 142–43; Lipsky (1956), 99–105; Shlaim (1999), 11; Laqueur (1976), 339.

19. Laqueur (1976), 339–42; Fromkin (2001), 277–78; Kister (2000), 7–9; Schechtman (1956), 207–30; Pedahzur and Perliger (2009), 11; Shlaim (1999), 11; Wasserstein (1978), 44.

20. Schechtman (1956), 322–23; Segev (2000), 123–25; Laqueur (1976), 241, 279; Morris (2008), 11; Wasserstein (1978), 63.

21. Schechtman (1956), 324; Dinur (1954–72), 1:517–20; Fromkin (2001), 446–47; Morris (2008), 11.

22. Storrs (1939), 342; La Guardia (2007), 60–61; Military Intelligence Division, report, Sept. 6, 1943, RG 65, 867N.20/211, NARA.

23. Reich (1996), 578–79; Rolef (1993), 318; Morris (2001), 95; Schechtman (1956), 295.

24. OSS R&A Report 1014; Wasserstein (1978), 65; Morris (2001), 95; Schechtman (1956), 327; Meinertzhagen (1959), 82; Segev (2000), 128; Newton (1948), 133–35; Krämer (2008), 208–10.

25. Keith-Roach (1994), 71; Storrs (1939), 342.

26. OSS Report 1014; Knight (2008), 215; Morris (2001), 95–96; Wasserstein (1978), 64; Meinertzhagen (1959), 79–80; Newton (1948), 133; Segev (2000), 132–33.

27. Schechtman (1956), 338. For a detailed account of the arrest and trial, see 329–37; Fromkin (2001), 446; Morris (2001), 96; Segev (2000), 139; Wasserstein (1978), 65–69; Wasserstein (1992), 244; Schechtman (1956), 329–38; Keith-Roach (1994), 71–72; Mattar (1988), 16–18; Morris (2001), 97.

28. Bauer (1966), 182; Dinur (1954–72), 1:154.

29. Dinur (1954–72), 1:154, 667–69; Morris (2001), 99; Segev (2000), 208–20.

30. *Times*, April 27, 1920; Wasserstein (1978), 71; Meinertzhagen (1959), 79–80, 84–88.

31. Wasserstein (1978), 71–72; Wasserstein (1992), 244; Meinertzhagen (1959), 87–88.
32. Wasserstein (1992), vii–viii, 247; Fromkin (2001), 269; Shepherd (1999), 13–14; Stein (1961), 103.
33. Wasserstein (1992), 247; Bentwich (1991), 64; Shepherd (1999), 56; Sherman (1997), 55; Storrs (1939), 349.
34. Hurewitz (1976), 23–24; Sherman (1997), 11, 32; Wasserstein (1992), 252; "A History of Government House" (1983); Kroyanker (1994), 147; Goren (1998), 332; "Augusta Victoria Hospital."
35. RIIA (1976), 39; Caplan (1982), 3; Mattar (1988), 19 21; Wasserstein (1978), 92; Keith-Roach (1994), 86; Wasserstein (2003), 13; Morris (2001), 98.
36. Caplan (1982), 5; Wasserstein (1992), 255; Hadawi (1967), 58.
37. Bentwich (1977), 72; Knight (2008), 218; LeVine (2005), 144–45; Schlor (1999), 39.
38. Schlor (1999), 15; LeVine (2005), 134–36, 144, 146; Morris (2001), 45.
39. Azaryahu (2007), 37–38; Schlor (1999), 15, 40, 54; LeVine (2005), 135, 139.
40. Morris (2001), 101; Krämer (2008), 210.
41. Bentwich (1991), 69, 72; Fromkin (2001), 515; Keith-Roach (1994), 86–87; Knight (2008), 220–22; Krämer (2008), 210; LeVine (2005), 110; Morris (2001), 101; Wasserstein (1978), 100–101.
42. Wasserstein (1978), 100–102; Gilbert (1993), 11; Keith-Roach (1994), 87; Krämer (2008), 210–11; Morris (2001), 102; Wasserstein (1992), 256.
43. Porath (1974), 129; Keith-Roach (1994), 86–87; Gilbert (2007), 73; Makovsky (2007), 113–14; Wasserstein (1992), 256; Wasserstein (1978), 102–5; Caplan (1982), 10–11.
44. Porath (1974), 132.
45. Keith-Roach (1994), 84; Wasserstein (1992), 266.
46. Mattar (1988), 8–10, 25–27; Morris (2008), 6; Segev (2000), 160; Wasserstein (1978), 96–99, 143–46, 244; Porath (1974), 131.
47. Wasserstein (1978), 109; British White Paper, June 3, 1922, Cmd. 1700; RIIA (1976), app. 3, 155–59.
48. Fromkin (2001), 525; Gilbert (2007), 84–85; Makovsky (2007), 118–19; Wasserstein (1992), 260; Fromkin (2001), 525–26; Gilbert (2007), 84–85; Makovsky (2007), 118–19; Caplan (1982), 21–22; Krämer (2008), 213–14; Morris (2001), 103–4; RIIA (1976), 40–42; Wasserstein (1978), 118–19.
49. Moore (1974), 71–73; RIIA (1976), 151–55.
50. Bentwich (1932), 71; Fromkin (2001), 524; Schechtman (1956), 378–79; Meinertzhagen (1959), 106–7; Wasserstein (1978), 109; Porath (1974), 131–32.

CHAPTER 2: THE SEEDS OF TERROR

1. Knight (2008), 223–26; Keith-Roach (1994), 88; Sinclair (2006a), 16, 19–21; RIIA (1976), 43.
2. Lesch (1979), 80–83; Porath (1974), 134.
3. Bentwich (1961), 84; Keith-Roach (1994), 98; Newton (1948), 233, 235; RIIA (1976), 42–43; LeVine (2005), 109.
4. RIIA (1976), 44; Bentwich (1961), 77, 82; Migdal (1980), 29; LeVine (2005), 85; Wasserstein (1978), 159–60.
5. Friedman (1986), 290n14; Ben-Arieh (1986), 3, 8, 328; Diness (1993), 10; Mor-

dechai Eliav (1997), 21, 30, 45–46; Sanders (1983), 3–4, 11–18; Moscrop (2000), 1–4; Storrs (1939), 321.

6. Kroyanker (1994), 143–44, 146–47, 155, 157; Storrs (1939), 455–57; Keith-Roach (1994), 101; *Independent*, Dec. 10, 1992; Storrs (1939), 321–22.

7. Kroyanker (1994), 143, 146, 150, 155, 157.

8. Schlor (1999), 65, 77; LeVine (2005), 89, 100; Azaryahu (2007), 39; Storrs (1939), 443; RIIA (1976), 43.

9. Seikaly (2002), 2–7, 47, 49, 61, 72, 74; Krämer (2008), 199–200.

10. RIIA (1976), 43; Wasserstein (1978), 159–60; Schlor (1999), 62; Wasserstein (2003), 14; Gilbert (1993), 13; Porath (1974), 134, 254–55.

11. Kelly (1980), 7; Porath (1974), 265–73; Mattar (1988), 33, 35–36, 49; Krämer (2008), 216–18.

12. Keith-Roach (1994), 119.

13. *Times*, Aug. 27, 1927; Keith-Roach (1994), 117–18; Krämer (2008), 225; Wasserstein (1978), 222–23; Guinn (2006), 25–28; RIIA (1976), 44; Storrs (1939), 359, 307.

14. Storrs (1939), 359; *Times*, Aug. 27, 1927; Krämer (2008), 227; Porath (1974), 260–62, 266–67; Marlowe (1959), 113–14; Mattar (1988), 35, 38–40; Newton (1948), 236–37; Samuel (1929), 39–46; Wasserstein (1978), 131, 223–26; Keith-Roach (1994), 118–20; Bentwich (1961), 90; Morris (2001), 112–13.

15. Mattar (1988), 45; Wasserstein (1978), 226–27; Keith-Roach (1994), 120.

16. Bentwich (1961), 84; Schechtman (1961), 92, 94–95; Mattar (1988), 45; Wasserstein (1978), 227–28.

17. Mitchell Cohen (1987), 141–43; Krämer (2008), 191; Laqueur (1976), 345; Shlaim (1999), 11–12, 16.

18. Jabotinsky (2007), 42–43.

19. Mitchell Cohen (1987), 141; Schechtman and Benari (1970), 1:33–35; Kister (2000), 15; Krämer (2008), 191; Laqueur (1976), 359–61; Wasserstein (1978), 229n3.

20. Niv (1975), 1:127; Mitchell Cohen (1987), 154.

21. Keith-Roach (1994), 122; Krämer (2008), 230; Samuel (1929), 49; Schechtman (1961), 120; Schechtman and Benari (1970), 1:256; Wasserstein (1978), 229; Mattar (1988), 46.

22. Keith-Roach (1994), 122; Bell (1977), 1; Samuel (1929), 49–50, 58; Edward Horne (1982), 134; Mattar (1988), 46; Wasserstein (1978), 229–30.

23. Samuel (1929), 58–61; Newton (1948), 236–38.

24. Bentwich (1961), 91; RIIA (1976), 45; Samuel (1929), 64, 87–96, 101; Wasserstein (1978), 230–32.

25. Keith-Roach (1994), 122–23; Krämer (2008), 231.

26. Walter S. Shaw et al. to Lord Passfield (colonial secretary), report, March 12, 1930, NA, CO 733/177/4.

27. Keith-Roach (1994), 123; Bentwich (1932), 185; Wasserstein (1978), 232; Samuel (1929), 101–14; Director (Department of Health), to Lord Passfield, report, Jan. 2, 1930, NA, CO 733/180/4.

28. Horne (1982), 35, 56, 60–61, 134; Sinclair (2006a), 21–22; Wasserstein (1978), 168, 232; Keith-Roach (1994), 123; Morris (2001), 113; Shaw et al. to Passfield, report, March 12, 1930; Bentwich (1932), 186; *Times*, Aug. 26, 1929.

29. Aharon Reuven Bernzweig and Breine Zuch Bernzweig to "My dear children," letter, Sept. 2, 1929, trans. from the Yiddish by Helen G. Meyrowitz and Dr. Meyer Greenberg and published as "Hebron scroll," *Jerusalem Post*, Aug. 26, 1989; Samuel (1929), 118; Segev (2000), 325–26; *Times*, Nov. 8, 1929.

30. "Hebron scroll," *Jerusalem Post*, Aug. 26, 1989; *Times*, Nov. 8, 1929.

31. "Hebron scroll"; *Times*, Nov. 8, 1929; Wasserstein (1978), 234.
32. *Times*, Nov. 8, 1929; "Tidyings," A. E. Smith Coggins Ltd. (Autumn 1966), 35, DS.126, Cafferata Papers; Director (Department of Health), report of disturbances, Jan. 2, 1930, NA, CO 733/180/4; Samuel (1929), 120; "Hebron scroll."
33. "Hebron scroll"; Shaw et al. to Passfield, report, March 12, 1930; "Tidyings," 35.
34. J. Macqueen (senior medical officer) in Chancellor to Lord Passfield, Report on Disturbances at Motza on August 24 and Later, Jan. 2, 1930, NA, CO 733/180/4, app. Ia; Samuel (1929), 113–14, 124; Krämer (2008), 232–34; Morris (2001), 115; Segev (2000), 324; Shaw et al. to Passfield, report, March 12, 1930; Edward Horne (1982), 146–47.
35. Shaw et al. to Passfield, report, March 12, 1930; Director (Department of Health), report of disturbances, Jan. 2, 1930; *Times*, Nov. 8, 1929; Samuel (1929), 132.
36. Director (Department of Health), report of disturbances, Jan. 2, 1930; Gilbert (1993), 13; Bentwich (1961), 72.
37. Newton (1948), 239–40; RIIA (1976), 45–46.
38. RIIA (1976), 45–46.
39. Newton (1948), 241; Laqueur (1976), 49; RIIA (1976), 45–46, 48n1.
40. RIIA (1976), 49.
41. Wasserstein (1978), 233; Shaw et al. to Passfield, report, March 12, 1930; Edward Horne (1982), 137–54; note on the Palestine Police Force, Dec. 1946, NA, CO 537/2269.
42. Edward Horne (1982), 159–60; Sinclair (2006a), 29–31, 35n106, 190.
43. Sinclair (2006a), 106; RIIA (1976), 50.
44. Bowden (1977), 156; Sinclair (2006a), 190, 206; Shaw et al. to Passfield, report, March 12, 1930; COS Subcommittee, report, Nov. 1929, CAB 24/209; CP 343 (29), Nov. 28, 1929, NA, CAB 24/2-7; Edward Horne (1982), 161-63.
45. Sinclair (2006a), 190.
46. Morris (2001), 116; Keith-Roach (1994), 128–29; Laqueur (1976), 492–93; Segev (2000), 335–36; RIIA (1976), 50–55; Krämer (2008), 235.
47. RIIA (1976), 45; Morris (2001), 117; Segev (2000), 329–30; Krämer (2008), 234.
48. Porath (1974), 272; Meinertzhagen (1959), 141; Krämer (2008), 237; Mattar (1988), 50; Wasserstein (1978), 240.
49. Shaw et al. to Passfield, report, March 12, 1930; Kurzman (1983), 174; LeVine (2005), 112.
50. Bentwich (1961), 91; Wasserstein (1978), 229, 233; Dinur (1954–72), 2:299–404; Morris (2001), 119–20; Schechtman (1961), 442–43.
51. Dinur (1954–72), vol. 2, 255, 259, 292, 416; Kister (2000), 27–28.
52. Schechtman and Benari (1970), 1:289; Luttwak and Horowitz (1975), 9; Schechtman (1961), 443–44; Kister (2000), 29–31; Laqueur (1976), 374; Dinur (1954–72), 2:429–30; Niv (1975), 1:163–64.
53. Schechtman (1961), 444; Pedahzur and Perliger (2009), 12–13; Dinur (1954–72), 2:426–32; Niv (1975), 1:263–78.

CHAPTER 3: RED DAYS OF RIOTS AND BLOOD

1. Esco (1947), 2:661–62; Connell (1964), 187; Bentwich (1932), 230; Keith-Roach (1994), 137, 142–43; Marlowe (1946), 133–34; Seikaly (2002), 72–73.
2. Keith-Roach (1994), 143; Sherman (1997), 65; Shepherd (1999), 127, 136; Hurewitz (1976), 36.

3. Wauchope to Ormsby-Gore, letter, June 24, 1936, NA, CO 733/297/3; Fergusson (1970), 32; Michael J. Cohen (1978), 12; Keith-Roach (1994), 132, 195; Shepherd (1997), 38, 162, 183–85; Chaim Weizmann (1949), 2:345; Pearlman and Ben-Gurion (1965), 72.
4. Shepherd (1999), 38.
5. Esco (1947), 2:662–63; Evans (2005), 14–16; Bauer (1974), 163.
6. Gilbert (2007), 108; Hurewitz (1976), 27; Marlowe (1959), 130; McCarthy (1980), 36; Wasserstein (1979), 11; Porath (1977), 2:82; Lachman (1982), 53; Lesch (1979), 68; Esco (1947), 2:662; Marlowe (1946), 131, 136.
7. CP 343 (29), Nov. 28, 1929, NA, CAB 24/207; Shepherd (1999), 193; Lachman (1982), 56; Krämer (2008), 259; Chancellor to Passfield, letter, Feb. 22, 1930, NA, CO 733/190/5.
8. Porath (1977), 2:40–43; Marlowe (1946), 132; Laqueur (1976), 493–94; Krämer (2008), 234–35, 254–55; Edward Horne (1982), 186.
9. Edward Horne (1982), 187–90.
10. Ibid., 186–91; Porath (1977), 2:44.
11. Edward Horne (1982), 193–95; Imray (1995), 93–94; Porath (1977), 2:45; Shepherd (1999), 181–82.
12. Imray (1995), 94–95; *Time*, Nov. 6, 1933; Edward Horne (1982), 196–99; Porath (1977), 2:45.
13. Edward Horne (1982), 201–3.
14. Marlowe (1946), 133; Edward Horne (1982), 203–4; Mohammad Amin Husseini (chairman, Arab Supreme Committee) to Wauchope, letter and manifesto by the Supreme Arab Committee to the Noble Arab Nation (attached), April 27, 1936, NA, CO 733/297/2; Porath (1977), 2:45.
15. Lachman (1982), 53–54; Krämer (2008), 259; Mattar (1988), 66.
16. Krämer (2008), 260; Lachman (1982), 59–60; Lesch (1979), 108; Porath (1977), 2:133; Sayigh (1997), 2; Segev (2000), 359–61.
17. Krämer (2008), 261–62; Lachman (1982), 60; Mishal and Sela (2000), 16; Porath (1977), 2:133–34; Segev (2000), 361; Sayigh (1997), 2.
18. Krämer (2008), 259–60; Lachman (1982), 63–64.
19. Mattar (1988), 30, 67; Mishal and Sela (2000), 16; Lachman (1982), 64; Segev (2000), 361; Porath (1977), 2:133–35; Lesch (1979), 108; Krämer (2008), 262.
20. Krämer (2008), 262; Lachman (1982), 61–67; Porath (1977), 2:134–35; Segev (2000), 361–62; Esco (1947), 2:784; Marlowe (1946), 144–45.
21. Porath (1977), 2:136; Segev (2000), 362; Krämer (2008), 262–63; Lachman (1982), 71.
22. Bowden (1977), 190; Hroub (2000), 5, 11; Krämer (2008), 262; Lachman (1982), 71, 86–88; Lesch (1979), 114; Marlowe (1959), 138; Mattar (1988), 67–68; Mishal and Sela (2000), 16, 30–31, 225n4; Porath (1977), 2:136, 142; Sayigh (1997), 2; Segev (2000), 362; Esco (1947), 2:784.
23. Lesch (1979), 114; Keith-Roach (1994), 146; Bowden (1977), 190; Teveth (1987), 512, 544; Lachman (1982), 72; Porath (1977), 2:142; Segev (2000), 362.
24. H. P. Rich (deputy inspector general, CID) to John Hall (chief secretary), letter, secret PPF assessment, Dec. 14, 1935, NA, CO 733/297/1; Porath (1977), 2:137, 142; Mattar (1988), 68; Mishal and Sela (2000), 16, 225n4.
25. *Palestine Post*, April 17, 1936; Niv (1975), 1:273–74; Chen (2009), 95; Morris (2001), 128; Krämer (2008), 271.
26. *Times*, April 20, 21, and 22, 1936; Michael J. Cohen (1978), 10–12; Gilbert (1993),

18; Hillel Cohen (2009), 95; Edward Horne (1982), 206–7; Lesch (1979), 114–15, 217; Lapidot (1996), 54; Marlowe (1946), 150–51; Mattar (1988), 68; Morris (2001), 128–29; Niv (1975), 1:242; Porath (1977), 2:142, 162–64; RIIA (1976), 28–29; Simson (1937), 187–89.

27. Al-Husseini to Wauchope, letter, April 27, 1936.

28. Hillel Cohen (2009), 98.

29. Lachman (1982), 57–58; Porath (1977), 2:131–32.

30. Wauchope to Ormsby-Gore, letter, June 7, 1936, NA, CO 733/297/2; précis of General Dill's dispatch No. C.R./Pal/1026/G, Oct. 30, 1936, NA, WO 32/9401; *Palestine Post*, June 22, 1936, Esco (1947), 2:793; Mattar (1988), 74–76; Shepherd (1999), 184–85; Bowden (1977), 173; Keith-Roach (1994), 185; Simson (1937), 189, 194–95.

31. Wauchope to Ormsby-Gore, letter, June 7, 1936; *Times*, April 23 and May 2 and 6, 1936; Bowden (1975), 147; Gilbert (1993), 18–19; Keith-Roach (1994), 184–85; Morris (2001), 130–31; Porath (1977), 2:178 84; Simson (1937), 196–97.

32. Esco (1947), 2:794; Mattar (1988), 76; Keith-Roach (1994), 187–88; Wauchope to Ormsby-Gore, letter, June 7, 1936.

33. Bowden (1977), 186; Lachman (1982), 52; Morris (2001), 129; Porath (1977), 2:142; Marlowe (1946), 153; Marlowe (1959), 139–40; Hurewitz (1949), 87; Philip Jones (1979), 86; "The Most Underrated Books and Authors, from the *Times Literary Supplement*, 1977"; Simson (1937), 331; Beckett (2001), 216; Notes on Tactical Lessons of the Palestine Rebellion, 1936, March 1, 1937, NA, AIR 5/1244.

34. Wauchope to Ormsby-Gore, letter, June 7, 1936.

35. Marlowe (1946), 135; Simson (1937), 170–71, 173, 180–81, 198.

36. Simson (1937), 182, 198; Bowden (1977), 172; Edward Horne (1982), 206; précis of General Dill's dispatch No. C.R./Pal/1026/G, Oct. 30, 1936.

37. Porath (1977), 2:183–85; précis of General Dill's dispatch No. C.R./Pal/1026/G, Oct. 30, 1936; Notes on Tactical Lessons of the Palestine Rebellion, 1936, March 1, 1937; Anglo-American Committee of Inquiry, "Report of the Anglo-American Committee of Inquiry (1946), Appendix V. Palestine—Public Security"; *Times*, June 9, 1936, June 26, 1937, and July 6, 1936; Marlowe (1946), 158–63, 200; Newton (1948), 287–89; Morris (2001), 130–32; Segev (2000), 399; Hughes (2009), 322–23; RIIA (1976), 89; memorandum of comments by the high commissioner on General Dill's report on events in Palestine from Sept. 15 to Oct. 30, 1936, NA, WO 32/4178; Simson (1937), 209–11, 218–19.

38. Esco (1947), 2:797; Krämer (2008), 274.

39. Esco (1947), 2:797; Marlowe (1946), 163; RIIA (1976), 96; General Dill's dispatch, Oct. 30, 1936, NA, WO 32/9401; Mattar (1988), 79; Morris (2001), 134–35; Sherman (1997), 103.

40. Précis of General Dill's dispatch No. C.R./Pal/1026/G, Oct. 30, 1936; Esco (1947), 2:797; Marlowe (1946), 166–67; Morris (2001), 135; Porath (1977), 2:300; Notes on Tactical Lessons of the Palestine Rebellion, 1936, March 1, 1937; Michael J. Cohen (1978), 12–15; CP 225 (36), Aug. 26, 1936, NA, CO 733/297/4; app. 1, Wauchope to Ormsby-Gore, secret dispatch, Aug. 22, 1936, NA, CO 733/297/4; Simson (1937), 286; Connell (1964), 188; Hughes (2009), 319.

41. Mattar (1988), 73; Who's Who of Palestine: Jewish Politicians and Personalities, Political Reference Library, CID HQ, Jerusalem, Sept. 1944, 70, 73, 132, MSS Medit. S20 (4), Catling Papers; Teveth (1987), 543–44; Sherman (1997), 94.

42. Kurzman (1983), 210; Teveth (1987), 543–44.
43. Teveth (1987), 548–49; Bransten (1970), 82; Bar-Zohar (1968), 55.
44. Luttwak and Horowitz (1975), 12; Kurzman (1983), 210; Who's Who of Palestine, 121; Teveth (1987), 550.
45. Dinur (1954–72), 1:426–28; Samuel Katz (1968), 15; Shindler (2010), 191–92; *Times*, July 23, 1936; Levine (1991), 98; Niv (1975), 2:209, 269–76.
46. Kister (2000), 45; Niv (1975), 2:269–71; Shindler (2010), 194; Pearlman and Ben-Gurion (1965), 77; Levine (1991), 100; Schechtman (1961), 447.
47. Levine (1991), 96–97; Samuel Katz (1968), 15; Bauer (1966), 184; Niv (1975), 1:283–84, 286–87.
48. Schechtman (1961), 445.
49. Niv (1975), 1:282–84; Schechtman (1961), 444; Levine (1991), 99–100, 104; Shindler (2010), 194.
50. Levine (1991), 99–101.

CHAPTER 4: TERROR AGAINST TERROR

1. Michael J. Cohen (1978), 12–13; RIIA (1976), 90–91; Sherman (1997), 103; Teveth (1987), 556–57; *Palestine Royal Commission: Report 1937*, Cmd. 5479, 503.
2. Michael J. Cohen (1978), 12–14; Esco (1947), 2:797–98; Marlowe (1946), 173–74, 178; Mattar (1988), 80; Morris (2001), 138; Porath (1977), 2:220–21; RIIA (1976), 90–92; Sherman (1997), 105; Teveth (1987), 556–58.
3. RIIA (1976), 97; Keith-Roach (1994), 188–89; Mattar (1988), 80; Porath (1977), 2:224–25.
4. Bar-Zohar (1968), 56–58; Marlowe (1946), 178; Mattar (1988), 80; Porath (1977), 2:230; Schechtman (1961), 445–46; Golan (2003), 81; Niv (1975), 1:276–78.
5. Niv (1975), 1:276–78; Levine (1991), 102; Shindler (2010), 194.
6. Levine (1991), 103, 105; Bar-Zohar (1968), 67.
7. Levine (1991), 101, 107; Niv (1975), 1:297–99; Schechtman (1961), 447.
8. Bauer (1966), 184; Levine (1991), 107; Niv (1975), 1:298–99; Lapidot, "Restrain [*sic*] and Retaliation"; Schechtman (1961), 447–48.
9. Niv (1975), 1:298–99; Schechtman (1961), 448–51; PICME Paper 2, Aug. 30, 1943, NA, WO 169/8311; Cavendish (1990), 17; Levine (1991), 111–12; OSS R&A Report 2612, Oct. 13, 1944, RG 226, NARA; Lapidot (2001), 73–74; Bauer (1973), 14–15.
10. Niv (1975), 1:298.
11. Keith-Roach (1994), 189–90; Marlowe (1959), 142; Sherman (1997), 106; *Palestine Royal Commission: Report 1937*, 554.
12. Hillel Cohen (2009), 122–23; Hurewitz (1976), 79–80; *Palestine Royal Commission: Report 1937*, 544–48; Morris (2001), 139; Marlowe (1959), 145; Porath (1977), 2:228–32; RIIA (1976), 104–5.
13. Michael J. Cohen (1978), 34–38; Hurewitz (1976), 77–78; RIIA (1976), 105–6.
14. Krämer (2008), 284–85; Hurewitz (1976), 81; Wauchope to Dill, letter, Dec. 15, 1936, NA, WO 32/4178; Connell (1964), 187; Marlowe (1959), 184; Porath (1977), 2:233; Lachman (1982), 81.
15. *Palestine Post*, Sept. 28, 1937; *Times*, Sept. 28 and 29, 1937; Segev (2000), 7; Shepherd (1999), 117, 191; Keith-Roach to Battershill, memorandum, Oct. 9, 1937, NA, CO 935/21.

16. Keith-Roach to Battershill, memorandum, Oct. 9, 1937; Battershill to Ormsby-Gore, report, Oct. 14, 1937, NA, CO 935/21.
17. Keith-Roach to Battershill, memorandum, Oct. 9, 1937; Battershill to Ormsby-Gore, report, Oct. 14, 1937; Lachman (1982), 81–82; Marlowe (1946), 185–87; Porath (1977), 2:235–36; Keith-Roach (1994), 190; Mattar (1988), 82–83; RIIA (1976), 113; Segev (2000), 426.
18. Bowden (1977), 227–28; Porath (1977), 2:233–34; Simson (1937), 309–11.
19. Battershill to Ormsby-Gore, report, Oct. 14, 1937; Porath (1977), 2:237.
20. Précis of General Dill's dispatch No. C.R./Pal/1026/G, Oct. 30, 1936; *Palestine Post*, Oct. 29, 1937; Porath (1977), 2:238–39; *Times*, Nov. 11, 1937; Sherman (1997), 106–7.
21. Lapidot (2001), 73–74; Schechtman (1961), 449; Niv (1975), 2:17; Pearlman and Ben-Gurion (1965), 72.
22. Schechtman (1961), 450–51; Niv (1975), 2:17; Golan (2003), 84.
23. Golan (2003), 83–84; Samuel Katz (1968), 25–26; Levine (1991), 112–13; Niv (1975), 2:18–20; Schechtman (1961), 448–49; Shindler (2010), 195.
24. Levine (1991), 115–16; Niv (1975), 2:34–38.
25. Niv (1975), 2:38; Lapidot, "Restrain [*sic*] and Retaliation."
26. Niv (1975), 2:41–42.
27. *Times*, Nov. 16, 1937; Levine (1991), 117–19; Shindler (2010), 196; Narrative Despatches from the High Commissioner for Palestine to the Secretary of State for the Colonies Reporting, Sept. 26, 1937, to Dec. 31, 1938, NA, CO 935/21; Niv (1975), 2:38–42; Esco (1947), 2:876; Borisov (1947), 11; Samuel Katz (1968), 24–25, 31; Levine (1991), 119–26; Lapidot, "Restrain [*sic*] and Retaliation"; Kister (2000), 54–55; Morris (2001), 147.
28. Lectures for Recruits, n.d., 47/60 008-447, IIA; Niv (1975), 1:224; Shamir (1994), 20–21.
29. Connell (1964), 191; RIIA (1976), 116, 188, 191; Report on the Operations Carried Out by the British Forces, April 7, 1938, NA, WO 32/9401; Anglim (2005), 13; Porath (1977), 2:215–16; Sherman (1997), 108.
30. Kroizer (2004), 122; Knight (2008), 255, 268; Bowden (1977), 171; Wavell to Lord Halifax (secretary of state for war), report on the operations from Sept. 12, 1937, to March 31, 1938, April 7, 1938, NA, WO 32/9401; Marlowe (1946), 190; Edward Horne (1982), 206; Connell (1964), 192.
31. Shepherd (1999), 204; Kroizer (2004), 123.
32. Kroizer (2004), 123–24; Hughes (2009), 331; Knight (2008), 266; Segev (2000), 428; Sinclair (2006a), 107; Sinclair (2006b), 53; *Palestine Post*, Nov. 9 and 18, 1937; Shepherd (1999), 206; Philip Jones (1979), 243.
33. Sinclair (2006a), 107–10; Sinclair (2006b), 53–54; Sir Charles Tegart and Sir D. Petrie, report, Jan. 24, 1938, NA, CO 733/383 75742/38; Kroizer (2004), 118, 124.
34. Tegart and Petrie, report, Jan. 24, 1938.
35. Ibid.; Edward Horne (1982), 474; Knight (2008), 268.
36. La Guardia (2007), 405; Ashkenazi, "Beneath Mandate-Era Nazareth Fort There's a Massive Surprise"; La Guardia, "Jericho Jail Creates Own Modern History"; Knight (2008), 269; Anglim (2005), 12; Edward Horne (1982), 236; Keith-Roach (1994), 191; Kroizer (2004), 128; Segev (2000), 428–29; Sinclair (2006a), 107.
37. Keith-Roach (1994), 191; Cahill (2009), 62; Duff (1953), 168; Shepherd (1999), 212.

38. Marlowe (1959), 4; Segev (2000), 416; Shepherd (1999), 191; Clarke Papers, 590; Marlowe (1946), 191–92; Reich and Goldberg (1996), 334–35; Bar-Zohar (1968), 6; Pearlman and Ben-Gurion (1965), 75.
39. Clarke Papers, 590; Sherman (1997), 111; Rymer-Jones Papers, 114, 134; Reich and Goldberg (1996), 334; MacMichael to MacDonald, telegram, June 9, 1938, NA, FO 371/21870 75156/38; Michael J. Cohen (1978), 66–68; Hurewitz (1976), 90–91.
40. Marlowe (1946), 196–97; Hurewitz (1976), 93; Esco (1947), 2:674.
41. Borisov (1947), 13; Gurion (1950), 31; Golan (2003), 94; Marlowe (1946), 198; Segev (2000), 385; Niv (1975), 2:61–63.
42. Niv (1975), 2:61–63.
43. *Palestine Post*, May 29, 1938; Bethell (1979), 41; Gilbert (1978), 200; Golan (2003), 94; Gurion (1950), 32–33; Marlowe (1946), 198–99; Memorandum on the Comparative Treatment of the Arabs During the Disturbances of 1936–39 and of the Jews During the Disturbances of 1945 and Subsequent Years, June 19, 1947, NA, FO 371/61938 E 5862/5862/31; Niv (1975), 2:63.
44. MacMichael to MacDonald, report 8, July 14, 1938, NA, CO 935/21; petitions and appeals, June 13, 16, and 23, July 1 and 4, 1938, NA, FO 371/2188; Niv (1975), 2:63–64; Borisov (1947), 13; Gilbert (1978), 200; Gurion (1950), 36–38; Marlowe (1946), 198; Schechtman (1961), 469.
45. Ibid., 469, 473–74; Niv (1975), 2:64; Samuel Katz (1968), 35; Haber (1978), 171; Shindler (2010), 203; MacMichael to MacDonald, report 8, July 14, 1938; Bethell (1979), 41; Levine (1991), 130; Perlmutter (1987), 95; Shamir (1994), 27; Teveth (1987), 665; Golan (2003), 94.
46. Levine (1991), 130; Niv (1975), 2:68; Samuel Katz (1968), 36; Haber (1978), 119; Gurion (1950), 40; Schechtman (1961), 471, 473; Shamir (1994), 27; Shindler (2010), 204; Golan (2003), 94.
47. MacMichael to MacDonald, report 8, July 14, 1938; *Palestine Post*, June 30, 1938; Teveth (1987), 665–66; Segev (2000), 385; Kurzman (1983), 220; Pearlman and Ben-Gurion (1965), 76; Perlmutter (1987), 95.
48. MacMichael to MacDonald, report 8, July 14, 1938; Marlowe (1946), 199.
49. Schechtman (1961), 472–73; Shindler (2010), 203; Lapidot, "Restrain [*sic*] and Retaliation"; Golan (2003), 95; Niv (1975), 2:77.
50. Niv (1975), 2:73–75; Levine (1991), 130, 132, 152; Kister (2000), 56–57; "In the Service of the British Army"; Lankin (1992), 45–46.
51. Levine (1991), 1–17, 52–61.
52. Ibid., 67–68, 74–76, 81; Perlmutter (1987), 95; Lapidot, "Restrain [*sic*] and Retaliation."
53. Levine (1991), 132–33; Perlmutter (1987), 95.
54. Samuel Katz (1968), 36; Niv (1975), 2:72–73, 77; Gilbert (1978), 204; Levine (1991), 134; Schechtman (1961), 424; Schechtman and Benari (1970), 1:346, 355, 379.
55. MacMichael to MacDonald, report 9, Sept. 13, 1938, NA, CO 935/21; Niv (1975), 2:77–78.
56. MacMichael to MacDonald, report 9, Sept. 13, 1938; *Times*, July 7, 1938.
57. Debates, House of Commons, vol. 349, col. 404, June 28, 1939; MacMichael to MacDonald, report 9, Sept. 13, 1938; Marlowe (1946), 200; Niv (1975), 2:78; *Palestine Post*, July 6, 1938; *Times*, July 9, 1938.
58. *Times*, July 11, 1938; Porath (1977), 2:238; *Palestine Post*, July 10, 1938.

59. *Times,* July 11, 12, 14, 18, and 22, 1938; Niv (1975), 2:79; Porath (1977), 2:238, 364; Bauer (1973), 14.
60. *Times,* July 11, 1938.
61. Niv (1975), 2:91; MacMichael to MacDonald, report 9, Sept. 13, 1938; *Palestine Post,* July 24, 1938; *Times,* July 25, 1938; Keith-Roach (1994), 196.
62. Debates, House of Commons, vol. 349, col. 404, June 28, 1939; MacMichael to MacDonald, report 9, Sept. 13, 1938; George Wadsworth (American consul general, Jerusalem) to Secretary of State, letter, May 29, 1939, Army Intelligence, Palestine 3800, RG 165 G-2, NARA; Niv (1975), 2:79–80; *Times,* July 25, 1938; *Palestine Post,* July 26, 1938.
63. Niv (1975), 2:82, 90–91; Levine (1991), 137–38.
64. Gilbert (1987), 204; MacMichael to MacDonald, report 9, Sept. 13, 1938; *Palestine Post,* July 10 and 26, 1938; Hurewitz (1976), 92; Samuel Katz (1968), 37; Kister (2000), 558–59; Teveth (1987), 552; Levine (1991), 137; Schechtman (1961), 461–62; Segev (2000), 387.
65. Levine (1991), 136; Niv (1975), 2:93–94; *Palestine Post,* Aug. 28, 1938; Marlowe (1946), 201–2.
66. Niv (1975), 2:94, 112–13, 117–20; Schechtman (1961), 463–65; Bar-Zohar (1968), 68.

CHAPTER 5: DARK NIGHTS OF DESPAIR

1. Haining, Hostile Propaganda in Palestine in 1938, Dec. 1, 1938, NA, WO 32/4562; Hamilton (1981), 292; Anglim (2005), 13–14; Bowden (1977), 178, 207, 212.
2. MacMichael to MacDonald, telegram, June 9, 1938; MacMichael to MacDonald, telegram, Sept. 2, 1938, NA, AIR 2/3312; MacMichael to MacDonald, report 9, Sept. 13, 1938; Haining, Hostile Propaganda in Palestine in 1938; Haining to Leslie Hore-Belisha (secretary of state for war), report, April 24, 1939, NA, WO 32/9499; Bowden (1977), 233, 237; Hillel Cohen (2009), 137–39; Gilbert (2007), 141; Morris (2001), 149–50; Porath (1977), 2:238; RIIA (1976), 115; Keith-Roach (1994), 196.
3. Report on Operations, August 24, 1938, NA, WO 32/9497.
4. Report on Operations, Aug. 24, 1938, NA, WO 32/9497; Anglim (2005), 14; Hughes (2009), 352; Memorandum on the Comparative Treatment.
5. Note of conference at the Colonial Office on Sept. 7, 1938, NA, AIR 2/3312; Michael J. Cohen (1978), 66, 189; Howard (1989), 137.
6. MacMichael to MacDonald, report 10, Oct. 24, 1938, NA, CO 935/21.
7. Bowden (1977), 233–34; Keith-Roach (1994), 197; Marlowe (1946), 202; Shepherd (1999), 209.
8. Michael J. Cohen (1978), 51; Esco (1947), 2:879; Marlowe (1946), 203; Morris (2001), 150; Shepherd (1999), 210; Hurewitz (1976), 94; Keith-Roach (1994), 201; Knight (2008), 306; Sykes (1959), 131; RIIA (1976), 116.
9. RIIA (1976), 116–17; Morris (2001), 150; Porath (1977), 2:240.
10. Bowden (1977), 249; Hurewitz (1976), 94–95; RIIA (1976), 116; Porath (1977), 2:240–41; Despatch on Operations, April 24, 1939, NA, WO 32/9499.
11. Gilbert (2007), 143–44; CP 7 (39), Jan. 16, 1939, NA, CAB 24/282; Michael J. Cohen (1978), 94, 97–102; Michael J. Cohen (1988), 94, 102; Howard (1989),

127–28, 137–38; Chaim Weizmann (1949), 2:401; MacDonald to MacMichael, letter, Feb. 24, 1939, Tegart Papers, II/2; 94, 102; MacDonald to Haining, letter, Oct. 15, 1938, Haining Papers, I/2.

12. CAB 60 (38), Dec. 21, 1938, NA, CAB 23/96.
13. Gilbert (1978), 201; Porath (1977), 2:277–78; *Palestine Partition Commission: Report*, Cmd. 5854, Oct. 1938; Marlowe (1946), 150; Porath (1977), 2:280; *Palestine: Statement by His Majesty's Government*, Cmd. 5893, Oct. 1938.
14. Bauer (1973), 16–40; Michael J. Cohen (1978), 72–87, 94–102; Cabinet 60 (38), Dec. 21, 1938, NA, CAB 23/96; Porath (1977), 2:281–94; RIIA (1976), 119–26; Michael J. Cohen (1972), 169; CP 56 (39), Feb. 27, 1939, NA, CAB 24/284; CP 89 (39), April 21, 1939, NA, CAB 24/285; CP 56 (39), Feb. 27, 1939, NA, CAB 24/284; Teveth (1987), 670.
15. Bauer (1973), 20, 27; CP 56 (39), Feb. 27, 1939, NA, CAB 24/284; CP 89 (39), April 21, 1939, NA, CAB 24/285.
16. Hurewitz (1976), 100; RIIA (1976), 123–24; Chaim Weizmann (1949), 2:402, 407; Evans (2005), 683–84; Teveth (1987), 704.
17. *British White Paper: Statement of Policy*, Cmd. 6019, May 1939; *British White Paper: Summary of Land Transfer Regulations*, Cmd. 6180, Feb. 1940.
18. Hurewitz (1976), 102–3; Porath (1977), 2:292; Sherman (1997), 125; Esco (1947), 2:908; Wadsworth to Secretary of State, letter, May 29, 1939, RG 165, NARA; Anglim (2009), 15; Morris (2001), 157–58; Niv (1975), 2:233; Memorandum on the Comparative Treatment; Morris (2001), 157.
19. Krämer (2008), 294; CP 56 (39), Feb. 27, 1939, NA, CAB 24/284; CP 89 (39), April 21, 1939, NA, CAB 24/285; MacMichael to MacDonald, telegram, May 8, 1939, Cabinet 27 (39) May 10, 1939, app. 2, NA, CAB 23/99; Army Intelligence, Probable Local Reaction to Government Policy, May 15, 1939, NA, CO 733/406/75872/12.
20. Esco (1947), 2:909–10; Debates, House of Commons, vol. 347, cols. 1626–27 (MacDonald), May 18, 1939; *Palestine Post*, May 19 and 20, 1939; Niv (1975), 2:232; Teveth (1987), 719; Trevor (1948), 37–38; Bauer (1973), 66.
21. Wadsworth to Secretary of State, letter, May 29, 1939; *Palestine Post*, May 20, 1939; Esco (1947), 2:910; Teveth (1987), 719–20.
22. Laqueur (1969), 76–77; Who's Who of Palestine, 54; Bar-Zohar (1968), 62–63; Kurzman (1983), 224; Teveth (1987), 721; Bauer (1973), 47–48.
23. Teveth (1987), 722–23; Kurzman (1983), 224.
24. Bauer (1973), 53–61; Bauer (1966), 190–91; Niv (1975), 2:246–47; Segev (2000), 386.
25. Bauer (1973), 53–61; Bauer (1966), 190–91; Niv (1975), 2:246–47.
26. Teveth (1987), 721–22; Bar-Zohar (1968), 36.
27. Levine (1991), 163, 166–75; Niv (1975), 2:228–29, 232–36, 238–41.
28. Niv (1975), 2:238–41; *Palestine Post*, June 2, 1939.
29. MacMichael to MacDonald, report 3, July 21, 1939, NA, CO 935/22; *Palestine Post*, June 3, 9, and 11, 1939; Niv (1975), 2:241–42.
30. Wadsworth to Secretary of State, letter, June 28, 1939, in *FRUS, 1939*, 4:780; Wadsworth to Secretary of State, July 28, 1939, RG 165, NARA; Borisov (1947), 14–15; Tavin and Alexander (1982), 92; Stern (1978), 11–14.
31. Wasserstein (2003), 105–6; Tavin and Alexander (1982), 89–93.
32. Niv (1975), 2:247–48; Debates, House of Commons, vol. 349, col. 404 (MacDonald), June 28, 1939; Wadsworth to Secretary of State, letter, June 28, 1939,

in *FRUS*, 4:780; MacMichael to MacDonald, report 3, July 21, 1939; Wadsworth to Secretary of State, letter, July 28, 1939; *Palestine Post*, June 20, 1939; Pedahzur and Perliger (2009), 13.

33. Wadsworth to Secretary of State, letters, June 13 and 29, 1939, RG 165, NARA; Niv (1975), 2:245–46.
34. *Irgun Press*, no. 1/5, Aug. 1939, K-4 4/15, JI.
35. Debates, House of Commons, vol. 349, col. 448 (MacDonald), June 28, 1939; Memorandum on the Comparative Treatment; Morton (1957), 60; Golan (2003), 133; Ben-Yehuda (1993), 155; Niv (1975), 2:272, 275.
36. Niv (1975), 2:275–76; Morton (1957), 61; Ben-Yehuda (1993), 156.
37. Bethell (1979), 73; Levine (1991), 177; Niv (1975), 2:276, 281–82; Shindler (2010), 216–17.
38. *Palestine Post*, Sept. 4, 1939; Sykes (1965), 246.
39. "A Word of the Irgun Ha'Zvai Ha'Le'umi to the Hebrew Yishuv," in Niv (1975), 3:19; "Irgun Zva'i Leumi Statement on Crisis."
40. New Zionist Organization to Sir Harold MacMichael, letter, Sept. 5, 1939, NA, FO 371/23240; Schechtman (1961), 484–85; Niv (1975), 3:13–19; *Palestine Post*, Sept. 11, 1939; Levine (1991), 181–82; Shindler (2010), 218.
41. Baxter, minute, Jan. 31, 1939, NA, FO 371/23221.
42. Chaim Weizmann (1949), 2:405; Haining to Shuckburgh, letter, Aug. 13, 1939, NA, CO 733/395; Debates, House of Commons, vol. 347, col. 1997, May 22, 1939.
43. Hurewitz (1976), 124; Sykes (1965), 247; Eyres, minute, Oct. 11, 1939, NA, FO 371/23240 E6852/6/31.

CHAPTER 6: THE SHADOW OF DEATH

1. CID, HQ, Palestine Police, The Stern Group, Oct. 14, 1941, 47/11, HA; Bell (1977), 52; Heller (1995a), 61; Levine (1991), 183; Niv (1975), 3:15.
2. Heller (1995a), 59–60; CID, HQ, Palestine Police, Stern Group, Oct. 14, 1941; CID, HQ, Palestine Police, July 9, 1940, 97/115 S.o.I. 9, HA; Niv (1975), 3:15.
3. Heller (1995a), 60, 62–63, 66–69, 79–80; Niv (1975), 3:34–35, 39; Shindler (2010), 192; Jabotinsky (1975), 177; Shindler (2010), 196, 218; Brenner (1982), 114–15; Heller (1995b), 94–96.
4. David Brinn, "In Baghdad: The Story of David Raziel," *Jerusalem Post*, March 23, 1991; OSS R&A Report 2717, Dec. 1, 1944, RG 226, NARA; The Fighters for the Freedom of Israel, American Friends of FFI (n.d.), G-12/Z3, JI; Note on Jewish Illegal Organisations, Their Activities and Finances, MacMichael to Moyne, letter, Oct. 16, 1941, NA, FO 371/31378; Intelligence Review 13, HQ Palestine, Feb. 18, 1942, NA, WO 169/4334; Brenner (1982), 116; Frank (1963), 91; Golan (2003), 202; Heller (1995a), 84, 86; Heller (1995b), 94–95, 98–99; Hurewitz (1976), 165; Marton (1994), 48; *Ha'aretz*, Nov. 3, 1991; Shamir (1994), 32–35; Levine (1991), 185; Geula Cohen (1966), 7–8.
5. Alfasi (1991), 71; Heller (1995a), 61–62; Hurewitz (1976), 127; Levine (1991), 183–84; Niv (1975), 3:40–41; Sherman (1997), 152; Slutsky (1972), 125; Colonial Secretary, report, Jan. 1–31, 1940, WP (R) (40) 47, NA, CAB 68/4; CID, HQ, Palestine Police, Stern Group, Oct. 14, 1941; extract from PIC Paper, July 1945, NA, KV 2/2375, Jan. 22, 1946.

6. Brenner (1982), 116; Hurewitz (1976), 127; Levine (1991), 185, 187; Sherman (1997), 152; CID, HQ, Palestine Police, July 9, 1940; Heller (1995a), 62; Niv (1975), 3:34–38, 42–43; CID, Irgun Zvai Leumi (n.d.), 47/61, HA; intelligence summary, July 23, 1940, NA, WO 169/147; Bauer (1973), 133.

7. Heller (1995a), 71; Niv (1975), 3:45–46.

8. Niv (1975), 3:44; Frank (1963), 91; Baumel (2005), 8–13; Heller (1995a), 73–74.

9. Marton (1994); Geula Cohen (1966), 8; Lankin (1992); Shamir (1994), 33.

10. OSS R&A Report 2717; Intelligence Review 13, Feb. 18, 1942; Heller (1995a), 62; Shindler (2010), 189–90; Sir Isaiah Berlin, interview with the author, All Souls College, Oxford, April 1979; Golan (2003), 200; Baumel (2005), 13–14; Marton (1994), 49.

11. Bell (1977), 53; Heller (1995a), 74–75; Niv (1975), 3:47–51; Levine (1991), 188, 190; Schechtman (1961), 398; *Jerusalem Post,* March 23, 1991.

12. Levine (1991), 192; Alfasi (1991); Morton (1957), 112, 136; Geula Cohen (1966), 1, 232–33; Marton (1994), 51; Yalin-Mor (1973), 76–84; Heller (1995b), 90, 100, 103; Hoffman (2006), 5–7; Broido (1977), 198–203; Ford (1985), 224–30; Ivianski (1989), 146; Heller (1995a), 80.

13. OSS R&A Report 2717; Fighters for the Freedom of Israel; Heller (1995a), 79–80, 84, 86; Heller (1995b), 94–95, 98–99, 103; Hurewitz (1976), 165; Shamir (1994), 32–35; Shindler (2010), 145–47; Jabotinsky (1975), 177.

14. Heller (1995b), 85, 105; Heller (1995a), 83; Golan (2003), 199; Stern (1978), 58–59.

15. OSS R&A Report 2717; Geula Cohen (1966), 232–33; Frank (1963), 102–3; Heller (1995a), 79, 103; Heller (1995b), 105.

16. OSS R&A Report 2717; Geula Cohen (1966), 273; Lankin (1992), 29, 37; Shamir (1994), 23, 34; Heller (1995b), 91, 103; Marton (1994), 56.

17. Shamir (1994), 33; Marton (1994), 51–52; General Staff Intelligence, Palestine, Jan. 1–31, 1942, NA, WO 169/4334; Office of the Area Security Officer, Jaffa, "Irgun Zvei [*sic*] Leumi and the Stern Group," Aug. 22, 1941, 47/62, HA.

18. OSS R&A Report 2717; intelligence summary, Jan. 22, 1941, NA, WO 169/1037; Brenner (1982), 117; Golan (2003), 205–7; Heller (1995b), 98; CID, HQ, Palestine Police, July 9, 1940; CID, Intelligence Summary 31/41, Dec. 18, 1941, 47/125, HA; Saunders to MacPherson, Most Secret Memo: The Stern Group, Feb. 20, 1942, 47/7, HA; *Palestine Post,* Sept. 18, 1940; Hurewitz (1976), 165; Morton (1957), 112; Keith-Roach (1994), 212.

19. *Palestine Post,* Sept. 7, 8, and 11, 1940; *Times,* Sept. 22, 1940; Heller (1995a), 78; Jackson (2006), 101, 142; Sherman (1997), 153; Liddell Hart (1970), 109–11.

20. Heller (1995b), 91; Marton (1994), 50.

21. Brenner (1982), 115; Heller (1995a), 78–79; Morton (1957), 131; OSS R&A Report 2717.

22. CID, HQ, Palestine Police, Stern Group, Oct. 14, 1941; Heller (1995a), 84; Heller (1995b), 101; CID, HQ, Palestine Police, Intelligence Summary 23/40, March 21, 1940, 47/109, HA; Levine (1991), 186.

23. OSS R&A Report 2717; Shamir (1994), 34; Marton (1994), 56; Bell (1977), 64–65; Bethell (1979), 126.

24. Heller (1995a), 85–88; Marton (1994), 54–55.

25. Heller (1995a), 88; Marton (1994), 55; Nazi Report Regarding Establishment of Jewish State in Syria and Palestine, June 6, 1941, RG 59 890D.01/533, NARA.

26. Marton (1994), 55.

27. Liddell Hart (1970), 137, 172.

28. CID, HQ, Palestine Police, Stern Group, Oct. 14, 1941; General Staff Intelligence (GSI) Monthly Intelligence Summary 3, Jan. 1–31, 1942, NA, WO 169/4334; Golan (2003), 215–17, 228; Heller (1995a), 89; Hurewitz (1976), 165.

29. CID, HQ, Palestine Police, Stern Group, Oct. 14, 1941; Brenner (1982), 117; Golan (2003), 217; CID, HQ, Palestine Police, July 9, 1940; Note on Jewish Illegal Organisations; intelligence summaries, Jan. 22 and May 1, 1941, NA, WO 169/1037; Monthly Intelligence Summaries 3 and 4, Jan. 1–31 and Feb. 1–28, 1942, NA, WO 169/4334; Debates, House of Lords, vol. 123, cols. 68–69 (Lord Snell), June 2, 1942; Andrew (2009), 138; Security Summary 2, Dec. 5, 1941, NA, WO 208/1560.

30. Golan (2003), 217; Heller (1995a), 90–91; Memo: The Stern Group, Feb. 20, 1942, 47/7, HA; GSI Monthly Intelligence Summary 3, Jan. 1–31, 1942; Marton (1994), 55.

31. Memo: The Stern Group, Feb. 20, 1942; GSI Monthly Intelligence Summary 3, Jan. 1–31, 1942; Morton (1957), 136; Golan (2003), 222.

32. Golan (2003), 223–25; GSI Monthly Intelligence Summary 3, Jan. 1–31, 1942; Memo: The Stern Group, Feb. 20, 1942; SIME Summary 17, Jan. 29, 1942, NA, WO 169/1561; Heller (1995a), 96; Hurewitz (1976), 165; Morton (1957), 187.

33. Morton (1957), 110, 118, 137–40; Shamir (1994), 35; GSI Monthly Intelligence Summary 3, Jan. 1–31, 1942; Golan (2003), 224; Intelligence Review 9, Jan. 31, 1942, NA, WO 169/4334.

34. Morton (1957), 137–40; Bell (1977), 71; Golan (2003), 224; Shertok to Saunders, letter, Jan. 21, 1942, Z 4/15413 (490), CZA; Brenner (1982), 117.

35. *Ha'aretz*, Sept. 20, 2002; SIME Security Summary 17, Jan. 29, 1942; Intelligence Review 9, Jan. 31, 1942; Shertok to Saunders, letter, Jan. 21, 1942; *Palestine Post*, Jan. 27, 1942; Heller (1995a), 97.

36. Morton (1957), 141; Memo: The Stern Group, Feb. 20, 1942; Intelligence Report 12, Feb. 11, 1942, NA, WO 169/4334; *Palestine Post*, Jan. 27 and Feb. 3, 1942; Golan (2003), 226–27; Heller (1995a), 97; *Ha'aretz*, Sept. 20, 2002.

37. *Ha'aretz*, Sept. 20, 2002; Bell (1977), 71–72; Heller (1995a), 97; Keith-Roach (1994), 214; Golan (2003), 228.

38. Memo: The Stern Group, Feb. 20, 1942; Intelligence Review 13, Feb. 18, 1942, NA, WO 169/4334; Morton (1957), 144–45; *Ha'aretz*, Sept. 20, 2002.

39. Memo: The Stern Group, Feb. 20, 1942; Intelligence Summary 4, Feb. 1–28, 1942; *Palestine Post*, Feb. 13, 1942; Intelligence Summary 14, Feb. 25, 1942, NA, WO 169/4334 app. A; Fighters for the Freedom of Israel; Shamir (1994), 40–41; *Ha'aretz*, Sept. 20, 2002; Bell (1977), 72, 101n5; Bethell (1979), 128; Marton (1994), 58; Morton (1957), 146; Golan (2003), 232–33; Debates, House of Lords, vol. 123, cols. 68–69 (Lord Snell), June 2, 1942.

40. *Palestine Post*, Feb. 13, 1942; Shamir (1994), 41; Yalin-Mor (1973), 77; Bethell (1979), 128–29; Saunders to MacPherson, Memo: The Stern Group, Feb. 20, 1942, 47/7, HA.

41. OSS R&A Report 2717; Hurewitz (1976), 165–66; Bauer (1973), 132–33; Office of the Area Security Officer, Jaffa, "Irgun Zvei Leumi and the Stern Group"; New Zionist Organization's Offer a Month Ago to Cooperate in Weeding Out German Agents (n.d.), 47/111, HA; Levine (1991), 198–99.

42. Levine and Shimoni (1972), 225; Niv (1975), 3:71–73; Zweig (1986), 97; Chavkin

(2009), 30, 40–42; Dayan (1976), 42–51; Jeffery (2010), 353; Segev (2000), 452; Shepherd (1999), 216–17.

43. Saunders to Colonel Jennings, letter, June 12, 1942, NA, HS 9/1446/8; Chavkin (2009), 41; Jackson (2006), 110; Shepherd (1999), 217; Major H. Grant-Taylor (n.d.), NA, HS 9/1446/8.
44. Chavkin (2009), 41–42; Levine (1991), 198–99; Niv (1975), 3:73–74.
45. *Jerusalem Post*, March 23, 1991; Levine (1991), 198–99; Niv (1975), 3:73–74; Schechtman (1965), 95–114; Mattar (1988), 86–94.
46. Niv (1975), 3:74–76; Bauer (1973), 135; *Jerusalem Post*, March 23, 1991; Levine (1991), 200–201; Mattar (1988), 95.
47. *Jerusalem Post*, March 23, 1991; Levine and Shimoni (1972), 225; Mattar (1988), 97–107; Niv (1975), 3:76; Schechtman (1965), 114–66.
48. Niv (1975), 3:75–76; *Jerusalem Post*, March 23, 1991.

CHAPTER 7: THE REVOLT

1. CID, HQ, Palestine Police, Intelligence Summary 20/42, Nov. 2, 1942, 47/129, HA.
2. Gervasi (1979), 215; *Times* and *Independent*, March 10, 1992; Kushner (2003), 181; Begin (1977a), 123–25. According to Borisov (1947), 29, the reward was initially set at £8,000.
3. Sofer (1988), 4–7; *Jerusalem Post*, March 10, 1992; Perlmutter (1987), 11, 24; Shindler (2010), 19; "Estimated Number of Jews Killed in the Final Solution."
4. Haber (1978), 22; Hurwitz (1977), 12–13; Sofer (1979), 6; Perlmutter (1987), 34; Begin (1977b), 17–18.
5. *Independent*, March 10, 1992; Haber (1978), 23; Sofer (1988), 5.
6. OSS Report XL 18461, Subject: Biographical Information—Menahem [*sic*] Begin, Sept. 11, 1945, RG 226, NARA (an *L* or *XL* prefix to OSS documents indicates that the distribution of such material was restricted to only the U.S. government or military); Haber (1978), 24; Hurwitz (1977), 12; Perlmutter (1987), 40–41, 50, 53, 76; *Times*, *Jerusalem Post*, and *Independent*, March 10, 1992; Shindler (2010), 17; Begin (1977b), 53; Sofer (1988), 6–7.
7. Shindler (2010), 7, 184–85; Haber (1978), 46; *Jerusalem Post*, March 10, 1992; Perlmutter (1987), 57, 78; OSS Report XL 18461; Haber (1978), 47.
8. *Times*, March 10, 1992; Shindler (2010), 187, 204.
9. Shindler (2010), 206, 211; Gervasi (1979), 93–95; Haber (1978), 48–51; *Independent*, March 10, 1992; Perlmutter (1987), 85–89.
10. Shindler (2010), 7–9, 17, 215; Haber (1978), 51, 58–74; Niv (1975), 3:273; Perlmutter (1989), 103, 107–17; Gervasi (1979), 93–108, 113–24; Hurwitz (1977), 13; Sofer (1988), 11–13; Begin (1977a), 25; Begin (1977b), 128–29.
11. Begin (1977a), 23, 25; Begin (1977b), 216–18; Korbonski (1979), 375–76; Haber (1978), 85; Perlmutter (1987), 118–29; Sofer (1988), 57, 61.
12. Kochanski (2012), 191; Begin (1977a), 24–25.
13. Begin (1977a), 24–25; OSS Report XL 18461; Haber (1978), 85; Niv (1975), 3:274, 276; Sofer (1988), 57–58; Samuel Katz (1968), 83; Korbonski (1979), 376–77; Lankin (1992), 65; *Independent*, *Times*, and *Jerusalem Post*, March 10, 1992; Perlmutter (1987), 131–33.
14. Samuel Katz (1968), 82; Perlmutter (1987), 134–35; Lankin (1992), 47–60; Niv (1975), 3:270–72; Bell (1977), 56–58; Sofer (1988), 59; *Jerusalem Post*, March 10, 1992.

15. Niv (1975), 3:277; Haber (1978), 88; *Times*, July 28, 1995; Perlmutter (1987), 131–35; Shindler (2010), 218–19; Sofer (1988), 59; *Jerusalem Post*, March 10, 1992.

16. Begin (1977a), 25; Niv (1975), 3:274; Perlmutter (1987), 131–33, 135–36; Lankin (1992), 65–66; OSS Report XL 18461; Sofer (1988), 59, 62; Haber (1978), 96.

17. Hoffman (2006), 53; Marighella (1971), 61–97; Foley (1964), 47; Alistair Horne (1977), 95; Hacker (1976), 73; Wright (2006), 303; Niv (1975), 4:12.

18. Begin (1977a), 52; MacMichael to Stanley, telegram, Feb. 19, 1944, NA, FO 371/40125.

19. Begin (1977a), 38, 43 44, 16, Sofer (1988), 63; *Jerusalem Post*, March 10, 1992; Sika-Aharoni (2002), 71 (Sika-Aharoni was then a member of the Irgun who favored renewing the revolt); DSO Intelligence Summary 44, June 1–30, 1943, 47/149, HA.

20. Niv (1975), 3:276–77, 4:17; Begin (1977a), 62, 77–87; DSO Intelligence Summary 44, June 1–30, 1943; Perlmutter (1987), 144; Sofer (1988), 63; Haber (1978), 99.

21. Illegal Jewish Organisations, May 17, 1943, NA, FO 371/35034; PICME Paper 2, Nov. 8, 1944, NA, WO 169/15703; OSS Report 68179, March 30, 1944, RG 226, NARA; Pinkerton to Secretary of State, letter, Feb. 29, 1944, RG 165, box 3029, NARA; Niv (1975), 4:15; Perlmutter (1987), 141, 143, 145; Begin (1977a), 74.

22. Markovitzki (2004), 68–69; Shindler (2010), 146; Perlmutter (1987), 141; Begin (1977a), 107; Pinkerton to Secretary of State, letter, Feb. 29, 1944, RG 59, 867N.00/661, NARA; Niv (1975), 3:277–81; Haber (1978), 104–7; Tavin and Alexander (1982), 259–62.

23. PICME Intelligence Summary 21, Feb. 8, 1944, NA, PRO 169/15698; Niv (1975), 3:277, 4:11–12, 19–22; MacMichael to Stanley, telegram, Feb. 19, 1944; DSO Intelligence Summary 28, Feb. 1–29, 1944, NA, WO 169/15851; Debates, House of Commons, vol. 397, col. 1430 (Emrys-Evans), March 1, 1944; SIME Intelligence Report 171, Feb. 1, 1944, NA, WO 208/1562; OSS, R&A Report 2612, Oct. 13, 1944, RG 226 097.3 Z1092, NARA; Samuel Katz (1968), 83.

24. Niv (1975), 4:24; Debates, House of Commons, vol. 397, col. 1430, March 1, 1944.

25. Pinkerton to Secretary of State, Feb. 29, 1944, RG 165, box 3029, NARA; Shindler (2010), 219.

26. JICAME Report, April 12, 1944, RG 165, box 3025, Palestine 2710, NARA; Weekly Intelligence Review 37, Sept. 30, 1942, NA, WO 169/4334; Heller (1995a), 101, 103, 105, 107, 124; Brenner (1982), 118; CID, The Stern Group, May 4, 1942, 47/6, HA; Saunders to MacPherson, letter, June 18, 1942, CS 0/166/44, ISA; Third Infantry Division, intelligence review, Aug. 1946, NA, WO 275/57; Morton (1957), 149.

27. Shamir (1994), 38–39, 41–42; instructions issued by Saunders, May 29, 1942, CS 0/166/44, ISA.

28. JICAME Reports, March 4 and 23, 1944, RG 165, box 3031, Palestine 3810-4000, NARA; Palestine 2710, April 12, 1944, RG 165, box 3025, NARA; Shamir (1994), 38–44; Frank (1963), 124–25; Yalin-Mor (1974), 136–38; DSO Intelligence Summary 75, March 29, 1943, NA, WO 169/15851; Nov. 7 and 12, 1943, RG 226, box 31, folder 212, Washington CI and TSS Files, NARA; G-2 File Palestine 2710, Dec. 3, 1943, RG 165 Box 3025, NARA.

29. DSO Monthly Intelligence Summary 22, Aug. 1–31, 1944, NA, WO 169/9029; JICAME Report, March 1944, RG 165, box 3028, Palestine 3700, NARA; OSS R&A Report 2717; Brenner (1982), 119–20; Heller (1995a), 91; Shamir (1994), 35–38; Yalin-Mor (1974), 138–39.

30. DSO Monthly Intelligence Summary 28, Feb. 1–29, 1944, NA, WO 169/15851; Frank (1963), 116–18, 155–57; Heller (1995a), 122; Morton (1957), 167–68.

31. Heller (1995a), 104–5; interview with Professor Edward Ullendorff, Yarnton, England, Aug. 1987; Ullendorff (1988), 13, 117; Avriel (1975), 116–17; Bauer (1973), 244; Brenner (1982), 118; Frank (1963), 71, 110–11; Sherman (1997), 155–57; Wasserstein (1979), 143–57; DSO Intelligence Review 17, March 18, 1942, NA, WO 169/4334; J. S. Bennett and Sir A. Rucker, minutes, July 9, 1942, NA, FO 921/6; Bell (1977), 89–90.

32. Feb. 6, 1944, RG 226, box 31, folder 212, Washington CI and TSS Files, NARA; OSS R&A Report 2717; Debates, House of Commons, vol. 397, col. 1430, March 1, 1944; *Palestine Post*, Feb. 8, 1944.

33. SIME Intelligence Report 171; JICAME Report, April 12, 1944, Palestine 2710; McConnel to War Office, telegram, London, Feb. 23, 1944, NA, FO 371/40125; OSS R&A Report 2717; Military Attaché Report, March 18, 1944, RG 165, box 3025, Palestine 2340, NARA; Debates, House of Commons, vol. 397, cols. 1117–18 (Emrys-Evans), Feb. 25, 1944; Debates, House of Commons, cols. 1430–31, March 1, 1944.

34. MacMichael to Stanley, telegram, Feb. 25, 1944, NA, FO 921/147; Pinkerton to Secretary of State, letter, Feb. 29, 1944, 867N.00/661; SIME Intelligence Report 171; DSO Monthly Summary 28, Feb. 1–29, 1944, NA, WO 169/15851; OSS Report, March 2, 1944, RG 165, box 3035, Palestine 5940-5990, NARA; Esco (1947), 2:1040.

35. Pinkerton to Secretary of State, letter, Feb. 29, 1944, 867N.00/661; JICAME Report, March 29, 1944, RG 226, 67296, NARA; Wadsworth to Secretary of State, Washington, D.C., letter, June 29, 1939, RG 165, box 3028, Palestine 3800, NARA; Palestine Police Force Secret Report 59/1809/3/G.S., containing MacMichael to Moyne, telegram, Oct. 16, 1941, MSS Medit. S20 (210), Catling Papers; SIME Summary 2, Dec. 5, 1941, NA, WO 208/1560; DSO Intelligence Review 10, Jan. 28, 1942, NA, WO 169/4334.

36. MacMichael to Stanley, telegram, Feb. 25, 1944, NA, CO 733/456/75156/143/43; DSO Intelligence Summary 28, Feb. 1–29, 1944.

37. MacMichael to Stanley, telegram, March 24, 1944, NA, FO 371/40125 E1958/17/31; JICAME Report, March 4, 1944, RG 165, box 3031, Palestine 3810-4000, NARA.

38. OSS R&A Report 2717.

39. Thurston Clarke (1981), 28; minute of interview, Feb. 28, 1944, S 25/28, CZA.

40. Table of Contents, Rymer-Jones Papers; Cahill (2009), 65; Philip Jones (1979), 691; minute of interview, March 3, 1944, S 25/6202, CZA.

41. Minute of interview, March 9, 1944, S 25/6202, CZA.

42. OSS Report, Feb. 29, 1944, RG 165, box 3035, Palestine 5940–5990, NARA.

43. Ibid.

44. *Palestine Post*, March 23, 1944.

45. Debates, House of Commons, vol. 398, cols. 2017–18 (Stanley), April 5, 1944; JICAME Report, April 12, 1944, RG 165, box 3025, Palestine 2710, NARA.

46. JICAME Report, April 12, 1944; Niv (1975), 4:28–29; "Terrorist Outrage in Palestine" (n.d.), Cannings Papers, 2/2; *Palestine Post*, March 24 and 26, 1944.

47. JICAME Report, April 12, 1944; Niv (1975), 4:26–28; "Terrorist Outrage in Palestine"; *Palestine Post*, March 24 and 26, 1944.
48. JICAME Report, April 12, 1944; OSS Report, April 5, 1944, RG 165, box 3025, Palestine 2340, NARA.
49. JICAME Report, April 12, 1944.
50. PICME Summary 2, April 18, 1944, NA, WO 169/15699; Intelligence Notes 2, March 25, 1944, NA, WO 169/15911; OSS Report 67296, JICAME Report, March 29, 1944, RG 226, NARA.
51. OSS Report, March 2, 1944, RG 165, box 3025, Palestine 6000-6770, NARA; Nov. 12, 1943, RG 226, box 31, entry 120, Washington CI and TSS Files, NARA.
52. JICAME Report, April 12, 1944; Rymer-Jones Papers, 129; McConnel, Situation in Palestine, Jan. 11, 1944, NA, WO 169/15849; U.S. Army Intelligence (G-2), March 29, 1944, RG 165, box 3025, Palestine 2710, NARA; Sinclair (2006a), 108; Joseph and Rymer-Jones, minute of interview, March 9, 1944, S 25/6202, CZA; OSS Report, March 2, 1944, RG 165, box 3036, Palestine 6000-6770, NARA; OSS Report 67284, April 17, 1944, RG 226, NARA; Nov. 12, 1943, RG 226, box 31, Washington CI and TSS Files, NARA.
53. Pinkerton to Secretary of State, telegram, March 28, 1944, RG 59, 867 N.00/663, NARA; JICAME Report, April 12, 1944.
54. Begin (1977a), 63.
55. OSS Report 67296, March 29, 1944, RG 226, NARA.
56. C. W. Baxter (Colonial Office) to W. G. Hayter (British embassy, Washington, D.C.), letter, April 13, 1944, NA, FO 371/40125; JICAME Report, April 12, 1944; *Palestine Post*, March 26, 1944; Esco (1947), 2:1040; JICAME Report, April 4, 1944, RG 165, box 3029, Palestine 3800-5940, NARA; L. C. Pinkerton (consul general, Jerusalem) to Secretary of State, Washington, D.C., letter, March 31, 1944, RG 59 867N.00/671, NARA; minute of interview, March 27, 1944, S 25/28, CZA.
57. JICAME Report, April 12, 1944; MacMichael to Stanley, telegram, March 24, 1944; MacMichael to Stanley, telegrams, April 26 and 27, 1944, NA, CO 733/456/75156/151 A pt. I; PICME Summary 1, April 4, 1944, NA, WO 169/15699; JICAME Report 3564, March 4, 1944, RG 218, NARA.
58. Meeting at Colonial Office, March 30, 1944, NA, CO 733/456/75156/151 A; Churchill to Attlee and Eden, note, Jan. 12, 1944, NA, PREM 4 52/5; Gilbert (2007), 164, 167, 203; Makovsky (2007), 184–200; MacMichael to Stanley, telegram, April 27, 1944, NA, CO 733/456/75156/151 A pt. I; Bauer (1973), 321–22; Michael J. Cohen (1979), 359.
59. Note on Stern Group/Revisionists, April 11, 1944, Z 4/15297, CZA; "Labour Leader Demands Outlawing of Terrorists," *Palestine Post*, April 7, 1944. Identical criticism of the police had been made by Shertok at the above-mentioned meeting at the Colonial Office on March 30 (see extract of meeting at Colonial Office, March 30, 1944, NA, CO 733/456/75156/151 A) and by the Jewish Agency in 1942 and 1943. A pamphlet published in January 1942 in connection with Stern Group violence, for instance, argued that it was "the authorities who do not execute their duty [to] put an end to this terror either from fear or from a desire to divide the Jewish population [and therefore] are accountable for the innocent blood being shed." Quoted in DSO Intelligence Review 10, Jan. 28, 1942, NA, WO 169/4334; Weizmann to Martin, letter, April 12, 1944, NA, PREM 4/52/3; note on Stern Group/Revisionists, April 11, 1944; DSO Intelligence Summary 76, April 12, 1944, NA, WO 169/15851; PICME Summary 4, May 16, 1944, NA,

WO 169/15700; OSS R&A Report 2717; Pinkerton to Secretary of State, letter, Aug. 18, 1944, RG 59 867N.00/8-1844, NARA.

60. McConnel to War Office, telegram, May 8, 1944, NA, CO 733/456/75156/151 A pt. I; SIME Security Summary 181, May 11, 1944, NA, WO 208/1562; McConnel to War Office, telegram, May 9, 1944, NA, CO 733/456/75156/151 A pt. I.

61. Memorandum of conversation between Dr. Nahum Goldmann, Dr. Bernard Joseph, and Messrs. Murray, Merriam, and Wilson, Nov. 24, 1944, RG 59 867N.001/11–2442, NARA.

62. Robert Scott (Chief Secretary's Office, Jerusalem) to Bennett, letter, July 6, 1944, NA, FO 921/6.

63. DSO Intelligence Summary 83, July 16, 1944, NA, WO 169/15851; OSS Report 86556, July 20, 1944, RG 226, NARA; DSO Intelligence Summary 32, June 1–30, 1944, NA, WO 169/15851; OSS Report L39462, June 30, 1944, RG 226, NARA.

64. Office of the Counter Intelligence Corps (CIC), Beirut, Lebanon, July 10, 1944, RG 226, box 3D, folder 6, entry 120, Washington CI and TSS Files, NARA; OSS Report 86556.

65. CIC, Beirut, Lebanon, July 20, 1944, RG 226, box 32, folder 3, Washington CI and TSS Files, NARA; Lieutenant Nicholas Andronovitch (military intelligence, liaison officer, American consulate, Jerusalem) to Assistant Chief of Staff (G-2 USAFIME), memorandum, July 21, 1944, RG 226, box 32, folder 3, NARA; MacMichael to Stanley, telegram, July 27, 1944, NA, FO 921/147; *Palestine Post*, April 18, 1944; OSS Report 67296.

66. Begin (1977a), 121.

CHAPTER 8: CONSCRIPTED FOR LIFE

1. CIC, Beirut, Lebanon, July 10, 1944, RG 226, box 31, folder 6, Washington CI and TSS Files, NARA; Lieutenant Nicholas Andronovitch to Major E. M. Wright (JICAME), letter, June 23, 1944, RG 226, box 32, folder 2, NARA.

2. "Bergson Group"; Baumel (2005), 36–206; Lankin (1992) 64; Zaar (1954), 103–12.

3. OSS R&A Report 2612, Oct. 13, 1944, RG 226, NARA; *Palestine Statehood Committee Records, 1939–1949*; Baumel (2005), 200–206; "Hillel Kook (a.k.a. Peter Bergson) (1915–2001)."

4. April 2, 1944, RG 165, box 3031, Palestine 3810-4000, NARA; Baumel (2005), 17, 88–89; Hecht (1954), 523–37; Zaar (1954), 104.

5. Berlin (1972), 9; Philip Jones (1979), 13; Eyres and Hankey, minutes, March 28 and 29 and April 4 and 6, 1944, NA, FO 371/40125.

6. Pinkerton to Secretary of State, letter, March 30, 1944, RG 59 867N.00/668, NARA.

7. Frank (1963), 154–55; Heller (1995a), 122–25; Marton (1994); 52; Shamir (1994), 86; Sofer (1988), 66.

8. MacMichael to Stanley, telegram, March 26, 1944, NA, FO 921/153; JICAME Report, April 12, 1944.

9. PICME Paper 2, Nov. 8, 1944, NA, WO 169/15703; Shaw to E. B. Boyd, letter, May 22, 1944, NA, CO 733/466/75969/1; OSS R&A Report 2717; OSS R&A Report 2612, Oct. 13, 1944; *Palestine Post*, March 26, 1944.

10. OSS Report 67296; OSS R&A Report 2717; Heller (1995a), 131–32; Frank (1963), 35, 130–31; Brenner (1982), 133.

11. Heller (1995a), 122, 132–33; Yalin-Mor (1974), 189–93; Frank (1963), 131, 161–64; June 20, 1944, RG 226, box 31, folder 6, Washington CI and TSS Files, NARA.

12. European Unit, MID Branch, Subject, March 30, 1944, RG 165, box 3025, NARA; Hull to Kirk, telegram, April 5, 1944, in *FRUS, 1944*, Vol. 5 (1965), 867N.01/2299; Frank (1963), 123; Yalin-Mor (1974), 190–94.

13. Yalin-Mor (1974), 190–94.

14. Ibid.; Ben-Gurion to MacMichael, letter, Aug. 9, 1944, S 25/6828, CZA; OSS R&A Report 2717; Bell (1977), 90–91; Frank (1963), 161–69.

15. Aug. 10 and 24, 1944, RG 226, box 32, folder 2, Washington CI and TSS Files, NARA; Andronovitch to Assistant Chief of Staff, reports, Aug. 17 and 18, 1944, RG 226, box 32, folder 2, NARA; OSS Report 92897, Sept. 18, 1944, RG 226, NARA; MacMichael to Stanley, telegram, Aug. 12, 1944, NA, CO 733/457/75156/151 C.

16. OSS Report, Feb. 14, 1944, RG 165, box 3030, NARA; MacMichael to Stanley, telegram, April 26, 1944, NA, FO 921/147; PICME Paper 41, Sept. 2, 1944, NA, WO 169/15703; Boyd, minute, Feb. 21, 1944, NA, CO 733/456/75156/151A pt. 1; DSO Intelligence Summary 31, May 1–31, 1944, NA, WO 169/15851; SIME Intelligence Summary 185, June 7, 1944, NA, WO 208/1562; DSO Intelligence Summary 34, Aug. 1–31, 1944, NA, WO 169/15851; Pinkerton to Gordon Merriam (chief, Division of Near Eastern Affairs, Department of State, Washington, D.C.), letter, Sept. 29, 1944, RG 59 867N.00/9-Part 2944, NARA; Oct. 6, 1944, RG 226, folder 2, Washington CI and TSS Files, NARA; JICAME Report, Feb. 14, 1944, RG 165, box 3030, NARA; DSO Intelligence Summary 83, July 16, 1944, NA, WO 169/15851; PICME Summary 11, Aug. 22, 1944, NA, WO 169/15702.

17. MacMichael to Stanley, telegram, Aug. 29, 1944, NA, CO 733/457/75156/151C; PICME Paper 41, Sept. 2, 1944, NA, FO 921/147; copy of paper prepared for HM King Farouk, Aug. 1, 1944, NA, FO 141/981 727/18/44; King Abdullah to Tewfiq Pasha, letter, Aug. 11, 1944, NA, CO 733/461/75872/18A.

18. *Second World War* (1972), 9–10; Sykes (1965), 301, 304; Reich (1996), 357; James (1967), 396; Moyne to Foreign Office, telegram, Aug. 18, 1944, NA, CO 733/457/75156/151D.

19. MacMichael to Stanley, letter, Aug. 21, 1944, NA, CO 733/457/75156/151 C; Aug. 22 and 24, 1944, RG 226, box 32, folder 6, Washington CI and TSS Files, NARA; John R. Appleton (SACI-CIC Levant) to Chief (CIC, USAFIME, Cairo), Sept. 8, 1944, RG 226, box 32, folder 6, NARA; Debates, House of Commons, vol. 403, cols. 226–27 (Stanley), Sept. 27, 1944; *Palestine Post*, Sept. 29, 1944; PICME Intelligence Summary 11, Aug. 22, 1944, NA, WO 169/15702.

20. Moyne to Stanley, telegram, Aug. 26, 1944, NA, FO 921/153.

21. Brigadier Sir Iltyd Clayton (adviser on Arab affairs, Minister Resident's Office, Cairo), memorandum, Nov. 14, 1944, NA, FO 141/1001 1546/12/44G; C. G. Eastwood, minute, Aug. 29, 1944, NA, CO 733/457/75156/151 D; DSO Intelligence Summary 34, Aug. 1–31, 1944, NA, WO 169/15851; PICME Intelligence Summary 12, Sept. 5, 1944, NA, WO 169/15703; Aug. 22 and 18, 1944, RG 226, box 32, folder 2, Washington CI and TSS Files, NARA; Who's Who of Palestine, 147; Aug. 17, 1944, RG 226, box 32, folder 2, Washington CI and TSS Files, NARA; OSS Report 92746, Pinkerton to Secretary of State, letter, Aug. 18, 1944, RG 226, NARA; Carl Devoe (chief, Labor Section) to S. B. L. Penrose Jr. (chief SI), letter, Sept. 16, 1944, RG 226, box 73, NARA.

22. Andronovitch to Assistant Chief of Staff, Oct. 7, 1944, RG 226, box 32, folder 2, Washington CI and TSS Files, NARA; DSO Intelligence Summary 34, Aug. 1–31, 1944, NA, WO 169/15851.
23. Rymer-Jones Papers, 114, 134; *Palestine Post*, Aug. 30 and Sept. 1, 1944; Andronovitch to Assistant Chief of Staff, Sept. 1, 1944, RG 226, box 32, folder 2, Washington CI and TSS Files, NARA.
24. Rymer-Jones Papers, 129, 135; Major E. M. Wright, report, March 29, 1944, RG 165, G-2, box 3025, NARA; OSS Report L45127, Aug. 31, 1944, RG 226, NARA; Martin (2007), 153; Liddell Diary, vol. 11, Sept. 7 and 8, 1944, 30, 37–38, NA, KV 4/195; Wagner (2010), 45, 48; Kollek (1978), 38.
25. DSO Intelligence Summary 35, Sept. 1–30, 1944, NA, WO 169/15851.
26. Edward Horne (1982), 513–17, 596; Colonial Office, memorandum, Sept. 15, 1944, NA, CO 733/75015/55B/44; Rymer-Jones Papers, 124; OSS Report 67284, April 17, 1944, RG 226, NARA; Sinclair (2006b), 55–56; Begin (1977a), 117–19.
27. Shaw to Stanley, telegram, Sept. 2, 1944, NA, CO 733/477/75156/151C; PICME Intelligence Summary 13, Sept. 19, 1944, NA, WO 169/15703; Oct. 24, 1944, RG 226, box 32, folder 2, Washington CI and TSS Files, NARA.
28. DSO Intelligence Summary 35, Sept. 1–30, 1944, NA, WO 169/15851.
29. Ibid.; *Palestine Post*, Sept. 29, 1944.
30. Morton (1957), 118, 152–53, 173; DSO Intelligence Summary 35; Oct. 6, 1944, RG 226, box 32, folder 2, Washington CI and TSS Files, NARA; OSS R&A Report 2717; *Palestine Post*, Oct. 1, 1944; Bell (1977), 99; Thurston Clarke (1981), 26.
31. Oct. 6, 1944, RG 226, box 32, folder 2, Washington CI and TSS Files, NARA.
32. Thurston Clarke (1981), 25, 27–28.
33. Ibid.; Philip Jones (1979), 115; "Collection Level Description: Papers of Sir John Valentine W. Shaw"; Rymer-Jones Papers, 132.
34. Shaw to Stanley, telegram, Sept. 29, 1944, NA, CO 733/457/75156/151 F pt. 1.
35. Hankey, minute, Oct. 5, 1944, NA, FO 371/40127; Shaw to Stanley, telegram, Sept. 29, 1944, NA, CO 733/457/75156/151 F pt. 1; Oct. 24, 1944, RG 226, box 32, folder 2, Washington CI and TSS Files, NARA; William Boyd, minute, April 4, 1944, NA, CO 733/466/75969/1; General Sir Bernard Paget (commander in chief Middle East) to War Office, telegram, Oct. 3, 1944, NA, CO 733/466/75969/1; Sept. 15, 1944, RG 226, box 32, folder 2, Washington CI and TSS Files, NARA; Stanley to Shaw, Oct. 5, 1944, RG 226, box 32, folder 2, NARA.
36. WP (44) 559, Oct. 7, 1944, NA, CAB 66/56/9; WM 134 (44), Oct. 9, 1944, NA, CAB 65/44; Oct. 24, 1944, RG 226, box 32, folder 2, Washington CI and TSS Files, NARA; OSS Report L51004, Dec. 24, 1944, RG 218, NARA.
37. Oct. 24, 1944, RG 226, box 32, folder 2, Washington CI and TSS Files, NARA.
38. Shaw to Stanley, telegram, Oct. 2, 1944, NA, WO 208/1705.
39. Ibid.; Stanley to Shaw, telegram, Oct. 13, 1944, NA, FO 921/153; Shaw to Stanley, telegram, Oct. 18, 1944, NA, FO 371/40127 E6485/17/31.
40. PICME Fortnightly Summary 15, Oct. 17, 1944, NA, WO 169/15703; *Palestine Post*, Oct. 12, 1944.
41. Gilbert (2007), 164, 167, 203, 222; Vera Weizmann (1967), 194; Gilbert (1986), 744; Berlin (1972), 23, 37, 53, 57, 63; Debates, House of Commons, vol. 347, cols. 2168–69, May 23, 1939; Makovsky (2007), 184–85, 191, 200, 202–10; Ignatieff (1998), 118–19; Michael J. Cohen (1978), 162; WP (43) 178, April 28, 1943, NA, CAB 66/36.

42. WM 92 (143), July 2, 1943, NA, CAB 65/39.
43. Barnes and Nicholson (1988), 897.
44. Michael J. Cohen (1978), 167–73; P(M) (44) 6, Jan. 22, 1944, NA, CAB 95/14; WM 18 (44), Jan. 25, 1944, NA, CAB 65/45; Churchill to Attlee and Eden, note, Jan. 12, 1944; Makovsky (2007), 208–9; Ignatieff (1998), 119.
45. OSS Report 100219, Oct. 15, 1944, RG 226, NARA; PICME Monthly Intelligence Summary 16, Oct. 31, 1944, NA, WO 169/15703.
46. PICME Intelligence Summary 16, Nov. 5, 1944, NA, WO 169/15851; Rymer-Jones to Shaw, letter, Nov. 3, 1944, 47/20, HA.
47. PICME Intelligence Summary 17, Nov. 11, 1944, NA, WO 169/5703; Rymer-Jones to Shaw, letter, Nov. 3, 1944; Michael J. Cohen (1988), 167.
48. OSS Report 100219, Oct. 15, 1944, RG 226, NARA; Rymer-Jones to Shaw, letter, Nov. 3, 1944; OSS R&A Report 86, Nov. 13, 1944, RG 226, NARA; PICME Intelligence Summary 17; OSS Report L48831, Nov. 8, 1944, RG 226, NARA; Michael J. Cohen (1988), 167–68; DSO Intelligence Summary 36, Oct. 1–31, 1944, NA, WO 169/15851; Oct. 26, 1944, RG 226, box 32, folder 2, Washington CI and TSS Files, NARA; Esco (1947), 2:1046.
49. OSS Report 100219; Bauer (1973), 324–25; Borisov (1947), 34; Michael J. Cohen (1988), 159; Niv (1975), 4:97–99; DSO Intelligence Summary 86, Aug. 27, 1944, NA, WO 169/15851; PICME Intelligence Summary 12, Sept. 5, 1944; DSO Intelligence Summary 36, Oct. 1–31, 1944; Rymer-Jones to Shaw, letter, Nov. 3, 1944; Nov. 6, 1944, RG 226, box 32, folder 223, Washington CI and TSS Files, NARA.
50. Heller (1995a), 135–36; Bauer (1973), 323–24.
51. Gilbert (1986), 742–44; June 20, 1944, RG 226, box 31, folder 213, Washington CI and TSS Files, NARA; July 21, 1944, RG 226, box 31, folder 120, Washington CI and TSS Files, NARA; Aug. 10, 1944, RG 226, box 31, folder 214, Washington CI and TSS Files, NARA; An Estimate of the Possibility That the Jews in Palestine May Use Force in 1944 to Achieve Their Political Aims, PIC/86, July 19, 1944, NA, WO 208/1705; Colville (1972), 258; Liddell Diary, vol. 11, Oct. 27, 1944, 201.
52. Colville (1972), 260–61; Dec. 11, 1945, RG 226, box 31, folder 4, Washington CI and TSS Files, NARA; Colville (1972), 260–61; Sykes (1965), 308; Pearlman and Ben-Gurion (1965), 74–75; Vera Weizmann (1967), 195.
53. Gort to Stanley, telegram, Nov. 4, 1944, NA, CO 733/457/75156/151 F pt. 1; Oct. 26, 1944, RG 226, box 32, folder 2, NARA; memorandum, Nov. 2, 1944, Blenkinsop Papers.
54. DSO Intelligence Summary 56, June 9, 1943, NA, WO 169/9029; PICME Intelligence Summary 3, June 15, 1943, NA, WO 169/8310; PICME Intelligence Summary 16, apps. A and B, Oct. 31, 1944; Shaw to Stanley, telegram, Oct. 27, 1944, NA, FO 921/147; Pinkerton to Gordon Merriam (chief, Division of Near Eastern Affairs, U.S. Department of State), letter, Oct. 20, 1944, RG 59 867N.00/668, NARA; Oct. 24, 1944, RG 226, box 32, folder 2, Washington CI and TSS Files, NARA; "To the British Soldier in Palestine!" (n.d.), Fraser Papers.
55. Debates, House of Lords, vol. 123, cols. 191–93, June 9, 1942; Saidel (2012); Bar-Zohar (1968), 71; Kurzman (1983), 233–34; Michael J. Cohen (1978), 111–12; Geula Cohen (1966), 60–61; Esco (1947), 2:1030–32; Heller (1995a), 106, 123; Wasserstein (1979), 153–55; Wasserstein (1982), 77–80; DSO Intelligence Summary 91, app. A, Nov. 5, 1944, NA, WO 169/15851.
56. Sir Edward Bridges, note, Nov. 3, 1944, NA, PREM 4/52/1; Martin to Gater, letter, Nov. 4, 1944, NA, PREM 4/52/3.

57. Martin to Gater, letter, Nov. 4, 1944; The Whole of Western Palestine (short minutes of meeting held on Nov. 4, 1944), WA; Gilbert (2007), 222–25; Gilbert (1986), 1048–50; Makovsky (2007), 213–16; Chaim Weizmann (1949), 2:436–37.
58. Weizmann to Rabbi Silver, letter, Nov. 7, 1944, WA; Whole of Western Palestine.

CHAPTER 9: THE DEED

1. Frank (1963), 172, 176–78, 194; Bell (1977), 74, 93.
2. Bell (1977), 93; Frank (1963), 172–74, 180; Shamir (1994), 52–53.
3. Frank (1963), 168–69, 178, 180, 184–85, 192, 194; Bell (1977), 93; Shamir (1994), 53; Frank (1945), 64.
4. Confession of Sadovsky, pt. I3, signed Yuzbashi Miralali, April 24, 1945, O'Sullivan Papers; O'Sullivan, Murder of Lord Moyne, July 22, 1945, O'Sullivan Papers; SIME Summary 229, May 9, 1945, app. A, NA, KV 5/29; April 24, 1945, RG 226, box 31, folder 215, Washington CI and TSS Files, NARA; Frank (1963), 185–89, 194.
5. Shamir (1994), 51–52; Shamir (1995), 333; Frank (1963), 189; Heller (1995a), 137; SIME Intelligence Summary 229, May 9, 1945, app. A; Gerold Frank, "The Most Hunted Man in Palestine," *Liberty: The Magazine of a Free People*, Oct. 12, 1946, in NA, FO 371/52563 Oct. 30, 1946.
6. Confession of Sadovsky, pt. 2, p. 1 [*sic*], 2–4, April 22, 1945; Confession of Sadovsky, I4, 3, April 26, 1945; Frank (1963), 196–202.
7. Confession of Sadovsky, pt. I3, 2, April 24, 1945; Fowler, North, and Stronge (2011), 54; "Nagant Model of 1895 (Belgium-Russia)"; Confession of Sadovsky, pt. 2, p. 1 [*sic*], 3, April 22, 1945.
8. Confession of Sadovsky, pt. 2, p. 1 [*sic*], 3, April 22, 1945, pt. I5, 2, April 27, 1945, pt. I3, 2, April 24, 1945, pt. I4, 3, April 26, 1945; Fowler, North, and Stronge (2011), 54; "Nagant Model of 1895 (Belgium-Russia)"; Laboratory, Police HQ, Jerusalem, to Giles, letter, Nov. 12, 1944, NA, CAB 104/254; Russell Lewa (commandant, Cairo City Police) to His Excellency Mahmoud Ghazali Bey (director, Public Security), letter, Nov. 15, 1944, NA, CAB 104/254; Bell (1977), 99; Edward Horne (1982), 285; Morton (1957), 153.
9. Confession of Sadovsky, pt. 2, p. 1 [*sic*], 3, April 22, 1945; O'Sullivan, Murder of Lord Moyne; PICME Fortnightly Summary 13, Sept. 19, 1944, NA, WO 169/15703.
10. Confession of Sadovsky, pt. I4, 1, April 26, 1945; O'Sullivan, Murder of Lord Moyne; Frank (1963), 194; Manning (1988), 132; Bird (2010), 172; Hassan, "Lost Age of the Salon de Thé"; Sutherland (1999), 110.
11. Confession of Sadovsky, pt. I4, 3, April 26, 1945.
12. Ibid.; O'Sullivan, Murder of Lord Moyne.
13. Confession of Sadovsky, pt. I4, 3, April 26, 1945; SIME Intelligence Summary 229, app. A.
14. Confession of Sadovsky, pt. I4, 3, April 26, 1945.
15. Frank (1963), 39–44, 51–57, 69–70; Shamir (1994), 22; Bell (1977), 93.
16. Frank (1963), 209–10, 55–57, 60–61, 91–99, 114–16, 127–28, 137–40, 147, 161, 207–13; Shamir (1994), 52–53; Frank (1945), 64; Marton (1994), 97.
17. Frank (1963), 213, 220–23; Confession of Sadovsky, pt. II, p. 1 [*sic*], April 22, 1945; *Egyptian Mail* (Cairo), Jan. 12, 1945, in OSS Report 0109787, RG 266, NARA; Saidel (2012).

18. Frank (1963), 213, 222–23; *Egyptian Mail,* Jan. 12, 1945; Confession of Sadovsky, pt. I5, April 27, 1945.
19. Frank (1963), 224–225; Bell (1977), 95.
20. Confession of Sadovsky, pt. II, p. 1 [*sic*], April 22, 1945.
21. Ibid., pt. I5, April 27, 1945; SIME Intelligence Summary 229, app. A.
22. Lewa to Ghazali Bey, letter, Nov. 15, 1944; Confession of Sadovsky, pt. II, p. 1 [*sic*], April 22, 1945; Bell (1977), 99; Frank (1963), 22; Marton (1994), 96–97.
23. Frank (1963), 22–23.
24. Assistant Provost Marshal, report, Cairo, Nov. 1944, NA, FO 921/211; *Times,* Nov. 7, 1944; Bell (1977), 96–97; Frank (1963), 22–24; Frank (1945), 68; Gurion (1950), 49–50; Marton (1994), 97; Nedava (1965), 8–13.
25. *Egyptian Mail,* Jan. 12, 1945; Debates, House of Commons, vol. 404, col. 1269 (Churchill), Nov. 7, 1944; *Times,* Nov. 7 and 8, 1944; *Palestine Post,* Nov. 7, 1944; Bell (1977), 97; Frank (1963), 24–25; Frank (1945), 68; Gurion (1950), 50; Marton (1994), 97–98; Nedava (1965), 13–14.
26. *Times,* Nov. 8, 1944; Bell (1977), 97–98; Frank (1963), 25.
27. WM (44) 46, Nov. 6, 1944, NA, CAB 65/44; *Palestine Post,* Nov. 7 and 10, 1944; Frank (1945), 66; *Times,* Nov. 8, 1944.
28. Stanley to Churchill, note, Nov. 6, 1944, NA, PREM 4 51/11; Vera Weizmann (1967), 194–95; Chaim Weizmann (1949), 2:437.
29. Peter Clarke (2008), 83; Debates, House of Commons, vol. 404, cols. 1269–70, Nov. 7, 1944; *Times,* Nov. 8, 1944.
30. Weizmann to Churchill, letter, Nov. 7, 1944, Z 4/14484, CZA; Rose (1986), 396.
31. Gort to Stanley, telegram, Nov. 4, 1944, NA, CO 733/457 75156/151F pt. 1; CID Report, Nov. 14, 1944, NA, CO 733/457 75156; Lev-Ami (1978), 240.
32. CID Report, Nov. 14, 1944; A. J. Kellar, Visit to the Middle East, Feb. 4, 1945, NA, KV4/384; OSS R&A Branch 1090.86, Nov. 13, 1944, RG 226, 097.3 Z1 092, NARA; Michael J. Cohen (1988), 168–70; Slutsky (1972), 535; Statement of the Executives of the Jewish Agency and Vaad Le'umi, Nov. 7, 1944, Z 4/14484, CZA.
33. OSS R&A Branch 1090.85, Nov. 11, 1944, RG 226 097.3 Z1 092, NARA; unnamed captain (Palestine Police Force), Report on Murder of Lord Moyne, Nov. 7, 1944, NA, CAB 104/254; *Times,* Nov. 8, 1944.
34. Unnamed captain (Palestine Police Force), Report on Murder of Lord Moyne; Governorate, Cairo, to Giles, telegram, Nov. 8, 1944, NA, FO 141/1001 1546/43/44G; Debates, House of Commons, vol. 404, col. 1539 (Eden), Nov. 9, 1944; Cairo to Foreign Office, telegram, Nov. 8, 1944, NA, FO 921/209; OSS 104558 JICAME Report, Nov. 14, 1944, RG 226, NARA.
35. OSS R&A Branch 1090.85; Frank (1963), 31; Statement Given by Eliahu Beth Tzouri [*sic*] and Eliahu Hakim on Their Examination by the Procurateur General, Nov. 10, 1944, NA, FO 141/1001 1546/43/44G; Frank (1963), 31–32; translation from Hebrew, Nov. 10, 1944, NA, FO 141/1001 1546/43/44G.
36. Liddell Diary, vol. 11, Nov. 13, 1944, 249.
37. Stanley to Gort, telegram, Nov. 8, 1944, NA, WO 208/1706; Wavell (1943), 113.
38. Gort to Stanley, telegram, Nov. 10, 1944, NA, CO 733/466/75998/6; memorandum, Arms Searches in Palestine, Nov. 1944, NA, CO 733/466/75998/6.
39. WM 149 (44), Nov. 13, 1944, NA, CAB 65/44/20.
40. Cornwallis to Eden, telegram, Nov. 13, 1944, NA, CAB 104/254.
41. Clayton, memorandum, Nov. 14, 1944.
42. Smart, minute, Nov. 16, 1944, NA, FO 141/1001.

43. OSS Report L49926, Nov. 21, 1944, RG 226, NARA; Smart and Clayton, minutes, Nov. 16, 1944, NA, FO 141/1001; Steger to Secretary of State, Washington, D.C., letter, Nov. 9, 1944, RG 59, 867N.00/11–944, NARA.
44. Churchill for Stanley, note, Nov. 17, 1944, NA, CAB 127/270.
45. War Cabinet Planning Staff, JP (44) 286, Nov. 15, 1944, NA, CO 733/466/75998/6.
46. Bennett and M. I. Hamilton, minutes, Nov. 22, 1944, NA, FO 921/154.
47. Debates, House of Commons, vol. 404, cols. 2242–43, Nov. 17, 1944.
48. Gort to Stanley, telegram, Nov. 20, 1944, NA, FO 921/154.
49. OSS Report 107581; OSS R&A Report 1090.86; OSS Report L49680; Lev-Ami (1978), 241, 244; Michael J. Cohen (1979), 370; *Zionist Review*, Nov. 24, 1944; Nov. 22 and 24, 1944, RG 226, box 32, folder 223, Washington CI and TSS Files, NARA; Bar-Zohar (1968), 76; Brenner (1982), 114; Slutsky (1972), 535–36; DSO Intelligence Summary 28, Feb. 1–29, 1944.
50. Killearn to Foreign Office, telegram, Nov. 18, 1944, NA, FO 921/154; Minister Resident's Office to Eden, telegram, Nov. 19, 1944, NA, WO 208/1706; WP (44) 675, Nov. 23, 1944, NA, CAB 66/58/28.
51. Gort to Stanley, Nov. 21 and 22, 1944, NA, FO 141/1001.
52. Killearn to Eden, telegrams, both sent on Nov. 23, 1944, NA, FO 141/1001.
53. WP (44) 678, Nov. 23, 1944, NA, CAB 66/58/28.
54. WM (44) 155, Nov. 24, 1944, NA, CAB 65/48; WP (44) 678, Nov. 23, 1944, NA, CAB 66/58/28, containing annex 4; Army Council Secretariat ACSB 1198, Nov. 24, 1944, NA, WO 32/10260; Martin to Churchill, note, Nov. 20, 1944, NA, PREM 4/51/11; Stanley to Gort, telegram, Nov. 27, 1944, NA, FO 921/154.

CHAPTER 10: TEARS OF BEREAVED MOTHERS

1. WM (44) 155, Nov. 24, 1944, NA, CAB 65/48; E. E. Bridges (cabinet secretary) to Churchill, memorandum, Nov. 29, 1944, NA, CAB 127/270.
2. Rymer-Jones Papers, 129, 139, 135; WP (44) 678, Nov. 23, 1944, NA, CAB 66/58/28; Liddell Diary, vol. 11, Nov. 25, 1944, 282.
3. Stanley to Gort, telegram, Nov. 27, 1944, NA, WO 208/1706; General Sir Bernard Paget (commander in chief, MEF), Middle East Forces Review, 1945, NA, WO 169/22881.
4. Gort to Stanley, telegram, Nov. 4, 1944, NA, CO 733/457 75156/151F pt. 1; WP (44) 678, Nov. 23, 1944, NA, CAB 66/58/28; Gort to Stanley, telegram, Nov. 30, 1944, NA, AIR 20/4962.
5. Andrew (2009), 352; Andrew (1986), 489; le Carré (1979), 6–7, 10, 11, 13, 15. *Call for the Dead* was first published in 1961.
6. Walton (2008), 438; Liddell Diary, vol. 8, Aug. 25, 1943, 162, NA, KV 4/192; Liddell Diary, vol. 6, Sept. 23, 1942, 791, NA, KV 4/190; Wagner (2010), 44–45.
7. Liddell Diary, vol. 11, Sept. 7 and 26, Oct. 21, 25, and 26, and Nov. 24, 1944, 30–31, 108, 186, 191, 199, 281; Walton (2008), 438–39, 448; Wagner (2010), 32, 44.
8. Liddell Diary, vol. 9, Jan. 8, Feb. 22, and March 7, 1944, 88, 216, 256–57, NA, KV 4/193; Liddell Diary, vol. 11, Sept. 7 and 26 and Oct. 23, 1944, 30–31, 108, 191.
9. Kellar, Visit to the Middle East, 1, 19.
10. A. J. Kellar, Report on Visit to SIME and CICI Organisations, 10–11, April 1944, NA, KV 4/384; Kellar, Visit to the Middle East, 5, 8–9.

11. Kellar, Visit to the Middle East, 5, 8–9; Malatzky (1995), 31.
12. Kellar, Visit to the Middle East, 5, 8–9.
13. Ibid., 9–10.
14. Ibid., 10.
15. Ibid., 13–15.
16. Eden to Killearn, telegram, Nov. 30, 1944, NA, FO 921/154.
17. Ibid.; Gort to Stanley, telegram, Nov. 28, 1944, NA, CO 733/456 75156/143/43; Gort to Stanley, telegram, Nov. 28, 1944, NA, FO 921/147; Gort to Stanley, telegram, Dec. 1, 1944, NA, AIR 20/4962; OSS Report L49682, Nov. 11, 1944, RG 226, NARA; OSS Report L49680; OSS Report 106212, Dec. 1, 1944, RG 226, NARA; OSS Report 106841, Dec. 12, 1944, RG 226, NARA.
18. Liddell Diary, vol. 11, Dec. 9, 1944, 320; Wagner (2010), 105; Rymer-Jones Papers, 127.
19. Gort to Stanley, telegram, Dec. 7, 1944, NA, PREM 4 52/3.
20. Weizmann to Churchill, message, Dec. 18, 1944, WP (44) 746, NA, CAB 66/59.
21. Dec. 24, 1944, RG 226, box 32, folder 3, Washington CI and TSS Files, NARA; Monthly Record of Palestine Situation in the Middle East, Jan. 1, 1945, NA, WO 169/19592; Eastwood, minute, Jan. 9, 1945, NA, CO 733/457 75156/151J; DSO Intelligence Summary 96, Jan. 14, 1945, NA, WO 169/19758; OSS Report 112479, Jan. 20, 1945, RG 226, NARA; Shaw to Dawe, letter, Dec. 22, 1944, NA, CO 733/457 75156/151J; Gort to Stanley, telegram, Dec. 30, 1944, NA, CO 733/457 75156/151J.
22. Lankin (1992), 99–101, 108; Bell (1977), 133; Samuel Katz (1968), 84; Slutsky (1972), 538.
23. Shaw to Dawe, letter, Dec. 22, 1944; Bauer (1973), 320–24, 327–33; Lev-Ami (1978), 241; Brenner (1982), 126–27.
24. Bauer (1966), 203; Heller (1995a), 138; Bauer (1973), 329–30; Begin (1977a), 150–51; Frank (1963), 152–53; Lev-Ami (1978), 257; Niv (1975), 4:96–98; Giles to Shaw, letter, April 24, 1945, NA, CO 733/457 75156/151J; Slutsky (1972), 539. Kollek put the figure at closer to a thousand in Marton (1994), 100.
25. OSS Report 117056, Feb. 17, 1945, RG 226, NARA; OSS Report 121721, March 22, 1945; DSO Intelligence Summary 40, Feb. 1–28, 1945, NA, WO 169/19758; Gort to Stanley, March 1, 1945, NA, CO 733/457 75156/151J; Meridor (1955), 1–3; Feb. 16, 1945, RG 226, box 32, folder 223, NND867120, Washington CI and TSS Files, NARA; Lev-Ami (1978), 251–52; Slutsky (1972), 538, 540.
26. DSO Intelligence Summary 94, Dec. 17, 1944, NA, WO 169/15851; PICME Intelligence Summary 20, Dec. 26, 1944, NA, WO 169/15703; OSS Report 113511, Jan. 16, 1945, RG 226, NARA; Lev-Ami (1978), 246; Meridor (1955), 3; OSS Report 121721, March 22, 1945, RG 226, NARA; Begin (1977a), 152.
27. Eastwood, minute, Jan. 9, 1945, NA, CO 733/457 75156/151J; DSO Intelligence Summary 96, Jan. 14, 1945, and DSO Intelligence Summary 97, Jan. 28, 1945, NA, WO 169/19758.
28. OSS Report L52732, Jan. 27, 1945, RG 226, NARA; OSS Report 11706, Feb. 17, 1945, RG 226, NARA; DSO Intelligence Summary 40; OSS Report 113511; OSS Report 114279, Feb. 1, 1945, RG 226, NARA; OSS Report 122540, March 21, 1945, RG 226, NARA; DSO Intelligence Summary 97; OSS Report 121721; Giles to Shaw, letter, April 24, 1945.
29. PICME Intelligence Summary 23, Feb. 6, 1945, NA, WO 169/19592; DSO

Intelligence Summary 97; Gort to Stanley, telegram, March 1, 1945; OSS Report XL5863, Jan. 27, 1945, RG 226, NARA; DSO Intelligence Summary 40.

30. Gort to Stanley, telegram, March 1, 1945; Intelligence Summary 8/45 in Giles to Shaw, April 24, 1945.

31. DSO Intelligence Summary 97; PICME Intelligence Summary 23, NA, WO 169/19592; Gort to Stanley, telegram, Jan. 31, 1945, NA, CO 733/456 75156/143/43; Lev-Ami (1978), 250; Slutsky (1972), 538; OSS Report XL 5863; Bell (1977), 134.

32. Slutsky (1972), 539; OSS Research and Analysis Branch Field Memorandum 253 (FR-466), June 8, 1945, RG 84, Post Files Cairo, 800 Palestine 150, NARA; Dayan (1976), 57; interview between Giles and Kollek, June 18, 1945, S 25/6202, CZA; PICME Intelligence Summary 28, April 17, 1945, NA, WO 169/19592; OSS R&D Memorandum 253, Cairo, April 1945, RG 84, box 150, NARA; Marlowe (1959), 195.

33. Marlowe (1959), 195; PICME Intelligence Summary 28; Bauer (1966), 203–4; Bell (1977), 135–36; Niv (1975), 4:116–17; Running Diary of Political Developments in Palestine from Jan. 1, 1945, to Dec. 31, 1945, NA, CO 537/1828; Lev-Ami (1978), 254; OSS Report 136238, June 23, 1945, RG 226, NARA.

34. Whole of Western Palestine; Berlin (1972), 57, 62; interview with R. H. S. Crossman, Oct. 19, 1958, Monroe Papers; Army Council Secretariat, April 11, 1945, NA, WO 32/10260; Bauer (1973), 328–29, 350; Michael J. Cohen (1988), 172; Wasserstein (1982), 80–82.

35. Hankey, minute, Oct. 5, 1944; Whole of Western Palestine; Wasserstein (1982), 81–82; Berlin (1972), 58; Chaim Weizmann (1949), 2:438.

36. Wasserstein (1982), 82; Gilbert (1986), 1047–48; Peter Clarke (2008), 386.

37. Michael J. Cohen (1988), 172.

38. Slutsky (1972), 540.

39. Benjamin (1952), 3; Saidel (2012).

40. PICME Intelligence Summary 18, app. B, Nov. 28, 1944, NA, FO 921/154; Shamir (1994), 52.

41. Wasserstein (1982), 78–79; extract from a speech by the Late Lord Moyne in the House of Lords, June 6, 1942, NA, FO 921/154; Bar-Zohar (1968), 71; Esco (1947), 2:1029–30; Teveth (1987), 791–93; Debates, House of Lords, vol. 123, col. 198, June 9, 1942; Peter Clarke (2008), 90–91.

42. Sykes (1965), 305.

43. Benjamin (1952), 3–4; Geula Cohen (1966), 60–61; Yalin-Mor (1974), 213; Golan (2003), 280; Gurion (1950), 48–49; Marton (1994), 94; Shamir (1994), 52; WM 21 (44), June 1, 1944, NA, CAB 65/42/29, where the countries stated are Yugoslavia, Romania, Czechoslovakia, and Poland while Hungary is not mentioned; Foreign Office to Ankara, telegram, June 3, 1944, NA, FO 921/227; Weissberg (1958), 167; Foreign Office to Washington, telegram, July 19, 1944, NA, FO 921/228, for details of Eichmann's offer and Brand's role in communicating it; Wasserstein (1982), 77–80.

44. Confession of Sadovsky, pt. I5, 13, April 27, 1945; Statement Given by Eliahu Beth Tzouri [*sic*] and Eliahu Hakim, Nov. 10, 1944; Frank (1963), 31–32.

45. Marton (1994), 95, 96–97; *Svivot* (1990), 156–57; Zaar (1954), 115; Benjamin (1952), 4; Esco (1947), 2:1048–49.

46. Eliahu Bet-Tsouri to M. Bethzoury, letter, Nov. 15, 1944, NA, FO 921/211; Hakim to parents, letter, Dec. 1944, NA, FO 921/211; report from the comman-

dant of the Cairo City Police on interrogation of prisoners, Nov. 8, 1944, NA, FO 921/209; OSS Report 104558; OSS Report 115394, Feb. 17, 1945, RG 226, NARA.

47. Bet-Tsouri to M. Bethzoury, letter, Nov. 15, 1944; Hakim to parents, letter, Dec. 1944; OSS Report L52842, Jan. 17, 1945, RG 226, NARA; PICME Intelligence Summary 23.

48. *Egyptian Mail*, Jan. 11 and 12, 1945, and *Egyptian Gazette* (Cairo), Jan. 11, 1945, in OSS 0109787 NND 750140 (n.d.), RG 226, NARA; Frank (1945), 66, 68; Bell (1977), 97; Frank (1963), 24–25; Shamir (1994), 52–53; OSS Report 112099, Jan. 16, 1945, RG 226, NARA

49. Frank (1966), 244, 252; *Egyptian Gazette*, Jan. 14, 1945; Frank (1945), 69; Shamir (1994), 54.

50. Major Branch to Director, British Military Censorship, letter, Jan. 12, 1945, NA, FO 141/1006; OSS Report 112099; *Egyptian Gazette*, Jan. 15, 1945, in OSS Report 0109787.

51. Churchill to Eden, note, Dec. 3, 1944, NA, PREM 4 51/11; Eden to Killearn, telegram, Dec. 5, 1944, NA, FO 141/1001; Michael J. Cohen (1988), 161–62.

52. Churchill to Eden, note, Dec. 3, 1944; Eden to Killearn, telegrams, Dec. 5, 1944, and Jan. 28, 1945, NA, FO 141/1001; Killearn to Eden, telegram, Feb. 9, 1945, NA, PREM 4 51/11.

53. Killearn to Eden, telegram, Feb. 9, 1945; extract from telegram 296, Killearn to Foreign Office, Feb. 9, 1945, NA, KV 5/29; Churchill and Eden to Killearn, telegram, Feb. 12, 1945, NA, KV 5/29.

54. O'Sullivan, Murder of Lord Moyne; SIME Summary 229, May 9, 1945, app. A; telegram 296, Feb. 9, 1945; April 24, 1945, RG 266, box 31, Washington CI and TSS Files, NARA; Bell (1977), 100.

55. Wasserstein (1982), 76n23; Shamir (1994), 55; Golan (2003), 280.

56. Hakim to parents, letter, Dec. 1944.

57. *New York Times*, June 19 and 26, 1975; *Times*, June 26 and 27, 1975; Shamir (1994), 55.

CHAPTER 11: WIDER HORIZONS

1. Giles to Shaw, top secret letter, May 26, 1945, RG 226, box 32, folder 223, Washington CI and TSS Files, NARA; Vera Weizmann (1967), 199; Gilbert (2007), 242; *Palestine Post*, May 9, 1945; Colonel Oliver Stanley, speech to the Foreign Policy Association, New York City, Jan. 19, 1945, CS POL/5/45, ISA; Chaim Weizmann (1949), 2:434–35; Makovsky (2007), 224–25.

2. Army Council Secretariat ACSB1398, Brief for the Colonial Secretary, April 11, 1945, NA, WO 32/10260; Peter Clarke (2008), 84–93, 387–88; Morrison to Churchill, note, Feb. 26, 1945, NA, PREM 4/51/2; Douglas Harris (reconstruction commissioner, Palestine), memorandum, Aug. 1945, NA, FO 371/45379; Bullock (1983), 172; Colville (1987), 246; Gilbert (1988), 8:15.

3. Begin (1977a), 177.

4. Gort to Stanley, telegram, May 30, 1945, NA, CO 733/456/75156/43/143; extract from SIME Intelligence Report 230, June 3, 1945, NA, KV 5/29; Andronovitch to Assistant Chief of Staff, May 17, 1945, RG 226, box 32, folder 3, Washington CI and TSS Files, NARA; Edward Horne (1982), 291; Niv (1975), 4:162–64; Shertok

to Weizmann, memorandum of interview with Scott, May 22, 1945, Z 4 15/252, CZA; Gort to Stanley, telegram, May 23, 1945, NA, CO 733/457/75156/151J; Mathieson to Kellar, letter, July 15, 1946, containing Palestine: Terrorist Outrages, 1945–46, 1, NA, CO 537/1715.

5. Intelligence Summary 1, May 19, 1945, NA, WO 169/19744; Hunloke to Kellar, telegram, May 15, 1945, NA, KV 5/34; Eastwood to Dawe, note, May 15, 1945, NA, CO 733/456/75156/151A pt. 1; Paget, Middle East Forces Review, 1945, 11; Andronovitch to Assistant Chief of Staff, May 17, 1945; OSS Report 130559, May 19, 1945, RG 226, NARA; extract from SIME Intelligence Summary 230; Begin (1977a), 55; Niv (1975), 4:163; Trevor (1948), 131.

6. Underwood to Kellar, telegram, May 15, 1945, NA, KV 5/34; Hunloke to Kellar, telegram, May 15, 1945; Mathieson to Kellar, letter, July 15, 1946; Andronovitch to Assistant Chief of Staff, G-2 USAFIME, May 17, 1945.

7. Liddell Diary, vol. 12, April 14, 1945, 244, NA, KV 4/196; War Cabinet COS Committee, Dec. 1, 1944, NA, AIR 20/4959 COS (44) 861 (0); NA, AIR 20/4959 COS (44) 861 (0), app. B; SIME Intelligence Summary 221, Feb. 2, 1944, NA, KV 5/34; Willestead to Kellar, letter, Feb. 28, 1945, NA, KV 5/34; Joint Intelligence Committee assessment, Jan. 11, 1945, in OSS Report XL8799, April 28, 1945, RG 226, NARA; Jan. 23, 1945, NA, PREM 3 296/9 COS Committee COS (45) 63 (0).

8. Gort to Stanley, telegram, March 20, 1945; Rymer-Jones to Eastwood, letter, April 16, 1945; Gort to Stanley, telegram, June 3, 1945; Stanley to Gort, June 15, 1945; Rymer-Jones to Eastwood, letter, June 15, 1945. All in NA, CO 733/451 75015/55B.

9. Paget to COS, telegram, Jan. 8, 1945, NA, CO 968/96/2; Joint Planning Staff, report, Jan. 18, 1945, JP (45) 30 (Final), NA, CO 968/96/2; Colonel W. R. Rolleston, minute, Jan. 16, 1945, NA, CO 968/96/2.

10. Rolleston, minute, Jan. 16, 1945; Joint Planning Staff, report, Jan. 18, 1945.

11. Eastwood, minute, Jan. 18, 1945, NA, CO 968/96/2; Joint Planning Staff, JP (45) 30 (Final), Feb. 15, 1945, NA, AIR 20/4959.

12. E. E. Sabben-Clare, minute, Feb. 8, 1945, NA, CO 968/96/2.

13. Gort to Stanley, telegram, May 30, 1945, NA, CO 733/456 75156/43/143; Esco (1947), 2:1049–50; Vera Weizmann (1967), 199; Gilbert (2007), 242; Joint Intelligence Committee, Jan. 11, 1945, in OSS Report XL8799; Trevor (1948), 142–43.

14. Giles to Shaw, letter, April 24, 1945, NA, CO 733/457 75156/151J; Lev-Ami (1978), 256; Andronovitch to Assistant Chief of Staff, letter, June 19, 1945, RG 226, box 32, Washington CI and TSS Files, NARA.

15. Shertok to Weizmann, memorandum of interview with Scott, May 22, 1945; OSS R&A Memorandum 253.

16. Shertok to Weizmann, memorandum of interview with Scott, May 22, 1945.

17. Ibid.; interview between Giles and Kollek, June 18, 1945.

18. Weizmann to Churchill, letter, May 22, 1945, WA; Churchill to Weizmann, letter, June 8, 1945, WA; Weizmann to Churchill, letter, June 13, 1945, WA; Gort to Stanley, telegram, May 23, 1945.

19. Mathieson to Kellar, letter, July 15, 1946; Shaw to Hall, letter, Aug. 24, 1945, NA, CO 733/456 75156/75; Rymer-Jones Papers, 139; Bell (1977), 136; Edward Horne (1982), 292; Wagner (2010), 121; Trevor (1948), 132.

20. Pinkerton to Secretary of State, Washington, D.C., letter, July 20, 1945, OSS Report XL14438, RG 226, NARA; Government of Palestine, memorandum, April 24, 1946, NA, CO 537/1828; Shaw to Hall, letter, Aug. 24, 1945.

21. Colville (1972), 263–64; Andronovitch to U.S. Army HQ, Middle East, telegram, June 24, 1945, RG 226, box 31, folder 4, Washington CI and TSS Files, NARA; *Palestine Post,* June 7 and Aug. 6, 1945.

22. Michael J. Cohen (1988), 176; Grigg, memorandum, June 17, 1945, NA, FO 371/45378.

23. Memorandum, CP (45) 55, July 2, 1945, NA, PREM 3 296/10.

24. COS Joint Planning Staff, JP (45) 167, July 10, 1945, NA, CO 733/463/75872/131; Mordecai Allen, report, April 11, 1945, RG 226, box 31, folder 213, Washington CI and TSS Files, NARA; Harold Beeley, minute, July 10, 1945, NA, FO 371/45378.

25. Michael J. Cohen (1978), 178; copy of a minute (COS 100635) for General Ismay to Churchill, July 12, 1945, NA, CO 733/463/75872/131; Stanley to Churchill, minute, July 13, 1945, NA, CO 733/463/75872/131.

26. Michael J. Cohen (1982), 20; "1945 Labour Party Election Manifesto"; Churchill (1956), 6:536–37; Gilbert (1988), 105–7; Harris (1982), 262.

27. Bullock (1983), 55; Peter Clarke (2008), 367; Harris (1982), 37, 252–53; Taylor (1965), 477.

28. Bullock (1960), 1:3–5, 15–57, 156–58, 572, 651; Bullock (1960), 2:3–5; "Ernest Bevin (1881–1951)"; Bullock (1983), 123, 56; Taylor (1965), 141n4, 478; Harris (1982), 294.

29. Moran (1966), 266; Michael J. Cohen (1982), 19.

30. Bullock (1983), 44; Peter Clarke (2008), 365; Goldsworthy (1971), 10; Louis (1986), 4–5.

31. Bullock (1983), 48, 165–66.

32. Ibid., 47, 164; Hurwitz (1976), 215; Louis (1986), 4; Michael J. Cohen (1986), 80; Harris (1982), 389.

33. Andronovitch to Assistant Chief of Staff, Aug. 3, 1945, RG 226, box 32, folder 223, Washington CI and TSS Files, NARA; DSO Intelligence Summary 46, Aug. 1–31, 1945, NA, WO 169/19758; Bagon (2003), 61–62; Bethell (1979), 202; *Fighting Judea,* Oct. 1945, K-4 3/15, JI; interview with Kollek, Aug. 18, 1945, NA, KV 5/34; Bauer (1966), 203–5; Peter Clarke (2008), 387–89; Rose (2009), 71–72.

34. Michael J. Cohen (1982), 22; Dugdale (1973), 224; Bullock (1983), 166.

35. Goldsworthy (1971), 14; Bullock (1983), 435; Dugdale (1973), 224; Michael J. Cohen (1982), 22.

36. Harris (1982), 390; Freundlich and Ganin (1996); Bullock (1983), 48, 173; Peter Clarke (2008), 388; Michael J. Cohen (1978), 184; Bauer (1966), 204.

37. Bullock (1983), 167, 173; Peter Clarke (2008), 387; Freundlich and Ganin (1996); Kurzman (1983), 260–61.

38. Talk on British Foreign Policy, Nov. 21, 1946, Archives of the Council on Foreign Relations; Bullock (1983), 49, 51, 54; Peter Clarke (2008), 314, 365, 367, 386; Creech Jones to Elizabeth Munro [sic], letter, Oct. 23, 1961, box 32/6, Creech Jones Papers; Dockerill (1988), 14, 31; Monroe (1961), 11.

39. Bullock (1983), 50; Morgan (1984), 511; Bartlett (1972), 9, 11.

40. Harris (1982), 270–71, 275–76; Michael J. Cohen (1982), 29; Bartlett (1972), 11–12; Bullock (1983), 50; Monroe (1963), 152–53; Dewar (1984), 14.

41. Chiefs of Staff Committee Note on JP (45) 145 (Final), Aug. 9, 1945, NA, WO 193/973; Alan Brooke, minute, Aug. 7, 1945, NA, WO 193/973; Aug. 7 and 8, 1945, NA, WO 193/973.

42. COS Joint Planning Staff, JP (45) 167, July 10, 1945, NA, FO 371/45378; Admin-

istrative Directive to C-in-C, MEF, Aug. 9, 1945, NA, WO 106/2326; Peter Clarke (2008), 365.

43. Palestine Committee: Report by the Lord President of the Council, Sept. 8, 1946, CP (45) 156, NA, CAB 129/2.

44. Shaw to Hall, letter, Aug. 24, 1945.

45. Ibid.; 400th A.M.E.T., April 11, 1945, RG 226, box 31, folder 213, Washington CI and TSS Files, NARA; Andronovitch, report, Aug. 11, 1945, RG 226, box 31, folder 4, Washington CI and TSS Files, NARA; Paget, report, Aug. 16, 1945, NA, FO 371/45379; Beeley and Baxter, minutes, Aug. 21 and 22, 1945, NA, FO 371/45379.

46. CP (45) 156, Sept. 8, 1946, NA, CAB 129/2.

47. CP (45) 185, Sept. 10, 1945, NA, CAB 129/2; Syrian Ministry of Foreign Affairs to HM Legation, Damascus, letter, Aug. 12, 1945, NA, CO 733/456/75156/151 A pt. 2; Eastwood, minute, Aug. 25, 1945, NA, CO 733/456/75156/151 A pt. 1; CID, Tel Aviv, Aug. 27, 1945, 62, ISA; Shaw to Hall, telegram, Aug. 18, 1945, NA, CO 733/451/75015/55B; W. W. Clark, note, Aug. 25, 1945, NA, CO 733/451/75015/55B; J. M. Martin to F. J. Bradstreet (crown agents), letter, Aug. 30, 1945; Bradstreet to Martin, letter, Sept. 4, 1945, NA, CO 733/451/75015/55B; Gater to Sir Henry Markham, Admiralty, letter, Sept. 28, 1945, NA, CO 733/451/75015/55B; Blaxland (1971), 30–33; Charters (1989), 88; Wilson (1949), 4–5; Paget (1976), 241. A wartime British infantry division comprised approximately 17,500 men. British War Office and U.S. War Department (2005), 23–24.

48. Begin (1977a), 177; Shaw to Hall, telegram, Aug. 18, 1945; DSO Intelligence Summary Extract, Aug. 17, 1945, NA, KV 5/34; Mathieson to Kellar, letter, July 15, 1946; DSO Intelligence Summary 46; DSO Intelligence Summary 113, Sept. 9, 1945, NA, WO 169/19758; Lieutenant Colonel J. V. Prendergast to Kellar, letter, Sept. 5, 1945, NA, KV 5/2; Geula Cohen (1966), 75; Heller (1995a), 151; Livni (1987), 134; Niv (1975), 4:176.

49. OSS Report XL25355, Oct. 30, 1945, RG 226, NARA; interview with Kollek, no. 4, Sept. 15, 1945, NA, KV 5/29; interview with Kollek, Aug. 18, 1945; Andrew (2009), 356; DSO Intelligence Summary Extract, Aug. 27, 1945, NA, KV 5/29.

50. OSS Report XL25355; DSO Intelligence Summary 47, Sept. 1–30, 1945, NA, WO 169/19758; Paget to Brooke, telegram, Oct. 30, 1945, NA, WO 106/3107; Begin (1977a), 181.

51. Weizmann to Attlee, letter, Sept. 21, 1945, NA, PREM 8/88; Attlee to Weizmann, letter, Sept. 28, 1945, NA, PREM 8/88.

52. Telegram 1 to London from Sneh in Jerusalem, Sept. 23, 1945, in *Palestine: Statement of Information Relating to Acts of Violence*, Cmd. 6873 (1946), 4.

53. Diaspora Headquarters of the Irgun Zvai Leumi, *Background of the Struggle for the Liberation of Eretz Israel: Facts on the Relations Between the Irgun Zvai Leumi and the Haganah* (New York: Information Department, American League for a Free Palestine, Inc., 1947), 6–7; interview with Kollek, DSO, HQ Palestine, Oct. 20, 1945, NA, KV 5/34; extract from SIME Report, Oct. 30, 1945, NA, KV 5/34; Begin (1977a), 184–87; Niv (1975), 4:179–81; telegram 5 to London from Jerusalem, Nov. 1, 1945, in *Palestine: Statement of Information Relating to Acts of Violence*, 5; OSS Report XL23242, Oct. 6, 1945, RG 226, NARA; OSS Report XL25259, Oct. 17, 1945, RG 226, NARA; Golan and Nakdimon (1978), 110; Bauer (1963), 205; Heller (1995a), 152; Kister (2000), 124–25; Livni (1987), 139; Rose (2009), 85; Shamir (1994), 58–59; Slutsky (1972), 854–57; Zadka (1995), 58–59.

54. Wagner (2010), 129–30; Bar-Zohar (1968), 82–83; Gort to Hall, telegram, Oct. 10, 1945, NA, CO 733/456/75156/151 A pt. 1; Paget, Middle East Forces Review, 1945, 11; Trevor (1948), 152–53.

55. OSS Report XL21545, Oct. 18, 1945, RG 226, NARA; Malcolm P. Hooper (American consul, Jerusalem) to Secretary of State (Byrnes), letter, Oct. 29, 1945, in OSS Report XL29671, RG 226, NARA; telegrams Nos. 6 and 7 to London from Jerusalem, Oct. 12 and 14, 1945, in *Palestine: Statement of Information Relating to Acts of Violence*, 6; Esco (1947), 2:1201–2; Bell (1977), 145.

56. Trevor (1948), 153; Scott to Mrs. Robert Scott, letter, Oct. 6 and 14, 1945, Scott Papers.

57. Gort to Hall, telegram, Oct. 17, 1945, NA, FO 371/45381; Colville (1972), 236, 266; Rymer-Jones Papers, 140; Bond (1991), 34; interview by Mr. Lloyd Phillips, April 29, 1969, 28, Scrivenor Papers; Rymer-Jones Papers, 135; Colville (1972), 260, 264–65; Grigg to Churchill, letter, Jan. 27, 1945, NA, PREM 4/52/3; Pearlman and Ben Gurion (1965), 74–75.

58. Colville (1972), 264–65; Rymer-Jones Papers, 135.

59. Colville (1972), 263–66; Gort to Hall, telegram, Oct. 13, 1945, NA, AIR 20/4962; OSS Report XL21545.

60. Trevor (1948), 157.

61. *Palestine: Statement of Information Relating to Acts of Violence*, 3–5; Gort to Hall, telegram, Nov. 1, 1945, NA, CO 733/456/75156/151A pt. 1; Gort to Hall, telegram, Nov. 2, 1945, NA, AIR 20/4962; Debates, House of Commons, vol. 415, cols. 785–88 (Hall), Nov. 2, 1945; Paget, Middle East Forces Review, 1945, 11; Cabinet Defence Committee DO (45) 12, Nov. 5, 1945, NA, PREM 8/627 pt. 1; *Palestine Post*, Nov. 2, 1945; Blaxland (1971), 31; Niv (1975), 4:183; Slutsky (1972), 858–60; Trevor (1948), 157–58.

62. Marlowe (1959), 201; *Palestine: Statement of Information Relating to Acts of Violence*, 5; *Palestine Post*, Nov. 2, 1945; Trevor (1948), 158.

63. Halifax to Bevin and Attlee, telegram, Oct. 3, 1945, NA, FO 800/484 Pa/45/9; Truman to Churchill, memorandum, July 24, 1945, NA, FO 800/484 Pa/45/1; Bullock (1983), 164; Michael J. Cohen (1982), 55.

64. Michael J. Cohen (1982), 56–57; Bullock (1983), 174–77; Harris (1982), 391–92; Attlee to Truman, telegram, Sept. 14, 1945, NA, PREM 8/89.

65. Creech Jones to Elizabeth Munro [*sic*], letter, Oct. 23, 1961; Halifax to Bevin, telegram, Oct. 4, 1945, NA, FO 371/45380; Bevin to Halifax, telegram, Oct. 12, 1945, NA, FO 800/484 Pa/45/13.

66. Bullock (1983), 176; CM (45) 40, Oct. 11, 1945, NA, CAB 128/1; Bevin to Halifax, telegram, Oct. 12, 1945; Abdullatif Salah (president of the National Bloc) to Shaw, letter, Nov. 3, 1945, NA, CO733/457/75156/151B; Paget, Middle East Forces Review, 1945, 10; Trevor (1948), 159.

67. Bevin to Halifax, telegram, Nov. 6, 1945, NA, PREM 8/627 pt. 1; Halifax, aide-mémoire, Nov. 6, 1945, in *FRUS Diplomatic Papers 1945* (1969), 867N.01/11-645, 812–13.

68. *Palestine: Statement of Information Relating to Acts of Violence*, 6; Giles to Shaw, top secret letter, Oct. 27, 1945, 115/45, HA; Trevor (1948), 158–59.

69. OSS Report XL26254, Nov. 8, 1945, RG 226, NARA; Blaxland (1971), 31; Trevor (1948), 159.

70. Rymer-Jones Papers, 140; *Palestine Post*, Nov. 4, 1945; Colville (1972), 266.

71. Colville (1972), 267; *Palestine Post*, Nov. 4, 1945.

72. Hurewitz (1976), 236–37.
73. *Palestine Post*, Nov. 14 and 15, 1945; Cunningham to Hall, telegram, Dec. 1, 1945, Cunningham Papers, I/1; Bullock (1983), 181; Trevor (1948), 160–61.

CHAPTER 12: TO DEFEND AND TO GUARD FOREVER

1. Slutsky (1972), 860; *Palestine Post*, Nov. 15 and 16, 1945.
2. Hooper to Byrnes, telegram, Nov. 15, 1945, 824, in *FRUS, 1945*; Scott to Hall, telegrams, Nov. 16 and 17, 1945, Cunningham Papers, I/1; memorandum, April 24, 1946, NA, CO 537/1828; Debates, House of Commons, vol. 415, cols. 2521–23 (Hall), Nov. 16, 1945; *Palestine Post*, Nov. 15 and 16, 1945; Blaxland (1971), 32–33; Dewar (1984), 20; Slutsky (1972), 860–61; Wilson (1949), 26–28; Trevor (1948), 161–63.
3. Scott to Hall, telegram, Nov. 16, 1945, NA, AIR 20/4962; *Palestine Post*, Nov. 18, 1945; Wilson (1949), 28–29; Slutsky (1972), 860–61; Trevor (1949), 162.
4. Proclamation by the Officer Administering the Government, Nov. 15, 1945, Fraser Papers; Trevor (1948), 163; Slutsky (1972), 861; *Palestine Post*, Nov. 16 and 18, 1945.
5. Ahron David Sobel to Fitzgerald, letter, Nov. 23, 1945, CS POC/30/45, ISA.
6. Letter, Dec. 3, 1945, NA, FO 371/45387.
7. Ibid.
8. Ibid.
9. HQ Palestine, Jerusalem, Appreciation of the Likely Reaction of the Jews to BROADSIDE, Nov. 15, 1945, NA, WO 169/19745.
10. The Reverend V. J. Pike to Chaplain General, London, in MEF Report 34, Feb. 12, 1946, NA, WO 169/22932.
11. Wilson (1949), xiii; Farran (1950), 372–73; Anderson (1947–48), 201.
12. Blaxland (1971), 27; Gater to Markham, letter, Sept. 28, 1945, and Shaw to Eastwood, Nov. 26, 1945, NA, CO 733/451/75015/55B.
13. Stanley to Gort, letter, June 15, 1945; F. J. Bradstreet (crown agents) to J. M. Martin (assistant undersecretary, Colonial Office), letter, Sept. 4, 1945; Gater to Markham, letter, Sept. 28, 1945; Trafford Smith to A. J. D. Winnifrith (Treasury), letter, Jan. 9, 1946; W. W. Clark, minute, Dec. 4, 1945; Gater to Cunningham, Dec. 6, 1945; Rymer-Jones to Eastwood, June 15, 1945. All in NA, CO 733/451/75015/55B.
14. Extract from Conclusions of DO (45) 12th Meeting, Nov. 5, 1945, NA, AIR 20/4962; Blaxland (1971), 32–33.
15. Debates, House of Commons, vol. 415, col. 2330 (Hall), Nov. 15, 1945; First Division, Directive 9, Nov. 7, 1945, NA, WO 169/19656; A Year as an Intelligence Officer, S 25/6910, CZA; Farran (1950), 345; Wilson (1949), 19.
16. Extract from Conclusions of DO (45) 12th Meeting, Nov. 5, 1945, NA, WO 32/10260.
17. General HQ, Middle East, to Cabinet Offices, telegram, Nov. 14, 1945, V/4, Cunningham Papers; Cabinet Defence Committee DO (45) 31 Report by the Chiefs of Staff, Nov. 19, 1945, NA, PREM 8/627 pt. 1; Brief for the Secretary of State DO (45) 31 ACSB, Nov. 21, 1945, NA, WO 32/10260.
18. Ismay to Attlee, minute, Nov. 29, 1945, NA, PREM 8/83; E. E. Sabben-Clare, minute, Nov. 29, 1945, NA, CO 968/96/2; Cabinet Defence Committee DO (45) 17th Meeting, Dec. 12, 1945, NA, CO 968/96/2.

19. Tuchman (1962), 22; Creech Jones to N. Ollerenshaw, letter, April 10, 1947, NA, CO 733/477/75156/151A/47; Memorandum on the Comparative Treatment.

20. Memorandum on the Comparative Treatment.

21. Barnett (1960), 79–80; Churchill (1956), 3:80; Craster (1991), 203; Fergusson (1970), 124–25; Mead (2007), 110; *Times*, Feb. 1, 1983.

22. Craster (1991), 203–7; "The True Story of How Auchinlek Removed Alan Cunningham from Command of the Eighth Army in November 1941" (written by Montgomery's hand), BLM 54, Montgomery Papers; Churchill (1956), 3:445–46; Gilbert (1983), 1242; Danchev and Todman (2002), 208, 211, 257–58, 261, 331, 433–34; Mead (2007), 112; Fearne (1757), 130.

23. Christmas Eve 1945, Lloyd Phillips Papers, 4/2; Rymer-Jones Papers, 142; interview by Lloyd Phillips, 29–30, Scrivenor Papers; Craster (1991), 207; Crum (1947), 224; *Times*, Nov. 9, 1945.

24. Ullendorff (1988), 113, *Daily Telegraph*, April 17, 2011; *Palestine Post*, Nov. 12 and 22, 1945; Pearlman and Ben-Gurion (1965), 81–82; *Times*, Nov. 10, 1945; Crum (1947), 224.

25. Cunningham to Bevin, note, Nov. 1945, Cunningham Papers, VI/1.

26. Pearlman and Ben-Gurion (1965), 81.

27. Kimche (1954), 113–22; Bauer (1970), 3–42, 66–99; Debates, House of Commons, vol. 416, cols. 2067–68 (Hall), Dec. 3, 1945; Cunningham to Hall, telegram, Dec. 1, 1945, Cunningham Papers, I/1; Heller (2003), xiv; Slutsky (1972), 860–65; Trevor (1948), 163–73; Wilson (1949), 30–33; *Palestine Post*, Nov. 27, 1945.

28. *Palestine Post*, Nov. 27, 1945.

29. Ibid.; Trevor (1948), 171.

30. *Palestine Post*, Nov. 27, 1945.

31. Wilson (1949), 32–33.

32. Heller (2003), 118; Slutsky (1972), 864.

33. DSO Intelligence Summary 3, Dec. 1945, NA, WO 169/19758; Illegal Jewish Military Organisations, Nov. 28, 1945, NA, FO 371/45386; CID Report, Dec. 14, 1945, 47/152, HA; Kellar to Martin, letter, Dec. 13, 1945, NA, KV 2/1435; Heller (2003), 118; Inner Zionist Council Meeting, Nov. 26, 1945, NA, WO 169/19745.

34. Palestine Sessional Papers, Secret Minutes of the 22nd Meeting, Nov. 14, 1945, NA, CO 814/41; Cunningham to Shaw, letter, Nov. 29, 1945, Cunningham Papers, V/4.

35. OSS Report XL32214, Dec. 6, 1945, RG 226, NARA; Bell (1977), 150; Cunningham to Hall, telegram, Dec. 4 and Nov. 28, 1945, NA, FO 371/45388; Halifax to Bevin, Nov. 30, 1945, NA, FO 371/45388; Kellar, note, Dec. 20, 1945, NA, KV 2/1435.

36. Cunningham to Shaw, letter, Dec. 20, 1945, Cunningham Papers, VI/1.

37. GHQ MEF, Review 41, Jan. 4, 1946, NA, WO 169/22882; Robertson to Kellar, note, Jan. 7, 1946, NA, KV 2/3428; Robertson to Trafford Smith, letter, Jan. 11, 1946, NA, KV 2/3428; *Palestine Post*, Dec. 28 and 30, 1945; *Times*, Dec. 28 and 29, 1945; Bell (1977), 151–52; Edward Horne (1982), 294; Slutsky (1972), 865–66; Trevor (1948), 175.

38. *Palestine Post*, Dec. 30, 1945; *Times*, Dec. 31, 1945; Bell (1977), 152; Slutsky (1972), 865; Wilson (1949), 35; note of interview, Dec. 28, 1945, Cunningham Papers, V/1; Cunningham to Hall, telegram, Dec. 29, 1945, NA, PREM 8/627 pt. 1; GHQ MEF, Review 41; Trevor (1948), 175.

39. *Times*, Dec. 31, 1945; Bell (1977), 151; Edward Horne (1982), 295, 312.
40. Note of interview, Dec. 28, 1945; Cunningham to Hall, telegram, Dec. 30, 1945, NA, PREM 8/626 pt. 1; Robertson to Trafford Smith, letter, Jan. 10, 1946, NA, KV 2/1435.
41. Trevor (1948), 176.
42. Cunningham to Hall, telegram, Dec. 29, 1945, Cunningham Papers, I/1; Cunningham to Hall, telegram, Dec. 29, 1945, NA, PREM 8/627 pt. 1.
43. CM 1 (46), Jan. 1, 1946, NA, CAB 128/5.
44. Slutsky (1972), 866; Paget to Brooke, telegram, Jan. 2, 1946, NA, WO 169/22882; Robertson to Trafford Smith, letter, Jan. 10, 1946, NA, KV 5/34; Jewish Telegraphic Agency, *Daily News Bulletin*, Dec. 28, 1945, NA, KV5/29; extract, Jan. 4, 1946, NA, KV 2/2375.
45. Garfield (2004), 162; Peter Clarke (2008), 397, 402–3; Rosecrance (1968), 35; Paget, Middle East Forces Review, 1945; Anglo-American Committee of Enquiry, JP (46) 15 (Final), Jan. 21, 1946, Cunningham Papers, V/2.
46. Top Secret: Jewish Military Organizations, Oct. 7, 1945, Morris Papers, 1/1/2; CID Report, Dec. 14, 1945; OSS Report XL32214; Scott to Martin, draft letter, Jan. 3, 1946, NA, CO 733/463; extract from DSO, HQ Palestine, Jan. 28, 1946, NA, KV 5/29; Gyles Isham to Kellar, Feb. 11, 1946, NA, KV 5/29; Palestine: Irgun Zvai Leumi, Feb. 21, 1946, NA, KV 5/34; FMI 3-07.22 (2004), 1–3; Thiel (2011).
47. Robertson to Trafford Smith, letter, Jan. 10, 1946, NA, KV 5/34; Robertson to Colonial Office, letter, Jan. 25, 1946, NA, KV 5/34; Robertson to Trafford Smith, letter, Feb. 4, 1946, NA, KV 5/34; extract from reports dated Jan. 24 and 30, 1946, NA, KV 5/34; GHQ MEF, Cairo, Military Intelligence Review 44, Jan. 25, 1946, NA, WO 169/22882; Jewish Terrorist Outrages Since His Excellency's Arrival in Palestine (n.d.), Cunningham Papers, V/4.
48. CID Report, Feb. 1946, 47/35, HA; Irgun Zvai Leumi, Feb. 21, 1946, NA, KV5/34; The Rival Forces in Palestine (n.d.), Morris Papers, 1/1/2.
49. Lieutenant Colonel H. A. Wickstead (DSO, HQ Palestine) to Kellar, letter, Jan. 14, 1946, NA, KV 5/29; Kellar to Trafford Smith, telegram, Feb. 19, 1946, NA, KV 5/29.
50. Trafford Smith, minute, Jan. 9, 1946, NA, CO 733/451/75015/55B.
51. Charteris, Fortnightly Newsletter 6, Jan. 1946, NA, WO 275/63; Haifa Sector, HQ Third Parachute Brigade, Preliminary Intelligence Summary, Jan. 27, 1946, NA, WO 261/216; Gyles Isham to Kellar, telegram, Feb. 11, 1946, NA, KV 2/3428; Palestine and Transjordan, Monthly Summary 4, DSO, HQ Palestine, Jan. 1946, NA, WO 169/23031; Baghdad to Foreign Office, telegram, Feb. 8, 1946, NA, CO 537/1768.
52. Gale (1968), 160; Meade (2007), 154; D'Arcy, Directive on the Degree of Force to Be Used in Internal Disturbances in Palestine, Jan. 11, 1946, NA, WO 275/16.
53. OSS Report XL45057, Feb. 8, 1946, RG 226, NARA; *Palestine Post*, Jan. 20 and 21, 1946.
54. GHQ MEF, Military Intelligence Review 44, NA WO 169/22882; Slutsky (1972), 866–67; *Palestine Post*, Jan. 21, 1946.
55. Trevor (1948), 182–86; Edward Horne (1982), 243.
56. Military Court Procedures (n.d.), Brebber Papers, II/1; *Palestine Post*, Jan. 29, 1946; Trevor (1948), 182–86.
57. Mathieson to Kellar, letter, July 15, 1946, containing Palestine: Terrorist Out-

rages, 3–4; HQ Palestine, Fortnightly Intelligence Newsletter 8, Feb. 2–16, 1946, NA, WO 169/23021; Jewish Terrorist Outrages Since His Excellency's Arrival in Palestine; Niv (1975), 4:229; Cunningham to Hall, telegrams, Jan. 31 and Feb. 1, 1946, Cunningham Papers, I/1; Charteris, memorandum, Jan. 11, 1946, NA, KV 5/34; CID Report, Feb. 1946; Palestine: Irgun Zvai Leumi, Feb. 21, 1946.

58. Cunningham to Hall, telegram, Feb. 1, 1946; HQ Palestine, Fortnightly Intelligence Newsletter 8, Feb. 2–16, 1946; minute of interview, Feb. 19, 1946, S 25/28, CZA; Rival Forces in Palestine; Rymer-Jones Papers, 132, 143, 144; HQ Palestine, Operational Instruction 22, Jan. 10, 1945, NA, WO 169/19743; Cunningham to Hall, telegram, Jan. 31, 1946.

59. Cavendish (1990), 20; "Gyles Isham"; Isham to Kellar, telegram, Feb. 11, 1946, NA, KV 2/3428; Director General to D.B., minute, March 26, 1945, NA, KV 5/29; Gort to Stanley, telegram, March 19, 1945, NA, CO 537/457/13 75156/151K; Eastwood and A. C. Jones, minutes, March 21, 1945, NA, CO 537/457/13 75156/151K; Top Secret Policy Regarding Suspected Jewish Terrorists in HM Forces, Aug. 1945, NA, CO 537/457/13 75156/151K; G. M. Liddell (director B Division, MI5) to A. Canning (deputy assistant commissioner, Metropolitan Police, Special Branch), letter, Jan. 15, 1946, NA, KV 2/3428.

60. Petrie to Maxwell, letter, April 2, 1945, NA, KV 5/29; Kellar, Reports on Visits to SIME and CICI, Feb. 1945, NA, KV 4/384.

61. Petrie to Maxwell, letter, April 2, 1945; Top Secret Policy Regarding Suspected Jewish Terrorists in HM Forces; Martin to Gates, minute, Aug. 20, 1945, NA, CO 537/457/13 75156/151K; J. C. Robertson (for Kellar) to D. Bates (Colonial Office), top secret letter, Nov. 10, 1945, NA, CO 733/457/13; Measures Undertaken by MI5, NA, CO 733/457/13; J. C. Robertson to D.B., note, Oct. 31, 1945, NA, KV 2/3428; Robertson to Brigadier E. R. Haylor (HQ, British army on the Rhine), Feb. 15, 1946, NA, KV 2/3428; Kellar to SIME, secret telegram, Feb. 16, 1946, NA, KV 2/3428; Walton (2008), 448; Petrie to Maxwell, letter, April 2, 1945; Killearn to Bevin, telegram, Nov. 19, 1945, NA, KV 5/29.

62. Isham to Kellar, secret telegram, Jan. 5, 1946, NA, KV 2/3428; Robertson to Trafford Smith, letter, Jan. 11, 1946; Robertson to T. E. Bromley (Foreign Office), letter, Jan. 15, 1946, NA, KV 2/3428; Shaw to Hall, telegram, Feb. 13, 1946, NA, KV 5/29; Liddell to Canning, letter, Jan. 15 and Feb. 14, 1946, NA, KV 5/29; Kellar to Bromley, Jan. 15, 1946, NA, KV 5/29; Kellar to Lieutenant Colonel F. H. W. Gore (War Office), Jan. 16, 1946, NA, KV 5/29; Kellar to Martin, Jan. 22, 1946, NA, KV 5/29; Robertson to Haylor, Feb. 15, 1946, NA, KV 5/29; Lieutenant Colonel H. A. Wickstead (DSO, HQ Palestine) to Kellar, letter, Jan. 14, 1946, NA, KV 5/29; Robertson to Trafford Smith, Feb. 15, 1946, NA, KV 5/29; D'Arcy to SIME, Feb. 15, 1946, NA, KV 5/29; R.A.P. to AIG (CID), Feb. 24, 1946, O'Sullivan Papers; Mathieson to Kellar, letter, July 15, 1946, containing Palestine: Terrorist Outrages, 4; HQ Palestine, Fortnightly Intelligence Newsletter 8; "Tidyings," 35; *Palestine Post*, June 25, 1946; Segev (2000), 474–75; Paget to Candle Jerusalem et al., telegram, Feb. 20, 1946, NA, KV 5/29.

63. Cunningham to Hall, telegram, Feb. 19, 1946, Cunningham Papers, I/1; CM (46) 17, Feb. 21, 1946, NA, CAB 128/5.

64. Crum (1947), 45, 82, 120, 162; Crossman (1947), 117; Anglo-American Committee, box 11, March 14, 1946, Leahy Papers, RG 43, NARA; Roberts to Kellar, telegram, Feb. 11, 1946, NA, KV 5/29; Mathieson to Kellar, letter, July 15, 1946, containing Palestine: Terrorist Outrages, 4; Jewish Terrorist Outrages Since His

Excellency's Arrival in Palestine; Begin (1977a), 237–41; Gurion (1950), 65–67; Niv (1975), 4:239–41; Blaxland (1971), 34; *Palestine Post*, March 7, 1946; HQ Palestine, Armed Raid on Sarafand Camp on March 6, 1946, March 15, 1946, NA, WO 169/23021.

65. Crossman (1947), 118; Crum (1947), 160–61.
66. Michael J. Cohen (1982), 96–102; Heller (2003), 28, 80; Dugdale (1973), 226–30; Chaim Weizmann (1949), 2:441; Vera Weizmann (1967), 202; *Times*, March 7, 1946; Nachmani (1980), 1; Brutton (1996), 25; Lloyd Phillips to the Reverend A. Lloyd Phillips, letter, March 2, 1946, Lloyd Phillips Papers.
67. *Palestine Post*, March 7, 1946; Crossman (1947), 15–16; Crum (1947), 5–6. In addition to Crossman, the British delegation included Sir John Singleton, a London high court judge; the Labour peer Lord Morrison; Major Reginald Manningham-Buller, a Conservative Party MP; Wilfrid Crick, a banker; and Sir Frederick Leggett, a labor mediator. Among the American members were Judge Joseph C. Hutcheson Jr., a distinguished Texas jurist; Dr. James G. McDonald, formerly the League of Nations high commissioner for German refugees and subsequently America's first ambassador to Israel; Frank W. Buxton, a Pulitzer Prize winner and newspaper editor; Dr. Frank Aydelotte, the director of Princeton University's Institute for Advanced Study; a former ambassador to Italy named William Phillips; and Bartley C. Crum, a corporate lawyer.
68. Nachmani (1980), 1.
69. Anglo-American Committee, box 11, March 14, 1946, Leahy Papers; Crum (1947), 219–20; Nachmani (1987), 171–74.
70. Crossman (1947), 157–58; Anglo-American Committee, box 11, March 14, 1946, Leahy Papers; OSS Report XL49021, March 22, 1946, RG 226, NARA; Hall to Cunningham, telegram, April 11, 1946, Cunningham Papers, I/1; Nachmani (1987), 178–79.
71. Crum (1947), 262–83; Crossman (1947), 165–87; Michael J. Cohen (1982), 104–5; Cunningham to Hall, March 30, 1946, NA, CO 733/75156/151A pt. 1; Kellar to Trafford Smith, letter, Jan. 21, 1946, NA, KV 5/33.
72. Government of Palestine, *Palestine Railways: Report of the General Manager on the Administration of the Palestine Railways and Operated Lines and on the Ports of Palestine for the Year 1946/47* (Haifa: Warhaftig's Press, 1948), 12, box 1, files 13–16, Scrivener Papers; Mathieson to Kellar, letter, July 15, 1946, containing Palestine: Terrorist Outrages, 4; Jewish Terrorist Outrages Since His Excellency's Arrival in Palestine; Bell (1977), 159; Trevor (1948), 199–200; HQ British Troops, Palestine and Transjordan, Fortnightly Intelligence Newsletter 12, March 31 to April 14, 1946, NA, WO 169/23022.
73. Chiefs of Staff Joint Planning Staff, JP (46) 68 (Final), April 9, 1946, NA, AIR 20/4963.
74. *Anglo-American Committee of Inquiry* (1946), 5, 44–48, 76–85; Report of Anglo-American Committee, April 22, 1946, NA, FO 371/52521.
75. *Anglo-American Committee of Inquiry* (1946).
76. Cabinet Defence Committee DO (46) 14, April 24, 1946, NA, WO 32/10260.

CHAPTER 13: ONLY DEATH WILL FREE US

1. HQ Palestine, Fortnightly Intelligence Newsletter 13, April 15–28, 1946, NA, WO 169/23022; Cunningham to Hall, telegram, April 26, 1946, NA, KV 5/29;

Washington Registry SI Intelligence Field Files, Report 401, April 29, 1946, RG 226, box 19, file 22, folder 1, NARA; Wilson (1949), 46; *Palestine Post,* April 26 and 28, 1946; *Times,* April 27, 1946; Niv (1975), 4:263–64; Trevor (1948), 201.

2. Washington Registry SI Intelligence Field Files GP Palestine, Report 401, April 29, 1946, RG 226, box 19, file 22, folder 1; Lloyd Phillips to Reverend A. Lloyd Phillips, letter, April 28, 1946, Lloyd Phillips Papers, 4/2; *Times,* April 29, 1946.

3. Record of a meeting on April 26, 1946, Cunningham Papers, V/4.

4. Wilson (1949), 47; *Times,* April 29, 1946; Trevor (1948), 201–2.

5. Mitchell (1969), 56; Blaxland (1971), 36; GHQ MEF, Cairo, Military Intelligence Review 57, April 26, 1946, NA, WO 169/22882; Wilson (1949), 45, 48; Trevor (1948), 202; HQ South Palestine District, Intelligence Summary 1, May 11, 1946, NA, WO 169/23057.

6. Farran (1950), 345–46; J. Abbott to Barbara Castle, letter, April 28, 1946, NA, CO 733/456/75156/151A pt. 1; "A Soldier's Will," n.d., S 25/6910, CZA.

7. Captain R. H. Medley to Kellar, letter, May 7, 1946, NA, KV 5/29.

8. CP (46) 173, April 27, 1946, NA, CAB 129/9; Byrnes to Truman, telegram, May 9, 1946, Leahy Papers, 56, RG 218, NARA.

9. Meeting on April 28, 1946, May 6, 1946, NA, FO 371/52521; CM (46) 38, April 29, 1946, NA, CAB 128/5; Minutes of 8th Meeting, May 3, 1946, NA, FO 371/52520.

10. Ovendale (1979), 419; Michael J. Cohen (1990), 129–30; Bevin to Byrnes, letter, May 1, 1946, NA, FO 371/52519.

11. Byrnes to Truman, telegram, May 9, 1946; CC 092 Palestine (5-3-46), Section 2, JIC 355, May 18, 1946, Leahy Papers, 56, RG 218, NARA.

12. Bevin to Attlee, telegram, May 1, 1946, NA, AIR 20/4963; Debates, House of Commons, vol. 422, cols. 195–99, May 1, 1946; *Palestine: Statement of Information Relating to Acts of Violence,* 8–9.

13. Cunningham to Hall, telegram, April 29, 1946, NA, PREM 8/627; Minutes of 8th Meeting, April 30, 1946, NA, FO 371/52520.

14. DSO Intelligence Summary 8, May 1946, NA, WO 169/23031; HQ South Palestine District, Intelligence Summary 1, May 11, 1946, NA, WO 169/23057; Kellar to Trafford Smith, letter, May 14, 1946, NA, KV 5/29; extract from report, May 18, 1946, NA, KV5/34; Rymer-Jones Papers, 149; D'Arcy to Lieutenant General Sir Evelyn Barker, letter, May 31, 1946, D'Arcy Papers; Women of Jaffa to Cunningham, letter, May 6, 1946, CS POL/9/46, ISA; Munira Darwich El Asir et al. to High Commissioner, letter, May 8, 1946, CS POL/9/46, ISA; "The Youth Qaalquilya" to High Commissioner, petition, May 15, 1946, CS POL/9/46, ISA; District Commissioners Office, Galilee District, Fortnightly Report for April 30, 1946, NA, CO 537/1707.

15. Ismay to Attlee, telegram, May 4, 1946, and Bevin, note, May 8, 1946, NA, FO 371/52525.

16. COS Committee (46) 77, May 15, 1946, NA, CO 537/1697.

17. Minutes of a staff conference, May 16, 1946, NA, FO 371/52525; COS Committee (46) 95, June 19, 194, NA, FO 371/52530; Hall to Cunningham, telegram, June 16, 1946, Cunningham Papers, I/1.

18. Michael J. Cohen (1982), 116–23; Slutsky (1972), 879; HQ Palestine, Intelligence Newsletter 16, June 9, 1946, NA, WO 169/23022; *Daily Telegraph,* June 7, 1946; Guela Cohen (1966), 191–201; Begin (1977b); Heller (1995), 42, 92, 106, 108, 111; Shindler (2010), 146, 211, 219; DSO Intelligence Summary 9, June 28, 1946, NA, WO 169/23031; *Jewish Standard,* June 14, 1946, NA, KV 5/35.

19. GHQ MEF, Intelligence Newsletter 64, June 14, 1946, NA, WO 169/22882; DSO Intelligence Summary 9; Shaw to D'Arcy, letter, June 15, 1946, D'Arcy Papers; *Jewish Standard*, June 14, 1946; Slutsky (1972), 879; Hall to Cunningham, telegram, June 16, 1946.

20. Charteris, memorandum, June 23, 1946, NA, WO 275/40; A. J. Kellar, Report Middle East Visit, July 1946, NA, KV 4/18; GHQ MEF, Weekly Intelligence Review 65, June 21, 1946, NA, WO 169/22882; *Palestine Post*, June 13, 1946; Bethell (1979), 243–44; Bullock (1983), 277–78; Michael J. Cohen (1982), 117–18; DSO Intelligence Summary 9; Slutsky (1972), 879.

21. Gurion (1950), 67, 70–75; Trevor (1948), 208–9; Begin (1977a), 241–45; Bethell (1979), 244; Washington Registry SI Intelligence Field Files, Report 473, June 16, 1946, RG 226, box 19, file 22, folder 3, NARA.

22. Cunningham to Hall, telegram, June 20, 1946, Cunningham Papers, I/1; Bethell (1979), 245. A different version of the story credits the acquisition of the list to a sympathetic British officer. See Dekel (1959), 96, 127–38; Trevor (1948), 211–12n14; Pa'il and Pinhas (2003), 206.

23. Charteris, memorandum, June 23, 1946; DSO Intelligence Summary 9; Allon (1970), 146–61; Slutsky (1972), 880–86.

24. Charteris, memorandum, June 23, 1946; DSO Intelligence Summary 9; Jewish Telegraphic Agency Bulletin, June 19, 1946, NA, KV 5/35; Mathieson to Kellar, letter, July 15, 1946, containing Palestine: Terrorist Outrages, 7; Jewish Terrorist Outrages Since His Excellency's Arrival in Palestine; *Palestine Post*, June 18, 1946; Bethell (1979), 246; Slutsky (1972), 886–87; Cunningham to Hall, letter, July 1, 1946, NA, CO 733/456/75156/151A pt. 2.

25. Charteris, memorandum, June 23, 1946; Jewish Telegraphic Agency Bulletin, June 19, 1946; Mathieson to Kellar, July 15, 1946, containing Palestine: Terrorist Outrages, 7; Jewish Terrorist Outrages Since His Excellency's Arrival in Palestine; *Times* and *Palestine Post*, June 19, 1946; Begin (1977a), 245–46; Bethell (1979), 246–47; Gurion (1950), 76–78; Wilson (1949), 55–56; extract from DSO report, June 15, 1946, NA, KV 5/34.

26. Palestine Post, June 21, 1946; Jewish Telegraphic Agency, *Daily News Bulletin*, June 25, 1946, NA, KV 5/35; Washington Registry SI Intelligence Field Files, Report 491, June 26, 1946, RG 226, box 19, file 22, folder 3, NARA; Slutsky (1972), 887; *Palestine Press Review*, June 26, 1946, NA, WO 275/108; *Palestine Post*, June 21 and 25, 1946; Barker to D'Arcy, letter, May 31, 1946, D'Arcy Papers.

27. Mead (2007), 58–60; Bell (1977), 159; Fergusson (1970), 39–40; Barker to Weizmann, letter, June 18, 1946, S 25/6908, CZA.

28. Charteris, memorandum, June 23, 1946; *Daily Telegraph* and *Times*, June 22, 1946; *Palestine Post*, June 23, 1946; Trevor (1948), 215; Hamilton (1986), 633–34; Montgomery (1958), 378–79, 381.

29. The Palestine Police Force Annual Administrative Report, 1946, NA, CO 814/40; Stephen Brooks, note, Imperial War Museum, Nov. 20, 1986, Montgomery Papers; Hamilton (1986), 109, 127, 267, 341, 621, 636, 665; Montgomery Diary, pt. 1, chap. 3, "Palestine First Tour, June 9–26, 1946," BLM 175/1, Montgomery Papers; Montgomery (1958), 378; Montgomery to Dempsey, letter, Aug. 5, 1946, BLM 211/9, Montgomery Papers; Montgomery to Hall, letter, Aug. 6, 1946, BLM 211/10, Montgomery Papers; Golani (2010), 183.

30. Hall to Cunningham, telegram, Dec. 29, 1945, Cunningham Papers, I/1; Cunningham to Hall, telegram, Dec. 30, 1945, NA, PREM 8/627 pt. 1; Howard (1983), 253.

31. Montgomery, "Palestine First Tour"; "True Story of How Auchinlek Removed Alan Cunningham from Command of the Eighth Army in November 1941"; "Supersession Lt. Gen. Sir Alan Cunningham as Commander Eighth Army, November 1941," BLM 54, Montgomery Papers.

32. Barnett (1960), 239; Lewin (1976), 501; Atkinson (2003), 418; Hamilton (1986), xv, 623.

33. Hamilton (1986), 636–37; Montgomery, "Palestine First Tour"; Montgomery (1958), 381.

34. Shaw to D'Arcy, letter, June 15, 1946.

35. Montgomery, "Palestine First Tour."

36. Montgomery (1958), 381–83.

37. Cunningham to Hall, telegram, June 19, 1946, Cunningham Papers, I/1; extract from DSO report, June 17, 1946, NA, KV 5/35; Washington Registry SI Intelligence Field Files, Report 474, June 19, 1946, RG 226, box 19, file 22, folder 3, NARA; Military Action to Be Taken to Enforce Law and Order in Palestine, June 22, 1946, NA, WO 275/29; Trevor (1948), 215.

38. Cunningham to Hall, telegram, June 19, 1946.

39. CP (46) 238, June 19, 1946, NA, CAB 129/10; COS (46) 76, June 19, 1946, and Secretary, Chiefs of Staff, to Gater (Colonial Office) and Sir Orme Sargent (Foreign Office), letter, June 19, 1946, NA, FO 371/52530.

40. Harriman to Truman, telegram, June 19, 1946, in *FRUS, 1946* (1969), 7:63; Cunningham to Hall, telegram, June 21, 1946, Cunningham Papers, I/1.

41. CM (46) 60, June 20, 1946, NA, CAB 128/5; *Palestine: Statement of Information Relating to Acts of Violence*, 3–10.

42. CM (46) 60, June 20, 1946; Attlee to Bevin, telegram, June 20, 1946, NA, CAB 127/270.

43. Cunningham to Hall, telegram, June 20, 1946; Military Action to Be Taken to Enforce Law and Order in Palestine.

44. *Palestine Post*, June 28, 1946; GHQ MEF, Intelligence Review 65, June 21, 1946, NA, WO 169/22882; Charteris, memorandum, June 23, 1946.

45. *Palestine Press Review*, June 19, 26, 20, and 21, 1946, NA, WO 275/108; DSO Intelligence Summary 9; GHQ MEF, Weekly Intelligence Review 66, June 28, 1946, NA, WO 169/22882.

46. Jewish Telegraphic Agency, *Daily News Bulletin*, June 25, 1946; *Palestine Post*, June 21, 1946; *Daily Telegraph*, June 25, 1946; *Jewish Chronicle*, June 28, 1946; Bell (1977), 164–66; Begin (1977a), 245–46; Bethell (1979), 247–48; Trevor (1948), 214; Washington Registry SI Intelligence Field Files, Reports 481 and 482, June 20 and 27, 1946, RG 226, box 19, file 22, folder 3, NARA.

47. Brutton (1996), 35; Wilson (1949), 57; Operation Agatha, Operation Instruction 68, June 1946, Cunningham Papers, V/4; Cunningham to Hall, telegram, June 25, 1946, Cunningham Papers, I/1.

48. Mead (2007), 116–21; Montgomery to Dempsey, personal directive, June 27, 1946, NA, WO 126.

49. Wilson (1949), 58–59; Cunningham to Hall, telegram, June 29, 1946, NA, FO 371/52534; Report on Operation Agatha, June 20 to July 1, 1946, NA, FO 371/52547; Charters (1989), 117–18; Rose (2009), 107.

50. Report on Operation Agatha; Who's Who of Palestine, 54, 68, 106, 121; Heller (2003), 130; Trevor (1948), 216–18.

51. Report on Operation Agatha; Begin (1977a), 204; Charters (1989), 118; Wagner (2010), 163; Dekel (1959), 25, 142–45; Dempsey to Montgomery, telegram, July 4,

1946, NA, WO 216/194; Zadka (1995), 139; Memorandum on Jewish National Institutions in Acts of Violence, 1947, Catling Papers; App. 39, HQ Palestine, Oct. 1946, Catling Papers; Wilson (1949), 60–61.

52. Appendix A: Narrative of Events by Parachute Brigade on Operation Agatha, July 1, 1946, NA, WO 275/29; Barker to D'Arcy, letter, July 2, 1946, D'Arcy Papers; Montgomery to Dempsey, telegram, July 3, 1946, BLM 211/4, Montgomery Papers; note of interview, July 20, 1946, NA, CO 537/1822; Dempsey to Montgomery, telegram, July 4, 1946; Report on Operation Agatha; CM 63 (46), July 1, 1946, NA, CAB 128/6; Kellar to Trafford Smith, letter, Jan. 10, 1946, NA, KV 2/1435; Washington Registry SI Intelligence Field Files, July 5, June 30, and July 15, 1946, RG 226, box 19, file 22, folders 3 and 4, NARA; Barker to D'Arcy, letter, July 1, 1946, D'Arcy Papers; Michael J. Cohen (1982), 85; Zadka (1995), 140; Bauer (1966), 207; Charters (1989), 118; Dr. Weizmann at a Jewish Agency meeting (n.d.), RG 226, box 19, file 22 folder 3, NARA; Laqueur (1992), 258; Cunningham to Hall, telegram, June 27, 1946, NA, FO 371/52534.

53. Report on Operation Agatha; Dugdale (1973), 237; Cunningham to Hall, telegram, June 29, 1946, Cunningham Papers, I/1; notes of an interview, July 1, 1946, Cunningham Papers, V/1; notes of an interview, July 3, 1946, Z 4/S226, CZA; *Palestine Press Review*, July 8, 1946, NA, WO 275/108; Geula Cohen (1966), 223; Michael J. Cohen (1982), 87; Meir (1973), 64–65; Sherman (1997), 179–80; Vera Weizmann (1967), 205; Brutton (1996), 36; Barker, Operational Instruction 67: Military cum Police Operations, June 17, 1946, NA, WO 275/13; App. A, July 1, 1946, NA, WO 275/29; Rose (2009), 108–9; Wilson (1949), 60; Third Infantry Brigade Report on Operation Agatha, app. D2, July 3, 1946, NA, WO 261/679; Barker to D'Arcy, letter, July 2, 1946; Fortnightly Intelligence Newsletter 18, June 24 to July 7, 1946, NA, WO 275/63.

54. Rose (2009), 109; Report on Operation Agatha; Third Infantry Brigade Report on Operation Agatha, app. D2; Meir (1975), 195; Dekel (1959), 145–46; Dugdale (1973), 237; Trevor (1948), 219–24; Vera Weizmann (1967), 204–6.

55. Vera Weizmann (1967), 207–8.

56. *Palestine Press Review*, July 8, 1946; Report on Operation Agatha; Mitchell (1969), 57.

57. Notes of an interview, July 3, 1946; Michael J. Cohen (1982), 88.

58. Debates, House of Commons, vol. 424, cols. 1795–97, July 1, 1947.

59. *Manchester Guardian*, July 1, 1946; Inverchapel to Bevin, telegram, July 3, 1946, NA, CO 537/1737; Attlee to Truman, telegram, June 29, 1946, in *FRUS, 1946*, 7:639–40.

60. Hall to Cunningham, telegram, July 4, 1946, NA, CO 537/1737; Lloyd Phillips to His Reverend A. Lloyd Phillips, letter, July 7, 1946, Lloyd Phillips Papers, 4/2; HQ Palestine and Transjordan, Fortnightly Intelligence Newsletter 34 (n.d.), NA, WO 261/566; Washington Registry SI Intelligence Field Files, Report 505, July 9, 1946, RG 226, box 19, file 22, folder 3, NARA; Vera Weizmann (1967), 207–8; Baumel (2005), 200.

61. Inverchapel to Bevin, telegram, July 8, 1946, NA, CO 537/2287; Cunningham to Hall, July 11, 1946, NA, CO 537/2287; Haifa District Fortnightly Report for June 16–30, July 4, 1946, NA, CO 537/1707; *Palestine Press Review*, July 2, 1946, NA, WO 275/108.

62. CM 76 (46), July 11, 1946, NA, CAB 128/6; Memorandum on Jewish National Institutions in Acts of Violence, 1947, app. 20, Account of an Interview, July 12,

1946; Cunningham to Hall, telegram, July 14, 1946, Cunningham Papers, I/1; Washington Registry SI Intelligence Field Files, July 15, 1946; Dr. Weizmann at a Jewish Agency meeting; DSO Intelligence Summary 9, June 1946, NA, KV 5/30; Washington Registry SI Intelligence Field Files, Report 509, July 12, 1946, RG 226, box 19, file 22, folder 3, NARA; Extract DSO Palestine, July 10, 1946, NA, KV 5/30; Robertson to Deputy Commander Burt (Special Branch, New Scotland Yard), letter, June 21, 1946, NA, KV 2/3428; H. A. R. Philby (MI6) to Liddell, letter, June 25, 1946, NA, KV 2/3428; Colonel Maurice Oldfield (SIME) to Kellar, telegram, July 2, 1946, NA, KV 2/3428; H. J. Seeger to Kellar and Isham, letter, July 6, 1946, NA, KV 2/3428; Kellar to Burt, letter, July 9, 1946, NA, KV 2/3428.

63. Montgomery to Dempsey, telegram, July 3, 1946, NA, WO 216/194; Dempsey to Montgomery, telegram, July 4, 1946; Kellar to Trafford Smith, letter, July 9, 1946, NA, KV 2/1435; Memorandum on Jewish National Institutions in Acts of Violence, 1947, containing CID HQ PPF, Jerusalem, Memorandum on the Participation of the Jewish National Institutions in Acts of Lawlessness and Violence, July 31, 1947.

64. Bauer (1966), 207–8; Wilson (1949), 61; Heller (2003), 130; Brenner (1982), 131–32; Golan and Nakdimon (1978), 114; Sherman (1997), 179–80.

65. Note of interview, July 20, 1946, NA, CO 537/1822; Vera Weizmann (1967), 205–6; Dugdale (1973), 238; Laqueur (1992), 262; Dekel (1959), 142–47; Michael J. Cohen (1982), 87; Thurston Clarke (1981), 96; Cunningham (1948), 485.

66. Dempsey to Montgomery, telegram, Nov. 16, 1946, NA, WO 216/194; Washington Registry SI Intelligence Field Files, Report 491; Bell (1977), 168; Trevor (1948), 224; *Times*, July 20, 1946; *Palestine Post*, July 21, 1946.

67. *Times*, July 22, 1946; note of interview, July 20, 1946, NA, CO 537/1822.

68. Washington Registry SI Intelligence Field Files, Report 510, July 15, 1946, Report 500, July 1, 1946, and Report 505, July 9, 1946, RG 226, box 19, folder 3, NARA; The Voice of Fighting Zion, broadcast of July 7, 1946, NA, KV5/34; Washington Registry SI Intelligence Field Files, June 30–July 15, 1946, RG 226, box 19, file 22, folder 3, NARA.

69. Palestine: Anglo-U.S. Report—Military Implications, July 10, 1946, NA, PREM 8/627 COS (46) 188 (0).

70. Anglo-U.S. Report—Military Implications, Report by the Chiefs of Staff, July 10, 1946, NA, FO 371/6571 E6571/4/g. 31 CP (46) 267; CM (46) 67, July 11, 1946, NA, CAB 128/6.

71. Monroe (1961), 29; Lieutenant Colonel Prescott (DSO, Jerusalem) to Kellar, letter, July 17, 1946, NA, KV 5/30; extract from DSO report, July 10, 1946, NA, KV 5/35; Washington Registry SI Intelligence Field Files, Report 510; Lloyd Phillips to Reverend A. Lloyd Phillips, letter, July 7, 1946.

CHAPTER 14: DEFENSE AND CONQUEST

1. Top Secret: Area Surrounding Headquarters Palestine, Jan. 1945, NA, WO 169/19849; Barker (2006), 56; Borisov (1947), 131; Cavendish (1990), 19; Thurston Clarke (1981), 36–37, 48–49, 94–95, 105; Crossman (1947), 118, 122; Hirst (1978), 108; Montefiore (2011), 461, 477; *Daily Telegraph*, July 23, 1946; Roman (2007), 34; Sherman (1997), 163, 165, 180; Vilnay (1948), 68.

2. Oz (2004), 3; Montefiore (2011), 462; Sherman (1997), 163, 165.

3. Roman (2007), 33; Vilnay (1948), 60; Barker (2006), 55–56; James (1967), 287–88.
4. Thurston Clarke (1981), 37; *Jerusalem Post International Edition*, Oct. 18, 1981; Roman (2007), 35; Sherman (1997), 165.
5. Thurston Clarke (1981), 29, 37; Montefiore (2011), 477; Crossman (1947), 118; Begin (1977a), 52, 212; Aviezer and Nakdimon (1978), 115.
6. Begin (1977a), 83–84, 213–15; O'Sullivan, Destruction of the King David Hotel, Dec. 6, 1946, O'Sullivan Papers; summary of letter from DSO, Palestine, July 26, 1946, NA, KV 5/36; Robertson to Trafford Smith, letter, July 29, 1946, NA, CO 537/1715; Aviezer and Nakdimon (1978), 115–16; Barker (2006), 55; Bell (1977), 168–69; Niv (1975), 4:277–78.
7. Begin (1977a), 121, 215; Thurston Clarke (1981), 83–85; Edward Horne (1982), 300–301; Bethell (1979), 257–58; O'Sullivan, Destruction of the King David Hotel.
8. Begin (1977a), 217.
9. Thurston Clarke (1981), 39–45.
10. *Times*, Sept. 17, 1977; Thurston Clarke (1981), 51–52, 89, 94–95.
11. Memorandum on Jewish National Institutions in Acts of Violence, 1947, app. LVa, J. P. I. Fforde (assistant inspector general, CID) to Sir Henry Gurney (chief secretary), letter, July 1947, containing "The Truth About the King David," National Military Organisation, July 22, 1947; Niv (1975), 4:277–78; Aviezer and Nakdimon (1978), 115–16; Begin (1977a), 215–16; Thurston Clarke (1981), 97–99.
12. Memorandum on Jewish National Institutions in Acts of Violence, app. LVa, July 22, 1947; Begin (1977a), 218; Bell (1977), 168–69; Thurston Clarke (1981), 123–24, 160; Heller (1995), 161; Niv (1975), 4:277–78.
13. Assistant Inspector General J. P. I. Fforde to Shaw, letter, Aug. 16, 1946, NA, CO 537/2290; Barker to Hall, telegram, July 22, 1946, Cunningham Papers, I/1; "La Regence," Dec. 13, 1946, Morris Papers, II/1; *Manchester Guardian* and *Palestine Post*, July 23, 1946; Begin (1977a), 218–19; Bethell (1979), 258–59; Thurston Clarke (1981), 163–66, 169, 180–81; Niv (1975), 4:279–80.
14. Fforde to Shaw, letter, Aug. 16, 1946; Cunningham to Hall, letter, Dec. 20, 1946, NA, CO 537/2290; Barker to Hall, telegram, July 22, 1946; "La Regence"; *Palestine Post*, July 23, 1946; Bethell (1979), 259; Thurston Clarke (1981), 170, 172–76, 233; Niv (1975), 4:279.
15. Fforde to Shaw, letter, Aug. 16, 1946; Brutton (1996), 46–47; Thurston Clarke (1981), 188–89, 196–99, 206–7; Bethell (1979), 260–62; Aviezer and Nakdimon (1978), 116.
16. Fforde to Shaw, letter, Aug. 16, 1946; Cunningham to Hall, letter, Dec. 20, 1946; "La Regence"; Aviezer and Nakdimon (1978), 116–17; Bethell (1979), 261–62; Brutton (1996), 46; Edward Horne (1982), 302; Thurston Clarke (1981), 196–99, 206–7.
17. Bethell (1979), 261; *New York Times*, Sept. 26, 1981.
18. Fforde to Shaw, letter, Aug. 16, 1946; "La Regence"; *Palestine Post*, July 23, 1946; Bell (1977), 171–72; Bethell (1979), 259–63; Brutton (1996), 46–47; Thurston Clarke (1981), 183–88, 200, 203–4, 221; Niv (1975), 4:280–82.
19. Fforde to Shaw, letter, Aug. 16, 1946; Scott to Mrs. Robert Scott, letter, July 28, 1946, Scott Papers; Cunningham to Hall, telegram, Aug. 3, 1946, NA, CO 537/1708; *Palestine Gazette*, Aug. 6, 1946, Shaw Papers; Thurston Clarke (1981), 222; Cunningham to Hall, Aug. 4, 1946, NA, CO 733/467/76046; *Times*, Sept. 17, 1977; Palestine: Cost of Terrorist Damage and Illegal Immigration, Brief for

Creech Jones, April 1947, NA, CO 537/2300; Sir John Gutch (assistant secretary, Middle East Department), minute, April 1947, NA, CO 537/2300; *Palestine Post*, July 23, 1946; *Jerusalem Post International Edition*, Oct. 18, 1981. See the calculator at MeasuringWorth.com, http://measuringworth.com/calculators/exchange/result_exchange.php.

20. Cunningham to Hall, telegram, Aug. 3, 1946; *New York Times*, Sept. 26, 1981; *Times*, July 20, 2006; *Jerusalem Post*, July 26, 2006; Segev, "The Spirit of the King David Hotel."

21. Bethell (1979), 258, 261; Begin (1977a), 219.

22. Ymedad, "Yehuda Avner's Scarlet Pimpernel"; Aviezer and Nakdimon (1978), 117.

23. Begin (1977a), 221.

24. OSS Report GP150, July 24, 1946, RG 226, box 19, file 22, folder 3, NARA; HQ British Troops in Palestine and Transjordan, G Branch, Historical Record, July–Sept. 1946, NA, WO 261/562; Extract: Appreciation of Situation Palestine, July 24, 1946, NA, KV 5/36; S. Prescott for DSO, HQ Palestine, to Kellar, letter, July 27, 1946, NA, KV 5/36; "Irgun Issues 'Communiqué on Attack'" (n.d.), NA, KV 5/36.

25. OSS Report 518, July 23, 1946, and OSS Notes on the King David Hotel Bombing, July 24, 1946, RG 226, box 19, file 22, folder 3, NARA; Robertson to Trafford Smith, letter, July 29, 1946; Trevor (1948), 228; *Manchester Guardian*, July 23, 1946; Vera Weizmann (1967), 209; *Palestine Press Review*, July 23, 1946, NA, WO 275; *Palestine Post*, July 24, 1946.

26. Begin (1977a), 223–24; Thurston Clarke (1981), 243.

27. Begin (1977a), 224; Bethell (1979), 263; Thurston Clarke (1981), 245; Aviezer and Nakdimon (1978), 118; Niv (1975), 4:282.

28. Begin (1977a), 224; OSS Report 535, July 31, 1946, RG 226, box 19, file 22, folder 3, NARA; Sharif to Isham, letter, Dec. 19, 1946, Sir Gyles Isham Papers, I.215, NRO; Robertson to Trafford Smith, letter, Aug. 8, 1946, KV 2/1435; Thurston Clarke (1981), 245.

29. Palestine: Jewish Reaction to Blowing Up of King David Hotel, Aug. 12, 1946, NA 5/36; Memorandum on Jewish National Institutions in Acts of Violence, 1947, app. LVa, Fforde to Gurney, letter, July 1947, containing "The Truth About the King David"; *Background of the Struggle for the Liberation of Eretz Israel: Facts on the Relations Between the Irgun Zvai Leumi and the Haganah* (1947), 10–12.

30. Borisov (1947), 133; Medoff (2002), 40; Baumel (2005), 186; Ziff (1948), 486.

31. High Court of Justice, King's Bench Division, the Hon. Mr. Justin Hilberry, 1948 S.No. 3790 Sir John Shaw v. Wm. B. Ziff, Donald George Port Trading as Jason Press and S. T. Botolphs Publishing Co. Ltd., April 12, 1949, Shaw Papers; Shaw to Isham, letter, Jan. 18, 1972, Isham Papers, I.184; Cavendish (1990), 19; Thurston Clarke (1981), 190–91, 260; Rose (2009), 115–16.

32. Shaw to W. L. Dale (deputy legal adviser, Colonial Office), letter, Sept. 26, 1951, Shaw Papers; Shaw to Messrs. W. H. Allen & Co. Ltd., letter, Sept. 3, 1951, Shaw Papers.

33. Niv (1975), 4:282–83; Shaw to Isham, letter, Jan. 18, 1972.

34. Bethell (1979), 263; Thurston Clarke (1981), 260.

35. Third Parachute Brigade, Quarterly Historical Report, July–Sept. 1946 (n.d.), NA, WO 261/700; Historical Record, July–Sept. 1946: The Attack on the King David Hotel—July 22, 1946 (n.d.), NA, WO 261/562.

36. OSS Report, July 24, 1946, RG 226, box 19, file 22, folder 3, NARA; Thurston Clarke (1981), 204–5, 211–13; Historical Record, July–Sept. 1946: The Attack on the King David Hotel.
37. Barker to D'Arcy, letter, July 29, 1946, D'Arcy Papers; Thurston Clarke (1981), 203–6, 211–13.
38. Fforde to Shaw, letter, Aug. 16, 1946; Cunningham to Hall, letter, Dec. 20, 1946; Thurston Clarke (1981), 222; Rose (2009), 116.
39. Debates, House of Commons, vol. 425, cols. 1877–80, July 23, 1946; Begin (1977a), 52; Fortnightly Intelligence Newsletter 20, NA, WO 261/562; HQ Palestine, July 22 to Aug. 4, 1946; Sherman (1997), 183; *Daily Telegraph* and *Manchester Guardian*, July 23, 1946.
40. Cunningham, note (n.d.), Cunningham Papers, IV/2; Shaw to Hall, telegram, July 22, 1946, Cunningham Papers, I/1; CM (46) 72, July 23, 1946, NA, CAB 128/6.
41. Montgomery to Dempsey, telegram, July 23, 1946, NA, WO 216/194; Montgomery, Confidential Annex DO (46) 23, Minute 6, July 22, 1946, BLM 211/6, Montgomery Papers.
42. CM (46) 72, July 23, 1946, NA, CAB 128/6; Top Secret: Operations in Palestine—Illegal Zionist Armed Forces in Palestine and the Complicity of the Jewish Agency (n.d.), NA, CO 537/1715; Hall to Cunningham, telegram, July 8, 1946, NA, CO 537/1715.
43. *Palestine: Statement of Information Relating to Acts of Violence*, 2–10; *Palestine Post*, July 25, 1946; *Times*, July 25 and 26, 1946; O'Sullivan, Destruction of the King David Hotel, Dec. 6, 1946; memorandum (n.d.), NA, CO 537/1715.
44. CM (46) 73, July 25, 1946, NA, CAB 128/6; Bullock (1983), 298; Michael J. Cohen (1982), 127–32.
45. CM (46) 74, July 29, 1946, NA, CAB 128/6.
46. Montgomery, Confidential Annex DO (46) 23, Minute 6, July 22, 1946; Montgomery to Dempsey, telegram, July 24, 1946, NA, WO 216/194; Cunningham to Hall, telegram, July 24, 1946, Cunningham Papers, I/1; CM (46) 75, July 30, 1946, NA, CAB 128/6; Hall to Cunningham, telegram, Aug. 5, 1946, NA, FO 371/52550.
47. Montgomery to Dempsey, telegram, July 24, 1946; 128/6 CM (46) 73, July 25, 1946, NA, CAB 128/6; Hall to Cunningham, July 7, 1946, Cunningham Papers, I/1.
48. *Palestine Post*, July 25, 1946; Bushinsky, "Early Years."
49. Inverchapel to Bevin, telegrams, July 30 and Aug. 3, 1946, NA, CO 537/2291; Debates, House of Commons, vol. 426, cols. 998–99 (the Reverend Gordon Lang), July 31, 1946; Meinertzhagen (1959), 214; Sherman (1997), 183; Barker, Order of the Day, July 25, 1946, Cunningham Papers, V/4.
50. Barker, Order of the Day, July 25, 1946; Cunningham to Hall, telegram, July 30, 1946, NA, CO 537/2291; Eban (1977), 62–63; Montgomery Diary, pt. 1, chap. 9, "The War Office Period, June 26 to August 19, 1946," BLM 175/1, Montgomery Papers.
51. *New York Times*, July 28, 1946; Inverchapel to Bevin, telegram, July 30, 1946; Montgomery to Dempsey, telegram, July 29, 1946, NA, WO 216/194; CM (46) 74, July 29, 1946, NA, CAB 128/6; *Times*, July 29, 1946; Montgomery, "War Office Period"; Montgomery to Dempsey, telegram, July 30, 1946, NA, WO 216/194.

52. CM (46) 75, July 30, 1946, NA, CAB 128/6; Debates, House of Commons, vol. 426, cols. 957–71, July 31, 1946; Montgomery to Dempsey, telegram, July 30, 1946; Dempsey to Montgomery, July 23, 1946, NA, WO 216/194; Montgomery to Dempsey, Aug. 3, 1946, NA, WO 216/194; Montgomery, "War Office Period"; *Palestine Post*, Aug. 9, 1946; Trevor (1948), 233n30.

53. Eban (1977), 63; Debates, House of Commons, vol. 426, cols. 957–1075, July 31, 1946.

54. Debates, House of Commons, vol. 426, cols. 998, 1014–15, July 31, 1946; "Attitude in England to the Palestine Problem," in HQ Palestine and Transjordan, Fortnightly Intelligence Newsletter 20, July 22 to Aug 4, 1946, NA, WO 261/562; Peter Clarke (2008), 463; Mass Observation: Recording Everyday Life in Britain.

55. Debates, House of Commons, vol. 426, cols. 1232–317, Aug. 1, 1946.

56. CM (46) 73, July 25, 1946, NA, CAB 128/6; CM (46) 74, July 29, 1946, NA, CAB 128/6; Cunningham to Hall, telegram, July 27, 1946, NA, FO 371/52545; telegram, Aug. 3, 1946, Cunningham Papers, I/1; Barker to D'Arcy, letter, July 29, 1946; OSS Report GP 150, Aug. 1, 1946, RG 226, box 19, file 22, folder 9, NARA; Husseini to Bevin, letter, July 23, 1946, NA, FO 371/52543.

57. Krämer (2008), 298–99; Cunningham to Hall, telegram, July 27, 1946; Monthly Report on Situation, Cunningham to Hall, Aug. 3, 1946, NA, CO 537/1708; Cunningham to Hall, telegram, Aug. 3, 1946; C.-in-C. Middle East, Appreciation of Situation in Palestine, July 24, 1946, NA, KV 5/36.

58. Charters (1989), 170–76; French (2011), 33, 180–84, 196; Mockaitis (1990), 12, 41–43, 52, 160; Stubbs (2004), 1, 70–74, 159–68, 173–84, 254–58, 262–63; Dempsey to Montgomery, telegram, July 24, 1946, NA, WO 216/194.

59. French (2011), 106, 148; *Palestine Post*, Jan. 9, 1946.

60. Kitson (1971), 95; French (2011), 33; Rymer-Jones Papers, 132, 143–44, 149; Shaw to Crossman, letter, Aug. 2, 1946, Crossman Papers; CM (46) 75th Conclusions, July 30, 1946, NA, CAB 128/6; Barker to D'Arcy, letter, July 29, 1946.

61. Philby to Bromley, letter, July 8, 1946, NA, KV 5/36; Foreign Office to Shone, July 19, 1946, NA, KV 5/36; Shone to Foreign Office, July 21, 1946, NA, KV 5/36; Isham to Shaw, letter, Jan. 15, 1972, Isham Papers, I.184.

62. CM (46) 73, July 25, 1946, NA, CAB 128/6; Niv (1975), 4:278; Fforde to Shaw, letter, Aug. 16, 1946.

63. Wilson (1949), 66.

64. Cunningham to Hall, telegram, Aug. 1, 1946, NA, CO 537/2291; Sixth Airborne Division, Intelligence Summary 4, Aug. 9, 1946, NA, WO 275/58; Wilson (1949), 67–71; HQ Palestine, Historical Record, July–Sept. 1946, Operation Shark, Sept. 1946, NA, WO 261/562; Trevor (1948), 231; HQ Parachute Brigade, Sixth Airborne Division Report on Operation Shark, Aug. 15, 1946, NA, WO 261/700; Historical Record, Sept. 1946, NA, WO 261/562; Jewish Terrorist Index, 1947, O'Sullivan Papers.

65. The Irgun Zvai Leumi, Aug. 7, 1946, NA, KV 5/36; OSS Report GP150, Aug. 7, 1946, RG 226, box 19, file 22, folder 4, NARA; *Daily Express*, Aug. 2, 1946; Shamir (1994), 60–61; Bethell (1979), 271; Wilson (1949), 71.

66. Shamir (1994), 60–62; *Daily Telegraph*, Sept. 10, 1946; Brutton (1996), 50; Bethell (1979), 277.

67. Cassels, Special Message, Aug. 3, 1946, NA, WO 275/4; OSS Report GP150, Aug. 21, 1946, RG 226, box 19, file 22, folder 5, NARA; Blaxland (1971), 39;

Wilson (1949), 66–73; Trevor (1948), 23; Sixth Airborne Division Report on Operation Shark, Aug. 30, 1946, NA, WO 275/33A; Sixth Airborne Division, Summary 4, Aug. 9, 1946, NA, WO 275/58; Cunningham to Hall, telegram, Aug. 1, 1946.

68. Sixth Airborne Division Report on Operation Shark, Aug. 30, 1946; Sixth Airborne Division Operation Shark, July 29, 1946, NA, WO 275/31; CM (46) 74, July 29, 1946, NA, CAB 128/6; O'Sullivan, Destruction of the King David Hotel.

69. Dempsey to Montgomery, telegram, Aug. 2, 1946, NA, WO 216/194; Cunningham to Hall, telegram, Aug. 6, 1946, NA, FO 371/52628; OSS Report GP150, Aug. 14, 1946, RG 226, box 19, file 22, folder 4, NARA; *Palestine Post*, July 24 and Aug. 6, 1946; Trevor (1948), 223–24.

70. OSS Report GP150, Aug. 2 and 14, 1946, RG 226, box 19, file 22, folder 4, NARA.

71. Gale (1968), 167.

72. Sherman (1997), 187; *Palestine Press Review*, Aug. 7, 1946, NA, WO 275/108; Gale (1968), 167; Assistant Secretary (John Gutch), Colonial Office, note, July 27, 1946, CS D/27/46, ISA; Gutch to Chairman, Palestine Civil Service, letter, July 28, 1946, CS D/27/46, ISA; Chairman, Palestine Civil Service to Shaw, letter, Aug. 5, 1946, CS D/27/46, ISA; CM (46) 75, July 30, 1946, NA, CAB 128/6; CP (46) 310, Aug. 5, 1946, NA, CAB 219/12; Cunningham to Hall, telegram, July 25, 1946, NA, FO 371/52544; Cunningham to Hall, telegrams, July 26, 1946, Cunningham Papers, I/1; Aug. 1 and 3, 1946, NA, FO 371/52549.

73. *Palestine Post*, July 1, 7, 12, 14, and 16, 1946; CM (46) 77 Conclusions, Aug. 7, 1946, NA, CAB 128/6; T. Wikley, minute, Aug. 2, 1946, NA, FO 371/52551; Budapest to Foreign Office, telegram, Aug. 3, 1946, NA, CO 537/1737; John Russell (Warsaw) to Baxter, telegram, Aug. 2, 1946, NA, FO 371/52630; Cunningham to Hall, telegram, July 25, 1946; memorandum of conversation between Sir Walter Smart and Philip W. Ireland (Cairo legation), Aug. 8, 1946, RG 84, Post Files Cairo, 800 Palestine 150, NARA; Foreign Office to Hungarian Ministry of Foreign Affairs, telegram, Aug. 24, 1946, NA, FO 371/52630; H. J. Seager to H. E. Burley, letter, Jan. 6, 1947, NA, KV 5/31.

74. CM (46) 75th Conclusions, July 30, 1946; Peter Clarke (2008), 461; CP (46) 306, July 29, 1946, NA, CAB 129/12.

75. CP (46) 310 Annex I, Cunningham to Hall, telegram, Aug. 3, 1946, NA, CAB 129/12; Annex II, Montgomery to Attlee, memorandum, Aug. 3, 1946, NA, CAB 129/12; CM (46) 77, Aug. 7, 1946, NA, CAB 129/12; Hall to Cunningham, telegram, Aug. 5, 1946; Montgomery to Dempsey, telegram, Aug. 7, 1946, NA, WO 216/194; Montgomery to Attlee, note, Aug. 9, 1946, NA, FO 371/52627; Foreign Office to Bevin, telegram, Aug. 11, 1946, NA, FO 371/525628; Hall to Cunningham, Aug. 11, 1946, Cunningham Papers, I/2; Cyprus (Sir C. Woolley) to Hall, telegrams, Aug. 12 and 14, 1946, NA, FO 371/52627; Hall to Woolley, Aug. 14, 1946, NA, FO 371/52627.

76. Montgomery to Dempsey, telegram, Aug. 5, 1946, NA, WO 216/194.

77. Montgomery, "War Office Period"; Montgomery to Hall, letter, Aug. 6, 1946, BLM 211/10, Montgomery Papers.

78. SIME, Possibility of Jewish Terrorist Outrages Outside Palestine, Aug. 3, 1946, NA, KV 2/3428; top secret meeting held in Mr. Howe's room on July 24 to discuss security arrangements for the U.K. delegation to the peace conference in Paris, July 25, 1946, NA, KV 2/3428; Liddell to Roberts, telegram, July 24, 1946, NA, KV 2/3428; Dixon to Ashley Clarke, telegram, July 24, 1946, NA, KV 2/3428;

Kellar, report, Feb. 1945, NA, KV 5/34; Kellar, Reports on Visits to SIME and CICI, Feb. 1945; C. Douglas Roberts (SIME, Cairo) to Kellar, letter, May 11, 1945, NA, KV 5/29; Barr (2012), 275, 278.

79. Top secret meeting held on July 24, NA, KV 2/3428; Foreign Office (Dixon) to Alexandria, telegram, July 24, 1946, NA, KV 2/3428; Codrington to Dixon, telegram, July 26, 1946, NA, KV 2/3428; Hall to Cunningham, telegram, Aug. 17, 1946, NA, KV 2/3428; *Palestine Post*, Aug. 30, 1946.

80. Liddell to Roberts, telegram, July 24, 1946; Foreign Office (Dixon) to Alexandria, telegram, July 24, 1946; Roberts to Liddell, telegram, July 27, 1946, NA, KV 2/3428; Liddell to Harold Caccia, July 31, 1946, NA, KV 2/3428.

81. Extract from Jewish Telegraphic Agency, *Daily News Bulletin*, Aug. 15, 1946, NA, KV 5/30; Cunningham to Hall, telegrams, Aug. 18, 19, and 22, 1946, NA, KV 5/30; extract from *Jewish Standard*, Aug. 23, 1946, NA, KV 5/30; Kellar to Trafford Smith, letter, Aug. 27, 1946, NA, KV 5/30; Notes for Director General's Meeting with Prime Minister, Aug. 28, 1946, NA, KV 5/30; Captain S. Bales (DSO, Jerusalem) to Lieutenant Colonel M. Oldfield (SIME), letter, Aug. 28, 1946, NA, KV 5/30; *Times*, Aug. 13, 1946.

CHAPTER 15: BEATING THE DOG IN HIS OWN KENNEL

1. *New York Times*, Sept. 5 and 7, 1946, and Feb. 2, 1979; Medoff, "Ben Hecht's 'A Flag Is Born'"; "Paul Muni"; Baumel (2005), 219, 220; Zaar (1954), 201–2.

2. *New York Times*, Sept. 5, 7, and 15, 1946; Medoff, "Ben Hecht's 'A Flag Is Born'"; *New Yorker*, Sept. 14, 1946.

3. *New York Times*, Sept. 5 and 7, 1946; Medoff, "Ben Hecht's 'A Flag Is Born.'"

4. Medoff, "Ben Hecht's 'A Flag Is Born'"; Baumel (2005), 220.

5. Zaar (1954), 200; Medoff, "Ben Hecht's 'A Flag Is Born'"; Hecht (1954), 614; Baumel (2005), 220; *New York Times*, Oct. 1, 1946.

6. Hall to Cunningham, Oct. 2, 1946, Cunningham Papers, I/2; Harris (1982), 396; Hall to Cunningham, telegram, July 4, 1946.

7. Johan J. Smertenko to J. M. Martin (CO), letter, Dec. 21, 1945, NA, CO 733/461.7582/14B; Martin, minute, Jan. 3, 1946, NA, CO 733/461.7582/14B; R. Gallopin (director delegate, Comité International de la Croix-Rouge) to Hall, letter and report, Sept. 27, 1946, NA, FO 371/61872; French (2011), 165–66; Trevor (1948), 260.

8. HQ South Palestine District, Quarterly Historical Report for Quarter July–Oct. 1946, NA, WO 261/646; *Palestine Post*, June 21 and Aug. 21, 1946; Trevor (1948), 249–50.

9. Wilson (1949), 78–79; Trevor (1948), 252–54; OSS Report GP200, Sept. 4, 1946, RG 226, box 19, file 22, folder 5, NARA; *Palestine Post*, Aug. 29 and Sept. 3, 1946.

10. *Palestine Post*, Sept. 3, 1946; Trevor (1948), 253.

11. Captain H. Linklater, 317 Airborne Field Security Section Report, Aug. 1946, NA, WO 275/72; HQ South Palestine District, Intelligence Summary 14, Sept. 2, 1946, NA, WO 261/646; Cunningham to Hall, telegram, Sept. 22, 1946, NA, CO 537/1789; Wilson (1949), 60; French (2011), 177; Charteris, A Year as an Intelligence Officer, Sept. 1946, S 25/6910, CZA; HQ South Palestine District, Quarterly Historical Report HQ South Palestine District for Quarter July–Oct. 1946; Cunningham to Hall, telegram, Oct. 12, 1946, NA, FO 371/52655.

12. Interview, April 29, 1969, Scrivenor Papers.

13. Begin (1977a), 55; summary of a statement by Menachem Begin, Dec. 20, 1946, NA, WO 275/63.

14. HQ British Troops in Palestine and Transjordan, G Branch Historical Record, Jan.–Sept. 1946, NA, WO 261/526; Levenberg (1991), 622–23; *Times*, Sept. 9, 1946; *Daily Telegraph*, Sept. 10, 1946; *Jewish Standard*, Sept. 13, 1946.

15. Robertson to Trafford Smith, letter, Sept. 10, 1946, NA, KV 5/37; *Times*, Sept. 9 and 10, 1946; HQ British Troops in Palestine and Transjordan, G Branch Historical Record, July–Sept. 1946, NA, WO 261/526; Bulletin 211, Sept. 10, 1946, NA, KV 5/37; *Daily Telegraph*, Sept. 10, 1946; *Jewish Standard*, Sept. 13, 1946; Dorrill (2000), 54; Jeffery (2010), 689; A. F. Kirby, Report of the General Manager (Palestine Railways), 1946–48, 12, box 1, files 13–16, Scrivener Papers; Trevor (1948), 258.

16. Cesarani (2009), 22–23; Charters (1989), 46, 48; Rose (2009), 144; Trevor (1948), 258; Extract from DO (46) 145 pt. 1, War Office View, Nov. 1946, Montgomery Papers; Bulletin 211, Sept. 10, 1946; Debates, House of Commons, vol. 434, col. 35 (Churchill), March 3, 1947; Debates, House of Commons, vol. 441, cols. 2341–43 (Lever), Aug. 12, 1947; Montgomery (1958), 419.

17. OSS Report GP200, Aug. 28 and Sept. 4, 1946, RG 226, box 19, file 22, folder 5, NARA; *Times*, Sept. 14, 1946; Wilson (1949), 87; Report of the General Manager, 12, Scrivener Papers; Jewish Telegraphic Agency, *Daily News Bulletin*, Sept. 29, 1945, NA, KV 5/37.

18. Trevor (1948), 262; security minutes, Sept. 30, 1946, Cunningham Papers, IV/1.

19. Cunningham to Hall, telegram, Sept. 27, 1946, NA, CAB 127/280.

20. Dugdale (1973), 238; Michael J. Cohen (1982), 159.

21. Note of a meeting, Oct. 1, 1946, NA, CAB 127/280; Bevin to Attlee, telegram, Aug. 14, 1946, NA, CAB 127/280.

22. Note of a meeting, Oct. 1, 1946.

23. DO (46) 40, Memorandum, March 13, 1946, NA, CAB 131/2; DO (46) 27 Memorandum, March 2, 1946, NA, CAB 131/2; Ismay to Attlee, note, July 15, 1946, NA, CAB 127/280; Army Council CP (46) 281 ACSB/2097, July 22, 1946, NA, WO 32/10260.

24. Note of a meeting, Oct. 1, 1946; Hall to Cunningham, telegram, Oct. 2, 1946, Cunningham Papers, I/3.

25. Dugdale (1973), 240; Michael J. Cohen (1982), 159, 162–67; Louis (1984), 439–41; Bullock (1983), 304–5; Harris (1982), 395–96; *Times*, Oct. 7, 1946.

26. Antonius (1979), 13–412; Bird (2010), 18–19; *Times*, Dec. 8, 1984; Segev (2000), 469–70; Wasserstein (1978), 28–29, 182–88; Montefiore (2011), 463–64, 485; Rose (2009), 32; Cleveland, "George Antonius"; Hasson, "Jay Gatsby in Jerusalem"; *Economist*, Jan. 13, 2011; Barker to Antonius, letters, Oct. 11, 24, and 26, 1946, P/867, ISA.

27. Barker to Antonius, letters, April 14, 1947, and April 26, 1947, P/867, ISA.

28. Bethell (1979), 280; Kenneally (2008), 229–30; *Times*, Sept. 28, 2000; First Battalion, Welsh Guards, Quarterly Historical Report, Sept. 30, 1946, NA, WO 261/302; HQ, Officer Commanding Troops, Jaffa/Tel Aviv, Quarterly Historical Report, Sept. 30, 1946, NA, WO 261/129.

29. Mansfield to Kellar, letter, Oct. 26, 1946, NA, KV 5/31; notes on a conversation between the DSO and "Z," Oct. 7, 1946, NA, KV 5/30.

30. Cunningham to Creech Jones, telegram, Oct. 29, 1946, NA, CO 733/456/75156/151 A pt. 2; *Daily Telegraph* and *Palestine Post*, Oct. 25, 1946; Trevor (1948),

273–74; Wilson (2001), 140; interview with Lieutenant Colonel Richard Webb, Oct. 24, 1946, S 25/6910, CZA; Mitchell (1969), 59.

31. Mitchell (1969), 55; Wilson (2001), 140; Max Steinberg to Inverchapel, telegram, Oct. 24, 1946, NA, FO 371/52508; T. E. Bromley to Steinberg, letter, Oct. 31, 1946, NA, FO 371/52508; *Palestine Post*, Oct. 27, 1946; Bethell (1979), 280–81.

32. Cunningham to Creech Jones, telegram, Oct. 29, 1946; Wilson (2001), 148; Cassels to Barker, letter, Oct. 28, 1946, NA, WO 275/72; Linklater, 317 Airborne Field Security Section Report, Aug. 1946; HQ South Palestine District, Intelligence Summary 14.

33. Begin (1977a), 53–54, 56; Kenneally (2008), 227

34. Niv (1975), 5:54; Sir David Petrie (director general, MI5), Minute 44, March 30, 1946, NA, KV 5/4; extract from SIME, Aug. 14, 1946, NA, KV 2/3428; Kellar to Trafford Smith, letter, Aug. 26, 1946, NA, KV 5/30; Andrew (2009), 355–56; Cesarani (2009), 44–45; Walton (2008), 448–50; Notes for Director General's Meeting with Prime Minister, Aug. 28, 1946, NA, KV 3/41.

35. Extract, Jewish Telegraphic Agency, July 18, 1946, NA, KV 5/36; Isham to Oldfield, telegram, Sept. 2, 1946, NA, KV 5/37; H. L. Brown to Lieutenant Colonel the Hon. G. Eyres Monsell, letter, Sept. 7, 1946, NA, KV 5/37; Cesarani (2009), 45.

36. Cesarani (2009), 45; Samuel Katz (1968), 102; Bethell (1979), 191.

37. Sir Noel Charles (ambassador, Rome) to Bevin, telegram, Dec. 28, 1946, NA, CO 537/2295; Charles to Bevin, letter, Jan. 14, 1947, NA, FO 371/67796; Tavin (1986), 20–21; Samuel Katz (1968), 102; Cesarani (2009), 45.

38. Niv (1975), 5:56, 213; Sixth Airborne Division, Intelligence Summary 17, Nov. 8, 1946, NA, WO 261/656; "The Signal from Rome," Voice of Fighting Zion (n.d.), K-4 3/15, JI; *Times*, Nov. 5, 1946.

39. John O'Sullivan, Destruction of British Embassy, Rome by Jewish Terrorists, Nov. 1, 1946, Nov. 20, 1946, O'Sullivan Papers; Tavin (1986), 20–21; *Times*, Oct. 31, 1946; *Palestine Post*, Nov. 1, 1946; Cesarani (2009), 46; Niv (1975), 5:213–14.

40. "Signal from Rome"; Foreign Office to Bevin, telegram, Nov. 4, 1946, NA, FO 800/486 Pa/46/112; *Palestine Post*, Nov. 8, 1946.

41. O'Sullivan, Destruction of British Embassy; Charles to Bevin, telegram, Dec. 28, 1946, NA, CO 537/2295; aide-mémoire, Rome, Jan. 4, 1947, NA, FO 371/67796; Begin (1977a), 131–32; Samuel Katz (1968), 103.

42. O'Sullivan, Destruction of British Embassy; Charles to Bevin, telegram, Dec. 28, 1946; *Palestine Post*, Nov. 5, 1946; Cesarani (2009), 48; Samuel Katz (1968), 105; Johan J. Smertenko to Creech Jones, letter, Dec. 24, 194, NA, CO 537/2295.

43. Cunningham to Creech Jones, telegram, Dec. 28, 1946, NA, FO 371/67796; *Palestine Post*, Nov. 20, 1946; Charles to Bevin, telegrams, Dec. 28 and 29, 1946, NA, CO 537/2295; Rome to Foreign Office, telegram, Dec. 19, 1946, NA, FO 371/67796; Charles to Bevin, telegram, Jan. 4, 1947, NA, FO 371/67796; E. Iredell, minute, Jan. 23, 1947, NA, FO 371/67796; British Embassy, Rome, to Eastern Department, Foreign Office, letter, Oct. 22, 1947, NA, FO 371/67796; Begin (1977a), 131–32; Cesarani (2009), 48; Samuel Katz (1968), 106.

44. Western Department to Chancery, British Embassy, Rome, letter, March 3, 1947, NA, FO 371/67796; British Embassy, Rome, to Eastern Department, Foreign Office, letter, Oct. 22, 1947; O'Sullivan, Destruction of British Embassy; Cesarani (2009), 48; Charles to Bevin, telegram, Jan. 14, 1947, NA, FO 371/67796; E. M. Fitzgerald (CO), minute, Jan. 14, 1947, NA, CO 537/2295.

45. Rymer-Jones to Cunningham, letter, Dec. 13, 1946, Cunningham Papers, VI/4; Andrew (2009), 355; Burt (1959), 126; Attlee to Bevin, telegram, Nov. 4, 1946, NA, FO 800/486 Pa/46/111; Dixon to Consul General, minute, New York, Nov. 5, 1946, NA, FO 800/486 Pa/46/111; Morgan (1984), 396; Harris (1982), 396.

46. Burt (1959), 126; J. C. Robertson to Telfer Smollett, letter, Nov. 9, 1946, NA, KV 5/38; Robertson to Young, telegram, Nov. 13, 1946, NA, KV 5/38; Cesarani (2009), 49; Niv (1975), 5:54. In his memoirs, Montgomery describes the incident but incorrectly attributes the threat to Lehi. Montgomery (1958), 422–23.

47. Niv (1975), 5:54; *Evening News*, Nov. 11, 1946; *Times*, Nov. 12, 1946; *Palestine Post*, Nov. 11 and 13, 1946.

48. Rymer-Jones to Cunningham, letter, Dec. 13, 1946, Cunningham Papers, VI/4; Cesarani (2009), 49; *Times*, Nov. 14, 1946; Andrew (2009), 357–58; *Palestine Post*, Nov. 12, 1946.

49. Major R. Thistlewaite to SIME GHQ, MELF, letter, Nov. 5, 1946, NA, KV 5/38; O'Sullivan to Oldfield, letter, Dec. 16, 1946, NA, KV 5/38; Andrew (2009), 352.

50. Montgomery to Dempsey, personal directive, June 27, 1946, NA 216/194; Dempsey to Montgomery, telegram, Sept. 27, 1946, NA 216/194; Charters (1989), 185–86, 196.

51. Attack on Jerusalem Railway Station by the Irgun Zvai Leumi, Nov. 1, 1946, O'Sullivan Papers; Bethell (1979), 289; security minutes, Nov. 1946, Cunningham Papers, IV/1; PICME Intelligence Summary 68, Nov. 1, 1946, NA, WO 261/769; *Times*, Nov. 1, 1946.

52. Michael J. Cohen (1982), 159; *Times*, Nov. 1, 1946.

53. Cunningham to Creech Jones, telegram, Oct. 22, 1946, Cunningham Papers, I/3; Cunningham to Hall, telegram, Sept. 27, 1946, NA, CO 537/2287; *Palestine Post*, Oct. 23 and 24 and Nov. 6, 1946; Creech Jones to Cunningham, telegram, Oct. 24, 1946, NA, FO 371/52650; Cunningham to Hall, telegrams, Sept. 20, 25, and 27, 1946, NA, FO 371/52650; Cunningham to Creech Jones, telegrams, Sept. 25 and 27, 1946, NA, CO 537/2287; Cunningham to Creech Jones, telegram, Oct. 21, 1946, NA, CAB 127/280; Dugdale (1973), 240–41; Michael J. Cohen (1982), 160; *Times*, Oct. 23 and 30, 1946; Trevor (1948), 272; Sager (1985), 4–5; CP (46) 414, Nov. 1, 1946, NA, CAB 129/14; Sixth Airborne Division, Intelligence Summary 16, Nov. 1, 1946, NA, WO 261/656; James Pollack, District Commissioner Offices, Jerusalem, Fortnightly Report, Oct. 16–31, NA, CO 537/1707.

54. CM (46) 94, Nov. 4, 1946, NA, CAB 128/6; Creech Jones to Cunningham, telegrams, Oct. 28 and Nov. 1, 1946, Cunningham Papers, I/3; Sixth Airborne Division, Intelligence Summary 16; CM (46) 414, Nov. 1, 1946, NA, CAB 128/6.

55. Army Council CP (46) 414 ACSB/2199, Nov. 4, 1946, NA, WO 32/10260; Sixth Airborne Division, Intelligence Summary 17, Nov. 8, 1946, NA, WO 275/58.

56. Memorandum on the Historical Background to the Present Position in Regard to Jewish Immigration into Palestine, Nov. 8, 1946, NA, FO 371/52636.

57. Hall to Cunningham, telegram, Oct. 3, 1946, NA, CO 537/2287; CM (46) 94, Nov. 4, 1946, NA, CAB 128/6; *Palestine Press Review*, Sept. 13 and 15, 1946, NA, WO 275/108; H. L. Brown (MI5) to Trafford Smith, letter, Sept. 19, 1946, NA, KV 5/33; Cunningham to Hall, telegram, Oct. 2, 1946, NA, CO 537/1708; Monthly Report, Oct. 2, 1946, NA, CO 537/1708; PICME Intelligence Summary 69, Nov. 15, 1946, NA, WO 261/769.

58. Pollack to Gurney, fortnightly report, Nov. 19, 1946, NA, CO 537/1707; *Palestine*

Press Review, Sept. 13, 1946; HQ Palestine, Fortnightly Intelligence Newsletter, Nov. 9–22, 1946, NA, WO 275/63; Lloyd Phillips to the Reverend A. Phillips, letter, Nov. 5, 1946, Lloyd Phillips Papers, 4/2.

59. Government of Palestine, *Palestine Railways*, 13; Jewish Terrorist Outrages Since His Excellency's Arrival in Palestine; Wilson (1949), 82; *Palestine Post*, Nov. 7 and 10, and Nov. 8, 1946; Section 7, Dec. 1946, 10.684, CZA.

60. Cunningham, notes on points raised with Creech Jones, Nov. 14, 1946, NA, CO 537/1822.

61. Dempsey to Montgomery, telegram, Nov. 16, 1946, NA, WO 216/194; Jewish Terrorist Outrages Since His Excellency's Arrival in Palestine; Government of Palestine, *Palestine Railways*, 12–13; *Palestine Post*, Nov. 14, 1946.

62. Dempsey to Montgomery, telegram, Nov. 16, 1946.

63. Cunningham to Creech Jones, telegram, Nov. 19, 1946, NA, CO 733/456 75156/151A pt. 2; Government of Palestine, *Palestine Railways*, 13; Jewish Terrorist Outrages Since His Excellency's Arrival in Palestine; Phillips to the Reverend A. Phillips, Nov. 23, 1946, Lloyd Phillips Papers, 4/2 2; *Palestine Post*, Nov. 18, 19, and 20, 1946; Dempsey to Montgomery, telegram, Nov. 19, 1946, NA, WO 216/194.

64. Cunningham to Creech Jones, telegram, Nov. 19, 1946, NA, CO 537/728; Montgomery (1958), 418–19; Montgomery to Dempsey, telegram, Nov. 11, 1946, BLM 211/11, Montgomery Papers; Dempsey to Montgomery, telegram, Nov. 19, 1946.

65. Extract from DO 33 (46), Nov. 20, 1946, NA, WO 32/10260; Montgomery Diary, pt. 4, chap. 26, "Palestine—November 28/December 1, 1946," BLM 177/1, Montgomery Papers; Montgomery (1958), 419; Montgomery to Dempsey, telegram, Nov. 20, 1946, NA, WO 216/194; Creech Jones to Cunningham, telegram, Nov. 21, 1946, Cunningham Papers, I/3.

66. Press cutting from Jewish Telegraphic Agency, *Daily News Bulletin*, Nov. 20, 1946, NA, KV 5/31; *Manchester Guardian*, Nov. 21, 1946; Montgomery, "Palestine—November 28/December 1, 1946"; Government of Palestine, *Palestine Railways*, 13; *Palestine Post*, Nov. 20 and 21, 1946; Cunningham to Creech Jones, telegram, Dec. 9, 1946, NA, CO 733/456/75156/151A pt. 2; Montgomery to Simpson, telegram, Nov. 26, 1946, BLM 211/19, Montgomery Papers; H.E. security minutes, Nov. 20, 1946, Cunningham Papers, IV/1.

67. Dempsey to Montgomery, telegram, Nov. 21, 1946, NA, WO 216/194.

68. Cunningham to Creech Jones, telegram, Nov. 23, 1946, NA, CAB 127/280; Cunningham to Creech Jones, telegram, Nov. 26, 1946, Cunningham Papers, I/3; PICME Intelligence Summary 70, Nov. 29, 1946, NA, WO 261/769.

69. Cunningham to Creech Jones, telegram, Nov. 23, 1946.

70. Montgomery to Simpson, telegram, Nov. 26, 1946; Montgomery to Simpson, telegram, Dec. 2, 1946, BLM 211/21, Montgomery Papers; Hamilton (1986), 665–66; Montgomery (1958), 419–20.

71. Barker to Dempsey, telegram, Nov. 21, 1946, Cunningham Papers, I/3.

72. Montgomery (1958), 418–21; Montgomery to Simpson, telegram, Nov. 26, 1946.

73. Conference held at Government House, Jerusalem, Nov. 29, 1946, signed by Montgomery of Alamein, NA, CAB 127/281.

74. Cunningham to Creech Jones, telegram, Dec. 3, 1946, Cunningham Papers, I/3; Cunningham, note (n.d.), Cunningham Papers, IV/2; conference held at Government House, Nov. 29, 1946.

75. Cunningham (1948), 485–86.
76. Cunningham, "Letter to *Daily Telegraph* on Publication of Monty's Book" (n.d.), Cunningham Papers, V/4; Montgomery, "Palestine—November 28/December 1, 1946."
77. Ibid.

CHAPTER 16: BLUNTED BAYONETS

1. Clark (1978), 243; conference at Colonial Office, Jan. 3, 1947, Montgomery Papers; Cunningham to Creech Jones, telegram, Nov. 23, 1946; Cunningham (1948), 486; Hall to Cunningham, telegram, July 26, 1946, NA, CO 537/1697; Cunningham to Hall, telegram, Aug. 1, 1946, Cunningham Papers, I/2; *Palestine Post*, July 31, 1946.
2. Museum Staff (1995), 24; "Lt. Col. Sir Charles Wickham"; Edward Horne (1982), 561–62, 569–70; Jeffery (1997), 156; Killingray and Anderson (1992), 75; Ryder (1990), 40, 48, 79.
3. R. J. K. Sinclair (curator, Royal Ulster Constabulary Museum, Belfast, Northern Ireland) to the author, July 16, 1996; Sir Charles Wickham, report, Dec. 2, 1946, NA, CO 537/2269.
4. Montgomery, "Palestine—November 28/December 1, 1946"; Montgomery to Simpson, telegram, Dec. 2, 1946, BLM 211/21, Montgomery Papers.
5. Wickham, report, Dec. 2, 1946; Montgomery to Simpson, telegram, Dec. 2, 1946.
6. Charters (1991), 127; Charters (1979), 57; Edward Horne (1982), 556–57; W. N. Gray, PPF Administrative Report 1946, 1947, NA, CO 814/40.
7. Hamilton (1981), 305; Montgomery to Simpson, telegram, Dec. 2, 1946.
8. W. W. Clark, minute, Nov. 1, 1946, NA, CO 537/1699 75015/59; CP (45) 165, Sept. 10, 1945, NA, CAB 129/2; Edward Horne (1982), 335; Hall to Cunningham, telegram, July 26, 1946; Fergusson (1970), 201–2.
9. The British section had 2,993 to 2,460 men below its authorized strength. Note on the Palestine Police Force, Dec. 1946, NA, CO 537/2269.
10. Wickham, report, Dec. 2, 1946; Pinkerton to State Department, letter, March 29, 1946, RG 226, box 19, file 22, folder 3 GP-50, NARA; Gray, PPF Administrative Report 1946.
11. Killingray and Anderson (1992), 72–73; Edward Horne (1982), 516–17, 555, 596; McConnel, Situation in Palestine, Jan. 11, 1944; Jeffries (1952), 157; WM 158 (43), Nov. 19, 1943, NA, CAB 65/36; memorandum, Sept. 15, 1944, NA, CO 733/451/750515/55B/44; JICAME Report, March 23, 1944, RG 165, Palestine 2710, box 3025, NARA; JICAME Report, May 10, 1944, RG 165, Palestine 2700, box 3025, NARA; JICAME Report, March 29, 1944, RG 165, Palestine 2700, box 3025, NARA; OSS Report 67284, April 17, 1944, RG 165, Palestine 2700, box 3025, NARA; Pinkerton to State Department, letter, March 29, 1946; note, Jan. 24, 1938, Tegart Papers, II/2; Edward Horne (1982), 236–37; Churchill, memorandum, Nov. 29, 1944, NA, CAB 127/270.
12. Note on the Palestine Police Force, Dec. 1946; Pinkerton to State Department, letter, March 29, 1946; Edward Horne (1982), 52; Montgomery to Simpson, telegram, Dec. 2, 1946; Montgomery, "Palestine—28 November/1 December 1946"; Montgomery (1958), 420; Wickham, report, Dec. 2, 1946; Killingray and Ander-

son (1992), 75; Hamilton (1981), 300–302, 304–5; Hamilton (1986), 666–67; Wilson (1949), 16–17.

13. Wickham, report, Dec. 2, 1946; Hamilton (1986), 666–67.
14. Wickham, report, Dec. 2, 1946; Gray, PPF Administrative Report 1946; W. W. Clark, minute, June 26, 1947, NA, CO 537/2269; Trevor (1948), 295; HQ Palestine, Jerusalem, picture of the military layout in Palestine and Transjordan, Feb. 1947, RG 65/3588, ISA.
15. Moffat, Criminal Investigation Department, Dec. 2, 1946, NA, CO 537/2269; Wickham, report, Dec. 2, 1946.
16. Moffat, Criminal Investigation Department; Gray, PPF Administrative Report 1946; French (2011), 21–22.
17. Wickham, report, Dec. 2, 1946; Moffat, Criminal Investigation Department; Clarke, "A Quarter of My Century: The Author in September 1939," Clarke Papers; Rymer-Jones to MacPherson, letter, Dec. 21, 1943, NA, WO 208/1702; Trafford Smith, minute of meeting at the Colonial Office between Hall, Trafford Smith, Clark, and Rymer-Jones, Jan. 9, 1946, NA, CO 733/451 75015/55B; Edward Horne (1982), 475; David John Clark (1978), 150; French (2011), 26; Dekel (1959), 15.
18. Moffat, Criminal Investigation Department; Charters (1991), 127.
19. Moffat, Criminal Investigation Department; Wickham, report, Dec. 2, 1946.
20. Police Recruitment, Dec. 31, 1946, NA, CO 537/1697 75015/55B; Palestine Police: Notes for the Information of Candidates for Appointment as British Police Constables (n.d.), Edwards Papers; *Palestine Police as a Career,* July 8, 1946, Morton Papers, 1/1; IWM, "Palestine Police," Colonial Film: Moving Images of the British Empire, http://www.colonialfilm.org.uk/node/6717; Clarke, minute, Nov. 1, 1946; Palestine Police—note of Sir George Gater's discussions with Gray on Nov. 13, 1946, NA, CO 537/1699 75015/59.
21. *Palestine Post,* Dec. 4, 1946; *Times,* Jan. 1, 1947; Cunningham to Creech Jones, telegram, Oct. 22, 1946.
22. Cunningham to Creech Jones, telegram, Dec. 3, 1946, NA, CAB 217/281; Michael J. Cohen (1982), 160; Trevor (1948), 277.
23. *Palestine Post,* Dec. 5, 1946; Cunningham to Creech Jones, telegram, Dec. 5, 1946, Cunningham Papers, I/3; Dugdale (1973), 242–44; Trevor (1948), 289.
24. Creech Jones to Lieutenant Colonel W. H. Bromley-Davenport (MP), letter, Dec. 12, 1946, NA, CO 733/456 75156/151A pt. 2; Creech Jones to A. Moyle (MP), letter, Dec. 30, 1946, NA, CO 733/456 75156/151A pt. 2; M. Acton to Creech Jones, letter, Dec. 1, 1946, NA, CO 733/456 75156/151A pt. 2; Debates, House of Commons, vol. 431, c20w, Dec. 2, 1946; Debates, House of Commons, vol. 431, col. 942, Dec. 4, 1946; Garfield (2004), 321; First Battalion, the Royal Ulster, Quarterly Historical Report, Dec. 31, 1946, NA, WO 261/374; First Battalion, Argyll and Sutherland Highlanders, Quarterly Historical Report, Dec. 31, 1946, NA, WO 261/383; Eighth Infantry Brigade, Third Infantry Division, Quarterly Historical Report, Dec. 31, 1946, NA, WO 261/383; HQ South Palestine District, Quarterly Historical Report, Dec. 31, 1946, NA, WO 261/647.
25. Dempsey to Montgomery, telegram, Dec. 17, 1946, NA, WO 216/194; Montgomery to Dempsey, telegram, Dec. 18, 1946, NA, WO 216/194; Beeley, minute, Dec. 31, 1946, NA, FO 371/52571.
26. Military Procedures, 1945–47, Scale of Punishments (n.d.), Brebber Papers, 2/1; *Palestine Post,* Dec. 12, 1946; Niv (1975), 5:71; Trevor (1948), 294.

27. *Palestine Press Review*, Jan. 9, 1947, CS SF/685/39/397, ISA; Trevor (1948), 294–95; *Palestine Post*, Jan. 3, 1935, and March 12, 1939; Niv (1975), 5:71.
28. Begin (1977a), 231–32; Gurion (1950), 107; Niv (1975), 5:73.
29. Gurion (1950), 106; *Palestine Post*, Dec. 12 and 18, 1946; Trevor (1948), 294–95; Voice of Fighting Zion, broadcast on Jan. 22, 1947, of poster issued on Dec. 27, 1946, K-4 7/15, JI.
30. *Palestine Post*, Dec. 30, 1946; Bethell (1979), 291–92; Gurion (1950), 106–8; Niv (1975), 5:73–76.
31. Montgomery to Dempsey, telegram, Dec. 29, 1946, NA, WO 216/194; interview with Rabbi Fishman, Jan. 1, 1947, Cunningham Papers, V/1; Ben-Zvi to Gurney, letter, Dec. 27, 1946, CS D/160/40, ISA; Wilson (1949), 87; Cunningham to Creech Jones, telegram, Jan. 9, 1947, NA, CO 733/477 7516/151A.
32. Trevor (1948), 296; *Times*, Jan. 2, 1947; Grimwood to Trafford-Smith, letter, Jan. 11, 1947, NA, CO 733/477 75156/151A; telegram 1, Jan. 3, 1947, in Tauber (2012), 59–60.
33. *Daily Telegraph*, Jan. 2, 3, and 6, 1947; *Times*, Dec. 31, 1946, and Jan. 3 and 8, 1947.
34. Gurney to Creech Jones, telegram, Jan. 10, 1947, NA, CO 537/2289; summary of a statement by Begin, Dec. 20, 1946, NA, WO 275/63; Thistlewaite for Isham to Sir Percy Sillitoe (director general, MI5), letter, Jan. 3, 1947, NA, KV 5/38.
35. Creech Jones to Gurney, telegram, Jan. 9, 1947, NA, FO 371/61763; Gurney to Creech Jones, telegram, Jan. 11, 1947, NA, FO 371/61763; *Palestine Post*, Jan. 5, 1947.
36. Minutes of the 1st (47) Defence Committee Meeting, Jan. 1, 1947, NA, WO 32/10260; Michael J. Cohen (1982), 178, 180, 208, 177–83; Dugdale (1973), 243–45; Bullock (1983), 345; Peter Clarke (2008), 480–82; Vera Weizmann (1967), 212–13; Heller (2003), 156–57; MI6 to Colonial Office, memorandum, Jan. 20, 1947, NA, KV 5/38; Policy of Jewish Terrorists in Palestine forwarded by MI6, Jan. 2, 1947, NA, KV 5/31.
37. District Commissioner's Offices, Gaza, Fortnightly Report 189, Dec. 18, 1946, NA, CO 537/1707; District Commissioner's Offices, Jerusalem, Fortnightly Report, Dec. 19, 1946, NA, CO 537/1707; Sixth Airborne Division, Intelligence Summary 25, Jan. 3, 1947, NA, WO 261/656; Cunningham to Creech Jones, telegram, Jan. 3, 1947, Cunningham Papers, I/4; District Commissioner's Offices, Gaza, Fortnightly Report 187, Nov. 21, 1946, NA, CO 537/1707; PICME Intelligence Summary 70, Nov. 29, 1946, NA, WO 261/769; Secretary-General Arab League to Sir Ronald Campbell (ambassador, Cairo), letter, Dec. 26, 1946, NA, FO 141/1091 101/45846; Sixth Airborne Division, Intelligence Summary 19, Nov. 22, 1946, NA, WO 261/656; District Commissioner's Offices, Galilee, Fortnightly Report 188, Dec. 7, 1946, NA, CO 537/1707; PICME Intelligence Summary 71, Dec. 13, 1946, NA, WO 261/769; Fayiza Majeed to Cunningham, letter, Dec. 15, 1946, CS D/237/46, ISA; Sami Taha to Gurney, letter, Dec. 1946, CS D/237/46, ISA; Cunningham to Creech Jones, telegram, Dec. 24, 1946, NA, CO 537/1728; Cunningham to Creech Jones, telegram, Jan. 2, 1947, NA, FO 371/61761; Gurney to Creech Jones, telegram, Jan. 3, 1947, NA, FO 371/61761; Sixth Airborne Division, Intelligence Summary 21, Dec. 6, 1946, NA, WO 275/58; Sixth Airborne Division, Intelligence Summary 20, Nov. 29, 1946, NA, WO 261/656.
38. Montgomery Diary, pt. 5, chap. 33, "December 10, 1946, to February 3, 1947," BLM 178/1, Montgomery Papers; Montgomery (1958), 421.

39. Hamilton (1981), 293–94, 300–302, 304–5; Rose (2009), 45; Army Council Secretariat Minutes of the Meeting of the Defence Committee DO (46) 145, Jan. 1, 1947, NA, WO 32/10260.

40. Army Council Secretariat Minutes of the Meeting of the Defence Committee DO (46) 145, Jan. 1, 1947; Montgomery (1958), 421; interview with Rabbi Fishman, Jan. 1, 1947.

41. Note of conference, Jan. 3, 1947, Cunningham Papers, V/4.

42. CM (47) 6, Jan. 15, 1947, NA, CAB 128/9; Montgomery to Dempsey, telegram, Jan. 15, 1947, NA, WO 216/194; Creech Jones to Cunningham, telegram, Jan. 20, 1946, Cunningham Papers, I/4; Montgomery to Dempsey, telegram, Jan. 2, 1947, NA, WO 216/194; Dempsey to Montgomery, telegram, Jan. 16, 1947, NA, WO 216/194; *Times*, Jan. 4 and 6, 1947; Bell (1977), 186.

43. Fletcher-Cooke, "The Compulsive 'Cuppa'" (unpublished MS), 1971, 4, Fletcher-Cooke Papers; Tomlinson, Memoir: Jerusalem (n.d.), Tomlinson Papers; Graves (1949), 55, 57.

44. O'Sullivan, Annual Report for J2 Section, 1947, Jan. 26, 1948, O'Sullivan Papers; summary of recent searches in Palestine, Jan. 1947, NA, CO 733/477 75156/151; Niv (1975), 5:76, 86–87; John Gutch (assistant secretary, CO) to Cunningham, telegram, Jan. 14, 1947, Cunningham Papers, I/4; Montgomery to Dempsey, telegram, Jan. 16, 1947, NA, WO 216/194; Debates, House of Commons, vol. 432, cols. 1303–4 (Stanley), Jan. 31, 1947; Trevor (1948), 295, 300.

45. Montgomery to Dempsey, telegram, Jan. 16, 1947; Gurney to Creech Jones, telegram, Jan. 21, 1947, Cunningham Papers, I/4; Montgomery, "December 10, 1946 to February 3, 1947."

46. Debates, House of Commons, vol. 432, col. 1323, Jan. 31, 1947.

47. Niv (1975), 5:79–83, 88; Golan (2003), 94, 280–81; Rymer-Jones Papers, 110, 147; Barker to Montgomery, telegram, Jan. 9, 1947, BLM 210/7, Montgomery Papers; Begin (1977a), 254–55; Bell (1977), 161; Bethell (1979), 298; Gruner (1950), 83–98; extract from *Jewish Standard*, Jan. 3, 1947, NA, KV 5/38 OF 608/1; *Times*, Jan. 25, 1947; Begin (1977a), 255–56; *Manchester Guardian*, Jan. 8, 1947.

48. Dempsey to Montgomery, telegram, Jan. 21, 1947, NA, WO 216/194; Cunningham to Creech Jones, telegram, Jan. 21, 1947, Cunningham Papers, I/4; Barker, Operation Policy, Jan. 23, 1947, Cunningham Papers, I/4; note of a meeting at Government House, Jan. 21, 1947, Cunningham Papers, V/4; record of conference at GHQ MELF, Cairo, Nov. 25, 1946, BLM 177/5, Montgomery Papers; Debates, House of Commons, vol. 432, cols. 196–201 (Mackeson, Smithers, and Creech Jones), Jan. 22, 1947.

49. *Times*, Jan. 27, 1947; telegram 11, Jan. 27, 1947, in Tauber (2012), 67; Trevor (1948), 301–2.

50. Bethell (1979), 299; *Times* and *Palestine Post*, Jan. 28, 1947; Bell (1977), 188; Trevor (1948), 302.

51. Creech Jones to Cunningham, telegram, Jan. 29, 1947, NA, CO 537/3870; Cunningham to Creech Jones, telegram, Jan. 27, 1947, NA, CO 537/3870; Note of meeting, Jan. 27, 1947, Cunningham Papers, V/4; Barker to Antonius, letter, Jan. 31, 1947, P/867, ISA; Debates, House of Commons, vol. 432, cols. 772–76, Jan. 28, 1947; *Times*, Jan. 28 and 30, 1947.

52. *Times*, Jan. 4 and 29–31, 1947; *Palestine Post*, Jan. 29, 1947; Gurney to Creech Jones, telegram, Jan. 7, 1947, NA, CO 537/2294; Gurney to Creech Jones, telegram, Jan. 8, 1947, Cunningham Papers, I/4; Martin to Sir George Gater,

minute, Jan. 10, 1947, NA, CO 537/3870; Gurney to Creech Jones, telegram, Jan. 13, 1947, Cunningham Papers, I/4; Cunningham to Creech Jones, telegram, Jan. 21, 1947, NA, CO 537/2294; HQ South Palestine, Intelligence Summary 21, Jan. 13, 1947, NA, WO 261/171; Bethell (1979), 299–300; telegram 11, Jan. 27, 1947, in Tauber (2012), 67; Begin (1977a), 256–57.

53. Cunningham to Creech Jones, telegram, Jan. 30, 1947, NA, CO 537/2298; Bevin to Inverchapel, telegram, Feb. 7, 1947, NA, CAB 104/272; Wilson (1949), 121; *Times*, Jan. 28, 1947; Cunningham to Creech Jones, telegram, Jan. 29, 1947, NA, CO 537/3870; Fortnightly Intelligence Newsletter 34, Jan. 1947, NA, WO 275/63; quoted in Debates, House of Commons, vol. 432, col. 1977, Feb. 6, 1947; Barker to Antonius, Jan. 31, 1947, P/867, IDA; Dempsey to Montgomery, telegram, Jan. 29, 1947, NA, WO 216/194.

54. Montgomery to Dempsey, telegram, Jan. 30, 1947, NA, WO 216/194.

55. Creech Jones to Montgomery, Jan. 28, 1947, BLM 210/0, Montgomery Papers; Montgomery, "December 10, 1946, to February 3, 1947"; Montgomery to Dempsey, telegram, Jan. 31, 1947, NA, WO 216/194; Montgomery (1958), 422.

56. *Times*, Jan. 27, 1947; Debates, House of Commons, vol. 432, cols. 1306, 1326–27, 1345–49, Jan. 31, 1947.

57. Trevor (1948), 304–5; Wilson (1949), 102–3; Gurney, Chief Secretary's Office, Jerusalem, notice, Jan. 31, 1947, NA, WO 261/215; Gurney to All Department Heads, letter, Feb. 7, 1947, SF/50/47/A, Keating Papers, IWM; Barker to Dempsey, telegram, Feb. 1947, NA, WO 261/140; Third Parachute Brigade Operational Instruction 26, Feb. 1, 1947, NA, WO 261/215.

58. Cunningham to Creech Jones, telegram, Feb. 13, 1947, NA, CO 537/2294; Trevor (1948), 305, 306n69; *Palestine Post*, Feb. 2, 1947; Sherman (1997), 201–2.

59. Secretary of State George Marshall to Inverchapel, telegram, Feb. 6, 1947, in *FRUS, 1947*, 1030; Creech Jones to Attlee, note, Feb. 4, 1947, NA, CO 537/2298; security meeting, Feb. 5, 1947, Cunningham Papers, IV/2; Operation Fantail, Feb. 5, 1947, NA, WO 275/36; Lloyd Phillips to the Reverend A. Lloyd Phillips, letters Jan. 21 and Feb. 3, 1947, Lloyd Phillips Papers, 4/2.

60. Tomlinson, Memoir: Jerusalem; *Times*, Feb. 1, 1947; Sherman (1997), 201, 251.

61. HQ South Palestine District, Quarterly Historical Report for Quarter Ending March 31, 1947, app. B, April 24, 1947, NA, WO 261/171; Blaxland (1971), 44; Wilson (1949), 103; Tomlinson, Memoir: Jerusalem; *Times*, March 5, 1947.

62. Wilson (1949), 103; CP (47) 59, Feb. 13, 1947, NA, CAB 129/17; Fletcher-Cooke, "Sir Henry Gurney," April 18, 1963, Fletcher-Cooke Papers; Fletcher-Cooke, "Compulsive 'Cuppa,'" 6–8; Sherman (1997), 202; ; Lloyd Phillips to the Reverend A. Lloyd Phillips, letters, Feb. 17 and Feb. 22, 1947, Lloyd Phillips Papers, 4/2.

63. Fletcher-Cooke, "Sir Henry Gurney"; The Sports Club of Jerusalem Annual General Meeting, March 21, 1947, box 2/4, Keating Papers; Fletcher-Cooke, "Compulsive 'Cuppa,'" 6–8; interview with Ivan Lloyd Phillips (n.d.), Scrivenor Papers; Golani (2009), 3–6; Brutton (1996), 80–82.

64. Debates, House of Commons, vol. 432, cols. 1301–2 (Stanley), Jan. 31, 1947; CP (47) 59, Feb. 13, 1947, NA, CAB 129/17; HQ First Infantry, Quarterly Historical Report, Dec. 14, 1946, NA, WO 261/652; Montgomery Diary, pt. 4, chap. 33, "November 28, 1946, to December 1, 1947," BLM 177/1, Montgomery Papers; Montgomery, "War Office Period"; CM 22 (47) Feb. 14, 1947, NA, CAB 128/9; Blaxland (1971), 42.

65. Barker, Special Order of the Day, Feb. 12, 1947, NA, WO 275/4; Blaxland (1971), 44.

66. CP (59) 18, Feb. 13, 1947, NA, CAB 129/17; CP (47) 49, Feb. 6, 1947, NA, CAB 129/17; CM (47) 18, Feb. 7, 1947, NA, CAB 128/9; Louis (1984), 460.

67. Dugdale (1973), 249; *Times*, Feb. 11 and 12, 1947; CM (47), 22 Feb. 14, 1947, NA, CAB 128/9; *Newsweek*, Feb. 24, 1947; Hurewitz (1976), 272–73.

68. Treasurer, notes, March 6, 1939, Tegart Papers, II/1; Pimlott (1986), 389–90; Garfield (2004), 343–44, 347–52; *Palestine Post*, Feb. 12 and 13, 1947; *Times*, Feb. 14, 1947; Peter Clarke (2008), 476; Harris (1982), 335; Fauvell and Simpson, "History of British Winters."

69. CP (47) 49, Feb. 6, 1947, NA, CAB 129/17; Debates, House of Commons, vol. 432, col. 1349, Jan. 31, 1947; Debates, House of Commons, vol. 425, col. 1871 (Dalton), July 23, 1946; Sherman (1997), 190; CM (46) 90, Oct. 24, 1946, NA, CAB 128/6; CM (47) 9, Jan. 17, 1947, NA, CAB 128/9.

70. Pimlott (1986), 389; Peter Clarke (2008), 471–72; Michael J. Cohen (1982), 30; CM (47) 9, Jan. 17, 1947, NA, CAB 128/9; CM (47) 13, Jan. 28 1947, NA, CAB 128/9; Bullock (1983), 354; Morgan (1984), 333.

71. Gordon (1969), 132; Morgan (1984), 213; Peter Clarke (2008), 476–77; CM 22 (47), Feb. 14, 1947, NA, CAB 128/9.

CHAPTER 17: AN INSTRUMENT OF DEATH

1. Cunningham to Creech Jones, telegram, Feb. 24, 1947, NA, CO 537/2294; Trevor (1948), 310; Bullock (1983), 367; Peter Clarke (2008), 482–83; Debates, House of Commons, vol. 433, col. 989 (Churchill), Feb. 18, 1947; Debates, House of Commons, vol. 433, col. 1901 (Stanley), cols. 1938–39 (Ayrton Gould), cols. 1978–90 (Crossman), Feb. 24, 1947; *Times*, Feb. 15, 1947; *Palestine Post*, Feb. 16, 1947.

2. CM 22 (47), Feb. 14, 1947, NA, CAB 128/9; Debates, House of Commons, vol. 433, col. 989, Feb. 18, 1947; Cunningham to Creech Jones, telegram, Feb. 24, 1947; telegrams 13 and 14, Feb. 19 and 20, 1947, in Tauber (2012), 68–69; *Palestine Post*, Feb. 19 and 20, 1947.

3. Wilson (1949), 112–16; HQ Chief Engineer, Palestine and Transjordan, Palestine Pamphlet: Terrorist Methods with Mines and Booby Traps, Dec. 1946, 5–15, 10.684, CZA; Cunningham to Creech Jones, telegram, April 28, 1947, Cunningham Papers, I/4.

4. Cunningham to Creech Jones, telegram, Feb. 24, 1947; telegram 15, Feb. 20, 1947, in Tauber (2012), 69; *Palestine Post*, Feb. 21, 1947.

5. Wilson (1949), 13, 102–3; Blaxland (1971), 44; J. R. Cochrane (General Staff) to 283 Wing RAF, letter, Feb. 21, 1947, NA, WO 275/86; *Palestine Post*, March 4, 1947.

6. Telegram 17, Feb. 28, 1947, in Tauber (2012), 71.

7. *Times*, March 3, 1947; Niv (1975), 5:103.

8. Destruction of the Officers' Club (n.d.), O'Sullivan Papers; *Times*, March 3, 1947; *Palestine Post*, March 2, 1947; telegram 20, March 1, 1947, in Tauber (2012), 72–73; Niv (1975), 5:102–3; "Welcome to the Yeshurun Central Synagogue."

9. Cunningham to Creech Jones, telegram, March 2, 1947, NA, CO 537/2299; telegram 22, March 2, 1947, in Tauber (2012), 73–75; *Palestine Post*, March 2, 1947.

10. Cunningham to Creech Jones, telegram, March 2, 1947; MacMillan, "Palestine: Narrative of Events from February 1947 Until Withdrawal of All British Troops," July 3, 1948, MacMillan Papers; First Infantry Report on Operation Elephant, LeRay Papers.

11. Cunningham to Creech Jones, telegram, March 2, 1947.

12. MacMillan, "Palestine: Narrative of Events."

13. Operation Elephant, April 1947, LeRay Papers; CP (47) 107, March 16, 1947, NA, CAB 129/18; Ben-Gurion to Attlee, telegram, March 18, 1947, NA, FO 371/61900; Trevor (1948), 318n76; *Palestine Post* and *Manchester Guardian*, March 4, 1947; *Times*, March 3, 1947; *Palestine Gazette Extraordinary*, March 9, 1947, NA, KV 5/30; CP (47) 107, March 26, 1947, NA, CAB 129/18; Operation Elephant, April 1947, LeRay Papers; Gale (1968), 172.

14. *Palestine Post*, March 4, 1947; *Times*, March 17, 1947; Gale (1968), 172; Cunningham to Creech Jones, telegram, March 24, 1947, Cunningham Papers, I/4; Attlee to Crossman, letter, March 31, 1947, Crossman Papers; security meeting, Feb. 5, 1947, Cunning Papers; Director of Plans to Director of Joint Planning, report, March 21, 1947, NA, CO 537/2299.

15. Cunningham to Creech Jones, telegram, Feb. 13, 1947, NA, CO 537/2299; Dempsey to Montgomery, telegram, July 23, 1946; Sixth Airborne Division, Intelligence Summary 33, March 7, 1947, NA, WO 275/58; Sixth Airborne Division, Intelligence Summary 34, March 14, 1947, NA, WO 275/58.

16. Cunningham to Creech Jones, telegram, March 3, 1947, NA, CO 537/2299.

17. Begin (1977a), 93, 326; CP (47) 107, March 16, 1947, NA, CAB 129/18.

18. Samuel Katz (1968), 124; Begin (1977a), 319.

19. *Sunday Express*, March 2, 1947; *Manchester Guardian*, March 4, 1947.

20. Debates, House of Commons, vol. 434, cols. 34–37 (Silverman, Pickthorn, Cocks, Lindsay, Mackeson, Nicholson, and Churchill), March 3, 1947.

21. *Palestine Post*, March 3, 1947; Wilson (1949), 262; telegrams 23–27, March 4–9, 1947, in Tauber (2012), 75–78; Cunningham to Creech Jones, telegram, March 11, 1947, Cunningham Papers, I/4; Sixth Airborne Division, Intelligence Summary 34, March 14, 1947.

22. Telegrams 29–33, March 12–17, 1947, in Tauber (2012), 79–82.

23. Barker to Antonius, March 3, 1947, P/867, ISA; security conference, March 14, 1947, Cunningham Papers, IV/1; CP (47) 95, March 19, 1947, NA, CAB 129/17; Gale (1968), 173; E. M. Fitzgerald, minute, April 3, 1947, NA, CO 537/2287; Cunningham to Creech Jones, telegrams, March 11 and 14, 1947, NA, CO 537/2294; HQ British Troops, G Branch, Historical Record, Jan.–March, 1947, NA, WO 261/566; HQ Palestine, Fortnightly Intelligence Newsletter, March 1–14, 1947, NA, CO 275/64.

24. Montgomery Diary, pt. 7, chap. 43, "Palestine—February 3–June 21, 1947," BLM 180/1, Montgomery Papers; Cunningham to Creech Jones, telegram, March 14, 1947, NA, CO 537/2299; Gale (1968), 172–73; Director of Plans to Director of Joint Planning, report, March 21, 1947; Gale (1968), 172–73.

25. Cunningham to Creech Jones, telegrams, March 15 and 17, 1947, NA, CO 537/2299.

26. Cunningham to Creech Jones, telegram, March 17, 1947, NA, CO 537/2294; *Daily Telegraph* and *Palestine Post*, March 17, 1947; telegram 33, March 17, 1947, in Tauber (2012), 82; HQ Palestine, Fortnightly Intelligence Newsletter 38, March 15–28, 1947, NA, WO 275/64; Trevor (1948), 323; Sixth Airborne Divi-

sion, Intelligence Summary 35, March 21, 1947, NA, WO 275/58; Ben-Gurion to Attlee, telegram, March 18, 1947.

27. Cunningham to Creech Jones, telegram, March 16, 1947, NA, CO 537/2299; security conference, March 14, 1947; Operation Elephant, April 1947, NA, WO 261/653; Montgomery, "Palestine—February 3–June 21, 1947."

28. CM (47) 30, March 20, 1947, NA, CAB 128/9.

29. Debates, House of Lords, vol. 146, col. 3, March 3, 1947; CM (47) 30, March 20, 1947, NA, CAB 128/9.

30. High Commissioner's Report for Feb. 1947, March 18, 1947, NA, CO 537/2281; Sixth Airborne Division, Intelligence Summary 33, March 7, 1947, NA, WO 261/660; Sixth Airborne Division, Intelligence Summary 35, March 21, 1947; Secretary, Arab Union Club, Haifa, to Cunningham, letter, March 18, 1947, CS D/237/46, ISA; Gurney to Creech Jones, telegram, March 24, 1947, NA, CO 537/2299; Campbell to Bevin, telegram, March 24, 1947, NA, FO 371/61905.

31. CP (47) 107, March 26, 1947, NA, CAB 128/9; COS (47) 54, April 21, 1947, NA, CO 537/2299.

32. CM (47) 33, March 27, 1947, NA, CAB 128/9; Montgomery (1958), 423; CM (47) 33, March 27, 1947, NA, CAB 128/9; Cunningham to Gurney, telegram, March 24, 1947, NA, CO 537/2299; JP (47) 38 (0), March 25, 1947, NA, CO 537/2299; CP (47) 107, March 26, 1947, NA, CAB 128/9.

33. Lloyd Phillips to the Reverend A. Lloyd Phillips, letter, March 2, 1947, Lloyd Phillips Papers; Keating to Cyril Conner (director of Overseas Programme Services, BBC, London), letter, April 23, 1947, Keating Papers, IWM; Cunningham to Creech Jones, telegram, March 13, 1947, NA, FO 371/61905; interview with Ivan Lloyd Phillips (n.d.), Scrivenor Papers.

34. Chairman and Secretary to Gurney, letter, March 24, 1947, CS D/27/46, ISA; Gray to Gurney, letter, April 17, 1947, CS D/27/46, ISA; Debates, House of Commons vol. 436, col. 45 (Creech Jones to Mellor), April 17, 1947; Keating to Conner, letter, April 23, 1947; Cunningham to Creech Jones, telegram, April 4, 1947, NA, FO 371/61772.

35. HQ Sixth Airborne Division, Quarterly Historical Report for the Quarter Ending March 31, 1947, NA, WO 261/170; HQ Gaza, Quarterly Historical Report for the Quarter Ending March 31, 1947, April 1, 1947, NA, WO 261/170; Eban to Jewish Agency Executive, Address to the Imperial Defence College, memorandum, March 10, 1947, S 25/6908, CZA; Lieutenant Colonel H. Edinew to Gurney, letter, April 4, 1947, CS D/160/40, ISA; Meyerson to Commander, Eighth Infantry Brigade, letter, April 17, 1947, S 25/6910, CZA.

36. Tavin and Alexander (1982), 88–89, 95–96, 98–99, 133; "The Soldiers of the Underground to the Soldiers of the Occupation Army," March 1947, K-4 3/15, JI; "It's Worth Thinking About," March 1947, Jerusalem and the East Mission Papers.

37. Debates, House of Commons, vol. 435, col. 200, March 26, 1947; Debates, House of Commons, vol. 436, col. 1938 (Creech Jones), April 30, 1947; telegrams 35–42, March 19–31, 1947, in Tauber (2012), 86–87; Cunningham to Creech Jones, telegram, March 31, 1947, NA, CO 537/2301; *Palestine Post*, March 31 and April 1, 1947; Charters (1989), 192; Wilson (1949), 262.

38. Creech Jones to Dalton, draft letter, March 6, 1947, NA, CO 537/2279; *Palestine Post*, April 1, May 1, and July 1, 1947; *Times*, April 1 and 18, 1947; Gurney to Creech Jones, April 23, 1947, Cunningham Papers, I/4; John Higham, min-

utes, April 1 and 18, 1947, NA, CO 537/2279; Cunningham to Creech Jones, letter, April 11, 1947, NA, CO 537/2279; Cunningham to Creech Jones, telegram, April 24, 1947, NA, CO 537/2301; Cunningham to Creech Jones, telegram, April 24, 1947, NA, CO 537/1822; Financial Situation, May 18, 1947, NA, CAB 129/19; minutes by William Mathieson, April 18 and May 3, 1947, John Higham, April 19, 1947, Trafford Smith, April 25 and May 8, 1947, and Sir Thomas Lloyd (permanent undersecretary), May 8, 1947, NA, CO 537/2300; CM (47) 48 May 20, 1947, NA, CAB 128/9; CM (47) 48, May 20, 1947, NA, CAB 128/9; Debates, House of Commons, vol. 435, col. 1871 (Dalton), July 23, 1946, and col. 30 (Wilkes and Alexander), March 17, 1947; *Times*, Jan. 8, 1947; Gurney to Cunningham, telegram, Jan. 14, 1947, NA, CO 537/2300; Cunningham to Creech Jones, telegram, April 28, 1947.

39. Trafford Smith, minute, April 25, 1947.

40. Trafford Smith and Lloyd, minutes, April 25, 1947, NA, CO 537/2300; Trafford Smith, minute, Dec. 10, 1946, NA, CO 537/1825; Martin, minute, Dec. 16, 1946, NA, CO 537/1825.

41. CM (47) 33, March 27, 1947, NA, CAB 128/9; Gitlin (1974), 15; Montgomery (1958), 423.

42. Cunningham to Creech Jones, telegram, March 19, 1947, NA, CO 733/477/75156/151A; Debates, House of Commons, vol. 427, col. 90, written answers (Creech Jones), Oct. 10, 1946; Debates, House of Commons, vol. 436, col. 46, written answers (Creech Jones), April 17, 1947; Memorandum on the Comparative Treatment; French (2011), 92; Rymer-Jones Papers, 147; Bevin to Inverchapel, telegram, Jan. 1, 1947, NA, FO 371/61799; Inverchapel to Bevin, telegram, Jan. 6, 1947, NA, FO 371/61799; Inverchapel to Byrnes, letter, Jan. 8, 1947, NA, FO 371/61800; Barker to Antonius, March 24, 1947, P/867, ISA; *Manchester Guardian*, April 30, 1947.

43. Army Council Secretariat ACSB/2322, March 20, 1947, NA, WO 32/10260; Montgomery, "Palestine—November 28/December 1, 1946"; MacMillan, "Palestine: Narrative of Events"; CM (47) 33, March 27, 1947, NA, CAB 128/9; COS (47) 54, April 21, 1947, NA, CO 537/2299 75156/175.

44. Rymer-Jones Papers, 147; Trevor (1948), 312, 324, 334; Gitlin (1974), 14–15.

45. Gurion (1950), 120; Gitlin (1974), 104.

46. Trevor (1948), 334–35; CM (12) 47, Jan. 27, 1947, NA, CAB 129/9.

47. Lyrics and translation at http://www.stateofisrael.com/anthem/.

48. Annex 2 in app. C to First Parachute Brigade, Historical Report for Quarter Ending June 30, 1947, Report by Liaison Officer on Executions at Acre Gaol, April 15/16, 1947, NA, WO 261/697; *Times* and *Palestine Post*, April 17, 1947; Bell (1977), 197–98; Bethell (1979), 305–6; Gitlin (1974), 110; Gurion (1950), 128; Niv (1975), 5:125.

49. Bethell (1979), 306; Bell (1977), 196–98; Gitlin (1974), 109–10; *Palestine Post*, April 17, 1947; Gurion (1950), 126–28.

50. *Times*, April 17 and 18, 1947; *Palestine Post*, April 17, 1947; Begin (1977a), 268; Rymer-Jones Papers, 147; Debates, House of Commons, vol. 441, col. 266w (Creech Jones), Aug. 13, 1947; Gurion (1950), 128.

51. "We Demand P-O-W Status" (1947), K-4 3/15, JI; HQ First Infantry Division, Internal Security Instruction 5, April 14, 1947, NA, WO 261/180; Third Parachute Brigade Operational Order 37, April 18, 1947, NA, WO 275/23; extract from Gray to Gale, confidential note, April 14, 1947, NA, WO 261/180; Tim Jones (2005), 81–82; O'Sullivan, Annual Report for J2 Section, 1947.

52. Shiloni, "Machteret Ha-Ktifa Ha-Dimion v'Ha-Shoni ben Ha-Shaidim Ha-Palestinaim v'Oley Ha-Gardom."

53. Niv (1975), 5:48–49, 128, 130–31; *Palestine Post*, March 18, 1947; Golan (2003), 276; Yossi Katz (2010), 93; "Meir Feinstein," http://www.etzel.org.il/english/people/feinstein.htm.

54. Statement of the Accused Moshe Barazani, p/47/85, March 15, 1947, Brebber Papers, 3/1; *Palestine Post*, March 18, 1947; Niv (1975), 5:131–32; Golan (2003), 275; Yossi Katz (2010), 92.

55. Begin (1977a), 273–74; Bell (1977), 196, 199–200; Gurion (1950), 115–19, 132–34; Museum of the Underground Prisoners—Jerusalem; Niv (1975), 5:129–30; Trevor (1948), 337.

56. Gurion (1950), 13; O'Sullivan, Annual Report for J2 Section, 1947; "Obituary," *Palestine Police Magazine*, June 1947, 6, Cannings Papers; Barker to Antonius, April 26, 1947; Brutton (1996), 92.

57. Bethell (1979), 307; Dempsey to Montgomery, telegram, Jan. 18, 1947, NA, CO 537/3870; Weizman (1979), 9, 39–41.

58. Weizman (1979), 41; Bethell (1979), 307; Postal packet containing bomb sent to General Sir Evelyn Barker (n.d.), NA, EF 5/12; John Place to Inspector, Surrey Constabulary, letter, May 18, 1948, NA, EF 5/12; H. E. Watts, report, June 10, 1948, NA, EF 5/12; Barker to Antonius, June 8, 1947, P/867, ISA; *Daily Telegraph*, May 13, 1948.

59. Thistlewaite to Sir Percy Sillitoe (director general, MI5), letter, Dec. 6, 1946, NA, KV 5/38; Rymer-Jones to Cunningham, letter, Dec. 13, 1946, Cunningham Papers, VI/4; Robertson to E. W. Jones, Special Branch, Dec. 5, 1946, NA, KV 2/2251; extract from report forwarded by SIS, Jan. 2, 1947, NA, KV 2/2251; anonymous letter to H. J. Seager, MI5, Feb. 13, 1947, NA, KV 2/2251; Seager to MI6, letter, Feb. 18, 1947, NA, KV 2/2251; Jewish Extremist and Terrorist Activities, Meeting of Police Officers and ALOs, Jan. 7, 1947, NA, KV 3/41; suggested introductory speech by director general (n.d.), NA, KV 3/41; Burt (1959), 126; DSO, Palestine, to Robertson, telegram, Nov. 29, 1946, NA, KV2/2251; Robertson to Jones, letter, Dec. 5, 1946, NA, KV2/2251; extract by SIS (MI6), Jan. 20, 1947, NA, KV 2/2375.

60. Rymer-Jones to Cunningham, letter, Dec. 13, 1946; Yaacov Eliav (1984), 246; Andrew (2009), 357–58; Walton (2013), 97.

61. Palestine Police Force, Entry for Yacov Levstein in Jewish Terrorist Index, June 30, 1947, O'Sullivan Papers; Yaacov Eliav (1984), 17–18, 34–38, 61–74, 95–100, 103–5, 114–18, 123–27, 151–58, 160–65, 189–97, 230–34

62. Yaacov Eliav (1984), 240–42; Cesarani (2009), 85; Walton (2013), 97–98.

63. Yaacov Eliav (1984), 243–46; Cesarani (2009), 85–86.

64. Yaacov Eliav (1984), 86, 235–36, 246; Foreign Office to Washington, Paris, Rome, Brussels, The Hague, Belgrade, Budapest, Prague, Warsaw, Bucharest, Sofia, Athens, telegram, April 16, 1947, NA, CO 537/2295 75156/165; Duff Cooper to Bevin, telegram, April 17, 1947, NA, CO 537/2295 75156/165; Cesarani (2009), 84–85; Walton (2013), 98; *L'Indépendance: Organe des Combattants pour la Liberté d'Israël*, Jan. 1947, NA, FO 371/61751 E633/32/31.

65. Sûreté Nationale Police, report (n.d.), NA, EF 5/12; *Times* and *Daily Telegraph*, April 17, 1947; Andrew (2009), 357; Burt (1959), 126–27; Cesarani (2009), 86–87; Yaacov Eliav (1984), 242–43; Walton (2013), ix–xx, 98–99.

66. Translation of Stern Gang Pamphlet, April 24, 1947, NA, WO 275/109.

67. Letter Bombs, June 16 and 17, 1947, NA, EF 5/12; MacMichael, Kent County

Constabulary Report witness statement, June 4, 1947, NA, EF 5/12; R. H. White, Kent County Constabulary Report, June 5, 1947, NA, EF 5/12; S. H. C. Burley to H. E. Watts, letter, June 12, 1947, NA, EF 5/12; H. A. Mayes to HM Inspector of Explosives, letter, June 13, 1947, NA, EF 5/12; Dr. Watts, statement, June 24, 1947, NA, EF 5/12; Sixth Airborne Division, Fortnightly Newsletter 44, June 20, 1947, NA, WO 275/64; First Armoured Division, Intelligence Summary 2, July 2, 1947, NA, WO 261/650; Third Parachute Brigade, Intelligence Summary 2, Aug. 20, 1947, NA, WO 261/707; Rymer-Jones Papers, 151; Andrew (2009), 357–59; Yaacov Eliav (1984), 246–60; Walton (2013), 98–99; *Sunday Guardian*, Nov. 21, 1948; Burt (1959), 127–28; *Daily Express*, Aug. 25, 1948.

68. O'Sullivan, Annual Report for J2 Section, 1947; Anderson (1947–48), 203; Captain J. K. Linklater, 317 Sixth Airborne Field Security Report on the Attack on Acre Gaol, May 5, 1947, 115/77, HA; First Armored Division, Intelligence Summary 1, app. E, June 15, 1947, NA, WO 261/650; Wilson (1949), 123–24; Sixth Airborne Division, Intelligence Summary 42, May 14, 1947, NA, WO 275/60; Gitlin (1974), 79; Michael J. Cohen (1982), 242.

69. *Palestine Post*, May 5, 1947; Brundage (1962), 183–84; Holt (1966), 129.

70. *Palestine Post*, May 5, 1947; Bell (1977), 204–6, 211; Fergusson (1970), 216–17; García-Granados (1948), 163; Gitlin (1974), 24, 70; Edward Horne (1982), 383; Wilson (1949), 123.

71. Bell (1977), 116, 196, 204–9; Gitlin (1974), 56–65; Niv (1975), 5:135–37; Wilson (1949), 124.

72. Linklater, 317 Sixth Airborne Field Security Report, May 5, 1947; Bell (1977), 208–11; Niv (1975), 5:137, 142–43; Gitlin (1974), 77, 125.

73. Linklater, 317 Sixth Airborne Field Security Report, May 5, 1947; Bell (1977), 208–12; Niv (1975), 5:137–38.

74. Cunningham to Creech Jones, telegrams, May 4, 5, and 6, 1947, Cunningham Papers, II/1; Linklater, 317 Sixth Airborne Field Security Report, May 5, 1947; Bell (1977), 208–12; Niv (1975), 5:137–38; Wilson (1949), 123–27.

75. Begin (1977a), 94; Michael J. Cohen (1982), 242.

76. *Palestine Post*, May 6, 1947; Hecht (1954), 615–17; Fortnightly Intelligence Newsletter, 42, May 10–23, 1947, NA, WO 275/64.

77. Hecht (1954), 617; Zaar (1954), 240–41; Inverchapel to Bevin, letter, Jan. 6, 1947; Inverchapel to Byrnes, letter, Jan. 8, 1947; British Embassy, Washington, D.C., to Eastern Department, letter, April 10, 1947, NA, FO 371/61799 E2494/46/31; M. S. Beith, minute, May 19, 1947, NA, FO 371/61807 E4105/48/31; Montgomery, "Palestine—Feb. 3–June 21, 1947"; Debates, House of Commons, vol. 437, col. 1981 (Major Bruce), May 19, 1947; Louis (1984), 466; Zaar (1954), 241–43.

78. Louis (1984), 466.

79. *Manchester Guardian* and *Palestine Post*, April 30, 1947; Zaar (1954), 241–43; Fortnightly Intelligence Newsletter, 42.

80. Begin (1977a), 521; MacMillan, "Palestine: Narrative of Events."

CHAPTER 18: BURIED QUIETLY IN THE NIGHT

1. Louis (1984), 467; MacMillan, app. D: "Appreciation by GOC, Palestine on August 5, 1947," in "Palestine: Narrative of Events"; Hurewitz (1976), 290.

2. Gray to O'Sullivan, letter, May 14, 1947, O'Sullivan Papers; Michael J. Cohen (1982), 250.

3. Fergusson (1970), 204; Goodman, "Acharei 57 Shanaim"; Tim Jones (2001), 32; HQ Haifa, Redistribution of Intelligence Duties, Nov. 22, 1947, NA, WO 261/620.

4. D'Arcy to Barker, letter, May 31, 1946, D'Arcy Papers; Debates, House of Lords, vol. 147, col. 63 (Lord Altrincham), April 23, 1947; Gale (1968), 169; Fergusson (1970), 216–17; Wilson (1949), 124; Isham to Shaw, letter, Jan. 15, 1972, Isham Papers, I.184.

5. Clarke, minute, Nov. 1, 1946, NA, CO 537/1699 75015/59; note of Sir George Gater's discussions with Colonel Gray on Nov. 13, 1946, NA, CO 537/1699 75015/59; Cesarani (2009), 30; Sinclair (2006a), 114.

6. *Times*, Nov. 29, 1980; Dear (1995), 233–34; Fergusson (1970), 9–142, 143–98; Cesarani (2009), 30–32; Sykes (1959), 367, 433, 441; Tim Jones (2005), 75; Royle (1995), 252, 315; Fergusson (2009), 1–256; Fergusson (1946), 1–288.

7. Fergusson (1970), 198–200; The Palestine Police Force Annual Administrative Report, 1946, O'Sullivan Papers; Cesarani (2009), 32–33.

8. Fergusson (1970), 200–201; Charters (1979), 57; Edward Horne (1982), 564; *Times*, Nov. 29, 1980.

9. Secondment of Army Officers to Palestine Police, Fergusson, memorandum, Feb. 12, 1947, NA, CO 537/2270; Fergusson (1970), 200–204; Goodman, "Acharei 57 Shanaim."

10. Fergusson (1970), 210.

11. Fergusson, memorandum, Feb. 12, 1947; Rymer-Jones Papers, 151; Cesarani (2009), 59–60; Cunningham to Creech Jones, telegram, Nov. 23, 1947, NA, CAB 127/280; Montgomery to Creech Jones, minute, March 21, 1947, BLM 180/5, Montgomery Papers.

12. Edward Horne (1982), 558; Fergusson (1970), 210.

13. Edward Horne (1982), 564–65; Fergusson, memorandum, Feb. 12, 1947.

14. Fergusson (1970), 210–11; Clark, minute, Feb. 12, 1947, NA, CO 537/2270; Martin to Lloyd, minute, Feb. 13, 1947, NA, CO 537/2270; Lloyd to Sir Eric Speed, letter, Feb. 13, 1947, NA, CO 537/2270; Tim Jones (2001), 35; Tim Jones (2005), 76; Fergusson, memorandum, Feb. 12, 1947.

15. Clark, minute, Feb. 12, 1947; J. M. Martin, minute, Feb. 13, 1947, NA, CO 537/2270; Martin to Sir T. Lloyd, note, Feb. 13, 1947, NA, CO 537/2270; Lloyd to Speed, letter, Feb. 13, 1947; Speed to Lloyd, letter, March 6, 1947, NA, CO 537/2270; Lloyd to Speed, letter, March 11, 1947, NA, CO 537/2270; Fergusson (1970), 225; Bethell (1979), 302; Cesarani (2009), 80–82, 87–88; Twiston Davies (2006), 411; Foot (1966), 405; Goodman, "Acharei 57 Shanaim"; Dina Kraft, "British War Hero to Be Investigated Again for Murder of Jewish 'Terrorist,'" *Daily Telegraph*, March 28, 2009; Tim Jones (2001), 28, 30, 33–34, 36; Farran (1950), 345–47; Edward Horne (1982), 564–65; Sinclair (2006a), 114; O'Sullivan Diary, March 8, 1947, 72, O'Sullivan Papers.

16. Farran (1950), 348; Fergusson (1970), 225–26; Cesarani (2009), 88–89; Charters (1979), 58; Tim Jones (2005), 80.

17. Farran (1950), 348; Fergusson (1970), 226; Tim Jones (2005), 81.

18. Kitson (1971), 165; Cesarani (2009), 217; Foot (1966), 405.

19. Rymer-Jones Papers, 151; Charters (1979), 58.

20. Farran (1950), 349–50.

21. Fergusson (1970), 226; Cesarani (2009), 89.
22. Goodman, "Acharei 57 Shanaim"; H. E. Burley, Home Office, to H. J. Seager, MI5, letter, Dec. 31, 1946, NA, KV 5/31; Seager to Burley, Jan. 6, 1947; Cesarani (2009), 2–4.
23. K. P. Hadingham, Superintendent of Police, Jerusalem District, Report on the Alleged Abduction and Murder of Alexander Rubovitz [*sic*], and Subsequent Police Investigation, June 19, 1947, NA, CO 537/2302; Goldie Meyerson to Cunningham, letter, June 23, 1947, S 25/6200, CZA; Political Department, Jewish Agency, The Alexander Rubowitz Case (internal memorandum) (n.d.), S 25/6200, CZA; internal memorandum 14662/47, Oct. 17, 1947, S 25/6200, CZA; Gurney to Creech Jones, telegram, June 25, 1947, Cunningham Papers, II/2; *Palestine Post*, May 22, 1947; Avner (1959), 21; Brutton (1996), 82; Cesarani (2009), 1–6, 96–98; Charters (1979), 56, 59; Farran (1950), 10, 356–76; Fergusson (2009), 225–38; Koestler (1949), 148–49; Kraft, "British War Hero"; Mitchell (1969), 61–62; Niv (1975), 5:149.
24. Hadingham, Report on the Alleged Abduction; *Palestine Post*, May 22, 1947; Cesarani (2009), 6–7; Goodman, "Acharei 57 Shanaim."
25. *Palestine Post*, May 22, 1947; "X" to Mrs. Rubowitz, letter, May 23, 1947, S 25/6200, CZA.
26. Meyerson to Cunningham, letter, June 23, 1947; Political Department, Jewish Agency, Rubowitz Case; Cunningham to Creech Jones, telegram, July 9, 1947, NA, FCO 141/14284.
27. Edward Horne (1982), 170; Seniority List—British Superior Police Officers (n.d.), O'Sullivan Papers; Hadingham, Report on the Alleged Abduction.
28. Hadingham, Report on the Alleged Abduction; Goodman, "Acharei 57 Shanaim."
29. "Notes for Interrogating Officers" (n.d.), O'Sullivan Papers.
30. Hadingham, Report on the Alleged Abduction; Cunningham to Creech Jones, telegram, June 13, 1947, NA, CO 537/2302; Cunningham to Creech Jones, telegram, June 25, 1947, Cunningham Papers, II/1; Cesarani (2009), 96–97; Kraft, "British War Hero."
31. Creech Jones to Cunningham, telegram, June 19, 1947, NA, CO 537/2302; Cunningham to Creech Jones, telegram, June 20, 1947, NA, CO 537/2302; Gray to Gurney, letter, June 24, 1947, NA, CO 537/2302; Farran (1950), 351; Hadingham, Report on the Alleged Abduction; Cesarani (2009), 98–99.
32. Gray to Gurney, letter, June 24, 1947.
33. O'Sullivan Diary, June 3, 1947, 76–77, June 11, 1947, 77; Goodman, "Acharei 57 Shanaim"; Gray to Gurney, letter, June 24, 1947.
34. Hadingham, Report on the Alleged Abduction; Gray to Gurney, letter, June 24, 1947.
35. Edward Horne (1982), 474, 556; Goodman, "Acharei 57 Shanaim"; Cesarani (2009), 100–101.
36. Cesarani (2009), 100–101; Gray to Gurney, letter, June 24, 1947; Cunningham to Creech Jones, telegram, June 19, 1947, NA, CO 537/2302; Hadingham, Report on the Alleged Abduction; Farran (1950), 352.
37. Farran (1950), 351–60.
38. Ibid., 354–55; Fergusson (1970), 228–29.
39. Fergusson (1970), 229–32; Golani (2009), 21.
40. Damascus to Foreign Office, telegrams, June 9 and 10, 1947, NA, CO 537/2302; Farran (1950), 361–67; Fergusson (1970), 232–36.

41. Damascus to Foreign Office, telegrams, June 9, 10, and 12, 1947; Cunningham to Creech Jones, telegram, June 26, 1947, NA, CO 537/2302; Hadingham, Report on the Alleged Abduction; Fergusson (1970), 236; Farran (1950), 367, "Palestine Officers," Reuters, June 14, 1947, NA, CO 537/2302; C. A. P. Dundas (Damascus) to Cunningham, letter, June 17, 1947, NA, CO 537/2302.

42. Dundas to Cunningham, letter, June 17, 1947; Cunningham to Creech Jones, telegram, June 19, 1947; Summary of Evidence of Court of Inquiry into Escape of Major Roy Farran, June 23, 1947, NA, CO 537/2302; Cunningham to Creech Jones, telegram, Aug. 14, 1947, NA, CO 537/2302; Y. Ben-Zvi (president, Vaad Leumi) to Gurney, letter, July 22, 1947, S 25/6200, CZA; Political Department, Jewish Agency, Rubowitz Case; *Daily Telegraph* and *Palestine Post*, June 20, 1947.

43. Meyerson to Cunningham, letter, June 23, 1947; Political Department, Jewish Agency, Rubowitz Case; Gurney to Creech Jones, telegram, June 25, 1947; O'Sullivan Diary, June 18, 1947, 77; Cunningham to Creech Jones, telegram, June 19, 1947; Cunningham to Creech Jones, telegram, July 1, 1947, NA, CO 537/2302; Gray to Gurney, letter, June 20, 1947, NA, CO 537/2302; *Palestine Post*, Oct. 2, 1947; Edward Horne (1982), 170, 190, 550; Niv (1975), 5:149.

44. Summary of Evidence of Court of Inquiry into Escape of Major Roy Farran; Farran (1950), 367; Creech Jones to Cunningham, telegram, June 18, 1947, NA, CO 537/2302; various press cuttings, June 13–20, 1947, NA, CO 537/2302; *New York Herald Tribune*, June 13, 1947.

45. Political Department, Jewish Agency, Rubowitz Case; Attlee to Creech Jones, note, June 19, 1947, NA, CO 537/2302; Cunningham to Creech Jones, telegrams, June 19 and 26, 1947, NA, CO 537/2302; *Palestine Post*, June 24, 1947.

46. Creech Jones to Cunningham, telegrams, June 19 and 20, 1947, NA, CO 537/2302.

47. Farran (1950), 367–68; Recommendation, Findings, and Summary by Court of Inquiry, June 23, 1947, NA, CO 537/2302.

48. Gray to Gurney, letter, June 20, 1947; Recommendation, Findings, and Summary by Court of Inquiry; Cunningham to Creech Jones, telegrams, June 20, 25, and 26, 1947; *Palestine Post*, June 24, 1947.

49. Farran (1950), 368; *Palestine Post*, June 29, 1947; Wilson (1949), 131.

50. Ben-Zvi to Gurney, letter, July 22, 1947; *Palestine Post*, July 18, 1947; Cesarani (2009), 146, 155–56.

51. Cesarani (2009), 156; Gray to Gurney, letter, June 20, 1947; Cunningham to Creech Jones, telegram, July 1, 1947.

52. Cunningham to Creech Jones, telegram, July 17, 1947, NA, CO 537/2302; Gutch to S. J. Baker (Home Office), letter, July 18, 1947, NA, CO 537/2302; Baker to Gutch, letter, July 18, 1947, NA, CO 537/2302; Cunningham to Creech Jones, telegrams, July 17, 1, and 23, Aug. 5 and 14, Sept. 13 and 29, and Oct. 1, 1947, NA, CO 537/2302; Laurence Collins and Fearnley-Whittingstall to Creech Jones, letters, Aug. 5, 7, and 27, 1947, NA, CO 537/2302; Trafford Smith to Shapcott, letter, Sept. 9, 1947, NA, CO 537/2302; Shapcott to Trafford Smith, letter, Sept. 12, 1947 NA, CO 537/2302; Damascus to London, telegrams, Sept. 14 and 23, 1947, NA, CO 537/2302; Gurney to Creech Jones, telegram, Sept. 23, 1947, NA, CO 537/2302; Mathieson to R. M. Howe (Scotland Yard), letter, Sept. 22, 1947, NA, CO 537/2302; Howe to Mathieson, letters, Sept. 23 and 29, 1947, NA, CO 537/2302; Mathieson to Lord Russell (Lord of Session), letter, Sept. 29, 1947, NA, CO 537/2302; Cesarani (2009), 156; Ben-Zvi to Gurney, letter,

July 22, 1947, NA, CO 537/2302; Cunningham to Creech Jones, July 19, 1947, NA, CO 537/2302; Mathieson to Brigadier H. Shapcott (War Office), letter, July 21, 1947, NA, CO 537/2302.

53. *Times* and *Palestine Post*, Oct. 2, 1947.

54. O'Sullivan Diary, June 3, 1947, 76–77; "The Farran Case," *Statesman*, Oct. 11, 1947, NA, CO 537/2270; *Palestine Post*, Oct. 2, 1947.

55. *Palestine Post*, Oct. 3, 1947; Cesarani (2009), 175.

56. Farran (1950), 382; *Daily Express* and *Daily Telegraph*, Oct. 31, 1947; *New York Times*, Feb. 11, 1947.

57. Farran (1950), 351.

58. Gray to Gurney, letter, June 24, 1947.

59. Farran, 7th ed. (Jan. 1950); Cesarani (2009), 187; Goodman, "Acharei 57 Shanaim"; Clutterbuck, "Bertrand Stewart Prize Essay, 1960," 167, cited in Charters (1979), 58–59, 60n26; Mitchell (1969), 61–62.

60. Interview, Richard Clutterbuck with the author, Exeter, England, March 1979; Mitchell (1969), 61–62; Farran (2009), 351.

61. Bethell (1979), 303; Paget (1967), 167, 174.

62. Montgomery Diary, pt. 8, tour no. 3, chap. 51, "Palestine, June 21–August 8, 1947," BLM 181/1, Montgomery Papers.

63. Charters (1979), 57.

64. Blaxland (1971), 47; Cunningham to Creech Jones, telegram, June 25, 1947; MacMillan, "Palestine: Narrative of Events"; Meyerson to Cunningham, letter, June 23, 1947.

65. Fergusson (2009), 240; *Times*, Nov. 29, 1980.

66. Twiston Davies (2006); Kemp (1994), 19.

67. Laurence Collins and Fearnley-Whittingstall to Creech Jones, letter, Dec. 5, 1947, NA, CO 537/2302; R. H. Cowell Parker, affidavit, Oct. 27, 1947, NA, CO 537/2302; Laurence Collins et al. to Judge Advocate General, Nov. 6, 1947, NA, CO 537/2302; Fox-Strangways to Laurence Collins et al., letter, Nov. 15, 1947, NA, CO 537/2302; Creech Jones to Cunningham, telegram, Dec. 22, 1947, NA, CO 537/2302; Creech Jones to Cunningham, telegram, Feb. 2, 1947, NA, CO 537/3872; Cunningham to Creech Jones, telegrams, Feb. 9 and April 24, 1947, NA, CO 537/3872.

68. Avner (1959), 21–22; *New York Times*, Sept. 18, 1947, and May 4, 1948; *Evening News*, Oct. 16, 1947; clippings from *Daily Express*, *Daily Herald*, *Daily Graphic*, and *Daily Mail*, Oct. 31, 1947, NA, HO 45/21445; Outrages, 1947–48, Letter Bombs, Letter to J. S. Skelton (Home Office Section), May 12, 1948, and photographs, NA, EF 5/12; *Times*, May 4, 1948; Melman, "Heruti Code"; Cesarani (2009), 183–84, 192–93, 201–2; Goodman, "Acharei 57 Shanaim."

69. Baxter to Smith, letter, Feb. 25, 1947, NA, FO 371/61872; García-Granados (1948), 170; Smith to Lloyd, minute, May 23, 1947, NA, CO 537/2283; O'Sullivan Diary, March 18, 1947, 71.

70. Dempsey to Montgomery, telegram, May 20, 1947, NA, CO 537/2283; Bell (1977), 286–87; Niv (1975), 5:302–3; Shamir (1994), 63–69; Baxter to Smith, letter, Feb. 25, 1947.

71. E. M. Fitzgerald to Mathieson, minute, May 8, 1947, NA, CO 537/2283.

72. Edith Weiss to Trygve Lie (UN secretary-general), letter, June 30, 1947, NA, FO 371/61781; Begin (1977a), 283–86; Gurion (1950), 149–50; Lapidot, "Haviv Avshalom"; Lapidot, "Meir Nakar"; Lapidot, "Yaakov Weiss"; García-Granados (1948), 50–52; *Palestine Post*, June 17 and 18, 1947; Samuel Katz (1968), 159.

73. Voice of Fighting Zion, April 23, 1947, K-4 7/15, JI; First Armored Division, Intelligence Summary 1, June 15, 1947, NA, WO 261/650; HQ South Palestine District (Sarafand), Internal Security, June 2, 1947, NA, WO 261/172.

74 Begin (1977a), 283–84; telegrams 85 and 86, June 10, 1947, in Tauber (2012), 113–15, Tovin and Alexander (1982), 171.

75. Third Parachute Brigade, Operational Instruction 39, June 14, 1947, NA, WO 275/223; Montgomery, "Palestine, June 21–August 8, 1947."

76. First Armored Division, Intelligence Summary 2, July 2, 1947, NA, WO 261/650; *Times*, May 5, 1947; Niv (1975), 5:163–69; *Background of the Struggle for the Liberation of Eretz Israel* (1947), 14–19; DSO, Palestine, to SIME, telegram, July 29, 1947, NA, KV 5/38.

77. Cunningham to Creech Jones, telegram, July 9, 1947, NA, FCO 141/14284; Cunningham to Creech Jones, telegram 89, June 19, 1947, in Tauber (2012), 115–16; Begin (1977a), 291– 94; Bell (1977), 222–23; Brutton (1996), 98–99; García-Granados (1948), 118; Wilson (1949), 131.

78. *Times*, May 5, 1947; García-Granados (1948), 118–19; Samuel Katz (1968), 163; Niv (1975), 5:165–67; Montgomery, "Palestine, June 21–August 8, 1947"; Montgomery to Bellenger, letter, June 27, 1947, BLM 181/9, Montgomery Papers.

79. Montgomery, "Palestine June 21–August 8, 1947"; MacMillan, "Appreciation by GOC, Palestine on August 5, 1947."

80. *Background of the Struggle for the Liberation of Eretz Israel* (1947), 14–19; Niv (1975), 5:169–76; Michael J. Cohen (1982), 243.

81. Brigadier J. C. Bedford-Roberts, Broadcast to Be Given on May 12, 1947, Keating Papers, IWM; Eighth Infantry Brigade, Intelligence Summary 5, May 25, 1947, NA, WO 261/682; Lieutenant Colonel C. R. W. Norman to Major E. Sacharov, letter, June 27, 1947, S 25/6908, CZA.

82. Barker to Antonius, July 6 and Oct. 8, 1947, P/867, ISA.

83. Cunningham to Creech Jones, telegram, June 13, 1947.

CHAPTER 19: DRUNK WITH THE HANGMAN'S BLOOD

1. Louis (1984), 467; García-Granados (1948), 32; Marton (1994), 109.

2. Bullock (1983), 446; Michael J. Cohen (1982), 260–61, 265; Harris (1982), 397.

3. Samuel Katz (1968), 159; Cunningham to Creech Jones, telegrams, June 11 and July 9, 1947, NA, FCO 141/14284; García-Granados (1948), 38–44; *Palestine Post*, June 17, 1947.

4. García-Granados (1948), 44–46.

5. Louis (1984), 468; García-Granados (1948), 58–59.

6. García-Granados (1948), 53–62; Cunningham to Creech Jones, telegram, July 5, 1947, NA, FCO 141/14284; *Times* and *Palestine Post*, July 2, 1947; Begin (1977a), 286–87; Niv (1975), 5:374.

7. García-Granados (1948), 192–93.

8. Begin (1977a), 294–302; Samuel Katz (1968), 160–61; Niv (1975), 5:370–79; Report of Conference Between Representatives of the UNSCOP and the Commander and Two Other Representatives of the Irgun Zvai Leumi, June 24, 1947, LXIX/2, Jerusalem and the Middle East Papers.

9. Report of Conference, June 24, 1947; Pinkerton to Hull, letter, Sept. 23, 1944, RG 226, OSS 99327, NARA; Shaw to Stanley, telegram, Sept. 29, 1944; PICME Intelligence Summary 12, Oct. 3, 1944, NA, WO 169/15703; Shaw to Stanley,

letter, Oct. 12, 1944, NA, CO 733/461 75872/18A; "To Our Arab Neighbours," July 1947, G13.089, CZA, in Irgun Zvai Leumi, *The Hebrew Struggle for National Liberation: A Selection of Documents on Its Background and on Events Punctuating Its Course* (n.d.); Begin (1977a), 49–50; Sixth Airborne Division, Intelligence Summary 42, May 14, 1947, app. E, and 44, May 30, 1947, NA, WO 275/60.

10. García-Granados (1948), 152–56; Begin (1977a), 304–7; Samuel Katz (1968), 162–63; Niv (1975), 5:380–82.

11. Department of Public Information, United Nations, "Background Story on Palestine Report," Aug. 31, 1947, http://unispal.un.org/UNISPAL.NSF/0/2D17B1 0E29EBCB4B85256A76006DD2DA; Jewish Agency for Palestine (1947); Cunningham to Creech Jones, telegram, July 13, 1947, NA, FCO 141/14284; García-Granados (1948), 182–88; Niv (1975), 5:376–78; Louis (1984), 470–71.

12. Louis (1986), 21; Debates, House of Commons, vol. 439, cols. 958–66, June 30, 1947; *Times*, June 30, 1947; Peter Clarke (2008), 489, 501; Schenk (2010), 61–62.

13. Debates, House of Commons, vol. 439, col. 959, June 30, 1947; *Times*, March 4, 1947; *Daily Telegraph*, March 6, 1947; Creech Jones to Cunningham, telegram, June 25, 1947, NA, FO 371/61932 (there were 74,400 "operational troops" deployed to Palestine, of whom 32,000 were "administrative"; see Charters [1989], 88, 145–48); minutes of the conversation between Gurney and Horowitz, May 27, 1947, S 25/28, CZA.

14. Charters (1989), 196; Cunningham to Creech Jones, telegram, April 26, 1947, NA, CO 537/2279; CP (47) 161, May 18, 1947, NA, CAB 129/19; supplementary memorandum by the government of Palestine, including notes on evidence given to UNSCOP, July 12, 1947, 56, Keating Papers, IWM; Cunningham to Creech Jones, telegram, April 28, 1947; CM 48 (47) May 20, 1947, NA, CAB 128/9.

15. *Palestine Post*, July 4, 1947; Fighters for the Freedom of Israel; 80th Cong., 1st sess., H.J. Resolution 237 (Rep. Andrew Somers), July 11, 1947, NA, CO 537/2313; minutes, May 3–5, 1947, NA, FO 371/61753; Baxter to HM Consul General, New York, letter, June 3, 1947, NA, FO 371/61753; Louis (1984), 464.

16. *Palestine Post*, July 9, 1947; Samuel Katz (1968), 164; García-Granados (1948), 54–55.

17. Barker to Antonius, May 4 and June 11 and 19, 1947, P/867, ISA; Cunningham to Creech Jones, telegram, July 9, 1947; telegrams 92, 94, and 96, June 23, 26, and 30, 1947, in Tauber (2012), 118–21; Samuel Katz (1968), 163–64.

18. 1 Guard Brigade Report on Operation Tiger, Sept. 1947, NA, WO 261/667.

19. O'Sullivan, "Abduction of Sergeant Paice and Sergeant Martin by Jewish Terrorists at Nathanya, July 1947," Aug. 30, 1947, O'Sullivan Papers; Ofer Aderet, "The 'Cruel Revenge' That Helped Drive the British out of Palestine," *Ha'aretz*, Aug. 7, 2012, http://www.haaretz.com/news/features/the-cruel-revenge-that -helped-drive-the-british-out-of-palestine-1.456440; telegram 97, July 12, 1947, in Tauber (2012), 121–22. O'Sullivan, "Abduction"; *Palestine Post*, July 13, 1947.

20. CP (47) 208, July 19, 1947, NA, CAB 129/20; O'Sullivan, "Abduction"; *Palestine Post*, July 13 and 14, 1947; PALCOR News Agency, July 16, 1947, NA, CO 537/2299.

21. O'Sullivan, "Abduction"; PALCOR News Agency, July 16, 1947; *Palestine Post*, July 13 and 14, 1947; Niv (1975), 5:162; García-Granados (1948), 141; Wilson (1949), 132; Bell (1977), 228.

22. Bell (1977), 227–28; O'Sullivan, "Abduction"; Niv (1975), 5:277; Tauber (2012), 121–22n1.

23. CP (47) 208, July 19, 1947, NA, CAB 129/20; *Palestine Post*, July 15, 18, and 28, 1947; Wilson (1949), 132.
24. O'Sullivan, Annual Report for J2 Section, 1947; *Palestine Post*, July 17, 1947; telegram 99, July 17, 1947, in Tauber (2012), 122; Voice of Fighting Zion, July 16, 1947, K-4 7/15, JI.
25. Tauber (2012), 87–120; O'Sullivan, Annual Report for J2 Section, 1947; Charters (1989), 196; David John Clark (1978), 243; *Palestine Post*, July 29, 1947.
26. *Palestine Post*, July 30, 1947; Begin (1977a), 289; Gurion (1950), 187–89; Rose (2009), 162.
27. *Palestine Post*, July 29 and 30, 1947; Gurion (1950), 189–90; O'Sullivan, "Abduction"; *New York Times*, Aug. 1, 1947.
28. Debates, House of Commons, vol. 441, col. 635 (Creech Jones), July 31, 1947; O'Sullivan, "Abduction"; *Times, New York Times*, and *Manchester Guardian*, Aug. 1, 1947; Brutton (1996), 101–2; Niv (1975), 5:278–79; app. A to Sixth Airborne Division, Weekly Intelligence Summary 54, Aug. 17, 1947, NA, WO 275/60.
29. Begin (1977a), 290; O'Sullivan, "Abduction"; Bethell (1979), 337; Brutton (1996), 101; Rose (2009), 163–64; "Israel > Netanya > Ha'Alonim Park," http://www.panoramio.com/photo/51333330.
30. *New York Times, Jewish Chronicle*, and *Times*, Aug. 1, 1947; Wilson (1949), 132.
31. Cunningham to Creech Jones, telegram, July 31, 1947, NA, CO 537/2300; Third Parachute Brigade, Intelligence Summary 2, Aug. 20, 1947; Macatee to Marshall, telegram, Aug. 1, 1947, in *FRUS, 1947*, 5:1134; Cunningham to Creech Jones, telegram, Aug. 2, 1947, Cunningham Papers, II/2; Cunningham to Creech Jones, telegram, Aug. 2, 1947, NA, FCO 141/14284; *Palestine Post*, Aug. 1 and 4, 1947.
32. Cunningham to Creech Jones, telegram, Aug. 1, 1947, Cunningham Papers, II/2; High Commissioner's Monthly Report for July 1947, NA, CO 537/2281.
33. Note of an interview, July 31, 1947, Cunningham Papers, V/1; *Times*, Aug. 1, 1947; *Palestine Post*, Aug. 3, 1947; Cunningham to Creech Jones, telegram, Aug. 2, 1947, NA, FCO 141/14284.
34. Wilson (1949), 132; Cunningham to Creech Jones, telegram, Aug. 1, 1947, NA, CO 733/477 75156/151 A; Cunningham to Creech Jones, telegram, Aug. 2, 1947; *Times*, Aug. 1, 1947.
35. Cunningham to Creech Jones, letter, Nov. 15, 1947, NA, CO 733/477 75156/151 A; Brutton (1996), 102.
36. Sixth Airborne Division, Fortnightly Intelligence Summary 47, July 19–Aug. 1, 1947, NA, WO 275/64; *Times*, Aug. 2, 1947; *Palestine Post*, Aug. 3, 1947; minutes of security conference, Aug. 1, 1947, Cunningham Papers, IV/1; Cunningham to Creech Jones, telegram, Aug. 1, 1947, Cunningham Papers, II/2.
37. *Palestine Post*, Aug. 3, 1947; Cunningham to Creech Jones, telegrams, Aug. 1 and 2, 1947, Cunningham Papers, II/2; High Commissioner's Monthly Report for July 1947.
38. Debates, House of Commons, vol. 441, col. 2342 (Harold Lever), Aug. 12, 1947; JIC (47) 52 (0) Chiefs of Staff Committee, Joint Intelligence Subcommittee, Possible Future of Palestine, Sept. 4, 1947, NA, CAB 158/2; MacMillan to Crocker, Aug. 1, 1947, NA, CAB 158/2.
39. *Times*, Aug. 2, 1947; Creech Jones to Cunningham, telegram, Aug. 5, 1947, NA, CO 537/2299; CM (47) 69, Aug. 5, 1947, NA, CAB 128/10; *Daily Telegraph*, Aug. 7, 1947.

40. MacMillan to Bols, letter, July 26, 1947, NA, WO 275/84; *Times*, Aug. 1, 1947; Cunningham to Creech Jones, telegram, Aug. 4, 1947, NA, CO 537/2299.
41. Crocker to Simpson, telegram, Aug. 3, 1947, NA, WO 216; Cunningham to Creech Jones, telegram, Monthly Report for July (n.d.), NA, FCO 141/14284; telegrams 113 and 115, Aug. 2 and 5, 1947, in Tauber (2012), 134–35, 139.
42. Voice of Fighting Zion, Aug. 3, 1947, K-4 7/15, JI; Sixth Airborne Division, Intelligence Summary 48, Aug. 2–15, 1947, and 59, Sept. 1947, NA, WO 275/64; Tavin and Alexander (1982), 228–29.
43. Bellenger to Simpson, note, and Simpson to Bellenger, reply, Aug. 4, 1947, NA, WO 216/221; Cunningham to Creech Jones, telegram, Aug. 4, 1947, NA, CO 733/477 75156/151 A.
44. Cunningham to Creech Jones, telegram, Aug. 4, 1947, NA, CO 733/477 75156/151 A.
45. Gale, "Operation 'Tiger,'" July 28 and Aug. 2 and 6, 1947, NA, WO 216/181; *Times*, Aug. 6, 1947.
46. Telegrams 116, 117, 188, Aug. 5, 7, and 8, 1947, in Tauber (2012), 139–41; *Palestine Post*, Aug. 6 and 8, 1947.
47. Cunningham to Creech Jones, telegram, Aug. 7, 1947, Cunningham Papers, II/2.
48. Trafford Smith, minute, Aug. 12, 1947, NA, CO 537/2299; Mathieson to Charteris, letter, Aug. 28 1947, NA, CO 537/2299; Mathieson, minute, Aug. 28, 1947, NA, CO 537/2299; *Palestine Post*, Aug. 8, 1947; Crocker to Simpson, telegram, Aug. 3, 1947, NA, WO 216/221; Crocker to Cunningham, letter, Aug. 13, 1947, Cunningham Papers, V/4; Appreciation by MacMillan, Aug. 5, 1947, NA, WO 261/541.
49. Trafford Smith, minute, Aug. 12, 1947; Mathieson, minute, Aug. 26, 1947, NA, CO 537/2299; Mathieson to Charteris, letter, Sept. 10. 1947, NA, CO 537/2299; minutes of security conference, Sept. 26, 1947, Cunningham Papers, IV/1.
50. *Daily Express* and *Times*, Aug. 1, 1947; Sykes (1965), 382–83; Monroe (1961), 34; note of conversation, Aug. 4, 1947, NA, FO 371/61821.
51. Louis (1984), 464; *Times*, Aug. 1 and 2, 1947.
52. *Times* and *Palestine Post*, Aug. 5, 1947; Cesarani (2009), 179.
53. Sixth Airborne Division, Intelligence Summary 48, Aug. 2–15, 1947, NA, WO 275/64; Shomron Bloc Jewish Settlements to Gurney, letter, Sept. 7, 1947, CS D/160/40, ISA; Brigadier W. S. Cole to Gurney, letter, Oct. 27, 1947, CS D/160/40, ISA; District Commissioner to Chief Secretary, letter, Nov. 19, 1947, CS D/160/40, ISA.
54. Sixth Airborne Division, Intelligence Fortnightly Newsletter 48, Aug. 2–15, 1947; Monroe (1961), 34; Gurney to Cunningham, letter, Aug. 4, 1947, Cunningham Papers, VI/1.
55. *Manchester Guardian* and *Daily Telegraph*, Aug. 1, 1947; *Economist*, Aug. 9, 1947.
56. *Times*, Aug. 1, 1947; Debates, House of Commons, vol., cols. 2314–15, Aug. 12, 1947.
57. Debates, House of Commons, vol. 441, cols. 2328–29, Aug. 12, 1947.
58. Debates, House of Commons, vol. 441, cols. 2340–47, 2360–62, Aug. 12, 1947.
59. Beeley, minute, Aug. 17, 1947, NA, FO 371/61948; Mathieson to Donald MacGillivray (undersecretary, CO, and liaison officer, UNSCOP), telegram, Aug. 22, 1947, NA, FO 371/61786.
60. Wright, draft paper, Aug. 21, 1947, NA, FO 371/61948; Sir Gladwyn Jebb (assistant undersecretary and UN adviser, FO) and Sir Orme Sargent (permanent undersecretary, FO), minutes, Aug. 21 and 22, 1947, NA, FO 371/61948.

61. Note, Aug. 11, 1947, NA, PREM 8/623.
62. Quoted in Beeley, minute, Aug. 19, 1947, NA, FO 371/61948.
63. García-Granados (1948), 172–82; Gruber (1948), 17–59; Holly (1969), 191–259; Sykes (1965), 381–82; Wilson (1949), 134–35; Jeffery (2010), 693–94.
64. *Economist*, Oct. 18, 1947; Bethell (1979), 342–43; Hurewitz (1976), 140; Jeffery (2010), 694; Louis (1984), 464, 470; Sykes (1965), 381–84; Gruber (1948), 127–28; Holly (1969), 265–67; Wilson (1949), 137–39.
65. *Economist*, Oct. 18, 1947; Bethell (1979), 343; Hurewitz (1976), 140; Louis (1984), 464, 470; Sykes (1965), 383–84; García-Granados (1948), 182, 213.
66. Laqueur (1969), 108–12.
67. The Australian representative abstained from voting on either plan on the ground that a unanimous report had not been produced. García-Granados (1948), 242n2; Bullock (1983), 476.
68. *Times*, Sept. 1, 1947; *Economist*, Sept. 6, 1947; Creech Jones to Munro [*sic*], letter, Oct. 23, 1961, box 32/6, Creech Jones Papers.
69. CP (47) 262, Sept. 18, 1947, NA, CAB 129/21.
70. CP (47) 259, Sept. 18, 1947, NA, CAB 129/21.
71. Ibid.
72. CM (47) 76, Sept. 20, 1947, NA, CAB 128/10; Pimlott (1986), 414.
73. CM (47) 76, Sept. 20, 1947, NA, CAB 128/10.
74. Speech to Ad Hoc Committee on the Palestine Question, Sept. 26, 1947, box 31/3, Creech Jones Papers.
75. CM 86 (47), Nov. 11, 1947, NA, CAB 128/10.

EPILOGUE: ONLY THUS

1. Creech Jones to Munro [*sic*], letter, Oct. 23, 1961.
2. Creech Jones to Callaghan, letter, Nov. 30, 1961, box 32/3, Creech Jones Papers.
3. Brutton (1996), 96; O'Sullivan, Annual Report for J2 Section, 1947.
4. Nachmani (1980), 1; Gurney Diary, March 15–May 14, 1948, entry for March 25, 1948, 19, Gurney Papers.
5. Note of interview, July 31, 1947, Cunningham Papers, V/1.
6. *Irgun Press*, no. 1/5, Aug. 1939, K-4 4/15, JI.
7. Thurston Clarke (1981), 29, 37; Montefiore (2011), 477; Crossman (1947), 118; Begin (1977a), 52, 212; Aviezer and Nakdimon (1978), 115; Begin (1977a), 52.
8. Marlowe (1959), 226.
9. Cunningham (1948), 485; Notes for Talk to Secretary of State on July 20, 1946, Cunningham Papers, IV/2.
10. Paget (1967), 8 and 156.
11. Creech Jones to Ollerenshaw, letter, April 10, 1947; Memorandum on the Comparative Treatment.
12. *Palestine Post*, Aug. 4 and 5, 1947.
13. JP (45) 30, Feb. 15, 1945, NA, AIR 20/4959; Ismay to Attlee, minute, Nov. 29, 1945, PREM 8/83; Cunningham to Creech Jones, telegram, Aug. 31, 1947, NA, CO 537/2299.
14. Tim Jones (2005), 81–82; Charters (1989), 204.
15. Sinclair (2006a), 29; French (2011), 16, 19, 41; Killingray and Anderson (1992), 8.
16. Montgomery (1958), 378–79; HQ Palestine, Operational Instruction 67, June 17, 1946, NA, WO 275/13.

17. David John Clark (1978), 3.
18. French (2011), 19–20; Kellar, Visit to the Middle East, Feb. 1945.
19. Kitson (1971), xi.
20. Gale, "Operation 'Tiger,'" Aug. 2, 1947, NA, WO 261/181.
21. Begin (1977a), 53–54, 56.
22. Ibid., 54–55.
23. 80th Cong., 1st sess., H.J. Resolution 237 (Rep. Somers), July 11, 1947; minutes, May 3–5, 1947, NA, FO 371/61753; Baxter to HM Consul General, New York, letter, June 3, 1947; Zaar (1954), 230, 243; Louis (1984), 464.
24. Jerusalem to Chancery, Washington, D.C., telegram, Sept. 18, 1947, NA, CO 733/477/75156/151A.
25. Foley (1964b), 1–219; Grivas-Dighenis (1964a), 1–108; Marighella (1971), 61–97; Hacker (1976), 72–73.
26. Al-Bahri (2013), 77; Wright (2006), 303.

Bibliography

MANUSCRIPT SOURCES

NATIONAL AND OFFICIAL ARCHIVES

Archives of the Council on Foreign Relations, New York
Record of Meetings, 1946

Central Zionist Archives, Jerusalem
S 25 Departments of the Executives of the Zionist Organization and the Jewish Agency
Z 4 Records of the Zionist Organization and the Jewish Agency

Haganah Archives, Tel Aviv
HA Criminal Investigation Department, Palestine Police Force

Israel State Archives, Jerusalem
CS   Records of the Office of Chief Secretary, Palestine Government
P 867 Barker–Antonius Correspondence

Jabotinsky Institute, Tel Aviv
G-12 Records of the Irgun Zvai Le'umi
K-4   Records of the Lohamei Herut Yisrael

National Archives and Records Administration, Washington, D.C.
RG 43   International Conferences, Commissions, and Expositions, Papers of Admiral William D. Leahy (chief of staff to President Harry S. Truman)
RG 59   Post Files, Jerusalem
RG 84   Post Files, Cairo
RG 165 Records of the War Department, General and Special Staffs (Intelligence)
RG 218 Records of the U.S. Joint Chiefs of Staff (JCS)
RG 226 Records of the Office of Strategic Services
RG 319 Records of U.S. Army Staff (Intelligence)

National Archives, London
Air Ministry
AIR 2   Correspondence
AIR 5   Air Historical Branch Papers (Series II)
AIR 20 Unregistered Papers from Air Ministry Branches

Cabinet
CAB 23   War Cabinet and Cabinet Minutes
CAB 24   War Cabinet and Cabinet Memoranda
CAB 65   War Cabinet Minutes
CAB 66   Memoranda—WP and CP Series
CAB 67   War Cabinet Memoranda—WP(G) Series
CAB 68   War Cabinet Memoranda—WP(R) Series
CAB 95   War Cabinet Committees on the Middle East and Africa
CAB 104   Supplementary Registered Files
CAB 127   Cabinet Defence Committee
CAB 128   Cabinet Minutes
CAB 129   Cabinet Memorandums
CAB 131   Cabinet Defence Committee Minutes and Papers
CAB 134   Miscellaneous Committees Minutes and Papers

Colonial Office
CO 537   Palestine Supplementary Correspondence
CO 733   Palestine Original Correspondence
CO 814   Palestine Sessional Papers
CO 935   Confidential Print Middle East
CO 968   Defence Original Correspondence

Ministry of Technology
EF 5   Explosives Inspectorate General Correspondence and Papers

Foreign Office
FO 141   Embassy and Consular Archives Egypt Correspondence
FO 371   General Correspondence of the Political Departments
FO 800   Private Collections of Various Ministers and Officials
FO 921   Files of the Office of the Minister of State Resident in Cairo

Foreign and Commonwealth Office
FCO 141 Colonial Administration Records (Migrated Archives): Palestine

Home Office
HO 45   Registered Papers

Special Operations Executive Records
HS 9   Special Operations Executive (SOE)

The Security Service (MI5)
KV 2   The Security Service: Personal (PF Series) Files
KV 3   The Security Service: Subject (SF Series) Files
KV 4   Intelligence Organisation in the Middle East (SIME)
KV 5   The Security Service: Organisation (OF Series) Files

Prime Minister's Office (Premier)
PREM 3   Operational Papers
PREM 4   Confidential Papers
PREM 8   Correspondence and Papers

War Office
WO 32   Registered Papers, General Series
WO 106 Directorate of Military Operations and Intelligence
WO 169 War Diaries, Middle East Forces
WO 193 Directorate of Military Operations: Collation Files
WO 201 War of 1939 to 1945, Military Papers, Middle East Forces
WO 208 Directorate of Military Intelligence
WO 216 Papers of the Chief of the Imperial General Staff
WO 261 Middle East Land Forces: Quarterly Historical Reports
WO 275 Sixth Airborne Division

Weizmann Archives, Rehovot, Israel
Papers and Correspondence of Dr. Chaim Weizmann (in alphabetical order)

PERSONAL PAPERS

Blenkinsop, Frederick William Geoffrey, GB165-0030. Middle East Centre, St. Antony's College, Oxford.

Brebber, Major Alexander, GB165-0387. Middle East Centre, St. Antony's College, Oxford.

Cafferata, Colonel Raymond Oswald, GB165-0044. Middle East Centre, St. Antony's College, Oxford.

Cannings, Victor Henry Douglas, GB165-0386. Middle East Centre, St. Antony's College, Oxford.

Catling, Sir Richard. Rhodes House, Oxford.

Clarke, Brigadier Dudley W. Imperial War Museum, London.

Creech Jones, Arthur. Rhodes House, Oxford.

Crossman, Richard Howard Stafford, GB165-0068. Middle East Centre, St. Antony's College, Oxford.

Cunningham, General Sir Alan, GB165-0072. Middle East Centre, St. Antony's College, Oxford.

D'Arcy, Lieutenant General John, GB165-0075. Middle East Centre, St. Antony's College, Oxford.

Edwards, Stephen, GB165-0354. Middle East Centre, St. Antony's College, Oxford.

Fletcher-Cooke, John, GB165-0107. Middle East Centre, St. Antony's College, Oxford.

Fraser, Ronald. Rhodes House, Oxford.

Gurney, Sir Henry, GB165-0128. Middle East Centre, St. Antony's College, Oxford.

Haining, Lieutenant General Sir Robert Hadden, GB165-0131. Middle East Centre, St. Antony's College, Oxford.

Isham, Sir Gyles. Northamptonshire Record Office, Wootton Hall Park, Northamptonshire.

Jerusalem and the East Mission Papers, GB165-0161. Middle East Centre, St. Antony's College, Oxford.

Keating, Rex. Imperial War Museum, London.

Keating, Rex, GB165-0361. Middle East Centre, St. Antony's College, Oxford.

LeRay, Hugh Granville, GB165-0181. Middle East Centre, St. Antony's College, Oxford.

Lloyd Phillips, Ivan. Rhodes House, Oxford.

MacMillan, General Sir G. H. A. Imperial War Museum.

Monroe, Elizabeth, GB165-0207. Middle East Centre, St. Antony's College, Oxford.

Montgomery, Field Marshal Viscount of Alamein Bernard Law. Imperial War Museum, London.

Morris, Philip, GB165-0379. Middle East Centre, St. Antony's College, Oxford.

Morton, Desmond, GB165-0405. Middle East Centre, St. Antony's College, Oxford.

O'Sullivan, John J. Rhodes House, Oxford.

Rymer-Jones, Brigadier J. M. Imperial War Museum, London.

Scott, Sir Robert. Rhodes House, Oxford.

Scrivener, Rupert, GB165-0257. Middle East Centre, St. Antony's College, Oxford.

Scrivenor, Sir Thomas V. Rhodes House, Oxford.

Shaw, Sir John. Rhodes House, Oxford.

Tegart, Sir Charles Augustus, GB165-0281. Middle East Centre, St. Antony's College, Oxford.

Tomlinson, David, GB165-0360. Middle East Centre, St. Antony's College, Oxford.

DISSERTATIONS

Bagon, Paul. "The Impact of the Jewish Underground upon Anglo Jewry, 1945–1947." M.Phil. thesis, Oxford University, 2003.

Chavkin, Jonathan. "British Intelligence and the Zionist, South African, and Australian Intelligence Communities During and After the Second World War." Ph.D. thesis, Cambridge University, 2009.

Clark, David John. "The Colonial Police and Anti-terrorism: Bengal 1930–1936, Palestine 1937–1947, and Cyprus 1955–1959." D.Phil. thesis, Oxford University, 1978.

Knight, John L. "Policing in British Palestine, 1917–1939." D.Phil. thesis, Oxford University, Trinity Term, 2008.

Nachmani, Amikam. "British Policy in Palestine After World War II: The Anglo-American Committee of Inquiry into the Problems of European Jewry and Palestine, 1945–1946." D.Phil. thesis, Oxford University, 1980.

Wagner, Steven. "Britain and the Jewish Underground, 1944–46: Intelligence, Policy, and Resistance." Master's thesis, University of Calgary, 2010.

PRINTED SOURCES: PRIMARY

BRITISH COMMAND PAPERS

Cmd. 5479. *Palestine Royal Commission Report*. London: HMSO, July 1937.

Cmd. 5854. *Palestine Partition Commission: Report*. London: HMSO, Oct. 1938.

Cmd. 5893. *Palestine: Statement by His Majesty's Government*. London: HMSO, Oct. 1938.

Cmd. 6019. *British White Paper: Statement of Policy*. London: HMSO, May 1939.

Cmd. 6180. *British White Paper: Summary of Land Transfer Regulations*. London: HMSO, Feb. 1940.

Cmd. 6873. *Palestine: Statement of Information Relating to Acts of Violence*. London: HMSO, July 1946.

FOREIGN RELATIONS OF THE UNITED STATES

Foreign Relations of the United States, 1939. Vol. 4. Washington, D.C., 1955.

Foreign Relations of the United States, 1943, Vol. 3, *The Conferences at Washington and Quebec*. Washington, D.C., 1946.

Foreign Relations of the United States, 1944. Vol. 5. Washington, D.C., 1965.
Foreign Relations of the United States, 1945. Vol. 5. Washington, D.C., 1969.
Foreign Relations of the United States, 1945. Vol. 8. Washington, D.C., 1969.
Foreign Relations of the United States, 1946. Vol. 7. Washington, D.C., 1969.
Foreign Relations of the United States, 1947. Vol. 7. Washington, D.C.: U.S. Department of State, 1977.

HANSARD

Hansard, 5th Series, Parliamentary Debates.

REPORTS

Anglo-American Committee of Inquiry: Report to the United States Government and His Majesty's Government in the United Kingdom, April 20, 1946. Washington, D.C.: U.S. Government Printing Office, 1946.
Diaspora Headquarters of the Irgun Zvai Leumi. *Background to the Struggle for the Liberation of Eretz Israel: Facts on the Relations Between the Irgun Zvai Leumi and the Haganah.* New York: Information Department of the American League for a Free Palestine, Inc., 1947.
Jewish Agency for Palestine. *The Jewish Plan for Palestine: Memoranda and Statements Presented by the Jewish Agency for Palestine to the United Nations Special Committee on Palestine.* Jerusalem: Jewish Agency for Palestine, 1947.

PUBLISHED GOVERNMENT DOCUMENT

"Field Manual 3-07.22: Counterinsurgency Operations." HQ, Department of the U.S. Army. Washington, D.C., 2004.

MEMOIRS, AUTOBIOGRAPHIES, AND PERSONAL ACCOUNTS

Alanbrooke, Field Marshal Lord. *War Diaries, 1939–1945: Field Marshal Lord Alan-brooke.* Edited by Alex Danchev and Daniel Todman. London: Phoenix, 2002.
Anderson, Brigadier R. N. "Search Operations in Palestine: The Problem of the Soldier." *Army Quarterly* 55 (1947–48).
Avner. *Memoirs of an Assassin: Confessions of a Stern Gang Killer.* London: Blond, 1959.
Avriel, Ehud. *Open the Gates! A Personal Story of "Illegal" Immigration to Israel.* New York: Atheneum, 1975.
Barnes, John, and David Nicholson, eds. *The Empire at Bay: The Leo Amery Diaries, 1929–1945.* London: Hutchinson, 1988.
Begin, Menachem. *The Revolt: Story of the Irgun.* Jerusalem: Steimatzky, 1977.
———. *White Knights: The Story of a Prisoner in Russia.* Jerusalem: Steimatzky, 1977.
Ben-Gurion, David. *Recollections.* Edited by Thomas R. Bransten. London: MacDonald Unit 75, 1970.

Bentwich, Norman. *My 77 Years: An Account of My Life and Times, 1883–1960.* Philadelphia: Jewish Publication Society of America, 1961.

Berlin, Sir Isaiah. "Zionist Politics in Wartime Washington: A Fragment of Personal Reminiscence." Yaacov Herzog Memorial Lecture, Hebrew University of Jerusalem, Oct. 2, 1972. Jerusalem: Jerusalem Post, 1972.

Brutton, Philip. *A Captain's Mandate Palestine, 1946–48.* London: Leo Cooper, 1996.

Burt, Leonard. *Commander Burt of Scotland Yard.* London: Heinemann, 1959.

Cavendish, Anthony. *Inside Intelligence.* London: Collins, 1990.

Channon, Sir Henry. *Chips: The Diaries of Sir Henry Channon.* Edited by Robert Rhodes James. London: Weidenfeld & Nicolson, 1967.

Churchill, Winston S. *The Second World War.* Vol. 6, *Triumph and Tragedy.* London: Reprint Society, 1956.

———. *The Second World War.* Vol. 3, *The Grand Alliance.* London: Reprint Society, 1956.

Cohen, Geula. *Woman of Violence: Memoirs of a Young Terrorist, 1943–1948.* New York: Holt, Rinehart and Winston, 1966.

Courtney, Roger. *Palestine Policeman: An Account of Eighteen Dramatic Months in the Palestine Police Force During the Great Jew-Arab Troubles.* London: Herbert Jenkins, 1939.

Crossman, Richard. *Palestine Mission.* New York: Harper & Brothers, 1947.

Crum, Bartley C. *Behind the Silken Curtain: A Personal Account of Anglo-American Diplomacy in Palestine and the Middle East.* New York: Simon & Schuster, 1947.

Dalton, Baron Hugh. *The Political Diary of Hugh Dalton, 1918–40, 1945–60.* Edited by Ben Pimlott. London: Jonathan Cape, 1986.

Dayan, Moshe. *Story of My Life.* London: Weidenfeld & Nicolson, 1976.

Diness, Mendel J., et al. *Capturing the Holy Land: M. J. Diness and the Beginning of Photography in Jerusalem.* Cambridge, Mass.: Harvard University Press, 1993.

Duff, Douglas V. *Bailing with a Teaspoon.* London: John Long, 1953.

Dugdale, Blanche. *Baffy: The Diaries of Blanche Dugdale, 1936–1947.* Edited by N. A. Rose. London: Vallentine, Mitchell, 1973.

Eban, Abba. *Abba Eban: An Autobiography.* New York: Random House, 1977.

Eliav, Yaacov. *Wanted.* New York: Shengold, 1984.

Farran, Roy. *Winged Dagger: Adventures on Special Service.* London: Collins, 1950.

Fergusson, Bernard. *Beyond the Chindwin: An Account of the Wingate Expedition into Burma.* Barnsley: Pen & Sword, 2009.

———. *The Trumpet in the Hall, 1930–1958.* London: Collins, 1970.

———. *The Wild Green Earth.* London: Collins, 1946.

Gale, General Sir Richard. *Call to Arms: An Autobiography.* London: Hutchinson, 1968.

García-Granados, Jorge. *The Birth of Israel: The Drama as I Saw It.* New York: Knopf, 1948.

Garfield, Simon, ed. *Our Hidden Lives: The Everyday Diaries of a Forgotten Britain, 1945–1948.* London: Ebury, 2004.

Golani, Motti, ed. *The End of the British Mandate for Palestine, 1948: The Diary of Sir Henry Gurney.* New York: Palgrave Macmillan, 2009.

Graves, Richard. *Experiment in Anarchy.* London: Victor Gollancz, 1949.

Grivas-Dighenis, General George. *Guerrilla Warfare and Eoka's Struggle.* London: Longmans, 1964a.

———. *The Memoirs of General Grivas.* Edited by Charles Foley. London: Longmans, 1964.

Gruber, Ruth. *Destination Palestine: The Story of the Haganah Ship* Exodus, *1947.* New York: Current Books, 1948.

Hecht, Ben. *A Child of the Century.* New York: Simon & Schuster, 1954.

Hughes, Matthew, ed. *Allenby in Palestine: The Middle East Correspondence of Field Marshal Viscount Allenby, June 1917–October 1919.* Stroud, Gloucestershire: Sutton, 2004.

Imray, Colin. *Policeman in Palestine.* Devon: Edward Gaskell, 1995.

Katz, Samuel. *Days of Fire.* London: Doubleday, 1968.

Keith-Roach, Edward. *Pasha of Jerusalem: Memoirs of a District Commissioner Under the British Mandate.* London: Radcliffe, 1994.

Kenneally, John. *The Honour and the Shame.* London: Headline Review, 2008.

Kollek, Teddy. *For Jerusalem.* With Amos Kollek. New York: Random House, 1978.

Lankin, Eliahu. *To Win the Promised Land: Story of a Freedom Fighter.* Walnut Creek, Calif.: Benmir, 1992.

Laqueur, Walter. *Thursday's Child Has Far to Go: A Memoir of the Journeying Years.* New York: Scribner's, 1992.

Martin, Robin H. *Palestine Betrayed: A British Policeman's Memoirs (1936–1948).* Ringwood, Berkshire: Seglawi Press, 2007.

Meinertzhagen, Colonel Richard. *Middle East Diary, 1917–1956.* London: Cresset, 1959.

Meir, Golda. *A Land of Our Own: An Oral Autobiography.* New York: G. P. Putnam's, 1973.

———. *My Life.* New York: G. P. Putnam's, 1975.

Meridor, Ya'acov. *Long Is the Road to Freedom.* Johannesburg: NEWZO Press, 1955.

Mitchell, Colin. *Having Been a Soldier.* London: Hamish Hamilton, 1969.

Montgomery, Bernard Law. *The Memoirs of Field-Marshal the Viscount Montgomery of Alamein, K.G.* New York: World, 1958.

Moran, Lord. *Churchill: Taken from the Diaries of Lord Moran: The Struggle for Survival, 1940–1965.* Boston: Houghton Mifflin, 1966.

Morton, Geoffrey J. *Just the Job: Some Experiences of a Colonial Policeman.* London: Hodder & Stoughton, 1957.

Newton, Frances. *Fifty Years in Palestine.* London: Coldharbour Press, 1948.

Oz, Amos. *A Tale of Love and Darkness.* Boston: Houghton Mifflin Harcourt, 2004.

Pearlman, Moshe, and David Ben-Gurion. *Ben-Gurion Looks Back.* New York: Simon & Schuster, 1965.

Shamir, Yitzhak. "Mado'a ha-lehi hitnakshu b' Lord Moyne?" [Why did the Lehi assassinate Lord Moyne?]. *Ha'uma* [The nation] 119 (1995).

———. *Summing Up: An Autobiography.* London: Weidenfeld & Nicolson, 1994.

Storrs, Sir Ronald. *Orientations.* London: Ivor Nicholson & Watson, 1939.

Sutherland, David. *He Who Dares: Recollections of Service in the SAS, SBS, and MI5.* Annapolis, Md.: Naval Institute Press, 1999.

Tauber, Eliezer, ed. *Military Resistance in Late Mandatory Palestine: The Activities of the Jewish and Arab Military Organizations as Reflected in the Reports of High Commissioner General Sir Alan Cunningham.* Ramat Gan: Bar-Ilan University Press, 2012.

Tavin, Eli. "HaShagrirut HaBritit Be-Roma: HaMatara HaRishona shel HaHazit HaShnia" [The British embassy in Rome: The first target of the second front], *b'Eretz Israel* (Nov. 1986).

Ullendorff, Edward. *Two Zions: Reminiscences of Jerusalem and Ethiopia.* Oxford: Oxford University Press, 1988.

Weizman, Ezer. *On Eagles' Wings: The Personal Story of the Leading Commander of the Israeli Air Force.* Tel Aviv: Steimatsky, 1979.

Weizmann, Chaim. *Trial and Error: The Autobiography of Chaim Weizmann.* Vol. 2. Philadelphia: Jewish Publication Society of America, 1949.

Weizmann, Vera. *The Impossible Takes Longer: The Memoirs of Vera Weizmann, Wife of Israel's First President, as Told to David Tutaev.* New York: Harper & Row, 1967.

Wilson, Major R. D. *Cordon and Search: With 6th Airborne Division in Palestine.* Aldershot: Gale & Polden, 1949.

Yalin-Mor, Nathan. "The British Called Us the Stern Gang." *Israel Magazine*, Feb. 1973, 76–84.

———. *Lohamei Herut Israel: anashim, ra'ayanot, alilot* [Fighters for the freedom of Israel: People, ideas, deeds]. Jerusalem: Shikmona, 1974.

NEWSPAPERS

Daily Express (London)
Daily Graphic (London)
Daily Telegraph (London)
Davar (Tel Aviv)
Economist
Evening News (London)
Ha'aretz (Tel Aviv)
Illustrated London News
Independent (London)
Jerusalem Post
Jerusalem Post International Edition
Jewish Chronicle (London)
Jewish Standard (London)
Manchester Guardian
Newsweek
New Yorker
New York Herald Tribune
New York Times
Palestine Post (Jerusalem)
Scotsman (Edinburgh)
Sunday Express (London)
Sunday Guardian (Manchester)
Times (London)
Times Literary Supplement (London)

PRINTED SOURCES: SECONDARY

Abrahms, Max. "Why Terrorism Does Not Work." *International Security* 31, no. 2 (Fall 2006): 42–78.

Alfasi, Yitzhak. "Ma'arechet ha-yachasim ha-hadadi ben ha-Etzel ve ha-Lechi" [The relationship between the Etzel and the Lehi]. *Ha'uma* [The nation] 29, no. 105 (1991).

Allon, Yigal. *The Making of Israel's Army.* London: Vallentine, Mitchell, 1970.

Andrew, Christopher. *Defence of the Realm: The Authorized History of MI5*. London: Allen Lane, 2009.

———. *Her Majesty's Secret Service: The Making of the British Intelligence Community*. New York: Viking, 1986.

Anglim, Simon. *Orde Wingate: The Iron Wall and Counter-terrorism in Palestine, 1937–39*. Shrivenham, Wiltshire: Strategic and Combat Studies Institute, 2005.

Antonius, George. *The Arab Awakening: The Story of the Arab National Movement*. New York: Paragon, 1979.

Atkinson, Rick. *An Army at Dawn: The War in North Africa, 1942–1943*. New York: Owl Books, 2003.

Azaryahu, Maoz. *Tel Aviv: Mythology of a City*. Syracuse, N.Y.: Syracuse University Press, 2007.

Bahri, Nasser, al-. *Guarding Bin Laden: My Life in al-Qaeda*. With Georges Malbrunot. London: Thin Man Press, 2013.

Barker, James. "The Bombing of the King David Hotel." *History Today* 56, no. 7 (July 2006): 50–56.

Barnett, Correlli. *The Desert Generals*. London: William Kimber, 1960.

Barr, James. *A Line in the Sand: The Anglo-French Struggle for the Middle East, 1914–1948*. New York: W. W. Norton, 2012.

Bartlett, C. J. *The Long Retreat: A Short History of British Defence Policy, 1945–1970*. London: Macmillan, 1972.

Bar-Zohar, Michael. *Ben-Gurion: The Armed Prophet*. Englewood Cliffs, N.J.: Prentice-Hall, 1968.

Bauer, Yehuda. *Flight and Rescue: Brichah*. New York: Random House, 1970.

———. "From Cooperation to Resistance: The Haganah, 1938–1946." *Middle Eastern Studies* 2, no. 3 (April 1966): 182–210.

———. *From Diplomacy to Resistance: A History of Jewish Palestine, 1939–1945*. New York: Atheneum, 1973.

———. *My Brother's Keeper: A History of the American Jewish Joint Distribution Committee, 1929–1939*. Philadelphia: Jewish Publication Society of America, 1974.

Baumel, Judith Tydor. *The "Bergson Boys" and the Origins of Contemporary Zionist Militancy*. Syracuse, N.Y.: Syracuse University Press, 2005.

Beckett, Ian F. W. *Encyclopedia of Guerrilla Warfare*. New York: Checkmark, 2001.

Bell, J. Bowyer. *Terror out of Zion: Irgun Zvai Leumi, LEHI, and the Palestine Underground, 1929–1949*. New York: St. Martin's Press, 1977.

Ben-Arieh, Yeoshua. *Jerusalem in the 19th Century: The Old City*. New York: St. Martin's Press, 1986.

Ben-Gurion, David. "Britain's Contributions to Arming the Hagana [sic]." In *From Haven to Conquest: Readings in Zionism and the Palestine Problem Until 1948*, edited by Walid Khalidi. Beirut: Institute for Palestine Studies, 1971.

———. "Our Friend: What Wingate Did for Us." In *From Haven to Conquest: Readings in Zionism and the Palestine Problem Until 1948*, edited by Walid Khalidi. Beirut: Institute for Palestine Studies, 1971.

Benjamin, Leo. *Martyrs in Cairo*. New York: Imprint, 1952.

Bentwich, Norman. *England in Palestine*. London: K. Paul, Trench, Trubner, 1932.

Ben-Yehuda, Nachman. *Political Assassinations by Jews: A Rhetorical Device for Justice*. Albany: State University of New York Press, 1993.

Bethell, Nicholas. *The Palestine Triangle: The Struggle Between the British, the Jews, and the Arabs, 1935–48*. London: Andrew Deutsch, 1979.

Bird, Kai. *Crossing Mandelbaum Gate: Coming of Age Between the Arabs and Israelis, 1956–78.* New York: Scribner, 2010.

Blaxland, Gregory. *The Regiments Depart: A History of the British Army, 1945–1970.* London: William Kimber, 1971.

Bond, Brian. "Gort." In *Churchill's Generals*, edited by John Keegan. New York: Grove Weidenfeld, 1991.

Borisov, J. *Palestine Underground: The Story of the Jewish Resistance.* New York: Judea, 1947.

Bowden, Tom. *The Breakdown of Public Security: The Case of Ireland, 1916–1921, and Palestine, 1936–1939.* London: Sage, 1977.

———. "The Politics of the Arab Rebellion in Palestine, 1936–39." *Middle Eastern Studies* 11, no. 2 (May 1975): 147–74.

Breitman, Richard, and Norman J. W. Goda. *Hitler's Shadow: Nazi War Criminals, U.S. Intelligence, and the Cold War.* Washington, D.C.: National Archives, 2010.

Brenner, Y. S. "'The Stern Gang,' 1940–1948." In *Palestine and Israel in the 19th and 20th Centuries*, edited by Elie Kedourie and Sylvia Haim. London: Frank Cass, 1982.

British War Office and U.S. War Department. *The British Army, 1942.* Smalldale, U.K.: Military Library Research Service, 2005.

Broido, Vera. *Apostles into Terrorists: Women and the Revolutionary Movement in the Russia of Alexander II.* London: Maurice Temple Smith, 1977.

Brundage, James. *The Crusades: A Documentary Survey.* Milwaukee: Marquette University Press, 1962.

Bullock, Alan. *Ernest Bevin: Foreign Secretary, 1945–1951.* New York: W. W. Norton, 1983.

———. *The Life and Times of Ernest Bevin.* Vol. 1, *Trade Union Leader, 1881–1940.* London: Heinemann, 1960.

———. *The Life and Times of Ernest Bevin.* Vol. 2, *Minister of Labour, 1940–1945.* London: Heinemann, 1960.

Cahill, Richard Andrew. "'Going Beserk': 'Black and Tans' in Palestine." *Jerusalem Quarterly* 38 (Summer 2009): 59–68.

Caplan, Neil. "The Yishuv, Sir Herbert Samuel, and the Arab Question in Palestine, 1921–25." In *Zionism and Arabism in Palestine and Israel*, edited by Elie Kedourie and Sylvia Haim. London: Frank Cass, 1982.

Carr, Caleb. *The Lessons of Terror: A History of Warfare Against Civilians—Why It Has Always Failed and Why It Will Fail Again.* New York: Random House, 2002.

Cesarani, David. *Major Farran's Hat: Murder, Scandal, and Britain's War Against Jewish Terrorism, 1945–1948.* London: William Heinemann, 2009.

Charters, David A. *The British Army and Jewish Insurgency in Palestine, 1945–47.* New York: St. Martin's Press, 1989.

———. "British Intelligence in the Palestine Campaign, 1945–47." *Intelligence and National Security* 6, no. 1 (Jan. 1991): 115–40.

———. "Special Operations in Counter-insurgency: The Farran Case, Palestine, 1947." *Journal of the Royal United Services Institute for Defence Studies* 124, no. 2 (June 1979).

Clark, Christopher. *The Sleepwalkers: How Europe Went to War in 1914.* New York: HarperCollins, 2012.

Clarke, Peter. *The Last Thousand Days of the British Empire: Churchill, Roosevelt, and the Birth of the Pax Americana.* New York: Bloomsbury, 2008.

Clarke, Thurston. *By Blood and Fire: The Attack on the King David Hotel.* New York: G. P. Putnam's Sons, 1981.

Cohen, Hillel. *Army of Shadows: Palestinian Collaboration with Zionism, 1917–1948.* Berkeley: University of California Press, 2009.

Cohen, Michael J. "British Strategy and the Palestine Question, 1936–39." *Journal of Contemporary History* 7, no. 3/4 (July–Oct. 1972): 157–83.

———. "The Moyne Assassination, November 1944: A Political Analysis." *Middle Eastern Studies* 15, no. 3 (Oct. 1979): 358–73.

———. *Palestine and the Great Powers, 1945–1948.* Princeton, N.J.: Princeton University Press, 1982.

———. *Palestine: Retreat from the Mandate: The Making of British Policy, 1936–45.* London: Paul Elek, 1978.

———. *Palestine to Israel: From Mandate to Independence.* London: Frank Cass, 1988.

———. *Truman and Israel.* Berkeley: University of California Press, 1990.

———. "The Zionist Perspective." In *The End of the Palestine Mandate*, edited by Wm. Roger Louis and Robert W. Stookey. London: I. B. Tauris, 1986.

Cohen, Mitchell. *Zion and State: Nation, Class, and the Shaping of Modern Israel.* Oxford: Basil Blackwell, 1987.

Collins, Larry, and Dominique Lapierre. *O Jerusalem!* London: Pan Books, 1973.

Colville, John. *The Fringes of Power: Downing Street Diaries.* Vol. 2, *1941–April 1955.* London: Sceptre, 1987.

———. *Man of Valour: The Life of Field-Marshal the Viscount Gort, VC, GCB, DSO, MVO, MC.* London: Collins, 1972.

Connell, John. *Wavell: Scholar and Soldier.* New York: Harcourt, Brace & World, 1964.

Craster, Michael. "Cunningham, Ritchie, and Leese." In *Churchill's Generals*, edited by John Keegan. New York: Grove Weidenfeld, 1991.

Crenshaw, Martha. "The Causes of Terrorism." *Comparative Politics* 13, no. 4 (July 1981): 379–99.

———. "The Logic of Terrorism: Terrorist Behavior as a Product of Strategic Choice." In *Origins of Terrorism: Psychologies, Ideologies, Theologies, States of Mind*, edited by Walter Reich. Cambridge, U.K.: Cambridge University Press, 1992.

Cunningham, Sir Alan. "Palestine—the Last Days of the Mandate." *International Affairs* 24, no. 4 (Oct. 1948): 481–90.

Danchev, Alex, and Daniel Todman. *War Diaries, 1939–1945: Field Marshal Lord Alanbrooke.* London: Phoenix, 2002.

Davies, David Twiston. "Major Roy Farran." *"Daily Telegraph" Military Obituaries Book Two.* London: Grubb Street, 2006.

Dear, I. C. B. *The Oxford Companion to the Second World War.* Oxford: Oxford University Press, 1995.

Dekel, Efraim. *Shai: The Exploits of Hagana Intelligence.* London: Thomas Yoseloff, 1959.

Dewar, Michael. *Brush Fire Wars: Minor Campaigns of the British Army Since 1945.* New York: St. Martin's Press, 1984.

Dinur, Ben-Zion. *Sefer toldo ha-Haganah* [A history of the Haganah]. Tel Aviv: Ma'arhot, 1954–72.

Dockerill, Michael. *British Defence Since 1945.* Oxford: Basil Blackwell, 1988.

Dorrill, Stephen. *MI6: Fifty Years of Special Operations.* London: Fourth Estate, 2000.

Eliav, Mordechai. *Britain and the Holy Land, 1838–1914: Selected Documents from the British Consulate in Jerusalem.* Jerusalem: Magnes Press, 1997.

Esco Foundation for Palestine. *Palestine: A Study of Jewish, Arab, and British Policies.* Vol. 2. New Haven, Conn.: Yale University Press, 1947.

Evans, Richard. *The Coming of the Third Reich.* New York: Penguin, 2003.

———. *The Third Reich in Power.* New York: Penguin, 2005.

Fanon, Frantz. *The Wretched of the Earth.* London: Penguin, 1990.

Fearne, Charles. *Trial of the Honourable Admiral John Byng at a Court Martial.* London: Manby, Whiston, White, 1757.

Foot, M. R. D. *SOE in France: An Account of the Work of the British Special Operations Executive in France, 1940–1944.* London: HMSO, 1966.

Ford, Franklin. *Political Murder: From Tyrannicide to Terrorism.* Cambridge, Mass.: Harvard University Press, 1985.

Fowler, Will, Anthony North, and Charles Stronge. *The Illustrated Encyclopedia of Pistols, Revolvers, and Submachine Guns.* East Bridgewater, Mass.: World, 2011.

Frank, Gerold. *The Deed.* New York: Simon & Schuster, 1963.

———. "The Moyne Case: A Tragic History." *Commentary,* Dec. 1945, 64–71.

French, David. *The British Way in Counterinsurgency, 1945–1967.* Oxford: Oxford University Press, 2011.

Friedman, Isaiah. "The System of Capitulations and Its Effects on Turco-Jewish Relations in Palestine, 1901–1914." In *Palestine in the Late Ottoman Period: Political, Social, and Economic Transformation,* edited by David Kushner. Jerusalem: Yad Izhak Ben-Zvi Institute for the Study of Eretz Israel; Leiden: E. J. Brill, 1986.

Fromkin, David. *A Peace to End All Peace: The Fall of the Ottoman Empire and the Creation of the Modern Middle East.* New York: Holt, 2001.

Fyvel, T. R. "Wingate in Palestine." *Encounter* 64, no. 1 (1985).

Garfield, Brian. *The Meinertzhagen Mystery: The Life and Legend of a Colossal Fraud.* Washington, D.C.: Potomac, 2007.

Gervasi, Frank. *The Life and Times of Menachem Begin: Rebel to Statesman.* New York: G. P. Putnam's Sons, 1979.

Gilbert, Martin. *Churchill and the Jews: A Lifelong Friendship.* New York: Henry Holt, 2007.

———. *The Dent Atlas of the Arab-Israeli Conflict: The Complete History of the Struggle and the Efforts to Resolve It.* London: J. M. Dent, 1993.

———. *Exile and Return: The Struggle for a Jewish Homeland.* London: Weidenfeld & Nicolson, 1978.

———. *Winston S. Churchill: Finest Hour, 1939–1941.* Vol. 6. Boston: Houghton Mifflin, 1983.

———. *Winston S. Churchill: Never Despair, 1945–1965.* Vol. 8. Boston: Houghton Mifflin, 1988.

———. *Winston S. Churchill: Road to Victory, 1941–1945.* Vol. 7. Boston: Houghton Mifflin, 1986.

Gitlin, Jan. *The Conquest of Acre Fortress.* Tel Aviv: Hadar, 1974.

Golan, Aviezer, and Shlomo Nakdimon. *Begin.* Jerusalem: Edanim, 1978.

Golan, Zev. *Free Jerusalem: Heroes, Heroines, and Rogues Who Created the State of Israel.* Jerusalem: Devora, 2003.

Golani, Matti. "Palestine, 1945–1948: A View from the High Commissioner's Office." In *Britain, Palestine, and Empire: The Mandate Years,* edited by Rory Miller. Burlington, Vt.: Ashgate, 2010.

Goldhill, Simon. *Jerusalem: City of Longing.* Cambridge, Mass.: Belknap Press of Harvard University Press, 2008.

Goldsworthy, David. *Colonial Issues in British Politics, 1945–1961*. Oxford: Clarendon, 1971.

Gordon, Michael R. *Conflict and Consensus in Labour's Foreign Policy, 1914–1965*. Stanford, Calif.: Stanford University Press, 1969.

Goren, Arthur A. "Sanctifying Scopus: Locating the Hebrew University on Mount Scopus." In *Jewish History and Jewish Memory: Essays in Honor of Yosef Hayim Yerushalmi*, edited by John M. Efron and David N. Meyers. Hanover, N.H.: University Press of New England, 1998.

Graham-Brown, Sarah. *Palestinians and Their Society, 1880–1946*. London: Quartet, 1980.

Guinn, David E. *Protecting Jerusalem's Holy Sites: A Strategy for Negotiating a Sacred Peace*. Cambridge, U.K.: Cambridge University Press, 2006.

Gurevich, D., et al. *Statistical Handbook of Jewish Palestine*. Jerusalem: Department of Statistics of the Jewish Agency, 1947.

Gurion, Itzhak. *Triumph on the Gallows*. New York: American Memorial Committee for the Martyrs of Eretz Israel and Brit Trumpeldor of America, 1950.

Haber, Eitan. *Menachem Begin: The Legend and the Man*. New York: Dell, 1978.

Hacker, Frederick J. *Crusaders, Criminals, Crazies: Terror and Terrorism in Our Times*. New York: W. W. Norton, 1976.

Hadawi, Sami. *Bitter Harvest: Palestine Between 1914–1967*. New York: New World Press, 1967.

Hamilton, Nigel. *Monty: The Field-Marshal, 1944–1976*. London: Hamish Hamilton, 1986.

———. *Monty: The Making of a General, 1887–1942*. London: Hamish Hamilton, 1981.

Harris, Kenneth. *Attlee*. London: Weidenfeld & Nicolson, 1982.

Heller, Joseph. *The Birth of Israel, 1945–1949: Ben-Gurion and His Critics*. Gainesville: University Press of Florida, 2003.

———. *The Stern Gang: Ideology, Politics, and Terror, 1940–1949*. London: Frank Cass, 1995.

———. "The Zionist Right and National Liberation: From Jabotinsky to Avraham Stern." *Israel Affairs* 1, no. 3 (Spring 1995): 85–109.

Herf, Jeffrey. *Nazi Propaganda for the Arab World*. New Haven, Conn.: Yale University Press, 2009.

Hirst, David. *The Gun and the Olive Branch: The Roots of Violence in the Middle East*. London: Futura, 1978.

"A History of Government House." Reprinted from *UNTSO Magazine*, Nov./Dec. 1983.

Hoffman, Bruce. *Inside Terrorism*. New York: Columbia University Press, 2006.

———. "The Logic of Suicide Terrorism: Lessons from Israel That America Must Learn." *Atlantic Monthly*, June 2003, 40–47.

Hoffman, Bruce, and Gordon H. McCormick. "Terrorism, Signaling, and Suicide Attack." *Studies in Conflict and Terrorism* 27, no. 4 (July–Aug. 2004): 243–81.

Holly, David C. *Exodus 1947*. Boston: Little, Brown, 1969.

Holt, P. M. *Egypt and the Fertile Crescent, 1516–1922: A Political History*. Ithaca, N.Y.: Cornell University Press, 1966.

Horne, Alistair. *A Savage War of Peace: Algeria, 1954–1962*. Harmondsworth, U.K.: Penguin, 1977.

Horne, Edward. *A Job Well Done: A History of the Palestine Police Force, 1920–1948*. Leigh-on-Sea, Essex: Palestine Police Old Comrades Benevolent Association, 1982.

Howard, Michael. *The Causes of War*. London: Unwin, 1983.

————. *The Continental Commitment.* London: Ashfield, 1989.

Hroub, Khaled. *Hamas: Political Thought and Practice.* Washington, D.C.: Institute for Palestine Studies, 2000.

Hughes, Matthew. "The Banality of Brutality: British Armed Forces and the Repression of the Arab Revolt in Palestine, 1936–39." *English Historical Review* 124, no. 507 (2009): 313–54.

Hurewitz, J. C. "Review: Recent Books on the Problem of Palestine." *Middle East Journal* 3, no. 1 (Jan. 1949): 86–91.

————. *The Struggle for Palestine.* New York: Schocken, 1976.

Hurwitz, Harry. *Menachem Begin.* Johannesburg: Jewish Herald, 1977.

Hyams, Edward. *Terrorists and Terrorism.* New York: St. Martin's Press, 1974.

Ignatieff, Michael. *Isaiah Berlin: A Life.* New York: Henry Holt, 1998.

Ivianski, Zeev. "Fathers and Sons: A Study of Jewish Involvement in the Revolutionary Movement and Terrorism in Tsarist Russia." *Terrorism and Political Violence* 1, no. 2 (April 1989): 137–55.

Jabotinsky, Vladimir Z. "The Iron Wall, November 4, 1923." In *Israel in the Middle East: Documents and Readings on Society, Politics, and Foreign Relations, Pre-1948 to the Present,* edited by Itamar Rabinovich and Jehuda Reinharz. Waltham, Mass.: Brandeis University Press, 2007.

————. *The Jewish War Front.* Westport, Conn.: Greenwood, 1975.

Jackson, Ashley. *The British Empire and the Second World War.* London: Hambledon Continuum, 2006.

Jeffries, Sir Charles. *Colonial Police.* London: M. Parrish, 1952.

Jeffery, Keith. "Police and Government in Northern Ireland, 1922–1969." In *The Policing of Politics in the Twentieth Century: Historical Perspectives,* edited by Mark Mazower. Providence, R.I.: Berghahn Books, 1997.

————. *The Secret History of MI6.* New York: Penguin, 2010.

Jones, Philip. *Britain and Palestine, 1914–1948: Archival Sources for the History of the British Mandate.* Oxford: Oxford University Press, 1979.

Jones, Tim. *Postwar Counterinsurgency and the SAS, 1945–1952.* London: Routledge, 2001.

————. *SAS: The First Secret War—the Unknown Years of Combat and Counter-insurgency.* London: I. B. Tauris, 2005.

Katz, Shmuel. *Lone Wolf: A Biography of Vladimir (Ze'ev) Jabotinsky.* New York: Barricade, 1996.

Katz, Yossi. *A Voice Called: Stories of Jewish Heroism.* Jerusalem: Gefen, 2010.

Kedourie, Elie. *Inside the Anglo-Arab Labyrinth.* Cambridge, U.K.: Cambridge University Press, 1976.

Keegan, John, and Andrew Wheatcroft. *Who's Who in Military History: From 1453 to the Present Day.* London: Routledge, 1996.

Kelly, J. B. *Arabia, the Gulf, and the West.* London: Weidenfeld & Nicolson, 1980.

Kemp, Anthony. *The SAS: Savage Wars of Peace, 1947 to the Present.* London: Signet, 1994.

Killingray, David, and David M. Anderson. "An Orderly Retreat? Police and the End of Empire." In *Policing and Decolonization: Politics, Nationalism, and the Police, 1917–65,* edited by David Killingray and David M. Anderson. Manchester: Manchester University Press, 1992.

Kimche, John, and David Kimche. *The Secret Roads: The "Illegal" Migration of People, 1938–1948.* London: Secker & Warburg, 1954.

Kister, Joseph. *The Irgun (I.Z.L.): The Story of Israel's Underground Movement for National Liberation*. Tel Aviv: Ministry of Defence Publishing House and Museum Unit, 2000.

Kitson, Frank. *Low Intensity Operations: Subversion, Insurgency, Peace-Keeping*. London: Faber & Faber, 1971.

Kochanski, Halik. *The Eagle Unbowed: Poland and the Poles in the Second World War*. Cambridge, Mass.: Harvard University Press, 2012.

Koestler, Arthur. *Promise and Fulfilment: Palestine, 1917–1949*. London: Macmillan, 1949.

Korbonski, Stefan. "Unknown Chapter in the Life of Menachem Begin and Irgun Zvai Leumi." *East European Quarterly* 8, no. 3 (Fall 1979): 373–84.

Krämer, Gudrun. *A History of Palestine: From the Ottoman Conquest to the Founding of the State of Israel*. Princeton, N.J.: Princeton University Press, 2008.

Kroizer, Gad. "From Dowbiggin to Tegart: Revolutionary Change in the Colonial Police in Palestine During the 1930s." *Journal of Imperial and Commonwealth History* 32, no. 2 (May 2004): 115–33.

Kroyanker, David. *Jerusalem Architecture*. New York: Vendome Press, 1994.

Kurzman, Dan. *Ben-Gurion: Prophet of Fire*. New York: Simon & Schuster, 1983.

———. *Genesis 1948: The First Arab-Israeli War*. London: Vallentine, Mitchell, 1970.

Kushner, Harvey. *Encyclopedia of Terrorism*. Thousand Oaks, Calif.: Sage, 2003.

Kydd, Andrew H., and Barbara F. Walter. "The Strategies of Terrorism." *International Security* 31, no. 1 (Summer 2006): 49–80.

Lachman, Shai. "Arab Rebellion and Terrorism in Palestine, 1929–39: The Case of Sheikh Izz al-Din al-Qassam and His Movement." In *Zionism and Arabism in Palestine and Israel*, edited by Elie Kedourie and Sylvia Haim. London: Frank Cass, 1982.

La Guardia, Anton. *Holy Land, Unholy War: Israelis and Palestinians*. London: Penguin, 2007.

Lake, David. "Rational Extremism: Understanding Terrorism in the Twenty-First Century." *Dialogue-IO* 1, no. 1 (Spring 2002): 15–29.

Lapidot, Yehuda. *B'lahav ha-marad: kravot ha-Etzel b'Yerushalim* [The flames of the revolt: Etzel's battle for Jerusalem]. Tel Aviv: Ministry of Defense, 1996.

———. *Lidata shel machteret: ha'Etzel b'shanot ha-shloshim* [The birth of the underground: The Etzel in the 1930s]. Tel Aviv: Brith Hayalei Etzel, 2001.

Laqueur, Walter. *A History of Zionism*. New York: Schocken, 1976.

———. *The Israel-Arab Reader*. New York: Bantam, 1969.

Lawrence, T. E. *Seven Pillars of Wisdom: A Triumph*. Harmondsworth: Penguin, 1977.

Le Carré, John. *Call for the Dead*. New York: Bantam, 1979.

Legg, L. G., and E. T. Williams. *Dictionary of National Biography*. Oxford: Oxford University Press, 1959.

Lesch, Ann Mosley. *Arab Politics in Palestine, 1917–1939: The Frustration of a Nationalist Movement*. Ithaca, N.Y.: Cornell University Press, 1979.

Lev-Ami, Shlomo. *B'mavek u'vmared: Haganah, Etzel v' Lehi, 1918–1948* [By struggle and by revolt: Haganah, Etzel, and Lehi, 1918–1948]. Tel Aviv: Ministry of Defence, 1978.

Levenberg, H. "Bevin's Disillusionment: The London Conference, Autumn, 194▪ *Middle Eastern Studies* 27, no. 4 (Oct. 1991): 615–30.

Levine, Daniel. *David Raziel, the Man and the Legend: The Birth of the Irgun Zvai L a Jewish Liberation Movement*. Jerusalem: Gefen, 1991.

Levine, Evyatar, and Yaacov Shimoni, eds. *Political Dictionary of the Middle East in the Twentieth Century.* London: Weidenfeld & Nicolson, 1972.

LeVine, Mark. *Overthrowing Geography: Jaffa, Tel Aviv, and the Struggle for Palestine, 1880–1948.* Berkeley: University of California Press, 2005.

Lewin, Ronald. "Montgomery." In *The War Lords: Military Commanders of the Twentieth Century,* edited by Field Marshal Sir Michael Carver. London: Weidenfeld & Nicolson, 1976.

Liddell Hart, B. H. *History of the Second World War.* New York: Paragon, 1970.

Lipsky, Louis. *A Gallery of Zionist Profiles.* New York: Farrar, Straus and Cudahy, 1956.

Livni, Eitan. *Etzel: meevtzot v'machteret* [IZL: Operations and underground]. Jerusalem: Edanim, 1987.

Louis, Wm. Roger. *The British Empire in the Middle East, 1945–1951: Arab Nationalism, the United States, and Postwar Imperialism.* Oxford: Clarendon, 1984.

———. "British Imperialism and the End of the Palestine Mandate." In *The End of the Palestine Mandate,* edited by Wm. Roger Louis and Robert W. Stookey. London: I. B. Tauris, 1986.

Luttwak, Edward, and Dan Horowitz. *The Israeli Army.* London: Allen Lane, 1975.

Makovsky, Michael. *Churchill's Promised Land: Zionism and Statecraft.* New Haven, Conn.: Yale University Press, 2007.

Malatzky, Mendel. *Emet achat velo shtaim* [The one truth and not the other]. Tel Aviv: Yedioth Ahronoth, 1995.

Mallman, Klaus-Michael, and Martin Cuppers. *Nazi Palestine: The Plans for the Extermination of the Jews of Palestine.* New York: Enigma Press, 2010.

Manning, Olivia. *The Levant Trilogy.* Vol. 1, *The Danger Tree.* New York: Viking Penguin, 1988.

Mardor, Munya M. *Haganah—British Title: Strictly Illegal.* New York: New American Library, 1964.

Marighella, Carlos. *For the Liberation of Brazil.* Harmondsworth, U.K.: Penguin, 1971.

Markovitzki, Ya'acov. "Ha-mered: ha-tkafot ha-tasha oreroo et ha-mandat ha-briti" [The revolt: Attrition attacks destabilized the British mandate]. *Ha-uma* [The nation] 41, no. 151 (2004).

Marlowe, John. *Rebellion in Palestine.* London: Cresset, 1946.

———. *The Seat of Pilate: An Account of the Palestine Mandate.* London: Cresset, 1959.

Marton, Kati. *A Death in Jerusalem.* New York: Pantheon, 1994.

Mattar, Philip. *The Mufti of Jerusalem: Al-Hajj Amin al-Husayni and the Palestinian National Movement.* New York: Columbia University Press, 1988.

McCarthy, Justin. *The Population of Palestine: Population History and Statistics of the Late Ottoman Period and the Mandate.* New York: Columbia University Press, 1990.

Mead, Richard. *Churchill's Lions: A Biographical Guide to the Key British Generals of World War II.* Stroud: Spellmount, 2007.

Medoff, Rafael. *Militant Zionism in America: The Rise and Impact of the Jabotinsky Movement in the United States, 1926–1948.* Tuscaloosa: University of Alabama Press, 2002.

Migdal, Joel S. "The Effects of Regime Policies on Social Cohesion and Fragmentation." In Migdal et al., *Palestinian Society and Politics.*

Migdal, Joel S., et al., eds. *Palestinian Society and Politics.* Princeton, N.J.: Princeton University Press, 1980.

———, Shaul, and Avraham Sela. *The Palestinian Hamas: Vision, Violence, and Coexistence.* New York: Columbia University Press, 2000.

Mockaitis, Thomas R. *British Counterinsurgency, 1919–60*. New York: St. Martin's Press, 1990.

Monroe, Elizabeth. *Britain's Moment in the Middle East, 1914–1956*. London: Chatto & Windus, 1963.

———. "Mr. Bevin's 'Arab Policy.'" In *St Antony's Papers No. 11, Middle Eastern Affairs No. 2*, edited by Albert Hourani. London: Chatto & Windus, 1961.

Montefiore, Simon Sebag. *Jerusalem: The Biography*. New York: Knopf, 2011.

Moore, John Norton, ed. *The Arab-Israeli Conflict*. Vol. 3, *Documents*. Princeton, N.J.: Princeton University Press, 1974.

Morgan, Kenneth O. *Labour in Power, 1945–51*. Oxford: Oxford University Press, 1984.

Morris, Benny. *1948: A History of the First Arab-Israel War*. New Haven, Conn.: Yale University Press, 2008.

———. *Righteous Victims: A History of the Zionist-Arab Conflict, 1881–2001*. New York: Vintage, 2001.

Moscrop, John James. *Measuring Jerusalem: The Palestinian Exploration Fund and British Interests in the Holy Land*. Leicester, U.K.: Leicester University Press, 2000.

Mosley, Leonard. *Gideon Goes to War*. London: Arthur Baker, 1955.

———. "Orde Wingate and Moshe Dayan, 1938." In *From Haven to Conquest: Readings in Zionism and the Palestine Problem Until 1948*, edited by Walid Khalidi. Beirut: Institute for Palestine Studies, 1971.

Museum Staff. *The Royal Ulster Constabulary Museum: A Guide to the Collection*. Belfast: RUC Historical Society, 1995.

Nachmani, Amikam. *Great Power Discord in Palestine: The Anglo-American Committee of Inquiry into the Problems of European Jewry and Palestine, 1945–1946*. London: Frank Cass, 1987.

Nedava, Yosef. *Gardomim b'Kahir* [Gallows in Cairo]. Jerusalem: Achiasaf, 1965.

Newsinger, John. *British Counterinsurgency: From Palestine to Northern Ireland*. Basingstoke, U.K.: Palgrave, 2002.

Niv, David. *Ma'archot ha-Irgun ha-Zvai ha–Leumi* [Battle for freedom: The Irgun Zvai Leumi]. Vols. 1–5. Tel Aviv: Klausner Institute, 1975.

Oren, Michael. *Six Days of War: June 1967 and the Making of the Modern Middle East*. Oxford: Oxford University Press, 2002.

Ovendale, Ritchie. *British Defence Policy Since 1945*. Manchester: Manchester University Press, 1994.

———. "The Palestine Policy of the British Labour Party." *International Affairs* 55, no. 3 (July 1979): 409–31.

Pa'il, Meir and Pinhas, Yorman. *Ha-mivchan shel tenuat ha-tzioni: samchut manhigei ha-politi neged ha-mitpatrim* (The test of the Zionist movement: The authority of the political leadership versus the quitters, 1931–1948). Tel Aviv: Tcherikover, 2003.

Paget, Julian. *Counter-insurgency Campaigning*. London: Faber, 1967.

———. *The Story of the Guards*. London: Osprey, 1976.

The Palestine Police Force Close Quarter Battle: Revolvers, Automatics, and Submachine Guns—the Grant-Taylor Manual (1943). Boulder, Colo.: Paladin, 2008.

Pape, Robert A. *Dying to Win: The Strategic Logic of Suicide Terrorism*. New York: Random House, 2005.

———. "The Strategic Logic of Suicide Terrorism." *American Political Science Review* 97 no. 3 (Aug. 2003): 343–61.

Pappe, Ilan. *A History of Modern Palestine: One Land, Two Peoples*. Cambridge, U.K.: Cambridge University Press, 2004.

Pedahzur, Ami, and Arie Perliger. *Jewish Terrorism in Israel*. New York: Columbia University Press, 2009.

Perlmutter, Amos. *The Life and Times of Menachem Begin*. Garden City, N.Y.: Doubleday, 1987.

———. *Military and Politics in Israel*. London: Frank Cass, 1969.

Plowright, John. *The Routledge Dictionary of Modern British History*. London: Routledge, 2006.

Porath, Y. *The Emergence of the Palestinian-Arab National Movement, 1918–1929*. London: Frank Cass, 1974.

———. *From Riots to Rebellion: The Palestinian Arab National Movement, 1929–1939*. London: Frank Cass, 1977.

Reich, Bernard, and Joseph E. Goldberg, eds. *An Historical Encyclopedia of the Arab-Israel Conflict*. Westport, Conn.: Greenwood, 1996.

Rolef, Susan Hattis, ed. *Political Dictionary of the State of Israel—Supplement, 1987–1993*. New York: Macmillan, 1993.

Roman, Yadin. "The Grand Hotel of Jerusalem." *Eretz: The Magazine of Israel*, Feb. 2007.

Rose, Norman. *Chaim Weizmann: A Biography*. New York: Viking, 1986.

———. *"A Senseless, Squalid War": Voices from Palestine, 1945–1948*. London: Bodley Head, 2009.

Rosecrance, R. N. *Defense of the Realm: British Strategy in the Nuclear Epoch*. New York: Columbia University Press, 1968.

Royal Institute of International Affairs (RIIA). *Great Britain and Palestine, 1915–1945*. Westport, Conn.: Hyperion, 1976.

Royle, Trevor. *Orde Wingate: Irregular Soldier*. London: Weidenfeld & Nicolson, 1995.

Ryder, Chris. *The RUC: A Force Under Fire*. London: Mandarin, 1990.

Sager, Samuel. *The Parliamentary System of Israel*. Syracuse, N.Y.: Syracuse University Press, 1985.

Samuel, Maurice. *What Happened in Palestine: The Events of August, 1929, Their Background, and Their Significance*. Boston: Stratford, 1929.

Sanders, Ronald. *The High Walls of Jerusalem: A History of the Balfour Declaration and the Birth of the British Mandate for Palestine*. New York: Holt, Rinehart and Winston, 1983.

Sayigh, Yezid. *Armed Struggle and the Search for State: The Palestinian National Movement, 1949–1993*. Oxford: Clarendon, 1997.

Schechtman, Joseph B. *Fighter and Prophet: The Vladimir Jabotinsky Story—the Last Years*. New York: Thomas Yoseloff, 1961.

———. *The Mufti and the Fuehrer: The Rise and Fall of Haj Amin el-Husseini*. New York: Thomas Yoseloff, 1965.

———. *Rebel and Statesman: The Vladimir Jabotinsky Story—the Early Years*. New York: Thomas Yoseloff, 1956.

Schechtman, Joseph B., and Yehuda Benari. *History of the Revisionist Movement, 1925–1930*. Vol. 1. Tel Aviv: Hadar, 1970.

Schenk, Catherine R. *The Decline of Sterling: Managing the Retreat of an International Currency, 1945–1992*. Cambridge, U.K.: Cambridge University Press, 2010.

Schiff, Zeev. *A History of the Israeli Army*. San Francisco: Straight Arrow, 1974.

———chlor, Joachim. *Tel Aviv: From Dream to City*. London: Reaktion Books, 1999.

The Second World War: A Guide to Documents in the Public Record Office. Public Record Office Handbooks 15. London: Her Majesty's Stationery Office, 1972.

Segev, Tom. *One Palestine, Complete: Jews and Arabs Under the British Mandate*. New York: Holt, 2000.

Seikaly, May. *Haifa: Transformation of a Palestinian Arab Society, 1918–1939*. London: I. B. Tauris, 2002.

Shepherd, Naomi. *Ploughing Sand: British Rule in Palestine, 1917–1948*. London: John Murray, 1999.

Sherman, A. J. *Mandate Days: British Lives in Palestine, 1918–1948*. London: Thames and Hudson, 1997.

"Shihot im Dr. Pinhas Ginosar: al hanehonut lirzoah lema'an matara neala" [Talks with Dr. Pinhas Ginosar: On the willingness to assassinate for a superior cause]. *Svivot* [Surroundings], nos. 24–25 (1990).

Shindler, Colin. *The Triumph of Military Zionism: Nationalism and the Origins of the Israeli Right*. London: I. B. Tauris, 2010.

Shlaim, Avi. *The Iron Wall: Israel and the Arab World*. New York: W. W. Norton, 1999.

Sika-Aharoni, Ya'acov. "Le-olam loh tyiyeh milchemet achim" [There will never be a civil war]. *Ha-uma* [The nation] 39, no. 147 (2002).

Simson, H. J. *British Rule in Palestine and the Arab Rebellion of 1936–1937*. Edinburgh: Wm. Blackwood & Sons, 1937.

Sinclair, Georgina. *At the End of the Line: Colonial Policing and the Imperial Endgame, 1945–80*. Manchester: Manchester University Press, 2006a.

———. "'Get into a Crack Force and Earn £20 a Month and All Found . . .': The Influence of the Palestine Police upon Colonial Policing, 1922–1948." *European Review of History* 13, no. 1 (March 2006b): 49–65.

Slutsky, Yehuda. *Sefer Toldot Ha'Haganah: M'Hitnagdut l'Milchamag* [A history of the Haganah: From resistance to war]. Vol. 3, pt. 1. Tel Aviv: Am Oved, 1972.

Sofer, Sasson. *Begin: An Anatomy of Leadership*. Oxford: Blackwell, 1988.

Stein, Leonard. *The Balfour Declaration*. New York: Simon & Schuster, 1961.

Stern, Abraham. *B'dmi l'ad t'chaii* [In my blood you will live forever: Poems]. 5th ed. Tel Aviv: Yair Publishing House in Memory of Abraham Stern, 1978.

Strachan, Hew. *The Politics of the British Army*. Oxford: Clarendon, 1997.

Stubbs, Richard. *Hearts and Minds in Guerrilla Warfare: The Malayan Emergency, 1948–1960*. Singapore: Eastern University Press, 2004.

Sykes, Christopher. *Cross Roads to Israel*. London: Collins, 1965.

———. *Orde Wingate*. London: Collins, 1959.

Tavin, Eli, and Yonah Alexander, eds. *Psychological Warfare and Propaganda: Irgun Documentation*. Wilmington, Del.: Scholarly Resources, 1982.

Taylor, A. J. P. *English History, 1914–1945*. Oxford: Oxford University Press, 1965.

Teveth, Shabtai. *Ben-Gurion: The Burning Ground, 1886–1948*. Boston: Houghton Mifflin, 1987.

Trevor, Daphne. *Under the White Paper: Some Aspects of British Administration in Palestine from 1939–1947*. Jerusalem: Jerusalem Press, 1948.

Tuchman, Barbara W. *The Guns of August*. New York: Macmillan, 1962.

Vatikiotis, P. J. *The Modern History of Egypt*. London: Weidenfeld & Nicolson, 1969.

Vilnay, Zev. *Steimatzky's Guides: Jerusalem and Its Environs*. Jerusalem: Steimatzky's, 1946.

———. *Steimatzky's Palestine Guide*. Jerusalem: Steimatzky's, 1948.

Walton, Calder. "British Intelligence and the Mandate of Palestine: Threats to British National Security Immediately After the Second World War." *Intelligence and National Security* 23, no. 4 (Aug. 2008): 435–62.

———. *Empire of Secrets: British Intelligence, the Cold War, and the Twilight of Empire.* London: Harper Press, 2013.

Wasserstein, Bernard. "The Assassination of Lord Moyne." *Transactions of the Jewish Historical Society of England* 27 (1982): 72–83.

———. *Britain and the Jews of Europe, 1939–1945.* London: Institute of Jewish Affairs; Oxford: Clarendon, 1979.

———. *The British in Palestine: The Mandatory Government and the Arab-Jewish Conflict, 1917–1929.* London: Royal Historical Society, 1978.

———. *Herbert Samuel: A Political Life.* Oxford: Clarendon, 1992.

———. *Israel and Palestine: Why They Fight and Can They Stop?* London: Profile, 2003.

Wavell, General Sir Archibald. *Allenby, a Study in Greatness: The Biography of Field Marshal Viscount Allenby of Megiddo and Felixstowe, G.C.B., G.C.M.G.* New York: Oxford University Press, 1941.

———. *Allenby in Egypt.* London: Harrap, 1943.

Weissberg, Alex. *Advocate for the Dead: The Story of Joel Brand.* London: Andre Deutsch, 1958.

Wilson, David. *The Sum of Things.* Staplehurst, U.K.: Spellmount, 2001.

Wright, Lawrence. *The Looming Tower: Al-Qaeda and the Road to 9/11.* New York: Knopf, 2006.

Zaar, Isaac. *Rescue and Liberation: America's Part in the Birth of Israel.* New York: Bloch, 1954.

Zadka, Saul. *Blood in Zion: How the Jewish Guerrillas Drove the British out of Palestine.* London: Brassey's, 1995.

Ziff, William B. *The Rape of Palestine.* London: St. Botolph's, 1948.

Zweig, Ronald W. *Britain and Palestine During the Second World War.* Woodbridge, U.K.: Boydell Press for the Royal Historical Society, 1986.

WEB SOURCES

Anglo-American Committee of Inquiry. "Report of the Anglo-American Committee of Inquiry (1946), Appendix V: Palestine—Public Security." Jewish Virtual Library. Accessed June 18, 2013. https://www.jewishvirtuallibrary.org/jsource/History/Anglo16.html.

Ashkenazi, Eli. "Beneath Mandate-Era Nazareth Fort There's a Massive Surprise." *Ha'aretz*, Nov. 19, 2009. http://www.haaretz.com/print-edition/news/beneath-mandate-era-nazareth-fort-there-s-a-massive-surprise-1.4465.

"The Augusta Victoria Hospital: A History Shaped by Conflict." The Lutheran World Federation, Department for World Service—Jerusalem. Accessed June 18, 2013. http://.lwfjerusalem.org/about/history/.

"The Bergson Group." WymanInstitute.org. The David S. Wyman Institute for Holocaust Studies. Accessed June 18, 2013. http://wymaninstitute.org/special/bergsonexhibit/about.php.

"A Brief History." Mass Observation: Recording Everyday Life in Britain. The Mass Observation Archive. Accessed June 18, 2013. http://www.massobs.org.uk/a_brief_history.

Bushinsky, Jay. "The Early Years." *Jerusalem Post Magazine*, Nov. 29, 2007. http://www.jpost.com/Magazine/Features/The-early-years.

Cleveland, William L. "George Antonius." *Gale Encyclopedia of the Mideast & N. Africa*. Answers. Accessed June 18, 2013. http://www.answers.com/topic/george-antonius.

"Collection Level Description: Papers of Sir John Valentine W. Shaw." Bodleian Library. University of Oxford. Accessed June 18, 2013. http://www.bodley.ox.ac.uk/dept/scwmss/wmss/online/blcas/shaw-jvw1.html.

"Ernest Bevin (1881–1951)." BBC History. British Broadcasting Corporation. Accessed June 18, 2013. http://www.bbc.co.uk/history/historic_figures/bevin_ernest.shtml.

"Estimated Number of Jews Killed in the Final Solution." Jewish Virtual Library. Accessed June 18, 2013. http://www.jewishvirtuallibrary.org/jsource/Holocaust/killedtable.html.

Fauvell, D., and I. Simpson. "The History of British Winters." Netweather.tv. Accessed June 18, 2013. http://www.netweather.tv/index.cgi?action=winter-history;sess=.

"Five Ways to Compute the Relative Value of a UK Pound Amount, 1270 to Present." measuringworth.com. Accessed June 18, 2013. http://www.measuringworth.com/ukcompare.

"French Journalist Wins T. R. Fyvel Book Award." *Leicester Review of Books*, March 31, 2006. http://leicesterreviewofbooks.wordpress.com/2006/03/31/french-journalist-wins-tr-fyvel-book-award/.

Freundlich, Yehoshua, and Zvi Ganin, eds. *Political Documents of the Jewish Agency*. Vol. 1, *May 1945–December 1946*. Jerusalem: Hassifriya Haziyonit, 1996. Accessed June 18, 2013. http://www.archives.gov.il/NR/rdonlyres/DA9AE12E-1071-4F51-B115-091E7A0D3CD2/0/POLITICALDOCUMENTSvol11945.pdf.

"George Antonius (1891–1941)." Jewish Virtual Library. Accessed June 18, 2013. http://www.jewishvirtuallibrary.org/jsource/biography/antonius.html.

Goodman, Giora. "Acharei 57 shanaim: filuim b'parashat ha-rezach" [After 57 years: New information about the assassination]. *Ha'aretz Weekly Magazine*, Sept. 2, 2004. http://www.haaretz.co.il/misc/1.996137.

"Gyles Isham." IMDb. Accessed June 18, 2013. http://www.imdb.com/name/nm0410861/.

Hassan, Fayza. "Lost Age of the Salon de Thé." *Al-Ahram: Weekly On-Line*, April 3–9, 2008. http://weekly.ahram.org.eg/2008/891/li1.htm.

Hasson, Nir. "Jay Gatsby in Jerusalem." *Ha'aretz*, Sept. 3, 2009. http://www.haaretz.com/print-edition/features/jay-gatsby-in-jerusalem-1.8564.

"HaTikvah ('The Hope')." Israel's National Anthem. Stateofisrael.com. Accessed June 18, 2013. http://www.stateofisrael.com/anthem/.

"Hillel Kook (a.k.a. Peter Bergson) (1915–2001)." Jewish Virtual Library. Accessed June 18, 2013. http://www.jewishvirtuallibrary.org/jsource.biography/HKook.html.

"In the Service of the British Army." *Ha'aretz*, April 22, 2010. http://www.haaretz.com/weekend/magazine/in-the-service-of-the-british-army-1.284712.

"'The Kalaniots'—The 6th Airborne Division in Palestine." Britain's Small Wars. Accessed June 18, 2013. http://www.britains-smallwars.com/Palestine/6TH.htm.

Kedourie, Elie. "The Most Underrated Books and Authors, from *The Times Literary Supplement*, 1977." The Neglected Books Page. Accessed June 18, 2013. http://neglectedbooks.com/?page_id=145.

"Kidnappings, Beatings, Murders, and Hangings: Attacks by the Irgun and Stern Gang." Britain's Small Wars. Accessed June 18, 2013. http://www.britains-smallwars.com/Palestine/kidnap.htm.

La Guardia, Anton. "Jericho Jail Creates Own Modern History." *Arab News*, March 24, 2006. Accessed March 10, 2010. http://archive.arabnews.com/?page=7&section=0&article=79673&d=24&m=3&y=2006&pix=opinion.jpg&category=Opinion.

Lapidot, Yehuda. "Haviv Avshalom (1926–1947)." Jewish Virtual Library. Accessed June 18, 2013. http://www.jewishvirtuallibrary.org/jsource/biography/Avshalom .html.

———. "Meir Nakar (1926–1947)." Jewish Virtual Library. Accessed June 18, 2013. http://www.jewishvirtuallibrary.org/jsource/biography/Nakar.html.

———. "Restrain [*sic*] and Retaliation." *Welcom [sic] to the Irgun Site.* Accessed June 18, 2013. http://www.etzel.org.il/english/ac03.htm.

———. "Yaakov Weiss (1924–1947)." Jewish Virtual Library. Accessed June 18, 2013. http://www.jewishvirtuallibrary.org/jsource/biography/Weiss.html.

"Lt. Col. Sir Charles Wickham, K.C.M.G., K.B.E., D.S.O., Inspector General June 1922–August 1945." The Royal Ulster Constabulary George Cross. Accessed June 18, 2013. http://www.royalulsterconstabulary.org/wickham.htm.

"Medals: Campaigns, Descriptions, and Eligibility—Distinguished Service Order." Ministry of Defence (United Kingdom). Government of the United Kingdom, Dec. 12, 2012. Accessed June 18, 2013. https://www.gov.uk/medals-campaigns -descriptions-and-eligibility#distinguished-service-order.

Medoff, Rafael. "Ben Hecht's 'A Flag Is Born': A Play That Changed History." WymanInstitute.org. The David S. Wyman Institute for Holocaust Studies, April 2004. Accessed June 18, 2013. http://www.wymaninstitute.org/articles/2004-04 -flagisborn.php.

Melman, Yossi. "The Heruti Code." *Ha'aretz*, Jan. 14, 2005. http://www.haaretz.com/ the-heruti-code-1.147066.

"Meri Feinstein (1927–1947)." The Gallows. The Irgun. Accessed June 18, 2013. http://www.etzel.org.il/english/people/feinstein.htm.

Museum of Underground Prisoners—Jerusalem. Accessed June 18, 2013. http:// hamachtarot.blogspot.com/.

"Nagant Model of 1895 (Belgium-Russia)." World Guns: Modern Firearms— Handguns. Accessed June 18, 2013. http://world.guns.ru/handguns/double-action -revolvers/rus/nagan-arr-195-e.html.

"1945 Labour Party Election Manifesto." Archive of Labour Party Manifestos. Accessed June 18, 2013. http://www.labour-party.org.uk/manifestos/1945/1945 -labour-manifesto.shtml.

Oberholz, Mark. "Orde Charles Wingate (1903–1944)." Orde Charles Wingate. Accessed June 18, 2013. http://www.ordewingate.net/summarymain.html.

"Orde Charles Wingate—'Hayedid.'" Zionism and Israel—Biographies. Zionism and Israel Information Center. Accessed June 18, 2013. http://www.zionism-israel .com/bio/charles_orde_wingate.htm.

Oren, Michael B. "Orde Wingate: Friend Under Fire." *AzureOnline* 10 (Winter 2001). http://www.azure.org.il/article.php?id=279.

The Palestine Statehood Committee Records, 1939–1949. Wilmington, Del.: Scholarly Resources, 1999. Accessed June 18, 2013. http://www.gale.cengage.com/pdf/ scguides/palestine/palstateintro.pdf.

"Paul Muni." IMDb. Accessed June 18, 2013. http://www.imdb.com/name/ nm0612847/.

Saidel, Joanna. "Yitzhak Shamir: Why We Killed Lord Moyne," *Times of Israel*, July 5, 2012. http://www.timesofisrael.com/yitzhak-shamir-why-we-killed-lord-moyne/.

Segev, Tom. "The Spirit of the King David Hotel." *Ha'aretz*, July 23, 2006. http://www .haaretz.com/print-edition/opinion/the-spirit-of-the-king-david-hotel-1.193571.

Shiloni, Avi. "Machteret ha-ktifa ha-dimion ve-ha-shoni ben ha-shaidim ha-Palestinaim ve-oley ha-gardom" [The Velvet Underground: The resemblance and dissimilarity between Shahids and the ones who rose to the gallows]. *Ma'ariv*, Feb. 14, 2002. http://www.nrg.co.il/online/archive/ART/248/433.html.

Thiel, Joshua. "COIN Manpower Ratios: Debunking the 10 to 1 Ratio and Surges." *Small Wars Journal*, Jan. 15, 2011. Accessed June 18, 2013. http://smallwarsjournal.com/jrnl/art/coin-manpower-ratios-debunking-the-10-to-1-ratio-and-surges.

"Underground Prisoners Museum." ilMuseums. Accessed June 18, 2013. http://ilmuseums.com/museum_eng.asp?id=38.

United Nations Conciliation Commission for Palestine. "Note on Currency and Banking in Palestine and Transjordan." United Nations Information System on the Question of Palestine. July 18, 1949. Accessed June 18, 2013. http://unispal.un.org/UNISPAL.NSF/0/1280A68C84F565B5852573A7004FF70B.

"Welcome to the Yeshurun Central Synagogue." Yeshurun Central Synagogue. Accessed June 18, 2013. http://www.yeshurun.org.il/.

Ymedad. "Yehuda Avner's Scarlet Pimpernel." *Begin Center Diary*, March 13, 2008. Accessed June 18, 2013. http://begincenterdiary.blogspot.com/200803/Yehuda-avner's-scarlet-pimpernel.html.

Index

Illustration Credits

Insert 1

PAGE 1: Allenby enters Jerusalem: GB 165-0161 Jerusalem and East Mission Collection—PA 1/163/1 "Allenby entering Jerusalem, 9 Dec. 1917." Courtesy of the Middle East Centre, St. Antony's College, Oxford.

PAGE 2: Churchill and Lawrence: GB 165 0196 Sir Harold MacMichael Collection PA 1/617 "Churchill, Lawrence, and Abdullah at the Jerusalem Conference, 1921." Courtesy of the Middle East Centre, St. Antony's College, Oxford

PAGE 3: (top) Government House: Courtesy of the author; (bottom) British soldiers: Courtesy of Department of Defense—Museum Division, the Etzel in 1948 Museum

PAGE 4: (top) The Jewish Agency headquarters: Courtesy of the Imperial War Museum; (bottom) Palestine Police Force's Camel Corps: GB 165-0161 Jerusalem and East Mission Collection—Magic Lantern Slides 7/6/4 "Police Camel Patrol." Courtesy of the Middle East Centre, St. Antony's College, Oxford

PAGE 5: (top) Certificate issued by the Polish army: Courtesy of Department of Defense—Museum Division, the Etzel in 1948 Museum; (bottom) Irgun commander Menachem Begin: Courtesy of Department of Defense—Museum Division, the Etzel in 1948 Museum

PAGE 6: (top) Polish passport issued to Menachem Begin: Courtesy of Department of Defense—Museum Division, the Etzel in 1948 Museum; (bottom left) Portrait of Major Roy Farran: Courtesy of Special Forces Club; (bottom right) Lieutenant General Sir Evelyn Barker and Major Richard Gale with an unidentified staff officer: Courtesy of the Imperial War Museum

PAGE 7: (top) General Sir Alan Cunningham: Courtesy of the Imperial War Museum; (bottom) Field Marshal Sir Bernard Montgomery: Courtesy of the Imperial War Museum

PAGE 8: (top) Lord Moyne: Courtesy of Wikipedia commons; (bottom) Sir Harold MacMichael: Courtesy of the Library of Congress

Insert 2

PAGE 1: (top) Ramle train station: Courtesy of Wikipedia commons; (bottom) British embassy in Rome: Courtesy of the Library of Congress

PAGE 2: (top) The Yarmuk Bridge: Courtesy of the National Archives of the United Kingdom; (bottom) Farran family home in Codsall: Courtesy of the National Archives of the United Kingdom

PAGE 3: (top) Explosion at Jerusalem's King David Hotel: Courtesy of the Imperial War Museum; (bottom) wounded soldier on a stretcher: Courtesy of the Imperial War Museum

PAGE 4: Destroyed southwest corner of Jerusalem's King David Hotel: Courtesy of the Imperial War Museum

PAGE 5: (top) Plaque: Courtesy of author; (bottom) Palestine police examining identity papers: Courtesy of the Imperial War Museum

PAGE 6: (top) Interrogation by the Palestine police: Courtesy of the Imperial War Museum; (bottom) British soldiers search an unidentified Jewish settlement: Courtesy of Department of Defense—Museum Division, the Etzel in 1948 Museum

PAGE 7: Wanted poster: Courtesy of Wikipedia commons

PAGE 8: (top) Brigadier Johnson: Courtesy of the Imperial War Museum; (bottom) Palestine Police Criminal Investigation Department's offices: Courtesy of Department of Defense—Museum Division, the Etzel in 1948 Museum

Insert 3

PAGE 1: (top) The exercise yard at Acre prison: Courtesy of the author; (bottom) Acre prison: Courtesy of the author

PAGE 2: (top) Exercise yard at the central prison: Courtesy of the author; (bottom) Restored communal cell: Courtesy of the author

PAGE 3: (top) Gallows: Courtesy of the author; (bottom) Restored warden's office: Courtesy of the author

PAGE 4: (top) Tegart fort–cum–police station: Courtesy of Department of Defense—Museum Division, the Etzel in 1948 Museum; (bottom) A soldier: Courtesy of the Imperial War Museum

PAGE 5: (top) Mortars seized: Courtesy of the National Archives of the United Kingdom; (bottom) Vast quantity of arms and ammunition: Courtesy of the Imperial War Museum

PAGE 6: (top left) Package containing a bomb: Courtesy of the National Archives of the United Kingdom; (top right) Address label: Courtesy of the National Archives of the United Kingdom; (bottom) Letter bomb: Courtesy of the National Archives of the United Kingdom

PAGE 7: Headstones: Courtesy of the author; (bottom) Jerusalem British War Cemetery: Courtesy of the author

PAGE 8: Flag-lowering ceremony and honor guard: Courtesy of the Imperial War Museum

A Note About the Author

Bruce Hoffman is the director of the Center for Security Studies and director of the Security Studies Program at Georgetown University's Edmund A. Walsh School of Foreign Service. He is also a senior fellow at the U.S. Military Academy's Combating Terrorism Center. His previous books include *Inside Terrorism* (2006, 2nd ed.) and *The Failure of British Military Strategy Within Palestine, 1939–1947* (1983).

A Note on the Type

This book was set in Janson, a typeface long thought to have been made by the Dutchman Anton Janson. However, it has been conclusively demonstrated that these types are actually the work of Nicholas Kis (1650–1702), a Hungarian, who most probably learned his trade from the master Dutch typefounder Dirk Voskens.

Composed by North Market Street Graphics, Lancaster, Pennsylvania

Printed and bound by Berryville Graphics, Berryville, Virginia

Designed by M. Kristen Bearse

JERUSALEM
1946

KING DAVID HOTEL

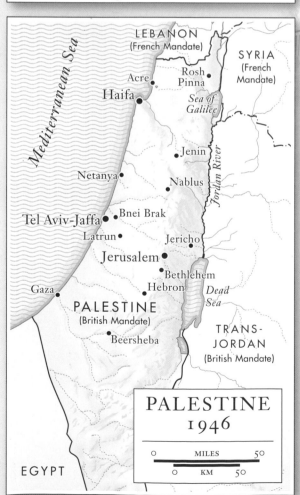

PALESTINE
1946

LEBANON
(French Mandate)

SYRIA
(French
Mandate)

Acre

Rosh
Pinna

Haifa

*Sea of
Galilee*

Jenin

Netanya

Nablus

Jordan River

Tel Aviv-Jaffa

Bnei Brak

Latrun

Jericho

Jerusalem

Bethlehem

Mediterranean Sea

Gaza

Hebron

*Dead
Sea*

PALESTINE
(British Mandate)

TRANS-
JORDAN
(British Mandate)

Beersheba

EGYPT

```
O        MILES        5O
O        KM           5O
```

NEW CITY

Schneller
Barracks

MEA
SHEARIM

STREET OF THE PROPHETS

JAFFA RD.

ZION
SQUARE

MAHANE
YEHUDA

AGRIPPA'S WAY

BEN YEHUDA ST.

KING GEORGE V AVE.

Goldschmidt
House

Jewish
Agency

REHAVIA

KATAMON